The Political Economy of American Industrialization, 1877–1900

In the late nineteenth century, the United States underwent an extremely rapid industrial expansion that moved the nation into the front ranks of the world economy. At the same time, the nation maintained democratic institutions as the primary means of allocating political offices and power. As the combination of robust democratic institutions and rapid industrialization is rarely found in world history, this book explains how development and democracy coexisted in the United States during industrialization. While most of the current literature falls into two discrete categories – studies of electoral politics emphasizing the local basis of party competition and purely economic analyses of industrialization – this book synthesizes politics and economics by stressing the Republican party's role as a developmental agent in national politics, the primacy of the three great developmental policies (the gold standard, the protective tariff, and the national market) in state and local politics, and the impact of uneven regional development on the construction of national political coalitions in Congress and presidential elections.

Richard Franklin Bensel is Professor in the Department of Government at Cornell University. He is the author of *Sectionalism and American Political Development, 1880–1980* (1984) and *Yankee Leviathan: The Origins of Central State Authority in America, 1859–1877* (1991).

D0897057

The Political Economy of American Industrialization, 1877–1900

RICHARD FRANKLIN BENSEL

Cornell University

CAMBRIDGE
UNIVERSITY PRESS

PUBLISHED BY THE PRESS SYNDICATE OF THE UNIVERSITY OF CAMBRIDGE
The Pitt Building, Trumpington Street, Cambridge, United Kingdom

CAMBRIDGE UNIVERSITY PRESS
The Edinburgh Building, Cambridge CB2 2RU, UK
40 West 20th Street, New York, NY 10011-4211, USA
10 Stamford Road, Oakleigh, VIC 3166, Australia
Ruiz de Alarcón 13, 28014 Madrid, Spain
Dock House, The Water Front, Cape Town 8001, South Africa

http://www.cambridge.org

© Richard Franklin Bensel 2000

First published 2000

Printed in the United States of America

Typeface Sabon 10/12 pt.　　*System* QuarkXPress [BTS]

A catalog record for this book is available from the British Library.

Library of Congress Cataloging in Publication Data
Bensel, Richard Franklin, 1949–
The political economy of American industrialization, 1877–1900 /
Richard Franklin Bensel.
p.　cm.
Includes index.
ISBN 0-521-77233-8
1. United States – Economic conditions – 1865–1918.
2. Industrialization – United States – History – 19th century.
3. Democracy – United States – History – 19th century.　I. Title.
HC105 .B45　2000
338.973′009′034–dc21　　　　　　　　　00-023677

ISBN　0 521 77233 8 hardback
ISBN　0 521 77604 X paperback

To WDDP

Contents

Tables

Maps and Charts

xv

Preface

This book is about the coexistence of democracy and development in the United States in the last decades of the nineteenth century. Democratic institutions and electoral practices were far from perfect; violence, fraud, and disfranchising legislation blemish the historical record, particularly after 1890 and particularly in the South. But we cannot understand the American political economy of that time without acknowledging the impact of popular sentiment on both the policy designs of the major parties and the construction of developmental institutions. Participation was high, political opinion was informed, organized insurgency was common, and people felt that the outcome of elections mattered. In all these ways, the late nineteenth century was a far more democratic era than the present and, compared with other developing countries then and since, the United States was well on the democratic side of the spectrum.

In this book, economic development is equated with industrialization: the transition from a predominantly agrarian to a predominantly industrial society, including the capacity to develop and export high-technology manufactured products in a competitive world economy. This is obviously a more demanding conception of development than some scholars would posit. The last condition, for example, is intended to exclude cases where industrialization occurs so slowly that a country can never compete with other advanced nations in the world economy. Here too, the United States was clearly at the upper end of the scale compared with other developing countries then and since.

The question set out in this book is how and why the United States in the late nineteenth century was able to simultaneously meet the demanding prerequisites of both economic development and a democratic process. By setting out the American case as an instance of democracy and development, this book points toward the possibility of cross-national comparison but also, more importantly, attempts to integrate politics and economics into one dynamic. The most important link between them is government policy. From the democracy side of the model, government policies are political demands originating in social groups and classes, articulated in platform appeals made by parties in elections, and enacted by popular representatives in office. From the development side, government policies either facilitate or hinder capital investment and the emergence of more efficient forms of production. Economic development thus imposes requirements on government policy: capital investment in industry must take place, organizational improvements in production must occur, and the size and quality of the market must not constrain either investment or technological innovation. Democracy imposes an equally important set of conditions: mass suffrage, the ability to freely propose policy alternatives, unrestricted entry of new political parties into electoral competition, and the control of government institutions by elected officials.

There was a solution to the democracy and development problem in the United States – an overlapping set of government policies that permitted both aggressive popular claims on wealth in electoral politics and high levels of capital accumulation and investment in industry. Most of the developing world has not been and is not now so fortunate. The policies that made democracy and development work in the United States were not written down in technocratic handbooks or academic treatises. They originated in the rough and tumble of a rich and diverse democratic politics and a pragmatic understanding of markets and investment by both capitalists and their sympathetic political agents. Because a solution existed, there could be a developmental agent mediating between democratic claims on wealth and the operating requirements of capital investment. That agent was the Republican party. As an organization, the Republican party was no monolith; party elites could not dictate a party line on economics or anything else. Party organizations in the individual states regularly chose to ignore or dissent from national party declarations when the latter impaired their competitiveness in local elections. And even party regulars, those who shared and supported the core policy principles of the organization, trimmed sail when election returns indicated a turn in popular opinion. But the Republican party nevertheless forged an effective political framework for economic development that turned back challenges from Democrats and insurgent third parties.

This framework rested upon three policies: tariff protection for industry, adherence to the international gold standard, and an unregulated national market for labor and production. The Republican party could never have implemented these policies on their own merits, largely because it was both the agent of industrial and financial elites and a mass popular organization. These two roles were in obvious tension, acutely so in the South, Plains, and West. In response, the party constructed a persuasive ideological vision within which these policies made sense to popular electorates and, equally important, made side payments to strategically located social groups that broadened and stabilized the party's role as developmental agent. What can be called the "tariff policy complex" became the most important source of side payments within the Republican program, providing revenue for a vast system of pensions for Union veterans who had served in the Civil War and protection for wool-producing farmers throughout the nation. While the protective tariff was in no way necessary to development in economic terms, it became politically essential as the popular backbone of the Republican program. The primary role of the tariff in American industrialization was thus to build a popular coalition for the Republican party, not to facilitate economic development. Because trade protection was not economically essential to American industrialization, the tariff could be left to Congress, which assembled protectionist coalitions out of the myriad of interests and groups that claimed favor in committee rooms and on chamber floors.

In effect, the protective tariff provided the Republican party with a political "surplus" upon which the Republicans drew as they constructed the other two economic legs of the developmental tripod: the national market and the gold standard. These policies were both far more politically vulnerable and economically essential than the tariff. The national market, for example, required the suppression of state and local attempts to regulate interstate commerce – a project that could only have been carried out by the Supreme Court. Insulated by life tenure appointments, Republican justices developed the required constitutional principles and doctrines that ruled out all but the most trivial state and local regulations of interstate trade. The gold standard required active management by the federal treasury and, thus, was an executive responsibility. While the executive branch was more insulated from popular pressure than Congress, presidents were much more susceptible to public opinion than the Supreme Court. In fact, the monetary system became the primary battleground over which developmental policy was fought, with Congress often in strong opposition to the conservative financial regime relentlessly pursued by Republican (and, as it turned out, Democratic) presidents.

The details and relationships elaborating this model have all been laid out in the opening and closing chapters and they need not be repeated here. However, several of the more important aspects of the model might be briefly noted. The first is the notion of the Republican party as a developmental agent, simultaneously anchored in a thoroughly democratic politics and yet responsive to the fundamental necessities of economic development as promulgated by the nation's industrial and financial elites. As a developmental agent, the Republican party could have been torn asunder by the conflicting demands of the electorate and the policy requirements of industrialization. That it survived and, in the end, prospered in this role was not the result of visionary genius. Republican success, instead, arose out of a process of pragmatic adjustment through which the party harvested political rent from benefit-rich and popular policies like the tariff and invested that return in contentious but elite-sponsored policies like the national market and the gold standard. Thus the party was a developmental agent in both political and economic senses of the term.

A second notion concerns the relative insulation of governmental institutions from popular politics and claims. Unpopular policies (those that cost more in electoral support than they return) will not be pursued unless they are economically essential. If they are essential, there will be unambiguous performance tests associated with their implementation (e.g., everyone could tell whether or not the United States was on the gold standard). However, if they are unpopular, the party is unlikely to provide much room for error (because it will try to minimize the political cost of these unpopular but essential policies). In fact, within the ensemble of national institutions, the most politically open branches will find it difficult, even impossible, to implement unpopular developmental policies. As the most politically open institution of the federal government, for example, Congress could be trusted only with the tariff (and almost single-handedly sabotaged the gold standard). What Congress would have done with the national market was never really tested; the Supreme Court had that leg of the developmental tripod largely to itself.

With respect to this relative insulation from popular pressure, the Constitution of course played a major role, both in separating powers among the three great branches of the national government and in imposing a federal design in the allocation of authority between the central government and the states. But the design of the Constitution did not somehow fortuitously mandate the division of developmental responsibility that actually took place. Policies could have been designed differently. For example, statutory bargains over the tariff in Congress could have been replaced by trade agreements with foreign nations negotiated by the executive branch. And constitutional doctrine was hardly written in stone. Dual sovereignty interpretations of the interstate commerce clause and substantive due process readings of the Fourteenth Amendment were creative acts of imagination, not rigid deductions from legal doctrine or hoary bequests from history. Within narrow limits, the Republican party was able to exercise discretion, both in assigning primary responsibility for developmental policies to the separate branches and in crafting constitutional doctrines made to order for American-style industrialization. Put simply, the Constitution did provide a fairly flexible framework within which the Republican party forged its developmental regime, but there is little in the American experience that suggests that a properly designed constitution is all a nation needs to guarantee that democracy and development will be compatible.

Finally, the notion that a political party, as developmental agent, can somehow transfer political rent from benefit-rich policies such as the tariff to costly policies such as the gold standard and national market seems to be worth highlighting. Without a party organization, the cross-subsidization of developmental policies could not have occurred; in fact, the protective tariff would not have been a developmental policy at all, but instead a dead loss weighing down industrialization. In explaining how the tariff politically subsidized economic development, we need a party organization bridging elite interests, policy implementation, government institutions, and popular opinion.

This short list does not exhaust the possible contributions to a theoretical understanding of the political economy of American industrialization. The reader will find several other notions emerging from the text, among them: the uneven pattern of regional development, interregional redistribution of wealth, and the transactional locus within which claims on income are made. Some of these serve to remind us that economic development is rarely a process that improves the condition of all regions or social groups in a society. The American South, for example, came out on the losing end of almost every developmental policy enacted in the late nineteenth century, and, within the South, northern-led industrialization victimized blacks more than any other group, despite their loyalty to the Republican party.

This explanatory model, I hope, plausibly explains what happened during American industrialization. As such, it has a very full agenda. For political historians, I attempt to retrieve the tariff and monetary policy from the scrap heap of history. For much too long, American politics during the Gilded Age has been presented as either focused on substantively unimportant disputes (the tariff and monetary policy allegedly ranking high on that list) or preoccupied with state and local cultural warfare over temperance and religion. Neither was the case. For economic historians, I try to make politics a major factor in American industrialization. Conventional explanations of industrialization have begun with an assumption that an unregulated national market existed in the United States, almost as a birthright of national existence. Unregulated national markets, however, are not like iron ore deposits or other natural endowments; they are politically constructed social realities. And how they are constructed and maintained presents analytical challenges at least as difficult and rewarding as any purely economic problem in this period.

For students of American political development, I present strong connections between ideological vision, popular response to partisan demands, and the underlying reality of the national political economy. As a scholarly community, we have often dismissed out of hand all but a handful of major political actors as mediocrities. Complex, internally coherent logic is disabling in a democracy; the sophistication we seek in ideological vision is instead to be found in the practice of politics. The Republican party, as a prime example, merits study not as the breeding ground for luminaries that somehow discovered the secret of a productive corporate-state relationship, but as a thriving nest of ambitious politicians who wrestled with the problem of democracy and development both as individuals and, together, as an organization. Politicians rarely risk their careers on intellectual theories that go much beyond what we really understand about economics or society. Nor should they. The problems the Republican party faced in reconciling popular politics with the few policies that were actually vital to American industrialization were already immense.

Finally, for those who study comparative development, I offer the United States as a case. In constructing this case, I have attempted to be as comprehensive as possible, but comprehensiveness clearly has no limits. Here, I hope, is a basis for comparing the American experience with other examples of successful (and unsuccessful) combinations of democracy and economic development. However, I do not attempt to carry out such comparisons. My goal is much more modest: to construct a political economic model of American industrialization that is both internally comprehensive and, when compared with other national cases, suggests parallels and differences. Put another way, the intent is to "walk up" this model to comparative possibility and leave it there.

I have incurred many debts in writing this book. The greatest of these is to my closest colleague, Elizabeth Sanders, who was preparing her own book (*Roots of Reform: Farmers, Workers, and the American State, 1877–1917*) during much of my own research. Only readers of our two books can settle the question of whether or not our interpretations have converged; I can only report that our debates are unfinished. For years, we have eaten our dinners while mulling over the importance of the gold standard to American industrialization and whether or not Bryan, as a president, would have been able to translate the 1896 Democratic platform into law. I don't recall what we ate but I do remember the footnotes to footnotes suspended in the air between us.

I began this book when I was still with the Graduate Faculty at the New School for Social Research. While they may not recognize the final product as the one they so vigorously debated at the time, I still welcome the opportunity to thank my colleagues in the Proseminar on State Formation and Collective Action for their advice and support: Guy Baldwin, Sven Beckert, Wayne te Brake, Perry Chang, Brian Daves, Elaine Fuller, Carmenza Gallo, Jeff Goodwin, Andrew Grossman, Michael Hanagan, Madeleine Hurd, Sadrul Kahn, Ira Katznelson, Dan Kryder, Fred Murphy, Andrew Schlewitz, Charles Tilly, and Nick Trippel. I must also thank John Gerring, Richard John, and Jonathan Kirshner for advice and criticism along the way. Just as I was putting the finishing touches on the manuscript, Laurinda Jackson helped me put the first chapter into perspective in a way that no one else could have done. Stephen Skowronek and Roger Ransom read the entire manuscript. Their generous advice and criticism once more reminded me of the virtues and folkways of a scholar's career. There are many maps in this book and for them I must thank Jacqueline Bow, who prepared the computer graphics, and Mindy Peden, who entered much of the data. Credit for the format underlying the maps goes to Carville Earle and Changyong Cao, *The Historical U.S. County Boundary Files, 1850–1970* (Baton Rouge: Department of Geography and Anthropology, Louisiana State University, 1991).

I wish to end this preface by acknowledging two very different debts. The first is to Frank Smith, the executive editor at Cambridge University Press. I warned him that the manuscript would be long but it turned out to be substantially longer than my original prediction. With what I took to be a deep sigh, he nonetheless added this volume to what I consider to be the most distinguished list of works on political and economic history in academic scholarship – a list for which he is largely responsible. I just hope that he will remember that sigh with amusement. The second debt is to a sibling. Academic politics can be rough and many scholars would rather withdraw than fight for the principles that make this an honorable career. This book is dedicated to my sister's courageous devotion to the values that make this a life worth living.

1

Introduction

IN THE LAST decades of the nineteenth century the United States underwent a rapid industrial expansion that moved the nation into the front ranks of the world economy. At the same time, robust democratic institutions formally allocated political power.[1] The primary purpose of this book is to explain how and why economic development and democratic institutions coexisted in the United States. This explanation stresses the intensity of popular claims on wealth, the openness of electoral politics, and the very high saliency of developmental policies underpinning industrial expansion.

The central problem is to explain why, in a democracy, popular claims for a class redistribution of wealth did not divert the stream of investment propelling industrial expansion. Such claims might have been anticipated, particularly from those classes and sectors most injured by industrialization. In fact, however, private capital accumulation in industrial plant and economic infrastructure was almost entirely unrestrained throughout the late nineteenth century. In explaining this result, four features of the national political economy play important roles: the regional nature of industrialization, the varying ways in which claims on wealth were pressed

---

[1] There are good reasons to believe that robust democratic institutions should, in most cases, preclude rapid industrialization. As Barrington Moore once said: ". . . there is no evidence that the mass of the population anywhere has wanted an industrial society, and plenty of evidence that they did not. At bottom all forms of industrialization so far have been revolutions from above, the work of a ruthless minority." *The Social Origins of Dictatorship and Democracy: Lord and Peasant in the Making of the Modern World* (Boston: Beacon Press, 1967), p. 506. The notion that democratic institutions might be incompatible with rapid industrialization in less-developed nations has been around for a long time. See, for example, Walter Galenson, ed., *Labor and Economic Development* (New York: John Wiley & Sons, 1959), pp. 16ff; Seymour Martin Lipset, *Political Man: The Social Bases of Politics* (Garden City, New York: Anchor Books, 1963), p. 29n.

in the different regions, the dynamics and structure of national party competition, and the susceptibility of the different branches of the federal government to popular political influence.

From the broadest perspective, robust democratic institutions and rampant industrialization were compatible because: (1) the agricultural sector that most heavily subsidized industrialization was the export-oriented southern plantation economy, and the South, as a region, was seriously disabled as a viable coalition partner in national politics during this period; (2) the structure of the national political economy led workers in the manufacturing belt to focus on interregional redistribution of wealth (from South to North) and intersectoral transfers of capital (from export-oriented agriculture to tariff-protected industry), rather than shop-floor contestation with capitalists over shares of industrial profits; and (3) the Republican party, as agent for northern industrialization, was able to both win elections and successfully administer a national developmental program. Summed up in a single sentence, democracy and development were compatible because the major groups most likely to pursue political claims on industrial profits, southern cotton producers and northern industrial workers, were unable to coalesce because they occupied antithetical positions within a national political economy restructured and influenced by the primacy of the Republican party.[2]

DEMOCRACY AND DEVELOPMENT

Economic development within democratic institutions has been rare because transitions from agrarian to industrial societies almost always generate intense conflict over the distribution of wealth.[3] Rapid transformation of a society from labor-intensive agrarian and artisanal production into energy- and machine-intensive industry necessarily requires vast amounts of capital. At the same time, nations on the threshhold of rapid industrialization usually contain large populations for whom food and shelter are immediate and pressing preoccupations. These preoccupations often emerge into politics as powerful demands for a sweeping redistribution of income; these demands have had a clear target because the rapid accumulation of capital in plant, equipment, and infrastructure exposes a

---

[2] For more on the complicated history of lower-class alliances in national politics between the end of Reconstruction and World War I, see Elizabeth Sanders, *Roots of Reform: Farmers, Workers, and the American State, 1877–1917* (Chicago: University of Chicago Press, 1999).

[3] See, for example, Edward Mueller and Mitchell Seligson, "Inequality and Insurgency," *American Political Science Review* 81:2 (June 1987): 425–451; Gunnar Myrdal, *Economic Theory and Under-Developed Regions* (London: Gerald Duckworth, 1957), pp. 82–83.

highly visible and potentially divertible stream of wealth. If such popular claims on wealth succeeded, capital formation could be seriously inhibited, thus precluding investment in industrial plant and supporting infrastructure. Thus, for industrialization to proceed, these claims must be suppressed or deferred.

Democratic institutions are more or less efficient transmitters of redistributive claims on wealth, because competition in electoral politics often produces at least one party that responds to the pressing material needs of impoverished classes and thus compels, in or out of power, the adoption of redistributive policies.[4] In less democratic or authoritarian regimes, however, redistributive claims can be repressed or deflected by political institutions specifically adapted for that purpose. In such regimes, capital formation and investment can be carried out by private or public institutions at the comparatively high rate needed to advance within the world economy. In contrasting the United States with other comparative cases, Walter Dean Burnham once said:

The take-off phase of industrialization has been a brutal and exploitative process everywhere, whether managed by capitalists or commissars. A vital functional political need during this phase is to provide adequate insulation of the industrializing elites from mass pressures, and to prevent their displacement by a coalition of those who are damaged by the processes of capital accumulation. This problem was effectively resolved in the Soviet Union under Lenin and Stalin by vesting a totalitarian monopoly of political power in the hands of Communist industrializing elites. In recent years developing nations have tended to rely upon less coercive devices such as non-totalitarian single-party systems of personalist dictatorship to meet that need, among others. The 19th century European elites were provided a good deal of insulation by the persistence of feudal patterns of social deference and especially by the restriction of the right to vote to the middle and upper classes.[5]

In sharp contrast, the political economy of the United States constrained the shape of party coalitions in such a way that policy competition between the major parties effectively substituted for institutional authoritarianism. Put another way, redistributive claims on wealth were discouraged by the nature of the social coalitions supporting competition between the major

---

[4] This conception of democracy focuses upon the formal characteristics of the political process. The crucial feature of a political system that defines it as "democratic" is the extent to which votes cast by a large electorate select officeholders who, in turn, shape government policy. For a now classic statement, see Robert A. Dahl, *A Preface to Democratic Theory* (Chicago: University of Chicago Press, 1963), esp. pp. 84–86.

[5] Walter Dean Burnham, "The Changing Shape of the American Political Universe," *American Political Science Review* 59 (1965): 24. As Burnham so ably describes in this article, the United States was a striking exception to this general pattern of authoritarian rule.

political parties.[6] These social coalitions, in turn, were decisively shaped by the underlying structure of the national political economy.[7]

The most influential factors shaping national party coalitions were wide regional imbalances in the pace and extent of economic development and a deep schism between agrarian and industrial elites in the United States that underpinned the inverted, sectionally based class structure of the party system. In many ways, uneven regional development lay at the foundation of both elite schism and party competition – so much so that, if pressed for a single factor explaining the absence of a major political movement for a radical redistribution of wealth during the late nineteenth century, that factor would be vast differences in the nature and trajectories of the nation's regional political economies.[8]

OVERVIEW OF AMERICAN INDUSTRIALIZATION

Industrialization transformed the United States from an agricultural, commodity-exporting dependency of Great Britain into an independent, leading force in the international system. In a number of ways, this rapid industrial expansion broke with prior patterns of growth in the United States.[9]

---

[6]   During the late nineteenth century, both economic growth generally and capital invest-
      ment in the industrial sector proceeded at a faster pace in the United States than almost
      anywhere else in the world. Angus Maddison, *Dynamic Forces in Capitalist Devel-
      opment* (New York: Oxford University Press, 1991), pp. 41, 49.
[7]   As used here, the "political economy" is a combination of *economy* and *state
      policy*. The *economy* is composed of all forms of material production and exchange.
      In capitalist nations such as the United States in the late nineteenth century, much of
      this activity was carried out by private actors in markets characterized by greater or
      lesser degrees of competition. The distribution of production and consumption results
      from the extent to which these actors can compete effectively with other actors and/or
      control the terms of exchange within their markets. *State policy* consists of the various
      interventions through which the government influences private production and
      exchange. State commands can shape markets and market relations in a number of
      ways by: altering the incentives motivating private actors; radically changing how
      markets are organized and who participates in them; or abolishing markets altogether,
      perhaps replacing them with government-sponsored production. The *political
      economy* is a dynamic organizing structure within society that shapes the potential
      replication of social groups and activities, permits or retards the emergence of novel
      forms of social organization, and thus determines the developmental trajectory of the
      nation. Within this conceptualization, *institutions* can be either creatures of the
      market and/or state policy or semiautonomous social forms within communities
      whose origins are only obliquely related to markets and states.
[8]   For a similar conclusion, see Linda Weiss and John M. Hobson, *States and Economic
      Development: A Comparative Historical Analysis* (Cambridge, Mass.: Polity Press,
      1995), pp. 219–223.
[9]   W. W. Rostow has called this period of rapid industrialization a "drive to techno-
      logical maturity." For the United States, he dates this period as bounded by the years
      1870 and 1910 by way of setting up comparisons with Great Britain (1830–70),

First, much of economic growth up until 1870 had been more or less extensive in nature, associated with the cultivation of new lands and their integration into the national economy. In the last three decades of the century, growth was increasingly intensive and transformational in character as agriculture more fully realized the productive capacity of the land, and, more important, the major locus of economic activity shifted from the farm to the city, from the cultivation of crops to the factory production of manufactured goods.

Second, economic growth in the late nineteenth century was much more uneven in its rate and sectoral characteristics than was the case previously. Until about 1870, for example, a description of the United States as an agricultural nation would have applied in many ways to all sections of the country, with the exception of some parts of the Northeast. In this earlier period, those sections with relatively large frontiers grew much more rapidly than long-settled regions. After 1870, sectional divergences in both the rate and type of economic growth widened considerably in ways that made American industrialization an extremely disjointed process in regional terms – so disjointed, in fact, that we could raise the question of whether or not economic development in the United States should be treated as a national process during this period.

Political conflict over industrialization intensified in the decades following the Compromise of 1877, the political settlement that ended Reconstruction in return for the elevation of Rutherford Hayes to the presidency. Less than two years later this settlement was followed by the return of the United States to the international gold standard – the culmination of a long process that began in 1865 and roughly paralleled the progressive abandonment of the effort to reconstruct the South. The abandonment of Reconstruction in fact facilitated the return of the United States to gold payments by reducing federal military expenditures, promoting resumption of cotton cultivation in the South, and, to most foreign observers at least, promising greater political stability for the nation as a whole.[10] In turn, the reduction in federal spending allowed the national government to contract the circulation of paper dollars (greenbacks), to repay a substantial portion of the

France (1870–1910), Germany (1870–1910), Sweden (1890–1920), Japan (1900–40), the Soviet Union (1900–1960), Italy (1920–40), Canada (1915–50), and Australia (1920–40). He gives slightly different dates for the "most rapid overall industrial growth, or the period when large-scale industry matured . . . Britain . . . 1819–1848; the United States . . . 1868–1893; Sweden . . . 1890–1920; Japan . . . 1900–1920; Russia . . . 1928–40." *The Stages of Economic Growth: A Non-Communist Manifesto*, 3rd ed. (New York: Cambridge University Press, 1990), pp. xviii, xxxix–xl, xliii, 9–10, 12–15, 40, 59, 71–72.

[10] For a description of these policies and their relation to resumption, see Richard Franklin Bensel, *Yankee Leviathan: The Origins of Central State Authority in America, 1859–1877* (New York: Cambridge University Press, 1990), chap. 4.

national debt that had been incurred during the Civil War, and to stockpile gold bullion in anticipation of a return to gold payments. The monetary discipline imposed by resumption and the subsequent maintenance of gold payments produced an extremely severe deflation – more severe, in fact, than was experienced by any other industrializing nation during the same period. The political consequences of this deflation were, from a developmental perspective, equally traumatic.[11]

The turn of the century brought both a final resolution of the great struggle over the gold standard in the form of the Gold Standard Act of 1900 and a refocusing of political debate on the territorial expansion of the United States. While many aspects of industrialization, particularly the growth of the nation's cities, continued to color national politics, new disputes over colonial acquisitions and the quieting of public debate over monetary policy marked very important turning points in American political development. While the great sections continued to struggle over which developmental trajectory the United States should follow, most politically viable alternatives would henceforth assume that the nation would continue to be a major industrial power and would accept policies closely related to that position, such as adherence to the gold standard, as uncontested realities.[12]

Three great developmental policies underpinned American industrialization in the late nineteenth century: the political construction of an unregulated national market, adherence to the international gold standard, and tariff protection for industry. The national market gave rise in the United States to the "modern multiunit business enterprise [which was] central to the process of modernization in the Western world." Taking for granted the political preconditions for the national market in the United States, Alfred Chandler has contended that American industrialization was an inevitabil-

---

[11]   For comparative trends in consumer prices between 1870 and 1913 for sixteen now advanced capitalist nations, see Maddison, *Dynamic Forces in Capitalist Development*, p. 174. Aside from the United States, only two other nations, Denmark and Great Britain, experienced a deflationary trend in consumer prices in this forty-year period, and the trend in the United States was significantly more severe than either one.

[12]   The consolidation of this industrial regime is often described in class terms. For example, Martin Sklar has described corporate reorganization and consolidation around the turn of the century, along with a myriad of other trends in American society, as the result of a more or less hegemonic social movement in which a neo-Marxist dominant class (the corporate business elite) guided modernization in the United States. "Periodization and Historiography: Studying American Political Development in the Progressive Era, 1890s–1916," *Studies in American Political Development* 5 (Fall 1991): 173–213; Steven Hahn, "Response to Sklar," in ibid.: 214–220. Also see James Livingston, "The Social Analysis of Economic History and Theory: Conjectures on Late Nineteenth Century American Development," *American Historical Review* 92 (February 1987): 70; and Lawrence Goodwyn, *Democratic Promise: The Populist Moment in America* (New York: Oxford University Press, 1976), pp. xii, 523–531.

ity, originating in the conjunction of a specific set of technological innovations and opportunities for large-scale production:

> The rise of modern business enterprise in American industry between the 1880s and World War I was little affected by public policy, capital markets, or entrepreneurial talents because it was part of a more fundamental economic development. Modern business enterprise ... was the organizational response to fundamental changes in processes of production and distribution made possible by the availability of new sources of energy and by the increasing application of scientific knowledge to industrial technology. The coming of the railroad and telegraph and the per-fection of new high-volume processes in the production of food, oil, rubber, glass, chemicals, machinery, and metals made possible a historically unprecedented volume of production. The rapidly expanding population resulting from a high birth rate, a falling death rate, and massive immigration and a high and rising per capita income helped to assure continuing and expanding markets for such production. Changes in transportation, communication, and demand brought a revolution in the processes of distribution. And where the new mass marketers had difficulty in handling the output of the new processes of production, the manufacturers integrated mass production with mass distribution. The result was the giant industrial enterprise which remains today the most powerful privately owned and managed economic institution in modern market economies.[13]

However, the modern business enterprise described in this passage arose within a largely unregulated national market that was politically constructed by the Supreme Court.[14] The members of that tribunal were selected by presidents and confirmed by senators who carefully noted both their devotion to party principles and "soundness" on the major economic questions of the day. Among the most important was the nominee's attitude toward regulation of interstate commerce by the individual states – if the states had been able to regulate interstate commerce, the national market would have been balkanized into much smaller units in ways that would have seriously retarded industrial consolidation during the late nineteenth century.[15] Thus policy design and political contestation significantly

[13] Alfred D. Chandler, Jr., *The Visible Hand: The Managerial Revolution in American Business* (Cambridge, Mass.: Harvard University Press, 1977), p. 376.

[14] On the primacy of the national market among the explanations offered for the early emergence of the modern business enterprise in the United States, see Chandler, *Visible Hand*, p. 498.

[15] The consolidation of a national market was a fairly common process among those nations with relatively advanced economies in the late nineteenth century. In addition to the United States, Belgium, France, Germany, Great Britain, and Switzerland all possessed by 1890 a national market for a broad range of products, accompanied by widespread reliance on wage labor, financial institutions for the mobilization of capital investment, and no significant "premodern restrictions" on trade. Of these six, the United States contained the largest national market, in terms of geographical extent, population, and size of economy. Cynthia Taft Morris and Irma Adelman, *Comparative Patterns of Economic Development, 1850–1914* (Baltimore: Johns Hopkins University Press, 1988), pp. 68–69.

shaped the realm Chandler and others imagine to have been a stateless economy. As a result, American industrialization was one outcome among a number of contingent possibilities.

The second great developmental policy was the federal government's adherence to the international gold standard which guaranteed exchange rate stability between the dollar and major foreign currencies, particularly the British pound. This guarantee removed a major source of uncertainty and risk from foreign investments in the United States and thus underpinned much of the relatively close integration of European and American capital markets.[16] While European investment in American railroad bonds and government securities was substantial, the most important result of this close integration was the retention of the vast profits generated by industrial corporations – wealth that might have been transferred abroad had the risk associated with American investments not been limited by the operation of the gold standard and its accompanying discipline on central state fiscal policy. That standard was attacked by Congress for much of this period, but the executive branch under presidents of both parties successfully defended gold in the political arena while competently administering the policy in financial markets.

The tariff protected American industry from foreign competition and thus aided rapid industrial expansion in the northern manufacturing belt. The agricultural exporting regions of the West and, particularly, the South were forced to buy manufactured goods from protected domestic producers while receiving prices for products, such as wheat and cotton, set by an openly competitive world market. The terms of trade under this tariff policy were thus set heavily against the South and West. In economic terms, what the tariff gave with one hand, it took away with the other; while the tariff certainly abetted capital accumulation in the industrial sector by raising prices on manufactured goods and thus increasing profits, the mass consumer base for those products, particularly in agriculture, was severely restricted by the redistribution of wealth the tariff imposed between the sectors. But in political terms, no other policy was as vital to the maintenance of the developmental coalition within the Republican party that supported all three policies. Despite episodic and largely ineffectual interventions by the executive branch, tariff policy was largely set by party coalitions in Congress. The Supreme Court played almost no role.

These three great developmental policies were mutually supporting and, thus, equally and inseparably necessary. In political terms, the protective tariff for industry, through its extensions into raw wool and the revenue it

---

[16]   As was the case with almost all nations prior to the late twentieth century, the United States internally generated "the great bulk of the savings needed for growth and industrialization." Kenneth Berrill, "Foreign Capital and Take-off," in W. W. Rostow, ed., *The Economics of Take-off into Sustained Growth* (New York: St. Martin's, 1963), pp. 286, 297.

provided for military pensions, was the central and indispensable element underlying the Republican coalition in the late nineteenth century. For that reason, the adherence of the United States to the international gold standard during this period is simply inconceivable without tariff protection – the political glue binding rural wool producers, Union veterans, and industrial labor to the Republican party and, thus indirectly, to gold. We can only speculate on the separate contributions of trade protection and the gold standard to industrialization (a staple of economic history); in practice, American adherence to the international gold standard politically depended on the protective tariff because the latter provided the foundation for the Republican coalition. For that reason, any late nineteenth-century combination of free trade and gold standard policies was politically impossible.

None of these developmental policies can be compared with counterparts in other nations without giving equal consideration to their interlocking political connections within the American party coalitions of the late nineteenth century. The protective tariff, for example, could not and did not stand alone; in order to impose high customs duties on manufactured goods, congressional tariff coalitions required the support of raw wool producers and Union pensioners. For its part, defense of the gold standard rested in important ways upon its thick insertion into the financial system by way of the national bank system. Left on its own, the nation's financial community in New York and other banking centers along the eastern seaboard would have been routed early and completely in the struggle over gold. The national bank system provided a strong political network that overlapped interests benefited by the protective tariff in much of the nation. Where this overlap was greatest, the Republican party emerged as the political vehicle for both the tariff and gold; in turn, the Republican coalition further deepened and strengthened political ties and policy logics that, considered separately on their own merits, would have otherwise been cast adrift.

Underlying both protectionism and gold was the most fundamental and characteristically American developmental policy of all, the political construction of an unregulated national market. Without the national market, both the gold standard and the protective tariff would have been useless, perhaps even pointlessly detrimental to the material well-being of the nation. This was also the most broadly conceived of the three developmental policies, demanding theoretical coherence without much day-to-day administration. For several reasons, the Supreme Court was particularly well-equipped to construct the national market. First, constitutional principles provided an effective framework for monitoring federal and state attempts to regulate corporate consolidation and interstate commercial transactions. Because the national market required no administrative activity beyond this close surveillance of state and federal policy, judicial review was a peculiarly well-adapted means of carrying out this responsibility. Second, as the least exposed of the three federal branches to societal influence, the Court was free to play the primary institutional role in the political construction of the national market. Hostile popular sentiment could only threaten Court doctrine over a period of years and then only if the mortality of justices was high enough to enable insurgent presidents to change the Court through new appointments. In addition to its political insularity, the Supreme Court was the only branch that had the power to span the divide between state and national authority. This combination of insularity and power made juridical construction of a national free market possible, even in the face of constant challenge by the individual states.

In strictly political terms, the protective tariff was the most important of the three developmental policies. Because the policy complex surrounding industrial protection rested on narrowly conceived and immediate material interests, the tariff defined numerous policy constituencies that required assembly into a prevailing legislative coalition.[17] Fragmented and decentralized in their representation of societal interests, both the House and Senate were particularly well-equipped to assemble these coalitions. Thus, Congress, the most societally penetrated of the branches, became the central institution for tariff policy.

The industrial tariff, along with its extensions into both an ever-expanding system of military pensions and protective duties on raw wool, became the primary policy foundation for the Republican party. Aside from the suppression of southern separatism, no other principle so defined the party's character and purpose. As for its economic impact on industrialization, the importance of the tariff rested on its redistribution of wealth from the agricultural to the industrial sector. Within the broad scope of that redistribution, policy coherence was not a salient consideration, leaving the Republican party free to build a diverse social coalition that included sheep ranchers and Civil War pensioners, as well as industrial producers.

Somewhere in between, less politically important than the tariff and less

---

[17] Minor parties sometimes declared the tariff to be merely a "technical issue," particularly when they felt that taking any position on industrial protection might destabilize their coalitions. With this partial exception, tariff policy was rarely evaluated on objective economic standards. Contemporary economic theory, in fact, strongly preferred free trade. However, whether or not free trade was more advantageous for American development was seen by most observers as beside the point, because the tariff played a much larger and more important role in structuring the social coalitions backing the major parties. The relevant test for tariff protection was thus whether or not the political viability of the Republican party was enhanced, not how economically well designed the policy was in actual practice. On the dominance of free trade as theory, see Edward C. Kirkland, *Industry Comes of Age: Business, Labor, and Public Policy, 1860–1897* (Chicago: Quadrangle Books, 1967), p. 187.

economically significant than the national market, was the gold standard. Here the abstract designs of monetary theory were not as central to policy as constitutional doctrines were to the construction of the national market. Instead, the policy test was relentlessly material and comparatively mundane: whether or not the Treasury could give gold upon demand to all those who presented currency and silver at the counter of one of the sub-treasury offices. While the gold standard was certainly discussed in highly theoretical terms, the day-to-day administration of the system was the greatest challenge facing monetary policy. Unavoidably, for that reason, the executive branch was the primary institutional agent for the gold standard's operation and defense. In terms of operation, the gold standard required more policy coherence than the tariff but less than the construction of a national market. In terms of political support, gold required more active intervention in national politics than the market but was much more constrained by the system's operating requirements than Congress was with reference to the tariff. In terms of societal penetration, the executive branch's relative autonomy permitted effective administration of the gold standard even when, as during Cleveland's second term, popular opinion was extremely hostile. On the other hand, the presidency, precisely because of its active participation in popular politics, was better equipped to promote the gold standard than the comparatively isolated judiciary. Neither Congress nor the Supreme Court could have negotiated the often convoluted moves that conduct of fiscal policy required under extreme political and economic stress. For all these reasons, when viewed from the perspective of democracy and development, the political economy within which the United States industrialized in the late nineteenth century was thoroughly grounded in the separation of powers between the three institutional branches of the central state.

The identification of the tariff, gold standard, and national market as the fundamental underpinnings of American industrialization rests on their interrelated importance to both politics and economics. In strictly economic terms, a host of additional factors, such as private property, could also be nominated, but because these were not politically challenged in the late nineteenth century, they can be taken as background features of the national political economy. Thus, the three developmental policies were fundamental in that they met two conditions: (1) they were central to the process of capital accumulation and investment that spurred on industrial expansion, and (2) they were strongly and persistently contested in national politics. The question then becomes how these policies were carried out in the face of these political challenges. The first part of an answer has been suggested in the brief survey of their institutional loci within each of the three federal branches. But the Supreme Court, the presidency, and Congress were in each instance policy-making bridges between popular claims and economic development.

POPULAR CLAIMS ON WEALTH

Popular claims on wealth focused on two very different aspects of the late nineteenth-century political economy. The first was the redistribution of wealth from agriculture to industry. Most popular claims associated with this redistribution targeted one or more features of the three great developmental policies: the tariff, the gold standard, and regulation of the national market. The second involved the distribution of income between labor and capital within each of the economic sectors. Here claims involved contestation over income shares within factories, plantations, and farms.

The radically uneven pattern of regional development structured the popular struggle over the redistribution of wealth from agriculture to industry. Industrialization was concentrated in the economic core of the nation, the manufacturing belt in the Northeast and Great Lakes littoral. Commodity agriculture remained the mainstay throughout the economic periphery of the South and West. This pattern made the flow of wealth from agriculture to industry an interregional movement as well as an intersectoral redistribution. In practice, each of the major developmental policies redistributed national income between the great sections. The increasing integration of the national market, for example, tended to eliminate small-scale factory production and petty merchants through-out the country, consolidating such activity in the much larger firms of the manufacturing belt. Within the economically advanced core, this was simply a consolidation of operations within the region. But for most of the South and West this process represented both a loss of locally controlled businesses and the transfer of wealth, through the repatriation of profits, from those sections toward the core. Thus, while underwriting the emergence of the large-scale modern business enterprise, the expanding national market also entailed a redistribution of wealth from the agricultural periphery to the manufacturing belt. The tariff reinforced this flow, particularly for heavy industry, by protecting domestic producers from foreign competition and thus enhancing corporate profits. The gold standard and the deflationary regime that it imposed on the nation through the mid-1890s directed wealth along very similar lines, more or less systematically redistributing assets from capital importers in the West and South to capital exporters in the East.

Those claims that involved contestation over income shares between labor and capital were much more local in character. While there were a great variety of such claims in the late nineteenth century, three of them stand out, dominating their respective regional economies and societies. In the northeastern and midwestern manufacturing belt, the archetypal struggle over income shares was between workers and capital on the industrial shop floor. Tens of thousands of industrial disputes, work stoppages, lockouts, and strikes raged throughout the northern manufacturing belt during this period and contributed to what became one of the most tumultuous and violent labor experiences in the history of industrialization.[18] Many of these disputes were resolved through judicial and military intervention.[19] Even so, labor issues seldom played a large role in either national politics or major party platforms; much more numerous and far more detailed were those platform planks devoted to the developmental policies that divided the interests of the industrial East and commodity-exporting South. In fact, one of the central problems of this period is explaining why the claims on wealth so poignantly expressed in industrial labor disputes failed to significantly influence major party competition in the late nineteenth century.[20] Northern labor clearly made strong and

[18] With respect to northern labor, Philip Taft and Philip Ross described the United States as having had "the bloodiest and most violent labor history of any industrial nation in the world." "American Labor Violence: Its Causes, Character and Outcome," in Hugh D. Graham and Ted R. Gurr, *The History of Violence in America: Historical and Comparative Perspectives* (New York: Praeger, 1969), p. 281. See pp. 281–304 for an overview of labor violence in the late nineteenth century.

[19] For a summary of the use of the national guard and federal troops in response to strikes and against workers generally, see David Montgomery, *Citizen Worker: The Experience of Workers in the United States with Democracy and the Free Market during the Nineteenth Century* (New York: Cambridge University Press, 1993), pp. 89–104. For a statistical survey of the use of federal troops and national guards in the United States during this period, see David Adams, "Internal Military Intervention in the United States," *Journal of Peace Research* 32:2 (May 1995): 200–203. Also see Gerald Friedman, "Strike Success and Union Ideology: The United States and France, 1880–1914," *Journal of Economic History* 48 (March 1988): 14.

[20] As Eric Foner puts it, "what needs to be explained is the coexistence in American history of workplace militancy and a politics organized around non-ideological parties appealing to broad coalitions." "Why Is There no Socialism", *History Workshop* 17 (Spring 1984): p. 59. P. K. Edwards notes that the American "strike rate has been very high compared with that of other countries, but its labour movement has been among the least radical in political terms." From his perspective, this pattern has been a "paradox of militancy combined with conservatism." *Strikes in the United States, 1881–1974* (New York: St. Martin's Press, 1981), p. 3. Also see Leon Fink, *Workingmen's Democracy: The Knights of Labor and American Politics* (Urbana: University of Illinois Press, 1983), p. xi; John Laslett, "Reflections on the Failure of Socialism in the American Federation of Labor," *Journal of American History* 50 (March 1964): 651. The most complete general overview is perhaps David Montgomery's *The Fall of the House of Labor: The Workplace, the State, and American Labor Activism, 1865–1925* (New York: Cambridge University Press, 1987). As Karen Orren emphasizes in her *Belated Feudalism: Labor, Law, and Liberal Development in the United States* (New York: Cambridge University Press, 1991), this lack of involvement in national party politics did not prevent labor from openly challenging the federal judiciary. Setting the conditions for governance of the industrial shop floor, judicial interpretation was heavily contested by labor and capital throughout the late nineteenth century. For a comparative perspective on class construction

persistent claims on the stream of wealth flowing into industrial expansion, but these claims were made on the shop floor and in the streets, rarely finding an echo in national politics.[21]

In the South, the archetypal claim on wealth involved a very different type of struggle between sharecroppers and tenant farmers, on the one hand, and planters and merchants, on the other. The focus of this struggle was the contractual forms and arrangements determining control of the cotton crop. In many ways this contestation was inextricably bound up with both race and national loyalty, with blacks comprising a disproportionate share of both sharecroppers and federal loyalists. For southern whites, the consolidation of planter and merchant influence within the cotton economy appeared to be a necessary step in gaining political autonomy from northern rule. In fact, elite influence in local areas and regional autonomy in national politics were often seen as just different sides of the same coin. Using both terror and economic intimidation to return to power throughout the South, former Confederate nationalists gradually disfranchised black and lower-class white voters so that, by the turn of the century, planters were once again a hegemonic force in regional politics. In the years just after the Compromise of 1877, Republicans bitterly complained of southern "atrocities" in their national party platforms, but these complaints became increasingly perfunctory as the years passed. In any event, platform demands which focused on suffrage and the conduct of elections did not begin to address the desperate situation of southern sharecroppers in their relations with planters and merchants. For the southern farmer, black or white, life was a continuous struggle with economic exploitation, grinding poverty, and diseases arising from dietary deficiencies and parasites.

The southern wing of the Populist party sought to connect regional political autonomy to a redress of agrarian class grievances by making the sharecropper and yeoman farmer the agent of resistance to northern economic

and politics in the United States, see Ira Katznelson, "Working-Class Formation: Constructing Cases and Comparisons," and Aristide R. Zolberg, "How Many Exceptionalisms?," in Katznelson and Zolberg, *Working-Class Formation: Nineteenth-Century Patterns in Western Europe and the United States* (Princeton, N.J.: Princeton University Press, 1986), pp. 3–41 and 397–455.

[21] For evidence that strike participation, as a percentage of the nonagricultural labor force, was much higher in the United States than in comparable European nations during the late nineteenth and early twentieth centuries and that strike-related violence was exceeded only by Czarist Russia, see Michael Mann, *The Sources of Social Power*, vol. 2: *The Rise of Classes and Nation-states, 1760–1914* (New York: Cambridge University Press, 1993), pp. 632–633, 644–647. At many points in his analysis, Mann also demonstrates that worker support for socialist parties and principles in the United States was much weaker than in comparable European nations. See, for example, pp. 634, 638. Also see David A. Shannon, "Socialism and Labor," in C. Vann Woodward, ed., *The Comparative Approach to American History* (New York: Basic Books, 1968), pp. 238–252.

exploitation. With this exception, the desperate conditions on the southern plantation, afflicting a sizable fraction of the country's population, never gave rise to significant claims on the wealth of the nation. Although more influential in southern local politics than shop-floor claims were in the North, class contestation over control of the cotton crop was almost completely ignored in national party competition.

On the recently settled western frontier, the archetypal claim on wealth involved yet a third kind of struggle. In this case, contestation was most intense over the terms under which the agents of eastern capital would integrate yeoman farmer settlers into the national economy. This integration assumed two primary forms: the extension of mortgage credit to settlers and the transportation of the commodities they produced to eastern markets. Much of the capital that underwrote farm mortgages in the West was imported from the East. In addition, many of the banks in the Plains and Mountain states, as well as the railroads that transported crops, were owned by eastern investors. The archetypal western claims on wealth thus tended to pit yeoman farmers against banks and railroad corporations that were often controlled by eastern interests. For a number of reasons these claims moved quite easily into local politics and, through third parties, into national politics. One was that yeoman farmers in the Plains and Mountain states were more economically independent than either eastern industrial workers or southern sharecroppers and were thus more likely to organize politically. But, more important, their class opponents in this struggle over income shares were primarily nonresident capital-holders who were represented in local politics by much less powerful agents. In terms of national politics, this was the one instance where claims on income shares within a sector more or less coincided with the redistribution of wealth between the nation's great regions. Only a slight refocusing of the lens of politics was required to transform local class claims into issues implicating the great developmental policies of the nation.

If the popular side in each of these archetypal struggles over wealth could have allied together in the late nineteenth century, American industrialization would have either been quite a bit slower or taken on a radically different form. Such an alliance was attempted by the Populists in 1892 and by the Democrats in both 1896 and 1900. In both cases, industrial workers refused their support while tension between the southern sharecropper and western yeoman producer made alliances between these two groups very volatile. It should be stressed that popular claims on wealth pervaded almost every aspect of late nineteenth-century American society and captured the attention of almost every community. Yet the way in which the national political economy was organized frustrated even the simple recognition of such claims in major party platforms and, even when they did emerge as platform demands, turned one or more elements of what could have been a national insurgency away from the struggle.

OVERVIEW OF THIS BOOK

Most of the current literature on the United States in the late nineteenth century falls into two general categories: electoral politics emphasizing the local basis of party competition and purely economic analyses of industrialization.[22] These literatures are almost hermetically isolated from one another in ways that have discouraged all but the most superficial answers to the question of why robust democratic institutions and rapid industrialization coexisted in the United States. In contrast to the existing literature, this book exposes strong connections between electoral party competition, central state institutions and developmental policy, and industrialization as a developmental process.[23]

These connections challenge some of the distinctive orientations of the now-reigning literatures. With respect to the literature on parties and voting, national developmental issues, not ethno-cultural conflict, are shown to be the dominant preoccupation of state party competition. With respect to the expansion of central state institutions, the integration of party organization into national policy administration is shown to have been a necessary element in the successful combination of democracy and development in the United States.

Finally, the literature on American economic history has long interpreted major features of industrialization, such as an unregulated national market, as historical "givens," placing them beyond politics and thus dismissing politics and central state policy as playing only superficial roles in economic expansion.[24] In sharp contrast, this book demonstrates the existence of popular challenges to each of the major developmental policies followed by

---

[22] The best recent synthesis of late nineteenth-century politics is Joel H. Silbey's *The American Political Nation, 1838–1893* (Stanford, Calif.: Stanford University Press, 1991), esp. pp. 225–232.

[23] But also see Walter D. Burnham's "The System of 1896: An Analysis," in *Evolution of American Electoral Systems*, ed. Paul Kleppner et al. (Westport, Conn.: Greenwood Press, 1981), pp. 147–202.

[24] For example, Chandler views federal regulation of the railroads and antimonopoly policies as unimportant factors in the expansion of the transportation network and consolidation of industrial production in the late nineteenth century. Otherwise his work assigns almost no political or governmental role in American industrialization before the Progressive Era. See his *Visible Hand*, pp. 13, 174–5, 331–333, 494–495. In his comparative study of the United States, Germany, and Great Britain, Chandler explicitly leaves the impact of government on the development of industrial capitalism to "historians of business-government relationships." *Scale and Scope: The Dynamics of Industrial Capitalism* (Cambridge, Mass.: Harvard University Press, 1990), p. 13. For a slightly more political account of the late nineteenth-century financial system, see Milton Friedman and Anna Jacobson Schwartz, *A Monetary History of the United States, 1867–1960* (Princeton, N.J.: Princeton University Press, 1963), pp. 3–188.

the United States. Analysis of these popular challenges, in turn, necessarily compels a reevaluation of both the developmental impact of national party competition (in terms of platform commitments) and the relative integration of party organizations into central state institutions. Politics and economic development were not separate processes, unfolding according to distinct logics; they were, instead, inseparably and intimately interconnected in ways that ultimately produced rapid industrialization within a robust democratic polity.

The following chapter lays out the social and economic topography of the United States during the late nineteenth century. The first part of the chapter describes the uneven regional pattern of economic development of the United States and provides explanations for its persistence. This description sets up an analysis of the national financial system emphasizing the importance of both intersectional capital flows and the varying extent of regional integration within the national financial system.

Building on these preceding discussions, Chapter 3 takes up questions related to the expression of class claims in politics by exploring the connection between national developmental policies and party competition within the individual states. This exploration challenges the prevailing notion that electoral politics in the late nineteenth century was predominantly local in nature and heavily colored by "ethno-cultural" conflict over issues such as temperance and secular education.[25] The reinterpretation proposed in this chapter resolves the long-standing paradox between the nature of national party competition (almost universally conceded to be focused on developmental issues such as the tariff and the monetary system) and the local basis of electoral behavior (which has been described as centered on locally framed issues of social norms and identity). Although ethno-cultural issues were certainly important in local politics during this period, an exhaustive survey of state party platforms between 1877 and 1900 demonstrates that a host of national developmental issues of many kinds in fact dominated state party declarations of principle, just as they did at the national level.

Following up on this discussion of platform demands, Chapter 4 demonstrates that most electoral behavior was shaped by developmental forces in ways that are incomprehensible in ethno-cultural terms. The chapter opens with an outline of the archetypal claims on wealth that characterized class conflict over income shares within each of the nation's major regions. The focus in this discussion is on these claims and their origin within the regional economy, whether or not they assumed an overtly political form. The sub-

---

[25] Some contemporary political historians have, in fact, subscribed to "ethno-cultural" interpretations of late nineteenth-century electoral behavior that almost entirely dispense with economic factors. See, for example, Paul Kleppner, *The Third Electoral System, 1853–1892: Parties, Voters, and Political Cultures* (Chapel Hill: University of North Carolina Press, 1979), pp. 10–11, 58–63, 366–373.

sequent analysis of election returns reveals the different ways this contestation over income shares influenced the construction of national party coalitions.

The next three chapters examine the politics of the three legs of the Republican developmental tripod: the unregulated national market, the gold standard, and tariff protection. Chapter 5 takes up the growth and consolidation of the national market, emphasizing the dominant role of the Supreme Court in the political construction of the market economy. Chapter 6 begins with a discussion of the institutional characteristics of monetary policy, later shifting to an analysis of legislative coalitions and the persistent support of the executive branch for the gold standard. This discussion establishes the strong connection between contestation over the monetary standard and economic development. Chapter 7 takes up the last of the major developmental policies, the tariff, examining the centrality of trade protection to the national Republican coalition. The conclusion provides a formal interpretive summary of the argument.

2

Uneven Economic Development
in the United States

AMERICAN industrial expansion in the late nineteenth century was extremely uneven, occurring almost entirely in the Northeast and in the midwestern states of Ohio, Indiana, Illinois, Wisconsin, and Michigan – what became known as the manufacturing belt of the nation. The South and West remained primarily agricultural sections, dependent on cotton and grains, livestock, and minerals. Although there were important links between these regions, each can be considered – in terms of the position of the United States in the world economy – as a distinct entity, both in terms of politics (e.g., the late nineteenth-century Populist revolt) and economics (e.g., the isolation of the South from the national capital market).

INDUSTRIALIZATION AND INCREASING IMBALANCES IN REGIONAL DEVELOPMENT

With the exception of small countries in which a unified national market is the natural product of constricted political boundaries, rapid economic development usually increases regional disparity in per capita wealth and income. American industrialization followed this rule. In 1840, before the transformation of the national economy, the great American sections were fairly close in per capita income. In fact, with a good harvest and a good price, the cotton crop could push per capita income in the South, slaves included, toward parity with the North.[1] But as industrialization picked up

---

[1] On regional disparities in per capita income and the late antebellum cotton boom, see Robert William Fogel, *Without Consent or Contract: The Rise and Fall of American Slavery* (New York: W. W. Norton, 1989), pp. 86–89, 95–97. The 1860 figures place southern per capita income, including slaves, a little less than 20 percent below the national average. Outside the Northeast, in fact, the per capita income of the slave South ran some 14 percent above that of the free states.

Table 2.1. *Sectional Per Capita Income as a
Percentage of the National Level, 1840–1900*

Section	1840	1880	1900
Northeast/Midwest	106	118	117
Plains and West	—	126	130
South	89	62	63
Nation	100	100	100

Source and note: Calculated from data in Richard
A. Easterlin, "Interregional Differences in Per Capita
Income, Population, and Total Income, 1840–1950,"
National Bureau of Economic Research, Conference on
Research in Income and Wealth, Studies in Income and
Wealth 24, *Trends in the American Economy in the
Nineteenth Century* (Princeton, N.J.: Princeton Univer-
sity Press, 1960), Appendix A. States included in the
South include all those that seceded into the Confeder-
acy plus Kentucky, Missouri, Oklahoma, and West Vir-
ginia. The Plains and West includes all states west of
Illinois and Wisconsin not included in the South. The
Northeast/Midwest includes all the remaining states. No
index figure is reported for the Plains and West in 1840
because the section in that year comprised less than
0.3 percent of the national population.

steam in the late nineteenth century, the terms of trade rapidly shifted
against the South (see Table 2.1). In the forty-year period between 1840
and 1880, southern per capita income actually declined while northern
income rose by more than 50 percent. Between 1880 and 1900, the relative position of the great American sections remained largely unchanged as
per capita income increased in all regions of the nation, but, in absolute
terms, income gains in the North continued to outstrip the South by a wide
margin.[2] While the devastation wrought by the Civil War accounts for some
of this southern retardation, postwar federal policies that systematically
redistributed wealth from the South to the North, such as the protective
tariff, military pensions, and adherence to the international gold standard,
were probably more important factors.[3]

[2] For regional per capita income data for 1880 and 1900, see Harvey S. Perloff, Edgar
S. Dunn, Jr., Eric E. Lampard, and Richard F. Muth, *Regions, Resources, and Economic Growth* (Baltimore: Johns Hopkins University Press, 1960), pp. 25–26.
[3] Adjustment for regional differences in cost of living would do little to reduce these
discrepancies. In 1880, for example, the cost of living in the states of Virginia, North

Imagining for a moment the national economy as one in which industry and agriculture were the only two pursuits, regional specialization at the turn of the century was nothing short of spectacular (see Table 2.2).[4] At one end, Rhode Island's per capita production of manufactured goods was almost twenty-nine times as great as the state's agricultural output. At the other end, North Dakota's agricultural production stood at more than seven times the state's industrial production. And there was bunching at these extremes. All of the nine states with the greatest manufacturing to agricultural production ratios bordered one another, extending from New Hampshire to the north to Maryland at the south. At the other extreme, the twenty-three states with the highest agriculture to manufacturing ratios fell into two regional clumps: all of the former states of the Confederacy (except Florida) plus Kentucky and West Virginia, and eleven states extending westward from Minnesota and Iowa to the Pacific Coast, excepting Montana and Washington. These two clumps would have been connected if Oklahoma had been a state rather than a territory.

Although they shared very high agriculture to manufacturing ratios, these two regions were otherwise very different. Aside from Utah, per capita income from agriculture in every western state was higher than every state in the southern clump. And the differences were, for the most part, very large: The dollar value of North Dakota's per capita agricultural production was more than four times that of the states of Alabama, Georgia, North Carolina, South Carolina, Virginia, and West Virginia. While the differences in manufacturing output were smaller, it was the South's low levels of agricultural income, not its low manufacturing output, that raised the ratio of manufacturing income above or even with that of the states in the northern clump. In fact, states like Illinois, Michigan, New Hampshire, and Maine – all of them heavily devoted to manufacturing – still reported per capita agricultural income levels as high or higher than that of a majority of the former states of the Confederacy. The South was, in fact, profoundly poor. While its comparative advantage lay in cotton, it was only an advantage because the region had to produce something or die.

To briefly illustrate this regional specialization, Arkansas and Connecticut can stand as typical southern and northeastern examples. In 1900, Arkansas had a population of about 1,300,000. Connecticut's population stood at 900,000. When the Census reported the value of manufacturing production by individual industries and states in 1900, Arkansas ranked

---

Carolina, South Carolina, and Florida equaled or surpassed corresponding levels in New England and were substantially higher than those in the midwestern states bordering one or more of the Great Lakes. Jeffrey G. Williamson and Peter H. Lindert, *American Inequality: A Macroeconomic History* (New York: Academic Press, 1980), pp. 323–325.

4   This stylization of the national economy sets aside the service sector which, within any region, merely attended primary producers.

Table 2.2. *Per Capita Value of Manufactured and Agricultural Products by State, 1900*

State	Per capita value of manufactures	Per capita value of agricultural products	Ratio of manufactures to agricultural products
Rhode Island	430	15	28.67
Massachusetts	369	15	24.60
New Jersey	325	23	14.13
Connecticut	388	31	12.52
New York	300	34	8.82
Pennsylvania	291	33	8.82
Maryland	204	37	5.51
New Hampshire	288	53	5.43
Delaware	246	50	4.92
Illinois	261	72	3.62
Maine	183	53	3.45
Ohio	200	62	3.23
Colorado	191	61	3.13
Washington	170	68	2.50
Michigan	147	61	2.41
Wisconsin	175	76	2.30
California	204	89	2.29
Florida	70	35	2.00
Montana	247	124	1.99
Indiana	150	81	1.85
Missouri	124	71	1.75
Vermont	168	98	1.71
Louisiana	88	53	1.66
West Virginia	78	47	1.66
Minnesota	151	93	1.62
Virginia	71	47	1.51
Utah	77	60	1.28
Kentucky	72	57	1.26
Oregon	112	93	1.20
North Carolina	50	47	1.06
Georgia	48	47	1.02
Tennessee	54	53	1.02
Nebraska	135	153	0.88
Alabama	44	50	0.88
South Carolina	44	51	0.86
Kansas	117	143	0.82
Arkansas	34	61	0.56
Texas	39	79	0.49
Iowa	74	164	0.45
Mississippi	26	66	0.39
Wyoming	47	131	0.36
Nevada	40	166	0.24
Idaho	25	113	0.22
South Dakota	32	172	0.19
North Dakota	29	206	0.14

Source: Calculated from data in *1900 Census of Manufactures*, pt. 1 (Washington, D.C.: U.S. Census Office, 1902), Table LXXIII, pp. clxxix–clxxx.

among the top five states only once (third of all the states in the value of cotton ginning). Connecticut, however, reached the top ranks in sixteen industries; the state ranked first in ammunition, brass and rolled copper, brass castings and brass finishing, brass ware, clocks, corsets, cutlery and edged tools, fur hats, hardware, needles and pins, and plated and britannia ware; second in sewing machines; third in both rubber and silk goods; and fourth in hosiery and woolen goods.[5]

THE MATERIAL FOUNDATION OF
ECONOMIC DEVELOPMENT

While economic development is inevitably a complex concept, it still should be clearly grounded in empirical reality. To describe the topography of American development in the late nineteenth century, five empirical dimensions have been selected: per capita value-added in manufacturing (in dollars), patents issued per 10,000 people, average interest rate on farm and home mortgages, per capita wealth, and the illiteracy rate among adult males.[6] These collectively cover the most salient dimensions of relative industrial development: the extent and depth of manufacturing activity, participation in technological change, integration into national and world capital markets, accumulation of wealth, and the skill level of the work force. Statistics on each were available by county – a necessary condition for their subsequent aggregation into congressional districts and trade areas. However, each of the five have shortcomings as empirical proxies for their respective developmental dimensions. As they are discussed in turn, the limitations of the census data will be acknowledged. However, taken together, these five appear to address most of the important dimensions and interdependencies of industrial development in the late nineteenth century with a concision that alternative measures would not improve on. The data on these five referents were subsequently aggregated into an overall "index of development" in which each county or alternative geographical unit can be assigned a single statistic indicating its relative "developmental level."

---

[5]   *1900 Census of Manufactures*, pt. 1 (Washington, D.C.: U.S. Census Office, 1902), pp. clxxxviii–clxxxix.

[6]   All but the last were taken from the *1890 Census* (illiteracy was taken from the *1900 Census*). For a description of the procedures and history of the 1890 census, see Carroll D. Wright, *The History and Growth of the United States Census* (Washington, D.C.: GPO, 1900), pp. 69–76, 177–199, 203–212, 221–227, 231–233, 278–304, 361–537, 584–606, 609–646, 684–691, 739–774, 779–786, 794–795, 802–809, 825–860, 874–894, 903–910. More generally, see Margo J. Anderson, *The American Census: A Social History* (New Haven, Conn.: Yale University Press, 1988), pp. 104–115. Anderson describes the 1890 census as "much more detailed" than previous censuses.

Per Capita Value-Added in Manufacturing

In gauging relative industrial development, the most obvious indicator is the amount of industrial activity. The 1890 federal census collected county level statistics on a number of dimensions related to manufacturing (here taken to be synonymous with industrial activity), among them the number of establishments, capital invested in the firm, numbers of workers, and value of production. Each, taken alone, presents significant problems. For example, the number of establishments, counting equally those that are very small and very large, seriously distorts the underlying comparison of industrial activity between counties with a few, very large steel plants and those with a large number of very small artisanal shops. Comparisons based on the number of manufacturing workers are preferable because they more appropriately weight the size of manufacturing establishments. But there are problems with associating employment figures with overall manufacturing productivity, particularly with assigning an appropriate discount for children under fifteen years of age who, in many regions, composed a sizable percentage of the work force. Data on total capital invested in manufacturing establishments improves on both the number of firms and the size of the work force but suffers from the absence of a discount for depreciation, a concept only poorly understood in the late nineteenth century and rarely given an explicit actuarial role in the calculation of capital accounts and operating profits.[7] Failure to include a discount for depreciation would overvalue the contribution of older firms compared with those more recently established, and thus overstate the amount of manufacturing activity in the more well-established regions of the nation. Finally, the value of industrial production improves on all of the above but still suffers from the fact that raw materials entering into industrial processes comprise very different proportions of the final output. Very little, for example, may be done to refine a diamond in the way of an industrial process, and yet the yield from the sale of that diamond, as an industrial product, will still be very great. On the other hand, the raw materials entering into the production of fine china may be very cheap, but, through the intense application of machinery and skilled labor, the output will also be extremely valuable.[8]

For all of these reasons, value-added in manufacturing appears to be the most appropriate referent for the relative significance of industrial activity within the various areas of the nation. The statistic is calculated by first

---

[7] On the relative accuracy of statistics on cost of materials, salaries and wages, and value of products produced, compared with those reporting capital investment, see *1900 Census of Manufactures*, pt. 1, pp. ccxiv–ccxvii. See, also, *1890 Census of Manufactures*, pt. 1 (Washington, D.C.: GPO, 1895), p. 49.

[8] On this aspect of the superiority of the value-added statistic over the gross value of production, see the *1900 Census of Manufactures*, pt. 1, p. ccxxxv.

determining the total value of all industrial production, including income from special orders (custom work) and repair, and then subtracting the cost of raw materials and intermediate goods used in the industrial process. The remainder thus includes the wages and salaries paid to the firm's work force, depreciation on capital utilized in the process, and profits (or losses) accruing to the owners of the enterprise.[9]

In 1890, the total value-added in manufacturing for the United States, aside from the territories and the District of Columbia, was $4,186,566,000, or $67.40 per capita.[10] The leading industrial states were all in the Northeast: Rhode Island ($191.74 per capita added in manufacturing), Massachusetts ($185.34), Connecticut ($167.71), New York ($140.10), and New Jersey ($114.34). The least industrial states were all in the South and West: South Dakota ($6.57), Mississippi ($6.70), Idaho ($8.97), Arkansas ($9.10), North Dakota ($10.62), North Carolina ($10.87), South Carolina ($11.34), Alabama ($15.07), Texas ($15.33), Tennessee ($18.04), and Georgia ($18.04). The most industrialized counties in the United States in the late nineteenth century included some of the largest in the nation (see Table 2.3). However, there are a few surprises. The most unexpected, perhaps, is Peoria, Illinois, which headed the list. The manuscript census for 1890 has been lost so the basis for this extraordinarily large figure, more than twice that of the second-ranking county, is unknown. However, federal taxation of the production of liquor distilleries, highly concentrated in and around Peoria, probably accounts for a major part of the total value-added in the county.[11]

---

[9] By subtracting the value of the raw materials and intermediate goods that enter into the production process, the statistic controls for their value. By combining paid wages and capital depreciation, the statistic takes into account the contribution of both. One possible downside is that the inclusion of profits and losses, because they are both accentuated by the movements of the business cycle and rather oblique to a conception of industrial activity as a feature of the social landscape, can be viewed as somewhat muddying. In practice, however, nothing can be done because returns to capital cannot be separately calculated from the evidence available. However, while much of American industry was very profitable in the late nineteenth century, the error introduced by the inclusion of profits and losses is probably small.

[10] Calculated from returns published in the *1890 Census of Manufactures*, pt. 1, pp. 336–639.

[11] The census returns for Peoria apparently included, as an extraordinarily large item, the payment of federal internal revenue taxes on distilled liquor, far and away the largest industry in the county. For that reason, the figure reported as "miscellaneous expenses" in the table on pp. 398–399 of the *1890 Census of Manufactures* is extremely large compared with other Illinois counties. In fact, of the 165 largest cities in the country in 1890, only New York, Chicago, and Philadelphia reported larger absolute totals under "miscellaneous expenses" than did Peoria. *Atlas of the World*, vol. 2 (United States) (Chicago: Rand, McNally, 1895), pp. 346–347. On the particular geological factors that made Peoria County one of the nation's leading distillery producers, see *Report of the Industrial Commission: Preliminary Report on Trusts and Industrial Combinations*, vol. 1 (Washington, D.C.: GPO, 1900), p. 201.

Table 2.3. *The Most Industrialized Counties in the United States:*
1890 Per Capita Value-Added in Manufacturing

County/Major city/State	Value-added (1890)
Peoria/Peoria/Ill.	$651.18
Hamilton/Cincinnati/Ohio	289.81
New York/New York/N.Y.	271.10
Philadelphia/Philadelphia/Penn.	253.68
St. Louis City/St. Louis City/Mo.	236.72
Providence/Providence/R.I.	225.44
Suffolk/Boston/Mass.	224.90
Hampden/Springfield/Mass.	221.89
Essex/Lawrence/Mass.	220.58
Passaic/Passaic/N.J.	217.84
New Haven/New Haven/Conn.	216.48
Cook/Chicago/Ill.	215.51
Essex/Newark/N.J.	210.63
Wyandotte/Kansas City/Ks.	203.80
San Francisco/San Francisco/Calif.	190.53
Bristol/Fall River/Mass.	187.95
Multnomah/Portland/Ore.	181.00
Worcester/Worcester/Mass.	180.77
Monroe/Rochester/N.Y.	179.33
Milwaukee/Milwaukee/Wis.	179.10

Note and source: All figures are calculated from returns published in the *1890 Census of Manufactures* (Washington, D.C.: GPO, 1895), pt. 1, pp. 336–639.

Only three of the counties on this list, Wyandotte (Kansas City, Kansas), San Francisco, and Multnomah (Portland, Oregon), lay outside the nation's manufacturing belt. Kansas City's leading industry, meat packing, arose out of the city's role as a processing center for a hinterland extending west as far as the Colorado border. For the Pacific Coast cities, their remote location allowed a wide variety of industrial activities to flourish because transportation costs more than compensated for the greater efficiency of industrial plants in the manufacturing belt. None of the leading industrial counties were in the South where most cities specialized in processing the agricultural production of their immediate hinterlands. In Texas, for example, the leading industry in ten of the twenty-eight principal towns and cities was the refining of grain in flour and grist mills. In eleven others, cotton played a major role: cotton compresses (6), cottonseed-oil mills (3), bagging and cordage (1), and cotton and wool cloth factories (1). All of these arose out of the locational advantage conferred by the community's proximity to the production of a bulky agricultural product.[12] Dozens of counties in the United States, many of them very small, reported no manufacturing activity of any kind in 1890.[13]

The least industrialized areas of the nation tended to clump in four regions: the densely populated cotton plantation counties of the Mississippi Delta, the equally well-settled lower Rio Grande valley of Texas, the recently opened territory of the western Plains, and the isolated counties of the lower Appalachians (see Map 2.1). The most industrialized areas, commonly termed the "manufacturing belt," comprised all of New England and most of the other northeastern states (with the exception of West Virginia). The belt ranged westward through Ohio and Michigan, and petered out just west of the Mississippi River.[14] A second industrial area took in the major ports and market centers of the Pacific Coast between the ocean and the Cascades and Sierra Nevada mountains. In the remainder of the nation, the distribution of manufacturing activity was spotty.[15]

Not surprisingly, the relative concentration of industry was fairly closely related to the extent that it was an urban activity (see Table 2.4). For example, iron and steel production and liquor distilling, each of them yielding over $200,000 a year in value-added per establishment, were highly concentrated in medium to large cities. Many iron and steel plants, in fact, generated the cities in which they were located.[16] For liquor distilling, which employed many fewer workers, the distribution of establishments was driven by the need to locate near the major consumer markets of the nation. The clustering of textile mills at the falls of rivers could also create medium-sized urban centers. For example, Fall River, Massachusetts, contained sixty-five cotton factories located along the outlet of Watuppa Pond which, as it drained toward Mount Hope Bay and the Atlantic Ocean, dropped

---

[12] William F. Switzler, *Report on the Internal Commerce of the United States, 1889* (Washington, D.C.: GPO, 1889), pp. 703–709, 737.

[13] About 1,600 counties recorded less than $10 per capita value-added in manufacturing in the 1890 census. Another 900 or so came in under the national average of $67.40. Only 119 were over $100. About 2,740 counties reported to the census (the count is not exact because some county units had to be merged to create equivalent units for calculating statistics for the other referents).

[14] For a description of the manufacturing belt in 1910 very similar to the one given here, see David Ward, *Cities and Immigrants* (New York: Oxford University Press, 1971), pp. 39–46.

[15] In Colorado, for example, most manufacturing in 1890 was related to grain production (e.g., flour mills), railroads (rolling stock repair and miscellaneous construction in support of operations), and mining (e.g., custom manufacturing of machinery and tools). Such activities, with the addition of lumber mills and cotton/tobacco processing, account for much of the intermittent distribution of manufacturing in rural counties outside the eastern manufacturing belt and the less-industrialized strip hugging the Pacific Ocean.

[16] See, for example, William Serrin, *Homestead: The Glory and Tragedy of an American Steel Town* (New York: Random House, 1992), pp. 32–36.

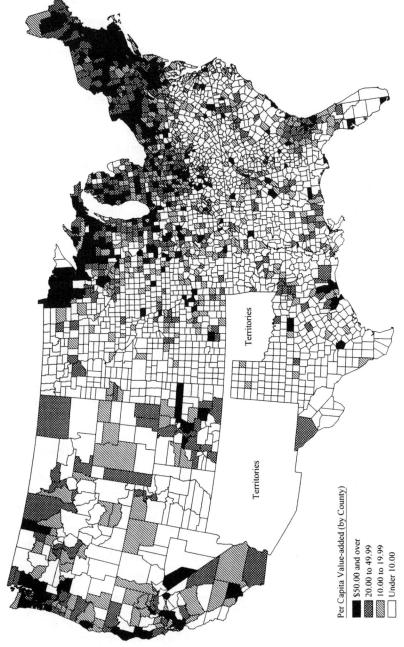

Per Capita Value-added (by County)

■ $50.00 and over
▨ 20.00 to 49.99
▧ 10.00 to 19.99
☐ Under 10.00

Territories

Territories

Map 2.1. Value-added in manufacturing, 1890. *Source: 1890 Census of Manufacturing* and the *1890 Census of Population.*

Table 2.4. *Leading Industries in the United States: Value-Added in Manufacturing, 1890*

Industrial sector	Total value-added	Number of establishments	Number of employees
Foundries/machine shops	$241,556,716	6,475	247,754
Printing and publishing	205,058,048	16,460	164,234
Lumber mill products	172,111,957	21,011	286,197
Carpentering	143,348,160	16,917	140,021
Iron and steel	135,176,505	645	152,535
Men's clothing/factory	122,172,752	4,867	156,341
Malt liquors	118,728,275	1,248	34,800
Cotton goods	113,068,745	905	221,585
Boots and shoes/factory	101,864,047	2,082	139,333
Brick and stone masonry	98,913,709	5,969	108,045
Distilled liquors	89,288,696	440	5,343
Flour and grist mills	79,819,184	18,470	63,481
Tobacco products	79,394,315	10,956	93,156
Finished wood products	78,754,718	3,670	86,888
Men's clothing/custom	75,724,514	13,591	86,143
Wagons and carriages	66,764,990	8,614	73,453
Wholesale meat packing	66,258,653	611	40,409
Railroad shops	62,900,172	716	108,585

Note and source: Because the figures reported in the table combine two separate entries in the source, some of the establishments may have been counted twice. Railroad shops comprise rolling stock repair and general construction by the railroad companies. Calculated from statistics in *Atlas of the World*, vol. 2: *United States* (Chicago: Rand, McNally, 1895), p. 345.

about 130 feet in the course of half a mile.[17] In the South, however, mill villages were much smaller, some of them surrounding but a single establishment. Railroad shops were also distributed more evenly throughout the nation. In this case, the association with major yards and the movement of rolling stock over the national network often placed their operations outside the nation's major metropolitan areas. But the major nonmetropolitan industries, in terms of number of establishments, value-added, and employment, were the processing of logs in lumber mills, the printing of newspapers, and the initial refining of the nation's major agricultural commodities (grain, cotton, and tobacco).

[17] *Lippincott's Gazetteer of the World* (Philadelphia: J. B. Lippincott, 1893), vol. 1, p. 1159.

Patent Activity and Technological Innovation

Patent filings record the amount of activity devoted to developing new technological solutions to problems associated with agricultural and industrial production. From this perspective, nineteenth-century inventive activity, as registered by the U.S. Patent Office, evidenced the relative accumulations of human capital, as well as the utilization of machines embodying new technologies and urbanization within the different regions of the nation.[18] As a group, these factors bear a strong family resemblance to one another; in fact, they are all so strongly intercorrelated as to be merely different facets of the same underlying phenomenon: a developed economy heavily dependent on the industrial utilization of advanced technological methods and machinery.[19]

In any given year, about 40 percent of patent applications were disallowed, usually on the ground that the claimed invention was not novel. Applications could also be disallowed on the basis of dysfunctionality or impracticality, but a persistent applicant, upon appeal, usually prevailed in such cases. Only the inventor, if alive, could apply for a patent, and all applicants were required to provide a model, drawing, and written specification of the invention. The original filing also required the payment of a fifteen-dollar fee. If the patent application was approved by the examiner, the inventor had to pay an additional twenty dollars to have it recorded. The invention was then protected for seventeen years.[20]

In 1892, the U.S. Patent Office granted 22,661 patents to American inventors.[21] For the nation as a whole, there were 3.65 patents issued per

---

[18] William H. Phillips, "Patent Growth in the Old Dominion: The Impact of Railroad Integration before 1880," *Journal of Economic History* 52:2 (June 1992): 389–400; Ross Thomson, "Learning by Selling and Invention: The Case of the Sewing Machine," *Journal of Economic History* 47:2 (June 1987): 433–445, and his *The Path to Mechanized Shoe Production in the United States* (Chapel Hill: University of North Carolina Press, 1989), particularly pp. 235–244.

[19] For a discussion of the intimate connections between technological innovation and the pace of late nineteenth-century industrialization in the United States, see Alfred D. Chandler, Jr., *The Visible Hand: The Managerial Revolution in American Business* (Cambridge, Mass.: Harvard University Press, 1977), pp. 240–244, 280–281. For a concise history of the U.S. Patent Office that emphasized the close connection between local levels of industrial development and the frequency of patenting, see the *Congressional Record*, 48:1:2408–2424, March 31, 1884. For a contemporary description of the patenting process, see *Appleton's Annual Cyclopaedia of 1883* (New York: D. Appleton, 1884), pp. 618–625.

[20] A good description of the history and operation of the patent office appears in the *New Americanized Encyclopaedia Britannica* (Akron, Ohio: Saalfield Publishing, 1903), vol. 11, pp. 2309–2323.

[21] *1892 Annual Report of the Commissioner of Patents* (Washington, D.C.: GPO, 1893), pp. 1–411. The annual report listed the name and residence of the inventor and a brief indication of the type of invention for which a patent was granted.

10,000 population. The leading states in terms of relative patent activity were all in New England: Connecticut (with 9.67 per 10,000 residents), Massachusetts (8.11), and Rhode Island (6.80). At the bottom of the national list were the southern states of Mississippi (0.42), Georgia (0.52), Alabama (0.68), Tennessee (0.74), Virginia (0.89), and Arkansas (0.90).[22] Hundreds of counties recorded no patents in 1892 and hundreds more reported only one or two. Of the counties recording five or more patents, thirteen possessed rates of activity greater than ten per 10,000 population. Most of these counties were large cities with diversified industrial bases (e.g., Boston, Chicago, Hartford, Newark, New Haven, Akron, and South Bend).

There are at least three shortcomings associated with the use of patents as an indicator of inventive activity. First, the administrative barriers for recording a patent were not very high; individuals willing to go to the trouble could often press an application to completion even when the proposed device was novel only in its unique impracticality. For that reason, those desiring a local reputation as inventors in their communities could almost literally buy patents for their ideas.[23] Since only one or two patents in a small county would give it a fairly high relative rate, the data for smaller counties sometimes recorded idiosyncratic filings only distantly, if at all, related to practical inventive activity.

Second, patent approval was not synonymous with patent protection. In infringement cases, the federal courts ruled invalid almost a third of patents approved by the Patent Office. In many of these cases, the invention was considered to be insufficiently novel or documented. Finally, rapidly expanding industrial corporations based on advanced technology sometimes indiscriminantly bought up relevant patents, whatever their source, in order to maintain control over their markets. Such a strategy tended to encourage the recording of patents that were not, in fact, innovative as a way of attracting the acquisitive attention of these companies.[24] Other

---

[22] For similar descriptions of the geographical pattern of patent activity in this and other years, see *Appleton's Annual Cyclopaedia of 1891* (New York: D. Appleton, 1892), p. 700; *Appleton's Annual Cyclopaedia of 1892* (New York: D. Appleton, 1893), pp. 616–617. The rankings of the states in terms of patent activity were remarkably stable over much of the nineteenth century. For these rankings in the years 1840, 1850, 1860, 1870, 1880, and 1883, see the *Congressional Record* 48:1:2415, March 31, 1884.

[23] Popular guides to patenting, complete with practical descriptions of the process and forms for filing, were published in the late nineteenth century. See, for example, W. B. Hutchinson and J. A. E. Criswell, *Patents and How to Make Money Out of Them* (New York: Fidelity Publishing, 1899). Such guides substantially reduced the cost of filing patent claims for individuals residing outside the major cities of the manufacturing belt.

[24] Such corporate strategies were public knowledge in the late nineteenth century. As the *Commercial and Financial Chronicle* reported, "the foundation patent [for the telephone industry] is running out but telephoning will not be free when it expires.

corporations raced ahead with technological innovations that might have warranted patenting but were not recorded because they represented only temporary intermediate solutions preceeding larger and more encompassing innovations. In the former case, corporate strategies probably generated too much patent activity, relative to actual technological development, and, in the latter, too little.[25]

For the nation as a whole, the pattern of patent distribution (see Map 2.2) was much like the one for manufacturing, with two important differences. First, in the North, patent filings were more evenly distributed than was the case for manufacturing, with largely agricultural counties in the western plains and many mountain regions (particularly those in which mining played a major role in the local economy) showing up as significant sites of inventive activity. While the major industrial regions in the North were still the dominant contributors to patent activity, the overall pattern was much less concentrated. Second, with the exception of central and west Texas and middle and southern Florida, large areas of the South reported almost no inventive activity whatsoever. Furthermore, manufacturing and patents appear to have been almost entirely uncorrelated in that region, which is surprising given the rather close relationship between the two in the North.

One of the reasons for including patents as an indicator of economic development is to distinguish a kind of "colonial" industrialization from an advanced economy. A "colonial" industry is one in which a low-cost work force and resource base is exploited without a deepening of the economic potential of the region; industry located in an advanced economy, on the other hand, often incorporates invention as a more or less routinized part of the industrial process. As a result, in an advanced economy, industrial operations both facilitate and come to depend on the expansion of auxiliary technological services such as professional training and research in universities, the fabrication of custom machinery, financial markets providing start-up capital for new products, and the legal services necessary for recording and adjudicating claims on creative productions.[26] The

The American Bell Telephone Company has from the beginning adopted the policy of buying every useful patent; and the licenses of this company will be in occupation of the territory, which is a strong point in their favor [as an investment]." June 27, 1885.

25 On patent litigation and corporate strategies, see Lawrence M. Friedman, *A History of American Law* (New York: Simon & Schuster, 1973), pp. 301, 380–381. On the diminishing reliance on patents by at least some high-technology firms, see Chandler, *The Visible Hand*, pp. 373–374.

26 Within the manufacturing belt, the agglomeration of local capital, utilization of technologically advanced machinery, custom fabricating and repair shops, and access to other support services created, in effect, a creative "soup" in which lone-wolf inventive activity thrived. Independent inventors were later largely replaced by professional technicians within research and development divisions of industrial corporations.

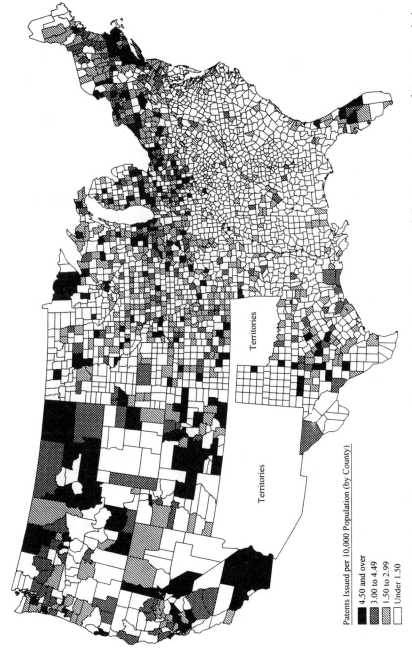

Patents Issued per 10,000 Population (by County)

■ 4.50 and over
▨ 3.00 to 4.49
▦ 1.50 to 2.99
☐ Under 1.50

Map 2.2. Distribution of patents, 1892. *Source: 1892 Annual Report of the Commissioner of Patents and the 1890 Census of Population.*

American South in the late nineteenth century was clearly a nonindustrial region. It was even more emphatically, in this sense, a colonial one.[27]

Adult Illiteracy and Human Capital

One of the major reasons that southern industrialization assumed a colonial form was the lack of skills in the local labor force. While such skills were not often required in mass production processes in the late nineteenth century, they were necessary to invention and the auxiliary services and institutions supporting technological development. And here the South was clearly lagging. While the Census did not systematically collect data on technical skills available in local labor markets, a good proxy, from a perspective of base expectations, is the literacy rate. In 1900, the Bureau of the Census enumerated the number of adult males over twenty-one who could read and write in any language (categorized as literate) and those who could neither read nor write (categorized as illiterate).[28] The South held all of the lowest rungs on the literacy ladder, starting with Louisiana (37.6% of all males of voting age were illiterate) and continuing with South Carolina (35.1), Mississippi (33.8), Alabama (33.7), Georgia (31.6), North Carolina (29.4), and Virginia (25.3). Many states reported illiteracy rates under 10 percent, the lowest among them were: Nebraska (2.5), Iowa (2.7), Kansas (3.4), Washington (3.4), Utah (3.7), Colorado (4.1), and Minnesota (4.1).[29]

Three broad patterns underlay the national distribution of illiterates. The

John Nader, "The Rise of an Inventive Profession: Learning Effects in the Midwestern Harvester Industry, 1850–1890," *Journal of Economic History* 54:2 (June 1994): 397–408.

[27] Perhaps the most striking exception to the otherwise overwhelming technological dependence of the South on northern inventive activity was in the area of cotton ginning. See William H. Phillips, "Making a Business of It: The Evolution of Southern Cotton Gin Patenting, 1831–1890," *Agricultural History* 68:2 (Spring 1994): 80–91.

[28] Those who could read but not write were also classified as illiterate. Because the census did not administer a test and, thus, relied on the self-description of respondents, literacy data is somewhat suspect. For example, respondents in some unknown percentage of cases undoubtedly felt social pressure to report an ability to read and write when, in fact, they could not do so. This problem was probably more serious in areas where literacy rates were already high (and the social stigma attached to illiteracy correspondingly greater) than in areas where rates were lower and than in the twentieth century (in which national literacy rates had risen across the board). Carl F. Kaestle et al., *Literacy in the United States: Readers and Reading since 1880* (New Haven, Conn.: Yale University Press, 1991), pp. 78–80.

[29] Because of the increasing interest in literacy tests as a voting qualification, the data were collected in this form for the first time. Before 1900, literacy figures are available only for those aged ten and over. See the *1900 Census of Population* (Washington, D.C.: GPO, 1901), pt. 1, tables XCIV, XCV, and 92, pp. cciii, cciv, ccv, and 970–1006.

first was the presence or absence of foreign-born males in the local population. While the illiteracy rate among native-born males (10.5%) was little different from that for foreign-born males (12.2), the rate for immigrants was marginally higher in the Northeast (15.3), and that discrepancy explains the absence of eastern states from the highest rungs of the literacy ladder.[30] However, this was but a minor deviation in the national pattern. More significant was the difference in illiteracy rates between the North and South. For native whites with native parents, the highest illiteracy rates were recorded in Louisiana (20.3), North Carolina (19.0), and Kentucky (15.5). In most northern states, the corresponding figure was well under 5 percent. However, the most significant factor was the extremely low literacy rates among nonwhite adult males. Almost half these men (46.8%) could not read and write in any language. And these rates were far higher in the South where nonwhites constituted a much greater proportion of the local population. Louisiana, for example, reported an illiteracy rate of 61.2 percent among nonwhites. In Alabama, Georgia, Mississippi, North Carolina, South Carolina, and Virginia, more than half of all nonwhite males (almost all the nonwhite population was black) were illiterate. In other parts of the country, local concentrations of Native Americans or Chinese sometimes produced comparable rates but, on the whole, nonwhite literacy rates were much higher than in the South. In the Northeast, for example, almost five out of every six nonwhites could read and write.[31]

In different ways, then, race and region shaped the national pattern of illiteracy. Race contributed to the distribution because the rate was always higher among nonwhites than whites, regardless of region. Region was important in two ways: First, because the illiteracy rate among nonwhites was much higher in the South, and, second, because most nonwhites were concentrated in that region. The illiteracy rate among southern blacks was largely a historical product in that the teaching of slaves to read and write had been socially discouraged and often illegal. In the postwar period, southern educational institutions failed to compensate for this inheritance, although there was a strong and positive pattern of increasing literacy among younger age cohorts. As a result, despite the fact that educational expenditures, already low compared with the rest of the nation, were increasingly diverted from black to white schools, literacy rates for younger blacks were steadily rising.[32] This diversion of educational expenditures

---

[30] Both rates were marginally higher than the corresponding proportions of adult males who were illiterate in England (three percent) and France (six percent) but comparable to Belgium (almost twelve, for army recruits). Kaestle, et al., *Literacy in the United States*, pp. 18–19.

[31] *1900 Census of Population*, Tables XCIV, XCV and CIV, pp. cciv–ccv, ccxvi. Almost nine of ten immigrant males of voting age (88.4%) could speak English.

[32] Robert A. Margo, *Race and Schooling in the South, 1880–1950: An Economic History* (Chicago: University of Chicago Press, 1990), pp. 6–9, 20–23, 33, 37, 43.

occurred even though southern blacks in many ways expressed a strong interest in educating their children. As one Georgia official noted, "the colored people manifest a great desire to have their children educated.... Their schools are overflowing whenever opened...." This was thus a supply-side failure.[33] Given the poverty of the region, the South could not have established an educational system as extensive or lavishly supported as that in the North. However, an educational system that could have eliminated illiteracy, for both races, was probably within the region's reach.[34]

All of these factors combined to produce the pattern depicted in Map 2.3. Illiteracy rates were highest in the southern black belt where cotton cultivation, tenancy, and the black proportion of the local population were all greatest. Beyond the black belt, in one of the one most strikingly regular social patterns recorded in the late nineteenth century, illiteracy rates shaded steadily downward. For example, the largely white uplands of the Ozarks and lower Appalachians recorded very high illiteracy rates, only marginally lower than those prevailing in the black belt. In rural areas of the North and West, however, illiteracy was rare.[35]

---

[33] Ibid., p. 45.

[34] The resource base for educational institutions varied greatly within the South. In upland and mountain regions, for example, poor whites could not have supported an adequate school system without state aid and, even if such a system had been established, would have had difficulty sparing their children from the fields in order that they might attend. In the much wealthier black belt, outside assistance was unnecessary for adequately supporting local schools but racial discrimination openly worked against the establishment of an effective system through a fair distribution of resources to black schools. Margo, *Race and Schooling in the South*, p. 37. Cursory inspection of literacy rates by county suggest that black and native white literacy rates were inversely related. For whites, illiteracy was highest in upland white counties, while black-belt whites had abundant resources to educate their children. However, black-belt whites refused to adequately fund black school systems, while, for reasons that are not clear, black literacy tended to be relatively higher in white upland counties.

[35] Other factors only slightly modify the otherwise stark national pattern. In the northern reaches of New England and New York, for example, the spillover of French Canadians – themselves an impoverished minority within Canada – appears to have marginally reduced literacy rates. As in the Northeast, lumber and mining operations along the northern border from Michigan to Washington tended to employ large numbers of often illiterate immigrants from a wide variety of nations. These lumber regions thus reported lower literacy rates than the surrounding agricultural counties. Immigrant work forces in the mining counties of the Mountain West accounted for the slightly higher rates in those areas as well. Counties containing Indian reservations also reported high illiteracy rates (e.g., the Dakotas and Montana). Similarly, Hispanic populations along the Rio Grande in southern Texas reported very high rates. It should be remembered that all of these ethnic groups, whatever their native tongue, could have been identified as "literate" if they could read and write in that language.

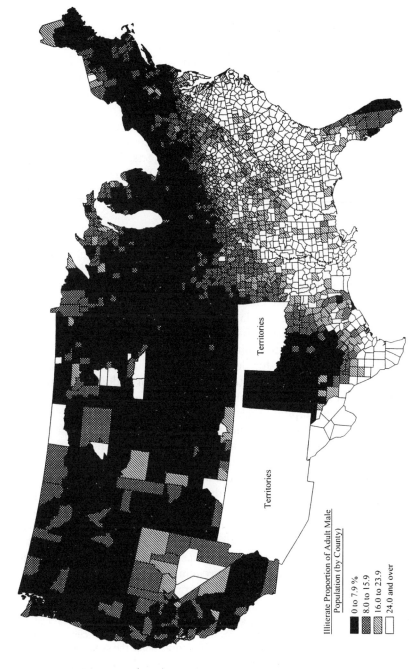

Illiterate Proportion of Adult Male
Population (by County)

■ 0 to 7.9 %
▨ 8.0 to 15.9
▧ 16.0 to 23.9
□ 24.0 and over

Territories

Territories

Map 2.3. Illiteracy among adult males, 1900. *Source: 1900 Census of Population.*

Accumulated Wealth and Capital Stock

At the onset of industrialization, the United States was predominantly an agricultural society, and most accumulated wealth was locked up in the capital stock of farms, plantations, and the transportation and commercial facilities that moved crops to market. During the late nineteenth century, this accumulated wealth, particularly in older regions east of the Mississippi and north of the Ohio, became a major source of capital underpinning industrial expansion and construction of the urban infrastructure. In the East such capital poured into local projects, both corporate and government, without crossing state lines. In the West, eastern capital was a major factor behind the rapid integration of the region into the national economy. In the South, there was little capital to be had, either native or imported.

Because much of the accumulated capital stock in the United States lay in the eastern agricultural sector and because the investment that drove industrial development moved between regions, the spatial distribution of tangible wealth increasingly diverged from the pattern of ownership of industry, railroads, and financial institutions. In the East, wealth statistics are a good referent for accumulated capital stock and, at the same time, accurately imply that local wealth-holders owned the property entering into the totals. However, because capital had been flowing out of the East and into the Midwest and West for decades, the data understate the extent of regional wealth by omitting eastern ownership of industrial plants and financial institutions in other regions. In the West, wealth statistics are again a good referent for capital stock but overstate local ownership because many of the wealth-holders for industry and banks resided in the East or Europe. With these reservations taken into account, wealth statistics are still indispensable for estimating the amount of capital per person that entered into productive activity in the late nineteenth century.

Although the tangible property of the nation had been recorded in prior enumerations, the data gathered by the 1890 census was both more complete and carefully collected. The result, after much approximation, placed a value of just over $65 billion on all tangible property in the United States (see Table 2.5). A little more than 60 percent of this total was accounted for by real estate (land with fixed improvements such as buildings but not including mines, telephones, telegraphs, or railroad property).[36] The second

---

[36] In some states railroad property (e.g., station houses, repair shops, and roadbed) was classified as real estate for the purposes of taxation, but state agencies did not separate out the value of such property in their reports. Since the census relied on state statistics for part of the valuation of this category, the inclusion of railroad property in some but not all cases introduced variation in the data between those states that included railroad assets and those that did not. The relatively high values placed on real estate in west Texas (see Map 2.4) was probably due to the fact that public land

Table 2.5. *Total Value of All Tangible Property in the United States, 1890*

Real estate, with improvements	$39,544,544,333
Railroads and rolling stock	8,685,407,323
Miscellaneous	7,893,708,821
Machinery of mills and inventories	3,058,593,441
Livestock on farms, farm implements	2,703,015,040
Mines and quarries, including inventories	1,291,291,579
Gold and silver coin and bullion	1,158,774,948
Telegraphs, telephones, shipping, canals	701,755,712
National total	$65,037,091,197

Source: *1890 Census of Wealth, Debt, and Taxation* (Washington, D.C.: GPO, 1895), p. 7.

largest entry, that for railroads and rolling stock, was much smaller, standing at about 13 percent of the total. A miscellaneous category, in which an estimate of $400 per house (for furniture, tools, and carriages) yielded about $5 billion of the total, was the third largest entry.[37] Other major items in this entry included the tangible property of national, state, and local governments, as well as merchant inventories and stocks of agricultural commodities held off the farm. The remaining categories contributed under 14 percent to the combined total.

Only the real estate entry was broken down by county by the census. But the effort and care with which the data were assembled was remarkable. Since the assessed valuations of taxable property were publicly available throughout the nation and subject to challenge (in that those who were overassessed had reason to appeal an assessment), the census relied on this data as a first approximation of the value of real estate and improvements.

in that region was owned by the state rather than the federal government. The value of unsold federal land was estimated by the census at $1.25 an acre throughout the country (evidently based on the nominal price of land under the Homestead Act). However, the census did not break down this entry by counties. Texas was both a frontier state (at least in its western portion) and held no federal land (because it entered the union as a previously independent nation, not a territory). In many of the unsettled western counties in Texas the value of vacant state-owned land appears to have been set at $2 an acre and included in the county figures. Because so few people lived in these counties, this produced abnormally high figures for per capita wealth. For a general description of the collection of wealth data, see *1890 Census of Wealth, Debt, and Taxation* (Washington, D.C.: GPO, 1895), pp. 7–11.

[37] Because it was applied throughout the country, this universal household estimate seriously overestimated the capital stock associated with southern homes while, less certainly, underestimating the stock of homes in the remainder of the nation.

However, this data had to be adjusted for varying relationships between the assessed and market valuations. So, as the first step in adjusting these statistics, the census sent questionnaires out to county and municipal officials asking them to estimate the relationship between the assessed and market value of real estate and improvements within their respective jurisdictions. In addition to these requests, the census sent out more than 25,000 questionnaires (more than eight, on the average, to every county in the nation) asking private and public individuals to independently estimate the same relationship. These reports were then checked against the estimates of the value of farm land independently recorded by the agricultural census. Finally, once the census had arrived at a tabulation of the value of real estate for every county, the reports were sent out to each of the respective governors, asking them to corroborate the estimates as best they could. In no case did the census attempt to independently estimate the value of real estate.

Although the procedures used to collect them are not without flaws, the data document one of the most important dimensions of relative economic development: the amount of fixed capital investment in land improvements, transportation facilities, and buildings (see Map 2.4). The total value of all real estate with fixed improvements, both public and private, came to about $637 per capita in 1890. The highest per capita value was reported in Washington State ($1,374), followed by Colorado ($1,339), California ($1,327), Oregon ($1,090), and New York ($970). As the census noted, the "valuation per capita of some counties situated in sections recently settled is relatively very high, owing it is thought, to a large portion of the property being held by nonresidents."[38] Most areas in the Pacific Coast states and the Mountain West were only recently settled, and the very high per capita values reported for these regions appear to indicate an exploitation pattern in which imported capital, from the East and Europe, generally outpaced human settlement. That pattern, for example, explains (1) the relatively high per capita value of real estate and improvements, (2) the relatively high proportion of adult males in the local work force and general population, and (3) the relatively high wages paid in order to attract workers.

All of these relationships were turned on their head in the South, and, as a consequence, per capita values were but a minor fraction of those in the West. In fact, the bottom five states in the nation were all southern: South Carolina ($153 per capita), Mississippi ($160), North Carolina ($172), Alabama ($178), and Arkansas ($202). Outside of west Texas and southern Florida (areas where western settlement patterns prevailed), only a few urban counties, such as those containing Atlanta, Birmingham, Chattanooga, Little Rock, and Savannah, recorded per capita real estate wealth much above the national average.

[38]   *1890 Census of Wealth*, p. 9.

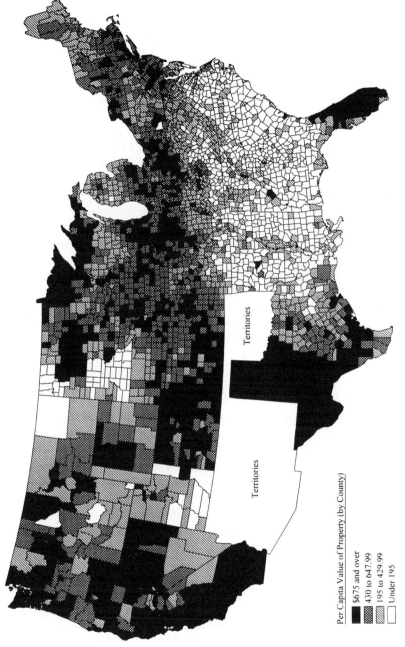

Per Capita Value of Property (by County)

■ $675 and over
▦ 430 to 647.99
▨ 195 to 429.99
☐ Under 195

Map 2.4. Value of tangible property, 1890. *Source: 1890 Census of Wealth, Debt and Taxation and the 1890 Census of Population.*

In 1890, about 120 counties reported per capita real estate valuations of $100 or less. Almost all of these were located in the South with the poorest among them primarily reliant on cotton. Another 600 or so reported per capita valuations of between $100 and $200. Although a slightly higher proportion of these were in the North and West, the vast majority of counties in this range were also located in the South. In fact, a majority of all southern counties reported valuations of under $200. As a measure of relative accumulated wealth in the region, this statistic was not misleading – the South neither possessed a significant indigenous stock of capital nor was investment flowing into the region from the East or Europe. And once it is recognized that real estate was the primary tax base for the support of public schools throughout the United States, the sheer material difficulty of establishing an adequate educational system, regardless of the biases introduced by race segregation and progressive disfranchisement of the lower classes, becomes apparent.[39] Without outside aid, the region faced a complex "chicken and egg" problem; to encourage economic development, the South needed to improve the educational system, but improving the educational system required an expanded tax base that only economic development could provide. The potential tax base for schools throughout the North and West was almost always at least twice as great as the average in the South and, for most counties, between three and seven times greater. Thus, the close similarity between the patterns in Maps 2.3 and 2.4 should come as no surprise.

Interest Rates on Home and Farm Mortgages

Economists have long postulated that, in a perfectly integrated and friction-free national market, interest rates would not vary from region to region or from locality to locality within regions. Operating on that assumption they have theorized that interest rates should be lowest within the most tightly integrated capital markets and steadily rise as regions become increasingly peripheral to those markets. Thus, the data on farm and home mortgages – the best such data source available from the 1890 census – is used here to indicate the relative integration of local communities and regions into the national capital market.[40] While these rates do not identify

---

[39] In his testimony before the Industrial Commission, for example, the black president of the Colored Normal, Industrial, Agricultural and Mechanical College of South Carolina lamented failure of the Blair bill in the Fifty-first Congress, a measure that would have provided federal subsidies to public education, because his state had reached the material limits of local taxation. *Report of the Industrial Commission: Immigration and Education*, vol. 15 (Washington, D.C.: GPO, 1901), p. 120.

[40] In a consensus summary of the literature, Howard Bodenhorn has proposed three general criteria for determining the extent of capital market integration among the

the direction of capital movements within the United States, they do summarize the relative integration of the nation's regions into the financial system by describing the terms upon which capital from all sources could be obtained.

Largely at the instigation of local chapters of the Single Tax League and a number of farm and labor organizations such as the Farmers' Alliance, the Patrons of Husbandry, and Knights of Labor, information on the interest rate and principal of home and farm mortgages was collected for the first time in 1890.[41] In collecting this data, federal enumerators, somewhat to their surprise, reported that rural residents readily responded to their questions. In the first round, however, the queries were restricted to whether or not the farm or home was mortgaged, ignoring the amount of the mortgage or the rate of interest. In the second round, a mail survey was sent out to the list of farms and homes that had reported a mortgage. The response rate was quite high to this survey and the census supplemented it with a house visit in most areas of the North and West where the householder or farm owner failed to answer. This procedure was considered quite sufficient in all the states of the union except Kentucky and the states of the former Confederacy (aside from Virginia). In those states, illiteracy among rural blacks and whites was so prevalent that special agents visited the individual counties and collected the necessary information from public officials. This procedure probably underestimated prevailing interest rates in the South to some extent, and this underestimation is the most significant draw-

---

nation's regions in the nineteenth century. Two are statistical: (1) equality or approximate equality of interest rates across the regions and (2) a high correlation of price movements across the regions over time (he particularly emphasizes the movement of short-term rates). The last criterion is both more qualitative and slightly oblique to the others: an efficiency standard based on the "fundamental characteristic of an efficient market [which is] that prices reflect the use of all relevant available information by market participants." "Capital Mobility and Financial Integration in Antebellum America," *Journal of Economic History* 52:3 (September 1992): 590–593. The use of mortgage interest rates as an indicator for capital market integration has the advantage of availability at the county level (and thus can be aggregated into congressional districts, trade areas, etc.). In addition, short-term rates were recorded only in active markets, of which, as Bodenhorn notes, there were very few in the South and West. (On the relative absence of active short-term markets in the postwar period, see *Commercial and Financial Chronicle*, March 20, 1886.) On the utility of interest rates as a referent for relative financial development, see John A. James, "Financial Underdevelopment in the Postbellum South," *Journal of Interdisciplinary History* 11 (Winter 1981): 444–445; John A. James, "The Development of the National Money Market, 1893–1911," *Journal of Economic History* 36 (December 1976): 878–897; Kerry A. Odell, "The Integration of Regional and Interregional Capital Markets: Evidence from the Pacific Coast States, 1883–1913," *Journal of Economic History* 49:2 (June 1989): 297–310.

[41] For a brief history of the popular call for the mortgage census, see *1890 Census of Farms and Homes: Proprietorship and Indebtedness*, vol. 13 (Washington, D.C.: GPO, 1896), pp. 3–4.

back in the data.[42] Otherwise, the data on mortgage rates applies to roughly the same form of debt throughout the nation and is therefore quite comparable from region to region.

In 1890, the average national interest rate on farm and home mortgages, computed on the total principal, was 6.65 percent. As economists would predict, Manhattan County, the heart of New York City and the site of the country's major financial and commodity markets, recorded the lowest interest rate in the nation (4.95%). The five states with the lowest interest rates and thus the most tightly integrated into the national capital market were Connecticut (5.47), New York (5.48), Massachusetts (5.49), Pennsylvania (5.49), and New Jersey (5.64). Occupying the topmost rungs of the financial hierarchy, these five capital-rich northeastern states had long been significant lenders to the remainder of the country, particularly the Plains and Mountain states. The latter, along with the Deep South, gathered at the bottom rungs of the financial ladder. Largely because of difficulties associated with determining risk along the western frontier (because local financial institutions were primitive, if they existed at all), the highest rates in the nation were recorded by the states of Montana (10.97%) and Idaho (10.66). Other western states were also high: Utah (9.83), Nevada (9.78), Washington (9.63), North Dakota (9.53), and South Dakota (9.52). Three southern states recorded rates greater than 9 percent: Florida (10.53), Mississippi (9.74), and Arkansas (9.44). While these rates were similar, in reality the southern and western states related to the national capital market in significantly different ways. In the West, capital was imported into the region in great quantities from the East and thus available, although expensive. Although rates were almost equally high in the South, capital was often simply unavailable.

Rising as a more or less simple function of distance from the nation's major financial markets in New York City, the distribution of interest rates

---

[42]   In many counties of the South, these public officials apparently reported, as the average rate of interest on mortgages, the highest rate of interest permitted under the prevailing usury law. For that reason and the fact that formal mortgages were relatively rare in the South generally (so that what might be called an active mortgage market can hardly be said to have existed), several southern states were recorded as having identical interest rates throughout their territory. In Arkansas, for example, 31 counties reported average rates of exactly 10 percent on farm mortgages (the usury ceiling), an additional 40 reported varying rates below 10, and only four counties reported rates above 10 percent. Many of these usury laws contained loopholes that made circumvention relatively easy and enforcement correspondingly lax. For that reason and because of the relative absence of active money markets in the South, the data on southern counties should be viewed both as a lower bound to interest rates and as a slightly creative result in which the picture conveyed of an "average rate" overrepresents the existence of a competitive and active market. *1890 Census of Farms and Homes*, pp. 4–7, 103, 113, 431. On the informality of southern and western mortgage loans and the consequent difficulty in ascertaining the actual, as opposed to nominal, interest rates, see *1890 Census of Real Estate Mortgages* (Washington, D.C.: GPO, 1895), pp. 7–11, 168.

displays a very regular geographical pattern (see Map 2.5).[43] For example, interest rates gradually rose with increasing distance westward of New York, the general pattern intermixed with small areas of locally lower rates in and around major cities such as Chicago, Milwaukee, St. Louis, and San Francisco. A number of risk and cost factors, related to the distance which capital had to travel from East to West, shaped this pattern. Some of these concerned the likelihood that electorates in capital-importing regions would permit the repayment of private and public debt. Others arose out of the higher servicing costs associated with packaging and marketing western mortgages in the East and Europe. In addition, the breadth and depth of the national financial system attenuated with distance, ultimately reaching the sparsely populated and capital-hungry expanses of the Rocky Mountains. There borrowers involved in highly profitable commercial operations (such as mining) bargained with local bankers who exploited their connections with eastern financial centers. The net results were very high interest rates and a thriving capital market.

Throughout American history, interest rates had always been relatively high on the frontier and steadily declined as settlement proceeded. Thus, the regional pattern of interest rates in 1890 simply reflected the historical regularity of most westward settlement; the distance gradient as one traveled west reflected the greater administrative costs, reliance on capital imports, and political risks that had always characterized the frontier and recently settled regions. Interest rates also rose across the South but the gradient was both steeper and relatively unrelated to frontier development.[44]

For the pricing of capital to have been equal across the nation's regions in the late nineteenth century, the South and West would have had to have matched the East in terms of the institutional efficiency of assessing

[43] The anomalies in Macon County (Alabama) and White Pine County (Nevada) involved very small numbers and may have been due to eccentricities in the local reports. Macon reported twelve mortgages averaging a little over $1,200; White Pine reported just two mortgages averaging a little under $7,000 apiece. In both cases, home mortgage rates were much closer to rates prevailing in the remainder of their respective states while farm mortgages were anomalously low. Calculated from data in *1890 Census of Farms and Homes*, pp. 430, 451. While the numbers in west Texas were also very small, the clumping pattern suggests a more systematic cause.

[44] As noted previously, the southern data should be interpreted as a lower bound for actual interest rates because of the evident tendency of local officials to report rates that conformed with state usury laws, regardless of what may have been the actual rates in their communities. This tendency, for example, explains the importance of state lines in the southern portion of the national pattern. For example, the abrupt transition between rates under 7 percent in Tennessee to rates over 8 percent in neighboring communities across the state's border to the south and west is almost certainly an artifact of the reports, not the actual pattern of rates on the ground. Similarly, the steep gradient along the Virginia–North Carolina border is probably an artifact of the reports. The Kentucky case is not so clear but there is a great deal of clumping in the data for that state around 6 percent as well.

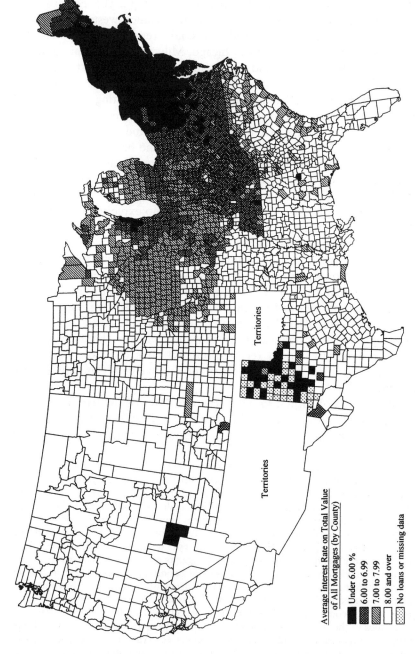

Under 6.00 %

6.00 to 6.99

7.00 to 7.99

8.00 and over

No loans or missing data

Territories

Territories

Map 2.5. Farm and home mortgage interest rates, 1890. *Source: 1890 Census of Real Estate Mortgages.*

the credit-worthiness of borrowers, the comparative impact of unforeseen economic conditions on the ability of borrowers to repay debt, the administrative costs associated with the servicing and management of loans, and the risk that local political units would intervene unfavorably to creditors. In other words, the very foundations of the political economies, in all their breadth, would have had to converge on the qualities that typified the eastern manufacturing belt. This conclusion, in turn, carries at least two important implications. First, a restructuring of the financial system, taken alone, would not have eliminated rate differentials between the regions. Second, these differentials in rates were and are a much more comprehensive referent for relative economic development than has been commonly understood. Instead of being solely a measure of integration into a national capital market, understood in purely financial terms, relative interest rates were in fact deeply embedded within and thus reflected the most fundamental characteristics of their respective regional political economies.

Summary: The Broad Index of Relative Economic Development

These five referents each describe a different aspect of late nineteenth-century industrial development. The most relevant, of course, are the data on per capita value-added in manufacturing because this statistic directly records the density of industrial activity. The data on patents complements this manufacturing statistic by discriminating between regions in which technological innovation accompanied industrial activity and those areas in which a more colonial pattern prevailed. In the latter, the absence of venture capital markets, auxiliary technical services, and professional training hampered innovation, producing a situation in which industrial processes were imported from other regions and local workers and producers of raw materials had to adapt to them. In the manufacturing belt, on the other hand, technological innovation was an ongoing activity in which local conditions in the labor market and the regional resource endowment continually fed back into the organization and design of the industrial process.

Adult male illiteracy complements the manufacturing data. While it would be easy to overestimate the importance of a skilled work force to industrial operations in the late nineteenth century and, in addition, to over-represent the connection between literacy and the acquisition of industrial skills, local investment in human capital still played a role in increasing the adaptability of workers to changing tasks and roles within the industrial process.[45]

---

[45] In addition, the complexity of the social infrastructure surrounding and supporting industrialization was probably constrained by high illiteracy rates – to cite just one example, the cooperation of the citizenry in obeying city ordinances and sanitary regulations depended in some part on their ability to read them.

Complementing all of the above, because it recorded both past capital accumulation (in the East) and the pace of capital investment (in the West), were the statistics on per capita wealth. The value of tangible real estate and fixed improvements underwrote local capacity to sustain growth: the ability of the local tax base to support government services and investment in infrastructure, the depth of local capital investment per worker (thus measuring, to some extent, relative capital intensity in local production), and the availability of indigenous capital as a source of investment. While, as was previously noted, this statistic does not distinguish between imported and native capital investment and thus introduces some ambiguity with respect to what exactly is referenced when comparing eastern and western communities, per capita wealth is very useful in recording the extremely large discrepancies between the capital endowments of the North and South. When combined with farm and home mortgage interest rates, which indicate the relative integration of regional financial markets, the precise relationship between the East and West in terms of the endogeneity of local capital endowments is easily untangled; those areas with high capital endowments and low interest rates relied on local investment while regions with high capital endowments and high interest rates depended on outside investment.

In part because the data usually contain minor systematic distortions of the conditions in local communities, each statistic is better viewed as a general, rather than precise, indicator of relative development along each of the five dimensions. For that reason, the developmental index constructed for each county rests on the determination of a simple relationship: the correspondence between the county's figure on each indicator and the national average. If, for example, the county reported a per capita value-added in manufacturing figure greater than the national average, the county was assigned a score of one; if equal or less, a score of zero. Corresponding scores were calculated for patents and wealth. With respect to illiteracy and interest rates, county figures lower than the national average indicated greater development and were awarded scores of one. All five scores were then added together, creating an overall developmental index ranging from five (a better than average score along each dimension) to zero (a worse than average score along each dimension).

Forty-eight counties in the United States had a developmental index of five, the highest possible score (see Table 2.6). Every one of them lay in the manufacturing belt of the nation, ranging from Boston in the northeast corner; Washington, D.C., and Louisville, Kentucky, in the south; and Milwaukee and St. Louis to the northwest and west. However, the greatest concentration of highly developed counties lay in a narrower region extending from the eastern seaboard north of Virginia to the western border of Ohio. New York State alone accounted for almost a third of the forty-eight counties. Most counties contained medium to large urban centers, although,

Table 2.6. *The Most Developed Counties in the United States, 1890*

County/State	1890 Value-added in manufacturing (per capita)	1892 Patents (per 10,000)	1890 Mortgage interest (%)	1890 Wealth (per capita)	1900 Adult male illiteracy (%)
Fairfield/Conn.	$170.79	9.20	5.40	$ 790.76	5.6
Hartford/Conn.	162.98	15.29	5.53	758.33	6.4
Middlesex/Conn.	107.55	7.34	5.67	663.25	4.8
New Haven/Conn.	216.48	12.25	5.46	823.60	6.3
Adams/Ill.	79.21	6.79	6.49	814.00	5.4
Cook/Ill.	215.51	11.89	6.45	1,311.90	4.0
La Porte/Ind.	72.06	3.77	6.63	773.91	5.1
Marion/Ind.	113.62	9.21	6.41	859.94	5.2
Jefferson/Ky.	147.16	5.41	6.01	867.30	10.7
Kenton/Ky.	154.87	4.43	6.00	721.52	7.6
Baltimore City/Md.	156.42	5.16	5.82	976.90	7.2
Hampden/Mass.	221.89	6.04	5.25	645.42	9.6
Middlesex/Mass.	157.70	9.07	5.58	746.76	5.0
Norfolk/Mass.	140.15	6.22	5.67	895.15	4.1
Suffolk/Mass.	224.90	11.22	5.18	1,564.10	4.5
Baraga/Mich.	158.43	6.59	6.64	619.82	10.7
St. Louis City/Mo.	236.72	7.70	6.15	864.81	4.1
Essex/N.J.	210.63	14.14	5.38	807.62	6.3
Hudson/N.J.	105.29	5.16	5.67	659.85	5.2
Mercer/N.J.	173.86	4.63	5.55	723.29	7.7
Passaic/N.J.	217.84	6.76	5.70	623.12	7.6
Albany/N.Y.	132.30	7.41	5.43	806.22	4.9
Cortland/N.Y.	85.84	3.84	5.79	639.96	2.5
Dutchess/N.Y.	77.81	4.75	5.16	688.02	6.4
Erie/N.Y.	149.65	3.68	5.72	891.30	5.2
Herkimer/N.Y.	111.19	5.04	5.69	809.93	3.8
Kings/N.Y.	141.95	8.10	5.21	902.49	4.6
Monroe/N.Y.	179.33	6.54	5.64	818.62	3.1
New York/N.Y.	271.10	9.31	4.95	1,733.75	7.7
Onondaga/N.Y.	119.07	9.71	5.60	710.65	4.1
Queens/N.Y.	77.17	4.22	5.62	851.47	5.4
Rensselaer/N.Y.	178.00	4.34	5.53	737.02	5.0
Richmond/N.Y.	126.46	6.00	5.75	649.91	4.4
Schenectady/N.Y.	112.16	6.71	5.63	729.52	5.5
Westchester/N.Y.	102.35	7.77	5.52	1,125.21	7.2
Cuyahoga/Ohio	158.43	9.36	6.23	755.92	5.1
Hamilton/Ohio	289.81	5.45	6.09	892.24	3.4
Stark/Ohio	104.98	9.15	6.37	712.10	3.0
Allegheny/Penn.	177.32	6.59	5.88	1,141.92	8.8
Beaver/Penn.	77.14	7.59	6.00	667.69	5.2
Delaware/Penn.	127.10	3.75	5.43	1,029.25	6.7
Philadelphia/Penn.	253.68	7.31	5.19	1,049.88	4.5
Bristol/R.I.	73.50	3.50	5.92	794.55	9.4
Providence/R.I.	225.44	7.88	5.81	970.36	9.3
Washington/R.I.	89.09	9.30	5.89	771.71	5.2
Ohio/W.Va.	136.61	4.33	6.02	989.57	4.7
Milwaukee/Wis.	179.10	6.99	6.17	829.42	4.1
Washington, D.C.	96.33	7.31	5.99	1,243.81	8.4

Note and sources: These are the 48 counties in the United States that scored above the national average with respect to per capita value-added in manufacturing, patents approved per 10,000 population, and per capita wealth in real estate and fixed improvements but below the national average in mortgage interest rates and adult male illiteracy. Thus, they all scored "five" on the developmental index (the highest level possible; see text). For sources, see previous tables in this chapter and the text.

particularly in the Northeast, these could be relatively small compared with others in the region. The major exception to the overall pattern was Baraga County on the Upper Peninsula of Michigan.[46]

Hundreds of counties scored zero on the developmental index (below the national mark on each of the developmental referents). In Alabama, all but two of the sixty-six counties were at this, the least developed, level (see Map 2.6). Mississippi was even worse – none of that state's counties recorded data above the national mark on any of the five developmental referents. In the rest of the Deep South, industrial development was equally retarded: in Arkansas (where 67 of the 75 counties scored zero), Florida (25 of 45), Georgia (151 of 158), Louisiana (55 of 59), North Carolina (92 of 96), and South Carolina (34 of 35). Because there were so many candidates for the list of least developed counties in the United States, the criteria were tightened in order to produce a ranking of manageable size (see the note to Table 2.7). The resulting list of twenty-five counties is dominated by the southern black belt; in fact, all twenty-five were located in just four states: Alabama, Georgia, Louisiana, and Mississippi. More than half were in Georgia. Despite their low level of economic development, twenty-two of the twenty-five were served by railroads – an indication of both the intensive extension of the network by 1890 and the thorough integration of the cotton South, regardless of its otherwise backward status, into the international economy.[47]

When combined into a single index of relative economic development, the regional patterns of these five indicators describe the broad division of the United States into what was then an advanced northeastern and midwestern industrial core and a comparatively stagnating southern periphery (see Map 2.7). In the manufacturing belt of the Northeast and Midwest, a rapid industrial expansion, accompanied by an equally rapid urbanization, dominated the pattern of economic growth. In the Plains and West, growth was driven by frontier settlement and expanding commodity grain cultivation. The South, however, was an entirely different world where only isolated areas were able to climb out of the deepest dungeons of the American economy: the Piedmont where expanding textile production underpinned light industrialization, the Birmingham district of Alabama with the construction of iron and steel plants, and the western frontier in Texas with

---

[46] Baraga contained a major Great Lakes port, L'Anse, that shipped out locally produced iron, lumber, fish, and slate. Although the township of L'Anse had a population of only 1,468 in 1890 (about half of the county's total), the port boasted a bank, newspaper office, a slate quarry, two churches, a graded school, two sawmills, and an iron dock. Additional sawmills were located in an adjoining township. *Lippincott's Gazetteer of the World* (1893), vols. 1 and 2, pp. 584 and 1606.

[47] The southern trinity of cotton, corn, and pork dominated the economic base of these counties. See *Lippincott's Gazetteer of the World* (1893), vols. 1 and 2. Information on the railroad network was taken from the maps in *Cram's Universal Atlas* (New York: George F. Cram, 1894).

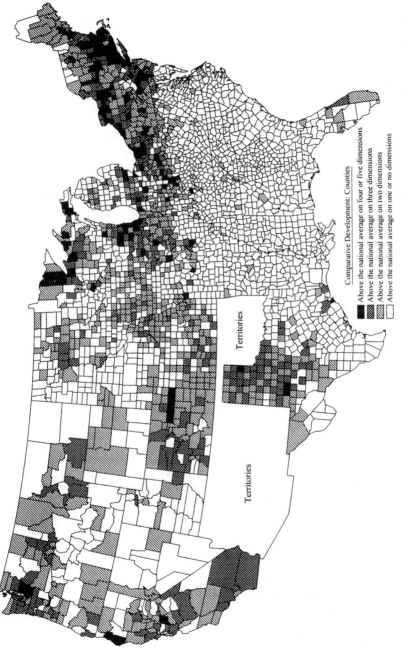

Map 2.6. Comparative level of U.S. economic development, by county. *Note*: Counties were compared with the national averages on five dimensions: per capita value-added in manufacturing, prevailing interest rates on mortgages, per capita wealth, per capita patent filings, and the proportion of literate adult males. The first four were calculated from the *1890 Census*; the last from the *1900 Census*.

Table 2.7. *The Least Developed Counties in the United States, 1890*

County/State	1890 Value-added in manufacturing (per capita)	1892 Patents (per 10,000)	1890 Mortgage interest (%)	1890 Wealth (per capita)	1900 Adult male illiteracy (%)
Greene/Ala.	$0.68	none	8.27	$ 90.95	60.0
Lowndes/Ala.	0.89	none	10.82	103.80	62.5
Perry/Ala.	0.41	none	9.60	115.10	51.4
Pickens/Ala.	0.22	none	8.00	120.84	42.7
Sumter/Ala.	0.78	none	8.01	89.61	53.7
Baker/Ga.	0.16	none	8.00	71.50	46.9
Chattahoochee/Ga.	0.00	none	8.00	123.42	44.5
Clay/Ga.	0.00	none	8.00	99.71	39.1
Columbia/Ga.	0.62	none	8.00	91.61	51.0
Early/Ga.	0.20	none	8.00	79.54	42.7
Glascock/Ga.	0.00	none	8.00	120.08	34.3
Harris/Ga.	0.71	none	8.00	111.04	39.5
Jones/Ga.	0.39	none	8.00	111.37	40.3
McDuffie/Ga.	0.80	none	8.00	124.78	46.9
Marion/Ga.	0.13	none	8.00	118.60	41.1
Miller/Ga.	0.00	none	8.00	105.25	41.4
Stewart/Ga.	0.64	none	8.00	113.12	45.5
Taliaferro/Ga.	0.82	none	8.00	102.77	44.7
Warren/Ga.	0.37	none	8.00	123.13	45.1
Avoyelles/La.	0.84	none	8.00	100.39	51.0
Richland/La.	0.20	none	8.00	104.89	37.4
St. Helena/La.	0.12	none	8.00	86.19	38.7
St. Landry/La.	0.77	none	8.00	120.68	61.2
Terrebonne/La.	0.20	none	8.82	102.52	55.4
Clay/Miss.	0.70	none	9.48	120.92	38.5

Note and sources: These are the 25 counties that (1) produced less than a dollar in value-added in manufacturing in 1890, (2) contained no inventors who had patents approved in 1892, (3) registered interest rates on farm and home mortgages of 8 percent or higher, (4) held real estate and fixed improvements of less than $125 per capita, and (5) exhibited illiteracy rates of greater than a third of all adult males. For sources, see notes to previous tables and the text.

the extension of cotton production. In his account of a funeral in a remote county in northern Georgia, Henry Grady poignantly described the consequences of this backwardness for one southern farmer:

They buried him in the midst of a marble quarry: they cut through solid marble to make his grave; and yet a little tombstone they put above him was from Vermont. They buried him in the heart of a pine forest, and yet the pine coffin was imported from Cincinnati. They buried him within touch of an iron mine, and yet the nails in his coffin and the iron in the shovel that dug his grave were imported from

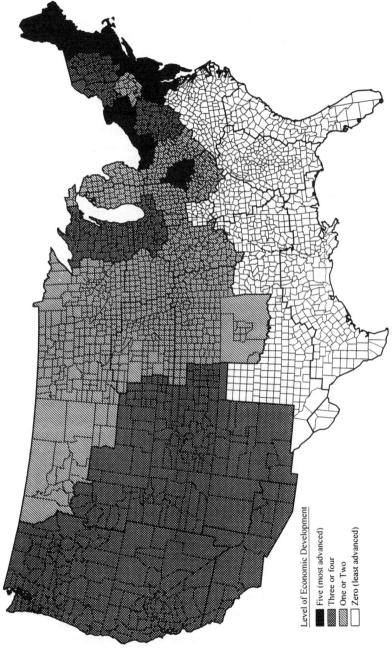

Level of Economic Development

■ Five (most advanced)

▨ Three or four

▧ One or Two

□ Zero (least advanced)

Map 2.7. Comparative level of U.S. economic development, by trade area. *Note:* For an explanation of the construction of trade area boundaries, see Richard Franklin Bensel, *Sectionalism and American Political Development, 1880–1980* (Madison: University of Wisconsin Press, 1984), pp. 421–426.

Pittsburgh. They buried him by the side of the best sheep-grazing country on the earth, and yet the wool in the coffin bands and the coffin bands themselves were brought from the North. The South didn't furnish a thing on earth for that funeral but the corpse and the hole in the ground.[48]

THE AMERICAN FINANCIAL SYSTEM

During this period, four primary forms of property and resources dominated the American political economy: private farms and plantations in the agricultural sector, entrepreneurial ownership of industrial firms, railroad corporations, and public services funded through the issue of government bonds. In terms of investment, each of these forms was capitalized in a different way. In agriculture, for example, most producers at some point mortgaged their land and improvements; the debt burden was usually heaviest just after the land was settled. In the Plains and Mountain states, lenders usually bundled these farm mortgages into interest-bearing securities and marketed them in the East through regional land and investment brokers.[49] In the South, in place of land mortgages, many sharecroppers and tenant farmers annually mortgaged their prospective crop. Most of these loans and their accompanying crop liens were small, entailed comparatively high risks to the lender, and thus carried high interest rates. In effect, local merchants borrowed from wholesalers and distributors by stocking their goods on credit and then, in turn, advanced these supplies to sharecroppers and tenants in return for a lien on the coming crop. Thus, in different ways, both western mortgages and southern crop liens were usually extended by local creditors who ultimately drew upon eastern capital.[50]

Although much larger in scale, American industrial and mercantile firms were also initially capitalized by drawing upon domestic capital. Although foreigners invested in a few industrial companies during the late nineteenth century, in some cases even owning the concerns outright, the overall level of foreign investment in American industry was minuscule.[51] Much of the

[48] Joseph J. Persky, *The Burden of Dependency: Colonial Themes in Southern Economic Thought* (Baltimore: Johns Hopkins University Press, 1992), p. 100.

[49] For a thorough overview and description of farm mortgages on the western plains, see Allan G. Bogue, *Money at Interest: The Farm Mortgage on the Middle Border* (Lincoln: University of Nebraska Press, 1955).

[50] For a description of the crop-lien system through which loans were made to southern sharecroppers and tenant farmers, see Roger L. Ransom and Richard Sutch, *One Kind of Freedom: The Economic Consequences of Emancipation* (New York: Cambridge University Press, 1977), pp. 81–168.

[51] Edward C. Kirkland, *Industry Comes of Age: Business, Labor, and Public Policy, 1860–1897* (Chicago: Quadrangle Books, 1967), p. 224.

growth of what became the Bell telephone system, for example, was funded by reinvesting profits.[52] Only in the late 1880s and 1890s, when the great consolidations and trusts began to appear, did industrial securities begin to enjoy easy access to organized public capital markets such as the New York Stock Exchange.[53]

Railroads, on the other hand, were the epitome of the modern business enterprise. Operated and capitalized as corporations almost from their birth, railroads became, aside from the bonds of the United States government, the most stable and popular investment property in the country. As the investment market in American railroad securities expanded and deepened, investment bankers on the East Coast, particularly New York, began to market them in Europe. Because European investors usually preferred bonds to stocks, most foreign investment in the emerging railroad system was passive, with American entrepreneurs retaining operating control of the lines. And, until the late 1890s, foreign investment was, with the apparently minor exception of United States government bonds and a sprinkling of state and local bonds after the war, concentrated in the railroad sector.[54] In the last decade of the nineteenth century, the American capital market expanded to include state and city bonds (which underwrote the construction of public schools, water systems, and public roads) and the corporate securities that flowed from railroad mergers and the rapid consolidation of industrial firms into vast combinations of vertically and horizontally

---

[52]   Chandler, *The Visible Hand*, pp. 373–374.

[53]   Banks were among the first non-railroad companies to receive broad access to the New York Stock Exchange; sixty-two were on the list in 1889. Among industrial companies and trusts, among the first to be listed were the Minnesota Iron Company and the Chicago Gas Trust (1888); the Consolidated Electric Light Company (1889); Edison General Electric Company, National Starch Manufacturing Company, American Tobacco, Brunswick, Distilling & Cattle Feeding, and National Linseed Oil (1890); and United States Rubber and Westinghouse Electric (1892). The number of new listings reached more than a dozen in 1893. Many of the early trusts were first traded in the New York Stock Exchange's "unlisted" department which did not require formal financial statements or revenue reports. The first of these was the American Cotton Seed Oil trust certificates in May 1886, followed by the Pipe Line certificates in March 1888. Then, in 1889, came a large influx: the sugar trust in February, the lead trust in March, the cattle trust and the Distillers & Cattle Feeder's Trust in June, and the American Pig Iron Storage Warrants in the last half of the year. By the end of 1889, sales in the unlisted department sometimes equaled or almost so the dollar volume on the regular list. *Commercial and Financial Chronicle*, March 10, 1888; January 5, March 30, June 29, July 13, 1889; January 4, June 28, 1890; January 3, 1891; May 7, December 24, 31, 1892; December 30, 1893; December 29, 1894; December 28, 1895; December 26, 1896; January 8, July 2, 1898; January 28, December 30, 1899.

[54]   Jeffrey G. Williamson, *American Growth and the Balance of Payments, 1820–1913: A Study of the Long Swing* (Chapel Hill: University of North Carolina Press, 1964), pp. 12, 96–97, 124, 135–136.

organized corporations.[55] Only the railroads, however, found a ready market abroad.[56]

Domestic Capital Movements

Even during the late nineteenth century, the manufacturing centers of the Northeast and Midwest exported capital because the extremely high profitability of the major industrial sectors created more wealth than could be absorbed in their expansion. Most of this excess profit flowed west, funding the settlement and rapid development of the agricultural and mining economy of that region. The greater part of this investment stream came from the Northeast, mediated by three types of institutions: savings banks, life insurance companies, and the major stock exchanges. Savings banks pooled the savings of individuals, large and small, into funds that could be invested in federal, state, and municipal bonds or corporate securities. Heavily regulated by state law in the late nineteenth century, these savings banks were gradually allowed to expand their holdings beyond the boundaries of their individual states and to extend the range of possible investment into corporate securities other than railroad bonds.[57] Restrictions on the withdrawal of their funds by depositors meant that savings banks, unlike other banking institutions from which deposits could be withdrawn on demand, could assume a long-term investment perspective. As a consequence, most of them held large and diversified portfolios of western securities. In 1886, New Hampshire savings banks, for example, held about a quarter of their total deposits in the form of investments originating in that state, another quarter in investments originating in the other New England states, and the remaining half apparently equally divided between the West and the rest of the nation. Aside from their holdings in railroad stocks and bonds (probably the major form of interregional investment in this period), most of the western total was held in the form of bundled farm mortgages

---

[55] For a general survey, see Mira Wilkins, *The History of Foreign Investment in the United States to 1914* (Cambridge, Mass.: Harvard University Press, 1989), esp. chaps. 5–16.

[56] Nathaniel T. Bacon, "American International Indebtedness," *Yale Review* 9 (November 1900): 265–285.

[57] In 1880, for example, Connecticut relaxed its regulations, allowing savings banks to invest in state bonds issued by Indiana, Kansas, Missouri, and Nebraska, in the municipal bonds of Chicago, Philadelphia, and Washington, D.C. (along with a few other cities), and in bonds issued by railroads that had paid dividends on common stock of 5 percent or more of their par value in the five previous years. In 1893, Connecticut again relaxed its regulations, greatly expanding the number of cities and states in which savings banks could place their funds. *Appleton's Annual Cyclopaedia of 1880* (New York: D. Appleton, 1881), p. 195; *Commercial and Financial Chronicle*, August 1882, *Investors' Supplement*: September 30, 1893.

and bonds issued by states, counties, or municipalities.[58] Although generally less dependent on long-term investments in the West than savings institutions, other state-chartered banks and trust companies also participated in this interregional flow of capital.

After 1880 or so, life insurance companies emerged as major players in the interregional movement of capital to the West.[59] Their rapidly expanding business dramatically increased the funds that these companies had to invest in income-producing securities. At the same time, the favored investment vehicle for these companies, the federal debt, was rapidly contracting. Since new issues of state bonds could not take up the slack, life insurance companies, like savings banks, were compelled to venture into new investments such as bundled real estate mortgages and city and county securities.[60]

Investment in both railroad and government bonds was centralized in the major stock exchanges of the nation. For instance, the financial communities of private banks and bond brokers that surrounded these exchanges often purchased the entire bond issue of western cities, counties, or states and then retailed the bonds to individual investors and savings banks. These communities provided similar services for the railroads, forming syndicates for the floatation of stock and bond issues in both the United States and Europe. Since many of these companies were extending their lines into the unsettled regions of the West, much of the movement of funds through the stock exchange was, in effect, an interregional transfer of capital.[61] There were, of course, strong interconnections between all of these institutions and the objects of their investment. Once capitalized on the major stock exchanges, for example, the railroads would construct their lines. As they did so, the roads earned their land grants and established a network for retailing farm land to settlers. The Burlington and Missouri River Railroad

[58] *Appleton's Annual Cyclopaedia of 1886* (New York: D. Appleton, 1888), p. 619.

[59] By 1888, the major eastern life insurance companies, particularly those headquartered in Connecticut (which permitted the companies to invest in western land mortgages), had transferred to the West some $180 million. *Commercial and Financial Chronicle*, January 21, 1888. Also see Bogue, *Money at Interest*, pp. 20, 81, 118, 227–228, 251.

[60] On the developing shortage of federal and state bonds, see *Commercial and Financial Chronicle*, April 1 and 15, 1882. That this shortage was a major reason for the liberalization of investment opportunities for savings banks under state regulations is indicated in the May 12, 1883, issue. In 1897, the total assets of savings banks stood at just over $2 billion and the publicly acknowledged assets of life insurance companies totaled about $1.5 billion. Kirkland, *Industry Comes of Age*, pp. 218–219.

[61] For example, in 1890 New York and Boston investors held a combined total of 279,166 shares in the Chicago, Burlington and Quincy. By comparison, Chicago stockholders residing in the main terminus of the road held only 3,104 shares in the line. William Cronon, *Nature's Metropolis: Chicago and the Great West* (New York: W. W. Norton, 1991), pp. 82–83.

Company went so far as to station salesmen in New York City, Glasgow, Liverpool, and London to attract settler-buyers, providing them with mortgages with very liberal rates of interest. Through such operations, railroad securities originally intended for the construction of the western lines could be transformed into farm mortgages for individual settlers.[62]

Other companies marketed farm mortgages directly to eastern investors and financial institutions.[63] These companies either sold farm and home mortgages on an individual basis, matching up western borrowers with eastern lenders for a fee, or bought mortgages on the company's own account, selling debentures to eastern creditors in order to raise the capital for these purchases. In the latter case, western mortgages were effectively bundled into new securities under the auspices and management of the company, thereby both spreading the creditor's risk and greatly reducing administrative costs. Before the early 1880s there were relatively few such firms engaged in this interregional movement of mortgage lending but the ensuing land boom in the Plains and West greatly increased both their number and size. In effect, these companies were engaged in arbitrage operations that exploited the large gap between mortgage rates in the East and West, thereby reducing to some extent the very high rates in the latter by making available millions upon millions of dollars of eastern capital.[64]

[62] In a pamphlet published in 1885 as a guide to immigrants, the Northern Pacific Railroad advertised for sale eight million acres within the Dakota Territory and promised to provide mortgages on up to 320 acres for actual settlers. The terms offered ten-year mortgages at 7 percent interest, one payment of interest and principal per year (the first year required interest only). With respect to both length and interest rate, such contracts were significantly better than settlers could usually obtain on the open market in the Territory. O. H. Holt, *Dakota* (Chicago: Rand McNally, 1885), p. 91. For a description of the generous terms under which credit was extended in land sales to Kansas settlers by the Santa Fe and Union Pacific, see *Fourth Biennial Report of the Kansas State Board of Agriculture: 1883–1884* (Topeka: T. D. Thacher, 1885), pp. 519–521.

[63] As the *Chronicle* pointed out, such companies were necessary intermediaries between eastern lenders and western borrowers because investment in real estate mortgages required close inspection of both the property and the title before a loan could be made. *Commercial and Financial Chronicle*, February 1882, *Investors' Supplement*.

[64] *Commercial and Financial Chronicle*, October 24, 1885. The *Chronicle* noted that "[s]tatistics as to the extent of this business are wholly wanting. . . ." The settlement of the Plains and Mountain West, promoted by this interregional movement of capital, both increasingly integrated these regions with eastern capital markets and provided more abundant local sources of funds. Both developments reduced the interest gradient between the East and West over time. For a description of this process from the perspective of a mortgage loan broker (who felt it necessary to explain why he was compelled to offer lower rates to eastern investors than he had previously), see Allen C. Mason, *Compendium of Information Concerning the City of Tacoma and Washington Territory* (Portland, Oreg.: A. Anderson, 1888), pp. 65–68,

Some of these firms became quite large. In 1889, for example, the Lombard Investment Company had branch offices for the examination and purchase of farm and home mortgages in Denver, Omaha, Wichita, St. Paul, Tacoma, Lincoln, Salt Lake City, Portland (Oregon), Concordia (Kansas), Sioux City (Iowa), and other locations near its headquarters in Kansas City. The territory covered by the company's agents included Iowa, Missouri, Wisconsin, Minnesota, southeast Dakota Territory, Nebraska, eastern Kansas, irrigated lands of Colorado, Oregon, Washington, western Idaho, Montana, Tennessee, Arkansas, Mississippi, and Utah. The leading cities in which home mortgages were purchased included Kansas City, Minneapolis, St. Paul, Omaha, Denver, Memphis, Lincoln, Sioux City, Wichita, Duluth, Tacoma, Portland, Chattanooga, Birmingham, Springfield, Nashville, Knoxville, Ogden, St. Joseph, and Fort Scott. The mortgages purchased in these cities, states, and territories were then sold through the Lombard Company's branch offices in New York, Boston, Philadelphia, and London. Transactions made at the American branches were telegraphed to the Kansas City home office so that the company could daily balance its books.[65] While this was the largest firm engaged in the interregional movement of mortgage capital, the characteristics of its organization were by no means unusual. In 1893, for example, nine of the eleven out-of-state financial corporations with business offices in Maine were companies headquartered in Arizona, Iowa, Minnesota, Missouri, and Nebraska – all of them, apparently, land mortgage brokers.[66]

As a result of all of these activities, most of the money capitalized into farm mortgages on the western plains between 1877 and 1895 appears to have originated in the eastern manufacturing belt.[67] Moving from east to west, the capital-rich position of the manufacturing belt gradually shaded into what became the capital-poor and capital-importing region of the Great Plains and Mountain West.[68] In fact, railroad expansion, town development, and the demand for farm mortgages made the rapidly settling West

---

109–110. For the years 1883 to 1888, Mason reported that he had negotiated $936,000 in real estate loans on property in the Washington Territory (about two thirds of this sum was located in and around Tacoma in Pierce County). The origin of the funds for these loans included New York State ($436,000, or 46.6% of the total), the New England states ($107,000, or 11.4%), and Pennsylvania and New Jersey (an additional $109,000, or 11.6%). In sum, about 70 percent of the total originated in the East. The eleven former Confederate states, by way of contrast, only provided $20,000, or a little over 2 percent of the total.

[65] *Commercial and Financial Chronicle*, December 28, 1889. For a detailed account of another such firm, the J. B. Watkins Land Mortgage Company, see Bogue, *Money at Interest*, pp. 77–204.

[66] *American Investments* 4:7 (July 1893): 311.

[67] See, for example, Bogue, *Money at Interest*, pp. 225–230, 250–251.

[68] Stuart Bruchey, *Enterprise: The Dynamic Economy of a Free People* (Cambridge, Mass.: Harvard University Press, 1990), pp. 272–349.

(excepting Arkansas, Louisiana, and Missouri) the major capital-importing region of the United States.

In all these respects, the American capital market was probably, after the British, the most sophisticated and extensive in the world. But it was still extremely uneven in geographical breadth and depth. And one of the most uneven elements in this market was the distribution of national banks. Organized around a pyramidal reserve system centered on New York City, national banks were the most unifying element of the late nineteenth century financial system. Thus, the distribution of national bank capital is a fairly good measure of regional linkages within the national financial system.

Capital invested in the national bank system was concentrated in two regions.[69] As might be expected, the largest portion of national bank capital was found in the Northeast, particularly Boston, Providence, Philadelphia, Pittsburgh, Baltimore, and many older, smaller urban centers in New England. To the west, a few of the mature river ports of the Ohio, particularly Cincinnati and Louisville, were also comparatively well endowed with national banks. The surprise comes on the western frontier where the organization of banks appears to have lagged only slightly behind the line of settlement. Given the steady criticism directed at the national bank system for its alleged inability to meet the credit demands of agrarian communities, the relatively dense concentration of banks near the frontier is remarkable.[70] More expected was the dearth of institutions throughout most of the South. Outside Texas (in which the distribution paralleled that in the western Plains states), only Nashville contained a relatively dense concentration of national banks.

When aggregated by trade area, this tripartite distribution of national

[69] As defined here, capital includes money that had been invested in a national bank through stock subscriptions plus the essentially identical bookkeeping entries for "surplus" and "undivided surplus," which represented profits that had been retained in the institution. For a general discussion of these terms, see the appropriate entries in Montgomery Rollins, *Money and Investments* (Boston: Southgate Books, 1907).

[70] Because of the prohibition on investment in farm and home mortgages, the relatively high threshold on capitalization (which was subsequently reduced), and other reasons, national banks were generally more viable as financial institutions in the low-interest-rate environment of the Northeast than in the high-interest-rate West. For that reason, the West tended to favor private banking institutions over national banks before 1880, while the situation was reversed in New England. *Appleton's 1880 Cyclopaedia*, p. 260. By 1900, however, the rapid expansion of the national banking system in the West had removed most of this imbalance. For a description of national bank formation in the South and West between 1880 and 1884, see *Commercial and Financial Chronicle*, May 17, 1884. For annual statistics on the total number of national banks in the United States between 1876 and 1907 as well as by region for the years 1882, 1891, and 1900, see Bruce W. Hetherington, "Bank Entry and the Low Issue of National Bank Notes: A Re-examination," *Journal of Economic History* 50:3 (September 1990): 670, 674.

Table 2.8. *Nonresident Ownership of National Bank Stock*
by Region, 1886

Region	Total number of national bank shares	Total number of shares held outside of region	Percent held outside region
New England	2,006,522	143,308	7.1
Eastern Middle	2,241,104	258,926	11.6
Southern Middle	1,017,735	41,160	4.0
Southern	403,887	54,960	13.6
Western Middle	926,358	74,478	8.0
Western	347,513	79,429	22.9
Far Western and Pacific	173,775	38,313	22.0
Nation	7,116,894	690,574	9.7
Selected states			
Wyoming	8,000	3,623	45.3
Dakota Territory	30,250	13,268	43.9
Louisiana	36,250	11,713	32.3
Minnesota	29,100	9,082	31.2
Missouri	29,000	8,725	30.1
Washington Territory	10,100	2,766	27.4
Nebraska	124,389	30,084	24.2
Montana	18,725	4,510	24.1
Kansas	63,382	14,622	23.1
Texas	76,050	13,297	17.5
Iowa	101,642	16,916	16.6
Colorado	24,350	4,017	16.5

Notes and sources: *Commercial and Financial Chronicle*, December 11, 1886.

bank capital is clearly evident (see Table 2.10). The major trade areas in New England, Boston and Hartford, had the greatest per capita holdings of national bank capital in the country. They were followed by the adjoining trade areas centered on Albany, Baltimore, New York, and Philadelphia, effectively completing the northeastern seaboard. All of these were major capital exporters within the national market. At this point the national bank hierarchy jumps to the west, taking in first Cincinnati, then Denver, Los Angeles, and Chicago. As will be shown, Cincinnati and Chicago were major conduits for the movement of capital to the West, while Denver and Los Angeles were at the receiving end of the interregional movement. The other western trade areas had slightly lower per capita holdings, but all of them were well above those in the South. At the very bottom of the national hierarchy were the trade areas centered on Richmond, Atlanta, Charleston (South Carolina), Evansville (Indiana), and New Orleans.[71] Like the region as a whole, all of these southern trade areas were effectively isolated from the primary east-west axis of capital transfer within the United States.

In the East, the formation of national banks, along with other financial institutions, was stimulated by a relative excess of capital.[72] The comparative safety of national banks and their strong connections with national banks in other major cities, particularly New York, provided a secure structure within which savings and profits could be collected and exported to other regions through investment in city and county bonds, common stock in railroads, or similar securities. At the receiving end in the West, national banks served as reputable platforms for the analysis of local investment opportunities and transfer of capital.[73] Because much of the capital on which western national banks were founded was provided by eastern investors, the very establishment of national banks frequently entailed an interregional transfer of funds (see Table 2.8).[74]

In sum, the distribution of national bank capital identifies many of the

[71] When aggregated by states instead of trade areas, the ten with the smallest per capita holdings of national bank capital were: Mississippi ($1.30), Arkansas ($1.94), North Carolina ($2.42), South Carolina ($3.21), Georgia ($3.27), West Virginia ($3.46), Alabama ($3.89), Florida ($3.93), Virginia ($4.18), and the Arizona Territory ($4.28). The ten states with the largest per capita holdings were Rhode Island ($76.92), Massachusetts ($60.74), Montana ($52.30), Connecticut ($46.77), Vermont ($30.43), Colorado ($28.70), Wyoming ($28.23), New York ($26.58), Washington ($24.06), and Maine ($23.00). The per capita holdings of national bank capital for the nation as a whole was $15.46.

[72] On the dearth of investment alternatives to national banks in the Northeast, see, for example, Naomi R. Lamoreaux, "Bank Mergers in Late Nineteenth-Century New England: The Contingent Nature of Structural Change," *Journal of Economic History* 51 (September 1991): 545–546. On the emergence of banks as institutional frameworks for the collection and mobilization of local capital, particularly as investment vehicles for kinship groups, see Naomi R. Lamoreaux, "Banks, Kinship, and Economic Development: The New England Case," *Journal of Economic History* 46:3 (September 1986): 647–667.

[73] In an advertisement placed in the *Commercial and Financial Chronicle*, for example, the First National Bank of Corning, Iowa, called attention to its specialization in the negotiation of farm mortgages in the Great Plains region for eastern "capitalists and private investors." June 28, 1884. In a slight variation on this theme, in 1888 the William C. Knox & Company established the United States Savings Bank in Topeka, Kansas, in order "to negotiate Western mortgages for savings banks and other investors at the East." August 4, 1888. For other examples of such services performed by western national banks for eastern investors, see Bogue, *Money at Interest*, pp. 69, 252–253.

[74] When the Iowa Savings Bank in Sioux City, Iowa, failed, a list of the shareholders revealed that almost $90,000 of the $250,000 of the bank's capitalization was owned by eastern investors. Those residing in Vermont alone owned over $50,000 in the bank's stock. *American Investments and Financial Opinions* 8:6 (June 1897): 234.

anchoring institutions for the thick ties that bound together the east-west axis of interregional capital movement, but the location of the banks does not, in and of itself, say much about the direction of the flow of capital between these two regions. For evidence of the direction of capital movements and their relative size we must turn to another source.

The Distribution of Bids Received for County and Municipal Bonds

In 1880, the total net indebtedness of American municipalities stood at $725 million. By 1902, the total debt had almost doubled, rising to $1.43 billion. Most of this money underwrote the construction of the major urban public services and utilities of the era: water systems, gas works and distributing lines, street railways, and, late in the century, central electric power plants and lines. Just as the development of the national railroad network knit together the separate regions of the country into a single national market, the emerging urban infrastructure provided the centrally produced and distributed services that made possible the huge agglomerations of people, factories, and commercial establishments associated with industrialization. The expansion of the national railroad network and the construction of this urban infrastructure were related in a second way as well. The fading away of the great railroad booms of the 1870s and 1880s left behind a vacuum in the national economy. Where railroad expansion had once been a driving force behind economic growth, the building of American cities now assumed a dominating role as municipal governments dug trenches for sewer and gas lines, laid down track for street railways, strung wire for electricity, and otherwise built up the common infrastructure of the urban environment.[75]

To fund the construction of this infrastructure, city and county governments issued bonds that in effect mortgaged future tax revenue. These bonds carried varying amounts of risk because counties and cities could fail to live up to the expansive visions of their residents and thus default on the debt that had mortgaged that future. Such visions were often disappointed in the western plains in the late nineteenth century. The town of Anthony, Kansas, for example, boasted a population of 3,574 in 1887. This was near the peak of the land boom that had been encouraged by a number of years of abnormally heavy rainfall.[76] Encouraged by

---

[75] Kirkland, *Industry Comes of Age*, pp. 237, 239.

[76] For Anthony, the land boom appears to have peaked in March 1887. Between March 2 and 16, the Anthony *Republican* proudly reported real estate transactions totaling $1,140,162. Jennie Small Owen and Kirke Mechem, eds., *The Annals of Kansas, 1886–1925* (Topeka: Kansas State Historical Society, n.d.), vol. 1, p. 34. In 1888, the assessed value of all real estate in the town was only $293,492. *Sixth Biennial Report of the Kansas State Board of Agriculture: 1887–1888* (Topeka: Clifford C. Baker, 1889), p. 203.

this boom, the town had issued about $170,000 in municipal bonds, about one third of the assessed valuation of the city in 1889. When the rain stopped, the surrounding agricultural district was thrown into a deep depression and many farmers abandoned their farms, fleeing the county and often the state. By 1896, Anthony's population had dropped to a little over a thousand people and the assessed valuation of property within the town limits was now only some $3,000 more than the total debt. To pay the interest and principal on its bonds, the town raised the tax rate on property to over 13 percent of its assessed value per year. In response, many of the remaining residents tore down their businesses and homes and rebuilt them just outside the town limits. Anthony was clearly and helplessly bankrupt.[77]

Cities and counties in the Mountain and Plains states often had very optimistic estimations of their future prosperity and they borrowed accordingly on the national capital market. In those areas where development did not proceed as expected, local governments subsequently attempted to rid themselves of a burden that, instead of financing the infrastructure for expansion, had become an incubus on what little development could be realistically achieved.[78] In these cases, local government officials often seized on their own errors as excuses for dishonoring bonds. State laws governing local bond issues were often complex and required a precision both as to format and procedure that, in practice, local politicians would have found difficult to implement correctly regardless of their attitude toward the financiers who bought their securities. In the actual case, many local officials, particularly in the southern and western periphery, were quite hostile to the eastern financiers who had bought their bonds and carefully inspected the procedural history with an eye toward any technical violation of the state laws that governed the issuance of these securities. When, as was almost always the case, some violation was discovered, local officials

---

[77] *Commercial and Financial Chronicle*, February 20, 1897. In Ulysses, the county seat of Grant County, there were only 65 people left in 1894 when the residents abandoned their lots, put their homes on wheels, and moved to a hilltop some three miles away in order to found New Ulysses. As in Anthony, the evacuation was provoked by astronomically rising tax rates as the town attempted to support a huge bonded debt. James R. Shortridge, *Peopling the Plains: Who Settled Where in Frontier Kansas* (Lawrence: University of Kansas Press, 1995), p. 143.

[78] The disappointment of local hopes sometimes produced violence, as well as bond defaults. In Kansas, for example, after the land boom began to bust in 1887 and 1888, disputes over which town would be the county seat led to several murders in Wichita, Sherman, and Stevens counties. In each case the state militia was ordered into the community to keep the peace. Although the towns that were competing for designation as the county seat were no more than hamlets, the business generated by an even minuscule civil establishment meant the difference between survival and extinction as a community on much of the western plains. *Appleton's Annual Cyclopaedia of 1888* (New York: D. Appleton, 1889), p. 460.

would happily declare that it would be illegal for their jurisdictions to honor bonds that had been inadvertently floated in violation of one or more formal requirements of the law.[79]

Although the lower state courts were sometimes sympathetic to the defaulting predilections of counties and municipalities, the federal courts usually favored bondholders. For example, when the Tennessee legislature repealed the Memphis city charter in order to allow the city to evade repayment of its debt, the federal courts declared the repeal to be invalid.[80] In 1878 alone more than thirty counties in Arkansas, more than a third of all the counties in the state, were ordered by the federal courts to honor their debts by enacting taxes dedicated to their repayment.[81] In Kentucky, the citizens of Muhlenberg County were so obstreperous that a federal court ordered the United States marshal, accompanied by an armed force of deputies, to protect a court-appointed officer as the latter attempted to collect the taxes necessary for the repayment of railroad bonds issued by the county some twenty-five years earlier.[82] Missouri counties, cities, and towns may have compiled the poorest repayment record. There the state legislature passed a bill that in effect would have encouraged county judges to resign when creditors pressed for repayment; left with no local officers upon whom to serve writs, federal court orders would have gone unenforced. The governor vetoed the bill.[83]

Wading through hundreds of municipal bond cases arising in these and other states, the U.S. Supreme Court upheld the validity of most bond issues and ruled that they must be honored.[84] But enforcement of such rulings was difficult and the attending litigation could be very expensive for bondholders. Recovery of principal and interest by creditors from defaulting jurisdictions could be time-consuming as well, ultimately requiring the hiring of political talent as well as legal skill.[85] As a result, bond issues in many southern and western jurisdictions required a careful estimation of

---

[79] One of the most blatant examples of such fiscal opportunism occurred in 1886 when Gunnison County, Colorado, stopped payment on its bonded debt. *Commercial and Financial Chronicle*, April 15, 1899.

[80] By disbanding the city, the Tennessee legislature hoped to leave nothing for the bondholders to litigate when their bonds were not paid. *Appleton's Annual Cyclopaedia of 1879* (New York: D. Appleton, 1886), pp. 826–829. But while the federal courts were, on the whole, more favorable to creditors, the active participation of the state legislature in local efforts to evade repayment of debts often conferred immunity to federal relief. See the criteria for enforcement laid down by the Supreme Court in *Barkeley vs. Levee Commissioners et al.*, *Appleton's 1880 Cyclopaedia*, pp. 11–12.

[81] *Appleton's Annual Cyclopaedia of 1878* (New York: D. Appleton, 1879), pp. 25–28; *Appleton's 1879 Cyclopaedia*, pp. 41–42, 46.

[82] *Appleton's Annual Cyclopaedia of 1893* (New York: D. Appleton, 1894), p. 424.

[83] *Appleton's 1879 Cyclopaedia*, pp. 643–646.

[84] Kirkland, *Industry Comes of Age*, pp. 67–68.

[85] For a more or less typical account of legal process for recovery of bonds issued by St. Clair County, Missouri, see *Commercial and Financial Chronicle*, May 6, 1899.

political risk that, in most cases, raised the interest rate well above the national average.[86]

Despite the relatively high level of political risk in the peripheral regions of the country, the market for local and state government securities increasingly became both formal in organization and national in scope during the late nineteenth century. Bond issues were described in national advertisements that invited offers to purchase from all parts of the country.[87] After these bids were received, the bonds were awarded to those who had placed the highest bids. In most cases, all of the bidders were publicly reported; in others, only the name of the highest bidder was published. There were thousands of such public advertisements and award announcements for bond issues in the late nineteenth century.[88] In the large majority of cases, the award announcements identified both the name of the bidders and city in which they were located. In many of the instances in which the location of the bidder was not given, the city could be identified from national financial directories or other sources.[89] This public financial record provides the most thorough evidence for the direction of interregional capital transfers available in the late nineteenth century.[90]

[86] In rare cases, local governments outside the South and West defaulted on debt obligations. For example, the cities of Elizabeth and Rahway in New Jersey effectively declared bankruptcy in 1879. *Appleton's 1879 Cyclopaedia*, p. 669; *Commercial and Financial Chronicle*, November 25, 1882; September 29, 1883; July 14, 1888; March 30, 1889.

[87] See, for example, the advertisement placed in the *Commercial and Financial Chronicle* by the treasurer of Cascade County, Montana, inviting bids for $200,000 of twenty-year bonds paying 4 percent annually. The county promised to deliver the bonds to any national bank in the nation at the request of the successful bidder. December 29, 1900.

[88] The four January 1899 issues of the *Commercial and Financial Chronicle*, for example, carried a combined total of 338 announcements of bond offerings, negotiations, and awards by state, county, and municipal governments.

[89] In compiling this data, information, including subsequent corrections and additions from other issues of the *Commercial and Financial Chronicle*, was recorded for all types of securities, including long-term bonds, temporary loans, and tax warrants. Both successful and unsuccessful bids were recorded. Successful bids represented actual transfers of capital from the winning bidder to the governmental authority. When added to unsuccessful bids, they represent the pool of credit from which local governments could draw. All the data was weighted by the face amount of the bond issue (not the sum realized by the acceptance of a bid, which was usually slightly higher or lower than the face amount). Joint bids by two or more bidders were divided equally among them. In cases where the state or local government refused to issue the bonds after the offering, the bids were still recorded as indicating credit availability. In those instances, governments usually refused to award the bonds because the bids were deemed too low or the state attorney general denied approval. However, if a successful bidder refused to take the bonds when properly awarded, information with respect to that bid was dropped from the data set.

[90] State laws, however, could privilege "in-state" bidders by clothing the issues with various forms of tax exemptions or other privileges that would apply only to bond-

When aggregated by trade area, the pattern describes a bipolar capital market. At one pole stood those trade areas that placed many more bids outside their boundaries than they received (see Table 2.9). Banks and other financial institutions located within the Cincinnati trade area, for example, placed almost $92 million in bids for county and municipal securities outside the trade area while receiving back, for its own issues, less than $6 million. The resulting ratio of exported to imported bids (16.14) was the highest of all the nation's trade areas. The Chicago and New York trade areas followed with ratios of almost 9. In total, Chicago exported almost $78 million in bids while importing from other trade areas a little under $9 million. The corresponding numbers for New York doubled those for Chicago, standing at almost $165 million and a little under $19 million. For its size, Cleveland posted large numbers on both sides: $89 million in exported bids and some $44 million in imports. Boston's figures were slightly smaller: $53 million in exports and $33 million in imports. The only other trade area to export more bids than it received was St. Louis (roughly $7.5 million and $5 million).[91] Setting St. Louis aside, the other five donor trade areas (New York, Boston, Chicago, Cleveland, and Cincinnati) had a positive financial trade balance of some $366 million with the rest of the nation. All the remaining trade areas had deficits and none were close to parity.

Most of the donor trade areas dominated their home markets as well. For example, New York banks and financial institutions provided 93.9 percent of the extraordinarily large value of all bids received for bonds issued within that trade area (see Table 2.9). In the country as a whole, banks and financial institutions located in the five donor trade areas placed over half of all bids for county and municipal bonds in all but two of the nation's trade areas. The two exceptions, Philadelphia and Baltimore, possessed fairly strong financial centers in their own right, although their firms rarely participated in the competition for bonds issued outside their respective regions. At the most general level, each of the donor trade areas shared a common pattern in that they tended to dominate the bidding in immediately adjacent trade areas as well as their own home market. The pattern was strongest for Boston, which clearly dominated the comparatively rich New England bond market (both the Boston and Hartford trade areas) and

---

holders within that state's jurisdiction. While such laws were undoubtedly on the books in at least some of the states, the patterns revealed in the data strongly suggest that their impact on bidding was slight.

[91] All of these figures exclude local bids for county and city bonds. New York trade area institutions, for example, bid about $289 million for securities issued within that region, a total excluded from both the export and import sides of the trade area's financial balance with the rest of the nation. The corresponding domestic markets for Boston, Chicago, Cleveland, Cincinnati, and St. Louis were $104, $44, $22, $19, and $3 million.

Table 2.9. *Regional Pattern of Bidding for County and City Bonds, 1899–1900*

			Distribution of bids received from donor trade areas			
Trade area of bond issuer	Bids received from New York (%)	Bids received from Boston (%)	Bids received from Chicago (%)	Bids received from Cleveland (%)	Bids received from Cincinnati (%)	Bids received from all five (%)
Boston dominant						
Boston	21.1	76.0	1.3	1.3	0.3	100.0
Hartford	24.3	60.8	1.0	2.8	0.7	89.6
New York dominant						
New York	93.9	1.7	0.6	3.1	0.3	99.6
Syracuse	57.5	5.3	2.7	11.5	3.1	80.1
Albany	40.0	23.2	1.7	10.2	2.0	77.1
Charleston	32.8	11.9	7.3	6.0	9.0	67.0
Pittsburgh	46.9	0.2	1.8	9.9	6.3	65.1
Scranton	24.6	6.3	1.6	23.2	9.4	65.1
San Francisco	19.1	6.0	18.3	14.7	5.2	63.3
New Orleans	33.7	1.5	4.1	7.3	12.7	59.3
Buffalo	34.5	7.9	0.6	11.3	1.8	56.1
Philadelphia	30.5	1.7	9.5	5.8	2.4	49.9
Memphis	16.7	1.1	13.8	12.1	5.5	49.2
Baltimore	21.0	0.4	8.8	3.8	0.7	34.7
Chicago dominant						
Chicago	2.6	0.1	83.3	1.9	8.7	96.6
Des Moines	0.3	0.1	48.8	17.8	6.7	73.7
Milwaukee	7.3	9.3	31.3	16.0	8.6	72.5

Omaha	2.5	4.7	34.8	15.5	8.4	65.9
Minneapolis	7.1	6.9	28.2	14.6	8.2	65.0
St. Louis	1.9	0.1	36.2	11.0	12.0	61.2
Atlanta	7.8	—	18.1	13.3	17.2	56.4
Kansas City	1.2	1.0	18.1	9.9	9.4	39.6
Cincinnati dominant						
Cincinnati	1.0	0.3	3.9	13.0	75.4	93.6
Cleveland	9.5	3.0	3.1	33.6	41.3	90.5
Richmond	12.7	1.9	16.7	18.9	23.2	73.4
Evansville	1.3	—	13.9	16.8	37.8	69.8
Columbus	0.3	1.2	5.5	21.7	40.8	69.5
Nashville	7.4	2.0	20.9	16.4	21.7	68.4
Louisville	0.9	4.9	10.3	16.3	29.5	61.9
Indianapolis	0.5	1.1	17.1	11.6	21.8	52.1
Cleveland dominant						
Denver	2.3	6.3	19.5	45.3	4.3	77.7
Grand Rapids	0.4	8.2	21.2	25.1	16.4	71.3
Detroit	7.3	13.3	14.3	20.1	15.9	70.9
Los Angeles	11.3	2.8	20.0	23.2	—	57.3

Notes and sources: Calculated from bids for county and city bonds published in the *Commercial and Financial Chronicle* during the years 1899 and 1900. All bids are weighted by the face value of the underlying bond issue. With respect to the movement of funds between regions, there were five trade areas that exported more capital than they received (the "donor regions" of Boston, New York, Chicago, Cincinnati, and Cleveland). Each of these donor regions led the bidding for bonds in differing sets of trade areas (e.g., Boston firms dominated the bidding in both its own and the Hartford trade areas). Trade area boundaries can be found in Richard Franklin Bensel, *Sectionalism and American Political Development, 1880–1980* (Madison: University of Wisconsin Press, 1984), p. 424.

provided almost a quarter of the bids for Albany bond issues. Participation by Boston firms dropped off sharply outside these regions. New York firms were similarly strong throughout the Northeast, particularly to the south and east of the Boston investment field. However, New York firms also strongly competed in many of the southern trade areas (Charleston, Memphis, New Orleans, and Richmond) as well as San Francisco on the Pacific Coast. This pattern reflected the city's traditional commercial ties with the major cotton export centers of the South and the mining economies of California and Nevada.[92]

Chicago firms likewise dominated many of the trade areas of the Midwest and Plains, with particular strength to the west of the city and region. Des Moines, Milwaukee, Minneapolis, Omaha, and St. Louis all fell well within the Chicago investment field. To the east, participation by firms located in the Chicago trade area was comparatively weak but still significant. Where Chicago dropped off, Cincinnati and Cleveland picked up: the former in Columbus, Evansville, Indianapolis, and Louisville and the latter in Detroit and Grand Rapids.[93]

In sum, bids for county and municipal bonds suggest a two-dimensional pattern of capital flow in the late nineteenth century. On the one hand, capital flowed horizontally through the national economy from the major urban centers of the manufacturing belt into the peripheral regions of the South and West.[94] The stronger current, by far, connected the East with the West. In fact, in much of the South, county and city bond issues appear to have attracted little or no interest in the national capital market. On the other hand, capital also flowed vertically through the national city hierarchy, from the major financial centers of the nation in New York, Chicago,

---

[92]   Individual financial houses often specialized, for one reason or another, in government securities from a particular region, and these regions were frequently at variance with the dominant pattern for firms in the city in which the house was located. The banking house of Winslow, Lanier & Co., for example, specialized in bonds issued by cities and towns in Illinois, Indiana, and Ohio – states that were not among those in which New York firms were generally strong players. *Commercial and Financial Chronicle*, January 4, 1879.

[93]   Of the five donor trade areas, the least localized distribution of bids originated in Cleveland whose firms produced a much flatter bidding pattern than any other region of the nation. Firms located in the Cleveland trade area, for example, placed bids for 10 percent or more of the total value of bonds issued in 24 of the nation's 34 trade areas. The comparable figures were: New York (16), Boston (5), Chicago (19), and Cincinnati (13).

[94]   This current was so strong that interest on government securities issued in the Plains and West was often paid exclusively through eastern institutions. For example, when the town of Anthony, Kansas, issued twenty-year, 6 percent bonds in 1890, arrangement was made for the semiannual interest to be paid through the First National Bank in New York City. See the advertisement for these bonds by the New York banking house of Griswold & Gillett in the *Commercial and Financial Chronicle*, July 5, 1890.

and Boston to smaller regional cities such as Albany, Buffalo, Detroit, and Milwaukee. For the most part, these two patterns reflect only the "wholesale" movement of capital through which firms purchased bond issues in their entirety in order to retail them to individual investors, savings banks, and other institutions.[95] Thus the bidding data do not reveal the final distribution of bonds as long-term holdings and, thus, the actual movement of capital out of the hands of final purchasers into the coffers of local governments.[96]

However, the retail distribution of these issues appears to have been quite localized in almost all cases. For example, Boston firms appear to have bid very competitively for bonds issued throughout New England both because they possessed more and better information concerning the authorities issuing these securities than was available to firms in more distant centers and because their retail customers in Boston and neighboring areas were also more comfortable holding these bonds than those issued some distance away. For these reasons, the bidding pattern tends to overrepresent the five donor trade areas as the final destination of bonds (as long-term holdings) and to underrepresent that role for smaller trade areas in the Northeast (such as Albany, Hartford, and Philadelphia). At the retail level, the latter probably had a positive financial trade balance with the remainder of the nation, along with the other five donor regions. However, the return of bonds to southern and western regions was unlikely because these were relatively attractive to eastern investors due to their high yields (even on a risk-adjusted basis), because the South and West lacked the extensive network of financial institutions that could have retailed these bonds to firms and individual investors, and because the periphery, by any number of alternative measures, was comparatively capital-starved. In sum, then, the bidding data reveal a complex movement of capital between the nation's regions in which, at the wholesale level, the major financial centers of the

[95] For example, the New York banking house of Griswold & Gillett publicly offered $726,000 of Kansas municipal and county bonds originally issued to support construction of an extension of the Chicago, Rock Island & Pacific Railroad Company within that state (*Commercial and Financial Chronicle*, December 31, 1887). For a representative list of city, town, township, county, school, and state bonds made available to investors by leading bond brokers, see *American Investments and Financial Opinions* 7:12 (December 1896): 524–525.

[96] In 1899, the city of Morganton, North Carolina, issued $5,000 in bonds to purchase the local, privately owned electric company. These bonds were taken by a Raleigh banking house and sold immediately to a regionally prominent firm in Chattanooga, which, in turn, transferred the bonds to a nationally active banking company in Chicago. From there, the bonds were probably sold in small lots to buyers in the Midwest and East. The first sale to the Raleigh firm, however, was the only one included in the data set and obviously understated to a considerable extent the interregional movement of capital that underpinned the North Carolina city's purchase. *Commercial and Financial Chronicle*, July 22, 1899.

manufacturing belt served as intermediaries between the capital-importing West and South and the capital-exporting communities distributed throughout the East.

SUMMARY OF THE NATIONAL FINANCIAL SYSTEM AND INTERREGIONAL CAPITAL FLOW

There were thus two distinct dimensions of capital transfer within the national financial system of the late nineteenth century. As discussed, the city hierarchy within the financial system placed some of the larger metropolitan areas in an intermediating role with regard to the interregional flow of capital. Brokers and bankers in these cities bought southern and western debt obligations, as well as those in the manufacturing belt, in order to retail them to smaller institutions and individual investors in the capital-rich East. The capital-rich areas of the nation, therefore, can be fairly easily divided into those which contained such intermediating metropolitan centers and those that did not. In Table 2.10, the trade areas containing these regions tend to stand out as those with relatively high percentages of bids for bonds issued in remote regions of the country (column two). When combined with the data on density of national bank capital (column one), all of the capital-rich trade areas can be divided into those with significant intermediating roles and those that were not directly involved in the interregional movement of capital. Similarly, the capital-poor regions of the nation can be easily divided into those that were relatively heavy importers of capital from the East and those that received very little investment from outside their region. The areas that heavily imported capital were comparatively well endowed with institutional connections to the remainder of the national financial system, exhibiting generally higher densities of national bank capital and issuing many more bonds, both by number and value, than those with weaker links. However, bonds issued by both types of capital-poor regions attracted bids from firms in distant trade areas while bonds issued by capital-rich regions tended to attract bids only from neighboring trade areas (see column three).[97]

Thus, the nation's regions can be divided into four broad categories:

---

[97]   The bidding data can be used to distinguish heavy-importing areas from those that imported only small amounts of capital. Ranked in declining order, the importing trade areas range from Minneapolis ($10.19 per capita in bids received from the capital-exporting manufacturing belt), through Los Angeles ($9.89), Evansville ($9.15), New Orleans ($8.52), Denver ($8.48), Louisville ($7.57), Kansas City ($7.35), Omaha ($6.30), Grand Rapids ($5.81), Des Moines ($4.95), Richmond ($4.62), San Francisco ($4.38), Nashville ($2.73), Memphis ($1.02), Atlanta ($0.89), and Charleston ($0.60). However, the reader should keep in mind that this data is restricted to the very last years of the nineteenth century and, for that reason, may misrepresent the volume and direction of capital flows in earlier periods.

Table 2.10. *Relative Integration of Trade Areas into the National Financial System*

		Financial indicators of relative integration		
		Bids for city and county bonds		
Trade area	National bank capital (per capita)	Bids offered for bonds issued in remote trade areas (% of all offers)	Bids received from firms in remote trade areas (% of all bids received)	Interest rate on farm and home mortgages (%)
New York	$32.54	27.4	5.9	5.29
Philadelphia	25.88	5.1	19.9	5.36
Hartford	48.54	27.3	5.1	5.43
Boston	51.36	17.7	24.0	5.64
Albany	24.65	10.8	18.4	5.68
Syracuse	16.24	1.6	80.1	5.74
Buffalo	8.77	10.9	45.3	5.77
Baltimore	21.26	2.9	34.9	5.78
Scranton	13.27	2.0	40.6	5.80
Pittsburgh	14.33	5.1	59.5	5.89
Cleveland	15.76	60.3	57.8	6.42
Louisville	15.24	—	36.4	6.56
Milwaukee	6.23	0.4	43.4	6.57
Cincinnati	19.98	65.1	19.8	6.64
Columbus	8.45	30.5	7.0	6.88
Richmond	3.23	—	73.7	6.93
Indianapolis	8.55	3.5	13.9	6.95
Detroit	10.27	29.1	53.2	6.96
Nashville	6.56	—	74.6	7.05
St. Louis	7.06	8.3	25.5	7.13
Evansville	6.11	—	76.5	7.15
Grand Rapids	10.74	—	52.8	7.26
Des Moines	7.75	—	29.6	7.41
Chicago	16.38	49.5	14.0	7.47
Omaha	13.41	—	78.7	7.97
Atlanta	3.31	—	59.9	7.99
Kansas City	11.71	3.6	48.2	8.14
Minneapolis	15.03	3.3	70.2	8.34
Memphis	7.41	—	52.0	8.62
San Francisco	8.67	—	67.3	8.69
New Orleans	6.19	—	66.3	8.69
Charleston	4.63	—	74.8	8.87
Denver	19.30	—	80.3	9.24
Los Angeles	18.42	0.6	59.6	9.83

Notes and sources: National bank capital was calculated as the sum of the entries for capital, surplus, and undivided profits as reported by the January 1891 edition of *Rand McNally International Bankers' Directory* (Chicago: Rand McNally, 1891). "Remote trade areas" were those that were not adjacent to the trade area either offering or receiving bids. For example, 27.4 percent of the value of all bids for city and county bonds made by firms in the New York trade area were made for bonds issued in regions that did not border the New York trade area. Dashes indicate that no firm in the trade area ever bid for bonds issued in a nonadjacent region. The percentages in the third column from the left indicate the proportion of all bids received from firms in remote trade areas. For example, 5.9 percent of the value of all bids made for bonds issued in the New York trade area were received from firms located in nonadjacent trade areas. Although there is no direct statistical relationship between the two middle columns, the striking inverse relationship between them should be expected because both proportions relate to the financial trade balance between the respective trade areas and the remainder of the nation. The source for bid information was the *Commercial and Financial Chronicle* for the years 1899 and 1900. Interest rates were calculated from data in *1890 Census Report on Farms and Homes: Proprietorship and Indebtedness* (Washington: GPO, 1896), Table 108.

Table 2.11. *Classification of Trade Areas with Respect to*
Intermediating Roles and Capital Flow

Capital-exporting regions		Capital-importing regions	
Trade areas with significant intermediating roles	Trade areas with no significant intermediating role	Well-integrated heavy capital-importing trade areas	Poorly integrated light capital-importing trade areas
New York	Philadelphia	Los Angeles	Atlanta
Boston	Hartford	Denver	Charleston
Cleveland	Albany	Minneapolis	Memphis
Cincinnati	Syracuse	Omaha	Richmond
Chicago	Buffalo	Kansas City	New Orleans
	Baltimore	San Francisco	Nashville
	St. Louis	Grand Rapids	
	Scranton	Des Moines	
	Pittsburgh	Louisville	
	Milwaukee	Evansville	
	Columbus		
	Indianapolis		
	Detroit		

Note: Trade areas with large concentrations of firms involved in the wholesale marketing of city and county bonds played "intermediating" roles in the national capital market. All other capital-exporting regions were placed in the second category. Capital-importing trade areas with large concentrations of national banks and other institutions with significant interregional connections were "well integrated" with the remainder of the national financial system. All other capital-importing regions were placed in the fourth category. Ranks within each category indicate the extent to which the trade area reflected the characteristics that typify each grouping. For example, of the five trade areas in the first category, New York most epitomized the intermediating, capital-exporting characteristics of the classification. The fit was least good with respect to Chicago.

capital-exporting trade areas with significant intermediating roles; capital-exporting areas lacking such roles; well-integrated, heavy capital-importing regions; and poorly integrated, light importing areas (see Table 2.11).

The first two categories divide the capital-rich East into first- and second-class metropolitan regions with the first-class areas containing those financial centers that played major intermediating roles in the movement of capital between regions. While the distinction between these two classes was economically important, it carried little political significance. All wealth-holders in the capital-exporting regions of the nation shared a common interest in the repayment of their loans and a minimization of inflation. Although the value of these loans varied within the manufacturing belt, it was the volume of interregional capital exports, not the presence or absence of intermediating institutions, that determined the relative response of eastern trade areas to threats to the gold standard and the national bank system. Thus little difference in political support for these conservative financial policies should be expected among the two major categories of capital-exporting regions.

The third and fourth categories divide the capital-importing regions of the nation and carry more political significance. While all capital-importing regions had at least some interest in adjusting the terms of financial trade between the nation's great sections and were, for that reason, more or less hostile to the gold standard, the political saliency of the financial system was much greater in heavy capital-importing regions than in those areas that imported little capital. In the latter, the protective tariff and other policies shaping the terms of trade in the national political economy were comparatively more important. While capital-importing regions were not divided with respect to the fundamental issues associated with capital flow in the United States, the relative dependence of importing regions on outside capital did shape the types of policies that trade area representatives advanced as redistributive claims in national politics.

Industrialization and International Capital Investment

While some of the county and city bonds issued in the late nineteenth century found their way to Europe, most of this capital movement was confined to the United States. However, foreign capital markets were extremely important for other kinds of capital investment, particularly railroad and, episodically, federal bonds. The sale of these securities to foreign investors promoted the consolidation of the American and European, particularly British, capital markets into one, fairly unified financial system. In the late nineteenth century, the integration of the United States into the world economy rested primarily on ties between finance capitalists, industrial manufacturers, and raw material distributors in the United States and their counterparts abroad. As was the case with most other important aspects of the American political economy in this period, these links were very unevenly distributed. In some parts of the nation, commercial and financial ties between firms in the United States and Europe were extremely strong and active. In others, they were almost entirely absent.

The laying of the undersea telegraph cables between the United States and Britain allowed commercial and financial information to move across the Atlantic almost instantaneously.[98] Well before the turn of the century

---

[98] "The leading money markets of the world have in late years entered into closer relations with one another than they have ever before held. This is the fact even as between European centres of trade, but is peculiarly true with regard to our own

such cables linked not only the United States and Europe but, in addition, had spread throughout the globe. Following for the most part the major shipping routes in the world economy, particularly those emanating from or otherwise involving Great Britain, multiple extensions of the oceanic cable system stretched across the North Atlantic between Ireland and Nova Scotia, linked Great Britain and Brazil via Lisbon and the Cape Verde Islands, and traveled through the Mediterranean, the Suez Canal, thence to India, Southeast Asia, China, Australia, finally terminating in New Zealand, New Caledonia, the Philippines, and the Pacific frontier of Russia. Other oceanic lines circumnavigated the southern half of Africa, knit together the islands of the Caribbean, and drove down the western coast of South America. These international cables complemented land-based telegraph networks which were comparatively dense throughout Europe, the United States, Argentina, and most of the British empire.[99]

The international telegraph network was expensive, and, as a result, most messages represented urgent commercial transactions or government orders. As both the most important commercial nation in the world and, because of its imperial possessions, the most expansive government administration, Great Britain was the center of the international telegraph network and responsible for much of its construction. But the United States, in both its domestic network and connections to trading partners in Latin America, was not far behind.

Because the messages that cable companies carried reflected the most substantial commercial links between the domestic and international economies, one way of gauging the relative extent of these links is to analyze the location of American firms that maintained addresses with a cable company. Because cable connections between the United States and the rest of the world were controlled by a handful of companies, most cable directories thus document the relative orientation of domestic trade areas toward

relations with the old world. Electricity [i.e., the Atlantic cable] and steam [i.e., steamships] have annihilated distance, while a common monetary basis [i.e., the gold standard] for exchanges, completes the union." *Commercial and Financial Chronicle*, December 31, 1881. Some years later the *Chronicle* added: ". . . any development in the United States, whether bearing on the crop outlook, or upon other things, is flashed over to Europe, and thus the markets are under world-wide domination, instead of under limited local influences. . . . Two things may be said to follow . . . first, an equalization of values in the markets of the world, and secondly a reduction and narrowing of the margin of profits." July 16, 1892. For a general discussion of the impact of high-speed communications on investor decisions and corporate operations, see Alexander James Field, "The Magnetic Telegraph, Price and Quantity Data, and the New Management of Capital," *Journal of Economic History* 52:2 (June 1992): 401–414.

99   For a detailed depiction of the international network, see the maps at the beginning of the *Atlantic Cable Directory of Registered Addresses* (New York: Atlantic Cable Directory and Code Company, 1898).

the international economy.[100] The 1898 edition of the *Atlantic Cable Directory*, for example, carried 5,532 separate listings for American firms. In per capita density, the New York trade area led the nation with slightly over thirty-five firms per 100,000 people (see Table 2.12). In absolute numbers, the New York trade area also contained the largest number of firms in the directory (1,486). As was the case for almost all of the nation's trade areas, the leading urban center in the region, New York City, was the site for the greatest number of firms.[101] In this instance, New York City firms comprised almost nine out of every ten in the trade area and 24 percent of the national total.

New York clearly stood apart as the primary entrepôt linking the European and American economies. The dominance of the port in the import/export trade of the United States conferred on the city's financial markets a dominant role in managing domestic and foreign investment. For example, among the nation's leading trade centers, New York City alone was responsible for almost half (380 of 842) of the finance capital addresses in the cable directory. This position carried with it several significant implications. First, New York had far stronger ties to London (and, to a lesser extent, other world financial centers such as Paris) than it had with most American cities. In fact, in terms of transactions, telegraph messages, commercial alliances between otherwise independent firms, intermarriage between members of the respective financial elites, cultural interchange of theatrical and operatic companies, and so forth, the links between New York and London were probably as thick as those between New York and any other American city. Because of the city's intimate relations with foreign economies, cultures, and peoples (the latter often settling in the city itself), many Americans viewed New York as an alien presence in both domestic society and the national political economy. The irony, repeated throughout history in many other places and times, was that this same alien presence

---

[100] In the *Atlantic Cable Directory*, for example, each of the firms listed was given a one-word "address" which, when combined with a similar word designating the city, served to identify the destination or origin of the message. For example, J. P. Morgan & Co. in New York City became, through use of the directory and the accompanying code dictionary, "Morgan Vederhoed." All of the firms were listed by name and city, assigned a code word, and allowed to briefly identify the chief business or businesses in which they were engaged. The geographical directory was, in addition, supplemented by a general commercial directory in which firms were identified by their line of business, regardless of location. For these reasons, the directory doubled both as a listing of addresses for the sending and receiving of messages and as a compilation of those firms in each line of business most heavily engaged in international trade or finance.

[101] The exceptions were in the Albany trade area (where Troy, New York, had more listings than Albany), Des Moines (with no listings at all in the entire trade area), and Nashville (where Birmingham, Alabama, had more listings). In the other 31 trade areas, the leading urban center was usually the location for half or more of all listed firms in the entire region.

Table 2.12. Level of Development and Relative Integration into the World Economy: Atlantic Cable Addresses in 1898

Trade area level of development (by category)	Addresses (per 100,000 population)	Distribution of firms with cable addresses in leading cities					
		Finance capital	Cotton	Grain	Meat	Other (including manufacturing)	Total addresses
5 (highest)	18.9	551 (65.4)	11 (21.6)	29 (19.5)	16 (34.8)	1,647 (60.1)	2,255 (58.9)
4	16.9	178 (21.1)	1 (2.0)	39 (26.2)	20 (43.5)	609 (22.2)	847 (22.1)
3	6.0	17 (2.0)		5 (3.4)	1 (2.2)	121 (4.4)	144 (3.8)
2	1.8	13 (1.5)		17 (11.4)	6 (13.0)	63 (2.3)	99 (2.6)
1	2.9	34 (4.0)	2 (3.9)	40 (26.8)	3 (6.5)	125 (4.6)	204 (5.3)
0 (lowest)	3.8	49 (5.8)	37 (72.5)	19 (12.8)		176 (6.4)	281 (7.3)
Nation	6.1	842 (100)	51 (100)	149 (100)	46 (100)	2,741 (100)	3,830 (100)

Note and source: The figures in the second column from the left give the number of Atlantic cable addresses for firms throughout the entire trade area as a ratio to every 100,000 people residing in that trade area. The figures to the right record, for the leading city in each trade area, the firms maintaining cable addresses by type of business. The "Finance capital" column includes all firms under the general heading of financial, insurance, and commission merchants, as well as real estate. The "Cotton" column includes all firms listed under the general entries for cotton (raw), as well as cottonseed and its manufactured products. The "Grain" column includes all firms listed under the general entry flours and cereals, in addition to those under grain and grain brokers. The "Meat" column includes all firms listed under livestock, canned and dressed meats, beef and pork packers, and packing house products. Duplicate listings for any firm in the business index were recorded only for the first designation in the general directory. The firms under the "Other" column are quite diverse but the vast majority are industrial manufacturers or the wholesale distributors of manufactured products. For both addresses and business categories, see Atlantic Cable Directory of Registered Addresses (New York: Atlantic Cable Directory and Code Company, 1898). Level of development is based on comparison of the trade area with the national average along five referents: per capita value-added in manufacturing, per capita patent filings, per capita wealth, prevailing interest rates for farm and home mortgages, and literacy rates for adult males. Category 5 included the following trade areas: Baltimore, Boston, Buffalo, Cincinnati, Cleveland, Hartford, New York, and Philadelphia; category 4: Chicago, Pittsburgh, and San Francisco; category 3: Albany, Denver, Los Angeles, Milwaukee, and Syracuse; category 2: Des Moines, Detroit, Grand Rapids, Indianapolis, Minneapolis, and Omaha; category 1: Columbus, Kansas City, Louisville, St. Louis, and Scranton; category 0: Atlanta, Charleston, Evansville, Memphis, Nashville, New Orleans, and Richmond.

was the cultural center that constructed much of the nation's very identity as a people.

Much more than half of the export and import trade of the United States moved across the docks ringing New York harbor.[102] As a consequence, port operations alone employed the brawn and talents of a very significant portion of the city labor force. But beyond the activity at the waterfront lay the vast commercial districts and warehouse facilities that underpinned the wholesale collection and distribution of goods that moved either into or out of the nation. Astride both of these was the financial district that financed much of the movement of goods and capital in both foreign and domestic trade. All three sectors, ranging from the mundane operations at dockside to the complex extrapolations of profit in hundreds of private banks and commercial emporia, fed on the stream of commerce through New York in ways that made tariff protection anathema to their interests. In addition, New York City was constantly exposed to foreign competition to a much higher degree than the nation's interior, where the much greater costs of overland rail transportation or river movement constituted a "natural" tariff against foreign producers.[103]

---

[102]   For a description of New York City's prominence as an export-import center, see the *Commercial and Financial Chronicle*, September 1, 1888. In reporting trade statistics for the 1887–88 fiscal year, the *Chronicle* noted that 65.0 percent of the value of all imports and 44.7 percent of all exports had passed over the city's docks. Also see the September 27, 1890, issue.

[103]   Analysis of the tariff often assumes that the impact of duties fell uniformly throughout the nation. This was, in fact, not true because transportation costs to the interior often provided more than adequate "natural" protection to producers located away from the coasts. The differences in regional impact, in turn, sometimes had direct political implications as well. For example, during debate over redemption of the trade dollar in 1884, a measure supported by silver interests in the West, James Belford, a Colorado Republican, warned his party colleague, William "Pig Iron" Kelley of Pennsylvania, that "Colorado needs no tariff on Bessemer steel. It costs $14 to ship a ton of Bessemer steel rails from the State of Pennsylvania to the State of Colorado. All the tariff that is there needed is the distance which the rails have to be conveyed." *Congressional Record* 48:1:2484, April 1, 1884. If members from eastern iron and steel districts did not support silver interests on the trade dollar bill, Belford warned that the West could easily abandon the protectionist coalition with respect to the iron and steel portions of the tariff (which, according to his calculations, Colorado producers did not need). The flip side was that the tariff often had its greatest impact on prices along the nation's coasts. In his testimony before the Industrial Commission, for example, Charles M. Schwab, president of the United States Steel Company, contended that a tariff on steel rails was necessary because American producers, given the greater cost of overland transport from eastern mills, could not compete in California markets with British producers who shipped rails as "ballast in outgoing ships." *Report of the Industrial Commission: Trusts and Industrial Combinations*, vol. 13 (Washington, D.C.: GPO, 1901), p. 456. Overland transport thus made the impact of the tariff highly variable across the country; coastal ports and their hinterlands were often adversely affected

Although New York was, in fact, the largest manufacturing center in the United States, most industries requiring protection from foreign competition had been purged from the city's economy long ago. As a result, much of the city's manufacturing base was either efficient compared with foreign producers or devoted to the production of high-value, cultural goods that both responded to and, increasingly, created the changing tastes of consumers in the rest of the nation. Publishing houses and the fashion district thus joined hands in the urban and domestic economy but required no protection from the rest of the world. In short, the heavy involvement of the city in the management of the nation's export/import trade effectively overrode the protectionist implications of its vast manufacturing base.

The strong links to foreign financial centers and the large financial community servicing investment markets and international trade within the city also made New York the leading defender of the international gold standard in national politics. Investors in Boston or Philadelphia often defended the gold standard by citing the potential depreciation of their securities if the system were abandoned – a static interpretation that only acknowledged creditor-borrower relations in the financial system. Although many members of the financial community were very wealthy and thus held large, long-term investments in stocks, bonds, and other assets, the New York commercial and financial establishment drew most of its wealth from trade. Thus, the vital role of the international gold standard in the trading of goods and financial securities was much more apparent and materially significant in New York City than anywhere else in the nation. For that reason, political agents representing New York, whether elected officials or financiers, often assumed a leading role in the design and operation of the financial system – a role that relegated other capital-rich regions and representatives to a limited, supporting position.

All of these factors combined in such a way as to make the New York trade area the only free trade/gold standard region of the nation. With respect to the tariff, the city went the way of the Democratic South. With respect to the gold standard, the city could stay with the Democrats, even though a majority of the party's members in Congress supported abandonment of gold, as long as the national leadership was agreeable. Grover Cleveland's three nominations for the presidency and two terms in office, for example, underscored both the importance of New York's balancing position in national politics and the region's commitment to free trade and gold (Cleveland, who came from New York State and well understood the

by a tariff that, in the interior of the country, had little or no influence on prices. For a brief discussion of the varying impact of the tariff on the domestic iron and steel industry, depending on type of product and geographical location, see *Industrial Commission: Preliminary Report on Trusts and Industrial Combinations*, vol. 1, p. 24.

city's interests, was a strong and loyal adherent to both policies). After the nomination of William Jennings Bryan, New York entered the political wilderness; although the city and region, along with the rest of the capital-rich East, tilted heavily toward McKinley in 1896, the Republican commitment to tariff protection prevented the city from ever joining the party. Of all the major commercial cities in the world (e.g., London, Paris, St. Petersburg, or Rome), New York may have been the most politically isolated and culturally alienated with respect to the remainder of the nation in which it was located.[104]

While other cities and regions shared a few of New York's entrepôt characteristics (e.g., Boston, Philadelphia, and Chicago), all of them were much closer in scale and composition to other trade areas in the manufacturing belt than they were to New York.[105] However, San Francisco was an exception in some ways. The city's relative isolation from what otherwise would have been the smothering influence of the major eastern commercial centers and the port's privileged, almost monopolistic position with respect to trans-Pacific trade gave rise to a very powerful financial community in the city. In fact, financiers and merchants may have dominated San Francisco politics to a greater extent than corresponding groups in any other major urban center, save New York.[106] Outside the eastern seaboard and San Francisco, the nation's industrial centers contained only a small number of

[104] New York was one of the few major entrepôts that did not double as the national capital of its country. As intended when Washington was selected as a site for the capital, this fact permanently separated the nation's commercial interests from politics in a way and to an extent not found in most comparable European states. In these other nations, state formation focused on a political capital that became the primary commercial center in part because the crown stimulated expansion of local financial and commercial interests. In terms of alienation, the closest parallel was in South America where Buenos Aires, over the strong but divided opposition of provinces in the surrounding Argentine hinterland, ultimately succeeded in constructing a state that almost exactly coincided with its natural trading region. New York, by comparison, played only a secondary (and often losing) role in the construction of the United States during the nineteenth century. These two facts, the separation of political and commercial centers plus the relatively insignificant role of New York in American state formation, reinforced the alien status of the city in the national political economy – a status that became enshrined in political rhetoric condemning the city for greed, exploitation, and disloyalty.

[105] In numbers of addresses registered in the cable directory, the ten leading cities in the United States were New York (1,335 listings), Chicago (474), Boston (298), Philadelphia (295), San Francisco (192), Pittsburgh (181), Buffalo (92), New Orleans (92), St. Louis (89), and Hartford (88).

[106] On the emergence of San Francisco as an advanced entrepôt and the factors supporting the city's anomalous development, see Odell, "The Integration of Regional and Interregional Capital Markets," 299–302. For a description of municipal politics in San Francisco during this period, see Philip J. Ethington, *The Public City: The Political Construction of Urban Life in San Francisco, 1850–1900* (New York: Cambridge University Press, 1994), pp. 287–407.

nonmanufacturing companies among the firms maintaining addresses in the cable directory.

In the agrarian periphery, the leading cities usually reported only a few listings and a much higher proportion of these were addresses for firms engaged in the wholesale marketing and distribution of the nation's major export commodities. For example, both New Orleans and Memphis were major participants in the cotton trade. Even comparatively small ports could be significant players in organizing cotton exports; Galveston, for example, reported eight firms specializing in raw cotton or cottonseed products. Kansas City, Minneapolis, and Evansville were similarly involved in the management of the wholesale marketing and distribution of grain.[107] Well over a third of all the cable addresses maintained by Richmond firms concerned some aspect of the tobacco trade. Meat and livestock products, on the other hand, were much more centralized within the manufacturing belt, with Chicago alone accounting for almost 40 percent of all firms located in the nation's leading centers.

In sum, two broad and general patterns governed the distribution of American firms participating in international trade and finance. On the one hand, the density of such firms declined more or less in tandem with relative development. Trade areas with low interest rates, high densities of national banks, and heavy involvement in interregional capital movements tended to have much higher densities of such firms than less well-endowed trade areas. On the other hand, the type of firms maintaining addresses in the nation's leading cities changed in significant ways across the spectrum from most to least developed regions. At the most developed end of the spectrum, the composition of firms was heavily weighted toward the financial and commercial houses that together comprised America's contribution to international finance capital. At this end, also, the absolute numbers of firms engaged in the wholesale marketing or distribution of major export commodities was relatively large, although they comprised but small fractions of the overall numbers of cable addresses. Most manufacturing firms were similarly located in these cities.[108] Among the least developed trade areas, the distribution of firms was heavily weighted (in absolute numbers) toward the wholesale marketing and distribution of agricultural commodities; relatively few financial or industrial firms maintained addresses.

New York City dominated the linkages that integrated the United States into the world economy. That dominance was particularly strong with respect to the integration of the national and international capital markets,

---

[107]   For a description of the internal organization of the grain trade, see *Report of the Industrial Commission: Distribution of Farm Products*, vol. 6 (Washington, D.C.: GPO, 1901), pp. 105–114, 121–135.

[108]   The "other" category in Table 2.12, although quite diverse (e.g., containing a significant number of wholesale marketers and distributors of raw tobacco in the case of Richmond), is primarily composed of manufacturers and the distributors of industrial products.

and the international exchange of manufactured goods. For meat, the organization of American trade was only slightly less concentrated in the nation's most developed regions and cities because animal products, in order to enter the export trade, had first to be manufactured and this operation usually took place within the more developed cities of the East and Midwest (particularly Chicago). The movement of grain, however, was more frequently organized on the periphery of the manufacturing belt.[109] Raw cotton was even more closely controlled by firms located in peripheral regions. In both cases, the firms specializing in the wholesale marketing and distribution of these commodities often diversified into financial activities closely associated with their mercantile operations; for that reason, the leading cities in the least developed regions had slightly higher numbers of financial institutions registering trans-Atlantic cable addresses than those regions a bit more advanced in overall development. However, the differences here are slight and do little to disturb the overall pattern.

In general, the integration of the manufacturing belt into the world system was controlled in all of its aspects by the major financial centers along the eastern seaboard. The movement of manufactured goods and money between the Plains and Mountain West and the international economy was also directed by these same eastern cities, but control of the grain trade was more localized within the western periphery. The South also exhibited this bifurcation of, on the one hand, eastern dominance over international capital markets and the movement of industrial goods and, on the other, indigenous control of trade in agricultural commodities. Thus the export relations of the periphery in the major commodity crops were often autonomous of the eastern financial centers while the operation of capital markets and distribution of industrial products were centralized in the core.

THE GOLD STANDARD AND INTEGRATION OF NEW YORK AND LONDON FINANCIAL MARKETS

The New York and London financial markets were the two most closely linked and integrated international centers in the world during the late

---

[109] Wheat was by far the most important of the grains. The two leading cities as locations for firms specializing in the international movement of wheat and the other grains were Chicago and St. Louis, with 26 and 21 cable addresses, respectively. Because of its location to the north of St. Louis, Chicago was the dominant center for the movement of spring wheat, while St. Louis marketed and distributed the winter crop. *Commercial and Financial Chronicle*, August 26, 1882. For a description of how grain transactions were executed using the trans-Atlantic cable, see *Commercial and Financial Chronicle*, June 12, 1880. For the regional organization of the grain trade, see *Industrial Commission: Distribution of Farm Products*, vol. 6, p. 77.

nineteenth century.[110] In addition to the gold standard, the linkages between these markets were strengthened by the increasing use of steam by trans-Atlantic vessels and the inauguration of suboceanic cable service. While demands for capital in the United States were routinely met by investors throughout Europe, close ties between American and European markets also meant that financial crises abroad were rapidly and easily transmitted to the United States. In describing the surprising impact of a speculative crisis in France on the American financial market, for example, the *Commercial and Financial Chronicle* exclaimed: "Each day's experience adds new proof of the commercial oneness of the world, under modern methods and appliances. Paris seemed quite a distance off and totally disunited from America a month ago; but we awoke one pleasant morning suddenly to learn that she was really our next-door neighbor."[111] Thus, in addition to the domestic business cycle and the annual rhythm of harvest demands for currency, American financial stability was also indirectly threatened by the same foreign events that roiled European markets. These events, for the most part, can be divided into three categories: (1) domestic business cycles within European economies, particularly Britain, that often drove interest rates up and down independently of business cycles in the United States; (2) threats of war between the major European powers which often led European investors to liquidate American investments as interest rates rose in Europe; and (3) financial crises in other parts of the world which, because these crises threatened the solvency of European financial institutions, similarly led foreign investors to liquidate their American holdings. All three of these, from the American perspective, were difficult to predict, produced stringency in the money market, increased short-term interest rates, and were quite independent of the rhythms of the domestic economy.

European markets, both in London and on the Continent, absorbed vast amounts of railroad bonds during the late nineteenth century. In many cases, because the initial placement of these securities was made abroad, the entire amount of an issue could be simply translated into an equivalent importation of foreign capital. These transactions were frequently so large that their impact on foreign exchange was anticipated.[112] For individual British investors the purchase of American securities had become so routine

---

[110]   On the unification of American and British financial, commodity, and labor markets, see Donald N. McCloskey and J. Richard Zecher, "How the Gold Standard Worked, 1880–1913," in Barry Eichengreen, ed., *The Gold Standard in Theory and History* (New York: Methuen, 1985), pp. 66–72, 76.

[111]   February 18, 1882.

[112]   For example, see the report of the sale of $3 million worth of Northern Pacific 6 percent bonds to German banks in the *Commercial and Financial Chronicle*, July 22, 1882. More generally, see November 4 and 11, 1882; January 20, 1883; May 31, 1884; April 16, 1892; and March 4, 1899.

by the late 1880s that an English Association of American Bondholders had appeared in London, advertising its mission as the registration of bonds, collection of dividends, and other services associated with trans-Atlantic investment.[113] Where large amounts of stock or bonds in specific companies were held by British investors, they often formed combinations of one sort or another in order to influence American corporate managers or otherwise protect their interests.[114] Still, the market in American railroad securities was very turbulent because company earnings were unpredictable, due to: the failure of most American companies to regularly publish financial statements; rapid expansion of the railroad network that constantly diverted traffic from one system to another; rate wars between companies that often followed the opening of a new competing line (these wars tended to reerupt as long as management of the companies remained in different hands); the prohibition of railroad pools by the Interstate Commerce Act and, to a much lesser extent, regulatory decisions by the Interstate Commerce Commission; variability in the size of the harvest which, for some railroads, comprised the larger part of their business; labor strikes which disproportionately targeted the nation's railroads during the late nineteenth century; and variability in weather conditions as an independent factor affecting the operation of the lines.[115]

Since most of this uncertainty was beyond the control of railroad managers, the accountability of the railroad companies to foreign investors, already committed to passive participation through their tendency to hold bonds rather than stocks, was generally weak. Despite these shortcomings, British investors in some cases came to exercise great influence over many lines in the United States, among them the Atchison, Topeka and Santa Fe; the Baltimore & Ohio; the Central Pacific; the Chicago, Milwaukee and St. Paul; the Erie; the Illinois Central; the Louisville and Nashville; the New York Central; the Norfolk and Western; the Northern Pacific; the Pennsylvania; and the Union Pacific.[116] As can be gathered from their names, many

---

[113] *Commercial and Financial Chronicle*, October 8, 1887.

[114] Bondholders were, however, in a particularly difficult position because they could directly influence corporate affairs only if the company entered bankruptcy. Since bonds were the investment vehicle of choice for foreign investors, their interest in profitable companies was only passive and their dissatisfaction with management could be expressed only by dumping their holdings. For descriptions of foreign bondholder committees organized for the Missouri, Kansas & Texas and, separately, for the Atlantic & Danville Railway, see the *Commercial and Financial Chronicle*, November 30, 1889; January 28, 1893.

[115] *Commercial and Financial Chronicle*, November 3, 1888.

[116] Kirkland, *Industry Comes of Age*, p. 69; Leland H. Jenks, "Britain and American Railway Development," *Journal of Economic History* 11 (Fall 1951): 376–377; Wilkins, *History of Foreign Investment to 1914*, pp. 198–228; *Commercial and Financial Chronicle*, May 11, June 1, August 17, September 21, 1889; January 23, 1892; April 4, 1896; February 6, 1897. Often this influence was mediated by

Table 2.13. *Regional and Foreign Holdings of*
Union Pacific Stock, 1884–1891

	In England	In Holland	Total foreign	In Massachusetts	In New York	Total United States
1884	13,289	31,675	51,748	238,268	263,065	NA
1885	29,567	42,075	79,997	228,630	244,197	NA
1886	82,616	53,785	142,332	208,601	203,084	NA
1887	62,546	51,355	118,272	201,882	239,736	NA
1888	67,745	60,713	132,479	197,773	210,789	NA
1889	110,876	55,805	171,003	157,905	233,218	NA
1890	153,089	39,935	199,836	150,148	218,567	408,671
1891	185,220	22,481	214,418	149,257	203,350	394,090

Source: Commercial and Financial Chronicle, April 30 and August 13, 1892. Share-holdings are as of December 31 of the respective years.

of the lines attracting foreign interest in this period were in the Plains and West. Foreign investment in railroads in other sections, particularly New England, was apparently light.[117] The Union Pacific was relatively visible and acceptable to foreign investors because the federal government continued to play a major sponsoring role as creditor. The Union Pacific was also the only railroad to regularly publish information on the residence of its shareholders. That data suggests some of the long-term trends in foreign (particularly British) ownership of American railroads between 1884 and 1891, as well as the concentration of shareholding in the northeastern United States (see Table 2.13).

European investment in the United States in 1899 has been estimated at over $3 billion.[118] While this was a large sum in absolute terms, foreign capital still played a secondary role in funding American industrialization; for example, even in the railroad sector, where European investment was

cooperation between pairs of private American and British banks, such as Kidder-Peabody and Baring with respect to the Santa Fe, and J. P. Morgan and August Belmont (the American representative of N. M. Rothschild & Sons of London) with respect to the St. Paul.

[117] Lance E. Davis and Robert J. Cull, *International Capital Markets and American Economic Growth, 1820–1914* (New York: Cambridge University Press, 1994), p. 24; Bacon, "American International Indebtedness," p. 266; Edward Chase Kirkland, *Men, Cities, and Transportation: A Study in New England History, 1820–1900* (New York: Russell & Russell, 1968), p. 339.

[118] Thomas C. Cochran and William Miller, *The Age of Enterprise: A Social History of Industrial America*, rev. ed. (New York: Harper Torchbooks, 1961), p. 137; Kirkland, *Industry Comes of Age*, p. 304.

heaviest, three quarters of all capital investment was contributed by Americans.[119] And, in fact, trans-Atlantic investment midway through the 1890s was transformed into a two-way street as the United States became, at the margin, a net creditor in the world economy.[120]

The Gold Standard and Industrial Expansion

The major factors that shaped the rapidly expanding and maturing American capital market during the late nineteenth century were the private ownership and control of almost all factors of production (e.g., natural resources, corporate institutions, and liquid capital), the integration of the domestic capital market with counterparts in Europe, and the extremely uneven pattern of regional development and economic growth. The first of these is a defining precondition for a capitalist economy and was never politically questioned during the late nineteenth century.[121] However, the integration of American and European capital markets, founded as it was on the operation of the international gold standard, was a focal point of political conflict. Similarly, proposals intended to redress imbalances between the regions, both in terms of their terms of trade with each other and within the world economy, were also primary staples of political conflict and party competition.

To understand just how radical proposals for change would have worked in the late nineteenth century, the relationship between industrialization and the financial system must first be described. American industrialization was supported by an abundance of capital originating in a high rate of personal savings by individuals, a high rate of reinvestment of corporate profits, and foreign investment.[122] All three depended on the stability of American finan-

---

[119] Kirkland, *Industry Comes of Age*, p. 70.

[120] Williamson, *American Growth*, pp. 11, 92; Davis and Cull, *International Capital Markets*, pp. 8–9, 79–107.

[121] Party platforms most commonly called for public ownership of the railroad, telegraph, and telephone networks, as well as control and operation of urban utilities. Aside from these sectors and other proposals to regulate fees charged by grain elevators, to abolish the national bank system (which would have left state-chartered institutions still operating), and to close down commodity exchanges that allowed trading in futures contracts, private enterprise was rarely the target of government controls in party platforms. Although socialist parties, after 1895 or so, were a minor exception, the foundational role of private property, as a general institution underlying the American economy, was just never mentioned in popular politics, let alone seriously threatened. See Chapter 3 for a thorough analysis of party platforms during this period.

[122] On personal savings, see Kirkland, *Industry Comes of Age*, p. 217; Raymond W. Goldsmith, *A Study of Saving in the United States* (Princeton, N.J.: Princeton University Press, 1955), vol. 1, pp. 4–5; Richard Sylla, Jack W. Wilson, and Charles P. Jones, "U.S. Financial Markets and Long-Term Economic Growth, 1790–1989," in Thomas Weiss and Donald Schaefer, eds., *American Economic Development in Historical Perspective* (Stanford, Calif.: Stanford University Press, 1994), p. 48.

cial markets which, in turn, rested on the stability of the dollar and the relative absence of political uncertainty with regard to government taxation,
military adventures, and other policies that might threaten the security of
investment.[123] Given the comparative breadth of the American national
market and the profitability of the modern corporation, capital investment
in the United States could realize very high real returns. However, even these
high returns could have been taxed or confiscated by punitive government
policies. In addition, the threat of other hostile government actions, particularly with respect to an abrupt change in the value of the dollar, was
always present, although the level of threat varied quite a bit over the course
of the late nineteenth century. Given these political threats and the capital
flight that would have ensued, the abundance of investment capital in the
late nineteenth century cannot be taken for granted. In fact, the unregulated openness of American capital markets was a clear response to these
threats and, thus, a major facilitating factor supporting capital investment.
Liquidity allowed individual investors, each independently and constantly
calculating the political risk attending their investments in the United States,
to immediately reduce their American holdings (sending funds to safer
havens abroad) if the political outlook darkened. In a very real sense, the
United States secured the confidence of investors by refusing to manipulate
or control international capital movements. The consequent integration of
New York financial markets into their London counterparts made the
United States economy in some ways a simple extension of the European
investment field.[124]

As commonly recognized at the time, the liquidity of American financial
markets was a precondition for large-scale foreign investment. In addition
and perhaps more important in some ways, these same characteristics were
a precondition for retention of individual savings and corporate profits in
the United States. Without liquidity and stability, the extraordinarily
large accumulations of capital arising from domestic savings and
profits might very well have been invested abroad, thus aborting rapid
economic expansion. In fact, foreign capital was far less important to
American development than domestic investment throughout the nineteenth
century.[125]

---

[123]   See, for example, the Duke of Marlborough's observations on the superiority of
American investments over those offered by Latin America, in *Commercial and
Financial Chronicle*, May 16, 1891.

[124]   For a description of American securities sold in London, Frankfurt, Berlin, and
Amsterdam capital markets, see *Commercial and Financial Chronicle*, July 5, 1890.
For the London Stock Exchange between 1870 and 1900, see Davis and Cull,
International Capital Markets, pp. 62–68.

[125]   Net foreign investment probably accounted for less than 5 percent of additions to
national capital stock between 1799 and 1900. Davis and Cull, *International Capital
Markets*, pp. 1, 17–19, 37–49, 115. Also see Robert E. Gallman, "Gross National
Product, 1834–1909," in National Bureau of Economic Research, *Output,*

Adherence to the international gold standard minimized the political risk associated with American investment in several ways.[126] Most important, the gold standard provided the foundation for the close integration of the New York and London financial markets by fixing the value of the dollar against the pound and thus eliminating fluctuations in the exchange rate.[127] Once this uncertainty was eliminated, it did not matter whether American securities or contractual agreements were denominated in dollars or pounds – regardless of how they were quoted or written, the terms meant gold.[128] As a result, both domestic and foreign investors could hold

Employment, and Productivity in the United States after 1860 (New York: Columbia University Press, 1966), pp. 14–15; Simon Kuznets, "Foreign Economic Relations of the United States and Their Impact upon the Domestic Economy: A Review of Long Term Trends," *Proceedings of the American Philosophical Society* 92:4 (1948): 233.

[126] Some authors have contended that the late nineteenth-century gold standard, viewed as an international system, was in reality a pound-based community because obligations denominated in British pounds supplemented gold as the international currency. See, for example, W. M. Scammell, "The Working of the Gold Standard," and A. G. Ford, "Notes on the Working of the Gold Standard before 1914," in Eichengreen, *Gold Standard*, pp. 104, 161. From the American perspective, this view is incorrect in that the United States Treasury exclusively held gold as backing for the dollar and thus behaved as if the pound were independently guaranteed by the British. There were several reasons, one major and one minor, why the United States did not hold reserves in the form of British pounds as backing for the dollar. The minor one was that the Treasury was not organized along the lines of a central bank and thus would have had difficulty conducting open-market operations in foreign exchange. But whatever difficulties might have hampered such operations were far from insurmountable. The major one was political; if the United States had fixed the dollar's value in terms of the British pound, the primacy of the foreign exchange function would have been laid bare (even though, because the British firmly adhered to the gold standard, the result would have been the same – a fixed value of the dollar in terms of gold). By exclusively denominating the dollar in gold, the government avoided identifying the nation's financial policy with a foreign power (Britain). Such an identification would have fatally undermined political support for the gold standard even though, in practice, the system would have functioned the same if the United States had held pound reserves in addition to gold. Even so, political opposition to the gold standard often cited American subordination to the British as an important reason to abandon the system (see Chapter 6).

[127] The historical record is littered with memorials in support of the gold standard's role in promoting trans-Atlantic market integration. See, for example, *Finance and Commerce: A Standard Weekly Review of Current Events* 5:23 (June 8, 1896): 501. On the integration of asset markets between the United States and Great Britain, mediated by the movement of gold, see Lawrence H. Officer, "The Remarkable Efficiency of the Dollar-Sterling Gold Standard, 1890–1906," *Journal of Economic History* 49:1 (March 1989): 1–41.

[128] As the *Commercial and Financial Chronicle* put it, "the permanent advantage of having in this country a single standard of value in harmony with the other great commercial nations of the world cannot be over-estimated in considering the prospective value of all our stocks, bonds and real estate securities. Such States as Texas, Colorado and Montana would scarcely have an existence to-day as wealthy

American securities without worrying whether central state exchange rate policies would unpredictably affect their value.

However, because adherence to the gold standard was itself a political decision, the gold standard merely replaced the dollar exchange rate as the major source of political risk for American investments.[129] The gold standard thus became the major stress point in the otherwise very investor-friendly structure of the American political economy. In response, both domestic and foreign investors minimized the information costs attending calculations of political risk by simply monitoring the size of the gold reserve in the United States Treasury. In practice, the gold reserve served as a proxy for the ability and willingness of the United States to maintain gold payments.[130] There was, of course, a downside to all this. If a large number of investors came to believe that abandonment of the gold standard was imminent, their consequent rush to liquidate investments in the United States could both overwhelm the financial markets of the period and push the nation off gold in what would have looked very much like a self-fulfilling prophecy.[131]

Because it was so important to American economic growth, political contestation over the gold standard became the single most important devel-

and flourishing communities except for the gold that has been contributed by New York and London to build their railroads and develop their mineral and other industrial resources." October 28, 1893. Also see Barry Eichengreen, "Editor's Introduction," in Eichengreen, *Gold Standard*, pp. 7, 9.

[129]   Great Britain was the only nation with a similarly unqualified commitment to the gold standard. All other gold standard nations placed at least some obstacles in the way of massive withdrawals from their bullion reserves. And Great Britain, as the largest creditor nation in the world, the beneficiary of a currency held by other nations as a substitute for gold, and a centralized financial system headed by the Bank of England, was in a position to draw in gold to replenish its reserves through any number of mechanisms, including raising interest rates or selling foreign securities. For Great Britain, all of these constituted material evidence of the nation's financial power and commitment to the gold standard as a creditor nation; through sheer financial strength, the British demonstrated that they could and would choose to adhere to gold. In contrast, as a borrower nation, credibility of American adherence to fixed exchange rates had to rest on its very vulnerability to gold withdrawals. This vulnerability permitted investors to react immediately to any central state policy threatening the nation's gold reserves and thus, in effect, held the viability of American capital markets hostage to the gold standard.

[130]   For an argument and analysis that presents adherence to the gold standard on the part of capital-importing nations as an accurate "signal of financial rectitude" which lowered the real costs of capital and, less certainly, increased its availability between 1870 and 1914, see Michael D. Bordo and Hugh Rockoff, "The Gold Standard as a 'Good Housekeeping Seal of Approval,'" *Journal of Economic History* 56:2 (June 1996): 389–428.

[131]   During the 1890s, for example, the crisis in confidence over gold redemption produced a general liquidation of American securities by foreign investors. *Commercial and Financial Chronicle*, May 4, 1895.

opmental issue in the late nineteenth century. Much of this struggle over money followed sectional lines because the volume of capital investment flowing between domestic regions was much greater than that moving between Europe and the United States. Agricultural regions, particularly the Plains and West, were heavy importers of capital in the late nineteenth century. Much of this investment flowed into mortgages on farm land, railroad construction, and bonds issued by state and local governments. Because of the shortage of capital in these regions and the substantial risks that creditors assumed, interest rates were relatively high. On the other hand, the more developed regions of the Northeast had become capital exporters. There interest rates were fairly low and capital markets were highly developed.

Investment capital thus moved into and through the United States in two distinct streams. One of these brought investment across the Atlantic from European capital markets and was strongly encouraged by the adherence of the United States to the international gold standard and the close integration of New York and London financial markets.[132] The other branch delivered investment capital from the relatively developed and capital-rich East into the developing regions of the western Plains and Mountain states.

THE ISOLATION OF THE SOUTHERN CAPITAL MARKET

The scholarly literature on the development of the American financial system has offered a wide variety of reasons for the relatively high interest rates in the South. One explanation attributes these rates to the lack of integration of the South into national capital markets. Because the South was starved for capital, investment opportunities in the region competed for a small pool of funds and thus drove rates up, far above the national average. Another line of argument assigns primary responsibility to the rural, agricultural characteristics of the region. Everywhere in the nation in the late nineteenth century interest rates in rural counties were higher than those in adjoining counties containing cities. This differential is primarily explained by the higher operating costs of loan services and banking generally outside urban centers (e.g., higher overhead, smaller size of average loans). As the most rural region of the nation, the South would have had, everything else being equal, higher interest rates than the North or West even in an integrated national capital market. But the agricultural base of the southern economy accentuated this differential in operating costs through the small size and low value of its farms. This meant that the

---

[132]   On British investment in the United States between 1870 and 1914, see Williamson, *American Growth*, pp. 144–147.

average size of farm mortgages was much lower than in other parts of the nation and that, as a consequence, operating costs for servicing them were even higher.[133]

Competition among lenders was further restricted by the relatively high rates of illiteracy among potential borrowers in such a way as to create local monopolies or oligopolistic markets for banking institutions and merchants. Finally, the small size of most southern farms, the impoverished condition of most rural producers, and their specialization in cotton accentuated the risk associated with a poor harvest; when the cotton crop failed, borrowers had no choice but to default on their loans. The compensation to lenders for this risk again took the form of higher interest rates.[134]

Given the importance of farm and home mortgages in banking operations, particularly in a rural region, this systematic retardation of the emergence of a mortgage market arrested the establishment of banking institutions and thus the development of southern capital markets. In turn, the underdevelopment of the southern financial network retarded industrial and commercial expansion by failing to provide sufficient intermediating institutions between northern capital holders and southern borrowers. Thus, because the potential profits of this intermediating function, taken alone, were not high enough to generate an adequate regional banking system, the arrested development of a mortgage market in the South was a very important factor underlying the isolation of the region from the rest of the American financial system. Thus the poverty of the region and its commitment to cotton cultivation were ultimately responsible for the absence of a capital market that could have otherwise facilitated industrial and commercial expansion in the South.

This focus on the centrality of southern poverty explains the coexistence of three patterns: (1) the restricted development of the southern banking system despite the low barriers to entry to banking under most state laws, (2) the small number of mortgage loans despite comparatively high average rates of interest, and (3) the failure of the banking system to fund attractive opportunities in industrial sectors such as textile manufacturing. The first two are consistent, in that the southern banking system, on the whole, was an appropriate market response to the high risks and limited opportunities available in the regional farm and home mortgage business.[135] In

---

[133] See, for example, Harold D. Woodman, *King Cotton and His Retainers: Financing and Marketing the Cotton Crop of the South, 1800–1925* (Columbia: University of South Carolina Press, 1990), pp. 349–352.

[134] For a good review of the influence of most of these factors, see John A. James, "Financial Underdevelopment in the Postbellum South," pp. 443–454.

[135] On the southern banking system as an appropriate response to the relative dearth of local capital and investment opportunities, see James T. Campen and Anne Mayhew, "The National Banking System and Southern Economic Growth: Evidence

many ways, in fact, the postwar southern economy required only small retailers of capital in a national market in which wholesaling was the rule. The difficulty regional manufacturers encountered in borrowing money followed from the others because the southern banking system did not generate large, intermediating institutions that could have drawn upon eastern capital. As a result, there were at least some extraordinarily profitable opportunities in the industrial and commercial sectors in the South that went unexploited because of the underdeveloped regional capital market.[136]

In fact, for all of these reasons, the South was probably better integrated into the national capital market before the Civil War than afterward. The antebellum concentration of cotton cultivation in larger, better capitalized productive units (i.e., slave plantations) allowed for a similar concentration in marketing and credit facilities (e.g., the cotton factor in major southern ports) which, in turn, allowed the latter to perform the intermediating functions so sorely lacking in the postwar period. In addition, the defeat of the Confederacy forced almost all southern banks to close their doors while the statutory requirements for erecting national banks and the dearth of capital in the region severely restricted the reemergence of banking institutions, particularly those that could have reestablished links with northern or foreign capital markets. The destruction wrought by the war plus the redistributive impact of the postwar political economy additionally contributed to the region's impoverishment and further inhibited the development of a regional capital market. When the relative absence of industrial resources in the South is added to all of these factors, any incentive for outside investors and financiers to relieve the isolation of the South through, for example, the establishment of banking facilities funded by eastern capital (as was the western experience) vanished.[137]

---

from One Southern City, 1870–1900," *Journal of Economic History* 48 (March 1988): 127–137.

[136] This can be said even though the South was a poor location for manufacturing and commercial development in the late nineteenth century. Because the South would have lagged northern industrial development in any case, the absence of intermediating institutions probably constituted only a minor constraint on regional expansion.

[137] On the relative integration of the South in the antebellum and postwar periods, as well as a summary of the causes for the deterioration, see Bodenhorn, "Capital Mobility and Financial Integration," pp. 585–610. On the whole, this deterioration appears to have almost entirely coincided with the Civil War. In the postwar period, the evidence points to a gradual, but painfully slow reintegration of the South into the national capital market. See, for example, James, "Development of the National Money Market," pp. 878–897. As James suggests, federal banking policy discouraged this recovery, at least until passage of the Gold Standard Act of 1900 (which halved capital requirements for establishing banks in small towns). However, as he also notes, state laws encouraging the chartering of banks alleviated the otherwise depressing impact of national bank regulations. However, southern states could offer

Investment in the region was also quite risky for political reasons. Ten of the eleven former Confederate states (all but Texas) repudiated at least some portion of their debt during the period following Reconstruction.[138] And some of the struggles over repudiation went on for years before a final settlement was imposed on bondholders. Georgia, for example, repeatedly repudiated a portion of its bonds by legislative act and public referendum, embedding prohibitions on repayment in both the statutory code and the state constitution. The most controversial and extended of the debates over repudiation began in 1870 in Virginia and finally ended in 1892 when the state scaled down the principal on its debt to 35 cents on the dollar. During the twenty-odd years of conflict over repayment, the controversy spawned a major political party within the state, sparked the formation of committees of bondholders in Britain who proposed to negotiate a solution, and instigated numerous rulings by both Virginia and federal courts on the arrangements through which the state attempted, by more or less transparent subterfuges, to avoid paying off its obligations.[139]

the opportunity only to establish state-chartered banks; they could not provide the capital for their creation nor remove the other obstacles in the national political economy that discouraged expansion of the southern financial system.

[138] Kirkland, *Industry Comes of Age*, p. 64. Kirkland mistakenly included Mississippi, along with Texas, as one of the southern states that did not repudiate. Although the state of Texas did not default on its debt, the cities of Austin, Fort Worth, and Houston, among other places, did refuse to pay either interest or principal on their obligations at one time or another. *Commercial and Financial Chronicle*, January 27, 1883; September 30, 1899; January 6, 13, 1900. For brief histories of debt repudiation within the southern states, see George W. Green, "Repudiation," in John J. Lalor, ed., *Cyclopedia of Political Science, Political Economy, and of the Political History of the United States* (Chicago: Melbert B. Cary, 1884), vol. 3, pp. 603–613; R. C. McGrane, *Foreign Bondholders and American State Debts* (New York: Macmillan, 1935), pp. 322–334. For discussions of the politics surrounding repudiation in the individual states of the South, see *Appleton's 1878 Cyclopaedia*, pp. 23–24, 768–770, 780–781, 820–824; *Appleton's 1879 Cyclopaedia*, pp. 562–563, 565–569, 686–688, 818–819, 826–829, 842–844; *Appleton's 1880 Cyclopaedia*, pp. 10, 269–270, 309–310, 480–481, 485, 582–583, 709; *Appleton's Annual Cyclopaedia of 1881* (New York: D. Appleton, 1882), pp. 32–33. A general survey is also available in *1880 Census of Valuation, Taxation, and Public Indebtedness* (Washington, D.C.: GPO, 1884), pp. 554–608. For articles describing the South Carolina debt controversy, see *Commercial and Financial Chronicle*, October 15, 22, 1892. The interest and principal on part of the South Carolina debt was still in default at the turn of the century. October 27, 1900. For articles describing the Arkansas debt controversy, see July 24, 1880; September 24, 1881; April 2, 1887; November 24, 1894. For articles describing the Tennessee debt controversy, see April 5, August 16, 1879; August 21, October 2, 1880; March 19, April 9, July 16, 1881; February 11, 25, March 4, May 20, 1882; February 10, September 8, 1883; May 9, 30, 1885; February 20, 1886.

[139] The antebellum debt also became entangled in the apportionment of the principal between Virginia and West Virginia, which had been created in 1863 out of the western portion of the state. Before repudiation, Virginia had the largest state debt

Since many of these disputes involved northern creditors, sectional feeling was often apparent in refusals to pay. In North Carolina, for example, Governor Zebulon Vance plainly made the political affiliation of creditors a reason for repudiation: "It is out of the question for us to attempt to pay [the state debt] at its face value. Indeed, I do not conceive that there is any moral obligation on us to do so, nor do our creditors expect it of us. Quite one half of our property upon which our bonds were based was wantonly destroyed by consent of a large majority of those who held them, and no court of conscience upon the earth would permit a creditor to destroy one half of his security, and claim full payment out of the remainder."[140] By justifying default as a partial redress for northern prosecution of the Civil War and Reconstruction, arguments such as this would have supported repudiation regardless of whether or not the bonds had been fraudulently issued. But political justifications for repudiation were probably redundant. Mississippi, for example, simply refused to pay back $7 million in bonds that had been issued before the war – a debt that was entirely free of any taint from Reconstruction politics.

Under the federal Constitution, no state could be compelled by the central government to honor its debt. The only sanction available to creditors was to deny future access to the capital market to any state that repudiated. In practice, of course, markets cannot enforce such an embargo; instead, the political risk attending southern obligations was adjudged to be so significant that the interest rates on new state bonds were practically prohibitive. This result, however, was in some ways redundant. The South was so impoverished that, irrespective of debt history or political sentiment, bond issues would have been small and would have run a serious risk of default on economic grounds.

Most of the heavy debts burdening the South had been run up during Reconstruction for political reasons. Although the visionary dreams of the Republican coalition of freedmen and poor whites had a clear economic component, embodied in the railroad projects they subsidized, these dreams were undeniably compromised by the patronage role they played in maintaining the party in power. Republicans who had mortgaged their states'

---

in the South. Kirkland, *Industry Comes of Age*, p. 64. Although a preliminary settlement was reached in 1891, delays in passing legislation enacting the agreement stalled its execution for some years afterward. The controversies surrounding the Virginia debt were also covered in detail by the *Commercial and Financial Chronicle* in many issues between 1879 and 1894. For a general survey of the politics of repudiation throughout the South, see C. Vann Woodward, *Origins of the New South, 1877–1913* (Baton Rouge: Louisiana State University Press, 1967), pp. 86–106.

[140] In his references to property destruction, Vance included emancipation of slaves by the Union. *Appleton's 1878 Cyclopaedia*, p. 626. For articles describing the North Carolina debt controversy, see *Commercial and Financial Chronicle*, June 11, 1887; November 10, 1894; May 27, 1899; *New York Times*, January 26, 1877.

futures in order to fund an unrealistic developmental program bought, in effect, political support from national and local elites. These elites, in turn, provided backing for what may have been the most sustained experiment in lower-class insurgency in American history. But this strategy worked no better in the American South than it works in contemporary Third World nations. Sooner or later the developmental projects arising primarily out of the needs of a political regime will fail, bringing down the regime with them. And, as is also the case with contemporary Third World nations, lenders held subsequent governments responsible for this debt regardless of their assessment of the earlier regime's legitimacy.

Thus, when southern Democrats defaulted on the debt run up by their Republican predecessors because, in their interpretation, the Republicans had been corrupt profligates who had squandered the future of their states behind a wall of Union bayonets, northern financiers were entirely unsympathetic. Whatever the shortcomings of the earlier regimes that had encumbered the southern states (and northern financiers shared many of the views of southern Democrats on the relative virtue of southern Republicans), the debt had to be paid. And, as is now the case with many Third World nations, it is an open question whether full repayment of the state debt would have made much sense in economic terms. On the one hand, default gave southern states more money to invest in developmental projects on a pay-as-you-go basis. But the region was poor and current revenue could provide only limited resources for development. On the other hand, honoring the debt in full would have conferred access to the national capital market on better terms, enabling southern states to borrow the money needed to fund development. However, full repayment of the debt would have consumed most or all of current revenue, so that the states would not have been able to borrow very much under this strategy either. The basic problem was that the South was poor.[141] And, given that fact and the hostility of southern whites to both Republicans and northern investors, defaulting on the Reconstruction debt made both political and economic sense.[142]

Another political reason for the isolation of the southern capital market

---

[141] This dilemma takes for granted the South's subordinate status within the national political economy. Repeal of federal policies such as the protective tariff would have reduced the interregional redistribution of wealth that retarded southern development. This reduction could have, in turn, reduced the frequency of default due to both economic causes and political hostility of southern electorates to northern investors.

[142] The South paid a very high price for this debt relief. In the 1893 amendments to the governing statute, for example, Connecticut regulators permitted the state's savings banks to invest in bonds issued by 26 states and hundreds of incorporated cities. This revision, however, continued the prohibition on investment in municipal, county, and state securities issued anywhere in the eleven former states of the Confederacy. *Commercial and Financial Chronicle,* September 30, 1893.

was federal bank policy. Because antebellum banks had committed their resources to the Confederacy, the financial system was destroyed when the North defeated southern armies. Only a few institutions survived the peace, most of them chartered as national banks by the federal government during the war. In addition, much of what capital the South had possessed had been physically destroyed or, in the case of slaves, liberated by federal edict. Throughout the rest of the nation, the emergence of the new national bank system restructured the financial economy as state-chartered banks called in their currency, took up national charters, and issued national bank notes. The South, however, had few surviving institutions that could convert to the new system.

Aggravating the problem was the relatively high capitalization requirements for establishing a national bank and the national ceiling placed on the total amount of national bank notes. Because the ceiling was reached before the South had reentered the Union, the section would have been discriminated against no matter how wealthy it had been. However, the South was too poor to have taken up many more national bank charters than it actually did before the ceiling was repealed. The relatively high capital threshold may have had a more substantial impact; the absence of national banks in the postwar South has been blamed for the merchant-lien system of crop loans that substituted for what might have otherwise been a more bank-centered organization of agricultural finance.[143] But this explanation is undercut by the fact that most crop loans supplied to sharecroppers and tenants by merchants were too small to attract the attention of banks, even where they existed.

The absence of national banks probably had its greatest impact on southern integration into the national capital market. The relatively high capitalization required for the issuance of national bank charters prevented the development of a regional financial network that might have linked local borrowers to the national capital market. Even so, southern poverty was probably still the more important factor; although facing the same high capital requirements, the Plains and West were able to charter many more national banks than did the South.

In sum, then, southern poverty underpinned almost every aspect of the region's weak integration into the national capital market. Poverty was

---

[143] This argument was most forcefully made by Ransom and Sutch in their *One Kind of Freedom*. Subsequent scholars have largely accepted their conclusion. See, for example, Steven Hahn, *The Roots of Southern Populism: Yeoman Farmers and the Transformation of the Georgia Upcountry, 1850–1890* (New York: Oxford University Press, 1983), pp. 172–173. Similar arguments have also been made by James, "Financial Underdevelopment in the Postbellum South," pp. 443–454; Hetherington, "Bank Entry," pp. 669–675. For an opposing interpretation, see John J. Binder and David T. Brown, "Bank Rates of Return and Entry Restrictions, 1869–1914," *Journal of Economic History* 51:1 (March 1991): 47–66.

directly responsible for underdevelopment of the regional financial system and the consequent absence of institutional intermediaries between local borrowers and northern capital. In addition, poverty reinforced the restrictive impact of national bank regulations on the expansion of the banking network in the region. Finally, poverty transformed the question of whether or not Reconstruction debts should be repaid into a largely irresolvable dilemma. Default by southern governments was not, of course, a positive factor in the development of the region.[144] But repudiation should be evaluated against the backdrop of a stultifying regional poverty which, in fact, made a decisive contribution to all the factors immediately underlying the isolation of the southern capital market.

For all these reasons, the persisting differential in interest rates between the South and the Northeast could not have been eliminated through the simple expansion of southern financial facilities. Instead, southern interest rates were higher for reasons only tangentially related to the dearth of banks: (1) the relatively greater risk that accompanied the movement of capital between regions (a movement that entailed the assessment of credit worthiness by intermediaries), (2) the relatively greater risk of default by borrowers (because of their generally weaker financial condition compared with similar borrowers in the East), (3) the smaller average size of southern loans and their wide dispersal across the region (entailing much higher servicing costs), and (4) the relatively greater risk that collection of debt would be frustrated by the intervention of state or local policies (e.g., moratoria on mortgage payments, failure to enforce contracts in the courts, or simple repudiation of their debts by state or local governments). While rates in the Plains and Mountain West were higher for similar reasons, the credit needs of local borrowers were met by the extension of the national bank system into that region, the role of railroads as agents in leading economic development, and the packaging of farm mortgages into securities issued

---

[144] As the *Commercial and Financial Chronicle* put the matter in its March 1, 1879, issue, just as the post-Reconstruction governments in the South began to default on their bonds: "Repudiating commonwealths do not prosper. If it is urged that prosperous ones pay their debts because they are rich, and repudiating ones dishonor theirs because they are poor; the answer is that repudiation prolongs the poverty and keeps off prosperity. States which disown public debts have a low commercial standard all through; they lack capital and enterprise for self development, and cannot attract vigor from the outside; they invariably languish in a condition of semi-paralysis and comparatively imperfect development.... True, capital and immigration, other things being equal, shun a heavily-burdened section; but repudiation is the heaviest burden, and the very last place they seek is that where there is not enough honesty, or wisdom, or enterprise, or pluck, to dispose of debt by working it out. Capital will avoid places where capital has been loaned and lost; emigration will not go where capital will not, and what is to be the result?" This disapproving commentary on the South stands in stark contrast to the welcome given the Territory of Dakota when the latter made an entry into the national capital market six years later (June 20, 1885).

by large land companies with access to eastern and European markets. The portion of the rate differential attributable to higher service costs was also probably lower because of the larger proportion of industrial loans (e.g., for mining operations) and larger size of agricultural units. Both factors would have raised the average size of loans in the West above those in the South and thus lowered servicing costs. But western obligations, because of the highly leveraged capitalization of the regional economy, probably carried risks arising out of unforeseen economic conditions as high or higher than those in the South. And, after the mid-1880s or so, the rate premium originating in political risk was probably as high or higher than that pertaining to the South.[145]

POPULAR CLAIMS ON CAPITAL ACCUMULATION

Over the last two decades of the nineteenth century, the nation followed the "yellow brick road," industrializing within the discipline and constraints of the international gold standard. As in other periods, the American financial system provided the structure within which trade and capital investment flowed domestically and between the United States and foreign nations. But the interconnected markets and institutions which comprised the financial system were unevenly deployed across the nation, deeply embedded within the capital-rich, industrial regions of the East and only lightly distributed in much of the South and West.

The uneven institutional foundation of the financial system reflected the larger regional division of the United States into what was then an advanced and developing industrial core, a rapidly settling western frontier, and a relatively stagnating southern periphery. Against this backdrop, popular claims on capital accumulation arose from those classes and economic sectors whose wealth and labor were appropriated for industrial expansion. Attacking tariff protection, corporate monopolies, and the gold standard, these claims focused on two highly visible streams of capital investment. One stream flowed directly from corporate profits enlarged by the operation of the protective tariff and industrial combinations ("trusts"). Successful attempts to reduce the tariff or break up industrial monopolies would have inhibited profits by affecting the competitive position of large

---

[145] For studies that have concluded that the highly uneven pattern of interest rates in the late nineteenth century can be explained by both regional differences in investment risk and the transaction costs associated with moving capital between donor and receiving regions, see Kenneth A. Snowden, "Mortgage Rates and American Capital Market Development in the Late Nineteenth Century," *Journal of Economic History* 47:3 (September 1987): 671–692; Barry Eichengreen, "Agricultural Mortgages in the Populist Era: Reply to Snowden," *Journal of Economic History* 47:3 (September 1987): 757–760. These studies, however, focus exclusively on economic risks and costs.

corporations. The realization of wage claims by industrial labor would have done so as well.

The second investment stream brought new capital from abroad. That importation, as well as the retention of domestic capital, required the maintenance of the international gold standard as a guarantee of the international exchange value of the dollar. Silver or paper money substitutes, from this perspective, would have reduced the supply of new capital in American markets by inflating the dollar, destabilizing the exchange rate, and thus destroying some of the most important links that unified the British and American capital markets.

The pattern of uneven regional development described in this chapter provided the setting for the emergence of these popular claims on wealth and their probable impact on the capital investment in industrial expansion. The next two chapters lay out the ways in which the parties responded to these popular claims by analyzing the policy basis of party competition and then describing how workers and farmers sought to expand their income shares in the different regions of the United States. As is shown, policy differences between industrial workers and periphery farmers over the structure of the national political economy ultimately frustrated challenges to the prevailing developmental regime of unregulated domestic markets, tariff protection, and conservative monetary policy.

3

Platform Demands, Party Competition, and Industrialization

THE AMERICAN political system was probably the most open and free-wheeling congregation of voters and parties on the face of the globe in the late nineteenth century. Eligible voters, under manhood suffrage almost all of them male, turned out in phenomenal numbers to cast their ballots. Competing for their affections, ambitious politicians constantly formed new party organizations, broke up old ones into factions, and led both into cross-party fusion agreements or coalitions. In the struggle for supremacy within the states and within the nation, almost all these parties, factions, and cross-party combinations presented official platforms to the electorate that conferred both identity and purpose on their sometimes ephemeral organizations. These platforms were complex political tracts, demanding from the voter a relatively high degree of sophistication in both politics and economics.[1] Intended, on the one hand, to attract voters to their cause and,

---

[1] For a review of the literature that represents late nineteenth-century policy divisions separating the major parties as superficial and inconclusive, see Joanne Reitano, *The Tariff Question in the Gilded Age: The Great Debate of 1888* (University Park: Pennsylvania State University Press, 1994), pp. xviii–xx. To cite just a few examples, Lawrence Goodwyn regarded both the tariff-centered electoral competition between the two parties before 1896 and the monetary contests thereafter as equally bereft of ideological substance. *Democratic Promise: The Populist Moment in America* (New York: Oxford University Press, 1976), pp. 7–9, 516. Thomas C. Cochran and William Miller similarly viewed the major parties as akin to large businesses that competed in politics only in the role of potential employers of government officials. *The Age of Enterprise: A Social History of Industrial America*, rev. ed. (New York: Harper Torchbooks, 1961), pp. 156, 165–166. As Paul Kleppner has concluded, traditional accounts "differ in their particulars and underlying values, but their legacy is a shared and still dominating motif: the politics of the Gilded Age were dull and sterile; they were evasive of the 'real' issues of the era, the questions arising from the massive economic and social transformations that were the hall marks of nineteenth-century America." *The Third Electoral System, 1853–1892: Parties, Voters, and Political Cultures* (Chapel Hill: University of North Carolina Press, 1979), pp. 4–5.

on the other, to shape public opinion with reference to actual legislation, party platforms translated popular sentiment into fairly clear public policy alternatives that unambiguously traced out the lines of class and sectional conflict.

The major purpose of this chapter is to present a descriptive analysis of state party platforms in the United States between the end of Reconstruction and the turn of the century. Given the importance of federal legislation as structuring context for industrialization, issues related to economic development dominated national party platforms in the late nineteenth century. While this should not be surprising, such issues also dominated party competition at the state level where, in fact, few opportunities to shape national development existed. The prevalence of developmental issues in state party platforms underscores the deep penetration of competing visions of national development into local politics. Both minor and major parties in state after state, year after year, devoted most of their platform demands to issues associated with national economic development, often relegating local problems to a rather desultory, secondary role among partisan concerns. This bias toward economic development was very pronounced, so pronounced that state planks tended to assume more detailed and committed positions on national economic development than did their respective national party conventions. And these planks were often bitterly contested in heavily attended state party conventions. These struggles were frequently so intense that the losers bolted, forming their own organization, platform, and candidate list for the coming election. There were dozens of such bolts in the late nineteenth century; the vast majority originated in contests over platform planks addressing one or more policy issues concerning national economic development or possible fusion arrangements with another party in which such issues were prominent.

STATE PLATFORMS

Participation in the state conventions that drafted platforms varied by party and period but many were mass assemblies.[2] The New England states, even

---

[2]   As is well known, economic and political development dominated the issues addressed by the national platforms of both the major and minor parties in the late nineteenth century. Because the content of these national declarations is both relatively familiar to scholars and discussed at many places in this and other chapters of the book, they are not taken up separately here. For a good review, along with evidence that national party platforms were subsequently enacted into federal law, see Benjamin Ginsberg, "Elections and Public Policy," *American Political Science Review* 70 (March 1976): 41–49. The platforms on which the individual state parties ran their campaigns were more detailed than and, often, at variance with these national declarations. Eastern Republicans, for example, had priorities very different from southern Republicans with respect to federal intervention in elections and from western Republicans with

with their small populations, were the site of many of the larger conventions. For example, the 1879 state convention of the Maine National Greenback-Labor party drew 910 delegates. In 1880, the Vermont Republican convention drew over 500.[3] In the South, disputes over repayment of the state debt produced some of the largest gatherings. The Tennessee Democratic party convention in 1880, for instance, drew 1,349 delegates. In the same year, the Virginia Readjusters, who had split off from the Democratic party over differences with respect to the state debt, drew over 500 delegates to their convention.[4] In fact, some of the largest state conventions involved bolts of one sort or another. In Kansas, for example, Democrats who dissented from their party's fusion with the Populists in the 1892 campaign called a separate convention that drew some 500 delegates representing over half the counties in the state. While this convention did not nominate a separate slate of candidates, the delegates did condemn major elements in the Populist platform such as the subtreasury plan and government ownership of the railroad system and recommended that party's defeat.[5] The largest conventions occurred between 1892 and 1896 when the silver issue divided many state parties. In Mississippi, for example, the 1895 Democratic convention attracted more than 1,200 delegates, all of whom had been elected in county caucuses.[6] Although the number of delegates was not reported in other cases, the votes cast on monetary planks or nominees in many state conventions often exceeded 500 and, in a few cases, 1,000.[7]

respect to monetary policy. These differences were adjusted in national conventions in such a way as to gloss over conflicts and highlight consensual positions which promised advantage over the opposition. But in state races, the parties were free to describe their own positions without compromising with the interests of other states. Although the parties often downplayed the differences between their state and the national platforms, the most common result was a more articulate and committed policy stance than the one assumed in national convention. For a general survey of national party platforms in the late nineteenth century, see John Gerring, *Party Ideologies in America, 1828–1966* (New York: Cambridge University Press, 1998), pp. 166–225.

[3] *Appleton's Annual Cyclopaedia of 1879* (New York: D. Appleton, 1886), p. 580. *Appleton's Annual Cyclopaedia of 1880* (New York: D. Appleton, 1881), p. 706.

[4] Tennessee Democrats apportioned county delegates on the basis of one for every hundred votes cast for Tilden in the 1876 presidential election. With delegations ranging in size from tiny Scott's lone delegate to Shelby (Memphis) County's 86, the apportionment at this convention may have been the most equitable of all party conventions during this period. *Appleton's 1880 Cyclopaedia*, pp. 679, 710–711.

[5] *Appleton's Annual Cyclopaedia of 1892* (New York: D. Appleton, 1893), p. 371.

[6] *Appleton's Annual Cyclopaedia of 1895* (New York: D. Appleton, 1896), p. 497.

[7] For example, over 1,700 votes were cast in the 1896 Indiana Democratic convention in a contest between gold and silver candidates for the gubernatorial nomination. In Iowa, the regular Democratic convention declared for free silver, recording over 900 votes on the issue. The bolting gold convention in the same state, held after Bryan's nomination, had about 700 delegates in attendance. In Texas, the regular

Monetary policy tore apart the Massachusetts Democratic party in 1878 when Benjamin F. Butler, a Republican congressman who advocated greenback monetary policies, was a leading contender for nomination as governor. Fearing that they would be denied entry, Butler's delegates arrived early and took possession of the hall on the day of the convention. They then nominated Butler as the party's nominee, but the State Democratic Committee declared this meeting illegal and issued a call for a new convention, giving as one of its reasons: "Mechanics' Hall . . . is in possession of a mob . . . which entered the hall by stealth and by force, by ladders through the windows and breaking down the doors; and . . . the Mayor of Worcester informs [the] Committee . . . that said hall can not be cleared and placed within the control of said Committee without force, and probably bloodshed. . . ." This convention met eight days later in Boston and nominated its own candidate for governor. However, Butler outpolled this "regular" nominee by a margin of almost eleven to one.[8]

In 1892, the Democratic party in Alabama was similarly split by rival claimants to the gubernatorial nomination, but there the scope of policy disputes was much wider and both candidates, at least at the beginning of the contest, were loyal members of the party. The incumbent candidate was Thomas Goode Jones, who also represented the state's traditional economic and party elite. Backed by the Alabama Farmers' Alliance, the insurgent was Reuben Kolb, a former Commissioner of Agriculture, who announced his candidacy almost a year before the state convention. Kolb and Jones contested county caucuses throughout the state for more than six months. As in most of the South, the Democratic party was far and away the best organized and largest party machine in the state. Jones, as governor and as the candidate of the conservative wing, thus possessed advantages that Kolb could not match in terms of organizational influence and tactical sophistication. Kolb's apparently immense popularity among the state's farmers – by far the largest group in both the state and the party – was still no match as the insurgent narrowly lost many of these county caucuses to Jones.

Democratic convention attracted some 1,000 delegates while almost as many attended the Populist meeting. *Appleton's Annual Cyclopaedia of 1896* (New York: D. Appleton, 1897), pp. 358–359, 362, 732–733.

8   However, Butler lost to the Republican candidate. *Appleton's Annual Cyclopaedia of 1878* (New York: D. Appleton, 1879), p. 534. The Massachusetts Democratic party in 1896 split again, this time into a popular faction favoring free silver and a state committee within which gold advocates were relatively strong. Some 500 silverites occupied the hall in Boston the night before the convention was to begin and refused to allow anyone else to enter. In response, the state committee convened in another building. The main issue between the two meetings seems to have been over control of the state organization, because both of them passed resolutions approving the national Democratic ticket and free silver. The gold Democrats subsequently bolted the party and formed their own ticket. *Appleton's 1896 Cyclopaedia*, p. 458.

Realizing that he would lose control of the state convention and charging that men supporting Jones had in several counties committed fraud, Kolb bolted the regular Democratic convention and called for an alternative meeting to be held on the same day. Both conventions met in Montgomery, both claimed to represent the Democratic party, and both secured the nomination for their respective candidates. Both conventions also announced detailed platforms that, with respect to national developmental issues, often put forward similar planks. The major differences between the two factions arose over class issues (e.g., suffrage, election laws, and local property taxation), monetary policy (e.g., the greenback leanings in the Kolb document), and race. The regular convention which nominated Jones placed their candidate on a platform that would have been considered fairly progressive in most parts of the nation. The Kolb convention was more radical, particularly with respect to voting and taxation of local property. Kolb's Jeffersonian Democrats, as they called themselves, later coalesced with the small Populist party in the state and came to dominate that organization as well. The state Republican party declined to nominate a state ticket and endorsed the insurgents, but Kolb still narrowly lost the general election.[9]

[9] The regular Democratic platform favored a tariff for revenue only, free coinage of silver, repeal of the federal tax on the notes issued by state-chartered banks, practical abandonment of the national bank system (by eliminating the note-issuing privilege), a progressive income tax, more strenuous rate regulation of railroads and telegraphs, and reform of the convict labor system. However, with respect to elections, the convention opposed federal intervention while favoring enactment of "such election laws as will better secure the government of the State in the hands of the intelligent and the virtuous, and will enable every elector to cast his ballot secretly and without fear or constraint." These proposals clearly targeted Kolb's largely illiterate and impoverished masses. For its part, Kolb's convention also supported reform of the convict labor system, a progressive income tax, and free coinage of silver while favoring, in addition, more rigorous enforcement of property taxes in the state, outright abolition of the national bank system, and the expansion of greenback currency until the circulation reached $50 per person. In place of the conservative restrictions on suffrage and voting promised by the Jones convention, the insurgents instead issued an appeal for interracial harmony: "We favor the protection of the colored race in their legal rights, and should afford them encouragement and aid in the attainment of a higher civilization and citizenship, so that through the means of kindness, fair treatment, and just regard for them, a better understanding and more satisfactory condition may exist between the races." After effectively merging with the Populists, Kolb's insurgents added planks calling for "a fair vote and a fair count" (the traditional Republican language for federal enforcement of southern elections), a prohibition on alien land ownership, and a tariff for revenue only (effectively matching the Democratic plank on this issue). For the planks and a brief account of the campaign, see *Appleton's Annual Cyclopaedia of 1892* (New York: D. Appleton, 1893), pp. 3–5. Also see Sheldon Hackney, *Populism to Progressivism in Alabama* (Princeton, N.J.: Princeton University Press, 1969), pp. 13–23.

The most violent convention occurred in 1898 in Colorado Springs, Colorado, when the Silver Republicans who had bolted their party over gold attempted to decide whether or not to fuse on a single ticket with the Democrats and Populists. The latter two parties, in fact, were meeting in the city at the same time for the purpose of perfecting fusion arrangements. The faction favoring fusion occupied the opera house where the Silver Republicans were to convene on the following day. They were then attacked by the antifusion wing in a struggle for possession of the hall. Some 150 shots were fired in the opera house, killing one man and wounding three others. A local court then ordered that neither faction could occupy the hall. The fusionists, led by Senator Teller, subsequently met the following day and agreed to ticket arrangements with the other silver parties.[10]

Many bolts were followed by a separate convention, platform declarations, and ticket nominations. There were at least sixty-six such bolts, involving both major and minor party organizations (see Table 3.1).[11] With respect to time, the pattern is anything but random. Only six party splits occurred before 1890 and all of those fell between 1877 and 1882. Repayment of the state's debt was the central issue in four of these party divisions. The other two, in Massachusetts, had greenback policy as one of several issues tainting Benjamin Butler's candidacy in the eyes of the party establishment. In the remainder of the 1880s no bolts were found.[12] With respect to the entire period, 1896 produced a very sharp spike with over half of all party divisions. Much smaller numbers of splits immediately precede and follow the Battle of the Standards. In terms of issues, monetary and financial policy account for the vast majority of all party splits.

---

[10] *Appleton's Annual Cyclopaedia of 1898* (New York: D. Appleton, 1899), pp. 136–137.

[11] This table unavoidably excludes a number of splits within state organizations, particularly for the Populists and Prohibitionists after 1895. For the Populists, the difficulty is primarily that many of the state organizations were very small to begin with, and when they divided into "middle-of-the-road" and fusion factions, they apparently failed to attract the attention of the yearly editions of *Appleton's Annual Cyclopaedia*. For the Prohibitionists, the problem in many instances involves the tracing of new party organizations with different names back to a prior dispute within the parent party. The contests between white and integrated factions within southern Republican organizations are probably underrepresented as well, although in their case the problem is that many did not hold conventions or, if they did meet, declare platforms.

[12] Before adoption of the Australian ballot, bolts could have an immediate impact on an election because all the bolting faction had to do was print its own tickets in order to present its case to the electorate. After the Australian ballot was adopted, for most states before the 1892 election, the major parties rapidly learned how to restrict access (e.g., through filing deadlines and other certification requirements) in such a way as to prevent bolting factions from going to the voters. However, as the pattern strongly suggests, the new ballot arrangement does not seem to have discouraged fragmentation among the state parties.

For the Democrats, the national party's endorsement of free silver alone provoked more than 70 percent of all state party divisions. For the Republicans, the proportion is just over half, if the Nevada bolt by the regular wing of the party is included.[13] Many of the other splits had national monetary policy as their backdrop. This was particularly the case with divisions occurring over fusion. In half a dozen instances, struggles by white and integrated factions for control of Republican organizations disrupted the southern parties. Because the party was rapidly becoming moribund in the region, these conflicts were of little electoral significance; they usually focused on representation at the national convention and rights to federal patronage.[14]

In sharp contrast with monetary questions, the tariff – the unshakable pillar of party identity for the Republicans and the object of unmitigated hostility for the Democrats – never provoked a party split; the electorate was already thoroughly divided along party lines and there were few dissidents left within either major party. Differences over labor policy also never split a state party organization. The most surprising absence is perhaps temperance, an issue that invoked intense ethnic and religious identities. As shown below, both of the major parties frequently inserted planks on alcohol in their platforms. In other instances, such planks were defeated in floor fights at the state convention. In addition, the parties often assumed contrasting positions on the issue, although the differences between them were sometimes narrow. Thus, the losers in a state convention (if they were Republican wets or Democratic drys) often had another party organization with which to ally if they bolted. Still, temperance appears to have never

[13] McKinley's nomination on a hard-money platform seriously stressed all of the western Republican party organizations. Many, as indicated in Table 3.1, split in two. Others donned fig leaves in the form of the national party's declaration that it would seek the holy grail of an international agreement on a bimetallic standard. Wyoming Republicans may have been unique when, in their August platform, the state party pointedly ignored the national convention and simply stated: "We favor the free coinage of gold and silver into standard money, as expressed in our former platforms, under such legislation as will guarantee that all our money shall remain on an equality." In fact, the state convention had bound its delegates to support McKinley for the party's presidential nomination and this plank was an attempt to square the circle, all the while emphasizing the tariff as the primary issue between the parties. Lewis L. Gould, *Wyoming: A Political History, 1868–1896* (New Haven, Conn.: Yale University Press, 1968), pp. 243, 249.

[14] Several of the splits in southern Democratic parties in 1896 also appear to have been motivated largely by the possibility of attracting patronage favors from Cleveland during his last year in office. Because the overwhelming majority of southern Democrats supported silver both before and after Bryan's nomination and because fusion with the Populists or Republicans was out of the question, gold dissidents merely nominated a slate of electors for the presidential ticket formed by the National Democrats who bolted the Chicago convention but, in all other respects, apparently sat out the election.

Table 3.1. *Factional Splits in State Party Organizations, 1877–1900*

State and year	Dividing issue or principle
Democrats	
Massachusetts (1878, 1879)	Party establishment bolts conventions controlled by supporters of Benjamin Butler and runs its own ticket.
Virginia (1879)	Differences over repayment of the state debt led to formation of the Readjuster party.
Tennessee (1880, 1882)	Whether to repudiate entirely the state debt or, instead, to negotiate a reduction with creditors.
South Carolina (1890)	Party establishment bolts convention controlled by supporters of Benjamin Tillman and runs its own ticket.
Alabama (1892, 1894)	Differences over the class elements in the Populist program, the losing faction later fuses with and becomes the leading element in the state Populist party.
Kansas (1892)	Bolt over the decision of the state organization to fuse with the Populists but no nomination of Cleveland electors.
Nebraska (1894)	Administration Democrats bolt convention and run their own ticket after the endorsement of silver. Their ticket is denied a place on the ballot.
Connecticut (1896); Florida (1896); Illinois (1896); Indiana (1896); Iowa (1896, 1897); Kentucky (1896); Louisiana (1896); Maine (1896); Maryland (1896); Massachusetts (1896, 1897); Michigan (1896); Mississippi (1896); Missouri (1896); Nebraska (1896); New Hampshire (1896); New Jersey (1896); New York (1896); North Carolina (1896); Ohio (1896, 1897); Pennsylvania (1896); Rhode Island (1896); Texas (1896); Vermont (1896); Wisconsin (1896, 1898)	The national party endorsement of free silver.
Kentucky (1899)	Split over an election law enacted the previous year.

Table 3.1. *(cont.)*

State and year	Dividing issue or principle
Populist	
California (1898); Iowa (1897, 1899, 1900); Kentucky (1900); Minnesota (1898); Nebraska (1900); Oregon (1900); South Dakota (1900)	Whether or not the party should fuse with the Democrats, the party splits into "fusion" and "middle-of-the-road" organizations.
Prohibition	
Indiana (1896); Massachusetts (1896); New Hampshire (1896)	Whether or not the platform should include declarations other than temperance, particularly endorsements of free silver.
Republican	
Virginia (1881)	Differences over whether and how the state debt should be repaid and, in that connection, over whether or not the party should fuse with the Readjusters.
Nevada (1892)	Regular Republicans bolt a convention controlled by silver advocates and nominate electors pledged to Benjamin Harrison.
Colorado (1896); Idaho (1896); Iowa (1897); Montana (1896); Nebraska (1896); South Dakota (1896); Utah (1896)	The national party endorsement of the gold standard.
Alabama (1898); Louisiana (1900); North Carolina (1896); South Carolina (1896); Tennessee (1900); Texas (1892)	Struggle for control of the state organization between white and integrated factions of the party.

Note: All splits in state party organizations in which the losing faction bolted the party, held a separate convention, wrote a platform, and nominated a slate of candidates are included. In some cases, the split continued into subsequent campaigns; these are also included. In other cases, what would have been the losing faction anticipated its loss by refusing to attend the regular party convention. In others, particularly for the major parties in 1896, the split occurred in response to the national organization's monetary stand. Where a separate convention or meeting of some kind was held in the state, resulting in a nomination of electors and declaration of principles, these are also included. The list is exhaustive in terms of its primary source, the yearly editions of *Appleton's Annual Cyclopaedia.*

sparked the formation of a renegade organization by the losing faction of a state party. When juxtaposed against the gold standard and national monetary policy, we can only conclude that temperance was an insignificant factor in the disruption and reformation of the party system of the late nineteenth century. Finally, national issues dominated those conventions that resulted in party splits; local questions, among them alcohol consumption, were just not as important to delegates attending state party conventions or to the electorates to which bolters would have had to appeal if they formed a new organization.

On the most general level, the distribution of bolts over time is very similar regardless of party, each one presenting a peak exactly at 1896. In addition, the dominant issue underlying these divisions was, for most parties, the national monetary system. For the Republicans, western parties divided over the national party's endorsement of gold. For the Democrats, eastern parties divided over the national party's endorsement of silver. For the Populists, who had no difficulty with monetary policy because almost everyone supported free silver, the problem was whether or not to fuse with the Democrats after 1896.[15] While this was not explicitly a monetary issue, the only reason it arose at all was because the Democratic national convention, under Bryan, had unequivocally endorsed silver. The important point here is that the actions of the other parties largely determined what dissidents would contemplate as alternatives when they lost or anticipated losing in their state party convention. From that perspective, the great Battle of the Standards disrupted party alignments throughout the nation and thus provided new political openings for dissidents. In that sense, there was a certain synergy that subsequently cascaded through most state party organizations as many party members bolted one way or another in response to Bryan's nomination and the free silver stand at the Democratic national convention. The emerging opportunity for Silver Republicans and Populists was fusion with regular Democrats (for Gold Democrats the usual choice was banishment to the political wilderness).

Regardless of whether the issues on which they waged the campaign were national or local, parties often followed through on these platform commitments by implementing their principles in legislation. Individual members, for example, often viewed their party's state platforms as binding,

---

[15]   For the Populists, two primary issues were involved in the decision of whether or not to fuse with the Democrats: the integrity of the party program (which would be largely narrowed to the silver plank from the much broader spectrum of insurgent proposals) and the continued existence of the party as an independent organization. In many ways, these were both summed up in the declaration against fusion in the 1898 Minnesota Populist "middle of the road" platform, the concluding sentence reading: "We refuse to get into the grave where the Greenback party lies, fused to death."

even in Congress.[16] At the state level, platform demands often moved into the statute books with dispatch if the party was in a position to carry through on its commitments.[17] Even out of power, party members at least pursued policy goals that honored platform commitments. This was particularly the case for the Populists for whom the enactment of platform demands was seen as a party-building strategy.[18] At the federal level, state legislatures sometimes felt that their electoral mandate justified instruction of the state's representatives and senators in Congress. In 1879, for example, the Arkansas legislature almost unanimously forwarded a detailed and extensive list of requests regarding the nation's monetary system:

Resolved, by the General Assembly of the State of Arkansas, That our Senators and Representatives in Congress be, and they are hereby, requested to vote for and support the following measures:

First. The unconditional repeal of the resumption act.

Second. The repeal of the act exempting United States bonds from taxation by the States.

Third. The repeal of all laws exempting greenbacks from taxation.

Fourth. The abolition and prohibition forever of all bank issues.

Sixth. The issue by the Government of *full legal-tender* paper money, receivable for all dues and demands, public and private, in amount sufficient to meet the wants of trade, said amount to be not less than thirty dollars per capita of the whole population of the United States, and provides by law that this paper money shall remain permanently in circulation, and equal before the law with the nation's gold and silver coin.[19]

---

[16] Western Republicans torn between the national party's commitment to gold and their region's demands for silver often stressed their loyalty to the state platform. See, for example, Oregon Rep. Binger Hermann's remarks in *Congressional Record* 51:1:6359, June 21, 1890.

[17] On the implementation of platform demands by the Populists in the 1897 Kansas state legislature, see Peter H. Argersinger, "Populists in Power: Public Policy and Legislative Behavior," *Journal of Interdisciplinary History* 18:1 (Summer 1987): 81–105.

[18] For the Populist agenda in the Idaho legislature, see William Joseph Gaboury, *Dissension in the Rockies: A History of Idaho Populism* (New York: Garland, 1988), pp. 71–84, 131–138, 257–262, 326–330, 411–412.

[19] *Appleton's 1879 Cyclopaedia*, p. 41. During the same year, the Alabama legislature instructed its congressional delegation to support repeal of the federal tax on bank notes issued by state-chartered institutions (p. 16); the Illinois State senate adopted resolutions endorsing free silver (pp. 478–479); the Indiana State house passed resolutions announcing the chamber's support for repeal of the federal resumption act, taxation of federal bonds and greenbacks, abolition of the national bank system, free coinage of silver, and an increase in greenback circulation to at least $30 per capita (p. 496); and, in Maine, the state senate passed a resolution endorsing the gold standard and urging Congress to enact any necessary supporting legislation, but the measure failed in the state house (p. 576). In 1878, the Louisiana legislature similarly directed the state's senators and congressmen to support passage of the Bland silver bill and to repeal the resumption act. *Harper's Encyclopaedia of United States History* (New York: Harper & Brothers, 1909), vol. 9, p. 366.

Observations on Platform Content and Analysis

For all these reasons, state platforms provide abundant evidence of the policy basis of party competition. However, the limitations must also be noted. First, many of the platforms that appear in the historical record are incomplete or have been paraphrased by editors in order to reduce the space required to publish them. In addition, when a party platform was not recorded, it is impossible in most cases to tell whether a party failed to propose one or whether the platform has been lost because it did not gain the attention of an editor. Although it is impossible to distinguish them from those that were never written, some platforms are undoubtedly missing from the historical record.[20] These are significant problems.

Three sources systematically recorded platform texts or summarized their contents during the late nineteenth century: the *Tribune Almanac*, *Appleton's Annual Cyclopaedia*, and *McPherson's Handbook of Politics*.[21] These sources tended to complement one another. For example, *McPherson's Handbook* stopped publishing extensive reproductions of state party platforms about the time that the *Tribune Almanac* decided to commit more space to their coverage. Although the first two sources apparently tended to economize on third-party platforms, often either radically editing their text or even failing to print them at all, *Appleton's Annual Cyclopaedia* was much more generous and evenhanded, often publishing the entire text of party platforms throughout the period. In all cases, the

[20] Southern Republican party organizations frequently failed to present a platform to the electorate. In at least four cases, the party did not meet at all: Delaware (1878), Georgia (1900), and Mississippi (1877 and 1900). In five more, the party neither wrote a platform nor nominated candidates for state office: Alabama (1880), Delaware (1886), Georgia (1888 and 1890), and Virginia (1877). In eight, the party wrote a platform but did not present candidates (these platforms were included in this chapter's analysis): Alabama (1878), Florida (1892), Georgia (1896), Mississippi (1889), and South Carolina (1878, 1888, 1890, and 1900). In ten more instances, in and out of the South, the party convention nominated candidates but declined to write a platform: Arkansas (1884), Maryland (1880), Mississippi (1880), and Rhode Island (1877–82 and 1891). Such irregularities were far less common in other parties and regions. The Democrats, for example, failed to draft a platform while nominating candidates in only two known cases: Georgia (1886) and Maine (1880). In the latter instance the state party fused with the Greenbackers in the gubernatorial race. The Connecticut Prohibition party declined to present a platform in 1882, but in their case, the major principle was already written into their name. Although the evidence is incomplete, the overall pattern is probably accurate; the Republican state parties were more likely, for one reason or another, to forgo a platform, and within that party, southern branches were most frequently irregular in this respect.

[21] See, for example, Edward McPherson, *McPherson's Hand-Book of Politics, 1878* (Washington, D.C.: Solomons and Chapman, 1878), pp. 152–167, and *Tribune Almanac and Political Register for 1892* (New York: Tribune Association, 1892), pp. 34–68. The 1897 platforms also drew on the *1898 Boston Journal Almanac* (Boston: Boston Journal, 1898), pp. 230–238.

editorial process often dropped minor or unusual planks while tending to report those that shaped, in the opinion of the editors, the state campaign. There is otherwise little evidence of editorial bias in the extent to which platforms were reprinted or summarized; editors in general strongly demonstrated an intention to serve as a public record as opposed to promoting a partisan or ideological advantage. In all, the complete text, major portions, or summaries were recovered for over 1,100 state party platforms announced between 1877 and 1900.[22]

With respect to content, the analysis of these platforms required additional care. For example, late nineteenth-century platforms in certain policy areas were often reflexive in that the parties blamed each other for more or less identical faults, depending on which of them was in power at the time.[23] In several areas of government administration, for example, platforms seem to make charges with little attention to the actual record of the incumbent party: waste in government spending, fraud or corruption in decision-making, and political abuse of the patronage system. These areas, the last in part excepted, were not closely analyzed because the same rhetoric was often simultaneously used by both parties – evidence that there was probably little difference between their behavior with respect to these issues and that electorates therefore did not rely on these planks in reaching their

---

[22] There were actually many more separate platforms published during these years. Platforms were included in the analysis only if they were announced as part of a campaign in which either the governor's chair or the presidency was contested. This restriction excluded at least some of the poorly attended party caucuses from being given equal weight with conventions in which more important offices and issues were at stake. In addition, in order to prevent states in which the gubernatorial elections were held every year from being given undue weight, party platforms were combined over consecutive two-year intervals (for example, the texts of Democratic platforms in Rhode Island for 1877 and 1878 were combined into one set of demands). Aside from the 1896 campaign, which reversed the position of many eastern Democratic parties on monetary issues, the parties tended to be very consistent in positions they assumed from year to year. For that reason, the consolidation of their texts also tended to reduce the incidence of missing planks, at least for those states that held gubernatorial elections every year or in odd-numbered years (they were combined with platforms announced in presidential elections).

[23] As an example of such a general indictment, remarkable only for its marginally stronger apocalyptic overtones, see this passage from the 1886 Tennessee Republican platform: "That we charge upon the Democratic party all the financial and industrial troubles now oppressing our people. That party has shown itself the enemy of the laboring-man and the friend of ignorance and pauperism; that party's rise to power has cast a dark shadow over the homes of the people, in which shadow strikes, riots, and destruction of life and property have impoverished labor, paralyzed capital, and alarmed patriots; and but for the certainty that with the present Administration the Democratic party will be turned out of power for another long term of years, the stagnation of business, the sufferings of the poor, the hoarding of capital, and the dearth of employment for labor would be so greatly increased as to threaten the very foundations of government."

voting decisions. In addition, many if not most state parties routinely announced their blanket endorsement of the national platform. If these general endorsements were taken at face value, the national orientation of the state party platforms would be predetermined by the analysis. For instance, a blanket approval of the Republican national platform would have to be interpreted as a specific endorsement of the protective tariff; in practice, such an interpretation would have automatically made the tariff far and away the most important issue separating the major parties in their respective state platforms. For that reason, blanket endorsements of the national platforms were not interpreted as approval for any particular policy. If the state parties did not specifically address an issue included in the national platform, they were recorded as assuming no position on that issue.[24]

Most platforms were very easy to analyze. The Republican, Democratic, and Greenback party platforms announced during the 1877 Iowa gubernatorial campaign, for example, were numbered, with a separate paragraph in each case devoted to a different policy stance. As was often the case, the Greenback platform was the most specific and clearly worded, with the first three planks reading:

1. We demand the unconditional repeal of the specie resumption act of January 14, 1875, and the abandonment of the present suicidal and destructive policy of contraction.

2. We demand the abolition of national banks, and the issue of legal-tender paper money, by the government, and made receivable for all dues public and private.

3. We demand the remonetization of the silver dollar, making it a full legal tender for the payment of all coin bonds of the Government, and for all other debts, public and private.[25]

As in these cases, the platform presented each position with an economy of language that effectively bridged, on the one hand, what could have been much longer tracts on a theory of money and, on the other, radically truncated campaign slogans (e.g., naming the greenback "the people's money"). When it appeared on the scene a decade later, the Populist party was also comparatively specific and direct in its claims. The major party platforms were less clear in many cases, relying on a kind of coded language to a greater extent than their minor party competitors. Intended to gloss over differences between factions in the convention and the party at large, these codes blurred together what could have been finer policy distinctions. In

---

24   In actuality, a state party that gave only a blanket endorsement to the national platform was often, in fact, opposed to one or more of the latter's individual planks. Disagreements on monetary issues with the national party, for example, were often glossed over with a simple endorsement of the national platform or of the administration's record (if the party held the White House).

25   *Appleton's Annual Cyclopaedia for 1877* (New York: D. Appleton, 1880), p. 399.

the analysis that follows, the policy categories through which the state party platforms are examined have been constructed in a way that maximizes the overall fit between platform planks and their topics. In that sense, the categories are inductively derived from their subject matter.

With respect to each individual policy, tables have been constructed in which the frequency of planks has been described for the two major parties and three minor parties (Greenback, Populist, and Prohibitionist). As has already been noted, in some cases these major or minor parties split into two or more factions. In those instances, the platform of the "regular" organization was recorded as the party's positions. Since most bolts took place either during or after a convention, identification of the regular organization was often unproblematic. Control of the convention hall was, unless very persuasive contradictory evidence was available, considered to be a conclusive indication of control of the party organization. In some cases, an insurgent faction that clearly captured the party organization by way of the convention was henceforward considered to be the regular party representative. In other instances, however, splits occurred before any convention met, with several factions claiming the party mantle. These cases were often settled on the basis of numbers in attendance, whether or not those calling the convention were in formal control of the party organization at the time, and other peripheral matters. After adoption of the Australian ballot, the regular party organization was usually defined as the one assigned the right to present candidates under the party's name.

Platform frequencies have also been calculated for five regions (the Northeast, Great Lakes, Plains, West, and South). Minnesota and Missouri were placed with the Plains states; Kentucky and West Virginia were grouped with the South. The remaining states were assigned along conventional regional boundaries. Platform frequencies were also separately analyzed in three temporal divisions (1877–88, 1889–96, and 1897–1900). These periods coincide with a number of temporal boundaries. For example, with respect to monetary politics, they stand in for the Greenback insurgency, silver insurgency, and the consolidation of the gold standard. They also match up rather well with periodization of the salience of tariff policy in national Democratic party politics. In the first period, the tariff was a partisan issue in Congress, but northern Democratic dissent in favor of protection was tolerated. In the second, Cleveland used presidential patronage and public declarations to bolster sentiment for lower duties in the party, while, in the House of Representatives, protectionist northern Democrats were punished for breaking party ranks. In the last, monetary issues and imperialism eclipsed the tariff as a party concern. Finally and most important, the periods line up with third-party histories so that the Greenback platforms are effectively separated from the Populist ones and, later, the fusion Populist period from the earlier third-party insurgency. In all of these periodizations, 1888 and, in particular, 1896 were transition years; there are almost equally good arguments for placing them on either side of the temporal divide they mark.

The examination begins with the three great developmental policies of the late nineteenth century: the construction of a national market, tariff protection for industry, and the international gold standard. Each of these entailed a complex of policy issues in addition to the overarching principle. In fact, most platform planks that dealt with economic issues can be placed under one of the great developmental policies. An analysis of claims on wealth follows this discussion of developmental policies. These claims neatly divide into those associated with industrial wage labor (e.g., with respect to convict labor, immigration, government intervention in strike activity, and the regulation of working hours) and those arising from the interests of agricultural producers (e.g., the subtreasury plan for marketing commodities and the prohibition of oleomargarine). Most planks addressing the claims of farmers, however, were inextricably bound up with the major developmental policies. In fact, when farm organizations themselves pressed such claims, they generally interpreted these policies as the primary reasons their income was depressed. While labor tended to press claims for a redistribution of wealth between workers and capital within the industrial sector (the parties reflecting this orientation in the construction of their platform planks), farmers tended to present claims for a redistribution of wealth between sectors, a redress of the bias toward industry within the national political economy.

Political issues are taken up next. These range from federal intervention in southern elections to the structure of federal-state relations, the adoption of the Australian ballot, direct election of senators, civil service reform, and woman suffrage. Many of these, as might be expected, involved highly charged class, sectional, and partisan issues. Others are significant solely because they appeared in state platforms fairly frequently; otherwise, comparatively little emotional vigor or rhetorical flourish colored their texts. Civil service planks, for example, tended to be both short and bland.

There then follows a brief examination of foreign policy issues, most of them related to the construction of a canal across the isthmus separating the Pacific Ocean from the Caribbean Sea and what became the Spanish-American War and its consequences. However, before the early 1890s, most platforms did not contain even a single plank devoted to any foreign policy other than those associated with economic development (such as the tariff or gold standard). Much more important were the ethno-cultural issues of the late nineteenth century: temperance, sectarian schools, ethnic or racial bigotry, and polygamy (as practiced by western Mormons). These issues sometimes carried clear economic or class implications, particularly with respect to the construction of partisan coalitions otherwise oriented toward national economic development. However, for the most part, they were a distinct and separate policy complex, one in which a white, Protestant, dry, and monogamous citizenry was promoted as the epitome of American identity. Although these were undoubtedly important issues that involved, in most cases, policies under the firm control of state governments, ethnocultural conflicts were distinctly secondary to the major conflicts over national economic development.

PLATFORM PLANKS AND THE CONSTRUCTION OF A NATIONAL MARKET

Although it was the most important factor in the construction of the national market, state conventions did not usually address constitutional demarcation of local and federal regulatory powers.[26] This subject was almost entirely, as has been noted elsewhere, the province of the United States Supreme Court; electoral or legislative politics rarely ventured onto the territory. However, there were two closely related aspects of the consolidating national market that drew frequent attention from platform makers: railroads and trusts. As discussed in Chapter 5, the expansion and consolidation of the railroad system provided the frame within which industrial corporations and commercial enterprise expanded into the national market. Without the railroad, the national economy would have developed within a much more limited and segmented market. In fact, without the railroad, most of the great industrial combinations of the period would not have been feasible.

Most state platforms addressed the consolidation and expansion of the railroad network through demands for the regulation of fares or, often, outright government ownership and control. While almost no platforms opposed government regulation outright, a few conventions couched their declarations in language that suggested little enthusiasm for close supervision. In 1885, for example, Virginia Republicans declared their party in favor of "every possible encouragement and aid to promote the construction of railroads and other facilities to open up the immense mineral and other resources of the western, southwestern, and other portions of the State ... against the suicidal Bourbon policy which sacrifices all our internal advantages and materials for self-advancement to outside interests and makes our ports and cities mere way stations and our territory a mere tributary and road-bed of convenient transit to the traffic of other States and their cities."[27] In the West, Republicans were less effusive but still notably reluctant to attack the railroads. The California Republican party in 1882,

---

[26] An exception was a plank adopted by the Mississippi Democratic party in 1877 and again in 1881: "Corporations of every description supervisable within constitutional limits by State authority, and subordinate to State legislation, in the interest and for the protection of the people."

[27] Also see the 1900 Arkansas Republican platform.

for example, declared "that railroad companies, the same as individuals, should be dealt with in fairness and without injustice" before emphatically demanding that they be regulated. In these cases, the silences or low-key appeals for regulation primarily arose out of a fear that aggressive demands for a reduction of rates would discourage investment in new track.[28] Railroad charges were, in fact, usually more extortionate in frontier states than in more developed parts of the nation where rampant competition between individual lines often drove rates far below profitable levels.

Some platforms were quite specific concerning how the railroads should be regulated. In 1880, for example, the Indiana National Greenback-Labor convention combined a demand for passage of the "Reagan bill," a precursor of what ultimately became the Interstate Commerce Act which was then pending in Congress, with a much more general call for "such other legislation as will force the transportation companies to become what the people designed them to be when they called them into existence, namely, the servants, and not the masters, of the people; aids to the development of the nation's resources, and not a power of a few men to build up an aristocracy of wealth, by crushing out all fair and honorable competition among business men." Most planks, however, were more general in nature, calling for the creation of a railroad commission, statutory regulation of fares and freight charges, or government ownership. For example, the 1890 platform of the Nebraska Independent party, formed out of a coalition of the Grange, the Farmers' Alliance, and the Knights of Labor, announced that the "railroad system, as at present managed, is a system of spoliation and robbery, and its enormous bonded debt at fictitious valuations is absorbing the substance of the people in the interest of millionaires; the General Government should own and operate the railroads and telegraph, and furnish transportation at cost, the same as mail facilities are now furnished; and our Legislature should enact a freight law which shall fix rates no higher than those now in force in Iowa." Many other platforms used the term "government control" or some variant in a way that blurred the distinction between regulation of private corporations and public ownership.[29] In other cases, government ownership was to follow the failure of regulatory legislation; if regulation succeeded in satisfactorily adjusting the

---

[28] In the Idaho State legislature during the 1890s, for example, Republicans and Democrats cited the discouraging impact on investment as their reason for strongly opposing Populist efforts to regulate railroad fares. Gaboury, *Dissension in the Rockies*, pp. 75–76.

[29] Government ownership and operation of the railroad and telegraph systems was publicly debated as an alternative to regulation throughout the late nineteenth century. For testimony by independent oil producers favoring government ownership of the railroads, see *Report of the Industrial Commission: Preliminary Report on Trusts and Industrial Combinations*, vol. 1 (Washington, D.C.: GPO, 1900), pp. 393, 730.

interests of the railroads and the public, the companies were to be left in private hands. In addition, many platforms added telegraph companies to their planks; in almost all cases where the telegraphs were included, the same treatment was demanded of them as of the railroads.[30] Sometimes the term "communication" was used, apparently to include emerging telephone networks in their scope. At other times, telephones were specifically named; this was particularly the case in the East where the networks first appeared. Many, if not most, platforms failed to distinguish between state and federal regulation of the railroads. This is not surprising since the United States Supreme Court was continually handing down decisions that moved the boundary between state and federal jurisdiction one way or the other. Consequently, popular demands for a government response to railroad predation were not particularly concerned with which federal level regulated or owned the carriers.

Table 3.2 displays the relative frequency of platform references to railroad regulation by party, region, and time period. This tabulation combines demands for regulation and government ownership because, as described previously, many state party platforms did not distinguish between the two policies. Demands for some form of government control of the railroad network were most frequently found in the Plains states. Almost half of all Republican state platforms in that region, for example, contained a demand for railroad regulation (although the Republicans very rarely called for government ownership of the network). This proportion was over three times as great as the national percentage of appearances. The Plains was also the leading region for the Prohibition, Greenback, and Populist parties. The "broad gauge," not inaptly named, wing of the Prohibition party embraced a wide range of policies in order both to make their central preoccupation, temperance, more attractive to the electorate and, separately, to present a more optimistic outlook on social engineering generally.[31] In many areas of

---

[30] As with railroads, government ownership of the telegraph lines was frequently discussed and promoted in public forums. For a report to the New York Board of Trade and Transportation endorsing government ownership of the telegraph system (as well as the journal's opposition to the proposal), see *Commercial and Financial Chronicle*, December 2, 1882. The International Typographical Union also supported government ownership. *Report of the Industrial Commission: Capital and Labor Employed in Manufactures and General Business*, vol. 7 (Washington, D.C.: GPO, 1901), pp. 284, 286–289, 291; *Report of the Industrial Commission: Transportation*, vol. 9 (Washington, D.C.: GPO, 1901), pp. 242–246, 266–272.

[31] The 1896 national convention of the Prohibition party split over the scope of the platform, particularly the question of whether the party should endorse free silver. When the "narrow gauge" faction prevailed, limiting the platform to a simple declaration favoring temperance, the "broad gaugers" bolted and nominated their own ticket. The latter was much less successful in the ensuing election, drawing about a tenth of all votes cast for the two prohibition parties. After this election, the "narrow gauge" faction appears to have captured most of the state party

Table 3.2. *Party Platforms Favoring Government Regulation or Ownership of the Railroads*

State party platforms containing railroad planks by region (%)

Party	Northeast	Great Lakes	Plains	West	South	Nation
Republican	5.5 (109)	9.3 (43)	47.6 (63)	14.8 (61)	6.5 (77)	15.3 (353)
Democratic	12.5 (112)	9.8 (41)	23.7 (59)	25.5 (55)	23.3 (103)	18.9 (370)
Prohibition	7.9 (63)	31.0 (29)	40.0 (20)	35.7 (14)	30.0 (20)	22.6 (146)
Greenback	40.0 (20)	27.3 (11)	81.8 (11)	0.0 (3)	30.0 (10)	41.8 (55)
Populist	44.4 (18)	57.1 (14)	60.7 (28)	31.6 (19)	20.0 (30)	39.4 (109)

State party platforms containing railroad planks by period (%)

Party	First period (1877–88)	Second period (1889–96)	Third period (1897–1900)	All years (1877–1900)
Republican	20.9 (139)	14.5 (145)	5.8 (69)	15.3 (353)
Democratic	20.7 (150)	13.4 (149)	26.8 (71)	18.9 (370)
Prohibition	9.5 (42)	39.7 (73)	0.0 (31)	22.6 (146)
Greenback	39.2 (51)	75.0 (4)	—	41.8 (55)
Populist	—	38.7 (75)	41.2 (34)	39.4 (109)

Note: The number of platforms on which the respective percentages were calculated appears in parentheses. Since the number will be the same in the tables reporting other planks, these entries will not be repeated. The regions were defined as follows: Northeast (New England, plus Delaware, Maryland, New Jersey, New York, and Pennsylvania), Great Lakes (Illinois, Indiana, Michigan, Ohio, and Wisconsin), Plains (Iowa, Kansas, Minnesota, Missouri, Nebraska, North Dakota, and South Dakota), West (California, Colorado, Idaho, Montana, Nevada, Oregon, Utah, Washington, and Wyoming), South (the former Confederate states plus Kentucky and West Virginia).

economic and social behavior, the party endorsed one form or another of rational, scientific adjustment, arbitration, or regulation of private conflicts. But this orientation, as in this case, often had a strong regional bias. Here northeastern Prohibition platforms were notably reluctant to include railroad planks in their platforms.[32]

organizations, thus explaining the precipitous drop in frequency of planks that did not directly or indirectly address alcohol. For a brief account of the convention and the content of the "broad gauge" platform, see *Appleton's 1896 Cyclopaedia*, p. 759.

[32] In 1899, for example, the Massachusetts Prohibition party refused to take a position on all issues involving commerce, the currency, or territorial expansion, declaring them "too important to be dealt with merely as party footballs, and kicked by scheming politicians backed by saloon interests." The platform then went on to say that such problems were best addressed by unprejudiced study, scientific methods, legislative debate, and judicial decision. The party's stand served three purposes at the

Demands for railroad regulation were far more central to the programs put forward by the Greenback and Populist parties; in fact, along with financial policy, such planks were an integral part of the developmental vision they proposed to the electorate.[33] Although agricultural producers were also dependent on the railroads in the South and West, the Plains states contained the largest numbers, both absolutely and as a proportion of the electorate, of yeoman farmers. Their direct contacts with a banking system and railroad network owned largely by eastern investors gave rise to a distinct form of claim-making that, as in this case, pulled all the parties toward such positions.[34] In fact, the distinct regional political economy of the Plains states was an important factor underlying the very emergence of the Greenback and Populist parties. In rather sharp contrast, state Republican parties proposed railroad planks ever less frequently as they consolidated their developmental visions around policies encouraging growth and economic development. With the revolution in party politics that followed Bryan's nomination in 1896, the Democrats moved in the opposite direction, thereby occupying some of the ground that the Greenbackers and Populists had previously held. This pattern was repeated in other policy areas.

Along with railroad regulation, calls for antitrust legislation were one of the few demands that directly addressed the consolidation of the national market.[35] From a developmental perspective, a "trust" was an industrial enterprise that exploited economies of scale within a national market, using the efficiencies created through mass production to control pricing and

same time: It accorded with the rationalist predisposition of the membership as one of the primary justifications for sobriety; it satisfied the "narrow-gauge" reorientation of the party that had been set in the 1896 national convention; and it avoided divisions within the membership that otherwise would have stressed what was already a very small organization.

[33] One related issue that played a minor role in party platforms concerned federal subsidies for international shipping lines. Most planks were written by the northeastern Republican parties where they appeared in almost a quarter of all platforms. Aside from that, only the southern Republican and northeastern Greenback parties made subsidy demands a minor feature of their platforms (with a frequency of about one in every ten platforms).

[34] For good examples of the grain market orientation of such demands, see the 1890 Minnesota Farmer's Alliance and 1892 Nebraska Republican platforms.

[35] With respect to the national market, a comparatively minor issue concerned the regulation of commodity markets. A few party platforms called for the regulation or, more commonly, complete abolition of commodity markets. But such planks were not a common element in state party platforms. The Republicans, for example, put such planks in fewer than 1 percent of their declarations. The Democrats were almost equally reticent. Populist parties inserted demands for the regulation or abolition of commodity markets in a little over 6 percent of all of their platforms; this was the highest such percentage but was closely followed by the Prohibitionists, who also much more frequently called for regulation than abolition.

entry into its field. This perspective was shared by most party platforms. For example, local industrial monopolies, which still existed in the period due to the balkanizing effects of transportation costs, were almost never referred to as "trusts."[36] Most antitrust planks contained very brief and general condemnations of trusts or monopolies with implied or explicit demands for some kind of government response.[37] In 1888, for example, Colorado Republicans declared "in favor of stringent State and national legislation prohibiting trusts and combinations of every kind and nature." Other planks were a little more focused. In 1888, Kansas Republicans, for example, went after the meat trust: "All so-called 'trusts' or combinations to monopolize food-supplies or control productions are dangerous to the interests of the people, and should be prohibited under the severest penalties of law. The 'trust' or combination of the packing-houses to drive out of business all other butchers, and thus control the cattle markets, is especially obnoxious and destructive to the interests of all classes of the people, and particularly to those in Western States." However, whether very general or narrowly framed, no state party ever adopted a plank defending either trusts or industrial consolidation; given the intense public hostility to trusts, public defenders were few and far between.[38]

[36]   Aside from Greenback platforms, most parties used "trust" interchangeably with "monopoly" and "combination." While use of the former term tended to displace the latter over the course of the late nineteenth century, they all appeared frequently in antitrust planks. Greenbackers tended to be more indiscriminate in referring to "monopoly" than the other parties. In their planks, "monopoly" often referred to the economic advantages that wealth conferred on the rich, regardless of how collusive they might be as a class. While other parties sometimes used "monopoly" in similar ways, especially when referring to land ownership, the term did not carry the same sense of class advantage and commitment to state intervention that accompanied Greenback platforms.

[37]   State antitrust legislation could be almost as sweeping as the planks adopted by the parties. For a description of the 1895 Texas law that was subsequently struck down by a federal district court, see *Commercial and Financial Chronicle*, February 27, 1897. The only exemption was that "this act shall not be held to apply to live stock and agricultural products in the hands of the producer or raiser, nor shall it be understood or construed to prevent the organization of laborers for the purpose of maintaining any standard of wages." As the journal wryly observed, the state legislature obviously intended that "the law was not to apply to the pursuits of the citizens of Texas."

[38]   Along with industrialists and financiers, organized labor was one of the most receptive major groups in American society. For example, the president of the Amalgamated Association of Iron, Steel and Tin Workers gave qualified support for the organization of the American Tin Plate Company as an "absolute necessity" in that "their combination of capital and direction under central superintendency" prevented a ruinous competition which would otherwise drive down wages. Later, when Samuel Gompers was asked: "If you were going to write a political platform to-day, then, to put the question straight, you would not begin by inveighing against trusts in the strongest language?," the AFL president evasively replied: "I have not been and am not likely to write platforms of political parties. That is something I am rather safe

Table 3.3. *Party Platforms Condemning Trusts and Monopolies*

State party platforms containing planks on trusts by region (%)

Party	Northeast	Great Lakes	Plains	West	South	Nation
Republican	11.0	16.3	41.3	19.7	11.7	18.7
Democratic	21.4	24.4	22.0	27.3	22.3	23.0
Prohibition	15.9	13.8	15.0	7.1	15.0	14.4
Greenback	10.0	9.1	18.2	0.0	10.0	10.9
Populist	11.1	28.6	39.3	10.5	16.7	22.0

State party platforms containing planks on trusts by period (%)

Party	First period (1877–88)	Second period (1889–96)	Third period (1897–1900)	All years (1877–1900)
Republican	8.6	17.2	42.0	18.7
Democratic	10.7	15.4	64.8	23.0
Prohibition	4.8	26.0	0.0	14.4
Greenback	11.8	0.0	—	10.9
Populist	—	18.7	29.4	22.0

The regional pattern with respect to antitrust planks was less pronounced than demands for railroad regulation (see Table 3.3). The Plains states still usually took the lead, by a large margin in Republican and Populist platforms. The Democratic and Prohibition parties, however, showed little regional variation in frequency. Antitrust demands appeared much less frequently in Greenback and Populist declarations. For the Greenbackers, this can be partially explained by the temporal distribution of their platforms; regardless of party, antitrust demands were generally concentrated in the late 1890s when the pace of industrial consolidation accelerated throughout the national economy.[39] The Populist pattern reflects the party's

from. I have not caught the fever yet, and trust to continue to live free from it." *Industrial Commission: Capital and Labor*, vol. 7, pp. 395–396, 654. On the general attitude of labor leaders toward the regulation of trusts, see Edward C. Kirkland, *Industry Comes of Age: Business, Labor, and Public Policy, 1860–1897* (Chicago: Quadrangle Books, 1967), pp. 395–396. Socialist parties, with their Marxist perspective on economic change, sometimes welcomed the emergence of trusts as a milestone on the path to the socialization of industry.

[39] *Commercial and Financial Chronicle*, January 7 and September 2, 1899. Also see Hans B. Thorelli, *Federal Antitrust Policy* (Baltimore: Johns Hopkins University Press, 1955), pp. 143–152, 358–368; William Letwin, *Law and Economic Policy in America: The Evolution of the Sherman Antitrust Act* (New York: Random House, 1965), pp. 85–87, 117, 137, 140.

emphasis on railroads and banks; Populists certainly did not favor industrial concentration but this issue also did not involve one of the market linkages between the yeoman farmer and the national economy. Along with the tariff, where the party maintained an even more studied indifference, antitrust legislation took second place to monetary inflation and railroad rates.[40] As was the case with railroad regulation, the Prohibitionists again displayed a precipitous drop in platform references after the narrow-gauge victory in the 1896 national convention.

Demands for both railroad and antitrust regulation were narrowly focused on their impact upon the national market. Aside from a few planks addressing the extremely dangerous working conditions in the operation of railroads and a few others that mentioned major strikes against the lines, railroad working conditions and wage claims just did not appear in state party platforms.[41] Given the very contentious relations between the railroad unions and the operating companies, this silence is remarkable and only underlines just how completely labor's claims on wealth were deflected from politics in the late nineteenth century. Only minor parties with radical agrarian leanings or socialist ideologies gave routine attention to claims on wealth arising out of the wage bargain between labor and capital.

TARIFF PLANKS

The most common topic addressed in major party state platforms was the tariff. Along with temperance, federal intervention in southern elections, and monetary policy, the tariff was also one of four broad policy areas in which the two major parties commonly assumed opposing positions. As discussed in Chapter 7, the tariff was the central political element in the policy complex that underlay the Republican developmental program. For that reason, the major parties often devoted more space to tariff planks than

---

[40] An exception that in some ways illustrates the norm was written into the 1899 Mississippi Populist platform: "We are opposed to trusts and combinations of capital whereby the fruits of labor are boldly stolen to build up colossal fortunes for the few; but we do not consider it possible to regulate or abolish them by State restrictive legislation. Trusts are founded upon the monopoly of public utilities, and the only solution of the trust problem is through the public ownership and operation of such public utilities." This skepticism concerning the regulation of privately owned corporations is very similar to the position assumed by the various socialist parties of the period.

[41] One of the exceptions was the 1893 Republican platform in Ohio which called for a state law compelling the railroads to use automatic couplers as a way of reducing injuries to employees. In fact, the Republicans more often included a plank on railroad safety than any other party. See, for example, the Republican platforms in Indiana (1888), Iowa (1889), Minnesota (1894), and Nebraska (1890). However, even these platforms did not generally address the exceedingly dangerous working conditions on the railroads that maimed or killed thousands every year.

they did to other issues, frequently making these planks the central element in major party platforms.[42] In fact, the tariff was such a prominent issue that it could completely dominate state contests in which the office, in formal policy terms, was entirely irrelevant.[43]

While discussions of tariff policy could be quite complex, most platforms were still very general. Early in this period, Democrats often clothed their opposition to protection as a demand for equitable markets. In 1878, for example, the Nebraska Democrats opposed "any and all protective tariffs, for the reason that no one industry can be protected except at the expense of all others, and for the reason that we desire perfect commercial freedom wherein we may sell where we can sell the highest and buy anywhere we can buy the lowest." In the following year, the Minnesota Democratic party was a little more emphatic: "The enormous tribute which the producers of the West are compelled to pay to the monopolists of the East by the present system of protection, is an intolerable burden and a gross injustice. We demand as a right that our people shall be allowed to buy and sell in the markets of the world untrammeled by vexatious and oppressive tariffs. We favor the speedy establishment of free trade as the permanent commercial policy of this country." However, in the industrial states of the East, the Democrats were much more restrained in their opposition to the tariff; many of them even embraced protection.[44] After Cleveland strongly committed the party to lower duties in 1888, state party endorsements of protection disappeared and many Democratic planks simply called for a "tariff for revenue only."

For Republicans, high tariffs were almost synonymous with patriotism. Protected by the tariff, industry would expand, both raising the wages of workers and furthering the economic development of the nation. Eastern Republican platforms were usually the most effusive, closely linking the tariff's benefits for industry and labor. However, emphatic endorsements

---

[42] One of every sixteen Democratic platforms, for example, blamed the tariff as partially or entirely responsible for the emergence of trusts and monopolies.

[43] The 1893 gubernatorial race in Ohio, for example, pit Republican William McKinley, who had authored the 1890 tariff act which bore his name, against a Democrat, Lawrence Neal, who had participated in the drafting of the plank condemning that act in the 1892 national Democratic platform. The tariff became far and away the most important issue dividing the two candidates despite the fact that, as governor, neither would have been able to shape tariff policy in any way. *Appleton's Annual Cyclopaedia of 1893* (New York: D. Appleton, 1894), p. 591.

[44] In 1882, for example, the Pennsylvania Democratic party declared "in favor of the protection of the industrial interests of Pennsylvania" but otherwise devoted most of the platform to civil service reform. Altogether, just over 4 percent of all Democratic state platforms endorsed tariff protection between 1877 and 1900 with the highest percentage in the Northeast (10.7) and none at all in the Plains and South. All but one of these platforms were adopted before Cleveland's 1888 presidential campaign unequivocally committed the Democrats to lower duties.

made western Republicans uncomfortable. In the Plains and West, Republican declarations often either restricted their endorsements to local products that benefited from protection or, in rare cases, even opposed high duties.[45] With little in the way of industry, a cotton economy that depended on exports, and few Union pensioners, southern Republicans were even more stressed by the tariff. With the development of the Birmingham iron and steel industry in the 1880s, the Alabama Republican party finally had something to point to in the way of local benefit. And Louisiana Republicans always had sugar cane, although the duty on sugar neither promoted much domestic industry nor was much at risk; both parties usually supported a sugar tariff because the duty so efficiently raised revenue for the government.[46] But the Republican party in other parts of the South had to scrabble for a rationale or ignore the policy altogether in their platforms.

Some northern Republican platforms, particularly those condemning the 1894 Wilson Tariff, placed the southern wing of the party in an even more exposed position. Abandoning all pretense that tariff protection was a national policy, for example, the 1894 Maine Republican convention charged that the Democratic tariff "surrenders the interests of Northern labor, while it protects those of the South." The New York Republican convention was much more harsh: "We denounce Northern Democratic Congressmen for permitting Southern members to protect the chief products of their section while removing or largely reducing protective duties on the products of the North; thus permitting the South, by legal enactment in time of peace, to destroy our prosperity and accomplish what it failed to do by illegal enactment in time of war." For their part, Pennsylvania Republicans described the Wilson Tariff as "sectional in its authorship, and . . . all too plainly aimed at Northern industries. It strikes Southern industries only where the same blow reaches greater Northern industries. It fosters the plantation system and destroys the farm. It is an attempt upon the part of the Free Traders of the South to reduce the industries of the North to the level of those of the South." After such declarations were noted in the southern press, these planks must have made party regularity very difficult for southern Republicans.

Republican state platforms sometimes attributed free trade sentiment to Anglophilia. The connection between lower tariffs and increased British exports of manufactured goods was sound. However, given the importance

---

[45]   For Republican demands for lower tariffs, see the 1877 and 1879 Iowa and the 1879, 1886, and 1888 Minnesota platforms. The Iowa planks were quite brief and comparatively circumspect. The Minnesota demands explicitly blamed protection for higher prices on consumer goods and lower prices for grain exports. In 1886, the party even endorsed the break in congressional discipline when a majority of the state delegation voted to bring a Democratic tariff bill to the House floor.

[46]   See, for example, the 1884 Alabama and 1888 Louisiana state platforms.

of Irish Catholics in party ranks, the accusation that the Democrats were Anglophilic was implausible. But weaning the Irish away from their Democratic moorings may have been the Republican intention nonetheless. In 1885, for example, Iowa Republicans spelled out the linkage in a way that no Irish sympathizer could possibly miss: "We are opposed to the British policy advocated by the Democratic party in this country under the guise of a tariff for revenue only. The English theory of free-trade . . . [that] has been so successfully used as a means to destroy the industries and oppress the people of Ireland, cannot be imposed for English interests upon the people of the United States. . . ."[47]

However, Republican platforms usually stressed more material reasons for supporting the tariff. For example, protection was extended to raw wool as a way of bringing farmers into the Republican fold.[48] Since raw wool was one of the few major agricultural products that faced effective foreign competition, the tariff on its importation had, in fact, a significant impact. And many farmers raised at least a few sheep and thus could personally identify with the policy. Just over 10 percent of all Republican platforms in the late nineteenth century explicitly mentioned the duty on raw wool. Republicans in Ohio, which led the nation in the number of sheep, demanded protection for raw wool in almost every platform. In the West, where there were fewer sheep but even fewer people so that the ratio of sheep to voters was much higher, almost a quarter of all Republican platforms referred to the wool schedule. In a very few instances, again either in Ohio or the West, the Democratic party also endorsed duties on raw wool but, more often, the Democrats denounced the tariff as an impediment to wool manufacturing.[49] With very rare exceptions, the other party organizations never mentioned wool. Still, compared with all other products protected by the tariff, raw wool drew far more attention in state party platforms than any other with almost all that attention restricted to Republican planks written in either Ohio or the West.[50]

[47] For other references to a link between British interests and free trade, see the 1885 Ohio, 1888 Maine, and the 1888 and 1894 California Republican state platforms. The Maine plank implied that the British Cobden Club had "taught" Grover Cleveland the free trade principles that he now strongly advocated in the current presidential campaign.

[48] For an example of farmer support for a tariff on raw wool, see the platform approved by the 1889 Farmers' Congress of the United States in which that demand was the most emphatic of the resolutions adopted. *Appleton's Annual Cyclopaedia of 1889* (New York: D. Appleton, 1890), p. 307.

[49] See the 1888, 1889, 1892, and 1896 Massachusetts and the 1887, 1888, and 1892 Rhode Island Democratic platforms.

[50] Western Republican platforms sometimes cited the duty on lead as well, asserting that the tariff kept out Mexican imports that otherwise would undercut the domestic market for that metal. See, for example, the 1890 Idaho and the 1892 Colorado and Montana platforms.

The inclusion of raw wool obviously could not solve all the problems that industrial protection raised for Republicans in agricultural regions. For example, Democrats often charged that high tariffs restricted grain exports by reducing foreign demand.[51] The Republicans responded by emphasizing the utility of the tariff as a means to negotiate lower trade barriers for American exports. In platforms, this response was often couched in the single word "reciprocity" which implied both negotiation and mutual advantage in bilateral trade agreements. In this way, both the advantages of industrial protection and foreign grain markets could be exploited at the same time, at least in theory. The Republicans proposed a reciprocity policy only once before 1888.[52] But, after Cleveland's vitriolic attacks on protection in the 1888 presidential campaign, the Republicans added demands for reciprocity to many of their tariff planks. Most were adopted in the Great Lakes and Plains states where grain production was greatest, but they were significant elements in party platforms elsewhere as well. While reciprocity planks appeared in over a third of all state Republican platforms announced between 1889 and 1896, all the other parties made fewer than half a dozen endorsements during the same period. Even more than raw wool, this policy demand was almost exclusively an internal adjustment of the Republican program made for the purpose of relieving strain within the party coalition.

Because the tariff was such a fundamental issue distinguishing the Republican and Democratic developmental programs, there was comparatively little regional variation in the frequency with which the state parties referred to protection (see Table 3.4).[53] A majority of the Republican platforms in all five sections explicitly endorsed tariff protection in some form or another, while a majority of Democratic statements opposed protection in all sections but the West. The most significant fact is that more than half of the Republican platforms in the South openly endorsed protection. Given the material interests of their social base, no southern Republican party should have ever backed a high tariff; in fact, given the major contribution of the tariff to the regional redistribution of wealth between the North and South, southern Republicans should have strongly opposed protection at almost every opportunity. That they were pulled so far from their moorings in the southern political

---

[51]   See, for example, the 1892 Ohio Democratic platform.

[52]   In the 1879 Minnesota Republican platform.

[53]   Party platforms were classified as favoring tariff protection when they endorsed purposes beyond revenue or indicated support for an increase in duties. Many planks, of course, simply and unambiguously endorsed protection. Platforms opposing protection usually called for a "tariff for revenue only" or supported a significant reduction in duties. Where the plank contained no other language, endorsements of the Wilson Tariff have been classed as opposed to tariff protection even though that act was not an across-the-board reduction in duties.

Table 3.4. *Party Platforms Containing Tariff Planks*

State party platforms favoring tariff protection by region (%)

Party	Northeast	Great Lakes	Plains	West	South	Nation
Republican	77.1	62.8	58.7	60.7	54.5	64.3
Prohibition	7.9	6.9	15.0	7.1	0.0	7.5
Greenback	25.0	9.1	0.0	0.0	0.0	10.9
Populist	0.0	0.0	0.0	0.0	3.3	0.9

State party platforms opposing tariff protection by region (%)

Democratic	54.5	63.4	71.2	40.0	60.2	57.6

State party platforms favoring tariff protection by period (%)

Party	First period (1877–88)	Second period (1889–96)	Third period (1897–1900)	All years (1877–1900)
Republican	53.2	83.4	46.4	64.3
Prohibition	2.4	13.7	0.0	7.5
Greenback	11.8	0.0	—	10.9
Populist	—	1.3	0.0	0.9

State party platforms opposing tariff protection by period (%)

Democratic	44.0	79.2	40.8	57.6

Note: As discussed in the text, there were a few Republican, Prohibition, and Greenback platforms that also opposed tariff protection.

economy is striking evidence of their client status within the national Republican party.[54]

The minor parties were much less preoccupied with the tariff than were the Republicans and Democrats. The Prohibition party supported protection in eleven platforms and opposed the policy in twelve more (the latter are not reported in Table 3.4).[55] The Greenback party platforms supported

[54] During Reconstruction, when the party had a wider and sounder base in the region, southern Republicans were not as subservient to their northern colleagues. Then southern Republican congressmen routinely opposed economic measures that appeared to conflict with their constituents' interests. Terry L. Seip, *The South Returns to Congress: Men, Economic Measures, and Intersectional Relationships, 1868–1879* (Baton Rouge: Louisiana State University Press, 1983), p. 6.

[55] The Prohibition party also attempted to neutralize the tariff issue by advocating the appointment of a commission of experts to "scientifically" set customs duties. Almost

tariff protection in only six platforms, five of them written in the Northeast. The party opposed the policy in four more, three of them in Plains state platforms. While all the minor parties downplayed the tariff compared with the Republicans and Democrats, the Populists maintained the most studied indifference. No Populist convention ever opposed the tariff and only one endorsed the policy. Given the length of Populist platforms, the aggressiveness with which the party otherwise presented its program to the electorate, and the relatively articulate construction of its demands, the party's deafening silence on the tariff was truly remarkable.[56]

Along with the tariff on raw wool, the maintenance and expansion of liberal pensions to Union veterans was an essential element supporting tariff protection. For almost the entire period between 1877 and 1900, the tariff was the largest single source of federal revenue while Union pensions were the largest single expenditure category in the federal budget. Given the Republican commitment to the gold standard, these two policies had to remain in rough balance.[57] For that reason, as interest on the Civil War debt declined with the repayment of principal and the refunding of high-interest bond issues at lower rates, increased spending on Union pensions became ever more attractive to the party as a way of balancing the budget (and thus preventing a Treasury surplus from dangerously contracting national bank reserves) while forestalling a reduction in customs duties. In fact, Republican planks favoring liberal expenditures on Union pensions followed much the same pattern as those favoring tariff protection (cf. Tables 3.4 and 3.5). While always much less prominent in party platforms than the tariff, pension planks were similarly much more common between 1889 and 1896 than either before or after.[58]

12 percent of all Prohibition platforms contained this plank in one form or another with the greatest concentration in the 1889–96 period. While none of the demands for a tariff commission came from conventions in the Plains or South, their frequency was fairly even throughout the rest of the nation.

[56] Although the 1897 platform announced by the "middle of the road" wing of the Populist party in Iowa was not silent on the tariff, the plank condemned the way in which tariffs were made while assuming no position on whether they should be high or low: "The trusts, the combines, the syndicates, the corporations all united to make the government an agency for the promotion of their special interests and welfare. They contributed millions upon millions to Mark Hanna's campaign fund, and having triumphed by the corrupt use of these vast sums they are now about to recoup themselves from the pockets of the people. The notorious, almost avowed, purpose of the tariff bill now under consideration in the [S]enate is to repay the trusts and the mine, the mill and the factory barons for their pecuniary aid to McKinley."

[57] See Chapter 6.

[58] A few southern Republican planks even endorsed state aid to Confederate veterans. See, for example, the 1890 Texas and 1898 Arkansas platforms.

Table 3.5. *Party Platforms Favoring Federal Pensions for Union Soldiers*

State party platforms containing pension planks by region (%)

Party	Northeast	Great Lakes	Plains	West	South	Nation
Republican	32.1	30.2	34.9	18.0	13.0	25.8
Democratic	14.3	24.4	18.6	9.1	1.0	11.6
Prohibition	4.8	13.8	25.0	0.0	0.0	8.2
Greenback	30.0	27.3	18.2	0.0	10.0	21.8
Populist	5.6	35.7	32.1	10.5	3.3	16.5

State party platforms containing pension planks by period (%)

Party	First period (1877–88)	Second period (1889–96)	Third period (1897–1900)	All years (1877–1900)
Republican	15.1	42.1	13.0	25.8
Democratic	4.7	20.8	7.0	11.6
Prohibition	4.8	13.7	0.0	8.2
Greenback	21.6	25.0	—	21.8
Populist	—	13.3	23.5	16.5

The Cleveland administration sought to reconcile the federal surplus, the tariff, the gold standard, and pensions by reducing both customs revenue and pension expenditures. This strategy spawned a host of planks calling for an "honest" or "just" pension policy.[59] Some planks explicitly cited the lax standards and more or less open corruption that had historically attended Republican administration of the system. In response, the Republicans described the Democrats as ungenerous, at best. At the other extreme stood the New York Republicans, who asserted in their 1894 platform that the Cleveland administration "treats the Union soldier as if the Grand Army badge were the badge of beggary and brigandage." In general, Democratic state platforms favored pension expenditures much less frequently than did the Republicans, regardless of region. In the South, almost no planks favoring Union pensions were written because

[59] While some platforms clearly and specifically indicated policy changes in federal pensions, most were very general. To be classified as favoring pension expenditures, planks must contain the word "liberal" or some other expansive adjective to describe administration of the pension system. Those declaring support for "just" or "honest" administration of the system were classed as neutral and thus omitted from the table. Reflecting the great popularity of Union pensions in the North, very few platforms outside the South suggested even minor reductions in spending or eligibility criteria.

the party's social base rested among Confederate veterans and Union pensioners were rare.[60] Much more common were hostile planks, such as the 1892 Georgia declaration that called for "a correction of the present pension system, which rests like a mammoth war tax on our section of the Union" or the Tennessee condemnation in the same year that viewed Union pensions as "a part of the general policy of the Government under the Republican rule to drain the South of its wealth and carry it to more favored sections." And although platform references to pensions and other benefits for Confederate veterans were not common, most southern states had provided at least some support by the turn of the century.[61]

The Greenback and Populist parties were comparatively indifferent toward the federal budget surplus and could thus endorse pension spending without addressing the tariff. However, they used their hostility to the gold standard to good effect, citing the deflationary impact of the monetary system during this period as a justification for increasing pension stipends. In addition, Union pension expenditures were an attractive means of distributing greenback currency amongst the citizenry because veterans were relatively evenly distributed with respect to social class. Thus the Iowa National Greenback platform in 1880 declared: "That the payment of the bonds in coin, originally payable in lawful money, was a gift to the bondholder, and the payment of the soldier in paper, when by contract payable in coin, was and is an unjust discrimination in favor of the bondholder; therefore we demand, in justice to the soldier, that he be paid according to contract." But as was the case with the major parties, Greenbackers and Populists were notably reluctant to favor Union pensions in the South and West where veterans were much more scarce than in the rest of the nation. The Prohibition party followed a similar pattern with the now familiar drop-off in references after 1896.

---

[60] The lone exception was the 1889 Virginia Democratic platform, which called for state aid to "men who were disabled in the service of the United States during the late conflict between the States, and the widows of those who lost their lives in such service." On the other hand, southern Democrats sometimes called for state aid to Confederate veterans.

[61] For the text of the Alabama Confederate pension act, see *Acts of the General Assembly of Alabama, 1884–1885* (Montgomery: Barrett & Co., 1885), pp. 157–158. For brief accounts of expenditures for Confederate veterans in Alabama and other southern states, see *Appleton's 1879 Cyclopaedia*, p. 421; *Appleton's 1880 Cyclopaedia*, p. 308; *Appleton's 1889 Cyclopaedia*, pp. 327, 612; *Appleton's Annual Cyclopaedia of 1891* (New York: D. Appleton, 1892), pp. 30–31, 301, 532, 535, 597, 819, 823; *Appleton's 1892 Cyclopaedia*, pp. 3, 305, 470, 788; *Appleton's 1893 Cyclopaedia*, pp. 7, 463, 498; *Appleton's Annual Cyclopaedia of 1894* (New York: D. Appleton, 1895), pp. 4, 550; *Harper's Encyclopaedia of United States History*, vol. 9, pp. 273, 520.

MONETARY POLICY AND THE NATIONAL FINANCIAL SYSTEM

The tariff had only one rival in the amount of ink spilt upon platform declarations: the monetary system. While the frequency of monetary and financial planks probably exceeded those endorsing or opposing the tariff, the policy focus of these planks was more diffuse. The status quo against which the parties addressed monetary issues was, of course, the gold standard. This was the case even in the years immediately preceding resumption when the nation had not yet resumed gold payments. But most opposition to gold was not unequivocally hostile. Instead, opponents often advocated the incorporation of greenback or silver policies that, they asserted, were compatible with the gold standard. This tendency meant that most planks endorsing silver or greenbacks did not openly attack gold. Some greenback declarations, for example, merely proposed expansion of the currency during the period immediately preceding resumption. While this position was surely detrimental to the resumption of gold payments, such planks can be seen as advocating policies that, inadvertently as it were, put at risk the gold standard while pursuing another goal.

A few silverites, for their part, apparently believed that the United States could actually, through government purchases of the metal, control the world price and thus determine the exchange ratio with gold. Such a belief was clearly more realistic in the early years of this period when the market price for silver was only slightly below parity with gold at the American ratio of 16 to 1. Late in the nineteenth century, when silver fell below 50 percent of parity, few people could have still believed that the United States could have regulated the price. In between those two extremes, the price of silver gradually declined so that distinguishing planks in which bimetallism might have been theoretically feasible from those in which hostility to gold can be unambiguously inferred is not easy.[62] Finally, greenbackers and silverites had more than a few differences, despite their shared problems with the gold standard; their mutual hostility to gold was often not enough to bring them together behind a single program. For all these reasons, planks referring to the competing monetary standards (greenback currency, silver, and gold) cannot be reduced to a single dimension without distorting the nature of platform declarations. However, if they had been so reduced to a single dimension, the frequency of platform references would have, in total, exceeded those for the tariff.

Planks approving the use of greenbacks ranged from those that simply opposed further contraction of the currency to others that advocated

---

[62] Many of the issues involved in late nineteenth-century monetary and financial policy are taken up in more detail in Chapter 6.

Table 3.6. *Party Platforms Favoring Greenbacks*

State party platforms containing greenback planks by region (%)

Party	Northeast	Great Lakes	Plains	West	South	Nation
Republican	0.0	0.0	0.0	0.0	1.3	0.3
Democratic	0.9	7.3	8.5	5.5	1.9	3.8
Prohibition	0.0	6.9	15.0	0.0	0.0	3.4
Greenback	85.0	36.4	36.4	66.7	30.0	54.5
Populist	33.3	28.6	32.1	31.6	16.7	27.5

State party platforms containing greenback planks by period (%)

Party	First period (1877–88)	Second period (1889–96)	Third period (1897–1900)	All years (1877–1900)
Republican	0.0	0.7	0.0	0.3
Democratic	2.0	4.0	7.0	3.8
Prohibition	0.0	6.8	0.0	3.4
Greenback	56.9	25.0	—	54.5
Populist	—	26.7	29.4	27.5

Note: This table records the frequency of planks that either supported expansion or opposed further contraction of the greenback currency, in addition to those declarations that advocated paper money as the nation's monetary standard.

active control of the money supply by the federal government. But almost all greenback planks were written into third-party declarations; the Republicans and Democrats were comparatively indifferent to greenbacks in any form (see Table 3.6).[63] In one sense, all of the Greenback party platforms favored paper currency as the monetary standard; that policy was, indeed, written into the party's very name and identity. But explicit declarations in favor of greenbacks, beyond simple endorsement of the national platform, were made only in a bare majority of the state platforms, most commonly in the Northeast. In fact, as seen below, there were several other policy areas in which the state Greenback parties announced positions more frequently. The Populists, who absorbed many former Greenbackers into their ranks, also wrote many planks favoring the use of paper currency. In both the

---

[63] The only Republican reference was a mild plank that appeared in the 1896 North Carolina platform. Democratic planks, however, were sufficiently common to draw complaints from Greenbackers. See, for example, the comments of Charles Brumm of Pennsylvania in House floor debate. *Congressional Record* 47:1:408, May 18, 1882. Also see the exchange between William Breckinridge, a Kentucky Democrat, and a Cincinnati Republican, Benjamin Butterworth. *Congressional Record* 49:1:7992, August 4, 1886.

Great Lakes and Plains states, for example, the Populists drafted greenback planks almost as often as did the Greenbackers before them.[64]

State party platforms rarely referred to silver as an alternative monetary standard; instead, almost all planks advocated an increase or decrease in coinage. In fact, most planks simply advocated free and unlimited coinage of silver at the ratio of 16 to 1 with gold. From the other end of the spectrum, it was fairly uncommon for party platforms to openly oppose silver coinage; such planks usually brusquely endorsed gold with a resolve that clearly ruled out any favor to silver. The compromise policy of limited silver purchases, enacted by Congress in the form of the 1878 Bland-Allison and the 1890 Sherman Silver Purchase Acts, was almost entirely ignored in platform declarations. When these policies were mentioned, it was usually to blame them, one way or another, for problems in the financial system. For silverites, the difficulty was not enough coinage under these policies; for financial conservatives, the problem was too much.

Over half of the Republican platforms written in the silver-producing western states endorsed silver coinage (see Table 3.7). Outside the West, the frequency of silver planks was comparatively low. In contrast, the Democrats made silver coinage a platform staple in every region but the Northeast, which never developed any appetite for silver even after Bryan's nomination had cleansed the state parties of gold advocates. In that region, Bryan's nomination and the national convention's declaration for free silver compelled those Democrats that remained within the party fold to perform a complete somersault. A comparison of the state platforms adopted before and after Bryan's nomination reveals that eleven state parties switched positions from gold to silver: Connecticut, Maine, Massachusetts, Michigan, Minnesota, New Hampshire, New Jersey, New York, Pennsylvania, Rhode Island, and South Dakota. Some of these switches were almost surreal. Before the national convention, for example, the New Jersey platform declared: "We are in favor of a firm, unvarying maintenance of the present gold standard. We are opposed to the free coinage of silver at any ratio, and to the compulsory purchase of silver bullion by the Government." Afterward, when Democrats met again to select a slate of presidential electors, the party insisted that free silver was "thoroughly Democratic and purely American, and with its enforcement we firmly believe that relief will come to the toiling masses and will advance the general prosperity of our country."[65] The Delaware party, in a transparently hypocritical attempt to evade conflict over the issue, explicitly retained their gold plank while endorsing the national ticket. The Vermont

---

[64] On the strong connections between the Greenback and later Populist parties, see Goodwyn, *Democratic Promise*, pp. 371, 482–483; Roscoe C. Martin, *The People's Party in Texas: A Study in Third Party Politics* (1933; rpt., Austin: University of Texas Press, 1970), pp. 70–72.

[65] Equally fascinating reversals were made in both Connecticut and New York.

Table 3.7. *Party Platforms Favoring Silver Coinage*

State party platforms containing silver planks by region (%)

Party	Northeast	Great Lakes	Plains	West	South	Nation
Republican	4.6	7.0	15.9	57.4	9.1	17.0
Democratic	16.1	41.5	54.2	80.0	45.6	42.7
Prohibition	3.2	20.7	15.0	28.6	5.0	11.0
Greenback	20.0	45.5	45.5	33.3	10.0	29.1
Populist	50.0	57.1	71.4	78.9	53.3	62.4

State party platforms containing silver planks by period (%)

Party	First period (1877–88)	Second period (1889–96)	Third period (1897–1900)	All years (1877–1900)
Republican	6.5	32.4	5.6	17.0
Democratic	21.3	59.1	53.5	42.7
Prohibition	0.0	21.9	0.0	11.0
Greenback	29.4	25.0	—	29.1
Populist	—	66.7	52.9	62.4

Note: These are planks that called for either limited or unlimited coinage of silver and/or remonetization of the metal as legal tender. In a few cases, demands for a bimetallism were included if the plank indicated a willingness to change the ratio of value between gold and silver in order to place the United States on such a dual standard.

and Wisconsin parties, both of which adopted strong gold planks before the national convention, appear to have declined to endorse either the national ticket or the platform after Bryan's nomination.

The distribution of planks over time also exhibits some striking differences between the two major parties. For the Republicans, silver becomes an important element in their state platforms in the middle period, only to drop off into insignificance after McKinley assumes office. Outside the West, many of these platforms were written in either 1893 or 1894 when Republicans opportunistically skewered the Cleveland administration for its hostility to silver. The party in effect blamed the economic depression of those years on administration policies such as repeal of the Sherman Silver Purchase Act which they would have pursued themselves, had they been in office. The Democrats, on the other hand, were always more favorable to silver than the Republicans, and the drop-off in frequency is much less after 1896 than for their opponents. Because of Cleveland's firm commitment to hard money, many of the state parties, in fact, were acutely uncomfortable with him as their party's presidential candidate.[66] As shown in Chapter 6, a majority of the Democrats in Congress favored silver throughout the late nineteenth century.

The distribution of silver planks within the Prohibition party mimicked that of the Republicans. As with other issues, the state organizations dropped silver as a platform issue once the narrow-gauge faction captured the national party. One of the truly great paradoxes of the period was the enthusiasm of Greenback parties for free silver coinage. The 1879 Minnesota National Greenback platform, for example, declared: "We are in favor of the free and unrestricted coinage of silver, upon the same terms and conditions as gold, and its retention as a full legal tender for all debts, public and private." However, the financial principles underlying the Greenback movement were quite formal and exact in their commitment to discretionary, government control of the supply of money as a tool for encouraging both monetary stability and economic growth. Free silver utterly abandoned that principle by making the supply of money dependent on the amount of the metal brought to the mints for coinage into dollars and subsidiary denominations. Nonetheless, almost half of the Greenback platforms in the Great Lakes and Plains states made silver coinage one of their demands.[67] The comparatively high frequency with which Greenback

---

[66] See, for example, the 1892 South Carolina Democratic platform which, after endorsing the Ocala platform of the Farmers' Alliance, then condemned Cleveland as a candidate forced on the party by "the money changers of Wall Street" and his nomination as "a surrender of the rights of the people to the financial kings of the country." As C. Vann Woodward notes, the convention then "carefully added that they would 'actively support' any candidate nominated, no matter what his platform." *Origins of the New South, 1877–1913* (Baton Rouge: Louisiana State University Press, 1967), p. 241. While an extreme example, the language in this declaration indicates just how natural and easy a thorough denunciation of Cleveland's hard-money proclivities came to the southern and western wings of his party. Where his candidacy was endorsed at all, parties in these regions wrote short, perfunctory planks.

[67] The 1879 Maine National Greenback-Labor platform combined free silver and discretionary control of the supply of paper currency as follows: ". . . we favor the unlimited coinage of gold and silver, to be supplemented by full legal-tender paper money, sufficient to transact the business of the country." Several conditions must be met for these policies to be compatible with one another. First, silver coinage must not outrun the indicated level of circulation. This condition is likely if the mint value of silver is set sufficiently high (at market parity with gold), but maintaining that value, in exchange for both greenbacks and gold, places a clear limit on the supply of paper currency. As a result, the financial policies necessary for maintaining the silver standard must closely coincide with the indicated level of circulation (otherwise the nation would be forced to choose whether to maintain the silver standard or manage the economy). Given the fluctuating world price for silver, along with the unpredictability of international trade movements and thus international exchange rates, this condition is highly unlikely to be met. Furthermore, the Maine plank in effect asserts that the nation could have been on both gold and silver standards simul-

parties adopted silver planks indicates just how thoroughly this movement accommodated a diverse amalgamation of insurgent elements, to the detriment of the doctrinal coherence and consistency with which it is sometimes credited. For the Populists, who were in many ways the direct inheritors of the Greenback movement, free silver was often the primary demand in their platforms. Given the extremely high frequency with which the state parties adopted such planks, even before 1896, fusion with the Bryan Democrats on the basis of that demand must have seemed natural to much of the movement.[68]

A central element in Greenback monetary theory attributed economic depression and instability to an inadequate supply of money. Thus frequent party demands for increased monetary circulation is no surprise (see Table 3.8). State platforms, in fact, demanded increased circulation with a slightly higher frequency than they called for greenback currency (cf. Table 3.6). Otherwise, the regional distribution of the two issues in Greenback platforms was very close. The Populist patterns on these two issues also paralleled each other. For the Republicans, Democrats, and Prohibitionists, the size of the money supply, as opposed to what it was made of, was never a salient policy issue.

Like the money supply and greenbacks, government bonds were also a major issue within Greenback orthodoxy. In the late nineteenth century, all financial theories highlighted the role of paper currency as interest-free debt. In effect, by providing money as a service to the public, the government received back an interest-free loan of goods and services. This aspect was

---

taneously. In 1879, this was possible, for at least a short time, if the United States had dedicated most of its budget to market stabilization of whatever ratio of value it chose to set between the two metals. But, in terms of greenback theory, such a policy would have been absurdly pointless because market stabilization, at whatever price, would have subsidized either gold or silver producers (by providing a higher price for their metal than the market set) while both limiting the supply of paper currency and drying up government funds that could have been spent on other policies. Finally, market stabilization of the gold-silver price ratio while attempting to manage total monetary circulation in such a way as to maximize economic growth was even more difficult than simply maintaining a silver standard and optimal circulation. If the extremely likely assumption is made that gold payments would have been abandoned under such conditions, it must also be assumed that going off gold would not have seriously damaged the national economy by drying up foreign investment and credit. Everything considered, this Greenback plank (and many others like it) set out one of the most internally incoherent and contradictory demands ever made in American political history.

[68] Lawrence Goodwyn overstates the resistance of Populist activists to free silver as a policy stance. However, the party's demands included many other issues that depended on its continued existence as an independent organization. For that reason, it was not free silver that the middle-of-the-roaders objected to but, instead, the practical reduction of the party's program to that one issue through fusion. *Democratic Promise*, pp. 432–434.

Table 3.8. *Party Platforms Favoring Increased Circulation*

State party platforms containing circulation planks by region (%)

Party	Northeast	Great Lakes	Plains	West	South	Nation
Republican	0.0	0.0	1.6	3.3	3.9	1.7
Democratic	1.8	14.6	10.2	5.5	12.6	8.1
Prohibition	1.6	13.8	10.0	7.1	5.0	6.2
Greenback	90.0	63.6	36.4	66.7	20.0	60.0
Populist	27.8	21.4	28.6	31.6	33.3	29.4

State party platforms containing circulation planks by period (%)

Party	First period (1877–88)	Second period (1889–96)	Third period (1897–1900)	All years (1877–1900)
Republican	0.7	3.4	0.0	1.7
Democratic	4.7	12.8	5.6	8.1
Prohibition	0.0	12.3	0.0	6.2
Greenback	60.8	50.0	—	60.0
Populist	—	34.7	17.6	29.4

Note: Only planks specifically opposing contraction of the money supply or demanding an expansion are included in this table.

a central element in the Greenbacker vision of the national government as a popular commonwealth, a commonwealth in which the people collectively furnished the material resources for government while simultaneously providing the primary policy lever for ensuring economic prosperity. Within this perspective, there was little reason to issue bonds or to continue to pay interest on those already sold. Greenbackers simply demanded that they be bought back with newly printed paper currency, a proposal that eliminated the debt at the same time that it expanded greenback circulation. The party attributed opposition to repayment of the debt to the rapacious greed of bankers and bondholders; this, too, fit in well with their hostility to financiers and wealth.

While the Greenback party emphasized the positive elements of debt monetization, the Populists and Democrats stressed the inequitable class advantages that accompanied gold-denominated principal and interest payments by the federal government. The Republicans had a very brief spurt of bond planks in the first half of the 1890s when Cleveland was forced to defend the gold standard by issuing millions of dollars in new federal debt. For eastern branches of the party, these planks, along with the silver demands made during the same years, rank among the most cynical ever written in American politics.[69] Overall, the distribution of bond planks by party, by region, and over time was very similar to the patterns for both greenbacks and increased circulation.

Although the gold standard stood at the center of the maelstrom over money, it was seldom openly denounced in state party platforms; most planks instead implied opposition to gold by advocating some other monetary system as a replacement.[70] The Republicans were the only party to consistently endorse the gold standard (see Table 3.9). A majority of the state party platforms in the capital-exporting regions of the Northeast and Great Lakes openly favored gold. In the West, state Republican party platforms favored silver over gold by a large margin, clearly presaging the problems those organizations would have with McKinley's 1896 platform and the administration's subsequent aggressive pursuit of hard money policy. South-

---

[69]   For the southern wing, however, this opportunity to denounce the gold standard and bonds while remaining within the national party fold was probably a liberating experience, one that the North Carolina Republicans exploited with relish in their 1896 plank: "We are opposed to the issue of interest-bearing bonds in time of peace, and we condemn the policy of President Cleveland and Secretary Carlisle in secretly making the sale of Government bonds to a foreign syndicate on such terms as to enable it to realize the enormous profit of $10,000,000, at the expense of the people."

[70]   These planks must be carefully interpreted because state platforms often included contradictory demands as the parties attempted to satisfy different constituencies. For example, the gold standard and free silver coinage were just not compatible given the structure of the international and national political economies of the period. Because the gold standard was relatively unpopular, the Republicans often attempted to say something favorable about silver while understating their more fundamental support for gold (particularly before 1896). In interpreting all party platforms, not just the Republican planks, the following principles guided their classification. First, if a state party platform explicitly endorsed the gold standard, then references to silver were set aside. In almost all contexts, "coin," "honest money," and "sound money" are interpreted as meaning "gold." In the few cases where these phrases were used by silverites or greenbackers, the terms merely asserted that those forms of money were as "honest" or "sound" as "gold" and thus could be easily distinguished from gold declarations. Because an international agreement on a bimetallic standard was so unlikely, demands that proposed such an agreement as a condition for abandoning the gold standard are simply interpreted as favoring gold. While these criteria might appear complex, in practice the vast majority of planks were easy to classify. For example, the 1879 Maine Democratic platform declared the party in favor of ". . . a currency of gold, silver, and paper, the paper to be kept at par with coin at all times, and . . . in favor of free, unlimited coinage of silver." As stated in the last clause, the priority was silver, and other policies, such as those necessary to maintain parity between gold and paper dollars, were subordinated to that clear and unqualified demand. Since those other policies were not well articulated and, in any case, would have been incompatible with free silver except under extraordinary conditions, they were clearly secondary declarations and were thus set aside in the analysis. Nonetheless, many monetary planks so thoroughly confused the issues and so successfully avoided any declaration of priorities that they were unclassifiable. These planks were omitted from the analysis in this section.

Table 3.9. *Party Platforms Favoring the Gold Standard*

State party platforms containing gold planks by region (%)

Party	Northeast	Great Lakes	Plains	West	South	Nation
Republican	59.6	55.8	47.6	18.0	27.3	42.8
Democratic	22.3	12.2	0.0	1.8	1.9	8.9
Prohibition	3.2	0.0	5.0	0.0	0.0	2.1

State party platforms containing gold planks by period (%)

Party	First period (1877–88)	Second period (1889–96)	Third period (1897–1900)	All years (1877–1900)
Republican	32.3	42.1	65.2	42.8
Democratic	4.7	17.4	0.0	8.9
Prohibition	4.8	1.4	0.0	2.1

ern Republicans were the most reticent regional wing of the party. Their dependency on the national party forced them to give lip service to the gold standard, but southern Republicans clearly preferred not to mention monetary policy at all. Almost all the Democratic platforms endorsing gold were written in the Northeast or Great Lakes regions. Northeastern Democrats, in fact, drafted slightly more gold than silver demands; as with the western Republicans and McKinley, this pattern forecast the problems that the regional wing would have with Bryan. Recognizing the prevalence of silver sentiment in their own national organization, however, northeastern Democrats generally preferred not to mention monetary policy in their state platforms even as their representatives voted for gold in Congress. Much more independent than southern Republicans were in their own party, northeastern Democrats were nonetheless almost as reticent on money. Prohibition parties rarely presented gold planks to the electorate. Greenbackers and Populists, not surprisingly, wrote none at all.

The national bank system was the single most important political constituency favoring the gold standard. In that role, the system itself came under heavy political attack. For the Greenbackers, hostility to national banks was both good politics and sound doctrine. As politics, demands for the system's abolition were a popular assault on the privileges of wealth. As doctrine, the note-issuing privilege assigned to these privately owned banks denied to the government the discretionary control over the supply of money that their theory demanded.[71] Furthermore, since national bank

---

[71] See, for example, the doctrinally correct 1881 Ohio Greenback platform.

Table 3.10. *Party Platforms Opposing the National Bank System*

State party platforms containing Planks by region (%)

Party	Northeast	Great Lakes	Plains	West	South	Nation
Republican	0.0	0.0	1.6	1.6	0.0	0.6
Democratic	8.0	14.6	16.9	12.7	15.5	13.0
Prohibition	6.3	27.6	15.0	7.1	0.0	11.0
Greenback	85.0	63.6	54.5	66.7	50.0	67.3
Populist	16.7	42.9	32.1	26.3	33.3	30.3

State party platforms containing planks by period (%)

Party	First period (1877–88)	Second period (1889–96)	Third period (1897–1900)	All years (1877–1900)
Republican	1.4	0.0	0.0	0.6
Democratic	12.7	14.1	11.3	13.0
Prohibition	0.0	21.9	0.0	11.0
Greenback	70.6	25.0	—	67.3
Populist	—	30.7	29.4	30.3

Note: All planks that called for either abolition of the national bank system or withdrawal of the note-issuing privilege are included.

notes were secured by deposits of federal bonds, the bankers drew interest on what could have been an interest-free public loan to the government. Compared with the Greenbackers, the Populists tended to emphasize the politics, as opposed to the doctrinal, side of the issue but otherwise frequently attacked the system. The Democrats less frequently assaulted the banks.[72] Aside from the Northeast where the frequency was slightly lower, the regional distribution of these demands was fairly even. There was little change over time as well. Reflecting the close relationship between the gold standard, the national bank system, and the Republican party – a relationship that in many ways was similar to the connection between Union pensions, the Grand Army of the Republic, and the party – the Republicans almost never wrote hostile planks. However, they also almost never wrote planks defending the system either, seven in all over the late nineteenth century. The Democrats drafted even fewer, only two.

As Tables 3.6–3.10 illustrate, planks on national financial and monetary policy were numerous, diverse, and interrelated. The connections between

[72]   A small percentage of state party platforms favored removing the 10 percent federal tax on bank notes issued by state-chartered institutions. Since the tax was prohibitive in practice, this demand was equivalent to permitting state-chartered banks to

them were generally mediated by the gold standard as the prevailing monetary policy. Support or opposition to gold often determined whether or not a party would even mention issues that were, in strictly economic terms, only distantly related to the operation of that standard. This was the case most obviously for the national bank system since, again in strictly economic terms, the gold standard would have worked at least as well without federally chartered banks. However, because the political economy surrounding the gold standard pragmatically directed much of the platform traffic around financial policy, gold supporters almost invariably defended the national bank system from the assaults of silverites and greenbackers. In contrast, the formalized and complex principles of greenback theory tended to dictate many of the positions assumed by both Greenbackers and Populists (and, to a much smaller extent, the Democrats). Greenback platforms, in fact, were often quite complex with three or four distinct policy declarations on separate financial issues. However, in the final analysis, the coherence of many platforms was severely compromised by the inclusion of silver demands. Populist planks tended to be shorter and even more oriented around silver coinage; however, they sometimes still contained greenback elements. On the whole, the Democrats exhibited much less doctrinal coherence, seldom adopting greenback positions and, when they did, adapting them in such a way as to maximize their political appeal at the expense of theoretical consistency.

LABOR PLANKS

In no area of public life was there a greater discrepancy between the frequency and intensity of popular claims on wealth and the response of political parties than in industrial labor relations. Tens of thousands of strikes, many of them violent, made the United States factory shop floor in the late nineteenth century one of the most bitterly contested labor arenas in world history. Yet the response of an extremely competitive party system that otherwise sought votes in every nook and cranny of the policy landscape was, at best, subdued.[73] While many party platforms addressed labor's

issue currency. The plank was only popular in the South where just under 15 percent of the platforms proposed abolition of the tax. Republican platforms favored retention, in effect continuing the prohibition on state-chartered bank notes, with the highest frequency in the Northeast (about 7% of the region's platforms). Although Greenback doctrine would have placed the party in opposition to note-issuing privileges for state-chartered banks, the issue was not salient during the years the party drafted platforms and thus was never mentioned. Largely because of their Greenback inheritance, however, the Populists wrote four planks opposing removal of the tax: Alabama (1894), Kansas (1894), Texas (1894), and Virginia (1893).

[73] Aside from vague denunciations of anarchy and communism as threats to public order, planks opposing labor's claims on wealth were much more rare than those

Table 3.11. *Party Platforms Favoring Labor Interests*

State party platforms containing labor planks by region (%)

Party	Northeast	Great Lakes	Plains	West	South	Nation
Republican	13.8	18.6	30.2	26.2	11.7	19.0
Democratic	29.5	26.8	18.6	27.3	7.8	21.1
Prohibition	4.8	3.4	15.0	7.1	0.0	5.5
Greenback	45.0	54.5	36.4	33.3	30.0	41.8
Populist	38.9	57.1	35.7	47.4	13.3	34.9

State party platforms containing labor planks by period (%)

Party	First period (1877–88)	Second period (1889–96)	Third period (1897–1900)	All years (1877–1900)
Republican	19.4	20.0	15.9	19.0
Democratic	20.0	18.1	29.6	21.1
Prohibition	7.1	6.8	0.0	5.5
Greenback	43.1	25.0	—	41.8
Populist	—	38.7	26.5	34.9

Note: Only planks containing a specific proposal that would have strengthened labor's bargaining position over wages and working conditions or directly improved those conditions through government regulation are included. Expressions of "good will" toward labor are excluded if not accompanied by a specific proposal. Pleas that labor and capital privately arbitrate their differences were also excluded if not accompanied by proposals either to make the outcome binding or to establish a government agency to oversee the process.

claims on an increased share of industrial wealth in one way or another, only two policy areas were mentioned frequently enough to be analyzed separately: the restriction of immigration and the regulation of convict labor. They are taken up below in this section. All other references to labor relations have been combined into one category (see Table 3.11). Where they presented any favorable labor demands at all, the party platforms generally had but one plank in which a general expression of sympathy for workers was expressed, followed by one or two brief proposals for government action. Many of these planks were very mild, calling, for example, for the collection of statistics by new state or federal bureaus of labor or

that favored worker's interests. One of the few exceptions appeared in the 1894 platform announced by the "Regular" faction of the Texas Republican party which approved of Cleveland's "action in interposing the national authority to suppress the late riots in Chicago and elsewhere."

nonbinding government arbitration of labor disputes. Because they would have, however slightly, strengthened labor's position in bargaining over wages and working conditions, these mild proposals are included in the analysis. Many other planks merely expressed concern for the intensity of disputes between labor and capital without recommending any specific government response. These planks were excluded.[74] Detailed platforms that advocated a general redress of grievances or a thorough reconstruction of the industrial shop floor were quite rare. The large majority of such demands were presented by the Greenback party in platforms that gave each policy a separate plank. The Populist party also presented rather strong demands favorable to labor but these tended to be less detailed even if more radical in rhetoric. The major party planks tended to be short, containing comparatively weak proposals.

As can be seen in Table 3.11, regardless of content, the parties presented labor planks to the electorate with widely varying frequencies. As might be expected, given their respective social bases in the manufacturing belt, the two major party distributions reveal a comparative tilt toward labor by Democrats in the Great Lakes and Northeast.[75] In the West, which contained large concentrations of relatively well-organized and active miners, both parties addressed labor issues with equal frequency. In the Plains states, the Republicans drew up a surprisingly high number of labor planks, both compared with the Democrats and in absolute terms. In the South,

---

[74] For example, the 1877 Iowa Democratic platform stated: "The rights of capital and labor are equally sacred, and alike entitled to legal protection. They have no just cause of quarrel, and the proper relations to each other are adjustable by natural laws, and should not be hampered by legislative interference." As noted in the text, such planks were excluded from the analysis.

[75] Many of the most detailed and favorable planks written by the Democratic party appeared in the Northeast during the heyday of the Knights of Labor. See, for example, the 1886 Pennsylvania Democratic platform which called for "the enlargement of the Bureau of Statistics, the abrogation of all laws that do not bear equally upon capital and labor, and the prevention of the hiring out of convict-labor; the adoption of measures providing for the health, and safety, and indemnification of injuries to those engaged in mining, manufacturing, and building industries; the enactment of laws by which labor organizations may be incorporated and arbitration extended and enforced, and a suitable apprenticeship act for the purpose of creating a better class of artisans and mechanics; the prohibition of the employment of children under fourteen years of age in workshops, mines, and factories; the strict and exact enforcement of the laws relating to pluck-me-stores and store-orders, and those relating to the accounting of industrial works; the appointment of inspectors to carry out these provisions, and a rigid enforcement of existing immigration laws, and [exclusion of] pauper, contract, and assisted immigration." For both Republicans and Democrats, the highest frequency of labor planks in state platforms occurred in the years 1885 and 1886 when the Knights became one of the broadest social movements in American history. Gerald Friedman reaches a similar conclusion in his *State-making and Labor Movements: France and the United States, 1876–1914* (Ithaca, N.Y.: Cornell University Press, 1998), pp. 109–110.

where industrial activity was far less important, labor planks were seldom written by either major party; there was a slight tendency for labor planks to be more frequent and favorable in Republican platforms but the differences were not great.[76] The radicalizing impact of Bryan's nomination explains the sharp rise in labor planks written in the last four years of the century in the Democratic party. The Prohibitionists began the period largely indifferent to labor's interests and ended it the same way. Where the party wrote planks addressing labor, most contained very mild requests for the establishment of agencies to oversee arbitration between labor and capital.[77] The contrast with the Greenbackers could hardly have been greater; the party often wrote detailed, vigorous labor planks that left little to the imagination. These were major components of Greenback platforms throughout the nation but were particularly prominent in the manufacturing belt. The Populists were only slightly less responsive, with a comparative tilt toward labor in the West where the party's alliance with miner organizations gave their platforms a particularly strong flavor.

Compared with their competitors, Greenbackers presented the closest approximation to a social democratic program most voters ever saw in the late nineteenth century. Because they thus embodied real possibilities, Greenback demands are worth closer examination. Near or at the peak of the movement's influence, for example, the 1879 Maryland Greenback convention offered the electorate the following labor proposals:

That the laborer is worthy of his hire; therefore equal payment should be made for like labor performed whether by males or females.

That Congress provide for the establishment of a labor bureau of statistics in every State.

That eight hours shall constitute a legal day's work.

That such laws should be enacted by the [state] Legislature as will secure proper ventilation and other necessary sanitary regulations of all inclosures wherein manual labor is performed.

That the employing of children under twelve years of age in any manufactory where manual labor is required be prohibited.

That debts due for labor performed shall be entitled to equally as stringent remedy for enforcement as any remedy tolerated by the State for the enforcement of any other debt.

Such planks were often combined with demands for the improvement of public education and other social reforms. In 1878, for example, Connecticut Greenbackers connected education to public recognition of the worker's contribution to society: "We demand a thorough reform in the

---

[76] One of the most detailed major party planks in the South appeared in the 1885 Virginia Republican platform, which was heavily influenced by the party's close links to the Knights of Labor.

[77] The party also tended to turn labor planks into temperance lectures. For an example, see the 1888 Indiana Prohibition platform.

system of public-school education, so as to establish agricultural, mechanical, and commercial schools in addition to our common schools; that all books should be procured at the expense of the State government, and that not less than one lecture per week be delivered upon the dignity of labor and its paramount importance in the affairs of men in every-day life." Other platforms demanded specific labor reforms but, just in case the prospective voter missed the general orientation of the party in the welter of detail, summarized the Greenback program in language that could have been borrowed directly from Marx. After such a list of demands, for example, the 1880 Illinois Greenback Labor convention concluded: "We are to embody in civil government the divine right of every laborer to the results of his toil, thus enabling the toiling producers of wealth to provide themselves with the means for physical comfort and the facilities for mental, social, and spiritual culture, condemning as unworthy in our civilization the barbarism which would impose upon the wealth-producers a state of perpetual drudgery as the price of bare animal existence." Other platforms mixed rhetoric and specific demands for reform into a single vision, for example, this plank from the 1880 Massachusetts Greenback platform:

That the hours of labor should be shortened, and the employment of young children in exhausting factory-labor be prevented; that labor-saving machinery is a boon of God to the sons and daughters of toil rather than an engine of torture to wring out larger profits for capital by bringing the laborer into heart-breaking competition with the muscles that never tire. The vast powers of nature are not harnessed by invention to secure even six percent dividends, but to relieve human slaves; not hours of toil, but the product of this new partnership of man with natural forces, should be the ruling compensation, and demand a new system of dividing the profits of capital and labor. We demand the rigid enforcement of the ten-hour law, now on the statutes of this Commonwealth relating to the employment of women and children, and we insist that the grasping corporation which filches an hour's labor from a thousand operatives deserves the same proportionate punishment meted out to lesser offenders.[78]

But, while poignant, Greenback planks usually did not name the class enemies of the worker or cite actual conflicts in which labor's claims were violated. As their inheritors, the Populists crafted many planks that were equally general in nature. In 1892, for example, the Colorado People's party convention issued "a declaration of war by the production classes against all forms of legislation which enable any man to exploit the labor of another." In 1894, to cite another example, the Kansas Populist party condemned "the policy of all the governing parties in this Nation whose legislation has favored capital and oppressed labor, and we hereby declare our sympathy with all toilers in their efforts to improve their

[78] An almost identical plank appeared in the platform written a year earlier by the Massachusetts party.

conditions, and demand such legislation as will result in removing some of the burdens of toil by shortening the hours of labor without lessening their daily wage."

But the Populists, unlike the Greenbackers before them, often took sides in some of the most violent and contentious labor disputes of their period. For example, the 1892 Minnesota Populist platform referred to the strike at the Carnegie steelworks by calling for a class alliance of workers and farmers: "We extend our sympathies to the oppressed workmen at Homestead and all over the United States, in their fight against the oppressions of monopolistic employers, and we urge them to join with us in an attempt to overthrow at the polls our common enemy, the monopolistic millionaires who are now, through their control of the Government and the industries of the country, rapidly and surely reducing the people to a condition of political and industrial slavery."[79] The strike by the American Railway Union that began at Pullman, Illinois, and later spread throughout much of the nation inspired another plank by Minnesota Populists, who announced in their 1894 convention: "In the United States it is not a crime for the great mass of the people to unite to improve their material condition by peaceful and lawful means; and we can not but regard the arrest of Mr. Debs and his associates as an unwise and unjust step, and a dangerous encroachment of the Federal judiciary upon the rights and liberties of the people." A year or so later, the Ohio Populist convention denounced prosecution of Debs as a treason to the Constitution of the United States because it denied the union leader his right to a trial before a jury of his peers. In fact, Debs became one of the folk heroes of the Populist movement even as he moved toward socialism. In 1900, for example, the "middle of the road" faction of the Iowa party chose Debs as its favorite for the party's presidential nomination.[80]

The other parties, however, fit labor demands into their own agendas in a way that stripped them of almost all radicalism. The Republicans, for example, offered "Protection and Prosperity" in which labor was offered tariff protection from competition with foreign workers. The Democrats responded with free silver as a panacea for unemployment. The Prohibitionists leaned heavily on government-enforced sobriety as the key to labor's well-being. The only parties to take up the full range of labor demands on their own terms were the Greenbackers and, slightly less so, the Populists.[81]

[79] Also see the 1892 Nebraska platform that used "Pinkertons" as a reference to the Homestead strike: "We are opposed to a system of government that allows corporations or individuals of the United States to employ Pinkertons or any other force to intimidate and coerce organized labor."

[80] *Appleton's Annual Cyclopaedia of 1900* (New York: D. Appleton, 1901), p. 310.

[81] Although the Knights of Labor were almost moribund by 1900, their favorable response to both the Populists in the early 1890s and Bryan Democrats in 1896 was remembered with some pride. See, for example, *Industrial Commission: Capital*

Table 3.12. *Party Platforms Favoring Restriction of Immigration*

State party platforms containing immigration planks by region (%)

Party	Northeast	Great Lakes	Plains	West	South	Nation
Republican	26.6	25.6	17.5	50.8	9.1	25.2
Democratic	6.2	7.3	6.8	36.4	2.9	10.0
Prohibition	20.6	6.9	20.0	28.6	25.0	19.2
Greenback	10.0	9.1	18.2	33.3	10.0	12.7
Populist	27.8	7.1	7.1	36.8	3.3	14.7

State party platforms containing immigration planks by period (%)

Party	First period (1877–88)	Second period (1889–96)	Third period (1897–1900)	All years (1877–1900)
Republican	20.9	36.6	10.1	25.2
Democratic	12.0	10.7	4.2	10.0
Prohibition	11.9	30.1	3.2	19.2
Greenback	11.8	25.0	—	12.7
Populist	—	17.3	8.8	14.7

Note: All proposals for restriction of immigration for reasons of health, moral character, illiteracy, political opinion, or racial origin are included in the table.

Under Bryan, the northern branches of the Democratic party also took up labor's torch.[82]

Immigration Planks

Of all the demands made by labor, the restriction of immigration into the United States was the one most commonly adopted in campaign platforms (see Table 3.12). From the worker's perspective, the flow of immigrants from abroad undercut the labor market, reducing wages and the

and Labor, vol. 7, p. 424. On close relations between the Knights of Labor and the Populists, see Selig Perlman, "Upheaval and Reorganisation (since 1876)," in John R. Commons et al., *History of Labour in the United States*, vol. 2 (New York: Macmillan, 1918), pp. 423, 491–495. Referring to the common platform agreed to by the National Farmers' Alliance (the precursor to the Populist party) and the Knights signed in St. Louis in 1889, Perlman said the "list of demands speaks volumes for the mental subjection of the Knights of Labor to the farmers' movement."

[82] Bryan's labor sympathies – and labor's rejection of him as a presidential candidate – is a major theme of Elizabeth Sanders's *Roots of Reform: Farmers, Workers, and the American State, 1877–1917* (Chicago: University of Chicago Press, 1999).

ability of labor to organize. The United States during most of this period had an almost unrestricted immigration policy; almost anyone who could pay their way could land on American shores. Over the course of the late nineteenth century, however, the countries of origin changed as immigrants from southern and eastern Europe displaced those from northern and western regions of that continent. This shift sparked demands for a more regulated immigration policy that would restrict what was considered unfair competition from the degraded workers from the Mediterranean, Balkan, and Slavic European nations. Reflecting a much broader societal concern with the racial composition of the American population, labor was only part of the movement for such restrictions.[83] Party platforms responded in two ways. First, the parties proclaimed that immigrants thought to be less useful to the American economy and to society – the diseased, the poor, the illiterate, and anarchists – should be barred from entry.

The second way that platforms responded was much narrower. Throughout the West, Chinese immigrants had become an important factor in the regional labor market, particularly in railroad construction and mining. For most western workers of European extraction, the Chinese were culturally and ethnically unacceptable as competitors in the labor market or colleagues in the workplace. Demands by western labor organizations for an absolute prohibition of Asian immigration produced a steady and, at times, thunderous drumbeat of protest throughout the region. When the political parties responded, their planks contained many of the most racist passages found in state platforms of the period – significantly more common, strident, and extreme, for example, than similar passages in southern Democratic planks.[84] While some of these demands were echoed in the East by the Knights of Labor, the American Federation of Labor, and a few of the state party platforms, they were much more prominent in the West where, in some instances, their frequency as political planks rivaled that of the

---

[83] For expressions of corporate opinion favoring immigration restrictions, much of it racially and politically inspired, see the *Commercial and Financial Chronicle*, May 28, June 25, August 13, 1887; August 25, 1888; September 13, 1890; July 30, 1892. On demands for a literacy test for immigrants as a way of restricting immigration from southern and eastern Europe, see Mark Wyman, *Round-Trip to America: The Immigrants Return to Europe, 1880–1930* (Ithaca, N.Y.: Cornell University Press, 1993), pp. 103–104. For an extensive list of organizations, including unions, that endorsed literacy tests for immigrants at the turn of the century, see *Report of the Industrial Commission: Immigration and Education*, vol. 15 (Washington, D.C.: GPO, 1901), pp. 68–70. For organized labor's hostility to many recent immigrants to the United States, see Gwendolyn Mink, *Old Labor and New Immigrants in American Political Development: Union, Party, and State, 1875–1920* (Ithaca, N.Y.: Cornell University Press, 1986), pp. 71–73, 79, 96–101, 118–129.

[84] For an exceptionally detailed declaration, see the 1882 California Democratic platform.

tariff and monetary policy.[85] Outside that region, sentiment was much more subdued.[86]

For several reasons, Republicans were more likely to adopt planks restricting immigration than any of the other parties. First, immigration barriers acted as a kind of protective tariff for labor, broadening and reinforcing the central theme of party policy. Second, the party generally attracted much more electoral support from native-born, Protestant workers of northern and western European extraction than from recent Catholic immigrants from the Mediterranean or Eastern Europe. For Republican workers, therefore, immigration barriers were not as likely to affect future arrivals of their family members and friends. For the Democrats, who drew much more of their support from recent immigrants deemed less wholesome, restriction tended to cut both ways: On the one hand, their workers tended to be unskilled and thus more immediately affected by competition from recent arrivals; on the other hand, many still had family and friends abroad who they would like to see join them in the United States. For these reasons, Democratic platforms were less likely to oppose immigration than Republican platforms regardless of region or time period. The Prohibition party tended to view immigration through a whisky glass; their demands for restriction usually emphasized presumed moral qualities and often called for more lengthy and stringent naturalization requirements so that the immigrant could not vote until properly acculturated. Although far more attuned to workers' interests than the Prohibitionists, Greenbackers and Populists gave only routine attention to immigration, compiling plank frequencies only slightly above those recorded by the Democrats and far lower than the Republicans (who were also much more strident). All of the parties wrote many more restrictive planks in the West where they also gave much more prominence to Asian immigration.[87] On the whole, the very serious depression of the early 1890s appears to have inspired more immi-

---

[85] The 1879 California New Constitution convention, for example, ordered that the phrase "Against Chinese immigration" be printed on their party's tickets immediately following the names of their candidates. *Appleton's 1879 Cyclopaedia*, p. 113. More generally, see Mink, *Old Labor and New Immigrants*, pp. 77–97; Rogers M. Smith, *Civic Ideals: Conflicting Visions of Citizenship in U.S. History* (New Haven, Conn.: Yale University Press, 1997), pp. 317, 359–369.

[86] Or even hostile; see, for example, this joint resolution passed in 1879 in Connecticut: "*Resolved*, by this General Assembly, that the proposed law now pending in the Congress of the United States, restricting Chinese immigration, is a flagrant violation of a sacred and honorable treaty, and is wholly inconsistent with the principles and traditions of our republic, and with the broad principles of human freedom; and it is our earnest hope that its provisions may not disgrace our statutes." *Appleton's 1879 Cyclopaedia*, p. 298.

[87] At least 25 major party state platforms contained a plank encouraging immigration into the state. All but four of these were southern, with eight written by Republicans and 13 by Democrats. Of these 21, Arkansas conventions wrote seven.

Table 3.13. *Party Platforms Favoring Abolition or*
Reform of Convict Labor

State party platforms containing convict labor planks by region (%)

Party	Northeast	Great Lakes	Plains	West	South	Nation
Republican	7.3	11.6	12.7	6.6	35.1	14.7
Democratic	8.9	12.2	13.6	5.5	15.5	11.4
Prohibition	0.0	3.4	5.0	7.1	15.0	4.1
Greenback	40.0	27.3	27.3	0.0	40.0	32.7
Populist	5.6	50.0	10.7	0.0	30.0	18.3

State party platforms containing convict labor planks by period (%)

Party	First period (1877–88)	Second period (1889–96)	Third period (1897–1900)	All years (1877–1900)
Republican	18.7	13.1	10.1	14.7
Democratic	16.7	8.7	5.6	11.4
Prohibition	7.1	4.1	0.0	4.1
Greenback	35.3	0.0	—	32.7
Populist	—	20.0	14.7	18.3

gration planks than were drafted in other periods. While very few platforms ever endorsed an open door for foreign immigration, that more or less remained American policy throughout the period with the prominent exception of Asians (who were excluded in a series of federal statutes).[88]

Convict Labor Planks

Demands for either the abolition or reform of convict labor were less common than immigration planks (cf. Tables 3.12 and 3.13). Labor's interest in the employment of convicts arose out of potential competition between what workers called "free labor," a term with origins in earlier antislavery movements, and prisoners either employed by the state or leased out to private citizens and corporations. As would be expected, the

[88]   The only endorsements for unrestricted immigration appeared in the 1879 Ohio Democratic platform (which was more concerned with German than American policy) and the 1879 Wisconsin Democratic platform. For discussion of legislative efforts to restrict immigration, including an analysis of congressional voting, see Claudia Goldin, "The Political Economy of Immigration Restriction in the United States, 1890 to 1921," in Claudia Goldin and Gary D. Libecap, eds., *The Regulated Economy: A Historical Approach to Political Economy* (Chicago: University of Chicago Press, 1994), pp. 223–257.

Greenback and Populist parties were more responsive than the major parties, although the Populists drafted their platforms later in the period when public concern over convict labor was clearly on the wane. In fact, every party distribution exhibits a declining frequency over time. Again, the Prohibitionists seem to have been the most aloof when labor's demands were on the table. The regional distribution of planks was fairly even for all parties except for the South where the proportion of platforms containing demands for abolition or reform was generally higher. For the southern wing of the Republican party, they were in fact much higher. The most interesting aspect of convict labor planks, however, was what they said and how what they said related to what actually happened when prisoners were employed by the state or leased to private contractors.

Throughout the late nineteenth century and well into the twentieth, convict labor was almost universal throughout the United States. In 1879, for example, the Massachusetts Bureau of Labor reported to the state legislature that 13,186 of the 29,197 prison inmates in the nation worked either under contract to private employers or under the direct supervision of prison authorities (what was known then as "on public account," an arrangement in which prison officials purchased raw materials and equipment, oversaw manufacturing operations, and marketed the product as a more or less state-owned industrial enterprise). Either way, convict labor came into direct competition with free labor outside prison walls. The average earnings of convicts, most or all of which went to support prison operations, was about 40 cents a day; free labor averaged about $2 a day. This difference, even after what must have been a heavy discounting for lower productivity for convict labor, presented a clear competitive alternative to the employment of free workers. While this degrading competition, in terms of wage scales for free workers, could be an important factor in local labor markets, on a national scale convict labor was insignificant; measured either in the value of total product or wages, convict labor represented far less than one third of 1 percent of national output.[89]

---

[89] For state laws governing convict labor, see *Report of the Industrial Commission: Labor Legislation*, vol. 5 (Washington, D.C.: GPO, 1900), pp. 167–213; U.S. Commissioner of Labor, *Second Annual Report: Convict Labor* (Washington, D.C.: GPO, 1886); *Appleton's 1879 Cyclopaedia*, pp. 600–601. In his testimony before the Industrial Commission, Rufus Wade, chief factory inspector in Massachusetts and former president of the International Association of Factory Inspectors, stated, "I have never yet seen wherein there was such a great amount done [with prison labor] as to affect the general production. I may be wrong, but it seems to me it would be a very small factor in the great falling of the wages in Massachusetts to-day." *Industrial Commission: Capital and Labor*, vol. 7, p. 76. One of the clearest cases in which convict labor was used to undercut the wage scale and working conditions of free workers occurred in Tennessee, where a coal mining company in 1891 leased prisoners to replace workers who refused to grant concessions. Woodward, *Origins of the New South*, pp. 232–234; Perlman, "Upheaval and Reorganisation," pp. 498–499.

Far more remarkable than the fact of their employment was the severely austere, sometimes barbaric conditions under which the prisoners lived, particularly in the South. The major reason for convict labor regimes, in fact, was to make prisons self-supporting. Another way to achieve the same goal was to reduce the costs of supporting the inmate population to levels matching their productivity either in the private economy or under state supervision. The result was a level of barbarity that is almost beyond modern imagination. In the space of less than a year during 1879, for example, 128 of the 285 South Carolina inmates leased to the Greenwood and Augusta Railway Company died. Another thirty-seven, over one in ten, had escaped what must have been seen by the convicts as a death sentence, to be imposed regardless of the gravity of their crime.[90]

While this example was exceptional in some respects, the annual death rate in southern prisons was usually quite high. In the years following 1880, for example, the death rate for prisoners in Alabama hovered at about 5 percent a year. This was actually an improvement; conditions in the state had previously been much worse. During Reconstruction, from 1867 through 1871, the death rate for convicts in Alabama had averaged over 20 percent per year (in 1870 alone, 41% of Alabama convicts died while in the custody of the state). The experience was a little better in Georgia, where reform efforts succeeded in reducing the rate from 4.72 percent annually (for 1874–76) to 2.42 (for 1877–79). In North Carolina, 142 of the state's 1,198 convicts died during the 1885–86 reporting period, prompting the governor to urge state supervision of prisoners leased out to the railroads.[91] The death rate for Mississippi convicts over the 1886–87 biennial averaged just over 12 percent a year. A study by a Mississippi investigating committee during this period reported that comparable death rates in midwestern state prisons ranged from 0.5 to just over 1 percent.[92]

Another notable feature of prison operations in the late nineteenth century was the racial and gender characteristics of the inmate population. In the South, for example, the overwhelming majority were black males, so much so that convict work gangs must have often resembled antebellum

---

[90]   *Appleton's 1879 Cyclopaedia*, p. 819.

[91]   *Appleton's Annual Cyclopaedia of 1881* (New York: D. Appleton, 1882), p. 7; *Appleton's 1880 Cyclopaedia*, p. 306; *Appleton's Annual Cyclopaedia of 1886* (New York: D. Appleton, 1888), p. 7; *Appleton's Annual Cyclopaedia of 1888* (New York: D. Appleton, 1889), p. 39; *Appleton's Annual Cyclopaedia of 1897* (New York: D. Appleton, 1898), p. 342.

[92]   *Appleton's 1888 Cyclopaedia*, pp. 562–563; Vernon Lane Wharton, *The Negro in Mississippi: 1865–1890* (New York: Harper Torchbooks, 1965), pp. 240–241. Also see William Cohen, *At Freedom's Edge: Black Mobility and the Southern White Quest for Racial Control, 1861–1915* (Baton Rouge: Louisiana State University Press, 1991), p. 226; Woodward, *Origins of the New South*, pp. 212–216.

slave labor.[93] In the later part of the period, after disfranchising legislation had removed most blacks from voter rolls in the South, most convicts were politically quite vulnerable.[94] Prison abuse, let alone poor diet and medical care, was the result. While race and gender clearly dominated the demographic characteristics of the prison population, in socio-economic terms these overlay an equally clear class bias. In the Alabama penitentiary in 1877, the previous occupation of just over half of all inmates had been that of a common laborer, and most of their crimes, just over 60 percent, had been those against property.[95]

The reality of convict labor in the late nineteenth century was that, everywhere, employment was arduous and cruel; in the South, it was murderous.[96] Yet most planks that urged the abolition or reform of convict labor systems cited not the barbaric conditions under which prisoners were worked but the (comparatively trivial) impact that prisoner-workers had upon the labor market. This was almost universally the case in northern

[93] In 1888, a committee appointed to inspect Mississippi prisons reported that the death rate for blacks was more than double that for whites and that mortality in the work camps of the Gulf and Ship Island Railroad Company "where convicts are supposed to be well" was three to six times higher than in the penitentiary hospital "where convicts are usually sick." *Appleton's 1888 Cyclopaedia*, pp. 562–563. For additional figures on black and white death rates for convicts over the period from 1880 to 1885, see Wharton, *The Negro in Mississippi*, p. 240.

[94] Wharton, *The Negro in Mississippi*, p. 239.

[95] *Appleton's 1879 Cyclopaedia*, p. 23. For additional information on the previous occupations of the Alabama prison population, see *Appleton's 1881 Cyclopaedia*, p. 7.

[96] Republican administrations had originally designed convict labor systems in the South with the intention that, as was true throughout the nation, prisoners were to pay for their own incarceration. However, the region was so poor and so dependent on the cotton economy that private employment of prisoners was confined to mining or lumbering, which was opposed because it brought them into direct competition with free workers, or plantations, where they could produce but little of value given the low price of cotton and their own slight productivity. Alternative employment on roads and other public works projects required state revenues that were already sorely pressed to provide schools and other essential services. Thus anywhere prisoners were employed brought very low returns, a situation that, in turn, explains some of the abuses of the system. Most southerners outside prisons were, in fact, underfed, suffered from serious dietary deficiencies, were debilitated by endemic disease, or threatened with violence from one source or another. While convict labor systems were undeniably far more brutal than they had to be, even seeming to attract particularly depraved sadists as guards, real improvement in the conditions suffered by prisoners could only, in all probability, have been achieved by letting them go. And for most of them, the improvement would have been noticeable only because the otherwise utterly deplorable conditions in the very bottom rung of the national class structure were better than prison. All of this is to say that southern Democrats, while obviously indifferent to the racism that made convict labor so brutal, were still hard pressed to find an alternative that did not present problems for workers outside the prison system.

and western states where, at least as measured by annual death rates, conditions inside and outside penitentiary walls appear to have been much less savage than in the South. But even in the South most planks urging abolition or reform ignored the inhumanity of convict labor systems. For example, the following demand placed before the electorate of Louisiana in 1888 by the Democratic party could have been at home in any state platform throughout the period: "We are opposed to the employment of the penitentiary convicts of the State in such manner as to bring the convict labor in competition with free labor." The state Republican party in the same election offered a plank that was almost indistinguishable: "We condemn the use of convict labor outside of public works, and demand that it shall not be allowed to come in competition with free labor." The orientation of the latter plank is particularly striking in that blacks, the most common victims of the system, composed the larger part of most southern Republican parties.

Most other Republican parties in the South, however, were more sensitive to the barbaric conditions imposed on prisoners. In 1886, for example, Arkansas Republicans declared: "We denounce the Democratic party of this State for . . . enacting and maintaining a system of criminal laws, which in cruelty surpasses that practiced in the middle ages, for permitting convict-labor to compete with honest workingmen. . . ."[97] Such declarations and the underlying reality of conditions in the South explain the comparatively large proportion of convict labor planks in the South adopted by almost all the major and minor parties. But, even in that region, most planks addressed unfair competition with free labor, not the conditions to which the prisoners were subjected. And outside that region, in very sharp contrast to the solicitude that northern Republican parties showed for the repression of suffrage rights for southern blacks, southern convict labor systems drew no comment at all. With the exception of a few Greenback and Populist planks, southern Republicans were on their own.

PLANKS ON THE DISPOSITION AND DISTRIBUTION OF LAND

With respect to labor's interests, as they were conceived at the time, one of the most closely related issues was the distribution of land. For centuries, the existence of vast tracts of unsettled land on the frontier had presented European and American settlers with an alternative to wage labor in eastern cities and towns. By the late nineteenth century, however, these lands were

---

[97] Also see the 1882 Alabama and the 1892 Georgia Republican platforms.

rapidly disappearing. In reaction, many planks were written into major and minor party platforms that demanded the reservation of remaining public lands for "actual settlers" as opposed to private land agents, timber companies, or railroad corporations. These demands were at the core of a number of related issues. For example, much of the territory beyond the Mississippi River had been granted to the railroads in return for the construction of track on the frontier. Many of these railroads had failed, in one way or another, to satisfy the terms of those grants. Thus arose many demands, particularly in the years just after the close of Reconstruction, for the return of "forfeited" land grants to the public domain from whence they would be available for homesteads.

Other planks proposed prohibitions on alien, corporate, or nonresident land ownership, policies that would, once again, reserve land for settlers. In closely related planks, a few very general demands were made for destruction of the "land monopoly" without much, if any, description of what was meant by the term.[98] As part of the "single-tax" movement, a few planks also proposed heavy levies on unoccupied, privately held land in order to compel their distribution to settlers.[99] Of all planks that had the disposition of land as their central focus, the mildest were those that demanded the preservation of the school lands that were intended to support the education of children residing on western homesteads. As in this plank drafted by the 1882 Pennsylvania Greenback convention, several of the different themes underlying land demands could be written into a single sentence in a way that made their ideological interconnections clear: "We are against the monopoly of the land, and demand the reservation of all public land, including the vast amount now forfeited by the great corporations, for actual settlers."

For the Greenbackers, the reservation of the frontier for homestead settlement was a major part of their general program for the readjustment of class privileges. Over half of all their state party platforms contained one or more demands related to land, with the greatest proportion in the Northeast where they focused their appeal on industrial workers, particularly in the iron and steel industry (see Table 3.14). In this region, Greenback demands carried much of the "safety valve" flavor of the traditional view of homesteads on the public domain as an alternative to oppressive wage

---

[98] One of the more specific references, which still leaves the term a little unclear, appeared in this 1879 Minnesota National Greenback plank: "We are earnestly opposed to all large landed monopolies, either by railroads, corporations, or private individuals, and believe that the public domain should be held exclusively for actual settlers, in moderate and reasonable quantities."

[99] On the single-tax movement in Washington State that dominated Democratic, Populist, and Silver Republican conventions in 1898, see Thomas W. Riddle, *The Old Radicalism: John R. Rogers and the Populist Movement in Washington* (New York: Garland, 1991), pp. 252–253, 264–265.

Table 3.14. *Party Platforms Concerning the*
Disposition and Distribution of Land

State party platforms containing land planks by region (%)

Party	Northeast	Great Lakes	Plains	West	South	Nation
Republican	5.5	14.0	23.8	24.6	3.9	12.7
Democratic	7.1	17.1	13.6	23.6	8.7	12.2
Prohibition	4.8	20.7	10.0	7.1	15.0	10.3
Greenback	75.0	36.4	54.5	0.0	40.0	52.7
Populist	22.2	35.7	14.3	42.1	16.7	23.9

State party platforms containing land planks by period (%)

Party	First period (1877–88)	Second period (1889–96)	Third period (1897–1900)	All years (1877–1900)
Republican	18.0	10.3	7.2	12.7
Democratic	14.0	12.1	8.5	12.2
Prohibition	11.9	13.7	0.0	10.3
Greenback	52.9	50.0	—	52.7
Populist	—	25.3	20.6	23.9

Note: This table includes platform demands for the reservation of public lands for settlement by "actual settlers"; for the prohibition or regulation of land ownership by nonresidents, aliens, or corporations; for a heavy tax on unoccupied private land holdings; for the destruction of the "land monopoly"; for the protection of lands dedicated to the support of public schools; and for the reassumption of federal ownership of lands previously granted to railroad companies and other concerns.

employment.[100] Populists were much less likely to write land planks, but such demands still appeared in almost a quarter of their platforms. The Republicans and Democrats were even less likely to respond to the closing of the frontier; only about one in eight of their platforms referred to the disposition and distribution of land. In comparison with the other parties, Republicans and Democrats tended to emphasize federal land policy. As a result, they shared a similar regional pattern, with land planks for the most part restricted to platforms written outside the Northeast and South. In these latter regions, federal lands were scarce and thus not a major factor

[100]   Benjamin Horace Hibbard called the public domain a "political and economic balance wheel" that, because it worked so well, was "imperceptible" in its operation. *A History of the Public Land Policies* (Madison: University of Wisconsin Press, 1965), p. 557. For a good example of Greenback attitudes, see the 1878 Massachusetts Independent Greenback platform.

in the economic and social development of local communities. Greenback and Populist parties, in contrast, made many class-related claims on land ownership that did not necessarily involve federal policy. Prohibitions on alien land ownership, for example, were more commonly a subject for state legislatures and other local governments.[101] When these prohibitions became mixed with single-tax proposals and other forms of class legislation, as was commonly the case for the Greenbackers and Populists, the proportion of land planks in the East and South increased compared with that for the major parties. While these planks, as a group, were drafted with fairly high frequency, the disposition of public lands was one of the fading issues of state and national politics in the late nineteenth century. Every party, save the Prohibitionists, wrote land planks with declining frequency between 1877 and 1900.

INCOME TAX PLANKS

As with land distribution, income tax planks clearly demanded greater economic equality. In August 1861, very early in the Civil War, the federal government instituted an income tax of 3 percent on all income over $800 per year. In July, 1862, this flat tax was replaced by a heavier, more progressive levy. Amended at various times, this law remained in effect until it expired in 1872. When the 1894 Wilson Tariff reimposed an income tax, the U.S. Supreme Court promptly struck down the new levy as unconstitutional; as a result, a federal income tax was never collected in the late nineteenth century.[102]

The politics surrounding the income tax arose out of its potential role in the political economy of industrialization. For example, the levy would have alleviated dependence on the tariff for federal revenue and thus might have enabled a reduction in customs duties. Free traders, particularly those with low or middling incomes, could therefore find the proposal quite attractive. Second, the tax carried clear class and sectional implications. The wealthy would carry most of the burden and most of the wealthy resided in the

---

[101] By 1900, some thirty states had passed restrictions on alien land ownership, the most stringent were in the Plains and Mountain regions, as well as the South. The Mountain states, however, tended to exempt mineral lands from their laws in order to attract foreign investment in the mining industry. Lance E. Davis and Robert J. Cull, *International Capital Markets and American Economic Growth, 1820–1914* (New York: Cambridge University Press, 1994), pp. 51–53.

[102] On the income tax case and more generally, see Louis B. Boudin, *Government by Judiciary* (1932; rpt., New York: Russell & Russell, 1968), pp. 206–261; Arnold M. Paul, *Conservative Crisis and the Rule of Law: Attitudes of Bar and Bench, 1887–1895* (New York: Harper Torchbooks, 1969), pp. 159–220; Willard L. King, *Melville Weston Fuller: Chief Justice of the United States, 1888–1910* (Chicago: University of Chicago Press, 1967), pp. 193–221.

Table 3.15. *Party Platforms Favoring an Income Tax*

State party platforms containing income tax planks by region (%)

Party	Northeast	Great Lakes	Plains	West	South	Nation
Democratic	4.5	9.8	16.9	9.1	19.4	11.9
Prohibition	1.6	10.3	10.0	0.0	10.0	5.5
Greenback	30.0	27.3	27.3	33.3	30.0	29.1
Populist	22.2	42.9	21.4	21.1	26.7	25.7

State party platforms containing income tax planks by period (%)

Party	First period (1877–88)	Second period (1889–96)	Third period (1897–1900)	All years (1877–1900)
Democratic	0.7	18.8	21.1	11.9
Prohibition	0.0	11.0	0.0	5.5
Greenback	29.4	25.0	—	29.1
Populist	—	26.7	23.5	25.7

Note: No Republican platform supported a federal income tax.

larger cities of the Northeast. Because the tariff was regressive, falling inordinately upon the low and middle income agricultural classes of the South and West, a partial substitution of a progressive income tax for protection would have redistributed wealth in at least three ways: from industry to agriculture, from upper to lower classes, and from the Northeast and Great Lakes states to the remainder of the country. And it was along these lines that the issue was engaged.[103]

The frequency with which the major and minor parties adopted income tax planks reflected these regional and class implications (see Table 3.15). For example, as the upper-class party of the nation's manufacturing belt, Republicans never supported an income tax in any of their state platforms.[104] Given the fact that the original, Civil War levy had been a Repub-

[103] In several respects, this conflict closely followed earlier alignments over federal taxation. See, for example, Richard Franklin Bensel, *Yankee Leviathan: The Origins of Central State Authority in America, 1859–1877* (New York: Cambridge University Press, 1990), pp. 329–341.

[104] Of the planks mentioning the income tax, all but five favored its adoption. Four of the five planks opposing the tax were Republican, three adopted by northeastern state conventions and one in the West. The only other exception was written into the 1894 New York Democratic platform: "We commend the efforts made by the Senators and Representatives in Congress from this State to avert the imposition of the present income tax."

lican measure and given the position of southern Republicans as the most underprivileged class in the national political economy, this unblemished silence eloquently testifies to the class, sectional, and sectoral commitments of the party in the national political economy. Within the Democratic party, the frequency with which the state parties endorsed an income tax more or less followed expected lines. The northeastern platforms were less likely to write income tax planks than those in the other regions; in sharp contrast, southern conventions wrote them into their platforms fairly often. The juxtaposition of southern Democrats, who represented upper-class planters but nevertheless backed an income tax, with southern Republicans, who represented black sharecroppers and lower-class mountain whites but nevertheless never wrote a plank, underlines both the importance of regional wealth disparities in the United States and the impact of the inverted class alignment in the national party system. Southern Democrats backed a federal income tax because, when connected to lower tariff duties, their region would be relieved of a heavy economic burden even if some of their wealthy constituents were compelled to pay a new tax.[105] Dependent on northern Republicans for support and afraid of alienating their cross-sectional party allies, southern Republicans simply stood mute when faced with a proposal that unmistakably benefited the class interests of their constituents. Because the class and sector commitments of the Greenbackers and Populists were both clear and uncompromised by organizational factors, both parties frequently supported an income tax with little variation across regions. The Prohibitionists, however, feared that the income tax might be used to reduce the internal revenue tax on liquor.[106] This possibility and the largely upper-class orientation of the movement, particularly in the Northeast, reduced the number of planks written by the party.

AGRICULTURE PLANKS

One of the most notable and, at first glance at least, unusual features of state platforms in the late nineteenth century was the infrequency with which they addressed specific agricultural issues. Even when they appeared, most references were rather bland proposals to prohibit the sale of

---

[105] Southern Democrats had much more difficulty with the imposition of a state income tax that would redistribute wealth between classes within the region. See, for example, the description of the unanimous repeal of a South Carolina income tax law that had been almost universally evaded by the wealthy, *Commercial and Financial Chronicle*, January 20, 1900.

[106] Other Prohibitionists opposed the internal revenue tax on alcohol because it appeared, at least passively, to endorse liquor consumption and, more materially, made the government dependent on the liquor industry. See, for example, the 1888 Massachusetts and New Hampshire platforms.

oleomargarine because of its competition with butter. The 1885 New York Democratic convention, for example, moved to "prevent the manufacture and sale of counterfeit compounds in simulation of genuine butter and cheeses. . . ." These planks were almost always narrowly framed. A little broader but more uncommon were planks that called for federal inspection of meat and other exports, as in this extract from the 1881 Iowa Republican platform: "That the position attained in our commerce by American meats and live animals demands the enactment of effective legislation by both the nation and the States for the suppression of such diseases as are calculated to interfere with this important feature of our foreign trade." Other policies, such as federal subsidies to land grant colleges and operation of agricultural stations, just did not appear in state platforms.[107] Only one reference to class relations in the agricultural sector appears in the entire record, a plank written by the 1880 North Carolina Republican convention denouncing "the laws known as the landlord and tenant acts, as devised for the benefit of a few and to oppress the humble and defenseless citizen."[108]

The absence of agricultural planks does not, of course, mean that farmers were apolitical in the late nineteenth century. In fact, they might have been the most self-consciously political class in the nation. But their goal was a thorough reconstruction of the national political economy, not the transformation of the sector into just one of what have become numerous interest groups within the federal and state policy systems. When compared with industrial labor in the same period, a bit of a paradox is revealed. Where labor generally shaved its claims in favor of incremental gains within the system, farmers advanced very broad proposals that targeted the pillars of national economic development. Of the two, labor should have been more easily transformed, even tamed, into one of the meek constituencies of federal and state bureaus. Instead, agriculture, almost by default, found an

[107] An exception, a bland expression of approval for a federal appropriation for agricultural stations, appeared in the 1888 Louisiana Republican platform.

[108] One surprise was the relative absence of planks supporting the subtreasury plan originally proposed by the National Farmers' Alliance as a means, all at the same time, of financing the storage of crops, expanding the money supply, and providing an alternative to the crop lien system of marketing and retail distribution. For a description of the plan, see Goodwyn, *Democratic Promise*, pp. 150, 152–153, and Chapter 6. As one of the primary policy bridges between greenback theory and the Populist program, Goodwyn assigns the plan great significance and notes its inclusion in the 1892 national platform. But, in the entire period analysed here, only six party platforms explicitly endorsed the subtreasury plan. Four of these, not surprisingly, were Populist: Idaho (1892), Iowa (1892), Oregon (1898), and Texas (1894). One more, the 1888 Texas demands proclaimed by a joint convention of the Texas Farmers' Alliance, Knights of Labor, and Union Labor party, was an important predecessor to the Populist movement. The last was the 1892 South Carolina Democratic platform that also gave a blanket endorsement to the 1890 Ocala Demands of the National Farmers' Alliance.

earlier and more comfortable accommodation within the policy systems of government.[109]

POLITICAL PLANKS

A number of purely political issues played either major or minor roles in nineteenth-century party programs. Five of these appeared as planks with fairly low frequencies: the power of the U.S. Supreme Court, civil service reform, the Australian ballot, direct election of U.S. senators, and woman suffrage. Far and away the major political issue in the late nineteenth century involved federal intervention in southern elections. Because of its fundamental role in shaping party competition, this subject is taken up separately. The other five issues made up a reform agenda that shared, in many respects, a common constituency.

Perhaps the most distinct of the five was the intense criticism directed at the U.S. Supreme Court and the federal judiciary generally for their use of injunctions in the suppression of strikes. These planks became a minor feature of party platforms only late in the century, particularly after the Pullman strike in 1894. They most frequently appeared in Populist platforms, although the Democrats were also active after Bryan's nomination in 1896.[110] Republicans, albeit infrequently, adopted planks defending the courts and injunctions.[111] Thus the issue was joined in almost purely class terms as one affecting the respective interests of industrial employers and workers.[112]

Civil service planks were much more common in party platforms (see Table 3.16). Almost all of them favored reform, although most were very short and perfunctory in their endorsements. As the *Commercial and Financial Chronicle* observed, in its review of the election that elevated James Garfield to the presidency: "The mention of [civil service reform] now almost excites a smile; and yet it is second to none, in its importance to the nation. A President or a Congress that effected a divorce of government office from politics, would leave a record worth having."[113] Garfield's

---

[109] Sanders, *Roots of Reform*; Kenneth Finegold and Theda Skocpol, *State and Party in America's New Deal* (Madison: University of Wisconsin Press, 1995), particularly chap. 3.

[110] In states where Bryan's nomination split the party organization, the silver wing often harshly criticized the court while bolting Gold Democrats condemned Bryan's opposition to injunctions.

[111] For a typical example, see the 1896 New Jersey Republican platform.

[112] For more on planks opposing injunctions and the power of the federal judiciary as well as overviews of the use of labor injunctions in the period, see Paul, *Conservative Crisis*, pp. 104–108, 225; *Report of the Industrial Commission: Labor Organizations*, vol. 17 (Washington, D.C.: GPO, 1901), pp. 602–615; Lawrence M. Friedman, *A History of American Law* (New York: Simon & Schuster, 1973), pp. 487–489.

[113] November 6, 1880.

Table 3.16. *Party Platforms Favoring Civil Service Reform*

State party platforms containing civil service planks by region (%)

Party	Northeast	Great Lakes	Plains	West	South	Nation
Republican	29.4	23.3	19.0	3.3	3.9	16.7
Democratic	21.4	9.8	7.9	3.6	6.8	11.4
Prohibition	15.9	3.4	0.0	7.1	0.0	8.2
Greenback	5.0	9.1	18.2	0.0	0.0	7.3
Populist	11.1	0.0	3.6	5.3	0.0	3.7

State party platforms containing civil service planks by period (%)

Party	First period (1877–88)	Second period (1889–96)	Third period (1897–1900)	All years (1877–1900)
Republican	30.2	5.5	13.0	16.7
Democratic	20.7	5.4	4.2	11.4
Prohibition	4.8	12.3	3.2	8.2
Greenback	5.9	25.0	—	7.3
Populist	—	2.7	5.9	3.7

assassination by a frustrated office-seeker early in 1881 made civil service proposals one of the most prominent features of major party platforms in the following eight years or so. After that, reform returned to the desultory role it had previously played. As with other issues in the late nineteenth century, civil service reform was a largely sectional and class issue. In regional terms, there were many more civil service planks in state platforms in the manufacturing belt than in the South and West. Northeastern Republicans, at the top of the national class structure, often embraced civil service proposals with some passion, while Greenbackers and Populists, as the class insurgents of the period, were largely indifferent to reform. At the very bottom of the national class structure, represented by the southern Republican parties, this indifference even turned into hostility.[114]

---

[114] Three of the five planks opposing civil service reform were written by southern Republican parties: Arkansas (1898), Tennessee (1898), and Virginia (1900). These all appeared very late in the period after southern Republicans had all but given up the struggle for power in their respective states (Tennessee was a partial exception). The hostility to reform reflected both their dependence on federal patronage when Republicans controlled the White House and the class interests of their constituents (who, because they were often illiterate, could not pass examinations). The other two planks, written by Democratic parties (Kentucky and Maryland, both in 1887), opposed civil service systems in principle.

The most episodic of all reform movements of the late nineteenth century was the Australian ballot which, within three or four years, transformed the way in which almost all Americans voted from the party ticket to the state-printed and -regulated ballot. References to the Australian system or, more generically, a "secret ballot" rose from none at all for the major parties before 1886 to almost a third of all platforms for the Republicans in the 1889–90 biennium. For the Democrats, almost half the platforms in the same period endorsed the reform. The Prohibitionists followed a similar pattern while the Greenbackers, who in some ways pioneered the concept in earlier years, ignored the idea when it became a national rage. Once almost all the states had changed over to the new system, platform references to secret voting precipitously dropped off so that in the years after 1892 there were only two planks devoted to the topic among all the major party platforms and none at all for the minor parties. As a platform topic, the Australian ballot was truly a blip, albeit a very bright one.

All of these reforms had a clear class bias. For the Supreme Court, the undemocratic use of the injunction and bench contempt proceedings clearly targeted workers as they pursued claims on the wealth of their employers. For the civil service, those who were illiterate or poorly educated were clearly excluded from employment where regulations and examinations were instituted. While not an open issue, the influence of this class bias can be unambiguously read off the pattern in platform adoptions. The Australian ballot had similar implications in that illiterate voters, left alone in the voting booth, would have difficulty selecting candidates. While the use of symbols and the shapes of letters in a name might help, the reform raised a barrier to electoral participation for those at the foot of the American class ladder, immigrants and illiterates.[115] And at times, class even outweighed the democratic principles usually favored by the insurgent parties. In 1892, for example, Texas Populists declared that their class enemies should be made ineligible for public office: "We favor such change in the constitution as shall prohibit national bankers and members of railway, telegraph, and telephone companies, and their attorneys, or who shall have held such positions within two years prior to an election, from holding any legislative or judicial office within this State."

Class considerations, not surprisingly, also colored proposals for the direct election of United States senators. The United States Senate, along

---

[115] The 1892 North Carolina Populist convention tried to square this circle: "We demand of our General Assembly at its next session the passage of a secret ballot law, with a provision in said law that will secure to voters who can not read an opportunity to vote." However, any arrangement that allowed illiterate voters to seek assistance in marking their ballot threatened to destroy the secrecy of their votes.

Table 3.17. *Party Platforms Favoring Direct Election of Senators*

State party platforms containing direct election planks by region (%)

Party	Northeast	Great Lakes	Plains	West	South	Nation
Republican	2.8	0.0	3.2	9.8	1.3	3.4
Democratic	8.9	19.5	25.4	38.2	4.9	15.9
Prohibition	9.5	24.1	20.0	50.0	10.0	17.8
Greenback	5.0	0.0	18.2	0.0	0.0	5.5
Populist	16.7	21.4	21.4	26.3	16.7	20.2

State party platforms containing direct election planks by period (%)

Party	First period (1877–88)	Second period (1889–96)	Third period (1897–1900)	All years (1877–1900)
Republican	1.4	4.1	5.8	3.4
Democratic	1.3	20.8	36.6	15.9
Prohibition	7.1	31.5	0.0	17.8
Greenback	5.9	0.0	—	5.5
Populist	—	21.3	17.6	20.2

with the Supreme Court, was one of the bulwarks of upper-class privilege among the ensemble of national political institutions. Indirect election through the state legislatures sometimes reinforced this role by providing a venue in which wealth, in the form of bribery, could operate upon selection. In most instances, the election returns governed the choice through the rather strong party organizations of the period. An unpopular senator could be a powerful drag on state and local tickets. However, where the state legislatures were closely divided with, perhaps, no single party holding a majority or the largest party splitting into factions, long deadlocks could ensue in which money, among other factors, could play a decisive role. Both the upper-class flavor of the United States Senate and sporadic corruption in the state legislatures gave rise to persistent demands for direct, popular election. Republicans were predictably indifferent to the reform (see Table 3.17). Democrats were much more favorably inclined, particularly in the Plains and West and after the Bryan revolution in 1896. Prohibitionists, with their long history of struggle with the "liquor lobby," also supported direct election, at least until the narrow-gauge coup in 1896. However, this reform was perhaps most identified with the Populists, who, regardless of region or time period, made the proposal a staple among the party's many demands.

The only one of these five reforms that did not carry a clear class bias

Table 3.18. *Party Platforms Favoring Woman Suffrage*

State party platforms containing woman suffrage planks by region (%)

Party	Northeast	Great Lakes	Plains	West	South	Nation
Republican	0.9	0.0	3.2	9.8	0.0	2.5
Democratic	0.0	0.0	0.0	3.6	0.0	0.5
Prohibition	44.4	55.2	80.0	28.6	20.0	46.6
Greenback	5.0	9.1	18.2	0.0	0.0	7.3
Populist	22.2	42.9	10.7	31.6	0.0	17.4

State party platforms containing woman suffrage planks by period (%)

Party	First period (1877–88)	Second period (1889–96)	Third period (1897–1900)	All years (1877–1900)
Republican	1.4	4.8	0.0	2.5
Democratic	0.0	1.3	0.0	0.5
Prohibition	23.8	58.9	48.4	46.6
Greenback	7.8	0.0	—	7.3
Populist	—	22.7	5.9	17.4

Note: Endorsements of woman suffrage that were restricted to municipal elections are not included.

was woman suffrage.[116] The preeminent factor behind enfranchisement demands was the very strong support given by women to temperance legislation.[117] The Republicans, however, avoided woman suffrage everywhere outside the West despite their generally favorable attitude toward temperance (see Table 3.18). In fact, in the West, the party was utterly indifferent to restrictions on alcohol while giving lukewarm support to woman suffrage, an inversion of the usual pattern (for temperance planks, see Table 3.21, below). For example, the almost unbroken silence on woman suffrage

[116] For a discussion of the social and political context within which women were denied suffrage, see Theda Skocpol, *Protecting Soldiers and Mothers: The Political Origins of Social Policy in the United States* (Cambridge: Harvard University Press, 1992), pp. ix–x, 20, 48, 51–52.

[117] In 1883, to take just a minor instance as example, the Iowa Woman's Suffrage Association adopted the following resolution as the central element of their platform: "That the votes of women are imperatively needed to promote the interest of temperance, purity, and peace, to give woman greater self-reliance, self-respect, and personal independence, and to secure to woman a 'fair-day's wages for a fair day's work.'" *Appleton's Annual Cyclopaedia of 1883* (New York: D. Appleton, 1884), p. 448.

by Democratic parties arose out of their opposition to temperance.[118] For the Prohibitionists, the reverse was true; indeed, woman suffrage was second only to temperance as a theme of the party's platforms throughout the country. The Prohibitionists fully expected women to bolster the cause whenever and wherever they could vote.[119] Populists made woman suffrage a familiar element in their platforms but at much lower rates; the connection to temperance was also much weaker, although evident where the party fused with the Prohibitionists. For the Populists, woman suffrage appears to have emerged from the much more equitable gender relations that characterized agrarian insurgent households and, separately, western communities.

NATIONALIZATION OF ELECTIONS

The question of whether the federal government should regulate and oversee state elections was far and away the most frequent and most bitterly contested of all purely political issues (see Table 3.19). The conflict arose out of Reconstruction, a policy which had more or less continued the Civil War with federal troops garrisoning southern towns and white terrorist bands roaming the countryside. After Reconstruction came to a close in 1877, this conflict crystallized into a party contest between southern Republicans and southern Democrats. Overlaying this party competition were alignments involving race, class, and national loyalty that sheared southern society along almost exactly the same lines that had struggled through the Civil War. The intensity of the claims associated with these cleavages and the relative absence of cross-cutting demands made the South the most violent and bitter political arena in the nation. People, usually blacks, died for their political beliefs in that region with a frequency much, much higher than anywhere else in the nation or at any other time in the nation's history.

For this and other reasons, federal intervention in southern elections was a major issue throughout the nation in the late nineteenth century. This was also one of very few issues, along with the tariff, monetary policy, and

---

[118]   In fact, the Democrats sometimes openly opposed suffrage for women. See, for example, this plank from the 1894 Kansas Democratic platform: "We oppose woman suffrage, as tending to destroy the home and family – the true basis of political safety – and express the hope that the helpmeet and guardian of the family sanctuary may not be dragged from the modest purity of self-imposed seclusion to be thrown unwillingly into the unfeminine places of political strife."

[119]   Women were allowed to vote in local elections much more often than in state or federal contests. In 1879, Iowa presented prohibition as a local question to the electorate, and in one Des Moines precinct where voting was recorded by gender, the women favored a ban on licenses for the sale of liquor by a vote of 477 to 3. *Appleton's 1879 Cyclopaedia*, p. 513.

Table 3.19. *Party Platforms Favoring Nationalization of Elections*

State party platforms containing nationalization planks by region (%)

Party	Northeast	Great Lakes	Plains	West	South	Nation
Favoring Republican	34.9	35.8	27.0	13.1	16.9	26.1
Opposing Democratic	29.5	17.1	16.9	9.1	27.2	22.4

State party platforms containing nationalization planks by period (%)

Party	First period (1877–88)	Second period (1889–96)	Third period (1897–1900)	All years (1877–1900)
Favoring Republican	40.3	20.7	8.7	26.1
Opposing Democratic	27.3	28.2	0.0	22.4

Note: Only planks explicitly calling for or opposing federal intervention in elections are included, with the addition of planks in which the rhetoric is so vigorous that an explicit position would have been redundant.

temperance, upon which the parties assumed opposing positions with any kind of regularity – on most issues in American politics, one party would favor a particular policy in their platform declarations, and the other, realizing that their opposing stance was not an asset in the election, would stand mute.[120] Programmatic and ideological links between individual policies were often thick, providing a foundation for the carefully crafted coalitions that rested on the intertwined constituencies and logics undergirding American party competition. In those cases where a policy was unpopular with the electorate but otherwise essential to the programmatic design of the party's platform, a party often chose to silently suffer the damage caused by passive identification with that position rather than disrupt their coalition with an opportunistic and sometimes insincere renunciation. On these four great policies, however, the major parties consistently declared opposing positions, even when, in particular states, these positions were unpopular. In that sense, these were the primary causes for which the parties fought, to which all other planks and issues were tributary.

---

[120] In the last five years of the century, a fifth policy could be added to this list: American imperialist expansion.

For the Republicans, federal intervention in southern elections was, all at the same time: a nationalist effort to protect blacks, the one remaining loyalist group in the South; an attempt to extend the centralizing power of the federal government into elections much as it operated in the national market, as a guarantor of regularity and rights; a partisan crusade to ensure the continued viability of southern Republican organizations; and a threat that could be bargained away to advantage in negotiations with southern congressmen and senators (as had happened in the Compromise of 1877 when Hayes had been elevated to the presidency in return for the withdrawal of federal troops in Louisiana and South Carolina).[121] These four purposes have been listed in the declining order of their public legitimacy and thus their likelihood of appearance in state platforms. As one of the purposes served by federal intervention, for example, the protection of the voting rights of southern loyalists was the most laudable and thus, usually along with a condemnation of former Confederates, the most likely to be cited in Republican platforms.[122]

The most poignant of all the Republican planks written on this issue came from the southern branch of the party for whom federal intervention promised survival in the face of otherwise overwhelming odds. Many of their declarations appear to have been written as pleas for aid, with a northern audience in mind. In 1878, for example, South Carolina Republicans declared: "We deem it inexpedient to nominate candidates for Governor and other State officers, because, owing to the condition of affairs in this State, occasioned by rifle-club rule and two years of Democratic supremacy, it is impossible for the Republican voters in many counties, without incurring great personal danger, to organize for the campaign or to vote at the election when held." In 1889, Mississippi Republicans withdrew their entire state ticket, explaining:

We knew that our votes would be stolen and our voters driven from the polls, but we hoped, in the larger towns and cities, at least, the semblance of free speech might

---

[121]   For the mixture of political opportunism and principle that characterized Republican attitudes, see J. Morgan Kousser, *The Shaping of Southern Politics: Suffrage Restriction and the Establishment of the One-Party South, 1880–1910* (New Haven, Conn.: Yale University Press, 1974), pp. 19, 24. Excellent overviews can be found in Stanley P. Hirshson, *Farewell to the Bloody Shirt: Northern Republicans and the Southern Negro, 1877–1893* (Chicago: Quadrangle Books, 1968), and Vincent P. De Santis, *Republicans Face the Southern Question: The New Departure Years, 1877–1897* (New York: Greenwood Press, 1969).

[122]   For typical examples, see the Maine (1877), Maryland (1879), Michigan (1880), Nebraska (1880), and Nevada (1878) Republican platforms. The 1878 Pennsylvania Republican convention, in condemning the payment of war claims to the South, made no distinction between loyalists or former Confederates, declaring that: "No conqueror should be forced to pay indemnity to the conquered. . . ." However, in the same platform, the party strongly supported federal protection of voting rights in the region.

still remain to us; but our candidates are not safely allowed to discuss or protest. We refer not only to such well-known slaughters as Kemper and Copiah, Linton and Carrollton, Wahalak and Vicksburg, Yazoo City and Leflore, but the nameless killing by creek and bayou, on highway and by-way. These are the Democratic arguments which crush us. We can do no more.

Such planks could not be usefully employed in the pursuit of political power within South Carolina and Mississippi; they had meaning and purpose only when read by northerners.

For their part, Democrats opposed federal intervention in state elections, describing the proposal as an undemocratic centralization of power in the federal government, as a partisan attempt to impose Republican regimes upon the southern states, as a denial of the rightful dominance of the white race, and as a policy that encouraged fraud and mismanagement of government affairs. As with the Republican purposes, these are listed in the declining order of their popular legitimacy. However, many platforms simply offered a shrill condemnation of Republican policy without distinguishing between these reasons. For example, the 1878 Nevada Democratic convention charged that the Republicans, "having impoverished and plundered the South, incited the animosities of race, inflamed the hates of sections, kept alive the passions of war and trampled upon the rights of the States, like a grinning hyena, [nonetheless promise] to go forward with the work of pacification." In the South, many Democratic platforms promised equal protection for both races under the law while strongly opposing federal intervention in elections.[123]

The frequency with which election planks were included in major party platforms declined fairly rapidly over the course of the late nineteenth century. At first, just after the end of Reconstruction, the Republicans included demands for federal intervention in a majority of platforms written outside the South. These planks gradually disappeared until around 1890 when the emergence of the Force bill in Congress led many state parties, in a more or less perfunctory manner, to again endorse federal intervention. After that, the issue played only a minor role in northern declarations. In some ways, the issue involved a complex dialogue between the party's industrial and southern wings in which the manufacturing belt organizations pragmatically proposed federal intervention as a means of undercutting their primary opponents in the national political economy, southern Democrats, while southern Republicans promised fealty to a national

---

[123] See, for example, the Florida (1880) and Mississippi (1877) platforms. In 1878, the Alabama Democratic party maintained that equal protection for blacks under the law could be achieved only through white supremacy: ". . . while we renew the pledges of protection to all the colored people, we recognize and hold essential that, without abridging the rights of any class, these great results have been achieved and can alone be maintained by the union of the great governing race – the white people of the land."

developmental program that otherwise involved the systematic impoverishment of their constituency. Early on, this tactic worked well for northern Republicans and they wrote demands supporting federal intervention
more often than northern Democrats found it advisable to oppose the
policy. Later, during the short period when the Force bill was before
Congress, the situation was reversed and northern Democrats, sensing an
electoral advantage, condemned a reopening of the question with more
alacrity than Republicans publicly embraced the proposal. Within the
South, planks proposing federal intervention could be written only with a
northern audience in mind, because white popular opinion was so hostile
that such planks could be written only if Republicans conceded the election. As their empty guarantees of equal rights amply document, southern
Democrats were also aware that northerners read their platforms but their
position conformed with white opinion and thus they wrote condemnations
of federal intervention much more frequently than Republicans supported
nationalization.

Minor parties were massively indifferent to federal intervention. The
Prohibition and Greenback parties, for example, never wrote a plank on
federal intervention, in either support or opposition. The Populists wrote
but one, a perfunctory call in the 1900 Minnesota platform for "a full, free,
and fair ballot and an honest count" in all the states. Federal intervention
addressed the most desperate political struggle of the day, between southern blacks and whites who bitterly fought elections in ways that resembled
racial war far more than democratic competition; nonetheless, insurgent
parties dismissed the issue as a prototypical "bloody shirt" dispute, a mere
distraction from the more salient problems of the period: silver coinage,
industrial and financial plutocracy, and temperance.[124]

---

[124]   One of the side issues involved in southern voting rights was a proposal, embodied
in what was called the Blair bill, for federal aid to education. This bill was primarily justified as a means of educating freedmen so that southern blacks could more
competently participate in governmental affairs. During the 1880s when the legislation was more or less constantly before Congress, federal aid enjoyed substantial
support in three very disparate regions and parties: the rather elite-oriented Republican parties of the Northeast which explicitly linked aid to voting rights, the southern Republican parties that would have been only too happy to have received
education subsidies on those terms, and southern Democrats who welcomed federal
support in principle but sought to detach aid from any qualifying conditions or regulations. For typical examples of each, see the 1881 Massachusetts and the 1886
Tennessee Republican platform, as well as the 1882 South Carolina Democratic
plank. Between 1877 and 1888 about one in every eight Republican platforms in
the nation contained planks supporting federal aid. Most of these appeared in platforms in the Northeast and South, while none at all were written in western or Plains
states. While these Republican declarations were interesting in their own right, they
sometimes paled when compared with southern Democratic demands which simultaneously recognized the relative impoverishment of the regional political economy
as a material base for an adequate educational system, the importance of education

As a separate issue, race segregation generally received little mention in state platforms, regardless of region or party. Almost all of the few references occurred in the South and most of those were vaguely worded.[125] Given the sweeping nature of some racial planks, explicit references to segregation were unnecessary. This was obviously the case for the 1896 Alabama Democratic platform: "It is our purpose to maintain a government in this State fair and just to all, under control of the white men of Alabama." In addition, segregation was also subsumed, as a practical matter, under federal intervention in elections.[126] Without such intervention, both parties understood that southern whites would ultimately reimpose a racial order on the region which would carry with it segregation and disfranchisement as a matter of course. For that reason, separate Republican protests against these consequences were seldom made in southern platforms.[127] Late in the period, however, after the remnants of the Republican party in many southern states began to split into white and integrated factions, the party became a less than faithful defender of black interests. Black Republicans, for example, called for a separate convention in North Carolina in 1896 to protest the "fraudulent nomination of Daniel L. Russell [the regular Republican nominee] for Governor of North Carolina – a man who has proclaimed to the world that negroes are largely savages, that all negroes follow rascals, and steal six days in the week and go to church on Sundays and pray it off; that nonproperty holders should not under any circumstances exercise the full privilege of citizenship; and because he foments racial strife and thereby jeopardizes our educational progress by subordinating all to corrupt politics and politicians. . . ." While declaring their continued loyalty to the Republican party, its national platform, and presidential ticket, the delegates at this convention nevertheless demanded "every negro in whose heart there is still a spark of self-respect and manhood to exert himself to the utmost to defend the honesty and integrity of the race by doing all in his power to defeat the election of D. L. Russell, whose name has become a stench to the humble, honest, and intelligent negroes throughout the land, and whose election would be a blot upon the fair name of the State of North Carolina." The convention then "heartily"

in southern development, and the class and racial implications of federal aid if accompanied by additional regulations and conditions. Only six Democratic planks in the entire nation ever referred to federal aid to education; all of them were written in the South and all but one favored national support. Also see Sanders, *Roots of Reform*, pp. 316, 486, n. 5.

[125] See, for example, the 1896 Florida Democratic platform.

[126] One prominent exception was lynching, which was condemned by a number of parties, particularly northeastern Republicans and both Republicans and Populists in the South. For a particularly blunt example, see the 1892 Arkansas Republican platform. *Appleton's 1892 Cyclopaedia*, p. 19.

[127] For a sampling of the exceptions, see the Louisiana (1892), Maryland (1887), Mississippi (1888), North Carolina (1900), and Texas (1892 and 1894) platforms.

recommended William A. Guthrie, the Populist nominee for governor, as "a suitable and worthy" alternative to Russell.[128]

For their part, the white factions in the Republican party often had difficulty in deciding what to do with their black compatriots. The 1894 "Lily White" Republican Texas convention proposed a remarkable plan combining segregation and imperialist expansion that could have been written only in the late nineteenth century:

That the negro race has earned and is as much entitled as any other race to domicile upon the North American continent and to citizenship within the United States of America. That whatever may be the condition of other races resident in the former slave States, it is a well-known fact that the political as well as the social condition of the negro race in some of said States is most unhappy and deplorable. That the said negro race can look to the Republican party only with any justified hope of relief from their present distressed condition. That to the end that said negro race may have an unobstructed opportunity, and be aided in their noble effort to prove to the other races of the world their capacity for national as well as for local self-government, this convention does hereby urgently recommend to the Republican party of the nation and of each State respectively zealous advocacy of the early purchase, for a just consideration, by the United States, of Lower California, Sonora, Chihuahua, Coahuila, Nuevo Leon, and Tamaulipas. That, after having acquired title to said territory the United States shall subdivide the same in such a manner as best insure its early development and enlightened Government. That the said territory be designated as a territorial republic.

To understand how such a solution – involving the treatment of the territory of another sovereign nation as a potential vessel for domestic policy – could have appeared natural, the logic and orientation of American politics toward international affairs must be examined.

---

[128] The first black conventions in the post-Reconstruction era were comparatively timid, but their demands became more specific and assertive later. See, for example, the 1877 declarations of a black convention in New Jersey. *Appleton's 1877 Cyclopaedia*, p. 554. In 1882, a black convention in Rhode Island strongly protested that the state Republican party took them and their interests for granted, even while eagerly seeking their votes. *Appleton's Annual Cyclopaedia of 1882* (New York: D. Appleton, 1883), p. 721. An 1883 national convention held in Louisville, Kentucky, was even more assertive. *Appleton's 1883 Cyclopaedia*, p. 776. Also see declarations adopted by black conventions in Maryland (1889), Texas (1889), Virginia (1890), and Delaware (1894). *Appleton's 1889 Cyclopaedia*, pp. 533, 791; *Appleton's Annual Cyclopaedia of 1890* (New York: D. Appleton, 1891), p. 850; *Appleton's 1894 Cyclopaedia*, pp. 239, 649. Most of these conventions stressed support for education and voting rights while condemning segregation and lynching. The undergirding for their demands was contained in their expressions of conditional loyalty to the Republican party; blacks rarely addressed Democrats or expected anything but grief from that corner of American politics.

PLANKS ON INTERNATIONAL DIPLOMACY AND WAR

For most of the late nineteenth century, foreign affairs were, at best, a minor preoccupation of the state party platforms. Aside from a sprinkling of planks recommending or condemning fishery treaties with Canada, expressing sympathy for the Irish in their long and continuing struggle for Home Rule, or assuming a position one way or another on annexation of Hawaii, state party conventions, like their national counterparts, were almost entirely devoted to domestic policies and controversies. However, the Spanish-American War, heralded by planks expressing sympathy for the rebels in the years just prior to the sinking of the *Maine*, produced an explosion of foreign policy declarations on a wide variety of topics. Since, when considered separately, few of these topics were ever mentioned in platforms with a frequency that matched even relatively mundane controversies on the domestic scene, all the foreign policy planks have been combined into one analysis (see Table 3.20).[129] The resulting display risks overstating the role of international diplomacy and war by including peripheral topics, such as relief for the starving people of Russia. However, the relative absence of foreign policy planks on any subject, however minor, is so striking in the early periods that the consolidation is justified. In any event, if considered separately, few of the foreign affairs planks were written with sufficient frequency to bear even superficial quantitative analysis, let alone presentation in a separate table.

[129] Planks included in Table 3.20 refer to at least one of the following topics: a Nicaragua Canal; sympathy for the Irish, including endorsements of home rule and land redistribution; denunciations of Russian persecution of Jews; relief for the starving people of Russia; annexation of Hawaii, including congratulations extended to the Hawaiian Republic; endorsements of the Monroe Doctrine; concern over the presence of British troops in Nicaragua; sympathy for Cuba, including endorsements of independence; positions for and against expansion of the Navy; construction of coastal defenses; endorsements of administration policy in Venezuela; approval or condemnation of the war with Spain, including administration conduct of the war; support or opposition to retention of conquered territories; use of the term "imperialism"; demands that alcohol be prohibited in conquered territories; sympathy or support for the Boers or South African republic; denunciations of the Puerto Rican tariff; opposition to foreign alliances; denunciations of the British; denunciations of Spain; protection of immigrants returning to Germany; demands for naval protection of ocean fisheries; support or opposition to a fishery treaty; demands for diplomatic firmness with Germany; support for international arbitration; demands for improvement of the consular service; support for the abolition of war; demands for protection of U.S. citizens imprisoned in foreign countries; and praise for the war record of the army and navy. The analysis does not include: demands for prohibition in the military canteen, support or opposition to a larger standing army, demands for higher pay for soldiers, support for the use of state militia or federal troops to protect the frontier from Indians, or immigration planks even where they refer to treaties with China.

Table 3.20. *Party Platforms Mentioning One or More Planks on*
International Diplomacy and War

State party platforms containing international planks by region (%)

Party	Northeast	Great Lakes	Plains	West	South	Nation
Republican	39.4	25.6	23.8	36.1	18.2	29.7
Democratic	25.9	34.1	23.7	30.9	19.4	25.4
Prohibition	9.5	3.4	15.0	14.3	5.0	8.9
Greenback	0.0	0.0	9.1	0.0	0.0	1.8
Populist	0.0	21.4	28.6	31.6	10.0	18.3

State party platforms containing international planks by period (%)

Party	First period (1877–88)	Second period (1889–96)	Third period (1897–1900)	All years (1877–1900)
Republican	8.6	32.4	66.7	29.7
Democratic	4.0	18.1	85.9	25.4
Prohibition	2.4	5.5	25.8	8.9
Greenback	2.0	0.0	—	1.8
Populist	—	4.0	50.0	18.3

Note: See note 129 for description of issues.

The spectacular eruption of foreign policy issues in American politics is clearly evident in the much higher frequency with which international affairs were mentioned in state party platforms after 1896. But even this tabulation overrepresents the significance of foreign concerns in earlier periods while understating their importance in the last. In the earlier years, for instance, Republicans often wrote planks that were clearly intended for home consumption even while formally engaging an international issue. In that vein, five of the party's twelve international planks written before 1889 expressed sympathy for the Irish or the construction of coastal defenses, the first an attempt to wean Irish Catholics away from the Democrats and the second entailing public works projects for the nation's seaboard cities.[130] After the end of the Spanish-American War, on the other hand, many Republican parties were satisfied with a simple, blanket endorsement of the

[130]   The following demand, written into the 1886 Nebraska Republican platform, is a typical example: "The sympathies of the Republicans of Nebraska are tendered to the people of Ireland and other portions of Great Britain in their struggle for home-rule, and they recognize in the contest for loyal freedom, waged by Parnell and Gladstone, a manly battle for human rights, against the assumptions of hereditary rulers and monopolists of land."

McKinley administration's policies. These endorsements were, under the procedures adopted in analyzing state platforms, excluded from the table even though they implied strong support for retention of captured foreign territory and imperialist expansion generally. In comparison, the Democratic percentage is a more accurate gauge in that their assault on imperialism and territorial expansion entailed explicit and often detailed planks on foreign policy issues. Only a few Democratic planks were excluded from the analysis after 1896 because they were too vaguely written.

Minor parties were much less interested in international diplomacy and war than either the Republicans or the Democrats. While the Prohibitionists wrote foreign policy planks with increasing frequency over the late nineteenth century, many of their demands were for either the arbitration of international disputes or the prohibition of alcohol in conquered territories. As was the case with domestic conflicts between labor and capital, a demand for arbitration of disputes with foreign powers was a rather transparent way of avoiding specific policy commitments in party platforms. And, while prohibition in the newly acquired possessions would have had substantive policy consequences, the proposal was otherwise but a simplistic way of incorporating the party's central preoccupation into what had become the hottest controversy facing the nation. The Greenback party wrote their platforms during what was perhaps the most tranquil period in American diplomatic history. As a result and with their characteristic commitment to plain-speaking, Greenbackers placed only one plank dealing with international affairs before the people during their entire history. That exception, as paraphrased by *Appleton's Annual Cyclopaedia*, was in the form of a resolution "extending the sympathies of the [1881 Iowa state] convention to the Land League of Ireland, and to all down-trodden people of the whole globe." Because the Irish Land League demanded a radical redistribution of land as a correction for the highly concentrated ownership pattern on the island, Greenbacker identification with the movement was natural. In the last years of the century, after the Spanish-American War, the Populists frequently drafted planks on foreign policy issues. Many of these sympathized with the Boers in their war with British imperialists and thus shared Greenbacker Anglophobic tendencies. Demands for free silver and against American imperialism, and sympathy for the Boers and Irish fit together very neatly in late nineteenth-century politics; the British stood at the center of the international gold standard, allied with the United States in such a way as to make American expansion feasible as an international adventure, and suppressed the Boers and Irish in their struggles, as the Democrats and Populists saw it, for liberty and democratic freedom.[131] The

---

[131] For Democratic condemnations of British influence as the inspiration for American imperialist policies, see platforms adopted in Iowa (1899), Massachusetts (1899), New Hampshire (1900), and Ohio (1899).

Republicans usually viewed discretion as the better part of valor when confronted with Anglophobic challenges, rarely mentioning the British in any way.[132]

TEMPERANCE

For more than three decades, ethno-cultural interpretations of late nineteenth-century American politics have dominated both history and political science. These interpretations have stressed the importance of religion and ethnic identity as the wellsprings of party ideology and loyalty. Some of these perspectives have, in fact, tended to rule out as insignificant all but the most fleeting of national controversies as important factors in voting behavior during the period. Instead, local issues such as whether alcohol consumption would be permitted and, if so, under what conditions have been presented as the preoccupying conflicts that divided voters and their parties. The explanations have contended that other issues, such as government support for parochial schools, Sabbath legislation, and naturalization of immigrants, overlapped with temperance in such a way as to reinforce a basic cleavage between Protestant, native-born Republicans and Catholic, foreign-born Democrats. Seen this way, American politics rarely generated class issues or parties because the electorate was divided along lines that cut obliquely through the social structure. Furthermore, national party organizations were, to a large extent, free to assume any position they wished on the great developmental issues facing the nation, as long as their careful maneuvering through the intricate, subterranean catacombs of ethnic identity and cultural icons brought them victory in locally oriented electoral contests.[133]

There are thus two primary implications to be drawn from this literature: that the parties went before the people as the bearers of cultural symbols and that party competition was largely centered in local affairs. Neither of these implications is borne out by the patterns of positions and demands embedded in state party declarations in the late nineteenth century. In fact, as evidenced by party platforms everywhere and anywhere between 1877 and 1900, American politics was unrelentingly focused on national issues, particularly those involving the major pillars of developmental policy.

[132]   A rather pointed exception was this plank adopted by the 1898 New Hampshire convention: "We commend the successful conduct of the war with Spain, a war prompted by the noblest sentiments of humanity. . . . It has brought about a better understanding between the two great English-speaking nations of the globe, whose united action will contribute to the maintenance in the twentieth century of a universal peace among civilized nations."

[133]   This is the unavoidable implication in Paul Kleppner's work. See, for example, *Third Electoral System*, p. 378.

Table 3.21. *Party Platforms Favoring or Opposing Temperance*

State party platforms containing temperance planks by region (%)

Party	Northeast	Great Lakes	Plains	West	South	Nation
Favoring						
Republican	44.0	27.9	38.1	1.6	5.2	25.2
Prohibition	100.0	100.0	100.0	100.0	100.0	100.0
Greenback	5.0	9.1	27.3	0.0	0.0	9.1
Populist	27.8	21.4	28.6	0.0	13.3	18.3
Opposing						
Democratic	34.8	26.8	45.8	7.3	1.0	22.2

State party platforms containing temperance planks by period (%)

Party	First period (1877–88)	Second period (1889–96)	Third period (1897–1900)	All years (1877–1900)
Favoring				
Republican	38.8	20.0	8.7	25.2
Prohibition	100.0	100.0	100.0	100.0
Greenback	9.8	0.0	—	9.1
Populist	—	20.0	14.7	18.3
Opposing				
Democratic	26.7	22.8	11.3	22.2

Note: All planks demanding prohibition or regulation of alcohol consumption were considered favorable to temperance with the exception of instances, all of them involving Democratic planks, where proposed regulations would have been less restrictive than those already enacted. A proposal to submit temperance reform to the electorate was excluded unless the party declared support or opposition to the proposal.

Of all the ethno-cultural issues of the late nineteenth century, those involving temperance were far and away the most important.[134] More than a quarter of all Republican platforms written during the period contained a plank on alcohol consumption, advocating either restriction or unconditional prohibition (see Table 3.21). More than a fifth of

---

[134] On temperance issues in American politics, see Ellis Paxson Oberholtzer, *A History of the United States Since the Civil War* (New York: Macmillan, 1931–1937), vol. 4, pp. 429–431, 581–585 and vol. 5, pp. 752–763. While restrictions on alcohol consumption were common throughout the United States, enforcement seems to have been fairly peaceful everywhere except South Carolina. There the implementation of a new state dispensary law was accompanied by mob violence in which a

Democratic platforms opposed, in one way or another, restrictions on alcohol consumption. Furthermore, the most durable minor party of the period, albeit a tiny one, took "Prohibition" as its name and, lest anyone mistake its purpose, distinctly called for an absolute ban on alcohol consumption in each and every platform the party ever wrote.[135] As a stand-alone issue, temperance produced some striking patterns in much of the manufacturing belt and the Plains states. In the South and West, however, alcohol was all but ignored by every party except the Prohibitionists. In addition, temperance exhibited high visibility and saliency early in the post-Reconstruction era but gradually declined in importance as the years passed. The decline was particularly striking for the Republicans but clearly evident in Democratic platforms as well. The Greenbackers were never very favorable to temperance, while the Populists, who sometimes allied with the Prohibitionists on a fusion platform, were only mildly receptive.

However, there were many signs that party organizations were often dragged unwillingly into temperance disputes. For example, the 1877 Republican convention in Maine was only too ready to declare that temperance "is now concurred in by so large a majority of the people that it is no longer a party question," a position the party would never had assumed with respect to the tariff. In 1880 the Vermont Democratic convention refused to endorse an antitemperance plank, preferring to go before the electorate with no position on alcohol. In 1890, when a temperance proposal was on the ballot in Nebraska, both the Republicans and an Independent ticket sponsored by the Farmers' Alliance rejected planks on alcohol. Similarly, after years of service as the most prominent advocate of temperance among all the state organizations of the Republican party, the 1893 Iowa convention finally declared: "Prohibition is no test of Republicanism. The General Assembly has given to the State a prohibitory law as strong as any that has ever been enacted by any country. Like any other criminal statute, its retention, modification, or repeal must be determined by the General Assembly, elected by and in sympathy with the people, and to them is relegated the subject to take such action as they may deem just and best in the matter of maintaining the present law in those portions of the State where it is now or can be made efficient, and give to the

---

number of people were killed, by military occupation of communities under a declaration of martial law, and by a reorganization of the state militia after many companies refused to obey the governor's mobilization orders. *Appleton's 1894 Cyclopaedia*, pp. 717–718.

[135] The party was so preoccupied by temperance that it sometimes introduced alcohol into otherwise totally unrelated policy issues. For example, the Pennsylvania convention in 1898, while expressing sympathy for Cubans, added that "in doing so we will not lose sight of our duty to the hundreds of thousands of ragged and starving of our own land, the victims of the merciless drink traffic, who with bitterness cry in vain for governmental protection from this worse than Spanish tyranny."

localities such methods of controlling and regulating the liquor traffic as will serve the cause of temperance and morality."[136]

Although a precise enumeration is impossible, planks on alcohol were probably more frequently rejected at state party conventions than almost any other issue in American politics during the late nineteenth century. However, in very sharp contrast to monetary issues, which sparked numerous bolts from state and national platforms, the losers in these party conventions never revolted. Alcohol was never sufficiently prominent or divisive to produce two competing tickets from a single party in the general election.

Ethno-cultural issues colored much of the politics of the late nineteenth century but the paint never reached very deep.[137] For the Prohibitionists, such issues justified their very existence and the party often linked alcohol to religion and morality in ways that were sure to offend Catholic voters even if the latter had been willing to vote dry. The 1888 New Hampshire Prohibition convention, for example, announced: "We believe in the right of the people to the enjoyment of a quiet Sabbath, and we request the railroad companies of the State to discontinue the running of Sunday trains. We oppose the publication and circulation of Sunday newspapers, and we call upon the Legislature to pass such laws as shall be best adapted to secure the people of the State from all forms of Sabbath desecration." Pronouncements of this sort were fairly common in Prohibition platforms. Ten years later a Kansas convention took a much more evangelical position: "We regard civil government as an ordinance of God, and recognize the Lord Jesus Christ as King of Kansas, and therefore believe that the administration of civil affairs should be in harmony with the law and in his spirit." However, parties that took religion, as opposed to alcohol or some other issue, as their foundational principle were very rare in the late nineteenth century.

---

[136]   Although he carefully notes the exclusion of the South and West from his study, Paul Kleppner's coverage of political competition in the Northeast and Midwest was still quite selective. In his index, for example, Kleppner recorded 578 page references to the individual states. Forty-three of these, more than any other state, were to Iowa where temperance policies were, indeed, more salient in party competition than anywhere else in the nation. *Third Electoral System*, pp. xvii–xviii.

[137]   Paul Kleppner, probably the major figure in the ethno-cultural school, came close to denying any connection between national policy stances and electoral alignments in the United States. See, for example, his discussion of the 1890 McKinley Tariff and changes in voting patterns between 1888 and 1890 and, also, the general discussion in his Chapter 9. *Third Electoral System*, pp. 304–306. In a subsequent work, he allowed that economic issues were more important in the latter part of the 1890s; *Continuity and Change in Electoral Politics, 1893–1928* (Westport, Conn.: Greenwood, 1987), p. xiv. Also see his *Cross of Culture: A Social Analysis of Midwestern Politics, 1850–1900* (New York: Free Press, 1970). For an attempt to subsume contention over the monetary standard within an ethno-cultural framework, see Richard Jensen, *The Winning of the Midwest: Social and Political Conflict, 1888–1896* (Chicago: University of Chicago Press, 1971), chap. 10.

While clear religious commitments were rare, moral concerns indirectly related to religion were prominent features of American politics. In 1896, the American Protective Association (APA), for example, claimed a membership of some two and a half million with another four million sympathetic voters.[138] Marching under a white banner upon which were emblazoned a schoolhouse flying an American flag and the motto "Teach Patriotism in the Public Schools," the APA opposed the election of Catholics to public office and demanded nonsectarian education, competency in the English language as a requirement for naturalization, restrictions on immigration, and governmental regulation of Catholic reformatories, hospitals, and other institutions. Founded in 1887, this secret organization required that prospective members swear that they would never employ a Catholic if a Protestant could be hired instead.[139] Not surprisingly, public demonstrations by the APA sometimes resulted in violent conflicts with the Catholic community.[140] While the APA almost certainly exaggerated its membership, perhaps wildly so, anti-Catholic sentiment was still strong. However, explicit religious bigotry remained outside the bounds of all political parties. No party ever endorsed either the APA or its distinctive demands, while at least sixteen platforms either explicitly or implicitly condemned the organization.[141]

Polygamy, practiced in Utah and Idaho by many Mormons, also inspired much debate and strong condemnation in other parts of the country. While the Democrats were more disturbed by anti-Catholic agitation, Republicans were particularly exercised by plural marriages. The 1881 Massachusetts convention, which wrote an extremely reformist platform in a number of respects, urged: "Immediate and stringent measures to suppress the crime of polygamy, which, under the guise of a precept of religion, is spreading over the Southeastern Territories and entrenching itself in defiance of law and morality, a rank offence and an increasing threat." Wisconsin Republicans, in their convention the same year, were more direct: ". . . polygamy must die. . . ." But polygamy was by now an old issue, having been fought over before the Civil War as one of the reasons why federal sovereignty over the western territories should be unrestricted (the other reason was the abolition of slavery). This history explains the way Michigan Republicans

---

[138]   Oberholtzer, *History of the United States*, vol. 5, pp. 426–430. More generally, see Donald Kinzer, *An Episode in Anti-Catholicism: The American Protective Association* (Seattle: University of Washington Press, 1964).

[139]   *Appleton's 1894 Cyclopaedia*, pp. 685–686; E. Benjamin Andrews, *The History of the Last Quarter-Century in the United States, 1870–1895* (New York: Charles Scribner's Sons, 1896), vol. 2, pp. 322–326.

[140]   For descriptions of such confrontations in Kansas City and Butte, Montana, see *Appleton's 1894 Cyclopaedia*, p. 495; Thomas A. Clinch, *Urban Populism and Free Silver in Montana* (Missoula: University of Montana Press, 1970), pp. 117–118.

[141]   Fifteen of these were written by Democratic conventions. The exception was inserted into the 1896 Republican platform in the state of Washington.

couched the issue in 1882: "From its organization until now the Republican party has denounced slavery and polygamy as 'twin relics of barbarism.' The first perished at the hands of the Republican party, shot to death on battle-fields and buried in amendments to the Constitution. The second disgrace of our civilization and our century must die. We demand that polygamy be destroyed." Polygamy was the prototypical "hurrah" issue of the late nineteenth century. Given the titillation and moral outrage plural marriages engendered among eastern voters, these were easy planks for the parties to write. The wonder is not that some of them did find their way into party declarations but that their numbers were so small.[142] In policy terms, the surprise is that polygamy was abolished in Utah only in the early 1890s; despite the overwhelming power of the federal government in this small territory and the wide consensus on the destruction of plural marriages, little in fact was done for almost forty years. The nation may have been titillated by unorthodox Mormon family structures but still had much more important developmental questions to settle.

COMPARISON OF FREQUENCIES OF PLANK APPEARANCE BY PARTY AND POLICY

The political agendas of state party organizations, with the exception of the Prohibitionists, were dominated by policies related to economic development throughout the late nineteenth century (see Tables 3.22, 3.23, and 3.24). For both Republicans and Democrats, the leading issue by a substantial margin was the protective tariff. Planks explicitly declaring support for the tariff led all other policies in Republican platforms in every region. Only after the 1896 election was the tariff displaced as the leading issue by declarations of support for McKinley's imperialist and gold standard policies.[143] The frequency of planks closely linked to tariff protection, such as tariff reciprocity and military pensions, tended to rise and fall with more general demands. Reciprocity promised to sustain and even expand export markets using protection as a bargaining chip. Military pensions, as the major expenditure item in the federal budget, were supported in large part by customs revenues and thus

---

[142]   Plural marriages were mentioned in only seventeen of the more than 1,000 platforms examined here: twelve Republican, three Democratic, and two Prohibition. In 1900, Iowa Populists attending the fusion convention also condemned slavery and polygamy in the Sulu Islands, an evident attempt to fasten the "twin relics of barbarism" on Republican-led imperialism.

[143]   The turn away from the tariff and toward imperialism was not something the Republicans brought about alone. When the National Association of American Manufacturers was formed in 1895, for example, the organization assumed no position on the tariff, neither favoring nor opposing protection. *Appleton's 1896 Cyclopaedia*, p. 448.

Table 3.22. *Relative Frequency of Appearance of Policy Planks in Republican Platforms*

Time period

First (1877–88)		Second (1889–96)		Third (1897–1900)		Overall (1877–1900)	
Tariff protection	53.2	Tariff protection	83.4	Foreign affairs	66.7	Tariff protection	64.3
Federal elections	40.3	Gold standard	42.1	Gold standard	65.2	Gold standard	42.8
Temperance	38.8	Military pensions	42.1	Tariff protection	46.4	Foreign affairs	29.7
Gold standard	32.3	Immigration	36.6	Trusts	42.0	Federal elections	26.1
Civil service	30.2	Tariff reciprocity	35.9	Shipping subsidies	19.7	Military pensions	25.8
Immigration	20.9	Foreign affairs	32.4	Labor	15.9	Immigration	25.2
Railroads	20.9	Silver coinage	32.4	Civil service	13.0	Temperance	25.2
Labor	19.4	Federal elections	20.7	Military pensions	13.0	Tariff reciprocity	19.3
Convict labor	18.7	Labor	20.0	Convict labor	10.1	Labor	19.0
Land distribution	18.0	Temperance	20.0	Immigration	10.1	Trusts	18.7
				Public works	10.1		

Region

Northeast		Great Lakes		Plains		West		South	
Tariff protection	77.1	Tariff protection	62.8	Tariff protection	58.7	Tariff protection	60.7	Tariff protection	54.5
Gold standard	59.6	Gold standard	55.8	Gold standard	47.6	Silver coinage	57.4	Convict labor	35.1
Temperance	44.0	Federal elections	35.8	Railroads	47.6	Immigration	50.8	Gold standard	27.3
Foreign affairs	39.4	Military pensions	30.2	Trusts	41.3	Foreign affairs	36.1	Foreign affairs	18.2
Federal elections	34.9	Temperance	27.9	Temperance	38.1	Labor	26.2	Federal elections	16.9
Military pensions	32.1	Immigration	25.6	Military pensions	34.9	Duty on raw wool	24.6	Military pensions	13.0
Civil service	29.4	Foreign affairs	25.6	Labor	30.2	Land distribution	24.6	Tariff reciprocity	13.0
Immigration	26.6	Civil service	23.3	Federal elections	27.0	Public works	21.3	Trusts	11.7
Shipping subsidies	22.9	Tariff reciprocity	23.3	Tariff reciprocity	27.0	Trusts	19.7	Labor	11.7
Tariff reciprocity	19.3	Duty on raw wool	20.9	Foreign affairs	23.8	Gold standard	18.0	Shipping subsidies	11.7
				Land distribution	23.8	Military pensions	18.0		

Note: Only planks supporting tariff protection, temperance, or federal intervention in elections were included in this table; there were in each instance only a few or no planks opposing the policy. The other policy positions associated with these planks have been described earlier in this chapter. Briefly summarized, gold standard planks contained explicit endorsements of that policy; civil service planks demanded reform; immigration planks asked for restrictions of some kind; railroad planks demanded regulation or government ownership of the lines; labor planks supported a favorable adjustment of worker interests in their competition with industrial owners; convict labor planks requested reform or abolition of the system; tariff reciprocity planks backed treaties with foreign nations in which duties would be mutually reduced; silver coinage planks endorsed mandatory coinage either under a fixed quota or the unlimited demand of those presenting the metal at the mint; trust planks condemned trusts or monopolies; planks addressing shipping subsidies always supported federal aid; public works planks supported federal projects; and foreign affairs planks contained either a demand for diplomatic action or a condemnation of a policy followed by a foreign nation, or favored an international policy to be followed by the United States. All of these were analyzed as mutually exclusive categories.

Table 3.23. *Relative Frequency of Appearance of Policy Planks in Democratic Platforms*

Time period

First (1877–88)		Second (1889–96)		Third (1897–1900)		Overall (1877–1900)	
Tariff protection	44.0	Tariff protection	79.2	Foreign affairs	85.9	Tariff protection	57.6
Federal elections	27.3	Silver coinage	59.1	Trusts	64.8	Silver coinage	42.7
Temperance	26.7	Federal elections	28.2	Silver coinage	53.5	Foreign affairs	25.4
Silver coinage	21.3	Temperance	22.8	Tariff protection	40.8	Trusts	23.2
Civil service	20.7	Senator elections	20.8	Senator elections	36.6	Federal elections	22.4
Railroads	20.7	Military pensions	20.8	Labor	29.6	Temperance	22.2
Labor	20.0	Income tax	18.8	Railroads	26.8	Labor	21.1
Convict labor	16.7	Foreign affairs	18.1	Income tax	21.1	Railroads	18.9
Land distribution	14.0	Labor	18.1	Federal bonds	14.1	Senator elections	15.9
National banks	12.7	Gold standard	17.4	Tariff and trusts	12.7	National banks	13.0

Region

Northeast		Great Lakes		Plains		West		South	
Tariff protection	54.5	Tariff protection	63.4	Tariff protection	71.2	Silver coinage	80.0	Tariff protection	60.2
Temperance	34.8	Silver coinage	41.5	Silver coinage	54.2	Tariff protection	40.0	Silver coinage	45.6
Labor	29.5	Foreign affairs	34.1	Temperance	45.8	Senator elections	38.2	Federal elections	27.2
Federal elections	29.5	Labor	26.8	Senator elections	25.4	Immigration	36.4	Railroads	23.3
Foreign affairs	25.9	Temperance	26.8	Foreign affairs	23.7	Foreign affairs	30.9	Trusts	22.3
Gold standard	22.3	Trusts	24.4	Railroads	23.7	Trusts	29.1	Income tax	19.4
Civil service	21.4	Military pensions	24.4	Trusts	22.0	Labor	27.3	Foreign affairs	19.4
Trusts	21.4	Senator elections	21.4	Labor	18.6	Railroads	25.5	Convict labor	15.5
Silver coinage	16.1	Land distribution	16.1	Military pensions	18.6	Land distribution	23.6	National banks	15.5
Military pensions	14.3	Federal elections	14.3	Income tax	16.9	Public works	21.8	State bank notes	14.6
				Federal elections	16.9				
				National banks	16.9				

Note: Only planks opposing tariff protection, temperance, national banks, federal bond issues, or federal intervention in elections are included in this table; there were in each instance only a few or no planks supporting the policy.

Table 3.24. *Relative Frequency of Appearance of Policy Planks in Minor Party Platforms*

Prohibition		Greenback		Populist	
Temperance	100.0	National banks	67.3	Silver coinage	62.4
Woman suffrage	46.6	Federal bonds	61.8	Railroads	39.4
Railroads	22.6	Money supply	60.0	Labor	34.9
Immigration	19.2	Greenback currency	54.5	National banks	30.3
Senator elections	17.8	Land distribution	52.7	Money supply	29.4
Trusts	14.4	Labor	41.8	Greenback currency	27.5
Tariff commission	11.6	Railroads	41.8	Income tax	25.7
National banks	11.0	Convict labor	32.7	Federal bonds	24.8
Silver coinage	11.0	Income tax	29.1	Land distribution	23.9
Land distribution	10.3	Silver coinage	29.1	Trusts	22.0

Note: Only planks opposing national banks and federal bond issues are included in this table. There were few or no planks on the other side of these issues written by the minor parties. "Money supply" planks endorsed an increase in the circulation of money.

intimately linked with protection both politically and programmatically. Thus three of the ten most frequent policy planks in Republican platforms in the late nineteenth century dealt with the tariff or closely related policies. In the Great Lakes and West, where protection of raw wool was a prominent demand, there were at least four tariff-related policies among the top ten (eleven in the latter case).[144] The centrality of tariff protection within the Republican program and as the foundational cement for the party coalition is clearly evident in both the tenor of these platform declarations and the overwhelming frequency with which they were written.

The only policy that rivaled the tariff was the gold standard. In fact, if planks supporting silver coinage and the gold standard were added together (under a common heading even though they represented mutually exclusive policies), "monetary standard" planks approached protection in frequency in the nation as a whole and exceeded the tariff in the Plains and West. However, even if combined, these monetary planks lacked the programmatic linkages and articulation associated with the tariff. Furthermore, as the contradictions between silver and gold policies amply demonstrated, monetary policy was often a divisive issue within the party, spawning organizational bolts throughout the western states and much distress elsewhere. The Republican party primarily supported gold because it was

[144] In constructing these tables, planks demanding protection for raw wool were enumerated separately from declarations of general support for tariff protection; however, in reality, all of the wool planks also contained general declarations as well.

an indispensable underpinning of industrial development, not because the issue brought the rich electoral dividends associated with protection.

Republican attitudes toward foreign affairs and federal intervention in southern elections moved in opposite directions over the course of the late nineteenth century. In the years immediately following the end of Reconstruction, state parties constantly called for renewed intervention in the South. The frequency of such planks dropped precipitously in the first half of the 1890s and almost disappeared after 1896. Foreign affairs, on the other hand, did not make the list before 1889 but rose rapidly in the succeeding two periods. In some ways, these coinciding but opposite trends reflected the increasing confidence of the Republican party as the developmental vehicle for industrial expansion. During the early years, when the party was forced to barter away the last remnants of federal military occupation of the South in return for the presidency, one of the reasons Republicans sought renewed federal intervention was to forestall the reemergence of former Confederate nationalists in the region. This desperate struggle conflated nationalism and party interests, as well as long-standing ideological commitments to black political and civil rights. Later the party succeeded in putting together a national coalition, largely based on the tariff and its extensions, that could compete with the Democrats even as the latter again came to dominate the South. At that point, Republicans began to experiment with imperialist policies such as the annexation of Hawaii. Imperialist expansion was compatible with the tariff in that they shared both a hard nationalist identity and exclusive control of consumer markets as major justifications for their pursuit. However, the party would have probably not moved as aggressively abroad had southern opposition continued to threaten the industrializing trajectory of the nation. In fact, the imperialist turn implicitly presumed that industrialization, as a dynamic process shaping the national political economy, was all but unstoppable after Bryan's defeat in 1896.

Against this backdrop, claims on wealth arising out of the industrial shop floor met a lukewarm reception within the Republican party. Within the manufacturing belt of the Northeast and Great Lakes, labor planks did not even break into the list of leading demands. In these regions, the party presented the tariff as its primary policy offer to labor. Southern Republicans, despite the lower-class base of the party and the negative impact of protection on the cotton economy, mentioned labor issues only as frequently as they demanded shipping subsidies for American ships plying international routes.[145] In the Plains and West, however, where class issues merged

---

[145] As described earlier, all planks that demanded some substantive change in the bargaining relationship between workers and owners were placed under the "labor" heading. For that reason, the category is about as broadly defined as possible, perhaps even exaggerating the frequency with which labor planks appeared by including purely administrative demands for the creation of state or federal bureaus of labor statistics.

more easily with demands for a redress of the sectional distribution of wealth, Republican state parties responded by complementing their tariff planks, which obviously promised but little benefit to workers in those regions, with more direct appeals to labor. Western parties, which were at odds with the national platform on a number of issues, were particularly responsive.

Like the tariff, labor issues spawned a number of related policy planks. One of these, restriction of immigration, was actually written into Republican platforms more frequently than the combined policies that fell under the more general and broader category. Here again the West led all regions, riding on the wave of anti-Asian sentiment with particularly strong appeals for the prohibition on Chinese immigration and, at times, the deportation of established residents. In the manufacturing belt, immigration planks were both milder and more general in nature. There an emphasis, usually implicit, was placed on how restrictions on the flow of immigrants into the United States would act as a kind of protective tariff for labor, thus bringing workers, from yet another angle, into the tariff fold. The other related policy was the reform or abolition of convict labor systems. This demand barely made the national list in the years before 1889, then disappeared during the early 1890s, emerging once more just before the turn of the century. While convict labor planks usually contained a demand for the elimination of unfair competition with workers outside the prison system, this was not the major reason southern Republicans wrote such demands with a frequency second only to the tariff. In the South, the sheer brutality of the system, along with the fact that blacks bore the brunt of abuse, made abolition of convict labor a matter of simple survival for many in the core constituency of the party.

When the leading demands in the nation overall are compared with the regional lists, the varying sectional foundations of the Republican party are clearly displayed. For example, in the Northeast, Republicans were disproportionately concerned with temperance, civil service reform, and shipping subsidies for international lines. Given the upper-class, business orientation of northeastern parties, the displacement of labor demands and criticism of trusts by civil service reform and shipping subsidies should be expected. In addition, the very high frequencies with which the tariff and gold were invoked should not be a surprise. In fact, with the exception of a tilt against lower-class Catholic immigrants, Republican platforms in the Northeast emphasized almost all of the classic policies of sectional redistribution that drove American industrialization: tariff protection, adherence to the gold standard, and military pensions. With respect to the national market, which was dominated for the most part by judicial proceedings as opposed to electoral politics, the northeastern parties were appropriately silent. The two leading issues there were regulation or government ownership of the railroad system and the elimination of trusts. Since such policies would have inhibited national market expansion and since opposing government intervention in both cases was politically unpopular, silence was the best the northeastern parties could do.

The Republican parties in the Great Lakes states produced a very similar pattern. The tariff on raw wool replaced shipping subsidies as the parochial claim while general tariff planks, temperance, and foreign affairs all exhibit relative declines. Corresponding increases in the frequency of reciprocity and wool planks represent attempts to compensate for some of the weakness of the tariff in the Great Lakes states but, on the whole, protection is still the central element in party coalitions. When the Great Lakes and Plains states are compared, however, the sectional stresses in the Republican party coalition are laid bare. Party organizations in the Plains states remained loyal to two elements in the Republican developmental program, the tariff and gold, but mightily dissented on the third, the national market. As a result, demands for railroad regulation and antitrust legislation were major factors in state party platforms. These planks, along with labor issues and demands for a more equitable distribution of land, emphasized the intersectional nature of class relations on the Great Plains, arising out of the massive financing of development by eastern and foreign capital-holders. Still, Republicans did not attack banks which, along with the railroads and land, were the major form of absentee investment in the region. Although Republican parties proposed a redress of grievances in the construction of the national market and thus attempted to reduce the upper-class profile of the party's national developmental program, they were never the insurgent party in the region.

Like their counterparts in the Plains states, western Republican parties also dissented from one of the orthodox development policies but deviated on the gold standard as opposed to the national market. In fact, the deviation was so great as to replace the gold standard with silver coinage, pairing the latter with tariff protection as the leading demands in western platforms. Immigration planks, the vast majority targeting Asian arrivals and residents, were a close third. Like their counterparts in the Great Plains, western Republicans attempted to soften their upper-class profiles with planks on labor and land. They also added a parochial claim of their own, public works, which in the arid western context almost always involved a demand for federal irrigation projects. Imperialism was also popular, promising to expand Asian markets for western goods shipped out of Pacific coast ports. However, the relative dearth of Union veterans in the young population of the West sparked a noticeable decline in references to military pensions. In the West, extensions of political support for the tariff depended on protection for wool and industrial minerals, not revenues to be spent on pensions. However, aside from these products, the West was so remote from the rest of the nation that the tariff was rendered largely irrelevant because transportation costs would have made foreign manufactured goods noncompetitive even under a free trade regime. In this, as in other ways, the West was a region apart in the late nineteenth century, almost exotic in the ways in which Republican parties of the region attempted to refine the national development program in local terms.

The most exotic region, however, was still the South where Republican parties attempted to survive by simultaneously espousing developmental policies that mimicked northeastern demands while making very few claims arising out of the distinct interests of their constituencies. Southern Republican platforms tended to be much shorter than those in other regions. The leading demand was for tariff protection which, in terms of the interests of sharecroppers and small farmers embedded in the southern cotton economy, was unavoidably a form of self-sacrificial blood-letting. This was equally true for the gold standard, military pensions (so few black Civil War veterans received benefits that, even in strictly racial terms, pensions drained wealth out of the southern black community), and shipping subsidies. All of these can be seen only as proffers to the Republican parties of the manufacturing belt which responded with comparatively strong support for federal intervention in southern elections. The western Republican parties, left out of this patron-client relationship for the most part, were indifferent to federal intervention while the party organizations in the Plains states were less supportive than those to the east. Southern Republicans, as dependent protectorates of the industrializing East, were so solicitous of property rights that the crop lien and other extreme forms of class exploitation in the South were very rarely addressed. Instead, the party focused on the violence to which the black community was subjected within the convict labor system and in exercising suffrage rights, with more infrequent but very strong condemnations of lynching as well. Although they were certainly salient problems confronting the southern black community and thus well meriting vigorous denunciations in Republican platforms, they provided the foil against which the absence of class-related property claims was starkly displayed. While a solution to their problems was probably beyond their grasp during the late nineteenth century, southern Republicans made the best offer they could make: diffidently deferring to the intersectional demands of the manufacturing belt, remaining silent on class exploitation within the cotton economy, and stressing only those issues of political rights and racial violence that were compatible with Republican ideology in the North (which was far more hostile to southern whites than it was friendly to southern blacks). No wonder many southern Republican leaders viewed Populist offers of interracial class insurgency with apprehension – such an alliance would have broken the umbilical cord with the northern wing of their party with little or no assurance that anything comparable would replace it. And no wonder: Even though the situation was one largely of their own making, southern Democrats viewed southern Republicans as an alien element in their region, an element allied with developmental policies that bled both black and white southerners of what little wealth they had.

In some ways Democratic platforms mirrored Republican demands and in other respects they varied. In terms of frequency of appearance between 1877 and 1900, five of the top ten Democratic positions were openly and consistently opposed to Republican claims: tariff protection, the gold standard, foreign affairs, federal intervention in elections, and temperance (see Table 3.23). Democratic proposals for abolition of the national bank system can also be juxtaposed to the certain but silent opposition of the Republican party, which had a very close class affiliation and policy relationship with the banks. Each of these Democratic alternatives was, with the exception of temperance, shaped in important ways by the Republican program (and vice versa) in a kind of electoral dialectic that can be seen in the roughly similar frequencies with which the two major parties wrote planks on these issues.

However, where the Republicans were comparatively silent on the national market, Democrats made antitrust legislation and railroad regulation fairly important elements in their platforms. The Democrats thus strongly opposed all three legs of the Republican developmental tripod, substituting free trade for protection, silver for gold, and government regulation for market-led economic integration. As a developmental alternative to the Republican program, this package clearly best suited southern Democrats who dominated both their region and the national party. In fact, seven of the leading issues in southern Democratic platforms either dissented from the major developmental policies guiding northern industrialization, presented related demands for the imposition of an income tax (which would have fallen much more heavily on the northeastern and Great Lakes states than elsewhere and could have been substituted for the tariff as a revenue source), or proposed abolition of the national banks (accompanied by the reemergence of a state banking system with currency-issuing privileges). Two of the three exceptions dealt with either federal intervention in elections or foreign affairs. In both cases, the party demanded political autonomy in the South unrestricted by northern intervention. This was, of course, immediately at issue in their opposition to a nationalization of elections but also underlay southern Democratic denunciations of imperialism which would otherwise seem quite anomalous.[146] With respect to convict labor, the party sought to allay worker fears of competition while utterly ignoring the brutality of the system itself. Although the

---

[146] During the years immediately following the end of Reconstruction, Democratic opposition to expanding the national army was intended to hamper the ability of the federal government to again intervene in southern elections. Because the party never lost sight of this possibility, many Democratic denunciations of imperialist "militarism" had nothing to do with the trampling of human rights in American colonies. Bensel, *Sectionalism and American Political Development*, pp. 88–101.

South was generally dry, temperance did not appear among the party's major demands.

Including the monetary standard, the southern Democratic and northeastern Republican lists overlap on only three issues, and on those they are in strong disagreement. Seen from this perspective, the two developmental visions of the sections animating the major parties were not only in conflict but they also tended to talk past one another. Northeastern Republicans demanded a federal government that would efficiently extend the unregulated national market within which industrial expansion would expand, adding a tinge of public morality in the form of temperance and immigration restrictions. Silent on morality or cultural norms, southern Democrats opposed almost everything else in the northeastern Republican agenda but added proposals to use the federal government to redistribute wealth between the sections through an income tax and restrain national markets through railroad regulation and antitrust laws. Where the Republican vision set out policies that provided a frame within which industrial expansion reshaped the national political economy to the advantage of northeastern interests, the southern Democratic program was much more defensive and, in some ways, a much less consistent hodgepodge of proposals that had only one consistent target – northern industry and finance – as a common link.[147] Thus, where northeastern and southern Republicans found much common ground arising out of their close patron-client relationship, northeastern Republicans and southern Democrats inhabited almost entirely different worlds in terms of their respective policy agendas.

---

[147] This reflexive Democratic negativism led Roswell Horr, a Michigan Republican, to observe on the House floor: "You gentlemen upon the Democratic side of this House have a method of opposing and finding fault with everything that is existing to-day. I have made a little list of the things I have listened to and heard you oppose on this floor. You are opposed to national banks. You are opposed to private banks. You are down on the railroads. You are down on all corporations. You are no friend of the bondholders. You are opposed to the tariff. You want to repeal the tax on whisky, and you would like to take the revenue tax off of tobacco. You are opposed to the improvement of our harbors. You are opposed to the defense of our cities and harbors. You want to reduce the Army. You want to cripple the Navy. You are opposed to home defenses. You are opposed to all laws and subsidies which would lead to ship-building, and which would benefit our shipping on the high seas. You are dissatisfied with the management of the Indian affairs; unhappy over our postal system; you find fault with our Supreme Court, abuse our public officials generally, and you are opposed to a fair election and an honest count. [Laughter on the Republican side.]

"Now, what institutions are you in favor of? I have tried to look up and see, but have found nothing that you really seem to unanimously favor except forgery, fraud, and free whisky. [Great laughter on the Republican side.] I may be mistaken, but it is certainly an unfortunate habit you have all fallen into of placing yourselves in opposition to everything in existence which contributes to the real welfare of the country." *Congressional Record* 46:3:732, January 18, 1881.

Northeastern Democrats, on the other hand, engaged their Republican competition on a much more common ground. Seven issues overlap between the two party lists. On four the two regional parties strongly disagreed: tariff protection, temperance, foreign affairs, and federal intervention in elections. But in three areas each of the two parties wrote planks that could have easily been mistaken for the other party's demands: the gold standard, civil service reform, and military pensions. The slight class bias between the two parties in the Northeast shows up only in the prominence of antitrust and labor demands on the Democratic side, juxtaposed against proposals for immigration restriction, tariff reciprocity, and shipping subsidies on the Republican. In the Northeast, the electoral base of the Democratic party was more heavily weighted by immigrants than anywhere else in the nation; Democrats were thus much more reluctant in that region to restrict immigration lest it divide families and friends by denying entry to later arrivals. In fact, some Republican proposals to restrict immigration referred to major ethnic groups in derogatory and insulting terms and, while Democrats were reluctant to openly oppose restrictions in principle, silence was a relatively effective way of conveying the same intention.

The wrenching impact of the Bryan revolution can be seen in the appearance of silver coinage near the bottom of the northeastern Democratic list. Declarations for silver in the northeastern Democratic parties, like praise for the gold standard in the western Republican organizations, emerged only after the parties had cleanly divided over the monetary standard in the 1896 national platforms. In both regions, but particularly for northeastern Democrats, these planks buttressed organizational claims for control of the state parties more than they indicated a reversal in interests within the local electorates. For example, New York Democrats originally adopted gold because the state and the Northeast generally depended on the gold standard as one of the primary pillars supporting their position in the national political economy. When Bryan won the nomination in 1896 and pushed the national party over to silver, the insurgent immigrant wing of the party in New York seized the opportunity to throw over the gold faction, led by prominent New York City financiers, in a class struggle for control of the party – a struggle that turned only opportunistically on the monetary standard. These kinds of struggles explain the appearance of both gold and silver on the Democratic list in the Northeast and, similarly, in the Republican West.

Democratic parties in the Great Lakes states wrote platforms that were fairly similar to those of their northeastern cousins. However, Democrats in this region had no problem with silver after 1896 since they had supported free coinage for at least two decades before Bryan won the nomination. The Democrats in the Great Lakes states were also slightly more inclined to raise class issues in their competition with Republicans, substituting, for instance, demands for the direct election of senators and a more equitable land distribution for the gold standard and civil service reform, which appeared on the northeastern list. While mild, both direct election and land planks emerged out of opposition to class privilege, either through the covert use of money in politics or the overt power of wealth in aggrandizing land holdings. There were thus deeper programmatic divisions, arising out of class issues, between Great Lakes Democrats and Republicans than existed between their counterparts in the Northeast. Both, however, pale against the stark and bloody divide between southern Democrats and Republicans.

Both Republicans and Democrats from the Plains states were preoccupied by the rampaging expansion of the unregulated national market. While the two parties in that region were as divided over tariff protection, the gold standard, temperance, and federal intervention in elections as their colleagues were in other regions, there was also remarkable convergence in areas devoted to market regulation. For instance, demands for railroad regulation and antitrust legislation were prominent among the leading issues in both party platforms. To these, the Democrats added abolition of the national bank system, unmatched on the Republican side. Both parties made labor demands a common feature of their platforms. Along with these the Republicans included land distribution, unmatched on the Democratic side. However, the Democrats added the income tax which highlighted, along with abolition of national banks, the intersectional nature of much of class competition on the Great Plains. For the Republicans, the problem was to somehow straddle this class alignment by emphasizing common interests with the East in national economic development. The Democrats were only too happy to stress the apparent inconsistencies between Republican support for both a developmental program that privileged eastern industrial expansion and an even-handed approach to local class competition. However, during the agricultural depression of the early 1890s, the Populists all but absorbed the Democratic party in much of the region by stressing the, albeit slighter, contradictions in the latter's view of the national political economy.

There was probably more convergence between the Democrats and Republicans in the West than anywhere else in the nation. The two parties both roughly agreed upon six prominent elements in their respective platforms: silver coinage, immigration restrictions, labor, land distribution, public works (primarily support for federal irrigation projects), and antitrust legislation. Unlike the remainder of the nation where the monetary standard was primarily a financial policy, silver in the West was also a commodity for which production subsidies could be gained through compulsory coinage. The consensus on silver, for that reason, was not over the monetary standard in principle but over parochial interest in a regional commodity. This was reflected, for example, in the ways in which western Republicans tried to maintain that compulsory coinage was both part of a reciprocal trade with the East in exchange for a protective tariff and, compared with gold, a more feasible basis for the financial system. Western Democrats had no problem with silver on either ground, as reflected in the extremely high frequency with which the metal was advocated in their platforms. This frequency was, in fact, higher than that of any other leading issue for any region for both major parties. (Only tariff protection in northeastern Republican platforms came close.) Most of these silver planks were as succinct as they were ubiquitous with, in many instances, a very simple "for free silver" summing up the party's position. The western parties disagreed most often over the tariff. However, where the Republicans worked very hard to extend support for protection by adding planks on raw wool and military pensions, the Democrats were fairly reluctant to mention the issue at all. In the other four regions of the nation, for example, opposition to the tariff was the leading issue in Democratic platforms; in the West, this plank ran a distant second with a frequency of appearance significantly below the other regions in absolute terms as well. As a counter to Republican emphasis on the policy complex surrounding the tariff, the Democrats emphasized regulation of the national market. This emphasis showed up in the much higher frequency of antitrust and railroad planks. But, even so, these were differences in nuance, not policy orientation.

Over time Democratic platforms followed trends similar to Republican patterns. For example, the tariff as an issue peaked during the first half of the 1890s, just as in the Republican party. Federal elections and foreign affairs again traced out opposing trajectories with the former's steady declines in platform appearances matched by increases in the latter. Monetary policy for both parties was a middling issue early on but rose to prominence after 1889. Temperance, on the other hand, declined steadily, even disappearing from the list of leading issues after 1896. In all these cases, the major party trends were in rough agreement even though the Republicans and Democrats assumed contradictory positions with respect to each policy.

But these frequencies sum up the platform characteristics of all the regional parties, and the differences between the regional wings of both parties are equally notable. In many respects, for example, there was more disagreement between the northeastern and western wings of the Democratic party than existed between the western Democrats and Republicans. And the regional convergence between the northeastern and southern Republicans defied their respective class bases in a way that was even more remarkable. The United States was a highly varied country in which local electorates were almost unrelentingly oriented toward national developmental issues. The state parties, in response, highlighted these developmental policies in their platforms but attempted to find some formula that would both strengthen their influence within the national party and, at the same time, maximize their competitive advantages at home. When the tension between these two impulses became unbearable, as it did over monetary policy for both northeastern Democrats and western Republicans, the state organizations were split asunder. One of the most important aggravating factors was the emergence of third parties whose agendas exploited the apparent contradictions that accompanied this straddling between regional and national politics and economies.

The Prohibitionists were the only minor party to persistently run candidates throughout the late nineteenth century. Although they were the weakest of the third parties, they nonetheless tugged the Republicans toward temperance by competing for the dry vote; this, in fact, may very well have been their primary purpose in many elections. In that sense, their task was done once they merely wrote their obligatory demands for a dry community and entered a slate of candidates. Winning elections on their own was just not a realistic goal for the party. Where the Prohibitionists managed to influence Republican platforms, the result probably encouraged the Democrats to exploit the Republican response by crafting relatively wet planks in opposition. Thus temperance as an issue in major party platforms owes some of its prominence to Prohibitionists' gadfly activities. Some of the other issues on this party's list were more or less related to their central preoccupation. For example, woman suffrage would have expanded electoral support for dry legislation. While the Prohibitionists lavished much praise on women as the bearers of western civilization through child-rearing and the natural sentiments characterizing their gender, the central ground for social and economic equality in Prohibitionist logic was the hostility of women to alcohol. Restrictions on immigration were likewise motivated by the tendency of Catholic, foreign-born citizens to oppose prohibition. The party, for that reason, not only advocated restrictions on arrivals but also often added demands for lengthy residency before naturalization, accompanied by language qualifications and other requirements. The eastern wing of the party tended to write very short platforms in which these were often the only issues mentioned. In the West, however, the state parties tried to extend their appeal by adding planks urging silver coinage, land distribution, and the abolition of national banks. The underlying logic supporting these longer platforms was two-fold: a need to associate temperance with popular demands that were clearly far more powerful than aversion to alcohol and a strong belief in the rational regulation of social and economic behavior. From the latter perspective, the party moved from regulating alcohol consumption and immigration to government intervention in the railroad network, antitrust legislation, and tariffs constructed by expert commissions. But all of these were comparatively minor influences on the construction of political coalitions in the late nineteenth century because the party was both so small and so completely identified with its hatred of liquor.

Although the Greenbackers were comparatively short-lived as a movement, they exerted far more influence on American politics. As arrays of policy demands, Greenback platforms were exceeded in their integrated and complex logics only by the rare socialist platforms that began to appear just before the turn of the century. Most of the leading planks in Greenback declarations, as their moniker suggests, demanded changes in the financial system and, in particular, the role of money in the national economy. Like the Populists, the Greenbackers rarely mentioned the tariff and, while both parties frequently wrote planks on railroads and other aspects of the national market, these varied from major party demands only in their frequency and stridency. Thus, of the three legs of the developmental tripod, the financial system became the most important target of Greenbacker and Populist platform writers. The four most frequent demands in Greenback platforms comprised a tight, coherent expression of the party's ideology and plan for monetary reform. The party, for example, demanded the abolition of national banks for two primary reasons: because the people alone, through the federal government, should control the supply of money, and because the national bank system was, in their eyes, a monolith of unwarranted privilege given over to aristocratic wealth. Like the national banks, federal bonds were unnecessary and a boon to the rich. They could, Greenbackers contended, be simply redeemed in paper money which would both eliminate interest payments to wealth-holders and expand the circulation of money in such a way as to encourage economic growth. Greenbackers, in fact, often made the expansion of money circulation a separate plank in their platforms, sometimes accompanied by a demand that the government monitor the money supply in order to modulate activity in the national economy. This plank returned the Greenbackers to their primary demand, which was for the abandonment of the gold standard with its comparatively rigid operating restrictions on the supply of money and the adoption of legal tender paper currency in its place. All of these demands, as a plan for the financial system and as a theory of monetary economics, made a lot of sense. In fact, the detail and articulation of monetary planks by the Greenbackers far exceeded the comparatively perfunctory endorsements of the status quo by the Republicans and the simplistic calls for "free silver" by the Democrats. The fly in the ointment was silver, which was so popular with agrarian electorates that more than a quarter of all Greenback state platforms endorsed the metal as an alternative to gold or a supplement to paper money. However, silver as a metallic standard would have imposed, after a one-step inflation of the dollar, the same strictures as gold on government manipulation of the money supply. Since government control over the circulation of money was the central ideological and operating principle of Greenback thought, silver was an alien weed in what was otherwise one of the most carefully tended and orderly programmatic gardens in American history.

Underlying much of the Greenback financial program was a clear and open hostility to wealth and privilege. This carried over into other realms as well and made the Greenbackers one of the most class-conscious parties ever to come before American voters. Their rhetoric dripping with contempt for the moneyed classes, a hypothesized monopoly on economic privilege, and, in some cases, the sanctity of property rights, Greenbackers issued calls for a more equitable land distribution, for labor legislation, for abolition of convict labor systems, and for the imposition of an income tax. Most Greenbackers were not socialists; they instead believed in market competition, but this was to be a competition among relative equals. No one, from their perspective, could be allowed to win on a scale large enough to affect the competition itself. While property rights in a worker's tools or a farmer's homestead were necessary and, in fact, positive features in the Greenback political economy, large estates and stock portfolios were threats to fair play that should be leveled through government intervention. In some ways, this also applied to the railroads, which necessarily entailed a massive investment of capital. If privately controlled, the railroads carried much of the same kind of threat that accompanied the national bank system, with the caveat that railroads performed a necessary social function where the national banks were simply superfluous boons to the wealthy. For this reason, Greenbackers often went beyond regulation and called for government ownership of the rail network, nationalizing it in much the same way that money would have been nationalized by abolition of the national banks. Unlike the major party platforms, Greenbacker railroad planks were much more concerned with class privilege than they were with the expansion of an unregulated national market.[148]

The Populists took up this program in the early 1890s with a fervor that made many of their platforms indistinguishable from those written by their Greenback predecessors. However, silver coinage, an inconsistent add-on in Greenback platforms, was now far and away the central demand of agrarian insurgents. The emergence of silver was accompanied by declining attention to the more orthodox elements of the Greenback program: demands for the abolition of national banks, government control of the money supply, a monetary system based on paper money, and the elimination or curtailment of federal bond issues. Where these topics found a place in Populist declarations, the planks were much briefer and longer on class rhetoric than on financial theory. However, the other class-conscious Greenback demands reemerged in the Populist program with roughly the same emphasis, although planks demanding a more equitable land distribution and the

---

[148] For a related but slightly different interpretation of the agrarian origins of Populist ideology, see Steven Hahn, *The Roots of Southern Populism: Yeoman Farmers and the Transformation of the Georgia Upcountry, 1850–1890* (New York: Oxford University Press, 1983), pp. 282–286.

abolition of convict labor declined in frequency. In their place, the Populists stressed the excesses of national market expansion by demanding regulation or government ownership of the railroad system and by making antitrust legislation one of the party's principles. However, compared with the regional and temporal variation in policy priorities within the major parties, these differences were truly minor. The Greenback and Populist demands have nine policies in common, with only the substitution of trusts for convict labor in the Populist rankings marring an otherwise complete agreement. This overlap is more extensive than any corresponding comparison between the major party lists, either regional or temporal. In other words, separated in time and by organizational identity, the Greenback and Populist parties still agreed more extensively on their common policy priorities than did, for example, the Democratic parties of the Northeast and Great Lakes. In fact, from that perspective, the major difference between the Greenbackers and Populists was that the former wrote longer and more detailed platforms. But the Greenbackers probably wrote the longest and most detailed platforms in American history (which explains why the party's plank frequencies in Table 3.24 are higher for that party than for any other).

PARTY PROGRAMS AND AMERICAN ECONOMIC DEVELOPMENT

In sum, the major parties repeatedly and consistently presented to the national electorate three visions of economic development. The Republican party advocated adherence to both the international gold standard and tariff protection, thus presenting an extremely harsh program of interregional redistribution that favored the industrial and financial core. The Democratic party also supported gold in presidential elections (until 1896) but consistently opposed tariff protection. These and other features of the Democratic program favored the export-oriented southern cotton economy as a dependent extension of European (primarily British) textile producers and thus envisioned development as an improvement in the regional terms of trade both within the United States and with the rest of the world economy. Third-party agrarian insurgency rejected the gold standard in favor of currency inflation, advocated more sweeping regulation of corporate consolidation and operations than the other parties, and rarely mentioned the tariff.

These alternative developmental paths or visions originated within the three great sections of the American political economy, each one attempting to bridge the gap between the regional alignment of conflict over income shares and the coalitional possibilities available to political leaders in national politics. From this perspective, the state platforms of the major

parties often represented attempts to adjudicate between national party programs with their unrelenting emphasis on the intersectional redistribution
of wealth and local demands for an adjustment of income shares between
upper and lower classes. But there can be no questioning of the tilt in this
adjudication – state platforms and party organizations heavily favored
national developmental policies over local class claims in the construction
of electoral demands.[149]

In fact, competing visions of economic development strongly shaped electoral alignments at all levels of American politics. One of the most important results was the deflection of class claims and cultural antipathy into
the sideshows of politics. The United States in the late nineteenth century
was a highly diverse nation in many ways: ethnic communities, religious
affiliations, and cultural traditions. Overlaying this diversity was a class
structure more starkly defined and harshly enforced than that in any other
period of American history. Yet cultural conflict produced only temperance
as a rather lukewarm and secondary political demand in state politics. And
only by combining a wide diversity of planks, many of them quite limited
in their scope and intent, does labor rise to an equivalent, minor role in
state politics.[150] In the states, as in the nation, political conflict instead raged

[149]   All minor parties deplored the salience of the tariff in American politics, although
most conceded the innate importance of monetary issues. Marxist parties, however,
denounced all issues involving the intersectional redistribution of wealth as manip-
ulative frauds. In 1896, for example, the New Jersey Socialist Labor party platform
concluded its list of demands with this passage: "The Socialist-Labor party repudi-
ates and warns the toilers of New Jersey against the damnable snares set by the
Democratic, Republican, and Populist parties in the shape of protection, free trade,
free silver, and gold standard, to catch the producers of all wealth and to further
exploit and rob them of what they produce, and urges the toilers to turn a deaf ear
to their cries and rally around the standard of the only party that stands for the
emancipation of labor from the competitive system of wage slavery that is crushing
humanity to-day."

[150]   For general discussions of labor in American politics during the late nineteenth
century, see Friedman, *State-making and Labor Movements*, pp. 94–98, 108–115,
183–192; Richard Oestreicher, "Urban Working-Class Political Behavior and Theories of American Electoral Politics, 1870–1940," *Journal of American History* 74
(1989): 1257–1286; David Montgomery, *Citizen Worker: The Experience of
Workers in the United States with Democracy and the Free Market during the
Nineteenth Century* (New York: Cambridge University Press, 1993), pp. 134–162.
Karen Orren stresses the role of labor in the courts, via strike litigation, as a major
and liberalizing influence on the late nineteenth-century American polity. The kinds
of transformation in the common law that she carefully documents can be seen as
apolitical claims on a larger share of industrial profits for labor; the absence of
electoral claim-making can be viewed as an outcome of working-class participation
in the intersectional redistribution of wealth between the industrial North and the
agrarian periphery. Thus the fact that labor's influence was largely deflected into
strike activity and thence into the courts, becoming a largely nonpartisan struggle
outside of electoral politics, is entirely compatible with the interpretation forwarded

over which vision of development would be imposed upon the United States.[151] And the most important features of that conflict were the inter-sectional redistributions of wealth that each entailed.

Recognition of the preeminence of developmental issues in both local and national politics transforms the sense of inevitability that often colors narratives of American industrialization into a highly contingent outcome that must be thoroughly reexamined. Political challenges to the course of American industrialization abounded in the late nineteenth century, assuming many different and often contradictory forms. While the Republican party was the primary developmental vehicle for industrialization, state organizations and regional wings of the party often dissented from major portions of the developmental program – even to the point of rupture. Furthermore, at the most crucial juncture in the period, involving defense of the gold standard through bond issues and repeal of the silver purchase act, Grover Cleveland, a Democrat, proved the most stalwart protector of the gold standard. And, in 1896, it was the movement of northeastern Democrats, many of them industrial workers, into the Republican party that swept McKinley into the White House. American politics had many enduring structural features in the late nineteenth century, among them: the foundational influence of radically uneven regional development on the alignment of the party

here. *Belated Feudalism: Labor, the Law, and Liberal Development in the United States* (New York: Cambridge University Press, 1991), pp. 19–28.

[151] Within this context, there are several ways to place Martin Sklar's *The Corporate Reconstruction of American Capitalism, 1890–1916* (New York: Cambridge University Press, 1988). On the one hand, Sklar's combination of neo-Marxism and modernization theory leaves little room for contingency in late nineteenth-century political and economic development. In his view, corporate capitalism and its attending ideologies were realized by an elite social movement that merely elaborated the working principles of a manifestly superior social formation. Because the masses were progressively persuaded that large corporate forms of production were benign, sympathetic political majorities in elections, Congress, and the courts were rarely in doubt. In short, American society was so thoroughly reorganized by the emergence of corporate capitalism that the success of industrialization as a political program was preordained. In fact, however, there is little evidence of hegemonic elite construction of political claims in party platforms before the turn of the century. The sheer diversity of party platforms provides abundant evidence of both attention to popular demands within the states and the lack of any overarching consensus on many of the most important economic issues of the day. This is true even within the parties. On the other hand, as applied to the period after the turn of the century, Sklar's interpretation has much to recommend it. McKinley's victories in the 1896 and 1900 presidential elections made the Republican vision of American development so dominant that the other parties were restricted to contesting its details. In the process, the Democratic and Populist visions of a full-blown, alternative political economy for the United States rapidly wasted away. In that context, Sklar's close attention to the political and economic thinking of Theodore Roosevelt, William Howard Taft, and Woodrow Wilson accurately stresses the emergence of a relatively consolidated and dominant corporate capitalist world view.

system, the role of the Republican party as the policy agent for industrialization, and the apportionment of developmental policies among the major branches of the federal government. But these are analytically and theoretically significant precisely to the extent that they survived the myriad of alternative ways in which claims could have been pressed within politics. In the next chapter, some of the most important of those electoral challenges are examined.

4

Claims on Wealth and Electoral Coalitions

MUCH of political conflict in the late nineteenth century was shaped by contending visions of the national political economy. The most powerful of these was the laissez-faire model of competitive capitalism that both figuratively and in reality liberated corporate-led industrialization. Like all ideological models, this vision served several purposes: It provided an interpretation of industrial expansion that made the process intelligible to the mass public; it legitimated that process by illustrating the beneficial aspects of capitalism as an organizing form for social energy and production; and it stipulated the place and available opportunities of individuals within society. Like all ideological models, the proffered explanations highlighted the leading role of the promulgators: the industrial and commercial elite of the nation. As such, this vision of the national political economy was both deeply rooted in material reality and selectively focused on particular aspects of that reality. As an interpretation of social possibility, this vision more closely resembled the status quo than alternatives, a competitive advantage of no insignificance in that the most important alternative ideological models both were programmatically incompatible and represented but a minority, in each case, of the electorate.

As the preceding discussion of platform demands demonstrated, the Greenbackers and Populists, as well as each of the major parties, constructed alternative political programs for American economic development. Each program possessed a clear, material foundation within a major portion of the national political economy; a logic within which a plan of political action could be legitimated; and a vision within which major elements of the electorate could identify both themselves and their interests. In tandem with the radically uneven pattern of regional development during this period, each of these party programs arose out of one of the major sections of the United States, either endorsing or opposing the laissez-faire vision of the political economy promulgated by the industrial and commercial elite of the East. But the origin of these ideological models lay much closer to home, in the immediate market transactions through which major portions of the regional population drew their wages or sold their produce. In the opening portion of this chapter, the material basis of class conflict within each of the major regions is described with an eye toward the way in which economic claims over income shares might have moved into national politics. The subsequent analysis of voting returns in the 1888, 1892, and 1896 presidential elections examines the extent to which these claims actually shaped voting decisions and national party coalitions during industrialization.

REGIONAL FOUNDATIONS OF INSURGENT IDEOLOGICAL MODELS

Three types of conflict over income shares, one within each of the great regions, were so widespread and intense that they became the foundation of local social and political competition. In each case, conflict focused on market transactions embedded within the economic sector producing the major commodities or goods exported from that region. In each instance, competing claims on wealth focused on political regulation of the conditions and terms under which these market transactions were executed. Since each of these sectors involved the major exports for their respective regions, these claims on wealth sometimes carried broader implications for the distribution of income between the great regions and between the United States and the world economy. Thus, these competing claims, in becoming major organizing factors in their respective regional political economies, also became potential sources of stress on even broader alignments in national politics.

The transactional locus of competition over income shares was the point at which labor, as a factor in production of the primary export good, was allocated a share of the proceeds of that good. Within each of the great regions, this locus of competition involved only a portion, albeit a large one, of the population and potential electorate. The classic case involved the factory shop floor where the wage bargain between the industrial worker and factory owner determined their respective shares of the firm's profits. Thus, in the manufacturing belt, labor and capital were arrayed in stark opposition to one another. On the western plains, however, labor and capital were usually combined in the hands of yeoman farmers. In this case, the transactional locus was not a wage bargain between workers and capitalists but, instead, a transaction in which commodity crops moved into the stream of national and international commerce. The southern plantation economy involved several alternative arrangements (arising out of share-cropping agreements, land rents, and the business operations of yeoman farmers) in which labor was allocated a share of proceeds from harvest of the cotton crop. In practice, however, the formal differences between these arrangements were often blurred in such a way that the transactional locus of the southern cotton economy was distinctly different from those either arising on the factory shop floor or involving the western homestead producer.

COMPETING CLAIMS ON CORPORATE PROFITS: THE WAGE BARGAIN IN NORTHERN INDUSTRY

Like all the great American regions, the political economy of the manufacturing belt in the Northeast and Midwest was complex, composed of a large and booming industrial sector, vast expanses of highly diversified and commodified agriculture, and dense commercial centers that handled the movement of goods and capital throughout the national market. Of all the transactions that composed the market economy of the rapidly industrializing regions of the nation, the most salient, in terms of both the contention associated with its organization and its impact on the lives of the citizenry, was the industrial wage bargain in which labor was exchanged for money.

Most American workers in the late nineteenth century labored for wages paid either by the hour or by the amount of product.[1] In some respects the wage bargain under which the worker was employed was primarily shaped by a freely competitive labor market in which workers could and did offer labor to employers. But in many instances the wage bargain was the outcome of many other factors and arrangements agreed upon, either implicitly or explicitly, by labor and management.[2]

There were several ways in which workers could shape the labor market and, thus, their wage bargain with capital. First, the supply of labor could be controlled in such a way as to decrease competition between workers for jobs. In the short run, many of the discriminatory and customary practices that excluded certain population groups from the factory or restricted their employment on the shop floor had this effect. But in the long run, which was not very long in the nineteenth century, open immigration laws meant that the most important factor affecting the labor supply was the

---

[1] For lists of unions that either prohibited or allowed members to work by the piece, as well as a discussion of why they individually assumed different positions with respect to this issue, see *Report of the Industrial Commission: Labor Organizations*, vol. 17 (Washington, D.C.: GPO, 1901), pp. liv–lviii.

[2] In some cases, for example, management would set a rate at which production would be paid to a group of workers who then collectively decided how that wage would be paid to their members. For a description of such an arrangement, see David Montgomery, *The Fall of the House of Labor: The Workplace, the State, and American Labor Activism, 1865–1925* (New York: Cambridge University Press, 1987), pp. 9–13; for a description of subcontracting in machine shops, see pp. 187–188.

movement of workers back and forth across the Atlantic Ocean.[3] As long as that movement took the form of ethnic groups closely identified with those already in the United States, support for restricting immigration was weak. Only with the changing composition of the flow, from northern and western to southern and eastern Europe after 1890 or so, did popular demands for immigration quotas and literacy tests begin to influence national politics.[4] Even then, the possibility of enacting such laws as a means of restricting competition in the national labor market remained remote until well into the twentieth century.

The second way in which workers could influence the allocation of shares between wages and profits was through government regulation. Through law some practices, such as the employment of children and women, could be prohibited and others, such as working hours, could be controlled. In addition, government intervention in the workplace could restructure routines and practices that contributed to the high injury and mortality rates of the late nineteenth century. While these policies did not regulate or raise wage levels directly, all of them promised, in one way or another, to increase the net return of employment to the worker.[5] To some extent, these regulations did make a difference in the way employers and employees bargained over wages and working conditions, but many laws were either poorly framed in ways that impeded enforcement in the courts or were weakly policed by underfunded and undermotivated government agencies.[6] However badly enforced, many labor leaders believed these statutes had an impact on the relative attractiveness of the different states to investors. For example, Samuel Gompers described repeal of an Alabama

[3]   Between 1850 and 1914, as much as a quarter of the European labor force may have crossed the Atlantic and permanently settled in the western hemisphere. Mark Wyman, *Round-Trip to America: The Immigrants Return to Europe, 1880–1930* (Ithaca, N.Y.: Cornell University Press, 1993), p. 48.

[4]   For a discussion of the increasing frequency with which immigration planks were inserted into party platforms during the late nineteenth century, see Chapter 3.

[5]   There were, in fact, no state or territorial laws fixing wage rates in the late nineteenth century. *Report of the Industrial Commission: Labor Legislation*, vol. 5 (Washington, D.C.: GPO, 1900), p. 23.

[6]   Examples of poorly formed labor laws and inadequate enforcement abound. For instance, see *Report of the Industrial Commission: Capital and Labor Employed in Manufactures and General Business*, vol. 7 (Washington, D.C.: GPO, 1901), pp. 26, 46, 54–68, 227–228. As the testimony of the witnesses appearing before the commission indicated, state labor officials were usually quite favorable to labor unions, government regulation of working conditions, and workers' rights generally. Where enforcement was lax it was not because the administration of the laws was placed in hostile hands. However, in some parts of the country, labor regulation was so weak as to be almost nonexistent. In North Carolina, for example, the state Commissioner of Labor was also the cashier of the Dime Savings Bank in Raleigh, normally a full-time occupation in itself. When asked about North Carolina labor laws, he replied, "We have got none in the State at all except" a statute modifying the fellow servant

law limiting work hours for children as an invitation to "Northern and English capital . . . the bill repealing the law might properly have been termed an act to sacrifice the lives of the children of Alabama in order that 6 percent dividends may be declared upon Northern capital."[7]

Finally, workers could organize into unions that then could expand wage shares through bargaining agreements with management.[8] This was the most direct strategy through which the wage bargain and all the other issues associated with industrial employment might be renegotiated to the benefit of workers.[9] Unions, of course, used strikes to compel management to come to the bargaining table, and in the United States, as in many other industrializing nations, strikes were a prominent feature of labor relations in the early stages of industrialization. Unlike most other industrializing nations, however, strike activity in the United States never made a transition from workshop claims directed at individual employers to political protest focused on government policy.[10]

In the United States, the peak in strike activity came relatively late, just

---

rule as it applied to railroad labor. The entire appropriation for the bureau was $1,100, including office expenses, and included no funds for employees other than the commissioner (pp. 499–500).

[7] *Industrial Commission: Capital and Labor*, vol. 7, p. 619.

[8] Then, as now, union organization could serve several purposes at the same time. While successful unionization could raise wage scales in a local industry, the raising of wages could also equalize wage costs between this locality and regions previously organized. For example, the secretary of the Memphis Industrial League charged that union organizers were sent into the north Alabama coal districts from Illinois in order to narrow differences in scales between the two regions. The secretary contended that unionization of southern labor would subsequently discourage economic growth by making investment of northern capital in the region less attractive. In his testimony before the Industrial Commission, Samuel Gompers reported that the American Federation of Labor maintained three full-time organizers devoted entirely to the unionization of southern workers and that their assignment was motivated, at least in part, by the organization's desire to establish a uniform national wage scale. *Industrial Commission: Capital and Labor*, vol. 7, pp. 579–580, 605.

[9] For a copy of what appears to have been a typical contract, at least in the shoe industry, see the agreement between the W. L. Douglas Shoe Company of Brockton, Massachusetts, and the Boot and Shoe Workers' Union, signed November 1, 1898. *Industrial Commission: Capital and Labor*, vol. 7, pp. 367–368.

[10] See P. K. Edwards, *Strikes in the United States, 1881–1974* (New York: St. Martin's Press, 1981), pp. 6–8; E. Shorter and C. Tilly, *Strikes in France, 1830–1968* (Cambridge, Engl.: Cambridge University Press, 1974); D. A. Hibbs, "Industrial Conflict in Advanced Industrial Societies," *American Political Science Review* 70 (1976): 1033–1058; Walter Korpi and Michael Shalev, "Strikes, Industrial Relations and Class Conflict in Capitalist Societies," *British Journal of Sociology* 30 (1979): 164–187. The United States began to compile official statistics on strike activity a decade or more before Canada and most European countries started keeping records. For a summary of what data is available from countries aside from the United States in this period, see U.S. Commissioner of Labor, *Twenty-first Annual Report: Strikes and Lockouts* (Washington, D.C.: GPO, 1907), pp. 777–916.

after 1900. This was because European immigrants continued to arrive in ever greater numbers in the decades following the transformation of the American economy from agriculture to industry in the late nineteenth century. Thus, because the United States continued to import rural Europeans who then became American workers, the socialization of new workers into the disciplined labor practices of industrial manufacturing lagged behind industrialization itself. And because the harsh reorganization of social relations associated with industrialization was experienced by the greatest number of workers just after the turn of the century, strike activity peaked in the opening decades of the twentieth century when most of the structural transformation of the national economy had already been completed.[11]

As a form of claim-making, the industrial strike of the late nineteenth and early twentieth century was usually a risky proposition. Before World War I, a substantial percentage of all strikes were not ordered by unions, and even where a union ordered a strike, many of the workers were not union members.[12] In fact the overall strike rate, in terms of per capita activity, was somewhat lower in highly organized sectors than in those where unions were relatively weak (see Table 4.1). Although variation within both highly and weakly organized industries was fairly wide, the general pattern was for strike frequency to decline with increasing union strength. In addition, the percentage of union-ordered strikes that failed was almost universally lower, regardless of industry. From the point of view of both workers and employers, the explanation for these patterns was the discipline associated with union organization – a discipline that transformed hot-headed, spur-of-the-moment walkouts of unorganized workers into a finely honed bargaining tool with which to shore up the long-term security and benefits of union members. For that reason, many employers actually preferred to deal with union representatives rather than unorganized workers.[13]

---

[11] For data and charts on the frequency of strike activity, see Edwards, *Strikes in the United States*, pp. 12–13, 254–256.

[12] Ibid., pp. 31–34. Most railroad strikes occurring between 1881 and 1894, for example, were not sanctioned by a union. Shelton Stromquist, *A Generation of Boomers: The Pattern of Railroad Labor Conflict in Nineteenth-Century America* (Urbana: University of Illinois Press, 1987), p. 44.

[13] Organized labor differed quite a bit on its attitude toward strikes. On one end of the spectrum was the Knights of Labor, which had always assumed, sometimes at odds with the wishes of its locals, a skeptical position. In 1880, for example, the national general assembly resolved that "strikes are, as a rule, productive of more injury than benefit to working people; consequently all attempts to foment strikes will be discouraged." *Industrial Commission: Labor Organizations*, vol. 17, p. 16. At the other end stood Samuel Gompers and the American Federation of Labor; in a paper delivered before the Congress on Industrial Conciliation and Arbitration in 1894, Gompers compared an "organization of labor which resolves that under no circumstances will it strike" to "a militia regiment which resolved that upon the breaking out of war it will disband." P. 696. For evidence that union sponsorship greatly

Table 4.1. *Strike Activity in Highly and Weakly Organized Industries, 1881–1900*

Industry	Strikes not ordered by unions (%)	Strikes that failed (%)		Annual number of strikers (per 1,000 workers)
		Unions	Not unions	
Highly organized				
Glass manufacturing	49.7 (374)	45.1	74.7	140.5
Tobacco	27.0 (1,509)	52.0	28.4	118.1
Ship building	45.0 (151)	38.7	58.5	76.6
Stone quarrying	28.5 (856)	28.4	42.0	56.8
Transportation	56.1 (1,262)	35.1	57.6	52.5
Brewing	9.9 (81)	4.6	40.0	45.8
Building trades	10.2 (4,440)	32.6	38.6	30.2
Machine manufacturing	33.6 (452)	31.4	64.1	25.7
Printing	14.1 (765)	47.5	68.1	15.5
Total	23.6 (9,890)	39.1	52.4	62.5
Weakly organized				
Coal and coke	48.1 (2,512)	47.9	56.3	297.3
Carpet manufacturing	67.2 (137)	47.4	61.4	124.0
Silk	53.7 (287)	53.4	56.9	83.0
Cotton mills	79.3 (512)	65.5	70.2	68.0
Brick	47.8 (184)	39.4	71.3	54.7
Rubber	76.8 (56)	76.9	62.8	46.7
Woolen mills	87.2 (289)	51.0	59.7	36.8
Boot and shoe	25.9 (862)	49.8	60.6	32.5
Paper manufacturing	81.4 (43)	50.0	82.9	2.8
Total	51.3 (4,882)	53.5	64.5	82.9

Note and source: Adapted from *Report of the Industrial Commission: Labor Organizations*, vol. 17 (Washington, D.C.: GPO, 1901), pp. cxxvii, 679. "Highly organized" industries are those in which union members compose a high percentage of the total work force; "weakly organized" industries are those in which union members represent a small percentage. Numbers of strikes by industry appear in parentheses.

However, few employers recognized unions as bargaining agents for their employees and fewer still would tolerate strikes as a bargaining tool. The

increased chances of success for strikes, see Gerald Friedman, *State-making and Labor Movements: France and the United States, 1876–1914* (Ithaca, N.Y.: Cornell University Press, 1998), pp. 129, 132–133, 138–139, 268.

net result was that late nineteenth- and early-twentieth-century strikes sometimes resulted in the mass firing of employees. This possibility meant that the stakes involved in a strike, from the worker's perspective, were very high at the turn of the century. In turn, these very high stakes, when added to the absence of a formal institutional structure and leadership, gave many strikes an almost apocalyptic quality that encouraged violence and discouraged compromise. Viewed against this backdrop, the comparatively high incidence of strike activity at the turn of the century should probably be translated into an even higher relative level of worker militancy.[14] In addition, a greater proportion of strikes in the late nineteenth century involved wage claims and demands for a reduction of working hours than in later periods when union recognition and other aspects of employment became relatively more important.[15] In sum, compared with strike actions after 1900, a much higher percentage of strikes in the late nineteenth century involved direct confrontations between workers and employers over their respective shares of income from industrial production. Many of these were stark confrontations unmediated by demands for union recognition, by strategic or tactical direction by union leaders, by other issues unrelated to wages or hours, or by state intervention or arbitration.[16] Although walkouts were particularly common in the building construction and coal-mining sectors, strike activity was fairly widely distributed throughout the industrial economy between 1881 and 1905.[17] However, strikes were rare in the agricultural sector and nonexistent in government employment.[18]

The office of the U.S. Commissioner of Labor collected and published information concerning the location and size of individual strikes occurring between January 1881 and June 1894.[19] Unlike information on strikes in later reports, this data can be tabulated by county; this was done for the

[14]   Other factors that would lend support to this interpretation would be the creation of strike funds once unions were established and the possibility of state intervention on the side of the unions (there was plenty of state intervention in support of employers in the late nineteenth century).

[15]   Edwards, *Strikes in the United States*, pp. 36–37. For a summary tabular description of the causes or goals around which workers struck against their employers between 1881 and 1894, see U.S. Commissioner of Labor, *Tenth Annual Report: Strikes and Lockouts* (Washington, D.C.: GPO, 1896), p. 29.

[16]   For a discussion of the changing characteristics of strike demands between 1881 and 1900 with respect to some of these issues, see Edwards, *Strikes in the United States*, pp. 90–96.

[17]   Ibid., p. 97.   [18]   Ibid., p. 98.

[19]   Carroll D. Wright, perhaps the leading statistician in the United States during the last quarter of the nineteenth century, was the U.S. Commissioner of Labor between 1885 and 1905; he was thus in charge of the collection of strike data. While there were unavoidable problems in collecting and collating information on the scale and with the detail that was attempted, the data is considered to be relatively accurate. See, for example, Edwards, *Strikes in the United States*, pp. 302, 305–309. For an

roughly ten-year period from January 1885 to June 1894.[20] By dividing the total number of strikers in a county by the population in 1890, the relative prominence of strike activity as a form of claim-making can be compared in detail across the nation (see Table 4.2 and Map 4.1).

As was the case with almost every other feature of the national political economy in the late nineteenth century, strike activity varied quite a bit from one region to another.[21] In terms of strikers per 1,000 people employed in nonagricultural occupations, the leading state or territory was Oklahoma (including the Indian Territory). All but twenty-seven of the 6,774 strikers in the territory were coal miners, the most strike-prone major occupational group in the country. In fact, workers employed in producing either coal or coke comprised 42.7 percent of all strikers in the United States between 1881 and 1900.[22]

Within the manufacturing belt of the Northeast and Midwest, approximately three of every four counties were the site of at least some strike activity; outside the manufacturing belt, the ratio was more or less reversed – not a single strike occurred in more than three of every four counties.[23] The three great urban centers in terms of strike activity also lay in the manufacturing belt: Pittsburgh (Allegheny County), Chicago (Cook County), and New York (the borough of Manhattan). New Orleans was the only other major urban center with more than 100 strikers per thousand.

exploratory discussion and analysis of the comprehensiveness of this data that raises some doubts, see Gary L. Bailey, "The Commissioner of Labor's *Strikes & Lockouts*: A Cautionary Note," *Labor History* 32:3 (Summer 1991): 432–440.

[20] Almost all strikes could be assigned within their respective counties, although in some cases, such as the larger coal strikes, the data gave multicounty districts as the location. In those cases, the number given for strikers was prorated among the counties in the district according to their shares of the respective work force. The compilation of strike activity presented here was comprehensive except for the larger railroad strikes that spanned multistate regions of the nation. In such cases, very few in number of strikes but significant in terms of number of strikers, there was just no way to determine the county distribution of employment along, for example, a particular railroad company's right of way.

[21] Because strikes, as opposed to lockouts, involved unambiguous claim-making by workers against the management of a shop or factory, the following analysis is restricted to strikes. For the distinction between strikes and lockouts in theory and some of the ambiguities in practice, see U.S. Commissioner of Labor, *Third Annual Report: Strikes and Lockouts* (Washington, D.C.: GPO, 1888), pp. 9–11.

[22] Calculated from data in U.S. Commissioner of Labor, *Sixteenth Annual Report: Strikes and Lockouts* (Washington, D.C.: GPO, 1901), pp. 180–267, 282. In Florida, the extremely high strike rate was produced by workers in the tobacco industry, primarily cigar-makers in Key West, Tampa, and Jacksonville.

[23] Because nonagricultural employment can be a tiny fraction of the local work force, calculating strike activity in terms of strikers per 1,000 people in the general population gives a much better idea of the prominence of such claim-making in the local political economy. For that reason, this statistic is used later in this chapter to analyze electoral coalitions.

Table 4.2. *States Ranked by Strike Activity, 1881–1900*

State or territory	Total number of strikers	Strikers (per 1,000 population)	Strikers (per 1,000 nonagricultural employment)
Pennsylvania	1,253,865	238.5	769.1
New York	1,008,945	168.2	495.0
Illinois	636,148	166.3	689.9
Florida	54,281	138.7	754.3
Oklahoma Terr.	6,774	109.6	968.4
Colorado	44,082	106.9	286.9
Massachusetts	219,430	98.0	240.4
West Virginia	74,683	97.9	719.4
Ohio	314,788	85.7	360.8
New Jersey	109,229	75.6	217.5
Wyoming	4,558	75.1	202.2
Rhode Island	21,030	60.9	145.8
Louisiana	59,557	53.2	323.7
Montana	6,682	50.6	117.0
Maryland	50,265	48.2	166.5
Wisconsin	79,947	47.4	236.1
Minnesota	58,720	45.1	212.1
Connecticut	31,721	42.5	116.9
Indiana	90,809	41.4	226.0
Idaho	2,975	35.3	167.6
Missouri	92,100	34.4	186.4
Iowa	63,791	33.4	205.9
Michigan	68,039	32.5	144.2
Washington	11,046	31.6	91.1
Dist. of Col.	7,024	30.5	70.7
Delaware	4,759	28.2	103.2
Alabama	41,133	27.2	242.6
California	31,006	25.7	76.1
Kentucky	45,897	24.7	169.9
Maine	16,335	24.7	92.9
Tennessee	42,870	24.3	192.3
New Hampshire	9,099	24.2	74.3
New Mexico Terr.	3,657	23.8	119.7
Vermont	7,087	21.3	94.7
Oregon	6,653	21.2	83.5
Kansas	23,449	16.4	116.3
Nebraska	14,027	13.2	70.9
Georgia	24,100	13.1	95.5
Utah	2,673	12.9	57.4
North Dakota	1,996	10.9	83.6
Virginia	16,016	9.7	54.8

Table 4.2. *(cont.)*

State or territory	Total number of strikers	Strikers (per 1,000 population)	Strikers (per 1,000 nonagricultural employment)
Texas	18,419	8.2	69.4
Arkansas	8,399	7.4	91.4
South Dakota	1,203	3.7	26.4
South Carolina	2,817	2.4	24.6
Arizona Terr.	137	2.3	7.0
Mississippi	1,821	1.4	17.7
North Carolina	786	0.5	4.7
Nevada	21	0.5	1.2
United States	4,694,849	75.0	331.3

Note and sources: For the total number of strikers by state, see *Sixteenth Annual Report of the Commissioner of Labor, 1901: Strikes and Lockouts* (Washington, D.C.: GPO, 1901), pp. 346–351. Nonagricultural employment was calculated by subtracting those employed in "agricultural pursuits" from the total number employed in "all occupations." Bureau of the Census, *Occupations at the Twelfth Census: 1900* (Washington, D.C.: GPO, 1904), Table XXII, p. lxxxviii.

With the exception of the coal fields of eastern Kansas and the port of Galveston, Texas, strikes were almost nonexistent throughout the tier of Plains states stretching from Canada all the way to Mexico. The West presented a more varied pattern in which mining areas, such as the silver lodes of Shoshone County in northern Idaho, were often the site of relatively intense strike activity but were surrounded by agricultural districts in which no strikes occurred. As was true in the nation as a whole, coal mines were important in the West (Sweetwater County, in the southwest corner of Wyoming and home of the Rock Springs mines that served the Union Pacific Railroad, was a noteworthy example), but copper, silver, and gold mining also underlay the strike pattern. However, as Nevada's record illustrates, much mining was carried on in the West with few or no strikes.

Coal-related strikes underlay the numerous counties exhibiting high activity along the Appalachian spine extending from the northern Pennsylvania border to central Alabama. In many cases, coal mining in this mountain region was intimately associated with iron and steel production; the two most prominent cases in this respect were the industrial complexes surrounding Pittsburgh and Birmingham, Alabama. Two cities in Tennessee, Chattanooga and Knoxville, provide less important examples. In some ways, also, the high levels of strike activity in the northern iron ore regions of Michigan, Minnesota, and Wisconsin can be seen as an extension of the

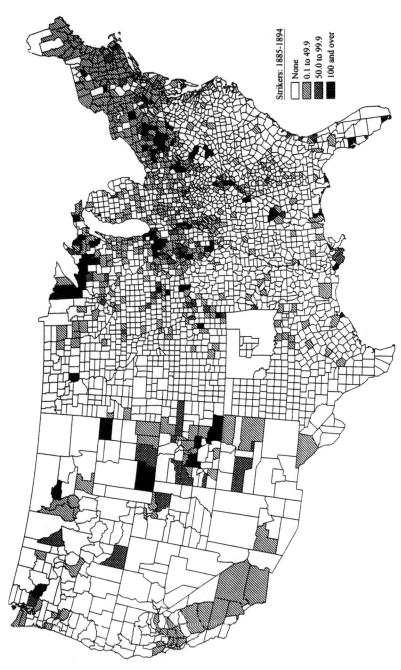

Map 4.1. Strike activity by county: number of strikers per 1,000 population, 1885–1894. *Source:* Calculated from population returns in *1890 Census* and strike data in *Strikes and Lockouts: Third Annual Report of the Commissioner of Labor* (Washington, D.C.: Government Printing Office, 1887), and *Strikes and Lockouts: Tenth Annual Report of the Commissioner of Labor,* vol. 1 (Washington, D.C.: Government Printing Office, 1896).

Strikers: 1885–1894

☐ None
▨ 0.1 to 49.9
▦ 50.0 to 99.9
■ 100 and over

iron and steel complexes to the South, particularly Chicago. The coal fields in south central Iowa, southern Illinois, and southeastern Ohio are also prominent in the national pattern. Outside the iron and coal districts of central Alabama and east Tennessee, strike activity in the South was largely concentrated along the coast with at least one strike occurring in every significant port (Norfolk, Wilmington, Charleston, Savannah, Jacksonville, Tampa, Appalachicola, Mobile, New Orleans, and Galveston). Otherwise very few strikes of any sort took place in this vast region. In terms of the overall national pattern, one broad feature is worthy of emphasis: Although strongly correlated with specific sectors within the industrial economy of the United States, relative strike activity was generally more diffuse than most other dimensions of economic development.[24] However, strikes were exceedingly rare in the southern cotton belt, site of a major transactional locus of another sort.

COMPETING CLAIMS ON THE COTTON CROP: THE CROP LIEN AND THE PLANTATION SYSTEM

The South was about as different a place from the manufacturing belt as it was possible for one nation to contain. There it was cotton that occupied the center of economic and social life, organizing institutions and politics in ways very different from the North and West. Five aspects of the South's political economy set the region apart from the remainder of the nation: dependence on cotton and agriculture generally, the export orientation of the economy, the extreme poverty of its people, the isolation of the labor and capital markets, and the distinctive character of social and political institutions. In many ways, cotton cultivation lay at the root of all of them.[25]

Cotton production was more thoroughly integrated in global markets than any other major sector of the American economy. The world price of the crop had been set at the Liverpool wharves for the better part of a

---

[24] See Chapter 2. For an alternative mapping of strike activity that displays the frequency of individual strikes by county between 1881 and 1894, see *Historical Atlas of the United States* (Washington, D.C.: National Geographic Society, 1988), p. 160. For the manufacturing belt between the same years, along with an extended discussion, see Carville Earle, *Geographical Inquiry and American Historical Problems* (Stanford, Calif.: Stanford University Press, 1992), chap. 9 (originally coauthored with Sari Bennett).

[25] On the dominant role of cotton production in the southern economy, see, for example, Michael Schwartz, *Radical Protest and Social Structure: The Southern Farmers' Alliance and Cotton Tenancy, 1880–1890* (1976; rpt., Chicago: University of Chicago Press, 1988), pp. 74–75. The isolation of the southern labor market is a major theme in Gavin Wright's *Old South, New South: Revolutions in the Southern Economy since the Civil War* (New York: Basic Books, 1986).

century and communicated from there across the Atlantic to points throughout the American cotton belt, everywhere that agents involved in marketing the harvest met the cultivators. In this respect, cotton production closely resembled the organization of grain production on the western plains. On the other hand, ownership of the means of production, particularly with respect to land, was generally separated from those who cultivated the crop. This separation of capital and labor transformed the major transactional locus of the cotton economy into an arrangement distantly resembling the cash nexus of the wage bargain on the eastern industrial shop floor. But while the eastern industrial shop floor was situated within a larger political economy abundantly supplied with capital and thoroughly integrated into the international financial system, the cotton South was comparatively isolated from both national and international capital markets. The transfer of ownership that accompanied the marketing of the cotton crop was, as a consequence, often transacted in exchanges that more closely resembled barter than cash, in part because the terms of interregional and international trade were so heavily set against the South that money left the cotton economy almost as rapidly as it was brought in to pay for the harvest.

Labor and capital came together to produce the cotton crop under three different systems: share-cropping agreements, rental contracts, and cultivation by owner-operators. Share-cropping agreements involved divisions of the harvest into shares between the landowner and the cultivator. The landowner provided the field and, depending on the agreement, the tools, horse or mule and feed, provisions for the sharecropper and his family, and/or seed necessary for producing the crop. In return, the cultivator (the sharecropper) promised to give over to the landowner a share of the harvest. The cost of provisions and, at times, other incidentals were deducted from the sharecropper's portion of the crop. Aside from these deductions, the division of shares between the farmer and the landowner was largely set by custom: one-half to landowner if he furnished the draft animal and tools, one-third if the sharecropper furnished the animal and tools. Because the most important terms in the contract were already set by custom and because the sharecropper was often illiterate, these contracts were usually not written down. The key to such agreements was the crop lien, a prior claim on the cotton harvest awarded to the planter or merchant who provided supplies and land to the sharecropper. Tenants who rented land paid cash for their acreage and provided their own supplies and tools.

Most cotton was produced on farms governed by either share-cropping or rental agreements, with all landless cotton farmers generally known as tenants.[26] Within the South, the percentage of farm families laboring under

---

[26] The high incidence of tenantry in southern agriculture was in some ways a direct result of the abolition of slavery. In effect, abolition forced the abandonment of collective cultivation of the soil; after a period of experimentation with alternative

tenantry arrangements was strongly correlated with the spatial topography of race, cotton cultivation, and soil type within the black belt.[27] Within that region, landholdings, often owned by descendants of former slave-owning planters, were large enough to support at least a few tenants and the yield from cotton was high enough to encourage specialization in that crop.

Throughout the South, then, tenantry was strongly and positively associated with the proportion of blacks in the local population, the value of farm land, the yield of cotton bales per acre cultivated, and, even when all these were taken into account, what had been the territorial limits of the antebellum plantation economy. As a distinct organizational form – an archetype – intensive cotton monoculture by farm operators who rented land for cash or cultivated for shares was solidly anchored within the traditional black belt of the antebellum South and its postwar extensions into Texas and Arkansas.[28] In the hill country and pine forests of the South, however, farmers were both less dependent on cotton as a primary cash crop and less reliant on merchants as provenders of credit. Although as impoverished as those in the black belt, producers in these regions participated in a local political economy that often emphasized, as claims on wealth, the terms under which cotton was marketed and transported over those arising from a struggle over control of the harvest (the primary preoccupation of the black belt). Because of their relative economic independence, up-country owner-operators were thus much more likely to pursue claims similar to demands

arrangements, contracts subsequently became the normal labor arrangement between producers and landlords. Because the best potential field hands strongly preferred the relative autonomy of tenantry to wage labor under the direct supervision of planters, comparatively few agricultural laborers were to be found. *1890 Census of Farms and Homes: Proprietorship and Indebtedness*, vol. 13 (Washington, D.C.: GPO, 1896), pp. 22–23. For a similar interpretation of the origins of the share-cropping system, see Roger L. Ransom and Richard Sutch, *One Kind of Freedom: The Economic Consequences of Emancipation* (New York: Cambridge University Press, 1977), pp. 57–67. Most scholars hold that the majority of blacks in the cotton belt worked cotton farms as sharecroppers, renters, or owner-operators. However, along the northern margins of the plantation economy many, if not a majority, occupied even lower rungs in the occupational hierarchy as common laborers. James R. Irwin, "Farmers and Laborers: A Note on Black Occupations in the Postbellum South," *Agricultural History* 64:1 (Winter 1990): 53–60.

[27] The terms "cotton belt" and "black belt" are used interchangeably. Both refer to the band of counties running in an arc through the middle of most of the former Confederate states from the Virginia-North Carolina border to east Texas. The first term emphasizes cotton production as a defining characteristic; the second stresses the high fertility of southern bottomlands, often darker in color than the soil types of adjoining regions. For a particularly careful statistical delineation of the southern cotton belt, based on the 1880 census returns, see Ransom and Sutch, *One Kind of Freedom*, pp. 273–283. On rare occasions the term "black belt" referred to regions in which the number of blacks outnumbered whites in the local population. For one such example, see William F. Switzler, *Report on the Internal Commerce of the United States, 1889* (Washington, D.C.: GPO, 1889), p. 36.

[28] *1890 Census of Farms and Homes*, pp. 23–24.

made by yeoman producers in the grain-producing West. In the black belt, sharecroppers and tenant farmers had much more pressing interests in eliminating the debt trap of the crop lien system.[29]

However, the expansion of the railroad network into the southern highlands in the postwar period remolded the economic and social structure of the uplands and piney woods. As the railroad pushed into the mountain fastness and the pine forest of the South, cotton followed close behind and, in their wake, the merchant and the crop lien.[30] The self-sufficient, classless society of the yeoman farmer was replaced by the cash nexus of the international cotton market, transacted over the counter at the nearest general store, with the subsequent eruption of all the class distinctions of advanced capitalist societies.[31] Most yeoman farmers fell into debt, mortgaging their land for supplies to tide them over until the next cotton harvest after poor crops, and many lost their land altogether, slipping into tenantry. In many ways this transformation of the uplands and pine woods brought those regions into closer alignment with the interests of the black belt in the national political economy. No longer isolated from the export-oriented operation of the cotton market and the international financial system's distribution of credit, the free trade and inflationary interests of the plantation system became the policy imperatives of the yeoman farmer as well.[32]

Thus, on the one hand, the expansion of cotton cultivation into the highlands tended to unify the South with respect to the structuring policies of the national political economy and, thus, as a force in national politics. On the other hand, cotton also created new class divisions within the internal politics of the region. White planters and merchants, the dominant class force in the black belt, stood at one end of the exchange that converted cotton into cash, while the white yeoman farmer stood at the other.[33] The resulting class division, separated by the transactional locus around which raged struggle over control of the cotton crop after harvest, was for the

---

[29] For broad descriptions of the emergence of merchant-centered sharecropping and the impact of lien crop laws, including the accumulation of land by merchants, see Steven Hahn, *The Roots of Southern Populism: Yeoman Farmers and the Transformation of the Georgia Upcountry, 1850–1890* (New York: Oxford University Press, 1983), pp. 173–203, and Schwartz, *Radical Protest and Social Structure*, pp. 22–39.

[30] In Hahn's words, "Over the short span of fifteen years [from 1865 to 1880], the Upcountry moved from the periphery into the vortex of the market economy." Hahn, *The Roots of Southern Populism*, pp. 10, 35–39, 142–143, 145, 148, 150–151, 158–159.

[31] Ibid., p. 27; Shawn Everett Kantor, "Razorbacks, Ticky Cows, and the Closing of the Georgia Open Range: The Dynamics of Institutional Change Uncovered," *Journal of Economic History* 51:4 (December 1991): 861–862.

[32] Hahn, *The Roots of Southern Populism*, p. 168.

[33] As claimants for competing portions of the cotton crop, merchants and planters also came into conflict with one another. See Jonathan Wiener, "Planter-Merchant Conflict in Reconstruction Alabama," *Past and Present* 68 (August 1975): 73–94.

white community a regional division as well, with the upland and piney woods in opposition to the dominant interests of the black belt.[34]

Within the central districts of the plantation system, this class struggle over control of the cotton crop turned on the politics of race, with largely black sharecroppers and cash tenants arrayed against white planters and merchants.[35] But here the positioning of black farmers as allies and dependents of the northern Republican party – imposed by the heritage of slavery and dynamics of the Civil War and Reconstruction – meant that class divisions within the black belt corresponded with national party alignments. While the politics of the South in the late nineteenth century was more fluid than this description suggests, the major alignments within the region tended to combine planters/merchants and white yeomen against black sharecroppers/renters with reference to national policies and to place planters/merchants against white yeomen and black sharecroppers/renters with regard to state and local policy disputes.[36] Thus differences over the structuring policies of the national political economy were embedded in a national party competition that tended to impose race cleavages in the South while state and local politics inscribed onto the statute books the outcome of class struggle over control of the cotton harvest.[37]

The Southern Farmers' Alliance became the organizational vehicle

[34] On the class organization of political contestation over the crop lien and other aspects of the postwar cotton economy, see Lacy K. Ford, "Rednecks and Merchants: Economic Development and Social Tensions in the South Carolina Upcountry, 1865–1900," *Journal of American History* 71:2 (September 1984): 294–318.

[35] At the turn of the century, the percentage of cotton farms operated by black landowners was but a fraction of the percentage operated by white owner-operators throughout the South. On the relative distribution of land ownership by race and personal wealth, see Ransom and Sutch, *One Kind of Freedom*, pp. 83–87. In Georgia, for example, almost 90 percent of all black-operated cotton farms were cultivated by tenants, but more than half of all white operators owned their farms. *1900 Census of Agriculture*, part II (Washington, D.C., 1902), pp. 408, 418–419.

[36] Without referring to race, Michael Schwartz has described this difference in perspective between the landless cultivator and the marginal yeoman. The tenant "related to the supply and selling systems almost exclusively through his or her merchant-landlord. He or she had little or no experience with marketing, selective buying, and transportation problems. His or her main concern centered around how to control, handle, or eliminate the merchant as a dominating influence. As a consequence, he or she was more easily organized to attack this visible enemy – the merchant or landlord – than the invisible enemy – the railroad. The yeoman, or former yeoman, on the other hand, had experiences with marketing and transport and perhaps with selective buying. Therefore, his or her vision of change included the possible reform of transport and merchandising systems." *Radical Protest and Social Structure*, pp. 186–187.

[37] In a different way, Michael Schwartz also distinguishes between the intrasectional alliances arrayed over control of the cotton crop and intersectional alliances deployed over the terms under which the South was integrated into the national political economy. See his *Radical Protest and Social Structure*, p. 13.

through which the largest mass of southern farmers attempted to redress their subordinate position within the cotton economy. Of all class insurgencies in the United States in the late nineteenth century, the Southern Alliance was the largest and carried the most potential for radical change in the form of economic production and patterning of income distribution.[38] In pursuit of these goals, the Alliance attempted to construct an entire array of economic and social institutions, free from the dominance of merchants and landowners, through which their communal and cooperative aspirations could be realized. As long as the Alliance thrived as a participatory organization, its central focus remained the reorganization of the economic system of the South through the establishment of an autonomous system for marketing the cotton harvest and for the cooperative purchasing of tools and supplies. The Alliance eschewed politics as long as these projects held out some hope of success. Their experiment ended in a failure that, in turn, propelled the explosive growth of the southern wing of the Populist party, itself a major exercise in radical insurgency but focused on capturing political institutions and turning them to lower-class purposes.

COMPETING CLAIMS ON THE MARKETING OF GRAIN:
INTERREGIONAL TRANSFER OF CREDIT AND
TRANSPORTATION OF THE HARVEST

In sharp contrast to the South's shackling ties to cotton cultivation, the factors engaged in northern and western grain production were radically free – almost too free – as they washed across the plains, first following westward the relatively humid conditions of the 1880s and then retreating before the comparatively arid climate of the 1890s. During the expansion between 1880 and 1890, the federal government sold enough public land to almost cover California twice over. Of this land, an area equal to three Missouris was put to the plow – over half located in the Great Plains.[39] This rapid settlement of the western fringes of the Great Plains and the fertile valleys and hills of the Far West greatly expanded national production of wheat, corn, and oats; their comparative advantage in grain production, in turn, was a major factor driving down cultivation of these crops all along the eastern seaboard and sharply limiting growth in other parts of the United States east of the Mississippi River.[40]

---

[38] See, for example, ibid., p. ix, 217; Lawrence Goodwyn, *Democratic Promise: The Populist Moment in America* (New York: Oxford University Press, 1976), pp. xi–xii, xviii–xix, 87–88, 100–113, 690 n. 33.

[39] Benjamin Horace Hibbard, *A History of the Public Land Policies* (Madison: University of Wisconsin Press, 1965), p. 541.

[40] Between 1879 and 1889, acreage in the Dakotas devoted to wheat cultivation multiplied almost twenty-fold, rising from 265,000 to 4,969,000. In the states of Illinois, Iowa, and Wisconsin, wheat acreage was more than halved, dropping from 8,216,000 to 3,571,000 acres. *1890 Census of Agriculture* (Washington, D.C.: GPO,

From a political perspective, the most important of the grains was wheat. Over the last quarter of the nineteenth century, the return from wheat cultivation in the United States first narrowed and then turned into, on the average, a loss. The harvest was unpredictable. In poor years, the crop might be small but the price high. In good years, the reverse might be true. And the harvest was not uniform across the United States, so that one region might do well at the expense of another during a poor year. Finally, one of the most important factors governing the price of wheat was the demand from Europe which, in turn, was largely determined by the quality of the crop there and economic conditions generally. Still, even given the highly uncertain climatic and market conditions under which wheat cultivation was undertaken, producers could calculate an average expected return.

The diverging destinies and interests of the eastern and western portions of the great corn and wheat belts of the North were shaped by several factors. Perhaps the most important, because it underlay most of the others, was the relative integration of eastern agricultural areas into the urban, industrial economy. Because they were close to comparatively wealthy urban markets, farmers in the East could choose to produce any number of a wide variety of crops and perishable products, such as eggs, milk, and vegetables.[41] Such diversification tended to limit the otherwise unavoidable risk that attended market fluctuations and the variability of the harvest. In addition, although switching between crops or other products could be expensive and time-consuming, eastern farmers could at least entertain the possibility; for other regions, the consolidation of the national market forced producers to increasingly specialize in those commodities in which their regions enjoyed a comparative advantage. Furthermore, because of the relative proximity of small factories and lumbering operations in the northern forests, eastern farmers could often supplement their farm income by working for wages in the off-season. Eastern farms were also usually older and better endowed with capital improvements such as farm structures and drainage systems for low-lying areas. Because their operations were well established, mortgages tended to be smaller relative to their overall capitalization, and even more important, the rate of interest on these mortgages was much lower than in the West. Finally, eastern farmers paid a smaller proportion of the market value of their crop to intermediaries generally and to the railroads in particular because the relative density of rural settlement, relative proximity to urban markets, and intense compe-

1895), p. 14. For a description of the impact of western settlement on wheat cultivation in Wisconsin, see John Giffin Thompson, *The Rise and Decline of the Wheat Growing Industry in Wisconsin*, Bulletin of the University of Wisconsin, no. 292 (Madison, 1909), pp. 71–102.

[41]   For a description of the organization of urban markets for farm produce in the United States, see *Report of the Industrial Commission: Distribution of Farm Products*, vol. 6 (Washington, D.C.: GPO, 1901), pp. 338–379.

tition between the railroads all combined to reduce such charges to a minimum.[42]

Western farms were at a disadvantage in all respects: Climatic conditions (e.g., relative aridity) tended to limit the range of commodities that the farmer could choose to plant; those same conditions also tended to introduce higher variability in the quantity and quality of the harvest, thus increasing risk; farm operations were both undercapitalized and burdened with heavy mortgages on which high rates of interest were imposed; farmers themselves tended to be isolated in rural communities with few, if any, opportunities for off-season employment; and railroad service was often monopolized by one carrier which imposed extraordinary charges on transport, above and beyond the heavier rates imposed by the longer distance to market.[43]

By 1885 or so, conditions significantly worsened along the outer fringes of the Great Plains where yields were even lower, mortgage rates were far higher, climatic conditions were more erratic, and transportation costs levied a much heavier toll. As the years passed, wheat farming became ever more precarious as an occupation throughout the nation, but nowhere were conditions worse than in the western portions of the Dakotas, Nebraska, and Kansas.

Like the southern planter, the grain producer hired labor to cultivate crops, but most of this labor was temporary or seasonal in character. For that reason, the wage bargain had few of the highly organized characteristics of that in the South. Few laws governed the wage bargain between agricultural laborers and their employers in the North and fewer still attempted to control the movement or contractual obligations of the field hand. Instead, the transactional locus around which redistributive claims arose involved the exchange of capital and marketing services between the grain producer, on the one side, and the railroads

---

[42] For example, a bushel of corn sold on the wholesale market for 39 cents on July 25, 1900. In Hutchinson, Kansas, some 670 miles by rail to the west of Chicago, a producer selling a bushel on that day would have received 25.4 cents; the other 13.6 cents would have been consumed in defraying the costs of distribution. Receiving about 31 cents a bushel, a producer in Media, Illinois, only some 190 miles to the west of Chicago, would have done much better; in this case, distribution charges consumed only 8 cents of the market price. *Industrial Commission: Distribution of Farm Products*, vol. 6, p. 9. Compared with southern cotton producers, western grain growers generally paid a much higher proportion of the value of their crop to the railroad. For freight charges on the movement of cotton to market, see pp. 179–185.

[43] For per-acre costs of wheat production in the various states and territories in 1893, based on separate surveys of 30,000 "leading farmers" and 4,000 "experts," see *Report of the Secretary of Agriculture for 1893*, 53d Congr., 2d sess., House of Representatives, Ex. Doc. 1, Pt. 6 (Washington, D.C.: GPO, 1894), pp. 515, 517. While these figures are not adjusted for yield, they still give some idea of the comparative costs of labor and capital inputs in the various regions of the nation.

and finance capitalists, on the other. In its most general terms, this transaction exchanged agricultural commodities for either cash or other goods, the terms of the exchange determining the respective income shares of the producer, on the one hand, and the mediating agents that marketed the crop in the national and international economy, on the other.

The archetypal transaction thus placed homestead cultivators of grains on the western plains on the one side, and financial agents marketing farm mortgages, the operators of grain elevators, and railroad officials on the other. The physical site of such exchanges was usually the community bank, the nearest grain elevator, or the local railroad station. But while these institutions were located in the producer's immediate neighborhood, they were often owned and controlled by capital holders in distant regions of the nation or even abroad. As a result, the western grain producer faced the agents of nonresident investors and corporations in a way quite unlike the situation on the industrial shop floor in the East or on a southern plantation. Because of the comparatively clear and direct involvement of these agents in their respective roles and the ubiquitous presence of such exchanges on the western plains, this transactional locus was very visible, in both the marketplace and politics.[44] While grain producers often pressed their claims through state legislatures, the interstate character of their transactions allowed these claims to move into national politics with exceptional ease and frequency.

In the beginning, the grain producer sought relief through state regulation of the railroads. In the late 1870s, this agrarian movement in the states north and west of Chicago was called "grangerism," after the National Grange that organized the farmer producers; the farmers themselves were labeled "grangers," and the rail lines subject to their attention were spoken of as the "granger roads." Throughout the last quarter of the nineteenth century the western extensions of the northern rail network in which granger agitation was most active were much less competitive than the eastern portions, and as a result, freight rates often carried a monopolistic surcharge.[45] Whenever grain prices dropped significantly, the proportion of

---

[44] As one farm editor put it, "there are three great crops raised in Nebraska. One is a crop of corn, one a crop of freight rates, and one a crop of interest. One is produced by farmers who by sweat and toil farm the land. The other two are produced by men who sit in their offices and behind their bank counters and farm the farmers." *Farmers' Alliance*, August 23, 1890, quoted in John D. Hicks, *The Populist Revolt: A History of the Farmers' Alliance and the People's Party* (1931; rpt., Lincoln: University of Nebraska Press, 1961), p. 83.

[45] In fact, the freight differential between transport in the East and in the West increased during the last quarter of the nineteenth century, conferring a gradually increasing advantage to eastern producers over the period. *Industrial Commission: Distribution of Farm Products*, vol. 6, pp. 7–8. However, rates generally declined everywhere in the late nineteenth century and, for that reason, probably made the railroads a grad-

the price in central markets, such as those in Chicago and New York, paid over to the railroads in order to move the crop tended to rise. In fact, very large crops tended to both reduce the market price (through superabundance) and raise railroad revenue (through increased freight traffic), thus associating low grain prices with higher railroad profits. For that reason, the producer did not have to look very far or very long to find a likely avenue for relief through reduction of railroad rates.[46]

Closely associated with the railroad but seldom controlled by the same interests was the grain elevator.[47] Grain elevators were managed by local proprietors who operated on their own account, agents for wholesale merchants who controlled the elevators as part of their grain-marketing operations, or cooperatives and associations owned by the grain producers themselves. Of the three types, the last was but a minor factor, while collusion between the first two was an ever-present possibility.[48] In 1901, for example, the Northern Pacific Railroad reported that at least one grain elevator was located at 156 of its country stations in the states of Minnesota and North Dakota. At sixty-six of these locations – over 40 percent – a local grain dealer or one of the major grain-buying firms in major cities to the east controlled the only elevator at the station. At another ten stations, there were two elevators, one controlled by a local grain dealer and the other by one of the major firms. In most other cases, some combination of local dealers and/or major firms controlled the two or three elevators at the site. Elevators controlled by farmers' associations, the only competitor to the local grain dealer or line firms, made an appearance at only eight stations, just over 5 percent of the total.[49] Almost all

ually less attractive target for redistributive claims. At least the *Commercial and Financial Chronicle* thought declining rate schedules should have had this effect. March 28, 1891.

[46] For example, the *Commercial and Financial Chronicle* cited prevailing low grain prices as a factor increasing the probability of "hostile granger legislation" and, thus, decreasing the investment attractiveness of the "Granger roads." December 13, 1884. For similar analysis of the investment prospects of the western railroads, including instances in which the journal viewed higher grain prices as alleviating hostility to the railroads, also see December 20, 1884; January 31, 1885; February 25, 1888; June 16, 1888; November 1, 8, 15, 1890.

[47] Although California and other parts of the Far West produced substantial quantities of grain, elevators were not used in the distribution of the harvest. Instead, the grain was moved by sack through warehouses. *Industrial Commission: Distribution of Farm Products*, vol. 6, pp. 96, 101.

[48] Elevators maintained by farmers' associations, however, were significant factors in Minnesota and the Dakotas. Ibid., pp. 8–9, 50–54, 60–70. The commission did not take a consistent position on the possibility of collusion. For a discussion of the farmer's grievances against the elevators, see Hicks, *Populist Revolt*, pp. 74–78.

[49] Calculated from data in *Industrial Commission: Distribution of Farm Products*, vol. 6, pp. 454–459. Warehouses were not included in these calculations. Conditions in Minnesota may have been more competitive; the secretary of the State Warehouse and Railroad Commission reported that there "is hardly a station in Minnesota now

grain was sold by producers before shipment to central markets and most of these transactions occurred either at the elevator or, less frequently, at a rail siding where the grain was loaded directly into a boxcar. Local purchases of grain were made on the basis of market quotations in Liverpool, New York, and Chicago, which were communicated at least daily over the telegraph.[50]

Both the railroads and the grain elevators were thoroughly enmeshed in contentious litigation in the federal courts over the extent of interstate commerce (and thus congressional authority over their operation) and the protection of the due process clause of the Fourteenth Amendment (and thus the quality of rate regulation by government with respect to the profitability of the roads).[51] For the grain producer in the Plains and West, the transactional locus at which the crop was sold was thus implicated in both state and federal regulation; in fact, grain producers often could not be certain which of these levels of government would become the one in which the federal courts would allow effective regulation. While the cotton producer was sometimes in a similar position with respect to the railroad network, the primary transactional locus for the cotton harvest was almost always beyond the reach of federal law because the crop was exchanged within the crossroads country store, under oral agreements made with either a planter or merchant with the terms structured by custom and tradition.

Deprivation drove much of the farming population of both the South and West into, first, the Farmers' Alliance and, subsequently, the Populist Party. The two regions shared a deep and enduring hostility to both the railroads and the banks. But in other respects their insurgencies differed, sometimes in important ways. For the Plains and West, insurgency was episodic, coinciding with drought and low commodity prices. The class enemies of the grain producer were viewed as distant, even alien financiers and corporate executives whose agents met the farmer at the bank window, railroad freight depot, or grain elevator. But the Plains and West were still entrained in the dynamics of northern industrialization in a way that made insurgency, for all of its heated rhetoric and radical legislation, more or less a temporary complaint concerning the terms within which the region would develop. With the return of higher commodity prices, the states of the Plains and West competed with one another with respect to their financial conservatism and economic promise under conservative developmental principles.

The South, on the other hand, was always depressed. Economic development was not the routine expectation of the communities that depended

but what has a farmers' cooperative elevator or some independent elevator of that character." *Report of the Industrial Commission: Transportation*, vol. 9 (Washington, D.C.: GPO, 1901), p. 370.

[50] *Industrial Commission: Distribution of Farm Products*, vol. 6, pp. 9, 56.
[51] See Chapter 5.

on cotton, rice, and tobacco cultivation. While the railroad companies were largely owned by investors in the North who, for that reason, could be viewed as alien exploiters, most sharecroppers and small farmers must have found it difficult to picture eastern financiers in the same way. For the fact was that little northern capital found its way into the South. In the Plains and West, many if not most of the thousands of national banks sprinkled throughout the region were originally capitalized, at least in part, with eastern money. In the South, there were both far fewer banks and less eastern participation in their capitalization.

Where the grain producer embraced the system while attempting to redress inequities within the market economy, the cotton producer often rejected the system itself, opposing protective tariffs, the national bank system, and military pensions as a northern-inspired design for redistributing wealth between the nation's great regions. Within the grinding poverty which accompanied this subordinate position in the national political economy, the class enemies of the small cotton farmer and sharecropper were the large planter and country merchant. These were neighbors, close to home and well known throughout the community. For all these reasons, political insurgency in the South was chronic and persistent when focused on the policy systems that underwrote northern industrialization; southern Democratic platforms routinely included planks that rejected these policy systems with a frequency that conferred a sheen of regional orthodoxy on what conservative northerners felt were benighted doctrines. On the other hand, the class antagonists for the cotton cultivator were frequently their own neighbors. When insurgent demands were focused on the transactional locus through which the cotton crop was moved to market, the result was a much more internally divided local politics than was the case in the Plains and West. Although complicated in deep and enduring ways by race, political radicalism in the South was in fact much more divisive, violent, enduring, and potentially transforming than anything that emerged on the western plains or mountains. To survive, the planter and merchant attacked, even more fervently than before, the policy systems supporting national industrialization while disfranchising blacks and poor whites in order to undercut the electoral basis of local insurgency.

THE TRANSACTIONAL LOCI OF THE GREAT ARCHETYPAL REGIONS

Each of these transactional loci, whether they involved the payroll office just off the factory shop floor, the purchasing agent at the western grain elevator, or the ledger displayed on the countertop of a southern country store, became the central and defining element in the way labor made claims on wealth within the major regions of the United States. When these claims moved into the political arena, each of these transactional loci became the pivot of intraregional class politics. In turn, local class politics helped shape the ways in which electorates pursued regional advantage within the national political economy. Such advantage, by redressing the terms of trade between the region and the rest of the nation, could expand the pie to be shared between the region's classes. The nation was, in effect, divided into distinct regional class structures. Each of them, in turn, focused both on local contestation over the division of wealth *within* the dominant sector and on national contestation over the direction and size of income flows *between* the regions.

In spatial terms, the conflicting interests arrayed at each of the three great transactional loci arose within the varying characteristics of industrial East, the grain-producing Plains and West, and the cotton South. To give a clear picture of how these types of conflicts were distributed within the nation and thus how pervasively they entered into political coalitions and competition, we can give each of them a set of statistical referents. Each set of referents defines, through its relationship with the other, an intersection of characteristics particularly relevant to one of the three transactional loci. For competition between capital and labor over industrial profits, for example, the coincidence of high levels of per capita value-added in manufacturing and low interest rates identify those localities in which workplace conflict would be expected to be the major form of redistributive claims made on wealth. These localities were both well integrated into the national and international credit systems, as evidenced by their comparatively low cost of credit, and deeply committed to industrial manufacturing within the interregional division of labor. For both reasons, the political economy of these areas presented extremely rich targets, in the form of corporate profits and abundant local capital, for those advocating a redistribution of wealth to the working class (see Chart 4.1).

In the South, the overwhelming dominance of the cotton crop and the organization of cultivation within the plantation system would theoretically lead us to expect that the intensity of claims on wealth would be shaped by both high levels of cotton production and high levels of share-cropping and tenancy. Counties scoring high on both per capita cotton production and nonowner cultivation arrayed large numbers of landless farmers against planters and merchants within the crop lien system. With respect to commodity grain production, we should expect that the intensity of claims on wealth, of owner-producers on the providers of credit and transportation facilities, can be traced through high interest rates and per capita production of grains. In these counties, large numbers of grain cultivators were arrayed against the agents of eastern capital and corporate wealth.

When displayed on a national map, the counties associated with each of these three types of claims on wealth clump together in very distinct regional concentrations (see Map 4.2). The Northeast is dominated by those

Chart 4.1. *Defining Criteria for Archetypal Claims on Wealth by Major Region*

I. Industrial shop floor: Claims by workers on corporate profits
Expected intensity of claim-making within category by locality*:
  High: $90 and over in per capita value-added in manufacturing and interest rates on mortgages at 5.49 percent or lower;
  Medium: $65 and over in per capita value-added in manufacturing and interest rates on mortgages at 5.74 percent or lower;
  Low: $40 and over in per capita value-added in manufacturing and interest rates on mortgages at 5.99 percent or lower;
  Bordering: Counties contain some manufacturing and a majority of the population in the bordering counties resides in counties falling in the above three categories.

II. Cotton plantation: Claims by sharecroppers/tenants on planters/merchants
Expected intensity of claim-making within category by locality*:
  High: 70 percent or more of farm families do not own the land they work and 400 or more pounds of cotton per capita (0.84 bales) is produced in the county;
  Medium: 50 percent or more of farm families do not own the land they work and 250 or more pounds of cotton per capita (0.53 bales) is produced in the county;
  Low: 30 percent or more of farm families do not own the land they work and 100 or more pounds of cotton per capita (0.21 bales) is produced in the county;
  Bordering: Counties produce some cotton and a majority of the population in the bordering counties resides in counties falling in the above three categories.

III. Commodity grain production: Claims by settler grain-producing farmers on the suppliers of credit and transportation facilities
Expected intensity of claim-making within category by locality*:
  High: Interest rates on mortgages at 8 percent or higher and 270 or more bushels of cereal grain per capita is produced in the county;
  Medium: Interest rates on mortgages at 7.75 percent or higher and 210 or more bushels of cereal grain per capita is produced in the county;
  Low: Interest rates on mortgages at 7.50 percent or higher and 150 or more bushels of cereal grain per capita is produced in the county;
  Bordering: Counties produce some cereal grain and a majority of the population in the bordering counties resides in counties falling in the above three categories.

* All localities (counties) were placed in the highest category warranted by their characteristics.

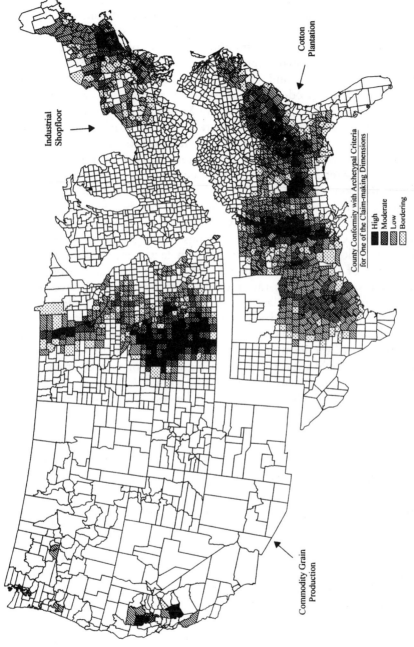

Map 4.2. Economic bases of archetypal claims on wealth: cotton, grains, and manufacturing. *Note*: See text for statistical criteria.

characteristics that should give rise to the clearest expression of shop-floor conflict in political competition: a combination of high densities of indigenous capital and value-added in manufacturing. The southern portion of the map more or less reflects the traditional confines of the cotton belt, partially redefined by the equal emphasis placed on landlessness. Both of these patterns in the Northeast and South are quite compact. This is not the case for commodity grain production. Some parts of the Pacific Coast states and eastern portions of Iowa, Minnesota, and Missouri are separated from the western plains, the central core of where we should expect claim-making over market transactions with capital and transportation.

None of the counties in these three great regions overlapped; given the statistical criteria used in their construction, this is not surprising. In addition, the boundaries for each of the regions were separated by wide distances in almost all cases; the exception was one isolated grain county in southeastern Missouri that was very close to the northern edge of the cotton region. Otherwise, the three regions were quite spatially distinct. More than a dozen states and territories, in fact, contained no counties meeting any of the statistical criteria defining these regions. Almost the entire expanse beginning at the northern boundary of the United States along the Great Lakes and arcing around to the southeast ending along Chesapeake Bay was devoid of such counties. This does not mean that claim-making along one or more of the transaction dimensions was not an important part of the local political economy in these regions, but it does mean that we should expect the organizing impact of such claim-making, as a contributing factor in the emergence of political platforms, policy choices, and coalition formation, should be less significant than in the respective central regions.

CLASS CONFLICT, REGIONAL REDISTRIBUTION OF WEALTH, AND NATIONAL PARTY COMPETITION

All of these conflicts within the local political economies of the great American regions influenced the competitive strategies of mainstream and insurgent party organizations. But as they entered into the calculations of national political actors and organizations, these archetypal claims became situated within a larger national political economy in which southern separatism and the great policy systems underwriting northern industrialization loomed as far larger issues. These issues, in effect, deflected local class claims into very different conflicts over the interregional distribution of wealth.

In the northeastern and midwestern manufacturing belt, conflict in the political economy centered on major aspects of the contractual relationship between labor and capital in the industrial sector: the wage bargain, working conditions, and the recognition of labor unions as negotiating agents for workers. Each of these carried more or less direct implications for the division of industrial profits into shares allocated to labor and to capital. While northern capitalists and workers agreed on the broad outlines of interregional redistribution (from the agrarian South and West to the industrializing Northeast and Midwest), the sharing of that appropriated wealth between capital and labor produced intense intraregional class divisions, with the Republicans slightly tilting toward capital and the Democrats toward labor. However, because interregional redistribution was the dominant force shaping the political system, most of the energy generated by contests over intraregional income shares did not find an outlet in party competition and remained confined in largely apolitical strike activity. Conflict between labor and capital thus remained a potent but unrealized source of stress on the broader alignments that characterized and drove major party competition during the late nineteenth century. In fact, explaining the relative passivity of labor on the national stage during this period is a major challenge. The explanation offered here emphasizes the coinciding interests of northern labor and capital within the larger national political economy and the success of the Republican party, as the major agent for northern industrialization, in realizing this potential consensus as a route to political power.

Throughout the southern black belt cotton production comprised half or more of all wealth generated by the local economy. In this region, the major site of conflict within the political economy was not the factory floor, as it was in the nation's manufacturing belt, but the cotton plantation. On the plantation, conflict was centered between black sharecroppers and tenant farmers, on the one side, and plantation owners and merchants, on the other. Most conflict over income shares focused on the legal enforcement of the lien against the cotton crop under which the sharecropper or tenant was lent supplies during cultivation, along with competition for control of the crop during the crucial transition from field to market. In both respects, control of the cotton crop became the major organizing factor in class-based competition in the southern regional economy. Somewhat similar conditions characterized other commodity crops, such as tobacco, rice, and sugar.

Race played an important role in the cotton belt, pitting black sharecroppers and tenants against white planters and merchants. This race alignment in the plantation economy, however, overlay the persisting cleavage between Union loyalists and Confederate separatists. Although southern blacks were tied to the Republicans through the party's role as a guarantor of civil and political rights (albeit an inadequate one), the inevitable result of their alliance with northern Republicans was that they were seen as the pliable allies of those who directed northern exploitation of the South. In addition, small landowning whites, who might have otherwise allied with black sharecroppers, had equally powerful interests, arising out of a common antipathy toward Republican-led development, that converged upon those of the plantation elite. Yet another barrier to black-poor white cooperation grew out of the economic dependence of blacks on white landowners and merchants; blacks were often intimidated by threats of economic retaliation into supporting candidates backed by the Bourbon elite. Thus, left alone, blacks overwhelmingly supported the Republican party and, where intimidation was successful, provided votes for upper-class whites. In neither case were they likely to be viewed by lower-class whites as possible allies. At the national level, all of these groups shared a common set of interests hostile to northern industrialization, interests that thus further discouraged the expression of southern class conflict in national politics.

In the grain-producing plains and mountain regions, single-family homesteads dominated the local economy. In this, the third of the great regions, the conflict-shaping transactions were those that linked these homestead producers to national and international markets. Of all these transactions, those involving access to eastern or foreign capital and the sale of agricultural commodities into the stream of interregional and international commerce were the most important. In the former case, the conditions under which local agents provided imported credit, for example, interest rates and the terms attending mortgage contracts, were the focus of conflict between debtors and creditors, farmers and financiers. In the latter case, the transportation of goods to market, necessarily involving at some stage the sale of these goods by producers to wholesale distributors, became the pivot of contention. Since the vast bulk of all transportation was by rail and since the railroad network in the West, as was true of the nation as a whole, was largely owned and controlled by eastern capital, the railroads too were locally operated by agents of outside capital. Thus, in both cases, the locus of conflict involved, on the one side, a comparatively large number of owner-producers and, on the other, much less numerous agents of eastern capital, either liquid (in the form of credit facilities) or fixed (in the form of railroad equipment, rolling stock, grain elevators, and stockyards). Thus, unlike the manufacturing and cotton belts, the central alignment within the western political economy paralleled divisions between that region and the East, between homestead owner-producers and the hired agents of outside capital.

This alignment, given the comparatively large number of homestead owner-producers, regularly produced overwhelming political majorities favoring local interests in the form of cheap and easy terms for capital and low-cost, heavily regulated marketing facilities. Several factors, however, either deflected or reduced political hostility to outside capital. In the first place, capital investment would not flow into or remain in regions where local regulation reduced returns below competitive opportunities in other areas. This potential market reaction constrained the passage of regulatory measures that sought to redress the interregional advantages the East appeared to enjoy.

An additional factor alleviating the political consequences of these opposing interests was the dependence of western producers on prosperous conditions in eastern manufacturing centers. Unlike the South, which produced an industrial raw material that largely sought markets abroad, the West sold foodstuffs to the laboring classes in eastern cities. The prosperity of these classes, under the Republican industrial program, thus strengthened the market for western produce to a much greater extent than was the case for southern cotton. In addition, cross-cutting elements of the Republican program, such as pension payments to Union veterans, land grants for railroad construction, and other developmental subsidies (particularly those involving water courses and harbors), served to reinforce the party coalition that had successfully prosecuted the Civil War in earlier years. For all these reasons, then, the central locus of conflict within the western political economy was more likely to move into national politics than the more localized conflicts involving income shares on the industrial shop floor or cotton plantation. And when this western conflict over marketing relations and arrangements did move into national politics, it tended to align the region with the South against the eastern manufacturing belt. But for most of the period between the end of Reconstruction and the turn of the century, western hostility to the agents of eastern capital was somewhat paradoxically embedded in a localized politics that coincided with widespread support for the national Republican party.

OVERVIEW OF INSURGENT MOVEMENTS IN NATIONAL POLITICS: 1877–1900

Between the end of Reconstruction and the turn of century, several political insurgencies threatened the prevailing pattern of capital accumulation underpinning American industrialization. The first of these was the Greenback party, which was as weak in electoral strength, at least in presidential elections, as it was strong in ideology. Peaking in the congressional elections of 1878 and the presidential contest in 1880, the Greenback party proposed a comprehensive reorganization of the national political economy that focused, in the first instance, on replacing the international gold standard with paper money issued by the federal government. But the Greenback platform was much more extensive and ambitious than this one plank and served as a wellspring for much of insurgent ideology long after the party had disappeared.[52] However, because its prowess at the polls was relatively slight, the Greenback movement is examined below in

---

[52] For a good survey of Greenback doctrine and its influence in American politics, see Gretchen Ritter, *Goldbugs and Greenbacks: The Antimonopoly Tradition and the Politics of Finance in America, 1865–1896* (New York: Cambridge University Press, 1997).

this chapter, along with the Socialist presidential campaign in 1912. These two campaigns, one in the form of prologue and the other as epilogue, are rather modest bookends to the main thrusts of political insurgency in this period: the Populist campaign in 1892 and the Bryan Democratic crusade in 1896.

As insurgent threats to the prevailing pattern of wealth accumulation and investment, these two campaigns represented different alternatives. The Populist party was the offspring of a genuine social movement, the Farmers' Alliance, one of the largest and most extensive grass-roots organizations ever to appear on the American stage. The demands made in national and state Populist platforms originated in both the movement's first-hand experience with the national political economy and ideological predispositions inherited from the Greenbackers. The Populist platform was, for these reasons, both rather specific in the remedies that the party sought for the prevailing inequitable distribution of wealth and rather broad with respect to the descriptive context into which these remedies were placed. But the Populists, even though their roots in large regions of the nation were relatively deep, were still much stronger on policy articulation than they were on vote-gathering. Their movement forcefully proposed an alternative trajectory for American development, but its realization depended on a union with the industrial worker that proved utterly barren when put to the test.

Much broader in terms of votes but somewhat shallower in ideology was the climactic Bryan campaign.[53] Although remnants of the Populist and Greenback visions of an alternative commonwealth decorate the 1896 Democratic platform, the primary issue in the subsequent campaign was the single demand for free coinage of silver. Although many scholars have both described the silver plank as simplistic and heaped ridicule on Bryan as its advocate, by 1896 free coinage meant much more than the substitution of one metal for another as the basis of the nation's monetary standard.[54] For much of the nation, opposition to the conservative orthodoxy represented by the international gold standard was an act of self-affirmation, implying strong and general support for reforms that would have alleviated the harsh political economy of rapid industrialization. In the case of the Bryanite Democrats, many of these other reforms were spelled out in the platform or in the party's legislative record.

But the differences between the Populists and Democrats were real. On the one hand, the Populists drew their strength from a grass-roots move-

---

[53] On the importance of the 1896 campaign as political threat to the dominant position of industrial elites, see Walter Dean Burnham, "The Changing Shape of the American Political Universe," *American Political Science Review* 59 (1965): 24–26.

[54] For a more favorable view of Bryan, see Elizabeth Sanders, *Roots of Reform: Farmers, Workers, and the American State, 1877–1917* (Chicago: University of Chicago Press, 1999), pp. 139–147.

ment – a movement that had tested much of its vision in cooperative organizations and had recruited members through argument and persuasion.
Ideological commitment and programmatic purity were in many ways the
party's organizational hallmarks. Except among elected party officials,
pragmatism was in rather short supply. On the other hand, the Democrats
were an established, major professional party long on pragmatism and
rather compromised by history with respect to ideological purity. Free
coinage, sometimes intermixed with greenback proposals, had coursed
through the party's veins for almost twenty years. Silver had also been
a weapon as the southern and eastern wings struggled for control of
the national party – an elite war waged, until 1896, almost exclusively in
Congress.

When the opportunity presented itself in 1896, free silver elements within
the Democratic party captured the presidential nomination for Bryan
because they believed (1) that his nomination would divest the party of
the more hidebound northeastern conservatives that had hitherto played
a role in party affairs much larger than their following warranted; (2)
that the addition of the Populist regiments to the Democratic army would
prove decisive in national competition with the Republicans, even allowing
for an exodus of gold Democrats; and (3) that much of the Populist platform, stripped of reform planks that threatened the southern plantation
elite, was a natural complement to the traditional Democratic emphasis
on redressing the terms of trade between agriculture and industry through
tariff reduction, local and state regulation of commerce, and a general
reduction in the central government's role in the national political economy.
By making an endorsement of Bryan the litmus test for party fealty, silverites consolidated their revolution in the highest councils of the party,
installing throughout the Northeast Irish Catholics (who cared nothing
for either gold or silver) in places vacated by Protestant goldbugs. Although
Bryan lost the 1896 election, there was to be no return to financial
orthodoxy.[55] In fact, the rapidly expanding national role of northeastern
Irish Catholics paved the way for the party's move toward anti-imperialism
in 1900 and, in later years, a more labor-oriented national program.[56]

---

[55] Free silver thus simultaneously was a demand that shifted leadership of the national
party toward the South and West and, within the Northeast, strengthened lower-class
ethnic groups in their struggle over control of the state and municipal party machinery. Paul Kleppner, *Continuity and Change in Electoral Politics, 1893–1928* (Westport, Conn.: Greenwood, 1987), pp. 107–108.

[56] For obvious reasons, Irish Catholics equated both the gold standard and imperialism with Great Britain, which still held Ireland in thralldom. In one sense, this equation had a rather simplistic quality: The mere suggestion of a parallel produced Irish
opposition. In another sense, the connection was more subtle. To the extent that such
a monetary regime could be directed by any nation, the international gold standard
was dominated by Great Britain and thus gave the English a pivotal role in the world
economy. Although one of the most important nations adhering to gold, the United
States still played second fiddle to the British. With respect to imperialist expansion,

In terms of economic development, these two insurgencies proposed different programs, both of them positioned as alternatives to the Republican system of protectionism, financial orthodoxy, and a consolidated national market. The Populists were silent on the tariff, opposed to the gold standard, and advocated government intervention in the marketplace at all levels of government. Silence on the tariff was largely tactical; forced to choose, a Populist party in power at the federal level would almost certainly have lowered duties. Abandonment of the gold standard would have severed the intimate ties between the London and New York financial markets and would have, in all probability, encouraged capital flight on a scale that would have hampered industrial expansion. However, government intervention, through a variety of policies, would have increased the availability of credit throughout the South and West. Some of these policies and others as well would have favorably altered the terms of trade between industry and agriculture from the perspective of small homesteads on the frontier and in the cotton belt. For all these reasons, the Populist vision outlined a cooperative commonwealth that would have privileged economic stability over growth, small producer independence over economies of scale, government intervention over laissez-faire, and a redistribution of wealth toward lower classes generally.

The traditional Democratic platform emphasized tariff reduction, home rule, and strict limitations on federal authority. As a developmental vision, traditional Democratic policies traced a trajectory that would have altered the prevailing terms of trade between agriculture and industry in much the same way as the Populists proposed. However, the Democratic party often opposed proposals for a class redistribution of wealth, particularly in the South. At the national level, Democratic platforms tacitly endorsed the gold standard as a concession to the eastern wing of the party while Democrats in Congress consistently provided heavy majorities for its abandonment. Compared with the Republican vision, the Democratic alternative would have reduced or eliminated much of the redistributive regional impact of federal policies such as tariff protection and military pensions while allowing the states to regulate more of the operations of national corporations. By restricting to some degree the consolidation of the national marketplace and reducing the ongoing redistribution of wealth underwriting industrialization, the Democratic vision would have lowered the overall rate of industrial expansion and enhanced incomes generated by the cotton economy. From this perspective, the addition of free silver in 1896 would have further

American policy was even more dependent on British favor – a hostile Great Britain could, through control of the oceans, deny the United States access to potential colonies. For Irish Catholics who wished that American policy would favor Irish independence, the first condition had to be regaining freedom of action for the United States with respect to Great Britain, freedom of action that both the gold standard and imperialism significantly comprised.

reduced the rate of industrial expansion; whether or not this reduction would have been accompanied by a increase in capital availability in the southern and western regions of the nation depends on the extent to which a Bryan administration would have adopted other features of the Populist vision. The Populists, through proposals such as the subtreasury plan, combined access to capital with wealth redistribution, favoring the independent small producer while providing a local source of credit. The subtreasury plan was most viable in the South, as both an ideological principle rooted in economic experience and a political claim on voter allegiance; however, southern Democrats were clearly reluctant to endorse this extension of the silver program. In the West, however, members of the party were much more open to such elaborations. In sum, there seems to be little doubt that the cooperative commonwealth proposed by the Populists would have been, under a Bryan administration, somewhat leaner. The emphasis would have been on redressing the prevailing redistribution of wealth between the regions; remedies for the inequitable distribution of wealth between classes within the regions and policies encouraging credit availability in the periphery would have been less important.

By addressing the class claims of industrial labor, Bryan also targeted workers in the manufacturing belt, thus exploiting class conflict in the East while attempting to unify all classes in the periphery.[57] On the whole, however, industrial workers shifted heavily toward McKinley and the Republican system. In fact, two aspects of American national politics stand out throughout this period: the almost complete absence of anything approaching a worker's party and the indifference with which industrial workers greeted coalition proposals put forward by agrarian insurgents. Dooming agrarian insurgency in national politics, the industrial worker thus became one of the mainstays of financial orthodoxy, tariff protection, and market consolidation. Though other policies also shaped labor's position in the northern party system, the tariff and gold standard policies of the Republican party drew many workers into its ranks and, in the end, effectively removed conflict over the industrial wage bargain from national politics even while strike activity rose to, by some accounts, the highest levels ever recorded in cross-national comparisons of industrialization. Throughout the industrial North, mass suffrage and violent claims on wealth in the workplace coexisted with broad support for the national Republican party – the developmental agent for capital accumulation and corporate consolidation. The result was a democratic political system in which the most powerful claims on wealth assumed an interregional character, arising out of conflicting claims through which commodity agriculture outside the manufacturing belt attempted to alter the developmental program driving industrialization. The deflection of claim-making by indus-

[57] Sanders, *Roots of Reform*, pp. 84, 143–146.

trial workers into relatively apolitical strike activity, away from national politics, was thus a major reason why robust industrialization and an open democratic polity coexisted in the American experience.

The purpose of this chapter is to outline the voting patterns that link these competing visions of economic development to the electoral coalitions supporting each of the major parties and their insurgent challengers. The analysis begins with an examination of the electoral alignments in the two most important contests, the Populist campaign in 1892 and Bryan's Democratic campaign in 1896. Both are analyzed through the lens of late nineteenth-century economic development, including strike activity (as a proxy for conflict between labor and capital). A subsequent section then compares the electoral patterns generated by the 1892 and 1896 elections with those of the 1880 Greenback and 1912 Socialist campaigns. Appearing both before and after the most powerful insurgencies of the period, the latter confirm the persistent strength of regional conflict over economic development in explaining the compatibility of democracy and development in the United States.

THE POPULIST CHALLENGE IN 1892

In 1892 the Republicans renominated Benjamin Harrison for president; the Democrats named, for the third time, Grover Cleveland. Because the platforms written by the major parties also resembled the declarations made four years earlier, the 1892 campaign was more or less a reprise of the 1888 contest. Although the earlier campaign had also centered on the tariff, the major parties now placed even more emphasis on protection. The Democrats had just blamed the worsening economy on the McKinley Tariff during the 1890 midterm elections and come away with a huge gain in the House of Representatives (86 seats) and a modest one in the Senate (two). But Republican losses had been even heavier than Democratic gains. Eight Populist congressmen, each of them replacing a Republican, entered the House in the new Fifty-second Congress; in the Senate the Populists took away two seats from the Republicans. For the next twelve years, until the Fifty-eighth Congress met in 1903, Populists sat in both chambers.

In Congress, the Populists were never a major force. Although they voted on legislation, the agendas set by the Democrats and Republicans in Washington rarely addressed the central themes of the Populist party. Marching to an entirely different tune, these Populists ignored the war over the tariff waged by the Republican and Democratic parties. Carrying their vision of a cooperative commonwealth of small producers into Congress, they were outsiders, silently feared and publicly ridiculed by their major party colleagues. Their strength lay in the country, in the states of the Plains and Mountain West at first and then the South. While they never controlled the

Table 4.3. *Summary of Level of Trade Area Development and
the 1892 Presidential Election Returns*

Trade area level	Percentage of all votes cast for				Vote total
	Democrat	Republican	Populist	Other	
5 (highest)	49.0	47.3	1.0	2.7	3,300,910
4 (high)	43.8	47.0	6.5	2.7	1,407,858
3 (middle high)	38.7	49.0	8.5	3.8	1,092,269
2 (middle low)	38.3	47.4	11.2	3.0	2,024,234
1 (low)	41.6	44.4	11.8	2.1	1,937,354
0 (lowest)	57.3	25.7	16.1	0.9	2,294,946

Sources: For definition of levels of development see Chapter 2. Election returns
for 1892 were taken from W. Dean Burnham, *Presidential Ballots: 1836–1892*
(Baltimore: Johns Hopkins University Press, 1955).

governor's chair and both chambers of a legislature at the same time in any
state, the Populists were for a decade or more the major agenda-setting
party organization in Kansas, Nebraska, North Carolina, Texas, and, for
shorter periods, elsewhere.

As an autonomous party, the Populists presented a candidate for president only once, in 1892. The party's nominee, James Weaver of Iowa, had
been the Greenback party candidate some twelve years before and had also
served a number of terms in the House of Representatives as a Greenbacker.
Running in every state but Delaware, Weaver drew more than a million
votes, almost 9 percent of all those cast, and carried five states (Colorado,
Idaho, Kansas, Nevada, and North Dakota). The Populist electoral vote
stood at 22 against Cleveland's 277 and Harrison's 145.[58]

The Populist Vote and National Economic Development

Viewed from the broadest perspective, support for Weaver in 1892 generally decreased with the relative development of the nation's various regions
(see Table 4.3). When the votes cast in the nation's eight most advanced
trade areas are aggregated, for example, approximately one in every 100

[58] In North Dakota, the Republicans managed to carry one of the three electors and
one of the two Populists subsequently defected to Cleveland. As finally cast in the
electoral college, then, North Dakota delivered one vote apiece to Weaver, Harrison,
and Cleveland. In Oregon, the Democrats and Populists fused on one elector who
subsequently gained more votes than any other. However, the Republicans won the
other three electors and Oregon's vote, as finally cast, thus stood at one for Weaver
and three for Harrison.

voters supported the Populist candidate in 1892. At the other end of the developmental spectrum, voters in the nation's least advanced trade areas supported the Populists with a frequency of one in every six. In between these two extremes, the pattern was quite regular with respect to Populist support, more or less gradually decreasing with relative development. The patterns for major party support were quite different. Cleveland's strength was concentrated at the very top and bottom of the development spectrum, particularly the bottom. The Democrats were weaker than the Republicans in all four developmental levels between these two extremes. Republican support, on the other hand, was remarkably steady through all of the top five developmental levels, collapsing only at the bottom. Support for parties other than these three was insignificant at every level.

This pattern is remarkable in several respects. First, the inverse relationship between relative development and electoral support for the Populist party is quite strong despite the fact that the degree of abstraction in these categories is very high. Of course, many other factors, some of them quite local in character, influenced support for the Populist party in 1892. While most had some connection to the political and economic processes associated with industrialization, the way in which their impact was felt in this election was often oblique to this general pattern, increasing Populist support in some regions and retarding the party in others. For example, fusion arrangements with the Democrats in many of the states of the Plains and Mountain West dramatically increased Populist electoral strength out of all proportion to what the party might have displayed had it been forced to run independently. While the attractiveness of fusion with the Populists depended, in part, on the third party's popularity within the state and thus could be traced back to the relevance of the Populist platform to local interests in the development of the national political economy, the Democratic party's decision to fuse was both very lumpy (in that the party could either choose to fuse or not with a dramatic impact on the Populist vote one way or another) and dependent on other factors, such as the historic relative strength of the Democratic party vis-à-vis the Republicans within that state.[59]

The other remarkable feature of the very general display in Table 4.3 is the comparative insensitivity of the major party vote to relative regional development. At the highest level of development, the Democrats ran ahead of the Republicans primarily on the strength of their showing in the New York trade area. New York City occupied an anomalous position in the national political economy that predisposed the city and much of the trade

---

[59] For an excellent discussion of the purely political factors that influenced relative Populist strength on western plains, see Jeffrey Ostler, *Prairie Populism: The Fate of Agrarian Radicalism in Kansas, Nebraska, and Iowa, 1880–1892* (Topeka: University Press of Kansas, 1993).

area to free trade and thus the Democratic party.[60] In 1892, this predisposition was reinforced by Cleveland's former service as governor of New York and his hard-money policies during his first term. At the least advanced end of the developmental spectrum, the Democratic party was overwhelmingly dominant, largely due to its strength throughout the cotton belt.

These broad patterns, however, gloss over wide variation within each of the developmental categories (see Table 4.4). At the highest level, for example, the Democrats enjoyed a 15 percent margin over the Republicans in the New York trade area and a 10 percent deficit in the Buffalo region. Among the "middle high" trade areas, Populist percentages ranged from over 50 to less than 1 percent. Clearly, the aggregation of such widely varying election outcomes into a single display fails to explain much of the national voting pattern in 1892. However, the fundamental purpose is not to explain the Populist or Bryanite voting patterns with precision. Such a quest would inevitably rely on different factors within the separate regions and states, and some of these factors, such as changes in rainfall in Kansas, would be difficult to generalize to other parts of the nation. Instead, the purpose of the analysis is to interpret the relationship between electoral support for these two insurgencies and national economic development in such a way as to provide a plausible explanation for the absence of a working-class party in national politics, the failure of attempts to establish a coalition between agrarian radicals and industrial workers, and major party indifference to claims on wealth accumulation in the industrial sector during this period. From this perspective, the analysis has begun with the most general connection between electoral support for the Populist party and relative economic development. This relationship is disaggregated in several ways.

As described in Chapter 2, the index of relative economic development is composed of five factors: value-added in manufacturing, patent activity, interest rates, wealth, and literacy. If the nation's trade areas are arrayed according to their relative performance on each of these individual factors (as in Table 4.5), the resulting patterns give a much more complete and detailed picture of the 1892 vote. In each case, for example, the highest Democratic percentage and the lowest Republican percentage fell in the bottom category. Other than this, the major party vote was only loosely, if at all, related to the five dimensions of the index. The closest relationship is between support for the Democratic party and increasing rates of illiteracy in the adult male population; otherwise, the major party patterns are weak. In strong contrast to the distribution of the major party vote, the Populist party vote usually displays a much stronger relationship with the

---

[60] For a discussion of New York City's anomalous place in the national political economy, see Chapter 2.

Table 4.4. *The Popular Vote in the 1892 Election:*
Economic Development and Party Strength

Trade area level of development	Percentage of all votes cast for				
	Democrat	Republican	Populist	Other	Votes cast
5 (highest)					
Baltimore	53.5	44.1	0.2	2.2	259,951
Boston	44.6	52.3	1.0	2.1	603,806
Buffalo	41.0	51.0	2.8	5.1	278,886
Cincinnati	50.0	46.1	1.8	2.1	274,105
Cleveland	47.2	47.1	2.2	3.4	273,990
Hartford	48.3	48.2	0.6	3.0	170,182
New York	55.9	40.7	0.6	2.8	882,127
Philadelphia	45.6	52.1	0.2	2.1	557,863
4 (high)					
Chicago	49.2	46.8	1.3	2.8	580,352
Pittsburgh	44.4	51.2	1.5	2.9	420,478
San Francisco	35.5	42.9	19.2	2.5	407,028
3 (middle high)					
Albany	42.8	52.3	0.8	4.0	308,591
Denver	2.0	44.1	53.3	0.6	133,601
Los Angeles	34.9	44.4	15.1	5.6	53,504
Milwaukee	48.8	45.5	2.1	3.6	360,410
Syracuse	39.6	53.6	1.6	5.1	236,163
2 (middle low)					
Des Moines	44.6	49.5	4.6	1.3	353,314
Detroit	46.6	46.9	2.9	3.7	287,375
Grand Rapids	39.0	49.1	6.6	5.3	190,261
Indianapolis	46.3	47.0	4.0	2.7	404,912
Minneapolis	32.2	46.9	16.8	4.0	468,752
Omaha	22.4	45.7	29.9	2.1	319,620
1 (low)					
Columbus	48.1	47.1	2.0	2.8	404,114
Kansas City	22.1	44.6	32.1	1.2	588,764
Louisville	51.3	42.3	4.7	1.7	208,590
St. Louis	51.9	42.1	3.9	2.0	534,653
Scranton	48.4	46.8	0.5	4.2	201,233
0 (lowest)					
Atlanta	55.1	24.5	19.8	0.6	428,171
Charleston	67.3	21.0	11.6	0.1	166,597
Evansville	47.7	41.0	9.5	1.8	129,898
Memphis	61.5	18.1	19.2	1.3	484,596
Nashville	54.8	23.6	20.1	1.5	214,526
New Orleans	62.3	17.8	18.9	1.1	378,142
Richmond	51.6	38.8	9.0	0.6	493,016

Notes and sources: In Louisiana, the Republicans and Populists fielded a fusion ticket that split the state's eight electors equally. That ticket's vote was apportioned between the two parties, half to each. For sources, see Table 4.3.

Table 4.5. *1892 Vote by Trade Area and Development Dimension*

1892 vote by trade area and value-added in manufacturing

Trade area	Democrat	Republican	Populist	Other	Vote total
Highest (above $145)	49.6	47.3	0.6	2.5	2,213,978
High ($74–$145)	45.4	47.0	4.5	3.1	2,382,903
Middle high ($43–$74)	46.4	47.4	2.7	3.5	2,220,573
Middle low ($25–$43)	40.4	46.7	10.3	2.6	2,026,787
Low ($17.81–$25)	37.1	40.5	21.3	0.1	1,697,895
Lowest (below $17.81)	58.9	20.6	19.4	1.0	1,505,435

1892 vote by trade area and patent activity

Trade area	Democrat	Republican	Populist	Other	Vote total
Highest (above 6.00)	50.5	46.0	0.9	2.6	2,236,467
High (3.88–6.00)	42.1	48.8	5.5	3.5	2,285,070
Middle high (2.90–3.88)	44.5	47.7	5.1	2.8	2,162,048
Middle low (2.10–2.90)	37.9	45.5	14.3	2.3	2,146,716
Low (0.90–2.10)	50.3	32.9	15.1	1.8	1,924,960
Lowest (below 0.90)	55.3	29.3	14.7	0.7	1,302,310

1892 vote by trade area and interest rate

Trade area	Democrat	Republican	Populist	Other	Vote total
Highest (5.65–5.29)	49.6	47.3	0.6	2.5	2,213,978
High (6.56–5.66)	45.7	49.0	1.7	3.6	2,187,882
Middle high (6.93–6.57)	49.6	44.7	3.4	2.3	2,111,997
Middle low (7.50–6.94)	47.8	43.6	6.1	2.5	2,114,939
Low (8.50–7.51)	32.6	40.6	24.8	1.9	1,805,307
Lowest (9.83–8.51)	50.0	27.5	21.0	1.5	1,623,468

1892 vote by trade area and wealth

Trade area	Democrat	Republican	Populist	Other	Vote total
Highest (850–1,433)	45.9	43.2	8.3	2.7	2,056,612
High (700–849)	43.6	49.5	4.3	2.7	2,164,362
Middle high (626–699)	42.9	47.8	6.3	3.0	2,228,593
Middle low (551–625)	40.0	47.0	10.4	2.5	2,308,860
Low (301–550)	53.5	33.8	10.4	2.3	1,996,834
Lowest (199–300)	55.3	29.3	14.7	0.7	1,302,310

Table 4.5. *(cont.)*

1892 vote by trade area and illiteracy

Trade area	Democrat	Republican	Populist	Other	Vote total
Highest (2.9–4.5)	39.9	47.8	9.1	3.2	2,465,175
High (4.6–6.3)	37.9	46.1	13.3	2.8	2,284,652
Middle high (6.4–7.1)	49.8	47.1	0.7	2.3	2,317,901
Middle low (7.2–9.1)	44.4	47.3	5.6	2.7	1,971,619
Low (9.2–25.0)	54.1	33.0	10.8	2.1	1,552,298
Lowest (25.1–30.8)	57.2	27.2	15.0	0.6	1,465,926

Note and sources: Each category groups together trade areas in such a way that the population of each one is as close as possible to one-sixth of the national population. For sources, see Table 4.3.

various developmental dimensions. This pattern is most pronounced with respect to interest rates and only slightly weaker with respect to value-added in manufacturing. The relationship is still clear in the case of patent activity but is only moderately visible with respect to wealth. Populist support displayed no pattern with respect to literacy.

These patterns are significant for several reasons. First, given the prominence of the tariff as an issue dividing the protectionist Republicans and free-trade Democrats, the absence of a relationship between value-added in manufacturing and support for the major parties is somewhat surprising. As described in other chapters, the tariff was the central part of an elaborate policy system that extended, through coalition arrangements, support for protectionism into many rural areas outside the manufacturing belt. The wool schedule, for example, transformed many otherwise disinterested farmers into fervent protectionists. The federal pension rolls did the same thing for Union veterans. Where there were very few factories, very few sheep, and very few Union veterans – in other words, the cotton belt – Republican strength collapsed and the Democrats surged. In addition, the tariff had a very different impact on national politics than it did at the local level. Within the national political economy, the tariff redistributed income between the industrial core and agricultural periphery. (Extensions of the policy complex surrounding the tariff were, in fact, intended to ameliorate this impact with respect to the Plains and Mountain West without, of course, doing anything at all for the South.) At the local level, the wealth thus redistributed into the industrial sector was the focus of competing claims by capital and labor. While capital could safely and consistently ally with the Republicans at both levels, labor was divided, drawn toward the Republicans with respect to the tariff in national policy and toward the Democrats in terms of claim-making on the industrial shop floor, where the states held sway. The votes of industrial workers were thus a major contributing factor in the relative competitiveness of the Democratic party within the manufacturing belt prior to 1896.

The second reason these patterns are remarkable is more straightforward. The Populist party was a political movement that persistently proposed a redress of the terms of trade between the nation's industrial and agricultural sectors and thus between the regions. Because the major federal policies affecting the terms of trade between the regions were the gold standard and the protective tariff, the high concentration of the party's electoral support in trade areas of high interest rates and low levels of manufacturing activity should come as no surprise.[61] As Paul Kleppner has contended, the western branch of the Populist movement was a revolt by a "semicolonial area of the country . . . against its urban-industrial imperium, the Northeast and eastern Midwest."[62] For the South, which had been in revolt one way or another for some time, the Populist movement simply restated long-standing regional demands with respect to the national political economy.

The 1892 Presidential Election and Strike Activity

Almost all strikes in the late nineteenth century involved claims by industrial workers against their employers.[63] In fact, such strikes were the major form of lower-class claims on the accumulation of wealth in the industrial sector. In the following analysis, the incidence of claim-making, in the form of strike participation between 1885 and 1894, is connected to support for the two major parties and the Populists in 1892. This analysis demonstrates the extent to which shop-floor contention was disconnected from worker alignments in national politics.

[61] There is a bit of a paradox in this explanation. The tariff played a large role in the way the major parties contested the 1892 election, and yet the election returns reveal only a weak relationship between value-added in manufacturing and support for the major parties. The Populists were silent on the tariff but their vote is highly and inversely correlated with industrial activity. The paradox is much more apparent than real, however; the Populists were silent because of the tariff's extensions into military pensions and the wool schedule, not because the party favored accumulation of wealth in the industrial sector. The problem for the party was that both sheep and Union veterans were concentrated in the Plains and Mountain West – regions where the Populists were otherwise quite naturally favored.

[62] *The Third Electoral System, 1853–1892: Parties, Voters, and Political Cultures* (Chapel Hill: University of North Carolina Press, 1979), p. 303. In similar terms, C. Vann Woodward described the coalition backing the Populist program as "a combination of exploited colonies against the exploiting empire." *Origins of the New South, 1877–1913* (Baton Rouge: Louisiana State University Press, 1967), p. 253. For a review of the literature on Populism that elaborates this and other themes, see William F. Holmes, "Populism: In Search of Context," *Agricultural History* 64:4 (Fall 1990): 26–58.

[63] See the first part of this chapter for a discussion of the types of issues and geographical pattern associated with strike activity in this period.

The Populists presented the most favorable program for the pursuit of claims on wealth by industrial workers in the 1892 election. None of the Democratic or Republican platforms, for example, could match the rhetorical blandishments of the Populist plank in the Minnesota state platform.[64] In Idaho, where a violent dispute wracked the silver mines in northern mountain valleys, the state Populist platform condemned "the action of the authorities both state and federal, in relation to the trouble now existing in Shoshone county between the mine owners and miners, and . . . we extend our hearty sympathy to the miners union in their unequal struggle."[65] In opposition, Republican state platforms usually emphasized the benefits of the protective tariff while the Democrats made somewhat vague arguments for economic stability.

If workers had focused on federal policies toward strikes and the claims associated with them (such as recognition of unions, the legitimation of sec-

[64] The Minnesota plank is quoted in Chapter 3 and can also be found in *Appleton's Annual Cyclopaedia of 1892* (New York: D. Appleton, 1893), p. 470. While the national platform contained several planks that openly appealed to what were at the time the most important political priorities of the labor movement, the program was still generally oriented toward farming interests in the nation's periphery. But even where, as in Minnesota, the state party adopted a platform that more than evenly balanced the respective concerns of labor and farmers, industrial workers still turned away from the Populists in droves. See, for example, Kleppner, *Third Electoral System*, pp. 283–285. In Montana, however, both the party's support for labor reforms and electoral support reflected the dominant influence of silver miners within the Populist party. When fusion accompanied Bryan's candidacy in 1896, the Populists brought miners into coalition with regular Democrats, including many of Montana's mine owners. The relative absence of labor strife in the state, unlike conditions in Idaho and Colorado, made this fusion arrangement rather placid. Thomas A. Clinch, *Urban Populism and Free Silver in Montana* (Missoula: University of Montana Press, 1970), pp. 50–51, 64–65, 122–123, 141, 170. Where the Populists came to power, they frequently followed through on their platform commitments by enacting laws that protected workers in their wage transactions with employers. For Kansas, see *Appleton's Annual Cyclopaedia of 1893* (New York: D. Appleton, 1894), p. 422; Peter H. Argersinger, "Populists in Power: Public Policy and Legislative Behavior," *Journal of Interdisciplinary History* 18:1 (Summer 1987): 97 n. 24. For a general overview of Populist policy-making, see Peter Argersinger, "Ideology and Behavior: Legislative Politics and Western Populism," *Agricultural History* 58 (January 1984): 43–58. For farmer sympathy and support for those columns of Coxey's Army that traversed the Plains and Mountain states, see *Appleton's Annual Cyclopaedia of 1894* (New York: D. Appleton, 1895), p. 380; William Joseph Gaboury, *Dissension in the Rockies: A History of Idaho Populism* (New York: Garland, 1988), pp. 103–110; Clinch, *Urban Populism and Free Silver in Montana*, pp. 88, 106–112; Hicks, *Populist Revolt*, pp. 323–324; Thomas W. Riddle, *The Old Radicalism: John R. Rogers and the Populist Movement in Washington* (New York: Garland, 1991), pp. 146–152. For a brief account of Populist support for striking miners in Alabama, see Sheldon Hackney, *Populism to Progressivism in Alabama* (Princeton, N.J.: Princeton University Press, 1969), pp. 61–62.

[65] Gaboury, *Dissension in the Rockies*, p. 40.

ondary boycotts, and the right to picket), there should have been at least some relationship between strike activity in the nation's counties and support for the Populist party. There was none. In fact, at the most general level, those regions of the country evidencing the highest levels of strike activity during this period were precisely the worst areas for the Populist party (see Table 4.6). For example, the Populist party drew almost 16 percent of the total vote in those counties in which no strikes were recorded between 1885 and 1894. The percentage drops by almost two thirds, to 5.5 percent, in those counties in which strike activity was very light. In the three highest categories of strike activity, the Populists drew shares of the total vote of a little over 3 percent – approximately one third of their national proportion.

When the nation's counties are regrouped with respect to their relative level of development, the pattern again demonstrates that Populist support was strongly related to economic advancement. Within each range of strike activity, from no strikes to a frequency of over 100 per thousand population, the Populist percentage almost invariably declined with increasing economic development. However, within each developmental category, strike frequency had almost no impact on Populist support. While the great majority of industrial workers were concentrated within the advanced regions of the manufacturing belt, most counties in the periphery had at least a few industrial workers (e.g., employed on railroads and in mines or lumber camps) and thus could, potentially at least, be the location of a strike. But very few strikes were recorded in the periphery. As a result, over one million votes were cast in counties which both scored zero on the developmental scale and recorded no strike activity (see the bottom portion of Table 4.6). By comparison, only 28,000 votes were cast in counties scoring zero and also recording very high levels of strike activity. The opposite pattern prevailed at the other end of the developmental scale. Only 2,000 votes were cast in the most advanced counties which also recorded no strikes during this period. But well over 600,000 were cast in those counties with very high levels of strike activity. Thus the summary pattern (the far right column of the table) connecting increasing Populist support with decreasing strike activity was entirely due to the weighting of votes cast within each developmental level.

The Populist percentages are so small for the most advanced regions of the nation that it can safely be presumed that the vast majority of all industrial workers in those counties opposed the party. However, while Populist support was substantial in the least advanced counties, it cannot be inferred that industrial workers were voting for the party with much higher frequency than in the advanced industrial core.[66] While worker support for

---

[66] There is, however, substantial evidence that the alliance between the Knights of Labor and the Populists was much stronger in the western periphery than anywhere else in the nation. In Nebraska, for example, some 12 percent of the Populist leadership

Table 4.6. *Strike Activity, Relative Economic Development, the 1892 Presidential Vote*

1892 Populist vote (%)

Strike activity	Developmental level						Total
	0	1	2	3	4	5	
No strikes	18.8	14.2	17.2	12.9	4.0	0.1	15.9
Low	9.5	8.1	6.0	5.5	2.7	1.1	5.5
Medium low	12.7	6.8	7.3	6.1	2.0	0.9	3.0
Medium high	24.3	8.3	7.0	4.0	8.8	0.7	3.6
High	9.2	9.9	6.2	3.2	2.2	0.8	3.1

1892 Democratic vote (%)

Strike activity	Developmental level						Total
	0	1	2	3	4	5	
No strikes	55.8	42.3	34.9	38.1	46.1	43.4	44.1
Low	55.0	47.3	41.5	43.8	45.0	46.2	44.8
Medium low	54.2	48.3	39.6	44.6	49.7	51.1	48.7
Medium high	43.6	46.6	42.8	44.4	37.8	49.3	46.3
High	49.4	41.3	46.9	45.9	42.9	55.6	50.8

1892 Republican vote (%)

Strike activity	Developmental level						Total
	0	1	2	3	4	5	
No strikes	24.7	41.4	45.3	45.5	45.8	53.1	38.1
Low	34.0	41.9	49.4	47.1	48.7	48.7	46.5
Medium low	32.5	42.1	50.0	46.0	46.3	45.8	45.9
Medium high	31.3	42.4	46.3	48.6	50.9	48.5	48.0
High	39.5	46.7	43.7	47.3	51.6	41.5	43.5

1892 presidential returns (total vote in thousands)

Strike activity	Developmental level						Total
	0	1	2	3	4	5	
No strikes	1,220	1,836	963	398	40	2	4,460
Low	183	620	922	847	644	220	3,436
Medium low	26	82	135	190	351	666	1,450
Medium high	7	118	155	83	216	817	1,396
High	28	141	185	95	77	679	1,204

Note: Strike activity categories are defined as follows: "Low" includes all counties in which the number of strikers between 1885 and 1894 was between 0.1 and 24.9 per 1,000 population in 1890; "medium low" includes all those between 25.0 and 49.9; "medium high" includes all those between 50.0 and 99.9; and "high" includes all those at or above 100.0. Within each category the votes of the counties were aggregated and it was upon these totals that the percentages were computed. See Chapter Two for a description of relative levels of economic development.

the party may have risen slightly with decreasing development, the vast bulk of the increase almost certainly arose out of the changing composition of the local political economy (e.g., increasing grain and cotton production which implied many more farmer-voters in those counties).[67] On the whole, then, the rejection of the Populist party by the industrial worker appears to have been both uniform throughout the nation, with the exception of western mining regions and small towns in the periphery, and particularly emphatic in regions where strikes were frequent.[68]

One interpretation of worker indifference and, often, hostility to the Populist party posits a basic contradiction between farmer and labor interests within the national economy. From this perspective, workers demanded higher wages, which could only push up the cost of goods that farmers bought in the marketplace. Farmers, on the other hand, wanted higher prices for their foodstuffs and fibers, such as cotton and wool; these higher prices could only increase the worker's expenditures on food and clothing.[69] The end result was a zero-sum game in which one side's gains could be balanced only by the other's losses. While such an interpretation is consistent with worker support for the Republican party as the primary proponent of a redistribution of wealth from the agrarian periphery to the industrial core, it tends to underestimate the impact of federal policy on income in the industrial sector and thus to undervalue the worker's positive commitment to the Republican developmental program. Simply put, workers not only rejected Populist appeals because they feared that their own income shares would be reduced; they also were strongly attracted to a developmental program that further increased the share of national wealth accruing to the industrial sector. When competing with industrial corporations for this wealth, workers both engaged in strike activity and, at the local level particularly, supported the Democratic party.[70] Faced with a choice between

belonged to the Knights of Labor. None of the Republican or Democratic leaders were associated with the Knights. Robert W. Cherny, *Populism, Progressivism, and the Transformation of Nebraska Politics, 1885–1915* (Lincoln: University of Nebraska Press, 1981), p. 69.

[67] In some instances, however, wage earners in the small towns and cities of the periphery responded very favorably to the party's appeals. Roscoe C. Martin, for example, concluded that it was an "indisputable" fact that most Texas workers voted Populist. *The People's Party in Texas: A Study in Third Party Politics* (1933; rpt., Austin: University of Texas Press, 1970), p. 68.

[68] After describing the Populist program in the 1892 campaign in more sympathetic terms than the contempt he assigned to Republican and Democratic promises, Samuel Gompers nonetheless declared the AFL neutral in the contest. See his "Organized Labor in the Campaign," reprinted in George B. Tindall, ed., *A Populist Reader* (New York: Harper Torchbooks, 1966), pp. 185–191.

[69] Melvyn Dubofsky, *We Shall Be All: A History of the Industrial Workers of the World* (New York: Quadrangle, 1969), pp. 13–14.

[70] Thus, Homestead, Pennsylvania, the site of one of the most violent strikes in American history during the summer of 1892, reported that over half of the voters in this heavily working-class community cast their ballots for Cleveland (543, or

open declarations of support for labor by the Populist party and the redistribution of wealth into the industrial sector favored by the Republicans, workers in the East and along the Great Lakes littoral overwhelmingly chose the latter, with the Democrats picking up the residual.

Support for the major parties was weakly related to strike activity, both at the national level and within each of the developmental categories. But the pattern was complex. For the nation as a whole, support for the Democratic party tended to rise with strike activity, although the difference between support within counties in which no strikes took place was only about 6 percent less than support in strike-prone counties. For the Republicans, there was also a tendency for support to increase, but this was even weaker than for the Democrats. When the national vote is disaggregated into developmental categories, however, a much stronger and more interesting set of patterns is uncovered. Within the least developed counties in the nation (zero on the scale), the Democratic share of the vote tended to decrease with rising strike activity. Republican support within the same category tended in the opposite direction, increasing along with shop-floor contention. Within the most advanced counties, these patterns were reversed, with Democratic support positively and Republican support negatively correlated with strike activity. In the middle four developmental categories, the pattern is less clear. In general the percentages in the table are consistent with the regional inversion of class alignments that characterized the two-party system in the late nineteenth century. The Democrats tended to represent lower-class elements in the electorate in the more advanced North (hence the party's relatively high percentages in strike-prone counties) and upper-class segments of the electorate in the South (hence the party's increasing dominance as strike activity declines among the least developed counties). The Republican pattern is equally consistent. The major difficulty with this interpretation is that working-class voters were often only a small part of the electorate in many parts of the nation. Even in highly developed, strike-prone regions, differences in major party shares of working-class votes could have been swallowed up by changes in the opposite direction by other classes in the electorate. Thus the pattern here is suggestive but far from conclusive.

The Populist vote primarily owes its theoretical significance to two features of the 1892 campaign: the sophisticated articulation of an alternative vision of national development in the party platform and the fact that, as

52.4%). Harrison followed with 401 (38.7%). A smattering of voters preferred the Prohibitionists (54, or 5.2%) with only a token number for the Populists (36, or 3.5%). The Socialist-Labor candidate was almost invisible (3 votes, or 0.3% of the total). These votes were cast in the three Homestead precincts where steelworkers employed by the Carnegie corporation worked and lived. *Smull's Legislative Hand Book and Manual of the State of Pennsylvania for 1893* (Harrisburg: E. K. Meyers, 1893), p. 497.

a national race, voters throughout the country were confronted with more or less the same set of options or choices. But the party's performance, although relatively good for a third-party effort, was weak enough that many voters who would have otherwise been inclined to cast a Populist ballot were dissuaded by the clear lack of competitiveness within their state. Such votes, in states where the Populists were almost certainly destined to run a poor third to the two major parties, would have been wasted. The Bryan vote in the 1896 election solved the problem of competitiveness in the time-honored tradition of American politics: by weakening the specificity and radical themes in the Populist list of demands.

BRYAN AND THE 1896 ELECTION

Compared with prior party declarations, the 1896 national Democratic platform was an insurgent platform. However, the claims the platform made were but pale shadows of the Populist demands upon which Weaver ran in 1892. These differing comparisons, one with the Democratic party's earlier declarations and the other with the Populist platform in 1892, have given rise to two contradictory interpretations of the extent and quality of insurgency behind Bryan's nomination and campaign. On the one hand, many contemporary observers and historians have viewed the Democratic platform as a hodge-podge combination of traditional party themes with a few Populist planks, particularly the free silver stand, tacked on in order to seduce the third party into a self-annihilating fusion.[71] On the other hand, the Democratic platform was clearly a major break with the past and, because the Republicans barely budged from their previous positions, dramatically widened differences between the two major parties. From this perspective, the 1896 platform appears to propose mass insurgency, only slightly circumscribed by competitive expediency. The first interpretation stresses cynical calculation and dissimulation, the second emphasizes ideological commitment tempered by a realistic assessment of political possibility.

Taken alone, an examination of the 1896 Democratic platform does not provide a basis upon which to choose between these two interpretations; everything depends on whether the stands are compared with prior Democratic platforms or the 1892 Populist demands. However, a pragmatic seduction of the Populist movement was compatible with the construction of a competitive major party insurgency. Ideological sincerity on the part of all of those who participated in both the Populist seduction and Bryan's nomination is not necessary for the subsequent campaign to be interpreted as an insurgent crusade. What does seem necessary is that the presidential

---

[71] See, for example, Ritter, *Goldbugs and Greenbacks*, pp. 57–61.

nominee, if he had been elected, would have faithfully supported the program outlined in the platform. And this consideration puts much of the weight of interpretation on an analysis of Bryan's political character.[72] As a leader of an insurgent party, for example, James Weaver was much less important to the Populists, both as the 1892 nominee and as a potential officeholder, than Bryan was to the Democratic party. Weaver ran on a far more explicit platform to which his party, if it had won office, would have held him accountable. Bryan's platform was both far less explicit, at least in its insurgent elements, and his party was far from united on much of the program that it outlined.

For these reasons, Bryan could have easily and understandably trimmed sail once in office. Although we will never know whether Bryan would have pragmatically moved to the political center, the weight of evidence seems to be to the contrary. Although substantial portions of his party were clearly indifferent or even opposed to the insurgent program and to his election, they were usually not in a position to affect the outcome. In the South, for example, conservative leaders who viewed the Populists and their program with distaste were nonetheless compelled to work for Bryan's election in order to maintain local political power.[73] In the Northeast, conservative Democrats committed to maintenance of the gold standard and other mainstream policies were either irrelevant because the Republicans were assured of victory in their states regardless of what they did or forced out of the Democratic party by local insurgents who, while caring little for most of the Bryan program, enthusiastically used loyalty to the platform as a means of purging the leadership. Bryan's election would have made a dramatic difference in the direction of the nation's subsequent political and economic development, but much of that difference would have been heavily contested even after his elevation to the presidency.

The Bryan Vote and National Economic Development

The 1896 campaign was one of the most intensely followed contests in history. Throughout the spring, the state Democratic and Republican parties met and selected delegations to their respective national conventions. Most of the state conventions took positions in favor or against free coinage of silver which, as has been discussed, was in some ways a shorthand for

---

[72] For a very negative evaluation of Bryan's grasp of the financial issues surrounding the free coinage of silver and, in fact, a summary evaluation of the candidate as one of those "men without ideas," see Goodwyn, *Democratic Promise*, pp. 389, 439, 453, 591, 681 n. 4.

[73] See, for example, Hoke Smith's decision to back Bryan, as explained in a letter to Cleveland, dated July 20, 1896. Allan Nevins, ed., *Letters of Grover Cleveland, 1850–1908* (Boston: Houghton Mifflin, 1933), pp. 450–451. As Cleveland's Secretary of the Interior, editor of the Atlanta *Journal*, active participant in Georgia politics, and sound-money advocate, Smith was torn in contradictory directions.

the entire agrarian program and in other ways an abandonment.[74] Because of the declared commitments of the state delegations, it was already very probable by late spring, weeks before the conventions would assemble, that the Republicans would commit their party to defense of the gold standard while the Democrats would declare for free silver.[75] Contrary to tradition, the major party controlling the White House met in national convention after the party out of power.[76] Thus the Republicans chose McKinley as their standard-bearer without knowing who would be the Democratic nominee. Although the Republicans also had splinter factions that dissented from one or more elements in the party's program, by and large the party possessed a substantial majority that consistently subscribed to each of the major planks. In many ways, these planks were so interrelated in their policy implications and political support as to constitute a kind of orthodoxy. Orthodox Republicans were high tariff protectionists, gold standard advocates, fervent supporters of military pensions to Union veterans, and believers in a comparatively unregulated and unfettered national market. As a program for national economic development, this had been their program since the end of the Civil War.[77]

The Democrats, on the other hand, were devoted to free trade (a tariff

---

[74] Citing free silver as shorthand for agrarian insurgency, as well as working-class claims on wealth, Paul Kleppner observes: "To urban trade unionists, or at least to some of their leaders, [free silver] meant limiting the power of the courts to issue injunctions ending strikes, freedom from repression by federal and state militia acting as agents of an industrial plutocracy, and the creation of a coalition uniting the country's laborers and farmers, its toiling producers. Of course, it was the very prospect of such possibilities that alarmed the 'goldbugs.' To them, 'free silver' was linked with repudiation of honestly incurred obligations, tramping armies of vagabonds, control by union dictators over the terms and conditions of work, strikes involving violence against property and persons, and a general breakdown of social order. Frightened out of proportion to the actual threat, they summed their fears by symbolically depicting 'free silver' as the inevitable prelude to anarchy...." *Continuity and Change*, p. 108.

[75] *Appleton's Annual Cyclopaedia of 1896* (New York: D. Appleton, 1897), p. 667; Kleppner, *Continuity and Change*, p. 109. The *Commercial and Financial Chronicle* closely followed the state conventions of both parties, lauding those that endorsed "sound money" and condemning the rest as subscribers to "financial lunacy." March 28, May 2, 16, 23, June 6, 13, 1896.

[76] This reversal was primarily a Democratic party decision in that the Democrats chose a July date after the Republicans had announced that their convention would be held in June. *Appleton's 1896 Cyclopaedia*, p. 666.

[77] While their respective stances on silver and the financial system generally were the most visible issues separating the two major parties in 1896, the Republicans laid almost as much emphasis on the protective tariff, first in nominating William McKinley (who was best known for his leadership role in crafting the McKinley Tariff in 1890) and in subsequently blaming the 1893 depression on Democratic efforts to repeal that tariff (efforts which had culminated in passage of the Wilson bill in 1894). Kleppner, *Continuity and Change*, p. 111. In Idaho, for example, where silver sentiment was overwhelming, regular Republicans almost exclusively focused their appeals on tariff protection. Gaboury, *Dissension in the Rockies*, p. 206.

for revenue only), a smaller and less political pension system, and a more decentralized regulation of the national market with more authority vested in the individual states. There were, to be sure, prominent dissenters from each of these policies, but the center of gravity within the party, both in Congress and in presidential races, incontestably lay in this direction and thus, in each case, in opposition to the Republicans. The exception had always been in monetary policy where the Democrats had been openly schizophrenic. In Congress, the party was clearly inclined, decisively so in most years, toward either a greenback monetary system or adoption of the silver standard; both involved rejection of gold. In presidential nominating conventions, however, the party had adopted ambiguous monetary planks upon which unapologetic gold standard advocates would run. These nominees were as committed to a defense of gold as anyone the Republicans put forward.

When put to the test in his second administration, for example, Cleveland proved perfectly capable of mobilizing the entire authority and resources of the presidency in maintaining the gold standard against the aggressive hostility of a majority of his own party in Congress. And, although Democratic organizations in many of the northern and western states tended to be more sympathetic to the industrial worker than their Republican counterparts, the party's presidential nominees and platforms were on the whole as indifferent to working-class claims on wealth as the Republican candidates. Certainly Cleveland's record toward labor, once in office, strongly indicated that the two parties were not far apart on this issue.

The importance of the 1896 election arises out of Bryan's break with what had been Democratic orthodoxy in presidential platforms and nominations on two issues: the gold standard and industrial labor. By endorsing silver, the party added one more major element to their vision of economic development, one that differed dramatically with the Republicans. In terms of regional programs, this change more closely aligned the Democrats with the periphery, both South and West, while eliminating one of the most important planks catering to the interests of industrial expansion. Otherwise, the class implications of the shift in position were not significant. With respect to labor policy, however, the platform broke new ground by emphasizing sympathy for the industrial worker. While the class implications here were clear, particularly when combined with the insurgent rhetoric in which the silver issue was often couched, the relative unimportance of the industrial political economy in the South and West largely restricted the potential impact of this stand to the manufacturing belt.

While clearly radical in its implications for redirecting the course of economic development, the Democratic strategy was also an obviously pragmatic attempt to solidify the party's strength in the southern and western periphery while splitting the industrial core along class lines. Below in this section, just how well Bryan was able to restructure the major party align-ment in these ways, raising the party's share of the electorate in the periph-ery while winning the labor vote in the industrial core, is analyzed in its broadest outlines. The short version is that Bryan succeeded, particularly in 1896, in solidifying the periphery while utterly failing to attract indus-trial workers. In fact, the industrial working class, to the extent that it evi-denced a change in position, strongly shifted to the Republicans.

The silver question deeply divided both major party conventions. In the Republican party, rejection of the minority report favoring free silver caused the entire delegations from Colorado and Idaho to bolt the convention, along with parts of the Montana, Nevada, South Dakota, and Utah con-tingents.[78] Although accompanied by emotional speeches and dramatic flourishes, this bolt was primarily driven by mining interests, which made opposition to silver impossible for any officeholder in the Mountain states.[79] In sharp contrast, only one southern delegation, North Carolina, voted for the silver plank even though many of the region's state Republican parties had cooperated with the Populists in local or national elections and even though the southern wing of the party held many sharecroppers and tenants who were otherwise drawn to the agrarian movement. None of the south-ern members joined the bolting delegates. In fact, 85 percent of the south-ern delegates voted to table the silver plank in what, considering the preferences of the members they represented, can only be viewed as obse-quious deference to the dominant eastern wing of the party.

A fight over the financial plank also took place in the Democratic con-vention but with a different outcome. There the silver forces prevailed. After the silver plank was adopted, those who favored gold did not bolt the con-vention but, instead, indicated their displeasure by abstaining on the vote that gave Bryan the party nomination. On that ballot, about 60 percent of the delegates from New England, along with the entire New York contin-gent and a scattering of members from Delaware, Maryland, Minnesota, New Jersey, and Wisconsin, sat on their hands. The fault lines in both con-ventions reflected the sectional divide that had dominated congressional votes on financial questions for decades (cf. Table 4.7 with Map 6.1).

With the exception of North Carolina where the Republican party had almost completely fused with the Populists, all the state delegations that supported silver in both conventions represented the Mountain and Pacific

---

[78] This bolt was no surprise. During Senate debate over a free silver bill four years pre-viously, for example, Senator Teller of Colorado had "given notice to 'the leaders of the Republican party' that if more than is now being done is not done hereafter for the silver industry 'four silver-producing States (including his own) will not hereafter be able to act in association with Republicans.'" *Commercial and Financial Chron-icle*, April 23, 1892.

[79] For an account of the convention proceedings that accompanied the bolt from the Republican convention, see *Appleton's 1896 Cyclopaedia*, pp. 667, 761–762.

Table 4.7. *Voting on the Silver Planks in the 1896*
Major Party Conventions

Delegation vote in the Republican convention	Delegation vote in the Democratic convention			
	Favored silver		Favored gold	
Favored silver	California Colorado Idaho Montana	Nevada North Carolina Utah Wyoming		
Favored gold	Alabama Arkansas Florida Georgia Illinois Indiana Iowa Kansas Kentucky Louisiana Michigan Mississippi	Missouri Nebraska North Dakota Ohio Oregon South Carolina Tennessee Texas Virginia Washington West Virginia	Connecticut Delaware Maine Maryland Massachusetts Minnesota New Hampshire	New Jersey New York Pennsylvania Rhode Island South Dakota Vermont Wisconsin

Notes and sources: Arizona Territory voted in favor of silver in both conventions. The delegations from Oklahoma Territory, the Indian Territory, and District of Columbia all supported gold in the Republican convention and silver in the Democratic. The New Mexico Territory delegation divided evenly in the Republican convention and supported silver in the Democratic. Alaska Territory voted for gold in both conventions. Most delegations voted as a unit in both conventions. The vote in the Republican convention was on a motion to table the silver plank. The vote in the Democratic convention occurred upon adoption of the majority report in favor of silver. For the roll call votes, see *Appleton's Annual Cyclopaedia of 1896* (New York: D. Appleton, 1897), pp. 761–762, 764.

West. All of the states in the Northeast, plus three from the upper Midwest, backed gold. The remaining delegations in the South, border states, and lower Midwest all voted for gold in the Republican convention and for silver in the Democratic.[80] Reflecting the bias of their respective parties both

[80] The vote on the adoption of free silver in the Democratic convention almost exactly followed the positions previously assumed in the declarations made by state conventions. Many of these declarations had left no room for vacillation by their delegates. Oregon, for example, had assumed a stance "unalterably opposed to the single gold standard," while Pennsylvania had called for "firm, unvarying maintenance" of the same thing. *Commercial and Financial Chronicle*, June 6, 1896.

inside and outside Congress, no delegation supported silver in the Republican convention and gold in the Democratic.

Neither major party had ever openly opposed the international gold standard in a presidential race. As a result, the political ground throughout the nation began to shift after the Democratic convention declared for silver. In the weeks following Bryan's nomination, over 100 daily Democratic papers of the major cities of the Northeast and Midwest abandoned the Democratic platform and candidate, many of them endorsing McKinley while restating their opposition to the protectionism that remained enshrined in the Republican declaration of principles.[81] In the Plains and Mountain West, on the other hand, the slide overwhelmingly favored the Democrats.[82] In the end, when the votes were finally counted in November, those states whose delegations had voted for gold in the Democratic convention tilted heavily toward the Republicans, compared with their historical loyalties. Traveling in the opposite direction, those states that had supported silver in the Republican convention tended even more strongly toward the Democrats in the presidential election. The tendency in those states that had split their positions, for gold in the Republican convention and for silver in the Democratic, favored the Democrats in regions far away from the money centers along the northeastern seaboard. In states located closer to these capital-exporting centers, the Republicans were often the beneficiaries of shifting loyalties.

Because the 1892 contest included the Populists, the best way to document the shift away from the Democrats in the industrial core and toward the party in the periphery is by comparing the party's respective shares of the total vote in the 1888 and 1896 elections.[83] Because the major party presidential candidates were identical in 1888 and 1892 and the party platforms were also similar, these two elections presented major party choices that were very much alike. As has been discussed, the 1896 election altered those choices in significant ways but, unlike 1892, was a two-party race.

---

[81] *Appleton's 1896 Cyclopaedia*, p. 668.

[82] By early August, for instance, twenty-five of the thirty-six formerly Republican papers in Idaho had endorsed Bryan, eight had remained with McKinley, and three were on the fence. Gaboury, *Dissension in the Rockies*, p. 204. On the other hand, in the South where almost all the press had previously been affiliated with the Democrats, a dozen or so of the major city papers refused to back Bryan. Woodward, *Origins of the New South*, pp. 286–287.

[83] As was described in the previous section, the Populists attracted many voters from the Democrats in the Plains and West and from the Republicans in the South. The return of these voters to their major party allegiance in 1896 would distort the impact of the Bryan campaign on the pre-Populist array of party strength. For example, in some western states where the Democrats endorsed Populist tickets in 1892, the Democratic vote jumped from nothing to over 50 percent in 1896. However, a comparison of Bryan's performance to Cleveland's in 1888 reveals that the net gain to the Democrats, relative to the Republicans in a two-party race, was much smaller.

Much changed in the United States between 1888 and 1896. The nation's population continued to grow at a prodigious rate. In regional terms, this expansion was very uneven, with rapid growth in many industrial cities and the Mountain West and steep declines on the western plains and some rural portions of the East. In addition, almost all areas of the United States changed over, as a means of recording votes, from political tickets distributed by political parties to the Australian ballot issued by state governments. Finally, many western states had been admitted to the Union after 1888, significantly reshaping the distribution of electoral influence in favor of many of the interests represented by Bryan's candidacy. For all of these reasons, comparison of the vote between 1888 and 1896 does not chart changes in the party affiliation of individual voters so much as it reflects the comparative tendencies of members of political economic communities to support one or the other of the two major parties.

In the most advanced regions of the nation, the Republicans in 1896 ran almost 10 percent ahead of their performance in 1888, shifting what had been a narrow plurality in the earlier contest into a massive landslide in the latter (see Table 4.8). The Democratic decline in these same trade areas was even greater than the Republican gain, as third parties slightly expanded their share of the vote. In general, Republican gains tended to be heavier in the most advanced regions of the nation and declined more or less steadily with relative development. The Democratic pattern was the inverse. The net impact of these shifts was to change what had been a murky relationship between development and major party strength in 1888 into a pattern in which the vote shares of the two parties was closely correlated with development. As a result, the Republicans enjoyed rather hefty majorities in all of the top four developmental categories, leaving the Democrats with a majority only at the bottom and a small plurality in the level just above.[84]

Most changes in the major party vote in the individual trade areas, not surprisingly, followed the broader national pattern (see Table 4.9). The four

---

[84]   For several reasons, the 1896 election was in fact much closer than it appears in Table 4.8. In the first place, many of the states in the Plains and Mountain West were admitted after the 1888 election and thus are not included in the comparison of changes in major party strength between that contest and the one in 1896. Although these states were small, Bryan's support in most of them was greater than in the nation as a whole. Second, the outcome in the electoral college could have been reversed with only slight changes in the popular vote. The electoral vote stood at 271 for McKinley and 176 for Bryan, a net advantage of 95 to the Republicans. The popular vote margin for the Republicans in Kentucky was 281; thus a shift of 141 votes from McKinley to Bryan there would have given twelve more electoral votes to the Democrats (a Democrat was actually elected as one of Kentucky's thirteen electors). A similar shift of 1,399 votes in California would have moved another eight into Bryan's column (one Democrat was actually elected there as well). Twenty-eight additional electoral votes would have been subtracted from the Republicans and

Table 4.8. *Summary of Trade Area Development and Change in Major Party Strength between 1888 and 1896*

Trade area level	Vote cast for major party candidates in 1888 (%)			Vote cast for major party candidates in 1896 (%)			Change 1888–96	
	Republican	Democratic	Total vote cast	Republican	Democratic	Total vote cast	Rep.	Dem.
5 (highest)	49.5	48.0	3,153,946	59.4	37.3	3,645,807	+9.9	−10.7
4 (high)	52.2	44.8	1,157,197	56.8	41.3	1,603,414	+4.6	−3.5
3 (middle high)	53.7	42.5	1,075,733	53.7	43.7	1,267,027	0.0	+1.2
2 (middle low)	51.4	43.9	1,825,149	53.3	44.7	2,228,294	+1.9	+0.8
1 (low)	47.9	46.7	1,908,744	48.7	49.9	2,289,874	+0.8	+3.2
0 (lowest)	37.7	60.2	2,242,864	36.1	62.1	2,474,679	−1.6	+1.9

Table 4.9. Development and Change in Major Party Strength between 1888 and 1896: Individual Trade Areas

Trade area level	Vote cast for major party candidates in 1888 (%)			Vote cast for major party candidates in 1896 (%)			Change 1888–96	
	Republican	Democratic	Total vote cast	Republican	Democratic	Total vote cast	Rep.	Dem.
5 (highest)								
Baltimore	47.3	51.0	255,463	54.9	41.9	299,134	+7.6	−9.1
Boston	54.3	43.2	565,667	69.0	26.8	614,309	+14.7	−16.4
Buffalo	54.6	40.7	275,386	59.3	37.7	307,603	+4.7	−3.0
Cincinnati	47.5	50.3	276,421	51.9	47.1	320,497	+4.4	−3.2
Cleveland	50.6	45.6	264,210	52.0	46.8	336,325	+1.4	+1.2
Hartford	49.3	47.5	158,197	65.3	30.3	177,790	+16.0	−17.2
New York	43.8	54.2	811,462	55.7	39.8	960,119	+11.9	−14.4
Philadelphia	52.0	46.2	547,140	64.1	32.9	630,030	+12.1	−13.3
4 (high)								
Chicago	51.9	44.7	476,585	59.2	39.2	757,045	+7.3	−5.5
Pittsburgh	53.8	43.4	406,114	58.7	39.1	509,519	+4.9	−4.3
San Francisco	50.4	46.8	274,498	48.5	49.3	336,850	−1.9	+2.5
3 (middle high)								
Albany	55.1	42.5	326,993	63.0	34.2	321,286	+7.9	−8.3
Denver	57.4	41.0	111,457	16.5	82.5	201,394	−40.9	+41.5
Los Angeles	53.6	41.7	50,234	48.9	47.9	69,542	−4.7	+6.2
Milwaukee	49.6	44.6	338,743	60.3	36.9	425,097	+10.7	−7.7
Syracuse	56.0	40.7	248,306	61.7	35.2	249,708	+5.7	−5.5

2 (middle low)							
Des Moines	51.9	325,540	55.2	43.3	410,136	+3.3	-1.8
Detroit	47.4	286,387	52.1	45.3	343,425	+4.7	-2.7
Grand Rapids	52.5	203,266	53.0	44.5	225,482	+0.5	+3.3
Indianapolis	49.7	387,758	51.6	46.9	469,445	+1.9	-0.7
Minneapolis	54.7	328,367	58.1	39.4	435,841	+3.4	0.0
Omaha	52.6	293,831	48.6	49.6	343,965	-4.0	+9.2
1 (low)							
Columbus	49.0	402,325	50.5	48.5	476,314	+1.5	+0.7
Kansas City	50.1	585,206	44.8	54.0	654,653	-5.3	+14.5
Louisville	46.8	210,131	53.4	44.5	266,444	+6.6	-7.3
St. Louis	44.3	506,844	47.2	52.2	650,340	+2.9	+0.6
Scranton	49.2	204,238	54.9	41.5	242,123	+5.7	-6.0
0 (lowest)							
Atlanta	61.9	353,147	40.5	57.3	382,964	+2.6	-4.6
Charleston	65.7	181,726	30.9	67.4	168,064	-2.8	+1.7
Evansville	52.3	125,957	45.2	53.5	153,517	-0.6	+1.2
Memphis	65.5	500,534	23.4	74.5	560,401	-5.1	+9.0
Nashville	58.4	211,703	39.4	58.3	249,241	-1.7	-0.1
New Orleans	65.3	375,343	31.9	65.6	439,229	+0.3	+0.3
Richmond	50.2	494,454	47.2	51.9	521,263	-2.2	+1.7

trade areas in which the Republicans made their best gains, for example, were all among the most advanced in the nation: Hartford, Boston, Philadelphia, and New York. Democratic gains were not so well distributed, however. The best trade area for the Democrats was Denver, where the complete collapse of the Republican vote in Colorado in 1896 more than doubled the Democratic percentage when compared with 1888. But Denver, with respect to its relatively high ranking on patent filings, wealth, and adult male literacy, was a comparatively developed trade area. Only slightly less anomalous were the favorable showings by the Democrats in the Omaha and Kansas City trade areas. What most of these anomalies and others not so remarkable had in common was a comparatively disadvantageous position in the national political economy with respect to the cost of capital.

In fact, when the nation's trade areas are regrouped according to their prevailing interest rates, the result is an almost perfect correlation between rates and support for Bryan (see Table 4.10). McKinley outperformed Harrison by almost thirteen percentage points in those trade areas with the lowest interest rates in the nation. In those trade areas with the highest rates, on the other hand, the Republican share of the vote declined by almost 6 percent. Everywhere the pattern was the inverse for the Democrats; higher interest rates were associated with Democratic gains, lower rates with losses. In 1888, the connection between interest rates and major party shares of the presidential vote had been murky at best, with only those trade areas with the very highest rates exhibiting a disproportionate tendency to support Cleveland. In sharp contrast, the 1896 contest was consistently and strongly aligned with the comparative cost of capital, with an almost two to one advantage for the Republicans in trade areas with the lowest rates and a greater than two to one advantage for the Democrats in trade areas with the highest rates. No other single measure of relative economic development more accurately traced the shift in major party vote shares over the two elections. In many respects, this should not be surprising, since the "Battle of the Standards," pitting gold against silver, made

added to the Democrats if 17,710 votes had been similarly shifted in four more states: Delaware, Indiana, Oregon, and West Virginia. Thus, if Bryan had attracted only 19,250 votes that were actually cast for McKinley and if these changes had been distributed with precision across the above six states, the electoral college totals in 1896 would have stood at 223 for McKinley and 224 for Bryan, thus electing the Democrat. By way of comparison, just over 300,000 voters would have had to shift from McKinley to Bryan in order to give the latter a majority of the popular vote. The popular and electoral votes cast in 1896 are conveniently displayed in the *1899 World Almanac* (New York: New York World, 1899), p. 427. Matthew Josephson presented a similar calculation in *The Politicos, 1865–1896* (New York: Harcourt, Brace & World, 1966), pp. 706–707, but included North Dakota in place of Delaware. H. Wayne Morgan also substituted North Dakota for Delaware in his *From Hayes to McKinley: National Party Politics, 1877–1896* (Syracuse, N.Y.: Syracuse University Press, 1969), p. 522.

Table 4.10. *Summary of Trade Area Interest Rates and Change in Major Party Strength between 1888 and 1896*

| Trade area interest rate | Vote cast for major party candidates in 1888 (%) | | | Vote cast for major party candidates in 1896 (%) | | | Change 1888–96 | |
	Republican (%)	Democratic (%)	Total vote cast	Republican (%)	Democratic (%)	Total vote cast	Rep. (%)	Dem. (%)
Lowest (5.65–5.29)	49.3	48.6	2,082,466	62.1	33.9	2,382,248	+12.8	–14.7
Low (6.56–5.66)	52.1	45.0	2,190,841	57.4	40.1	2,532,142	+5.3	–4.9
Middle low (6.93–6.57)	49.7	47.5	1,988,528	54.3	44.2	2,500,216	+4.6	–3.3
Middle high (7.50–6.94)	48.7	50.2	1,997,455	49.6	48.8	2,501,586	+0.9	–1.4
High (8.50–7.51)	48.8	44.7	1,560,551	47.8	50.4	1,817,423	–1.0	+5.7
Highest (9.83–8.51)	36.9	59.4	1,493,792	31.2	66.7	1,775,480	–5.7	+7.3

the financial system the central point of difference between the two parties. Where the two parties had almost matched platform planks in 1888 with respect to the nation's monetary standard, their differences could hardly have been more extreme in 1896.

The relationship between interest rates and voting returns held within trade areas as well (see Table 4.11). For those trade areas with the nation's lowest interest rates, the shift away from the Democrats between 1888 and 1896 in the major urban center was truly massive.[85] The Democratic share of the total vote in Hartford and Louisville, for example, declined by over 20 percent. In Boston and Philadelphia, the decline was almost as large with New York and Baltimore not far behind. Altogether, only nine of the thirty-four leading trade centers in the nation showed Democratic gains and five of those were in trade areas in which prevailing interest rates were above 8 percent. A similar pattern held for counties outside the major trade centers. When the vote is aggregated for counties with interest rates below the national average (6.64%), the shift away from the Democrats is far higher for these counties in trade areas with very low interest rates, turning gradually into Democratic gains at the other extreme. When the vote is aggregated for counties with interest rates above the national average, many of these Democratic losses turn into gains. Twenty-six of the nation's thirty-four trade areas contained at least some counties in which interest rates were higher than the national average; in sixteen of these, the Democratic share of the total vote increased between 1888 and 1896.

Thus relative interest rates structured much of the 1896 vote both within and between the nation's trade areas. As might be anticipated in any one-dimensional aggregation of the presidential vote, there are a few anomalies. For example, Democratic gains in 1896 were somewhat greater than expected in southern cities such as Atlanta, Nashville, and Richmond. Similarly, shifts toward Bryan in Denver, Minneapolis, and Los Angeles were all slightly higher than the remainder of their respective trade areas – a tendency that ran counter to the overall pattern. These anomalies aside, the connection between interest rates and changes in the Democratic share

---

[85]   It has long been known that Bryan did better in rural areas of the nation than in the cities. It has also been shown that the anti-Bryan bias with respect to cities in the national pattern resulted from the overwhelming proportion of the urban population residing in the industrial core and the equally overwhelming majorities that McKinley ran up in the East. However, this national pattern does not hold up when regions are examined separately. In the industrial core, for example, most cities cast higher percentages for Bryan than did their surrounding rural hinterlands. In the southern and western periphery, the pattern was the reverse – he did better in rural areas. William Diamond, "Urban and Rural Voting in 1896," *American Historical Review* 46 (January 1941): 281–305. As Table 4.11 demonstrates, both regional patterns were less pronounced in 1896 than had been the case eight years earlier when Cleveland, compared with Bryan, ran relatively stronger in eastern cities and relatively weaker in the rural areas of the South and West.

Table 4.11. *Interest Rates and Presidential Voting Patterns within the Nation's Trade Areas: Change in Democratic Party Percentage between 1888 and 1896 Elections*

Overall interest rate in trade area	Trade center	Counties under average national interest rate	Total vote cast in 1896	Counties over average national interest rate	Total vote cast in 1896
Under 5.51					
Hartford	−20.7	−16.3	141,727	No counties	NA
New York	−15.7	−13.5	651,887	No counties	NA
Philadelphia	−19.3	−9.5	385,193	No counties	NA
5.51–6.00					
Albany	−7.5	−8.4	280,452	No counties	NA
Baltimore	−13.9	−6.5	192,533	No counties	NA
Boston	−19.2	−16.3	131,310	−11.2	6,472
Buffalo	−9.0	−1.4	229,724	No counties	NA
Pittsburgh	−7.2	−3.1	394,721	−1.4	6,624
Scranton	−8.9	−5.5	210,518	No counties	NA
Syracuse	−6.0	−5.4	209,567	No counties	NA
6.01–6.64					
Cincinnati	−7.1	−4.3	52,026	−0.9	171,996
Cleveland	−0.8	+2.5	192,592	+0.2	62,243
Louisville	−22.1	−4.0	138,323	−4.8	80,849
Milwaukee	+1.5	−10.0	146,198	−8.8	214,093
6.65–7.00					
Chicago	−8.8	−6.0	51,347	−3.9	327,216
Columbus	−3.1	−1.0	126,141	−1.7	311,120
Detroit	−13.0	−2.5	33,942	+0.1	245,325
Indianapolis	−7.6	−1.6	6,293	+0.1	414,292
Richmond	+4.1	+0.5	267,793	+3.2	234,624
7.01–8.00					
Atlanta	+4.7	−2.7	89,713	−4.8	284,858
Des Moines	−2.1	No counties	NA	−1.7	391,690
Evansville	−2.5	−0.1	44,382	+2.8	93,838
Grand Rapids	−2.5	+1.8	4,141	+4.2	189,957
Nashville	+4.0	−0.5	141,041	−1.0	94,541
Omaha	−2.6	No counties	NA	+10.0	319,287
St. Louis	−0.7	−1.9	77,172	+2.1	456,172
Over 8.00					
Charleston	−21.8	No counties	NA	+2.1	165,422
Denver	+45.0	+30.5	1,431	+40.4	151,005

Table 4.11. *(cont.)*

Overall interest rate in trade area	Trade center	Counties under average national interest rate	Total vote cast in 1896	Counties over average national interest rate	Total vote cast in 1896
Kansas City	+1.0	No counties	NA	+15.2	614,791
Los Angeles	+6.9	No counties	NA	+5.5	31,691
Memphis	−7.0	+4.0	57,030	+9.8	490,199
Minneapolis	+2.9	No counties	NA	−0.4	387,553
New Orleans	+0.2	No counties	NA	+0.3	409,095
San Francisco	−3.2	+53.1	351	+3.8	273,377

Notes and sources: Trade center vote is for the county containing the major city for which the trade area is defined and named. In the other columns, the vote is aggregated for those counties under and over the national interest rate average. The vote cast in the trade center county is not included in these latter two categories.

of the total vote between 1888 and 1896 was very robust. The strength of the pattern, along with the relationship between development and changes in major party vote shares generally, demonstrates the primacy of inter-regional wealth redistribution among the major factors driving the Bryan campaign.[86]

---

[86] Paul Kleppner has stressed the importance of the 1893 depression and the subsequent Republican landslide in the 1894 congressional elections as the primary formative events in the emergence of the fourth electoral system. In the short term, this emphasis on voter reaction to the depression, in terms of blaming the Cleveland administration, has much to recommend it. Such reactions have been a staple of American politics for almost 200 years. The major shortcomings of his explanation, however, are that the depression was not limited to the industrial East but national in scope; yet Kleppner's statistical analysis indicates a very strong regional pattern in response to the depression – not a single county in New England, New York, New Jersey, Pennsylvania, Delaware, Ohio, West Virginia, Michigan, Indiana, or Illinois shifted toward the Democrats after 1892. In the Confederate South and the Plains and Mountain West, on the other hand, only a handful of counties shifted toward the Republicans (pp. 68–69). In addition, economic depressions, no matter how severe, do not result in major realignments of electoral coalitions unless there is a triggering policy response. In this case, the dramatic shift of the Democratic party toward silver and, to a lesser extent, the entire panoply of agrarian demands provoked a more or less enduring increase in Republican strength throughout the industrial East and Great Lakes littoral while adding voters to the Democratic coalition throughout the nation's periphery. Thus, the economic depression of 1893, Bryan's nomination in 1896, and the primacy of interregional wealth redistribution as a structuring principle in the national political economy combined to produce the very strong and persistent sectional realignment that he so well documents in his study. *Continuity and Change*, pp. 62–63, 66–89, 97–101.

The Bryan Vote and Strike Activity

The 1888 presidential returns exhibited almost no relation between relative strike activity and support for Cleveland as the Democratic candidate (see the right-hand column of Table 4.12). In 1896, the correlation between strike activity and Democratic support was higher but distinctively negative. Among the almost five million votes cast in counties in which no strikes had occurred, Bryan drew a clear and substantial majority over McKinley, running ahead of Cleveland by almost 3 percent. However, among all those counties in which strikes had taken place, Bryan lost ground compared with Cleveland. In the most strike-prone counties, Bryan's performance was abysmal, in each case losing by 7 percent or more of the total aggregate vote.[87]

Even where strike activity was high, however, workers who had actually participated in strikes probably constituted but a minority of all voters in the 1896 elections. Thus it is certainly possible that striking workers had cast a higher percentage of their votes for Bryan in 1896 than had been the case with respect to Cleveland in 1888. In that case, the explanation might have been that claim-making on the industrial shop floor led to increased Democratic support but was more than offset by conservative reaction in the remainder of the strike-prone communities. However, given the size of these shifts, the fact that most strikes were sympathetically viewed by the public at large, and the long history of strike activity in the United States (which argues against a sudden conservative reaction in 1896), workers probably moved toward McKinley in approximately the same rate as most other segments of the electorate.

As was the case with the Populist vote, the connection between change in Democratic support and the level of economic development was much stronger than that with relative strike activity. Very few strikes occurred in counties at the very bottom of the developmental scale, while most counties at the very top were the site of frequent and extensive strike activity. For these reasons, several of the cells in the lower left-hand corner and in

---

[87] Because the American Federation of Labor endorsed free silver in every national convention from 1893 through 1897, Bryan's nomination in 1896 appeared to bring the Democratic party into much closer alignment with the AFL than had been the case under Cleveland's leadership. In addition, while the Federation was officially neutral and at times took steps to enforce that neutrality, Gompers himself was accused of covertly aiding the Bryan campaign in 1896. Selig Perlman, "Upheaval and Reorganisation (since 1876)," in John R. Commons et al., *History of Labour in the United States*, vol. 2 (New York: Macmillan, 1918), pp. 510–514. With respect to the voting returns, there is no evidence that the programmatic declarations of the AFL or the covert sympathy of its leadership had any impact on working-class ballots. And the AFL was large enough to have made a difference in the returns. By 1899, the Federation contained, by Gompers's estimate from dues collection, more than 600,000 members with an additional 400,000 or so recently added to the rolls. Friedman, *State-making and Labor Movements*, pp. 40–41.

1888 Democratic Vote (%)

Strike activity	Developmental level						
	0	1	2	3	4	5	Total
No strikes	63.0	48.3	44.1	44.0	44.9	39.8	51.4
Low	51.4	48.3	43.2	45.6	45.2	45.4	45.7
Medium low	53.9	50.1	43.5	46.1	50.5	49.5	48.8
Medium high	56.3	48.6	46.1	44.7	41.1	48.2	46.8
High	46.4	46.9	46.6	45.5	40.5	52.3	49.2

1896 Democratic vote (%)

Strike activity	Developmental level						
	0	1	2	3	4	5	Total
No strikes	64.7	51.7	48.9	47.4	38.8	23.1	54.2
Low	51.5	49.8	41.9	42.6	37.9	35.2	42.9
Medium low	55.5	49.4	45.7	44.5	41.3	37.0	40.9
Medium high	48.8	48.6	45.4	45.7	44.9	35.5	39.8
High	49.2	48.7	46.7	41.6	32.4	40.0	41.9

Change in the Democratic vote, 1888–1896 (%)

Strike activity	Developmental level						
	0	1	2	3	4	5	Total
No strikes	+1.7	+3.4	+4.8	+3.4	−6.1	−16.7	+2.8
Low	+0.1	+1.5	−1.3	−3.0	−7.3	−10.2	−2.8
Medium low	+1.6	−0.7	+2.2	−1.6	−9.2	−12.5	−7.9
Medium high	−7.5	0.0	−0.7	+1.0	+3.8	−12.7	−7.0
High	+2.8	+1.8	+0.1	−3.9	−8.1	−12.3	−7.3

1896 presidential returns (total vote in thousands)

Strike activity	Developmental level						
	0	1	2	3	4	5	Total
No strikes	1,366	2,051	1,024	404	47	2	4,894
Low	215	705	991	958	708	236	3,813
Medium low	28	102	158	216	396	766	1,665
Medium high	10	136	182	101	243	973	1,646
High	33	196	205	109	93	857	1,494

Notes: Strike activity categories are defined as follows: "Low" includes all counties in which the number of strikers between 1885 and 1894 was between 0.1 and 24.9 per 1,000 population in 1890; "medium low" includes all those between 25.0 and 49.9; "medium high" includes all those between 50.0 and 99.9; and "high" includes all those at or above 100.0. Within each category the votes of the counties were aggregated and it was upon these totals that the percentages were computed. See Chapter 2 for a description of the index that provides the relative levels of economic development.

the upper right contain comparatively few votes upon which to compute Democratic support (see the bottom of Table 4.12). Keeping that in mind, the relationship between comparative development and changes in the Democratic vote is still fairly evident; within each strike level, the Democratic vote generally declined with increasing development in both 1888 and 1896. In 1896 this pattern was particularly strong as the vote in the most advanced counties in the nation shifted against the Democrats by more than 10 percent, regardless of how frequently strikes occurred.

When separated out by developmental levels, the 1888 returns do show a fairly strong relationship between strike activity and Democratic support at both extremes but in opposite directions. At the bottom of the developmental hierarchy (zero), for example, Cleveland drew a little under two thirds of the total vote in those counties with no strikes and less than half in those (very few) counties with high strike activity. In the most advanced counties in the nation the Democratic vote increased from a little under 40 percent in those with no strikes to over 50 percent in those with the greatest strike frequency. In 1896, the negative relation between strike activity and Democratic support in the least advanced counties is almost as strong as it was in 1888. The major change was the addition of one or two percentage points to the Democratic margin. The positive pattern in the most advanced counties also remains in place, relatively unaffected by the substantial Democratic decline across the board in these areas. This inversion of pattern in both elections is consistent with the sectional inversion of class alignments in the national party system in the late nineteenth century. From the standpoint of the industrial worker, the Democrats were the most likely advocate of interclass claims on wealth in the most advanced areas of the manufacturing belt; it thus would be expected, everything else being equal, that the party would do relatively well in strike-prone communities in the most developed counties. At the other end of the spectrum, where most of the least developed counties were southern, the Republicans were usually the most sympathetic vehicle for worker claims, with the Democratic party tending to represent elite interests.

Given these patterns and what is otherwise known about the political context of this period, it seems likely that industrial workers in the most advanced regions of the nation, regardless of strike activity, were no more or no less likely to shift against the Democrats in 1896. The Republican appeal to their interests in the prevailing sectional redistribution of wealth proved just as effective as it was for the remainder of their respective communities.

National electoral patterns throughout the late nineteenth-century United States were primarily organized around two broad alignments in the political economy. The grand sectional alignment set the stage for the broad redistribution of wealth between the regions that focused national politics on the tariff and monetary standard. The class alignment arose from the transactional locus within each of the great sections: between labor and capital in the East, between yeoman farmer and market agent in the Plains and West, and between sharecropper and planter or merchant in the South. These two great alignments provided the foundational structure within which the major parties and their insurgent challengers contended for power. However, when push came to shove, the grand sectional alignment thoroughly suppressed class conflict as an organizing influence on the course of American party competion, thus deflecting national politics from class claims that otherwise would have targeted the massive accumulation of capital in industrial plants throughout the East.

PROLOGUE AND EPILOGUE: THE GREENBACK AND SOCIALIST CAMPAIGNS

In all of the presidential contests between the end of Reconstruction and the beginning of World War I, there appeared at least one insurgent ticket that proposed a more or less radical alternative to the Republican developmental vision. In some elections, the radical alternative made only a token showing, such as in 1884 when, led by Benjamin Butler, the Greenback party collected only 1.7 percent of the national vote. Even less significant was the 1888 effort launched by the Union Labor party (1.3%). Much more important were the three Bryan campaigns in 1896, 1900, and 1908, although only the first might qualify as a radical insurgency. Aside from Bryan, three other campaigns were significant for their ideological coherence, the radical nature of their developmental vision, and the share of the national vote they were able to attract: the 1880 Greenback, the 1892 Populist, and the 1912 Socialist campaigns. The geographical distribution of their votes, along with Bryan's 1896 candidacy, are briefly compared in this section.

The 1880 Greenback party platform and ticket, as scholars have often noted, was in many ways a progenitor of the Populist campaign a dozen years later.[88] Organized in 1875, the Greenback party ran its first race in 1876, polling somewhat less than 1 percent of the total vote. In the congressional races in 1878, however, the party was a major force either when running alone or in fusion arrangements with one of the major parties.[89] Held just prior to resumption of gold payments in 1879, this election proved to be the party's high tide. While not quite anticlimactic for the Greenbackers, the 1880 presidential contest was nonetheless disappointing; James Weaver, who would run again as the Populist nominee in 1892, polled only

---

[88] For the impact of Greenback ideology on the emergence of Populism, see, for example, Goodwyn, *Democratic Promise*, pp. 82–83, 140, 241, 516.

[89] For a discussion of the 1878 elections, see Irwin Unger, *The Greenback Era: A Social and Political History of American Finance, 1865–1879* (Princeton, N.J.: Princeton University Press, 1964), pp. 374–395.

3.3 percent of the national ballots.[90] However, the party's opposition to resumption, to the national bank system, and to repayment of federal bonds in gold, along with proposals to regulate railroad rates, found a sympathetic audience throughout much of the midwestern and Texas plains, the Ozark Mountains, Michigan, the Tennessee River valley in Alabama, and the western half of Kentucky (see Map 4.3). In many of these areas, local chapters of the National Grange were active supporters of the party.[91] Planks favoring the eight-hour day and a prohibition on the importation of contract labor, along with labor conflict in eastern coalfields and railroads, drew the party votes in West Virginia and western Pennsylvania – the only major exceptions to the otherwise overwhelmingly agrarian composition of the Greenback vote.[92]

The much stronger campaign waged by the Populists in 1892 is immediately obvious when the maps of the two campaigns are compared (see Map 4.4 for the Populist vote). By 1892, six new states, in a bloc along the Canadian border from Minnesota to the Pacific Ocean, had been added to the Union, and in all of them, with the partial exception of Montana, the Populists did well. Although there was significant overlap in their areas of strength, the Greenbackers had drawn a proportionately greater number of votes in the East, including West Virginia, and some parts of the Midwest, particularly Iowa and Michigan. In all other regions of the nation, the Populists did better, with particularly striking increases in electoral strength throughout the South, Colorado, and the Far West. Iowa and, particularly, South Carolina stand out as anomalously weak in the overall pattern.[93]

Because Bryan was the nominee of one of the two major parties, depiction of his vote requires an entirely different scale (see Map 4.5). In the Greenback and Populist maps, the most heavily shaded counties were those in which the insurgent third parties drew 10 percent or more of the total

[90] Once the nomination of "sound money" candidates by the two major parties seemed assured, for example, the *Commercial and Financial Chronicle* became quite complacent. In its few comments on the campaign, the journal did not even mention the Greenbackers. See, for example, June 19, 1880; January 8, 1881.

[91] Implicitly aligning the organization with the Greenback movement, the 1877 National Grange convention had passed resolutions proposing the remonetization of silver and opposing resumption of the gold standard. Solon Justus Buck, *The Granger Movement: A Study of Agricultural Organization and Its Political, Economic and Social Manifestations, 1870–1880* (Lincoln: University of Nebraska Press, 1913), p. 114.

[92] Kleppner, *Third Electoral System*, pp. 268–269. For a detailed account of the interaction between labor and the Greenback party between 1876 and 1880, see Selig Perlman, "Upheaval and Reorganisation," pp. 240–251.

[93] The weakness of Populism in South Carolina is usually ascribed to the dominance of Benjamin Tillman and the strategic moves he made as he constructed his state Democratic machine. See, for example, Woodward, *Origins of the New South*, p. 261; Hicks, *Populist Revolt*, pp. 242, 246; Francis Butler Simkins, *Pitchfork Ben Tillman: South Carolinian* (Baton Rouge: Louisiana State University Press, 1967), pp. 206, 216.

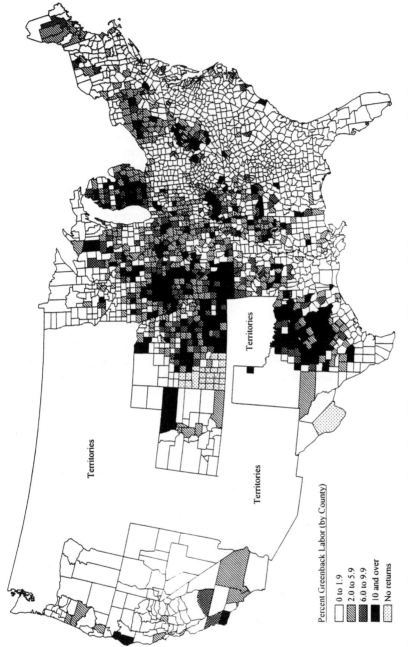

Percent Greenback Labor (by County)

☐ 0 to 1.9
▨ 2.0 to 5.9
▦ 6.0 to 9.9
■ 10 and over
▨ No returns

Territories

Territories

Territories

Territories

Map 4.3. Votes cast for the Greenback labor party, presidential election, 1880. *Source: 1880 American Almanac,* Walter Dean Burnham, *Presidential Ballots: 1836–1892* (Baltimore: Johns Hopkins University Press, 1955), and manuscript returns in individual state archives.

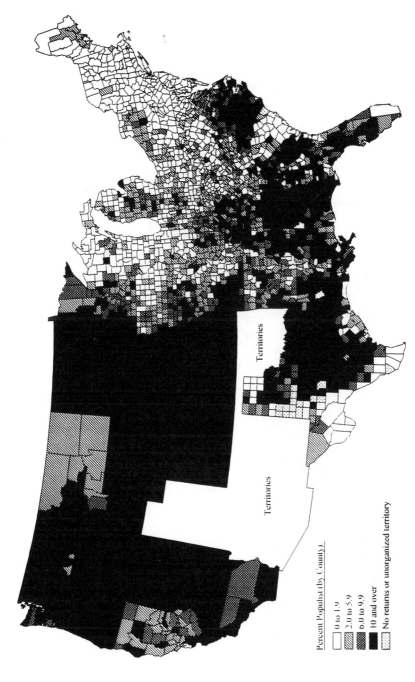

Map 4.4. Votes cast for the Populist party, presidential election, 1892. *Source:* Burnham, *Presidential Ballots.*

Percent Populist (by County)

- ☐ 0 to 1.9
- ▨ 2.0 to 5.9
- ▦ 6.0 to 9.9
- ■ 10 and over
- ⬚ No returns or unorganized territory

Territories

Territories

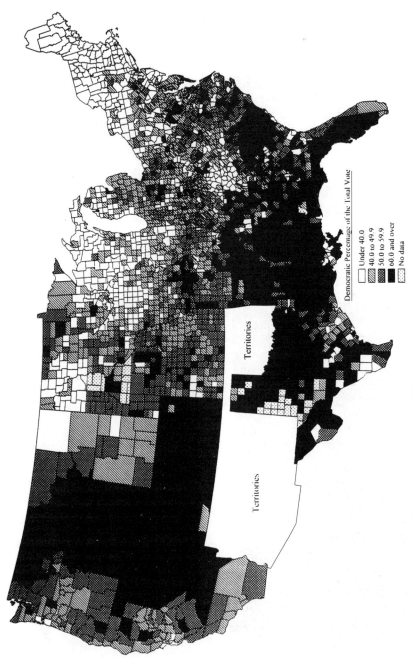

Democratic Percentage of the Total Vote

☐ Under 40.0
▨ 40.0 to 49.9
▦ 50.0 to 59.9
■ 60.0 and over
▨ No data

Territories

Territories

Map 4.5. Votes cast for William Jennings Bryan, presidential election, 1896. *Source:* Edgar Eugene Robinson, *The Presidential Vote, 1896–1932* (Stanford, Calif.: Stanford University Press, 1947). The Bryan vote in 1896 combines the Democratic and People's party tickets. In all but Texas, the source for the combined vote was the *1898 Boston Journal Almanac* (Boston: Boston Journal, 1898). For Texas, the source was the *1899 World Almanac* (New York: New York World, 1899).

vote. In the 1896 map, the most heavily shaded counties are those in which Bryan polled 60 percent or more of the vote. Given the analysis of the Bryan support presented earlier in this chapter, the national pattern should come as no surprise. At the most general level, there is much overlap with the Populist distribution of support, with the striking exception of South Carolina (where Democratic party leader Ben Tillman was only too happy to support Bryan in 1896 after spurning the national Populist ticket in 1892). Compared with both the Greenback and Populist votes, however, Bryan's support was much more closely related to the pattern of congressional opposition to the international gold standard between 1877 and 1900. In fact, the intersection between Bryan's electoral support and congressional voting on gold may have been the closest tie between popular voting behavior and legislative policy-making in history.[94]

Although the 1912 election otherwise falls outside the scope of this book, the performance of the Socialist party in that contest illustrates several important aspects of political insurgency in the late nineteenth century. First, before 1904, no party of any significance openly avowed socialist principles in American presidential elections. In fact, the first appearance of such a party was made only in 1888 when Socialist Labor mounted a campaign drawing just over 2,000 votes in New York State. The party offered a ticket nowhere else in the nation. In 1892, Socialist Labor offered a ticket in five states, all in the Northeast, and drew just over 21,000 votes (about a fifth of 1% of the national total). Running again in 1896, the party appeared in twenty states, polling some 36,000 votes (about a quarter of 1% of the national total). The Socialist Labor party continued to run tickets well into the twentieth century but never polled as much as a third of 1 percent of total vote. Far more important was the Socialist party, which ran Eugene Debs as its nominee in every presidential election from 1900 through 1912. The party's vote was only six tenths of 1 percent of the national total in 1900, but climbed to just under 3 percent in both 1904 and 1908. The best showing for the Socialist party, in fact for any party openly avowing socialist principles, came in 1912 when Debs polled just a hair under 6 percent of the national vote.[95]

The Socialist vote doubled in size for exactly one reason: In a dramatic turn about from previous policy, the party endorsed the private ownership of land by those who worked it. Prior to 1912, the Socialist party had slavishly followed Marx and Engels in condemning farmers to "the idiocy of rural life" in which class conflict was hopelessly muddled by preindustrial social formations; for that reason, orthodox socialists believed that agricultural producers would always lag behind urban workers in political sophistication and insurgent mobilization. They thus concluded that even

[94] See Map 6.1 and accompanying discussion in Chapter 6.
[95] Many of the election returns cited in this section can be found in *Congressional Quarterly's Guide to U.S. Elections* (Washington, D.C., 1975), pp. 276–284, 301–303.

transient concessions to agrarian radicals were to be avoided.[96] Victor Berger was an exception. In 1898, he included in the founding declaration of principles of the new Social Democratic party, the immediate forerunner of the Socialist party, five "Demands for Farmers" that almost copied planks that had previously appeared in Populist platforms throughout the South and West:

(1) government agricultural storage facilities; (2) telephone service and other communication services for rural communities; (3) public credit for local governments that wanted to undertake improvements such as irrigation; (4) uniform railroad charges for agricultural cargoes; and (5) an end to public land sales; government land should either be used for public purposes or "leased to farmers in small parcels of not over 640 acres, the state to make strict regulations as to improvement and cultivation."[97]

These demands, as otherwise sympathetic to farmers as they might seem, omitted any guarantee or endorsement of private landownership by agricultural producers. Even so, they sparked an internal "civil war" over doctrinal orthodoxy that raged throughout this period. In 1899, for example, a referendum of the party membership defeated the Demands for Farmers by a vote of 478 to 81.[98] Without a provision for private land ownership, the Socialist party denied itself access to the largest block of potentially insurgent voters in the nation.[99] Restricted to an urban, working-class, and professional base, the Socialists made only moderate progress between 1900 and 1912, most noticeably in Milwaukee where Berger led the party. There Berger hoped to extend the party into the outlying agricultural districts by moderating party principles on land and other agricultural issues as part of a larger, more pragmatic electoral strategy.[100] When the national party finally endorsed private land ownership in 1912, the number and proportion of farmers who responded to the party's call were much greater in the southern and western periphery than in the wealthier agricultural regions of the manufacturing belt (see Map 4.6).

Liberated from the doctrinal shackles that had prevented the party from

---

[96] Donald B. Marti, "Answering the Agrarian Question: Socialists, Farmers, and Algie Martin Simons," *Agricultural History* 65:3 (Summer 1991): 54. Even ostensibly moderate labor leaders, such as Samuel Gompers, shared this attitude toward farmers (p. 55).

[97] As paraphrased, with the exception of the last portion, in Marti, "Answering the Agrarian Question," p. 56.

[98] Ira Kipnis, *The American Socialist Movement, 1897–1912* (Westport, Conn.: Greenwood Press, 1968), pp. 67, 69–73.

[99] The national party convention in 1908, in fact, went out of its way to repel agricultural producers by explicitly including land among those means of production to be placed under social ownership. Marti, "Answering the Agrarian Question," p. 66.

[100] Ibid., p. 57.

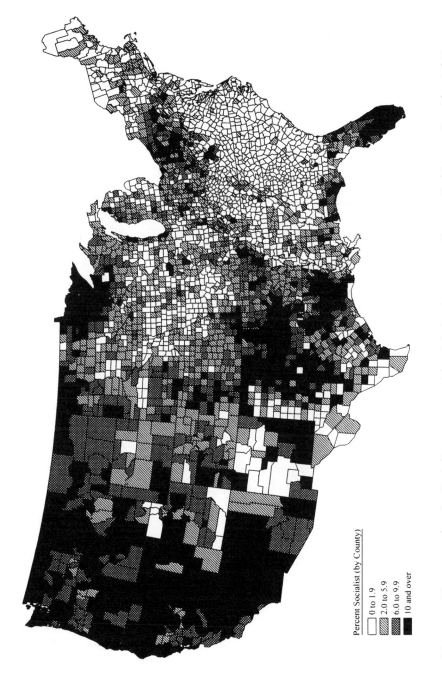

Percent Socialist (by County)

☐ 0 to 1.9
▨ 2.0 to 5.9
▦ 6.0 to 9.9
■ 10 and over

Map 4.6. Votes cast for the Socialist party, presidential election, 1912. *Source:* Robinson, *Presidential Vote, 1914 World Almanac,* and manuscript returns in individual state archives.

Table 4.13. *Top Ten Insurgent States in the 1880, 1892, 1896, and 1912 Presidential Elections (%)*

Greenback Labor 1880	Populist 1892	Democrat 1896	Socialist 1912
Texas (11.7)	Nevada (66.8)	Mississippi (91.0)	Nevada (16.5)
Iowa (10.0)	Colorado (57.1)	South Carolina (85.3)	Oklahoma (16.4)
Michigan (9.9)	Idaho (54.2)	Colorado (84.9)	Montana (13.5)
Kansas (9.8)	Kansas (50.3)	Utah (82.7)	Arizona (13.4)
Missouri (8.8)	North Dakota (49.0)	Nevada (81.2)	Washington (12.4)
W. Virginia (8.0)	Wyoming (46.2)	Montana (79.9)	California (11.7)
Mississippi (5.0)	Nebraska (41.5)	Idaho (78.1)	Idaho (11.3)
Nebraska (4.4)	South Dakota (37.8)	Louisiana (76.4)	Oregon (9.7)
Kentucky (4.3)	Alabama (36.6)	Arkansas (73.7)	Florida (9.5)
Illinois (4.2)	Oregon (34.3)	Florida (70.4)	Ohio (8.7)

Note and source: States are ranked by the percentage of their total vote cast for the indicated party. For the state election returns, see *Congressional Quarterly's Guide to U.S. Elections* (Washington, D.C., 1975), pp. 276–284.

exploiting the insurgent traditions of the South and West, the 1912 campaign produced an electoral pattern strikingly reminiscent of both the Populist and Bryan crusades. However, the Socialists were stronger in the coalfields and steel towns of western Pennsylvania, West Virginia, and eastern Ohio; they were also much weaker in the eastern half of the South where disfranchising legislation had forced many poor whites and blacks off the voting rolls. Aside from the eastern coal districts, the centers of Socialist strength lay in the mining and farming counties of the Far West beyond the Continental Divide, in the southwestern agricultural regions of Louisiana, Oklahoma, and Texas, in the iron ore ranges of northeastern Minnesota and northwestern Wisconsin, and in Florida. As in previous insurgent campaigns, western and southern states led the nation, and the Northeast was shut out (see Table 4.13). As before, the most recently settled states tended to be overrepresented, Arizona and Oklahoma prominent among the 1912 leaders. In 1892, Idaho, North Dakota, Wyoming, and South Dakota had just recently been admitted to the Union and were among the Populist vanguard. In 1896, Utah had voted for the first time and overwhelmingly supported Bryan. Political insurgency in late nineteenth- and early twentieth-century presidential elections tended to follow the frontier, particularly those areas in which imported capital from the East underpinned economic development. In sharp contrast, industrial workers, the shining hope of the more orthodox among the Socialist membership, appeared far more often in the enthusiastic ranks of regular Republicanism than they did among the heretical columns of insurgency.

An examination of the county returns between 1880 and 1912 isolates just one significant pocket of consistent insurgent strength (see Table 4.14). Among the 2,000 or so counties in the United States that cast ballots in all four elections, only twenty-six delivered consistently high levels of support to insurgent candidates. Among these twenty-six, the obvious outlier was Graham County in western Kansas. In many ways, Graham was no different from the dozens of counties around it; rainfall was erratic, the population was sparse and overwhelmingly rural, and boom and bust cycles severely tested the people in the 1880s and 1890s. Graham, however, did have an unusual settlement of blacks who had migrated, primarily from Kentucky, just before the great exoduster migration in 1879 and 1880. These blacks had taken up land in what was a planned colony in Nicodemus township (named for an ex-slave who was the first black in the United States to purchase his freedom). While blacks already comprised a majority of this township's population when the exoduster migration set in, they were hostile to the new arrivals and very few settled there. While the colony did not prosper, it did not die out either, making up about 16 percent of the county's population in 1885. It should be noted that this colony was primarily a commercial venture with little in the way of utopian or radical vision behind its founding.[101]

The twenty-five insurgent counties in Texas were roughly distributed in an arc around all but the northern side of Dallas and Ft. Worth, with a slightly heavier concentration to the southwest. They shared a number of developmental characteristics with Graham. For example, fifteen reported, as did the Kansas County, adult male illiteracy rates well below the national average in 1900. Like Graham, the Texas counties were relatively poor. Nineteen reported less per capita wealth in 1890 than the national average and all of these fell below the state average as well. Like Graham, too, interest rates in 1890 were comparatively high; all but one of the Texas counties reported rates on farm and home mortgage debt above the national average, and most were at 10 percent or above. Like Graham, residents in ten of the Texas counties filed no patents in 1892. Graham reported only two dollars per capita value-added in manufacturing in 1890, a tiny fraction of the national mark. Many Texas counties fell below even that level and none met or exceeded the national average. In sum, the most consistently insurgent counties in the United States between 1880 and 1912 were highly literate, comparatively and sometimes abysmally impoverished, saddled with extremely high interest rates, and exhibited only the very slightest traces of the rampant industrialization then taking place in the manufacturing belt.

[101] Jennie Small Owen and Kirke Mechem, eds., *The Annals of Kansas, 1886–1925* (Topeka: Kansas State Historical Society, n.d.), vol. 1, p. 9. *Sixth Biennial Report of the Kansas State Board of Agriculture: 1887–1888* (Topeka: Clifford C. Baker, 1889), pp. 176–177. James R. Shortridge, *Peopling the Plains: Who Settled Where in Frontier Kansas* (Lawrence: University of Kansas Press, 1995), pp. 89–90.

Table 4.14. *Counties Providing Consistently High Electoral Support to Insurgent Presidential Candidates, 1880–1912 (%)*

Counties	Greenback Labor 1880	Populist 1892	Democrat 1896	Socialist 1912
Kansas				
Graham	26.0	55.6	64.6	10.5
Texas				
Archer	28.1	14.5	85.5	12.8
Atascosa	11.5	50.4	92.5	10.6
Coleman	15.2	32.5	88.8	13.2
Comanche	14.1	50.9	93.5	21.8
Erath	19.6	44.7	81.4	15.5
Henderson	10.2	35.8	79.1	20.6
Hopkins	16.1	39.1	64.5	11.4
Jack	26.9	46.8	87.3	18.7
Johnson	15.2	32.8	85.1	11.8
Kaufman	23.8	10.7	75.7	10.0
Kimble	42.9	43.3	77.2	11.5
Leon	14.5	26.1	66.8	19.4
Limestone	26.6	28.2	79.3	10.2
McCulloch	19.5	36.6	81.0	17.0
Milam	16.8	39.1	67.5	17.5
Montague	20.1	25.1	91.1	15.9
Nacogdoches	24.8	47.8	76.7	16.3
Palo Pinto	13.5	39.8	90.0	20.6
Parker	22.3	32.1	86.6	16.9
Rains	29.1	51.4	77.4	30.6
San Saba	35.7	43.5	89.9	17.6
Somervell	14.8	53.6	96.6	27.0
Taylor	13.9	29.8	83.2	10.0
Van Zandt	24.3	44.9	82.9	29.1
Wood	26.8	25.9	76.6	17.3

Note and sources: This list includes all counties in the United States that cast at least 10 percent of their votes for the Greenback Labor party in 1880, the Populist party in 1892, and the Socialist party in 1912, as well as at least 60 percent of their votes for the Democratic party in 1896. For the 1880 and 1892 election statistics, the source was W. Dean Burnham, *Presidential Ballots, 1836–1892* (Baltimore: Johns Hopkins University Press, 1955). For Kansas, the Greenback party vote in 1880 was taken from the *American Almanac for 1888* (New York: American News, 1888). For most states, the source for 1896 and 1912 election statistics was Edgar Eugene Robinson, *The Presidential Vote, 1896–1932* (Stanford, Calif.: Stanford University Press, 1947). The Bryan vote in 1896 combines the Democratic and People's party tickets. In all but Texas, the source for the combined vote was the *1898 Boston Journal Almanac* (Boston: Boston Journal, 1898). In Texas, the source was the *1899 World Almanac* (New York: New York World, 1899). The Socialist vote in Kansas was taken from the *1914 World Almanac* (New York: Press Publishing, 1913). For Texas, the Socialist vote was taken from the Report of the Secretary of State.

Almost all of these counties, not surprisingly, were overwhelmingly dependent on agriculture. In Graham, corn, wheat, and other crops shared the field with cattle. In the Texas counties, cotton led the way with cattle close behind, followed by corn and hogs. Most of the very little manufacturing activity was devoted to cotton-ginning and, after 1890 or so, cottonseed processing in local market centers. In a few cases, flour mills were also present but these must have been very small compared with those in the northern plains. In one or two instances lumber mills made an appearance, but these, too, must have been comparatively tiny. Almost all of these counties were rapidly settled in the late nineteenth century with growth continuing after 1900. Although interest rates were high, there was evidently at least one bank in almost all communities. Compared with the rest of the South, capital was available but it wasn't cheap. Despite the poverty and recent settlement of these counties, there were an abnormally high number of high schools and private academies, again compared with the remainder of the South. Newspapers were common as well. Rains and Van Zandt were the only two counties that delivered more than 20 percent of their votes to each of the four insurgent campaigns and thus might be considered the most insurgent of the group, but other than the fact that they bordered each other, they were rather typical in their general characteristics.

Two of the Texas counties, Parker and Taylor, were a little more developed than the others. Weatherford, the Parker County seat, contained a number of newspapers and banks, Rutherford College, the Texas Female Seminary, cotton mills, cotton gins and compresses, flour mills, and a few coal mines. Weatherford's population of 3,369 in 1890 made it the largest city in any of these counties (including Graham), but it might be noted that the large majority of these counties did not hold a town of even a thousand souls. Taylor was the most urbanized, if the term can be properly used here, county; the city of Abilene, with a population of 3,194 in 1890, comprised almost half of the local population. Abilene held a number of national banks and newspapers, a Baptist college, a public high school, flour mills, and small factories and shops producing saddles, harnesses, ice, and miscellaneous iron products. The city was also a major collection point for grain and livestock.[102] In neither Weatherford or Abilene is there any evidence of working-class organization or political activity; in fact, in none of the counties, including Graham in Kansas, were there any recorded strikes during the period from 1885 to 1894.

The thick connections in both personnel and ideology between the Greenback, Populist, and Bryan campaigns explains the continuity between them

---

[102] The sources for much of the detailed information on these counties were the respective entries for both counties and county seats in *Lippincott's Gazetteer of the World*, vols. 1 and 2 (Philadelphia: J. B. Lippincott, 1893), and *Lippincott's New Gazetteer* (Philadelphia: J. B. Lippincott, 1906).

in these counties. However, sixteen years elapsed between Bryan and Deb's campaign in 1912, and most of the Socialist national leadership resided in the nation's manufacturing belt, far away from the regional redoubts of Populism. There is abundant evidence that many Populists turned to the Socialist party in the late 1890s and early 1900s. However, few Populists became Socialists until their own party had failed.[103] And the leadership of the Socialist Labor party, the only socialist organization in the field prior to 1898, was openly hostile to the Populists.[104] Before he announced his conversion to socialism, however, Eugene Debs warmly supported both the Populists and Bryan.[105] Writing after the latter's nomination in 1896, for example, Debs sent a congratulatory note:

My dear Mr. Bryan,
With millions of others of your countrymen I congratulate you most heartily upon being the People's standard bearer in the great uprising of the masses against the classes. You are at this hour the hope of the Republic – the central figure of the civilized world. In the arduous campaign before you the millions will rally to your standard and you will lead them to glorious victory. The people love and trust you – they believe in you as you believe in them, and under your administration the rule of the money power will be broken and the gold barons of Europe will no longer run the American government.[106]

Debs himself had been frequently mentioned as a possible standard-bearer for the Populist party in 1896. And in Texas in particular, the radical nature of the Populist platforms, combined with the wholesale movement of former Populist leaders into the new Socialist party around 1900, produced much continuity between the two organizations.[107] The migration of former Populists into the new Socialist party was evident in many other states as well.[108] As one, albeit unfriendly, Kansas paper put the matter in 1893: "All

[103] For example, Lawrence Goodwyn reported that fewer than twenty of the 1,300 delegates attending the 1896 Populist national convention were Socialists. *Democratic Promise*, p. 675 n. 1.

[104] Goodwyn, *Democratic Promise*, pp. 659–660 n. 2.

[105] Nick Salvatore, *Eugene V. Debs: Citizen and Socialist* (Urbana: University of Illinois Press, 1982), pp. 147–148, 157–161.

[106] In an accompanying note, Constantine states that "Bryan's defeat by William McKinley in 1896 was a contributing factor in Debs's public endorsement of socialism the following year." J. Robert Constantine, ed., *Letters of Eugene V. Debs: 1874–1912*, vol. 1 (Urbana: University of Illinois Press, 1990), pp. 120–122.

[107] Martin, *People's Party in Texas*, pp. 79–80. Martin provided a comparison of prior Populist voting strength in those precincts which voted Socialist in the 1912 race for governor. For an examination of the Populist origins of much of the Socialist vote in Lewis County, in the state of Washington, see Marilyn P. Watkins, *Rural Democracy: Family Farmers and Politics in Western Washington, 1890–1925* (Ithaca, N.Y.: Cornell University Press, 1995), pp. 113–122.

[108] On the movement of Populist activists in Idaho into the Socialist party after the turn of the century, see Gaboury, *Dissension in the Rockies*, pp. 419–421. For the state of Washington, see Riddle, *Old Radicalism*, pp. 257, 281–284.

Populists are not socialists . . . but all socialists . . . are Populists."[109] To the extent that Populists evolved into socialists, however, they were not doctrinally committed to socialized ownership of the land – that orthodox commitment, imported with other Eurocentric doctrinal exclusions of American yeomanry, was a major factor underlying the failure of a cross-class alliance between homestead and sharecropper agriculture, on the one hand, and the industrial worker, on the other.[110] However, as is shown repeatedly in this chapter, there was little indication of political insurgency on the part of the industrial worker, regardless of how claims on wealth were framed in party platforms.

CONCLUSION

The industrial worker chose instead to pursue claims on wealth through strike activity on the shop floor, combining rather apolitical strikes with support for the industrial tariff and other forms of intersectional redistribution in national politics. The absence of working-class radicalism did not mean that major party politics was an empty exercise in rhetorical obfuscation. In fact, the Republicans and Democrats offered very clear and competing visions of American economic development. The Republican program privileged the interests of the manufacturing belt with strong and largely unvarying commitments to both tariff protection and the gold standard. The center of the party's strength correspondingly lay in the nation's industrial core among the country's financial and corporate leadership. The industrial worker was divided between local and individual state policies that enabled effective claim-making in the workplace (e.g., eight-hour-day legislation and statutes encouraging union recognition) and the larger political economy of wealth redistribution between the southern and western periphery and the manufacturing belt. Positive local and individual state intervention into capital-labor relations tended to attract workers to state Democratic parties in the North, while the national campaigns tended to drive them into the Republican party. Barring economic crises, however, most industrial laborers, particularly skilled, native-born workers, remained loyal to the Republican party.

[109] *Topeka State Journal*, January 24, 1893, quoted in Peter H. Argersinger, *The Limits of Agrarian Radicalism: Western Populism and American Politics* (Lawrence: University of Kansas Press, 1995), p. 284 n. 23.

[110] That Eurocentric perspective on what should properly constitute political radicalism, as Lawrence Goodwyn noted, has long dominated the American academy as well: "As objects of study, the Populists themselves were to fall victim to the inability of twentieth-century humanists of various ideological persuasions to conceive that authentic political substance might originate outside such acceptable intellectual sources as the progressive, capitalist, middle classes or the European socialist heritage." *Democratic Promise*, p. 551. For a slightly different perspective, see Hahn, *Roots of Southern Populism*, p. 3.

The Democratic party presented a very different developmental program, one that privileged the interests of the commodity-exporting South. In Congress, a majority of the party's members and much of its leadership became very strongly committed to free trade and opposed to the gold standard. But the quadrennial national conventions were weighted toward the northern states where the party was comparatively weak (and thus lightly represented in Congress) and recognized that the party's southern base had to be expanded in order to win. For that reason, Democratic national conventions offered the North, particularly New York State, ambiguous formal endorsements of the gold standard in their platforms and practically unshakable commitments in the form of presidential candidates. Until the strategy was abandoned in 1896, this concession made the Democrats both competitive in national elections and hopelessly divided over financial questions once a Democrat won the presidency and subsequently confronted congressional party caucuses overwhelmingly hostile to gold. Bryan and the conversion to free silver would have eliminated that particular incongruency, had he been elected, but the party's concessions to agrarian insurgency may have promised even more serious problems with representatives of southern planters. Because the Democrats never won the presidency with an agrarian insurgent as the nominee, these problems never surfaced; instead, the regional wings of the party successfully deflected most local conflict over income shares in the South and West into proposals to redress disparities on the sectional redistribution of wealth.[111]

[111]   One of the net effects of the abandonment of gold in the 1896 Democratic platform was the increased congruence between sectional claims on wealth and the programs presented to the electorate by the two major parties. As a result of this increasing congruence and other factors, the general level of major party competition decreased throughout much of the United States as voters in the manufacturing belt increasingly gravitated toward the Republicans and those in the periphery toward the Democrats. Viewed from the broadest perspective, the interpretation proposed in the text is very similar to that forcefully outlined by Burnham, "Changing Shape of the American Political Universe," pp. 23, 24–26. Some of the major points of difference are, from the point of view of this book: (1) the more explicit connection between industrialization as an economic process and the structure of the party system; (2) the more contingent dependence of voting coalitions on programmatic commitments by the parties (e.g., realignments in voter allegiance tended to persist because the changing programmatic commitments that originally sparked voter shifts tended to persist – in practice, however, this is not much different from an interpretation that places more emphasis on "critical" elections as the progenitor of enduring party loyalties); (3) a less elitist approach in that it was the very structure of the national political economy that shaped both elitist and popular political positions and sentiment – although elites certainly offered their own, self-interested interpretations of competing party programs, those interpretations were largely persuasive to the mass public only to the extent that they were consistent with the actual operation of the national political economy; and (4) a less functionalist interpretation in that, while insulation of the process of capital accumulation in the manufacturing sector from popular political claims was a necessary and perhaps the most

The 1896 campaign turned the Democratic party into an insurgent vehicle in presidential politics. As such, the Democratic organization was imperfect, driven by southern Bourbons who, while radical in their opinions on the sectional distribution of wealth, were fairly orthodox concerning the class and racial organization of their region. However, there is no doubt that the Democrats, led by their southern wing, were the most progressive of the two major parties in national politics. In Congress this had been true since the end of Reconstruction.[112] In one sense, Bryan's candidacy merely brought the presidential nomination and platform into line with the congressional wing of the party and the large majority of the party's membership. In another sense, however, the new commitments in the national platform to silver and agrarian issues generally broke the back of the party over the "fault line" between the rapidly industrializing and capital-exporting East, on the one hand, and the agrarian and capital-importing South and West, on the other. From that perspective, the "System of 1896" opposed "the country's urban-industrial Metropole against its semicolonial Periphery" in such a way as to cleanse the party of inhibiting compromise with its eastern wing.[113]

The "Battle of the Standards" has often been dismissed as a sham conflict over which of two equally sterile metals would serve as the foundation for the monetary system. In fact, in its division of regions and individuals, no policy dispute cut as cleanly across the nation. To take a stand for gold was to be placed firmly in the ranks of the enlightened economic thought and interests of the eastern industrial core (and Europe as well). This was true whether the citizen lived in Beacon Hill or Wichita. In the East, gold sentiment was hegemonic, so much so that even the most unskilled worker must have felt its pull when McKinley faced off against Bryan. For many easterners, the continuing attraction of the Democratic party was that the more elitist elements had been purged from the organization because they would not support the new monetary plank, leaving control to more recent immigrant groups with strange names and religions. Within the eastern wing of the Democratic party, then, silver became a litmus test that

important element in American industrialization, that insulation was not thereby automatically called forth by the system – instead, the insulation of privately held wealth in industrial corporations was largely the result of favorable, but contingent, implications for coalition formation arising out of the extremely uneven course of American economic development. However, the differences between Burnham's interpretation and the one proposed here should not be overdrawn; this may be more complex, contingent, and centered in popular sentiment than Burnham's earlier and seminal work but most of these differences would probably have been incorporated into any elaboration of his earlier model.

[112] For a full exploration of the importance of southern Democrats to reform legislation in Congress from the end of Reconstruction through the Progressive era, see Sanders, *Roots of Reform*, esp. 314–386.

[113] Kleppner, *Continuity and Change*, pp. 36–37, 51.

identified class and nativity, things otherwise seemingly far removed from the logic of monetary policy.

In the West and South, gold identified the agents of eastern capital. Many were directly employed as representatives or officers of banks, insurance companies, or railroads. Others were formally independent of eastern wealth holders but practically ensnared in a web of market relations that inextricably connected their interests to those in the East. Most of these embattled gold bugs were small-town bankers, railroad agents, and commodity merchants, and even where they were not entirely persuaded by the merits of the case for gold, they were monitored into conformity by their eastern connections because financial heterodoxy was a sure sign of uncertain or unsound business methods. Outside Main Street, silver reigned supreme with scarcely a dissent in the more remote and poorer agricultural districts. Silver in that sense was a declaration of independence from the East, a demand for a level playing field between the sections within the ongoing rush to industrialization. Gold was the banner of developmental paternalism – the enlightened recognition that, while economic development may eventually improve conditions everywhere, the necessary sacrifice would always be disproportionately borne by the benighted sectors and communities of a nation.

For most of the nation, particularly for the eastern industrial core and the southern agrarian periphery, the alternatives of gold and silver stood in for much larger complexes of sectionally based claims on wealth; as a result, the "System of 1896" transformed the regional poles of uneven national development into political redoubts for the Republicans in the manufacturing belt and the Democrats in the South.[114] As the Republicans consolidated their grip over the burgeoning cities of the East, there was no doubt which section had won this first and only major conflict over the course of American industrialization.

[114]   Ibid., p. 71 and chap. 2 generally. See, also, Kleppner, *Third Electoral System*, p. 19.

5

Political Construction of the National Market

THE EMERGENCE of the United States as an advanced industrial nation was driven by the rise of the modern business enterprise as the primary organizational form of mass production.[1] Composed of many specialized operating divisions managed by a hierarchy of salaried executives, the modern business enterprise absorbed into its bureaucratic organization many of the allocating and coordinating functions previously performed by decentralized and often isolated markets in the preindustrial economy. Although the marketplace ultimately generated the price signals through which changes in demand were registered, in many sectors the modern business enterprise transformed arm's-length transactions between economic actors into institutional decisions concerning questions of supply, coordination of production, and distribution of goods. The engine behind the rise of the modern corporation was its ability to organize production of high volume, complex industrial goods more efficiently than smaller firms that had not similarly integrated resource-gathering and manufacturing tasks. For that reason, one of the major preconditions for the rise of the modern business enterprise was the existence of a large unregulated market; this market provided the raw materials and the consumer base through which to exploit the economies of scale for which the modern business enterprise was ideally suited.[2]

Arising between 1840 and the First World War, the managerial, multidivisional organization of the modern corporation was almost predestined to

[1] Robert E. Gallman, "Commodity Output, 1839–1899," in National Bureau of Economic Research, *Trends in the American Economy in the Nineteenth Century* (Princeton, N.J.: Princeton University Press, 1960), p. 40; Edward Chase Kirkland, *Industry Comes of Age: Business, Labor and Public Policy, 1860–1897* (Chicago: Quadrangle Books, 1967), pp. 278–305.
[2] Alfred D. Chandler, Jr., *The Visible Hand: The Managerial Revolution in American Business* (Cambridge, Mass.: Harvard University Press, 1977), pp. 1–11.

appear first in the United States. Possessing a large unregulated national market – aside from Britain, probably the largest such market in the world – the United States also presented the precise organizational challenge which, given the state of industrial technology in the early nineteenth century, most encouraged progressive evolution toward managerial capitalism. That organizational challenge arose out of the conjunction of three factors: the vast distances separating centers of supply and demand, the highly developed regional specialization in agricultural production, and the peculiar operating requirements of the railroad. The first two factors produced the demand for high-volume, long-distance freight that encouraged, more than any other national market in the world, the expansion of the railroad network. The last, particularly the problems of coordinating freight assignment in railroad yards and the movement of trains over great distances, drove railroad companies to first experiment with multiunit organizations and, then, once such organizations had demonstrated their utility, to ruthlessly exploit their potential for lowering transportation costs. American railroads were, for these reasons, the first modern business enterprises in the world, and from that sector, this novel form of economic organization spread throughout the expanding industrial and commercial sectors.[3]

This chapter describes the political construction of an unregulated national market in the late nineteenth century. Created through the intentional and purposeful exercise of central state authority against state and local challenges, the national market was neither a natural nor an inevitable feature of the American political economy.[4] This chapter also describes how, in the absence of political barriers to commerce, corporate consolidation became the major force driving the integration of the country's diverse regional economies into one system. While unifying the nation into one economy, the expansion of the national market also encouraged geographical specialization and, thus, regional differentiation within the United States.

The national market was a rapidly evolving and expanding system both in purely economic terms and in its political implications. In the early decades of the nineteenth century, most firms were quite small and the opportunities or occasion for local regulation of interstate trade were infrequent. With the emergence of the railroad after 1840, interstate trade began

---

[3] Ibid., pp. 13–14, 49, 76–87, 121, 124, 244–245.

[4] All national markets are, of course, consciously constructed economic spaces requiring facilitating central state policies. But in the case of the United States, this fact is almost routinely forgotten. For example, William Cronon never addresses the political origins and maintenance of the unregulated economic space in which Chicago mobilized and transformed the ecological environment of the Midwest in his *Nature's Metropolis: Chicago and the Great West* (New York: W. W. Norton, 1991).

to rapidly expand. Aside from the southern cotton belt, already integrated into the world economy, the railroad in many ways transformed the United States from a disparate collection of self-sufficient local communities into an integrated national market.[5] Just after the end of Reconstruction, this national market was still a highly circumscribed abstraction; even in the absence of political barriers, the rudimentary transportation and marketing networks of the nation did not permit the consolidation of industrial processes through which efficiencies of scale could be exploited. By the turn of the century, these networks, themselves subjected to corporate consolidation and reorganization, amply provided the means through which organizational and technological advances in the major industrial processes might be harnessed.[6] As the 1900 census pointed out, the "mainland of the United States is the largest area in the civilized world which is thus unrestricted by customs, excises, or national prejudice, and its population possesses, because of its great collective wealth, a larger consuming capacity than that of any other nation."[7] In many ways, the national market was a moving target, in the process of becoming an integrated system even as it attracted political challenges from peripheral communities absorbed into its network. As such, it was a political construction, not a natural endowment of the physical terrain or an inevitable artifact of the cultural predilections of the people. And, as a political construction, it was the product of politics and blood.

THE IMPACT OF THE CIVIL WAR ON THE EMERGENCE OF THE NATIONAL MARKET

The Civil War played a number of roles in the construction of the national market. Most important, Union victory suppressed southern separatism and forced the South back into what once again became the American nation. If the South had won the war, a substantial portion of what became the postwar national market would have been lost. In addition, the secession

---

[5] For a general discussion of the impact of the railroad on the economy and American society, see Cronon, *Nature's Metropolis*, pp. 74–80.

[6] On the consolidation of the national transportation and communication networks, see, for example, Thomas C. Cochran and William Miller, *The Age of Enterprise: A Social History of Industrial America*, rev. ed. (New York: Harper Torchbooks, 1961), p. 151.

[7] *1900 Census of Manufactures*, pt. 1 (Washington, D.C.: U.S. Census Office, 1902), p. lviii. For a rich overview of the social and economic topography of the United States in this period, see D. W. Meinig, *The Shaping of America: A Geographical Perspective on 500 Years of History*, vol. 3: *Transcontinental America, 1850–1915* (New Haven, Conn.: Yale University Press, 1998), particularly pp. 187–323.

of the South, along with capture of the federal government by the Republican party, broke a sectional deadlock in Congress that had hitherto prevented passage of measures such as the protective tariff, the Homestead Act, and the transcontinental railroad. All of these and a host of new policies, such as the national bank act, became structuring features of the postbellum political economy and, thus, the framework within which the industrialization and the expanding national market were to unfold.[8] Moreover, the Union war mobilization accelerated the commodification of major sectors of the United States economy that had previously been only partially integrated into the market. The northern war effort, for example, created a huge market for oats and pork that, in turn, stimulated speculation in the future prices of these commodities. One immediate outcome was the institutionalization of futures trading on the Chicago Board of Trade through the adoption of formal rules governing such contracts in 1865. Similarly, the need for a centralized market for the clearing of livestock transactions led, first, to the transfer of meatpacking operations from Cincinnati to Chicago and, subsequently, to the consolidation of livestock sales in the Union Stockyard.[9]

Over a longer term, Union victory vindicated principles of national sovereignty that were later forged into constitutional doctrines that suppressed state and local attempts to control "interstate commerce." These principles, crafted by Republican justices sitting on the United States Supreme Court, evolved into constitutional doctrines that prohibited the erection of barriers to national corporate operations. Finally, the electoral coalitions undergirding the major party system in the last quarter of the nineteenth century were to a large extent forged during and immediately after the Civil War. Although substantial continuity between the respective antebellum and post-Reconstruction party systems is readily apparent, the intervening Civil War hardened the alliances between the groups composing each of the major parties, renewed and extended their policy foundations in the national political economy, and created, in the southern freedman, a new and strategically located bloc of voters. In all these ways, the Civil War was an integral and fundamental contributor to the political construction and maintenance of the national market and, through that contribution, to the political economy of industrialization.

[8]   With reference to the transcontinental railroad, see Cronon, *Nature's Metropolis*, p. 301. With reference to the sectional deadlock and its disappearance with the beginning of the Civil War, see Richard Franklin Bensel, *Yankee Leviathan: The Origins of Central State Authority in America, 1859–1877* (New York: Cambridge University Press, 1990), pp. 88–93. On the impact of the Civil War on the rise of the industrial corporation, see Roger L. Ransom, *Conflict and Compromise: The Political Economy of Slavery, Emancipation, and the American Civil War* (New York: Cambridge University Press, 1989), pp. 279–284.

[9]   Cronon, *Nature's Metropolis*, pp. 124, 210, 230.

The National Market and Transformation of the West

The transformative forces associated with the national market worked their greatest influence on the Plains and West. There rapid sale of the public domain – the conversion of government holdings into private property – extended the free economic space of the national market westward and spurred on the commodification of the natural resource base of the region. Disposal of the public domain in the nineteenth century was highly cyclical, with short, explosive boom periods followed by longer stretches of relative quiescence. In 1836, the first of the land booms moved over 20 million acres into the national market. A national recession in 1837, brought on by President Andrew Jackson's refusal to accept private bank notes in payment for public land sales, brought that boom to a halt.[10] In 1855 and 1856, the second of the three great land booms occurred, taking about 35 million acres out of the public domain. This boom was also followed by a national recession, but in this case, the crash originated on Wall Street.[11]

During the third and last of the great land booms, the number of acres sold or otherwise given over to the private economy exceeded 16 million in every year from 1883 through 1887. Driven by a synergistic combination of heavy land sales and large regional importations of capital, western railroad construction added mileage to the national network at rates never before equaled in history. The St. Paul and Manitoba, for example, worked its construction crews in relays around the clock in an attempt to complete a route to Helena in the Montana Territory in time for the fall harvest. On August 11, 1887, the road laid down eight miles of new track in a single day.[12] As the nation's leading financial journal put it:

... the land speculation in the West and Southwest ... is following in the wake of the new railroad building and encouraged by the large immigration present and prospective, the sinews of war being provided by bond issues for local improvements, by mortgages on advancing town lots, and by other paper devices for raising money. ... In Kansas it is stated that the speculation keeps full abreast of the railroad surveys for routes, and as there is to be no lack of railroads in that State hereafter, there is hardly a square mile that has not its town lots for sale. ... It all looks a little fast to a conservative mind ...[13]

Unlike colonization, in which compact, organized groups of settlers occupied land in the name of a particular nation, most of the settlement of the

[10]   Roy M. Robbins, *Our Landed Heritage: The Public Domain, 1776–1936* (Lincoln: University of Nebraska Press, 1962), pp. 70–71.

[11]   James L. Huston, *The Panic of 1857 and the Coming of the Civil War* (Baton Rouge: Louisiana State University Press, 1987), pp. 14–24.

[12]   *Commercial and Financial Chronicle*, August 27, 1887.

[13]   Ibid., May 28, 1887.

West was driven by market forces that scattered migrants across the landscape, often in the wake of railroad construction or the removal of Native American tribes.[14] Laying down roads, platting lots in what were expected to become county seats, and locating sites for the public schools, these migrants attempted to replicate the political, social, and economic organization of more mature communities to the east. In some of its aspects, such as the provision of public domain lands for support of local schools, the framework within which these communities developed was set by the federal government. However, even though disposal of the public domain through sale, homestead settlement, railroad grants, and distribution to the states were all self-conscious central state policies, the net effect was only to place that land in private hands just about as fast as the expansion of the national market could put a price on it.[15] The federal government otherwise did little to guide western development. By 1890, the frontier – the original settlement of the public domain for the purpose of pursuing general, diversified agriculture – largely disappeared from the national political economy, persisting only in the western reaches of Kansas and North Dakota and in the Palouse region of the Pacific Northwest.[16]

Encouraged by immense grants of government land that were to be earned by the construction of new main line track into the plains and mountains, the railroads rapidly expanded westward beyond the Mississippi River. The most spectacular of these penetrations established the great transcontinental connections between the East and the Pacific Ocean – the Union Pacific, the Santa Fe, the Southern Pacific, and the Northern Pacific. More mundane but ultimately involving much heavier capital commitments was the backing and filling of the system, as companies constructed "feeder" lines and interbranch connections that both swelled the volume of freight and increased the efficiency of their operations. In addition and coincidentally, the land grant railroads became the premier promoters of western settlement, establishing land companies in order to market their holdings to prospective farmers and widely advertising the availability and attractiveness of the agricultural and commercial opportunities available along their rights of way.[17] The subsequent movement of people from the most remote points of Europe to the frontier of western settlement in the United States was remarkably efficient: On the average, transportation

---

[14] Benjamin Horace Hibbard, *A History of the Public Land Policies* (Madison: University of Wisconsin Press, 1965), p. 556.
[15] For a description of federal reservations of public land for support of the common schools, see Hibbard, *History of the Public Land Policies*, pp. 311–324.
[16] Ibid., p. 543.
[17] Kirkland, *Industry Comes of Age*, p. 60. Also see R. C. Overton, *Burlington West: A Colonization History of the Burlington Railroad* (Cambridge, Mass.: Harvard University Press, 1941); Paul W. Gates, *Fifty Million Acres: Conflicts over Kansas Land Policy, 1854–1890* (Ithaca, N.Y.: Cornell University Press, 1954), pp. 249–294.

from the furthest European capital to the railroad station nearest the new immigrant's land holdings cost about $70.[18] Because the process of transforming the settlement of western lands into the profitable movement of crops over company lines took years to complete, land sales and immigration were a very forward-looking factor in estimating a road's future returns. However, eastern investors still attempted to factor annual fluctuations in immigration into their valuations of land-grant railroad bonds and stock.[19]

Although the outlines of what became the national rail network were already in place by the end of Reconstruction, the network continued to expand through the last decades of the nineteenth century. Much of rail construction after 1877 was associated with system-building through which large regional carriers absorbed smaller competitors into their organizations, increasing their operating efficiencies by consolidating their combined operations and providing for more direct routes between points within their respective regions. Even before the last of the great merger waves in the railroad network, some companies had already reached a scale of operations that rivaled those of the federal government. In 1891, for example, the Pennsylvania Railroad employed over 110,000 workers, almost three times the number of men in the combined armed services of the United States.[20] The entire rail system, made up of many competing companies, was of course much larger.

By 1896, the United States contained 183,601 miles of rail line, not including some 60,000 miles in yards, sidings, and parallel track along main routes. Although the nation occupied only 6 percent of the land area of the globe and contained an even smaller share of the world's population, the mileage in the country's rail network represented approximately 42 percent of the world's total. In 1895, the total capitalization of American railroads was almost $35 billion, roughly 30 percent of the total capitalization of all the world's railways.[21] The amount of money received and spent by the railroad system was equivalent to about 15 percent of the nation's annual production of wealth and exceeded the combined total for all government expenditures, federal, state, and local.[22] Almost 800,000 men, over 3 percent of the nation's entire work force, were employed by the railroads.[23]

[18] Robbins, *Our Landed Heritage*, p. 270.
[19] *Commercial and Financial Chronicle*, April 21 and May 12, 1883.
[20] Chandler, *The Visible Hand*, pp. 88, 167, 204.
[21] *Appleton's Annual Cyclopaedia of 1897* (New York: D. Appleton, 1898), pp. 703–705.
[22] Ibid., p. 708. One estimate assigned one-fifth of the total wealth of the United States to the railroad system. *Appleton's Annual Cyclopaedia of 1885* (New York: D. Appleton, 1889), p. 677.
[23] The exact total was 785,034 in 1895, up from 418,957 in 1880. The wage and salary bill for these employees came to approximately a half billion dollars annually. *Appleton's 1897 Cyclopaedia*, p. 705. In 1882, during the great land boom, some 650,000

Table 5.1. *Traffic and Average Rates for the National Railroad Network,*
1880–1900

Year	Volume of traffic		Rates	
	Passenger	Freight	Passenger	Freight
1880	5.7	32.3	2.51	1.29
1890	12.1	80.0	2.20	0.92
1900	16.2	144.0	2.00	0.73

Source: Estimates in Albert Fishlow, "Productivity and Technological Change in the Railroad Sector, 1840–1910," in National Bureau of Economic Research, *Output, Employment, and Productivity in the United States After 1860* (New York: Columbia University Press, 1966), Table 1, p. 585. Traffic is measured in billions of passenger and ton miles. Rates are in terms of cents per passenger and ton of freight moved one mile.

As can be seen in Table 5.1, the volume of passenger traffic over the national railroad system almost tripled between 1880 and 1900 while freight traffic quadrupled. At the same time the cost of rail transport plummeted, particularly for freight.

As the railroad network expanded, the national market became ever more integrated as already developing patterns of interregional trade and economic diversification were extended.[24] Everywhere the railroad went, the local economy was reoriented and transformed in one way or another.[25]

workers were estimated to have been employed in the construction of new rail line but, unlike operating employment, the total varied widely with the construction cycle. *Appleton's 1885 Cyclopaedia*, pp. 678–679.

[24] Kansas was described as "the creature of the railway" and the *Commercial and Financial Chronicle* speculated that, if the railroads were to somehow disappear, "the continual existence of the present population on the soil would be impossible; a hegira, such as ancient populations frequently made in the face of famine, to some more favored locality must ensue; farms, villages, and cities would be abandoned and return to a state of nature, or to such a condition as a re-arrangement of the population on the basis of the distribution of products by primitive processes would necessitate." April 21 and May 12, 1883.

[25] As the *Commercial and Financial Chronicle* noted, the railroad was the most powerful agent operating on most parts of the late nineteenth-century economic landscape: "... when the railway is built, it remains as a permanent investment, an addition to the taxable wealth of the community, and is moreover the most powerful instrumentality in the growth and development of the districts in which it is located...." July 9, 1898. For a particularly useful survey of the impact of the railroad on the development of California cities and the state generally, see S. G. Brock, *Report on the Internal Commerce of the United States, 1890* (Washington, D.C.: GPO, 1891), pp. 174–187.

When, for example, the completion of the Northern Pacific in 1883 finally connected the Pacific Northwest with eastern markets by way of Minneapolis, the new line was reported to be "rapidly working a revolution in the business of the country. Relations long existing with San Francisco still retain a hold, but their grasp is gradually loosening, and the time is not far away when the people will only buy in California things which are produced there. The trade of the Northwest is turning eastward, where buyers have equal opportunities with the San Francisco houses which have heretofore supplied them." One of the "most conspicuous" effects was the stimulus the new connection gave to immigration: Four months after completion, immigrants were said to have been arriving in the Pacific Northwest at the rate of 40,000 a year.[26]

In many respects, the density of the rail network replicated the uneven topography of economic development. Where industrialization, urbanization, and investment in human capital were comparatively high, the network was very dense, in terms of miles of track both per capita and per square mile, and carried a great volume of traffic.[27] In less advanced regions, the rail system was less extensive. This relationship between relative development and railroad density, however, was somewhat stronger at the beginning of the post-Reconstruction period than at the turn of the century. The rapidly industrializing regions of the country added comparatively few miles to their already mature rail network in this period, while southern extensions of the system expanded much more rapidly (without, however, having much impact on the relative per capita income of the region or other general indicators of comparative development). The South, already well settled outside Texas, was clearly incorporated into the national market with little of what had been the historical benefits of that process. Much of the rapidly settling Plains and West, on the other hand, was laying down track hand in hand with a rapid improvement in most measures of relative national development.

In both the South and West much of the expansion of the rail network was primarily an extension of the great trunk lines that already dominated the East. This integration of the remainder of the country into the eastern network was accelerated by a number of developments such as the disappearance of river barriers to through rail traffic. The Mississippi, for example, was bridged at Rock Island in 1856, although a second bridge across the river was not constructed until 1865. The upper Ohio was

[26] *Appleton's Annual Cyclopaedia of 1883* (New York: D. Appleton, 1884), p. 613. Also see the 1887 annual report of the governor of the Washington Territory, reprinted in Allen C. Mason, *Compendium of Information Concerning the City of Tacoma and Washington Territory* (Portland, Oreg.: A. Anderson, 1888), pp. 13–15.

[27] A similar pattern held in Europe as well. See David S. Landes, *The Wealth and Poverty of Nations: Why Some Are So Rich and Some So Poor* (New York: W. W. Norton, 1998), pp. 258–259.

crossed during the Civil War at Steubenville, and in 1870, the lower Ohio was spanned at Cincinnati.[28] Other major rivers were spanned with increasing frequency. In April 1886, for example, the *Commercial and Financial Chronicle* reported that twelve bills proposing bridges over the Mississippi and Missouri rivers had been acted upon despite the fact that the Forty-ninth Congress was only midway through its first session.[29] In part because of the barrier imposed by the Ohio River, the southern rail system originally developed under a gauge different than that of the North – a width of five feet while northern railroads were four feet, eight and one-half inches. Although the difference was small, the disparity prevented the movement of northern engines and rolling stock on southern lines. The problem was not serious as long as freight had to be interchanged at river crossings. With the bridging of the nation's major rivers, however, the difference in widths became much more inefficient and, finally, the southern lines agreed to change over to the northern "standard" gauge. On May 31 and June 1, 1886, between 14,000 and 15,000 miles of track in the South, most of the line within the territory bounded by the Atlantic Ocean, the Gulf of Mexico, and the Ohio and Mississippi rivers, changed over, along with the wheels of engines, tenders, and freight and passenger cars.[30]

As the national network expanded and consolidated, the speed and volume of freight and passenger traffic moving between distant regions rapidly increased, compelling a corresponding national standardization of one of the most basic and familiar elements of local life: time. Prior to the imposition of national time zones in the United States in November 1883, the operating managers of railroad companies relied on the local time of the most important stations along their respective lines. As a result, they would in some instances rely on one standard for coordinating rail traffic along one part of a through route and another standard along another part. When operations had to be coordinated with lines controlled by other

[28] George Rogers Taylor and Irene D. Neu, *The American Railroad Network, 1861–1890* (Cambridge, Mass.: Harvard University Press, 1956), pp. 37, 41, 78.

[29] April 24, 1886. For a list and detailed description of railroad and highway bridges spanning the Mississippi between St. Louis and St. Paul and the Ohio River between Pittsburgh and Cairo, Illinois, in 1888, see William F. Switzler, *Report on the Internal Commerce of the United States, 1888* (Washington, D.C.: GPO, 1888), pp. 19–27, 551–558.

[30] Some of the lines with stronger connections with the North, such as the Illinois Central and the Chesapeake & Ohio, had previously converted to the northern standard. Their trackage is not included in the totals reported in the text. *Commercial and Financial Chronicle*, May 29, 1886. The *Chronicle* observed that "the South has been in a measure shut off from the rest of the country by this lack of uniformity." As the journal noted, the South was the last region of the entire North American continent to convert to standard gauge, both the Canadian and Mexican railroads having long operated at the northern standard. For a good description of how the conversion in gauge was carried out, see Taylor and Neu, *American Railroad Network*, pp. 78–81.

companies, these standards often had to be reconciled, on a more or less ad hoc basis, with those of the other company. By 1883, the multiplication of standards by the individual rail companies had created some seventy-five different time standards throughout the nation. In the Northeast, for example, passengers traveling from Boston to Washington, D.C., were compelled to reset their watches four times in order to keep on the same hour and minute as the engineer and conductor. From Boston to Providence, the governing standard for train traffic was that of Boston. From Providence to New London, Providence took over. From New London to New York, New York's time was the standard. From New York to Baltimore, Philadelphia's time coordinated traffic. And, along the last leg from Baltimore to Washington, the standard of the nation's capital governed train schedules. The net result of these four changes was to move the passenger's watch back just twenty-four minutes (Washington being just shy of a half hour slower than Boston). Because these standards followed only the rail line, these were not quite time zones – smaller communities still could and did keep to their own local times. Furthermore, along the boundary between the different schedules, a number of clocks could control the departure and arrival of trains going to and from different cities. From Hartford, Connecticut, for example, some trains left the station on Boston time and others left according to New York schedules.[31]

In the North, the railway system was primarily divided into two networks. The most highly capitalized, competitive, and profitable network was composed of the great trunk lines that ran from Chicago to the major Atlantic ports of New York (the New York Central and Erie), Philadelphia (the Pennsylvania), and Baltimore (the Baltimore and Ohio). These lines were the fastest, most heavily traveled long-distance lines in the nation.[32] Fanning out to the west of Chicago were numerous "feeder" lines running into cities such as Milwaukee, Minnesota, Omaha, St. Louis, and their rural hinterlands. The development of these networks was driven by the movement of crops from the interior of the nation to the Atlantic seaboard, where the harvest was transshipped to the major consuming markets of Europe.[33] For example, the St. Paul, Minneapolis and Manitoba was so dependent on moving the spring wheat harvest from western Minnesota and the Dakotas

---

[31] *Appleton's 1883 Cyclopaedia*, pp. 761–762. The new time zones were composed of consolidations of the various city-based schedules into regional territories. A map displaying the new time zones appears on page 763.

[32] Kirkland, *Industry Comes of Age*, p. 77.

[33] Noting that the movement of crops was "the sap of economic life" to the American railroad network, one investigation reported that 32 percent of all railroad freight (measured in ton-miles) was composed of grain over the five-year period from 1894 to 1898. *Report of the Industrial Commission: Distribution of Farm Products*, vol. 6 (Washington, D.C.: GPO, 1901), p. 37; for maps depicting the movement of grain, as well as a description, see pp. 45–47.

into Minneapolis that it was called a "one-crop road."[34] While most of the grain and meat grown in the United States was consumed domestically, many of the major urban markets for these products were also the leading points of departure for American exports, thus reinforcing the feeder and trunk line organization of the northern railroads.[35] All this traffic, combined with the impossibility of monopolizing the water routes over the lakes or over the Atlantic Ocean, made freight rates between Chicago and Liverpool more competitive than those prevailing over any other of the world's major trade routes.[36]

While bulk commodities moved east on this system, manufactured goods – both domestically produced and imported – and passengers, often immigrants, moved west. But because the trunk line system was constructed primarily to move grain to the seaboard, the majority of this traffic moved east, forcing the lines every year to return empty boxcars to the West in time to meet the annual harvest. By comparison, traffic over the transcontinental lines connecting the Pacific Coast to the rest of the nation was relatively light. Instead, these railroads divided their traffic between the upper reaches of the Missouri and Mississippi River basins (thus feeding into the Chicago terminals of the great trunk lines) and the western slopes of the Rocky Mountains, the Cascades, and the Sierra Nevada range (thus serving as both feeders and through lines for the major Pacific ports of San Francisco, Portland, and Seattle).

Driven by the movement of cotton, the southern rail network was comparatively decentralized. From the very beginning, each southern railroad almost invariably located its major terminal in one of the port cities of the Atlantic or Gulf coasts and, from there, extended branch lines into the upcountry cotton lands of the black belt, piedmont, and, late in the nineteenth century, the hills and mountains of the Appalachians and west Texas. With

---

[34] *Commercial and Financial Chronicle*, February 14, 1885.

[35] For comparing the freight structure of the American railroad network, the most important single rate – described as "the basis of all charges on grain and flour shipped from the West to the East" – was that quoted for the movement of grain and flour between Chicago and New York. *Appleton's 1897 Cyclopaedia*, p. 707. This was also the rate most commonly cited when the effectiveness of the great trunk line pools was discussed in the leading financial journals. When this figure declined to unprofitable levels, the rate was cited as evidence of the "breaking down" of the pool. When the figure held up, the pool was viewed as effective in maintaining rates.

[36] The later emergence of the Grand Trunk Railway in Canada as a major trunk line in its own right – one outside the regulatory powers of the Interstate Commerce Commission – also increased competition over these routes. *Commercial and Financial Chronicle*, May 11, 1889. Chicago's position as the common western terminal for eastern rail lines and, independently, the availability of the Great Lakes as a competing transport alternative combined to provide the lowest freight rates for the flow of western produce to the East. For an explanation of how these factors operated in such a way as to propel Chicago's emergence as the "gateway" for the development of the West, see Cronon, *Nature's Metropolis*, pp. 85–91.

the exception of the New York Central, which largely paralleled the pre-existing water route over the Great Lakes into the Erie Canal and thence to New York City, the rail system in the North created an entirely new set of routes and, thus, impressed new transportation alternatives upon the physical setting of the region. The southern network, in contrast, replicated a much more accommodating geography. Because most southern rivers ran directly to the Atlantic Ocean or Gulf of Mexico and were fairly evenly spaced around the coast, the topography gave rise to many separate ports, all of them serving as points of departure for the export of cotton to Europe: Wilmington, North Carolina; Charleston; Savannah; Jacksonville; Apalachicola, Florida; Mobile; and Galveston.[37] With the arrival of the railroad, most lines built their track from one of these cities into the southern interior, sometimes following the rivers that had originally given rise to the ports.[38]

Strategically placed at the mouth of the great Missouri-Mississippi river system, New Orleans was both the premier cotton port of the South and an entrepôt for the upriver ports of the North and West. Before the completion of the great trunk lines of the North in the 1850s, New Orleans had played a much larger role in northern trade along the Ohio and Mississippi rivers (most of the territory drained by the Missouri had not yet been settled). But the trunk lines diverted much of this trade to the East, and by the late nineteenth century, New Orleans was primarily a cotton port.

In fact, by 1895, waterborne transportation was an important competitor to the railroad only along the nation's coastline and over the Great Lakes/Erie Canal route from the Midwest into New York City. Along the latter, however, water competition set the rhythm of trunk line rates, determining whether the pools held up or broke down. From early April or so, when the ice on the lakes and along the canal broke up in the spring thaw, until late fall, when the water route froze up once more, railroad freight income from Chicago to the eastern seaboard was depressed by water competition.[39] During the winter months, when all freight movement was by

---

[37] A map of navigable rivers in the United States in 1890 was provided in the back pocket of *Preliminary Report of the Inland Waterways Commission*, 60th Cong., 1st sess., Senate Document no. 325 (Washington, D.C.: GPO, 1908).

[38] As the Industrial Commission put it, "the cotton territory is so situated that the main movement to market is from the center toward a circumference on which are located about twenty-five ocean and Gulf ports on the south and east, and interior gateways on north and west." By the turn of the century, almost all the annual harvest was transported by rail either to these ports or domestic mills. *Industrial Commission: Distribution of Farm Products*, vol. 6, p. 152.

[39] For a comparative summary of freight rates for wheat between 1870 and 1925 between Chicago and New York by rail, lake and rail, and water transportation, see Walter W. Jennings, *Introduction to American Economic History* (New York: Thomas Y. Crowell, 1928), p. 453.

rail, both freight rates and the pools tended to hold up comparatively well and the trunk lines usually reported good earnings.[40]

The railroad network underwent rapid consolidation in the late nineteenth century as smaller lines were absorbed into larger systems and bankrupt railroads were consolidated into new companies with much larger capitalizations and, the receivers expected, much more efficient operating units.[41] Consolidation usually proceeded in waves. In the early months of 1891, for example, mergers and takeovers in the railroad system so dominated the financial markets that rumor mongering reached somewhat absurd proportions.[42] The last great wave struck in the eighteen months between July 1899 and December 1900 when mergers involved over 25,000 miles of track, roughly equivalent to one-eighth of the national rail network. At the end of this period, only thirty-two companies controlled some 80 percent of the entire network. Of the survivors, almost all had established linkages, either through formal incorporation or company alliances, between the nation's interior and one or more of the Atlantic, Pacific, or Gulf ports – particularly striking testimony to both the raw competitiveness of the railroad sector with respect to long hauls and the importance of commodity exports as a driving force behind the construction of the national network.[43]

Driven by attempts to control rate competition, the railroad network consolidated into a small number of systems resting on interlocking stock hold-

[40] For general commentary on the relationship between the seasons and trunk-line profitability and traffic, see the *Commercial and Financial Chronicle*, April 14 and December 22, 1883; May 23, September 26, and December 5, 1885; November 26 and December 3, 1887; November 9, 1889; September 26, 1891; April 30, 1892. The usual pattern was five winter months of relatively strong trunk-line performance because waterborne competition was absent, followed by seven months of poor profitability and erratically observed pool agreements. Kirkland, *Industry Comes of Age*, pp. 104–105.

[41] For general commentary on the advantages of railroad consolidation, see the *Commercial and Financial Chronicle*, March 26, 1892. For a thorough overview of the expansion of the rail network, see H. T. Newcomb, "Railway Progress and Agricultural Development," *Yale Review* 9 (May 1900): 33–57.

[42] In its February 14, 1891, issue, the *Commercial and Financial Chronicle* criticized the New York *Herald* for the way in which it reported stories floating about the New York markets, maintaining that the newspaper had grouped "together somewhat grotesquely a number of rumors that have obtained wide publicity: 'That Jay Gould has bought the Chicago & Alton. That Calvin S. Brice has bought the 'Monon.' That John H. Inman has also bought the 'Monon' for the Richmond Terminal. That the Delaware Lackawanna & Western has acquired the New York Susquehanna & Western. That the West Shore has undoubtedly bought it likewise. That the Delaware & Hudson has also acquired it. That the Great Northern has bought the Stickney roads. That the Atchison has got the Denver & Rio Grande Western. That the Baltimore & Ohio has suddenly obtained the ownership of the Western New York & Pennsylvania.'"

[43] Chandler, *The Visible Hand*, p. 172.

ings and boards of directors. A small number of these share-holding communities of interest controlled some two thirds of the national rail network in 1906. However, with the exception of a tortuously twisted route reportedly under the control of the "Huntington party," no one company possessed the capacity to move freight from one coast of the United States to the other without delivering over the traffic to the management of another line.[44]

As the railroads relentlessly reduced transportation costs, a concomitant growth in interregional trade broke down the isolation of large portions of the nation's interior. This rapid increase in the long-distance movement of commodities and manufactured goods carried with it several interrelated consequences for the national market: (1) regions increasingly specialized in those economic sectors in which they had a comparative advantage in the production of goods and commodities in the national political economy; (2) local production of goods and commodities, previously protected by the isolation of regional markets from national competitors, now withered or vanished altogether; and (3) the economies of scale of mass-production methods became a practical possibility as industrial producers in the manufacturing belt drove out relatively high-cost local operators throughout the remainder of the nation.[45]

As transportation and communication systems expanded, consumer goods became standardized, along with emergence of brand names as guarantees of quality. Both developments encouraged purchase without prior personal inspection and, along with all-weather rail transportation, promoted replenishing of store inventories regardless of the season. These, in turn, dramatically reduced the seasonality of the great commercial markets in the nation's largest cities. In New York, for example, the "dry goods market, which used to open [in August], shows a fair movement especially on the part of the Southern merchants, though now-a-days the August buying is not so much of a feature any year as it was formerly. The telegraph and the habit of carrying small stocks has brought in the practice of distributing orders more through the year as new supplies are wanted. . . ."[46] Montgomery Ward, founded in 1872, became the first company to

---

[44]   Ibid., p. 174. *Commercial and Financial Chronicle*, September 20, 1884. While the Huntington route would have connected the two coasts by tying together portions of at least eight separate lines, the *Chronicle*'s description suggests that several portions were formally controlled by companies not managed by Huntington or his agents.

[45]   For an overview of the impact of expanding railroad network on the regional division of labor, see Harvey S. Perloff, Edgar S. Dunn, Jr., Eric E. Lampard, and Richard F. Muth, *Regions, Resources, and Economic Growth* (Baltimore: Johns Hopkins University Press, 1960), pp. 191–221. On the importance of national markets to industrialization, see, for example, William N. Parker, *Europe, America, and the Wider World*, vol. 2 (New York: Cambridge University Press, 1991), p. 244.

[46]   *Commercial and Financial Chronicle*, August 6, 1887.

sell a wide variety of consumer goods exclusively by mail. The company was supported by the Grange, then the largest agrarian organization in the country, as an alternative source of supplies for farmers otherwise dependent on the limited variety and, at times, exorbitant prices of the country merchant.[47]

The consolidation of the national market accentuated the pattern of uneven economic development by strengthening the spatial division of labor among the major regions while doing little, if anything, to lessen the wide disparity of wealth.[48] The transformative influence of rapidly declining transportation costs and industrial consolidation also had little effect on the regional isolation of the southern workers from the northern labor market.

The importance of the railroad to American industrialization can hardly be overstated. The railroad provided the means through which American commodities, particularly cotton, grains, and meat, could compete in world markets and thus allowed the various regions to specialize in their production. By exploiting the comparative advantage of these agricultural regions in the world economy, the United States was able to earn the foreign exchange that ultimately paid the toll on foreign capital. With that capital, the United States built the infrastructure, most important, the railroad network itself, that supported industrial expansion. Along with financial operations associated with the huge federal debt created by the Civil War, the sale of railroad bonds and stock was a major force behind the creation of national capital markets in the United States. When the great industrial trusts formally entered these markets over the last twelve years or so of the nineteenth century, they were ushered in by financiers who had built their reputations and banking connections on a business dominated by railroad and government securities. As American industrial corporations consolidated their operations into ever larger combinations, harnessing the economies of scale inherent in their respective sectors, they did not have to wait for a national capital market to develop or depend on foreign capitalists for assistance – the New York financial community was ready and waiting.[49]

---

[47] Chandler, *The Visible Hand*, p. 230.

[48] This consolidation also had a strong impact on the evolution of the urban hierarchy. For a discussion of the historical stages through which towns and cities evolved from their emergence on the frontier through their subsequent integration into the national market, see Edward K. Muller, "Regional Urbanization and the Selective Growth of Towns in North American Regions," *Journal of Historical Geography* 3:1 (1977): 21–39.

[49] The business generated on the New York markets by financial transactions connected with the railroads was truly enormous. In 1895, for example, American railroads were capitalized at about $11 billion, divided about evenly between stocks and bonds. Their combined total was fourteen times the national debt, and more than four times as large as the total indebtedness of all federal, state, and local governments. *Appleton's 1897 Cyclopaedia*, p. 706.

Among the most important changes furthering the consolidation of the national and international markets of the United States were those increasing the efficiency and volume of information. Modernization of the postal system, for example, relied on the speed and all-weather capacity of the railroad for long-distance hauls between market centers and as a complement to animal-based delivery to the nation's hamlets and crossroads. By the end of the century, with the steady growth of the railroad network throughout the country, the vast majority of all mail delivered between the nation's post offices moved at some point by rail. As early as 1870, the federal postal service had become both the largest such operation in the world and one of the most efficient.[50] The volume of mail varied quite a bit across the United States and appears to have been closely correlated with both literacy rates and per capita wealth. In letters mailed per capita, Colorado led the nation in 1880 with 55.2, followed by Wyoming (42.3), New York (41.6), Montana (40.2), Massachusetts (38.7), and Connecticut (38.2). The South lagged far behind; North Carolina was last in the nation with 5.8 letters per capita, only slightly bettered by the states of Mississippi (6.4), Alabama (7.0), South Carolina (7.2), Tennessee (7.3), West Virginia (7.9), and Arkansas (8.0).[51]

The railroad system also provided the routes over which the telegraph and, very late in the century, the telephone expanded. By following railroad rights of way and heavily depending on railroad messages for their revenues, the telegraph foreshortened commercial communication from a period of weeks and days to hours and minutes.[52] Having followed expansion of the railroad network for decades, the telegraph system was also more or less complete by 1870. The consolidation of the system into what

[50] For a brief account of administrative reorganization of the postal service between 1847 and 1870s, see Chandler, *The Visible Hand*, pp. 195–197. Also see Richard R. John, *Spreading the News: The American Postal System from Franklin to Morse* (Cambridge, Mass.: Harvard University Press, 1995). Although the United States had the cheapest postal rates in the world, the British system, probably the most advanced at that time, was both a little faster and, unlike the United States, provided door-to-door delivery in small towns. Given the much lower population density and much greater distances on the North American continent, however, the deficiencies in the American system were comparatively unimportant. *Commercial and Financial Chronicle*, January 30, 1886.

[51] Robert P. Porter, *The West: From the Census of 1880* (Chicago: Rand McNally, 1882), p. 75.

[52] The relationship between railroad operations and the emergence of the telegraph was so intimate that many of the first telegraph companies were in fact owned by the railroads. Chandler, *The Visible Hand*, p. 195. By the turn of the century, telegraph offices and, in much smaller numbers, telephone offices blanketed the nation with a density only moderately skewed toward the more advanced commercial and industrial regions. For statistics on this distribution, see *Report of the Industrial Commission: Transportation*, vol. 9 (Washington, D.C.: GPO, 1901), pp. 235–236.

became the Western Union company was extraordinarily rapid. Founded in 1851, Western Union first absorbed smaller companies at a feverish rate until 1863, at which time it, the American Telegraph Company, and the United States Telegraph Company shared most of the national market. In 1866, Western Union then took in these two companies as well, establishing a network of 75,000 miles and 2,250 offices throughout the nation.[53] This domestic network was supplemented when the Commercial Cable Company finished a second trans-Atlantic cable to Europe in 1884. The entry of the new company into competition with the previously monopolistic Western Union connection significantly increased the volume of messages sent between the New York and London capital markets, ultimately driving rates down to as low as 12 cents a word in 1887.[54] Within the United States, the rapid spread of the telephone network in the late nineteenth century further consolidated the national market by similarly increasing the flow of commercial information.[55]

While the railroad was transforming the American economy and society through ever lower transportation costs, the international market steadily became a more important factor driving the trajectory of industrialization in the United States. Responding to technological advances (such as the shift from wind to steam propulsion and from wooden to metal hulls) and the organizational development of international trade, oceanic shipping costs declined rapidly over all of the major world routes, including the North Atlantic, from the middle of the eighteenth century to the outbreak of World War I.[56] This decline in transportation costs was the major factor in the rapid convergence of commodity prices between the United States and Great Britain (and, by implication, the remainder of Europe) between 1870 and 1913. When combined with the decline in interior railroad rates, the drop was dramatic; for wheat traveling between Chicago and Liverpool – perhaps the longest, most heavily used transportation route in the world for a single commodity – the cumulative impact of cheaper transport was

---

[53] For discussions of the development of the telegraph network, see Chandler, *The Visible Hand*, pp. 197–200; Cochran and Miller, *Age of Enterprise*, pp. 115–116.

[54] *Commercial and Financial Chronicle*, December 27, 1884; August 6, 13, September 3, 1887.

[55] As early as 1885, the *Commercial and Financial Chronicle* noted the telephone's impact on urban commercial markets: "No invention for the facilitation of communication ever made such rapid progress. Ten years ago the very idea of using a wire for the conveyance of spoken words would have been scouted by ninety-nine out of every hundred scientific men. Six years ago the telephone was still in the stage of experiment to such an extent that most men regarded it as little more than a scientific plaything. Now it is in use in every city and large town in the country, and in every progressive city in the world. . . ." June 27, 1885.

[56] C. Knick Harley, "Ocean Freight Rates and Productivity, 1740–1913: The Primacy of Mechanical Invention Reaffirmed," *Journal of Economic History* 48:4 (December 1988): 851–876.

directly evidenced in the convergence of the price per bushel in those two markets. In the three years centering on 1870, wheat in Liverpool was 60.3 percent more expensive than in Chicago. In the three years centered on 1895, the difference was only 25.4 percent. Other commodities showed similar declines over the same period.[57] The natural tariff of the sea was breaking down just when American industry no longer needed protection from foreign competition.

RAILROAD REGULATION

Because of the centrality of the railroad to the American economy, the network was more heavily regulated than any other sector in the late nineteenth century. However, evaluation of the impact of those regulations, both federal and state, remains quite contentious. There are at least four areas of controversy: fundamental disagreements on how the railroads were faring before the government intervened, varying interpretations of the constitutional decisions handed down by U.S. Supreme Court, the inconclusive legislative history of the Interstate Commerce Act, and the ambivalent performance of the Interstate Commerce Commission once it was up and running. These are all taken up, but because railroad regulation, everything considered, had only a minor impact on the course of industrialization, the discussion is brief.[58]

One area of disagreement has to do with the effectiveness of voluntary pools organized by competing lines over heavily traveled routes.[59] These pools were intended to raise rates and share traffic in ways that would guar-

---

[57] Because transportation costs also declined between midwestern farms and Chicago but are not included in the Chicago-Liverpool calculations, the figures probably understate the convergence in price paid for wheat between the American farm and the British consumer. Kevin O'Rourke and Jeffrey G. Williamson, "Late Nineteenth-Century Anglo-American Factor-Price Convergence: Were Heckscher and Ohlin Right?," *Journal of Economic History* 54:4 (December 1994): 892, 897–902.

[58] Perhaps the most consensual conclusion concerning the impact of the Interstate Commerce Commission is that it helped stabilize railroad rates. See, for example, William F. Switzler, *Report on the Internal Commerce of the United States, 1889* (Washington, D.C.: GPO, 1889), pp. 10, 61. Paul W. MacAvoy, in fact, has argued that ICC regulation "tended to make more effective the [trunk line] cartel's control of the level of long-distance rates" between 1887–1893. *The Economic Effects of Regulation: The Trunk-Line Railroad Cartels and the Interstate Commerce Commission before 1900* (Cambridge, Mass.: MIT Press, 1965), pp. v, 119–153, 195.

[59] There is no doubt that such pools formed and reformed repeatedly throughout the United States. In the West, for example, what was called the Transcontinental Association was founded in 1881 in order to divide traffic between the Union Pacific and the Santa Fe, expanded to include the Texas and Pacific in 1882, expanded again to take in the Galveston, Harrisburgh and San Antonio in 1883, and, by 1890, included twenty-two lines among its membership. Brock, *Internal Commerce, 1890*, pp. 158–159.

antee the profitability of each of the lines. The cooperation of the participating roads could not be enforced in the courts but, before passage of the
Interstate Commerce Act in 1887, was not otherwise illegal.[60] The question
is whether these pools were effective. Some scholars point to the "Iowa"
pool as one that was both enduring and profitable.[61] Others single out the
pools established by the major trunk lines between Chicago and the major
eastern ports as episodically effective efforts at collusion (primarily
restricted to winter because shipping along the Great Lakes/Erie Canal route
undercut rate cooperation in the warmer months). Others interpret this
pool's episodic success as primarily an artifact of the market, not collusion,
because trunk line rates would have risen naturally in the winter months
when traffic was heavy with the harvest and the water route was frozen.[62]
Still others, willing to grant the pools some credit for raising rates, have
theorized that all such efforts over the long term were futile because extraordinary profitability always brought on the construction of new lines over
the pooled route as new competitors attempted to enter that artificially
maintained but profitable arrangement. As new lines were built, the profitability of pools inevitably dropped as the coordination problems among
the participating roads increased.[63] And, finally, there are those who conclude that the very thin profits generally available to the railroads in the
late nineteenth century inevitably led the weaker roads to chronically cheat
on both their shares and rates.[64] Once discovered, such defections brought

[60]   In discussing a suit filed by the Attorney General of Missouri intended to dissolve a
      pool between the various southwestern roads, the *Commercial and Financial Chron-
      icle* concluded, that in this particular instance, the ephemeral existence of such com-
      binations was a perverse advantage: "... a pool is scarcely more than a sentiment –
      the substance of things hoped for – an embodiment of a little potential energy. To
      bring such a creature into court would appear to be a very difficult task...." Sep-
      tember 18, 1886.

[61]   Kirkland, *Industry Comes of Age*, pp. 86–87.

[62]   MacAvoy, for example, has discovered "persistent cheating" by the individual roads
      belonging to the trunk line pool between 1875 and 1887. After the federal courts
      weakened the ICC, the cartel was again unstable from 1893 to 1900. *Economic
      Effects of Regulation*, pp. v, 39–109, 159–192.

[63]   See, for example, the complicated but intertwined strategies driving line extensions
      and construction over the route connecting Chicago with Minneapolis/St. Paul, the
      Commercial and Financial Chronicle, August 29, 1885. Profits, paranoia, and retri-
      bution are all cited in the *Chronicle's* discussion as possible motives on the part of
      the individual companies, but the net effect was expected to be a permanent reduc-
      tion in the profitability of operations over the route.

[64]   Chandler, for example, both describes the railroad pools organized during the late
      nineteenth century as among "the largest and most sophisticated cartels ever
      attempted in American business" and then concludes, in the very next sentence, that
      "these cartels rarely worked." *The Visible Hand*, p. 123. For a general discussion of
      the emergence of destructive competition between railroad lines and the failures of
      cartels, see pp. 133–143. For its part, the *Commercial and Financial Chronicle*
      observed that a "railroad war of the trunk lines is about as certain in recurrence as

on the pool's collapse.[65] For these analysts, the voluminous public evidence of such cheating by individual lines, the numerous bankruptcies throughout the system generally, and the frequent collapse of even the most carefully constructed collusive arrangements are sufficient proof that effective pools were but a fable – only nature could make the roads profitable by providing an abundant harvest.

Another area of controversy concerns the inconsistency of judicial decisions associated with railroad regulation in the late nineteenth century. In an important decision in 1877, the Supreme Court appeared to give the individual states fairly broad authority to regulate rail rates. Although fees for grain elevators was the central issue in the group of decisions jointly labeled as *Munn v. Illinois*, the court's opinion emphasized public interest considerations as justification for state intervention and included rail rates as well.[66] As the railroad system consolidated over the next nine years, the individual states both established railroad commissions with increasing frequency and discovered that their ability to control railroad rates was becoming ever more enfeebled by the increasing interstate nature of the system. Whether or not the states could have effectively intervened was rendered moot, however, by a second Supreme Court decision in 1886, *Wabash Railway v. Illinois*, which made regulation of interstate charges by the states impossible.[67] Proposals for federal regulation of interstate rates had been before Congress for many years; *Wabash* broke the stalemate.

In addition to the uneven judicial history of the period, the inconsistent attitude of the financial and commercial community toward government regulation has also sparked controversy. On the one hand, the nation's

the smallpox or the change of seasons. Periodically, and with many formalities, agreements are made between the rival parties and periodically, but without any formality, the agreements thus made are broken. . . . How childish is this marching up a hill and then marching down again every few months by our great railroads kings!" April 7, 1877. For an interpretation contending that the cartels were more or less effective in raising rates, see John J. Binder, "The Sherman Antitrust Act and the Railroad Cartels," *Journal of Law & Economics* 31 (October 1988): 444–445.

[65] For a contemporary example of pessimism with respect to many of these points, see the *Commercial and Financial Chronicle*, February 28, 1885. For a discussion of the impact of the varying strength of participants in the trunk line pool, see September 4, 1886.

[66] For summaries of this and related cases, see Louis B. Boudin, *Government by Judiciary* (1932; rpt., New York: Russell & Russell, 1968), pp. 387–394; Lawrence M. Friedman, *A History of American Law* (New York: Simon & Schuster, 1973), pp. 391–393; Bernard Schwartz, *A History of the Supreme Court* (New York: Oxford University Press, 1993), pp. 164–165. As Schwartz points out, *Munn* was never quite overturned in the late nineteenth century but, as constitutional doctrine, was not particularly relevant to subsequent Supreme Court rulings until it reappeared during the New Deal, over half a century after the decision had been originally handed down.

[67] Friedman, *History of American Law*, pp. 394–396. For a contemporary summary and analysis, see the *Commercial and Financial Chronicle*, October 30, 1886.

financial community and the railroads clearly supported the legalization of pools with reference to both rates and traffic over the major through routes. In fact, they continued to strongly support legalization long after the Interstate Commerce Act had altogether prohibited pools.[68] Many financiers and railroad officials would have gone even further and asked for government enforcement of these collective agreements between individual railroad companies. However, the commercial community in the terminal cities of these competitive routes usually preferred open competition as a means of holding down transport costs. To make things even more complicated, merchants in towns served by only one or two colluding lines were much more receptive to government intervention, particularly the regulation of rates over "short hauls" to competitively served larger cities.

Thus the merchant community itself was divided, with the commercial houses in the larger cities opposing government controls on rates because such regulation promised to reduce their freight advantage over smaller towns and merchants in those smaller towns taking just the opposite position.[69] But with respect to "short hauls," both financiers and railroad officials opposed government controls. This meant, for the most part, that the great commercial houses in the nation's major urban centers, on the one hand, and the financial community and the railroads, on the other hand, pursued almost entirely contradictory goals with respect to government regulation.[70] And as it turned out, the major regulatory intervention by the central state during this period, the Interstate Commerce Act, both prohibited pooling altogether and provided what, in combination with interpretive rulings in the federal courts, were only weak controls on "short haul" rates. Commenting on the bill just as it emerged from the conference committee between the House and the Senate, the *Commercial and Financial Chronicle* concluded that the proposed act was "so full of crudities" that its implementation would mean "ruin and disaster" for the railroads, mercantile interests, and the "great producing classes of the West."[71] While

---

[68] See, for example, an address by Charles Francis Adams to the Boston Commercial Club, partially reprinted in the *Commercial and Financial Chronicle*, December 22, 1888. Also see the issues of December 17 and 24, 1892; May 26 and December 15, 1894; December 4, 1897; April 9, 1898; December 2, 1899.

[69] See, for example, analysis of the positions assumed by merchants with reference to a major suit over rates in the *Commercial and Financial Chronicle*, July 2, 1898. Also see, for a description of the freight rate advantage enjoyed by firms in large cities, the testimony of a Chicago shoe manufacturer before the *Report of the Industrial Commission, Capital and Labor Employed in Manufactures and General Business*, vol. 7 (Washington, D.C.: GPO, 1901), p. 684.

[70] For an interpretation that emphasizes commercial and railroad sentiment as a major factor in passage of the Interstate Commerce Act, while downplaying agrarian support, see Kirkland, *Industry Comes of Age*, pp. 126–127.

[71] Even after applauding Cleveland's appointments to the Commission, the *Chronicle* could not resist condemning the entire effort. April 9, 1887.

presenting the very combination of principles most attractive to southern and western agrarians, the proposed act could have satisfied no one in the national business community save, perhaps, the great commercial houses on the eastern seaboard and at interior transportation nodes such as Chicago and St. Louis.

The legislative history of the Interstate Commerce Act provides some help with these issues. With respect to the initiation of federal intervention, the issue can be settled quite simply. Southern and western congressmen and senators were responsible for initiating legislative consideration of rate regulation and for keeping the issue alive before Congress in the years prior to passage. The most prominent legislator was Representative John Reagan, a Democrat from Texas who had served as Postmaster General of the Confederacy during the Civil War. Reagan was no friend of either eastern capital, commercial houses, or the railroads – in fact, he was routinely referred to as their scourge. In terms of proposed alternatives, however, the issue is less clear. Many businessmen, Charles Francis Adams among them, favored some sort of federal commission to study the major questions associated with rail regulation and then report their findings back to Congress. Under their scheme, the government would not regulate rates other than legalizing and, perhaps, enforcing pools while offering general advice to the country. Composed of the "right men," commissions would persuade the public of the relative virtues of such policies as opposed to the more radical controls that agrarians wanted to place on fares, rates, and capitalization.[72] Others, particularly the railroads, became enamored with the idea that a federal regulatory agency might set minimum rates, thus guaranteeing rates as profitable levels while allowing them to rise as market conditions warranted.[73]

Once created, the Interstate Commerce Commission (ICC) was never allowed to carve out its own destiny. With respect to the establishment of a summary process for the adjudication of complaints and enforcement of rulings, the federal courts insisted on substantive review of the commission's decisions and, through review, largely vitiated the entire project.[74] With respect to the maintenance of competition among the individual roads,

---

[72] *Commercial and Financial Chronicle*, March 18, 1882.

[73] Ibid., June 6, 1885. More generally, see Stephen Skowronek, *Building a New American State: The Expansion of National Administrative Capacities, 1877–1920* (New York: Cambridge University Press, 1982), chap. 5.

[74] See, for example, *Appleton's 1897 Cyclopaedia*, p. 708. The United States Supreme Court ruled in favor of the railroads in fifteen of the sixteen cases brought before it between 1887 and 1905. Cochran and Miller, *Age of Enterprise*, pp. 169–170. Also see MacAvoy, *Economic Effects of Regulation*, pp. 153–159, 164, 183–188, 204. In its annual report to Congress in 1897, the Interstate Commerce Commission stated that it "is hardly correct to say that the Supreme Court disapproved of the views of the Commission, for so far as appears from its opinion [in the latest round of cases] the Court never took pains to inform itself what the position of the Commission had

the prohibition on pooling worked quite well but, after passage of the Sherman Antitrust Act in 1890, was probably also quite redundant. In fact, when the traffic associations were banished from the land by the U.S. Supreme Court, it was the Sherman Antitrust Act, not the Interstate Commerce Act, that provided the requisite purchase within the law.[75] Even if the ICC itself had had a clear conception of what it was about in the late nineteenth century – which is very much in doubt – the agency was in no position to pursue that vision. Instead, the ICC floundered through the period as nothing so much as a major irrelevancy within the organized chaos of system-building that consolidated the national railroad system.[76] By the turn of the century, the commission was largely moribund and proposals to increase its authority enjoyed the almost universal hostility of the railroad companies.[77] Behind the failure of state and federal regulation stood the Supreme Court, striking down laws and regulatory orders as either unconstitutional transgressions on property rights or trespasses on interstate commerce.

As a result, state regulatory authority over railroad rates was hemmed in on two sides. On the one hand, the states could not regulate rates that covered freight or passengers moving in interstate commerce, thus restrict-

---

been." The Commission then concluded that, because of the Supreme Court's rulings, it had "ceased to be a body for the regulation of carriers." *Commercial and Financial Chronicle*, December 18, 1897.

[75] See *United States v. Trans-Missouri Freight Association*, 166 US 290 (1896). For a legal history of the Trans-Missouri case, see William Letwin, *Law and Economic Policy in America: The Evolution of the Sherman Antitrust Act* (New York: Random House, 1965), pp. 152–155, 167–172. For commentary and a summary of the decision, see *Commercial and Financial Chronicle*, March 27 and April 3, 1897. For an argument that this decision had little or no effect on freight rates in the long run because the railroads successfully resorted to secret rate agreements and concentrated markets through system consolidation, see Binder, "The Sherman Antitrust Act and the Railroad Cartels," pp. 443–468.

[76] However, contemporary observers often held that the Interstate Commerce Act encouraged the formation of vast systems under one corporate combination as a reaction to the statute's prohibition on pooling as a means of controlling rate competition. See, for example, the summary of testimony before the *Industrial Commission: Transportation*, vol. 9 (Washington, D.C.: GPO, 1901), pp. v–vii, lxvi–lxvii; *Commercial and Financial Chronicle* October 27, November 10, and December 22, 1888. Chandler also offers much the same judgment in his *The Visible Hand*, p. 144. Although the Interstate Commerce Act may have been a minor factor, the effectiveness of pools, even if they had been permitted, is at least somewhat suspect. The consolidation of the rail network appears, instead, to have been the product of massive bankruptcies by individual lines that created opportunities for Morgan and other major banking houses to reorganize them into large systems; the motivation behind these consolidations was the pursuit of operating efficiencies entirely independent of ICC regulations. See, for example, Chandler, *The Visible Hand*, p. 175.

[77] Chandler, *The Visible Hand*, p. 174.

ing their rate setting powers to intrastate charges.[78] On the other hand, the states were prohibited from setting rates so low as to prevent the companies from earning a fair return on their investment.[79] Since the determination of a fair return depended in part on how costs were allocated between short-haul, noncompetitive traffic within the states and long-haul, often intensely competitive traffic in interstate commerce (much of it over exactly the same track and utilizing the same stations and other facilities), judicial review of rate-setting by the states became a regular and important part of the process. Outside the manufacturing belt, the state railroad commissions themselves were often underfunded and relatively unprofessional bodies, unequipped to challenge legal counsel for the great railroad corporations in anything but the most blunt exercises of political power in the name of participatory democracy.[80] In the political side of this contest, the railroads were poorly armed; almost all of their owners resided outside the states of the South and West that regulated them.[81] Over the short term, the railroads had only the courts and hired retainers to defend their interests.[82]

---

[78] See, for example, the description of a case involving the question of whether the state of Illinois could compel the Illinois Central Railroad to stop a "fast mail train" running from Chicago to New Orleans at Cairo, Illinois. *Commercial and Financial Chronicle*, June 6, 1896. Just on the other side of this issue was an Ohio law, upheld by the U.S. Supreme Court, requiring trains running through the state to stop for passengers at all cities with 3,000 or more residents. April 29, 1899. States could also regulate the capitalization of railroads operating under their charters, safety features such as brakes and stoves, and the architectural design of stations.

[79] In this respect, federal court rulings imposed a "fair and reasonable" standard that would guarantee to the railroads, in the words of the *Commercial and Financial Chronicle*, the right to set rates that would cover "(1) the cost of the service, (2) fixed charges and (3) something for the stock." This standard originated in a circuit court review of the decisions of the Iowa railroad commission in 1888 and was elaborated and extended thereafter. July 28, 1888.

[80] Comparing the Iowa commission's official minutes to "a school-boy's diary" and charging that individual commissioners sometimes set rates without even consulting one another, let alone the railroad companies, the *Chronicle* concluded that the Iowa commission's performance "has not been an edifying one" and that such an informal and capricious body should not be "delegated care of the vast interests represented by the railroads." July 21, 1888. The *Chronicle*, of course, was not a friendly critic but its summary description of proceedings in the state commissions of the South and West is still more or less accurate.

[81] In the case of Iowa, for example, the *Commercial and Financial Chronicle* estimated that less than 2 percent of the stock of railroads operating within the state was owned by Iowa residents. August 11, 1888.

[82] After noting that railroad bondholders and the stockholders "live in the East, while their capital and their investments are located in the West, subject entirely to the control of those using the properties, and who have been taking advantage of that fact," the *Commercial and Financial Chronicle* cited with approval the intervention of railroad employees in the legislative process of states such as Kansas and Minnesota as a major, resident interest in favor of fair treatment. Employees, the journal argued, should support remunerative rates because failing railroads often attempted

Over the long term, the railroad companies could attempt to recover their capital through depreciation of assets by refusing to replace worn-out rail beds and other facilities.[83]

Over time, state regulation of rates sapped the financial strength of the southern and western railroads.[84] By 1894, most of the nation's railroads, weighted by the par value of their common stock, were paying no dividends.[85] In the ninth region laid out by the ICC that included Texas, Louisiana, and part of New Mexico, only $40,000 of some $234 million in common railroad stock paid out anything at all. In the remainder of the Southwest and in the Pacific Coast states the situation was little better – in those regions over 80 percent of common stock, weighted by par value, paid out nothing.[86] Many of the nation's railroads went into receivership and, through the bankruptcy process, were reorganized into larger and more efficient systems.

INDUSTRIAL AND COMMERCIAL CONSOLIDATION

Eclipsing even railroad expansion, the most dramatic evidence of a consolidating national market was the emergence of giant industrial corporations in the late nineteenth century. Exploiting the economies of scale made possible by the completion of the railroad and telegraph networks in the late 1870s and 1880s, these giant corporations brought together

to cut both wages and their labor force to the bone. March 7, 1891. Also see March 9, 1889; December 24, 1898.

[83] Over the long term, as the *Commercial and Financial Chronicle* seldom failed to remind its readers, the railroads could respond to confiscatory rates by failing to replenish their facilities, thus allowing them to fall into disrepair and ultimately suspending service within the state. Since no other road, given the same rate schedule, would replace the original lines, confiscatory rate-setting was, over this long term, equivalent to committing commercial suicide. But the problem was, as the journal noted, that the terms of political officials and the horizons of bankrupting farmers was much shorter than the time required to effectively withdraw fixed railroad investment from a state, so much so that the long-term impact of confiscatory regulation was usually a distinctly secondary consideration in rate-making decisions when grain prices were low. For general commentary on these aspects of the political environment of the South and West, see the issues of October 1, 1887; July 21, August 11, November 17, 1888; August 10, 1889; December 24, 1898. The journal was particularly critical of Texas, saying that the state was apparently determined to "repel capital" despite the fact that many "capitalists here in the East regard her resources with great favor and would be willing to invest their money freely in the State if they could receive assurance of fair treatment." March 16, 1895.

[84] Many separate factors drove the railroad system into financial decline over the last decades of the nineteenth century, among them: cutthroat competition between rival lines, construction of parallel routes that aggravated that competition, and speculative exploitation of some companies by their owners. Government regulation appears to have been an important factor only in the states of the Southwest and Plains.

[85] *Commercial and Financial Chronicle*, April 5, 1890.   [86] Ibid., September 1, 1894.

tremendous quantities of raw materials and capital along with the work force necessary to run modern industrial factories.[87] Closely following the founding of these behemoths was the emergence of combinations among them for regulating supply and prices. These combinations were intended to resolve some of the inefficiencies associated with uninhibited market competition in heavily capitalized industrial sectors. The major problem was that the national economy was subject to severe business cycles in which periods of rapid expansion were almost invariably followed by equally intense contractions. In theory, the efficient market response to declining demand was to restrict output, thus allowing markets to clear with little or no loss to the producer. With highly capitalized industrial corporations, however, the overhead costs associated with debt service, depreciation, and ongoing maintenance of equipment often made the restriction of output difficult; given these fixed costs, it often made more sense for individual firms to continue producing goods even as demand steadily declined. Vertical integration of the refining of raw materials and other intermediate manufacturing processes into a single corporation further increased fixed charges and thus reinforced the incentives to operate plant facilities regardless of market conditions.[88]

As the *Commercial and Financial Chronicle* put it, the "plant, once established, must be kept in operation, even though the returns do not pay interest or fully cover maintenance charges. It then becomes a life and death struggle with [the corporation] to maintain [its] position in the trade. . . ."[89] A few years later, the *Chronicle* declared, "We are far from believing that unrestricted competition is in these days a blessing to society. . . . The answer of the old school of economists is, Go on producing until none but the fittest survives, and then and by that method raise the price. . . . in these days such a policy only serves to push the weaker and the poorer to the wall and give survival to the rich and the strong, while on the other hand it does not protect and is not needed as a protection for the consumer. . . ."[90]

Heavy industry consolidated into a small number of firms in the years following the end of Reconstruction. The relatively small size of the pro-

---

[87] Chandler, *The Visible Hand*, p. 316. Also see Jeremy Atack, "Industrial Structure and the Emergence of the Modern Industrial Corporation," *Explorations in Economic History* 22 (January 1985): 29–52.

[88] Naomi R. Lamoreaux, *The Great Merger Movement in American Business, 1895–1904* (New York: Cambridge University Press, 1985), p. 32. In Chapter 3 of her book, Lamoreaux provides a lucid exposition of the economic imperatives underlying the tendency to "run full" regardless of the prices received for production.

[89] July 28, 1888. Responding to the same incentives that drove production generally, corporations increasingly sought to vertically integrate in order that production would never be interrupted by a lack of raw materials. Chandler, *The Visible Hand*, p. 282.

[90] May 7, 1892.

ducing community facilitated recognition of their common problems with relation to the business cycle and their potential resolution through collusion. The most primitive and least effective method of maintaining profitable production during a period of declining demand was a simple "price agreement" between the companies. Such agreements, however, almost always foundered because the courts would not enforce them.[91] Lack of an enforcement mechanism led corporations, sooner or later, to succumb to the overwhelming temptation to lower prices and thus capture market share while other firms honored their part of the agreement. The most common outcome, then, was for corporations to openly enter into such agreements and to privately undercut their implementation as soon as any significant market opportunity arose. In many cases, of course, no such opportunity ever emerged because all the companies, each expecting the others to cheat, waited for the others to raise prices first.[92]

The corporate "pool" was the next rung on the evolutionary ladder. A pool was slightly more enforceable in that it focused on restricting production instead of maintaining prices. In this case, corporations would agree to restrict output by assigning to each member of the pool a share of the market. Because production was often easier to monitor than prices, cooperating corporations could place more confidence in the pool's effectiveness than in price agreements. In 1887, for example, the manufacturers of steel rails agreed to production quotas, enforced by financial penalties imposed on those who exceeded their limit. This pool was apparently temporarily effective, in part because the heavy capital investment to produce such rails meant there were only a small number of producers in the United States and in part because the steel companies were able to gain the cooperation of their customers, the railroads, in helping to maintain the agreement.[93]

Where there were many producers, such as in anthracite coal mining, such pools – no matter how carefully crafted – inevitably succumbed to an often irresistible temptation for one or more companies to remain outside the pool, operate their plants at full capacity, and thus reap most of the benefits to be gained while other firms restricted production.[94] Like price

---

[91]   Hans B. Thorelli, *Federal Antitrust Policy* (Baltimore: Johns Hopkins University Press, 1955), p. 75.

[92]   In some cases such as in the wire-nail industry between 1895 and 1896, a price agreement among producers could raise profits over the short term only to come apart as the extraordinarily high returns attracted new firms into the sector. Lamoreaux, *Great Merger Movement*, pp. 68–74.

[93]   Kirkland, *Industry Comes of Age*, p. 202; Lamoreaux, *Great Merger*, pp. 76–83.

[94]   The most frequently formed pools between 1873 and 1896 were in the anthracite industry. Because the mines were often owned or leased by the railroads and were, in any case, dependent on rail transport for access to consumer markets, the railroad companies were in a position to allocate production quotas throughout the sector. Thus, the frequent breakdown of such pools was most directly caused by the desire

agreements the major drawback of pools, regardless of the industrial sector in which they formed, was that their agreements and enforcement mechanisms were unenforceable in the courts.[95]

Near the top of this evolutionary ladder was the trust. Under a trust, the control of various firms was assigned to a central agent by depositing sufficient numbers of shares of stock, along with their voting authorities, with that agent. At the time of its creation, the trust assigned market shares to the individual firms, guaranteed that the same price would be maintained across the sector, and otherwise promised to coordinate the affairs of the corporate community.[96] Although the trust was defined as an illegal restraint of trade by the Sherman Antitrust Act in 1890, this legislative measure had only a marginal impact on consolidation, both because the courts were reluctant to aggressively interpret its language and because the business community could and did respond by turning the trust into a formal consolidation of interests under a new, unified corporate organization.[97] Shortly before passage of the federal antitrust act, New Jersey had enacted a general incorporation law that permitted, on easy terms and under simple regulations, the formation of consolidated holding compa-

of one or more of the anthracite roads to increase traffic over their lines. Kirkland, *Industry Comes of Age*, pp. 202–203. In other cases, producers might temporarily join a pool while improving and expanding their operations and subsequently defect when they were able to compete effectively with other producers. For an example, see the description of Dow Chemical's participation in collusive arrangements with respect to the salt, bromine, and bleach markets in Margaret Levenstein, "Mass Production Conquers the Pool: Firm Organization and the Nature of Competition in the Nineteenth Century," *Journal of Economic History* 55:3 (September 1995): 575–611.

[95] Lamoreaux, *Great Merger Movement*, pp. 100–101.

[96] For a discussion of the economic incentives and business cycle conditions that drove this evolution from open competition to price agreements, pools, and, finally, trusts, see the *Commercial and Financial Chronicle*, July 28, 1888. For a summary history of the whisky trust that emphasizes this evolutionary path, see *Report of the Industrial Commission: Preliminary Report on Trusts and Industrial Combinations*, vol. 1 (Washington, D.C.: GPO, 1900), pp. 76–77. For similar analyses, see Chandler, *The Visible Hand*, pp. 315–320; Thorelli, *Federal Antitrust Policy*, pp. 72–80. As Thorelli points out, this evolutionary perspective on the trend from simple agreements to pools to trusts oversimplifies the history of corporate competition in the late nineteenth century; simple agreements, for example, were far and away the most common form of competitive restraint throughout the period.

[97] With reference to the capital market, trusts were almost always a mystifying and unusually risky investment. Because they refused to disclose their income or financial position, insiders possessed a strong advantage in what became a speculative, informal trading in trust certificates. For this reason alone, finance capitalists welcomed the transformation of the major trust organizations into consolidated corporations with periodic financial reports and regular listings of their securities on the major stock exchanges. See, for example, the *Commercial and Financial Chronicle*, September 28 and November 2, 1889.

nies.[98] The New Jersey law made the older trust form of organization obsolete because the new corporate form was a much more effective means of increasing operating efficiencies through centralizing administration and production. Thus, the Sherman Antitrust Act, in effect, only hastened the transformation of trusts into the corporate form.[99]

Critics of industrial consolidation have emphasized the interlocking directorates and close social communities that bound together American industry into what, from the outside, often appeared to be a monolithic class, living off the life blood of national commerce and ruthlessly exploiting the citizenry. In reality there were many chinks in this monolith, some of them bitterly contested crevasses into which the state and national governments were invited to move. One of those chinks was the fact that most trusts never established monopolistic positions in the national economy. Only four short years after its founding as a trust, for example, the American Cotton Oil Company faced significant competition from the Southern Cotton Oil Company. And even the most efficient industrial consolidations, such as the Standard Oil Trust, faced substantial competition whenever and wherever market opportunities opened up.[100]

In addition, industrial consolidations often imposed high, oligopolistic prices on intermediate goods or services sold to other large corporations. Conflict between these corporate producers and consumers, some of the latter as large as the industrial consolidations from which they purchased goods and services, could be quite intense. The following summary of Andrew Carnegie's denunciation of railroad practices provides a particularly apt example:

[98]   Christopher Grandy, "New Jersey Corporate Chartermongering, 1875–1929," *Journal of Economic History* 49:3 (September 1989): 677–692.

[99]   The rapid transition from trust to consolidated corporations was thus a response to several related factors in the economic environment: (1) the consolidated corporation enabled more effective and efficient management of the assets held by the enterprise; (2) public investors, an increasingly important source of the firm's capital needs, preferred corporate to trust securities; and (3) the legal standing of the consolidated corporation was more secure (because of the possibility of antitrust prosecution). With respect to the latter, the Supreme Court's interpretation of the Sherman Antitrust Act, combined with the availability of the New Jersey general incorporation law, actually encouraged mergers by appearing to legitimate the general corporation as the only viable strategy for coordinating production and pricing. Chandler, *The Visible Hand*, pp. 319–320, 330–333, 375–376. Over the long run, then, the economic imperatives associated with market competition would have accomplished the same thing as, in the actual case, did antitrust prosecution.

[100]   One reason these trusts rarely established monopolistic positions was that they tended to focus on maintaining a monopoly through the absorption of competitors, as opposed to maximizing the efficiency of their operations through consolidation of their operations. The former strategy would inevitably fail because the combination's practice of buying competitors out would encourage the constant emergence of new firms. Chandler, *The Visible Hand*, pp. 315–316, 320–327, 334–339.

In an effort to secure lower rates for his materials and products, Mr. Carnegie, the iron master, has been making a bitter warfare upon the transportation companies of the State of Pennsylvania. The attack has been in progress for some time, and while especially directed at the Pennsylvania Railroad, has incidentally embraced other roads. It was at first limited to newspaper interviews, speeches to his workmen, and public letters, but on Monday night of last week he read a carefully prepared paper before the Pennsylvania State Legislature at Harrisburg, which latter has attracted a good deal of attention. Though nominally relating to Pennsylvania's industrial progress and present advanced position, the chief feature of the discourse is its treatment of the railroad question. On that point, we are sorry to say, Mr. Carnegie is just as intemperate, injudicious and even incendiary as in any of his previous less formal statements.

The Pennsylvania is denounced as a gigantic monopoly; it is accused of violating the laws and the Constitution, of evading and treating with contempt orders of Court, of coercing the managers of rival lines, and of extorting millions of money each year to swell its surplus fund and then using those millions to perpetuate its hold upon the State.... In parts of the speech the language used, if it does not directly incite to violence, is yet capable of that construction, and calculated to have a very mischievous effect upon the ignorant and the vicious.... He ... suggests ... the enactment of a law making it compulsory upon the roads to give the same rates per ton per mile upon traffic within the State as are granted to the more distant points without the State, with a Railroad Commission to enforce this requirement. He also wants power to imprison "offenders," and suggests that solitary confinement would be a good thing for railroad officials....

It is so easy to create a feeling of hostility against corporations, and so difficult to allay that feeling after it has arisen, that we are surprised that a man of so much education, and especially one who lives in a glass house, should have resorted to any such methods to enforce his demand. Mr. Carnegie is a large manufacturer (he claims to employ nearly as many men as the Pennsylvania Railroad on its lines within Pennsylvania), a large capitalist, and a man capable of understanding and appreciating how unreasonable popular masses sometimes become under the agitation of a real or fancied grievance.... If to-day the Pennsylvania's profits and surplus are held up as an appropriate object for legislative or popular assault, to-morrow Mr. Carnegie's own millions and large annual income may share the same fate.[101]

The late nineteenth century was thus characterized by a massive consolidation of industrial production in the very midst of the economic transformation wrought by industrialization itself. During the early period, roughly from the end of Reconstruction until the late 1880s, this process was both relatively slow and dominated by trade association attempts to coordinate production and pricing. When these voluntaristic arrangements failed, pools formed and the great trusts arose. At the same time, the pace of consolidation quickened. But this middle period lasted only a few years, after which the Sherman Antitrust Act and the New Jersey

general incorporation law encouraged what appears to have been, in any
event, an inevitable shift to the holding company and, then, the general corporation as a centrally administered, multidivisional organization.[102] In the
last decade of the nineteenth century, this general corporate form came to
dominate the industrial landscape as the rate of consolidation steadily
increased. In the very last years of the nineteenth century the merger
movement in American industry peaked in a virtual orgy of horizontal
consolidation.[103]

While competition between producers in specific sectors was often dramatically reduced by industrial consolidation, the national market remained
about as competitive and unstructured by combinations as it had been at
the end of Reconstruction.[104] One factor behind this persistence of market
competition was the fact that many attempts at trust formation and industrial combination failed because they were mismanaged, attempted to consolidate in sectors lacking the economies of scale that could reward their
efforts, or were made obsolete by technological advances in their product
area.[105] Faltering on the part of the new combination for any of these
reasons immediately brought new competitors into the field and, often, as
in the case of General Electric in 1899, serious financial difficulties or even
bankruptcy.

An additional factor involved the expansion of the railroad network and
the transportation system generally. The consequent integration of isolated
regional markets into the national economy broke down many local oligopolistic or monopolistic arrangements about as rapidly as it allowed the
formation of centralized and consolidated national corporations.[106] Thus,
while industrial consolidation was encouraged at the national level, much
of that process involved the absorption of local noncompetitive markets
into the national economy – not the substitution of oligopoly for Smithian
competition. The rapid decline in the prices of industrial goods, such as

---

[102]   Lamoreaux suggests that the merger movement only hastened the inevitable emer-
gence of an oligopolistic organization of the marketplace in many industrial sectors.
Great Merger Movement, pp. 12, 159–180. For the impact of the New Jersey
Holding Company Act of 1888 on industrial consolidation, see Ralph L. Nelson,
Merger Movements in American Industry, 1895–1956 (Princeton, N.J.: Princeton
University Press, 1959), pp. 64–70.

[103]   Chandler, *The Visible Hand*, pp. 331–334; Lamoreaux, *Great Merger Movement*,
pp. 1–2; *Commercial and Financial Chronicle*, March 4, 1899; *1900 Census of Manufactures*, pt. 1 (Washington, D.C.: U.S. Census Office, 1902), pp. lxxv–xci; Thorelli,
Federal Antitrust Policy, pp. 294–303.

[104]   Of 93 major consolidations between 1895 and 1904 for which market shares can
be calculated, 72 subsequently controlled at least 40 percent of their respective
markets after merger and 42 of these controlled over 70 percent of their markets.
Lamoreaux, *Great Merger Movement*, pp. 2–5.

[105]   Ibid., pp. 138–142, 189–190.

[106]   For a discussion of manufacturing activity in Utah before and after the arrival of
the railroad, see Brock, *Internal Commerce, 1890*, pp. 877–884.

petroleum and steel products, which were the staple of the most concentrated sectors evidenced a third factor supporting continuing high levels of competition. At the onset of rapid industrialization, many of these sectors were unable to meet foreign, particularly British, competition and had emerged only behind the protective barriers of the tariff. As the new, consolidated corporations exploited efficiencies of scale attending horizontal and vertical integration, their cost structures dropped dramatically. As a result, the tariff, with respect to their products, became unnecessary because these corporations could now more than meet foreign competition. In fact, as these sectors began to export their production, at first tentatively and then with spiraling increases in volume, to Europe and throughout the world, the terms of competition were no longer solely or even primarily national.[107]

JUDICIAL CONSTRUCTION OF THE NATIONAL MARKET

Left to their own devices, the legislatures of the individual states would have erected significant barriers to the consolidation of the national market in the late nineteenth century. But the courts at both the national and state levels struck down many of these legislative barriers almost as fast as they were erected. The result was a complex pastiche of judicial doctrines through which both the state and federal governments were constrained in their attempts to regulate the nation's onrushing industrialization.

Contracts involving out-of-state insurance companies were a favored target of state regulation.[108] Often inadequately capitalized and possessing assets beyond the reach of the state courts, out-of-state insurance corporations were frequently required by states to guarantee, in one way or another,

---

[107] Kirkland, *Industry Comes of Age*, pp. 214–215.

[108] The Supreme Court consistently ruled that insurance contracts between a citizen of one state and a company in another state fell under the exclusive police power of the state in which the contract was written. Justice Joseph P. Bradley summarized in an opinion applying the commerce clause to express agencies: "The [present] case is entirely different from that of foreign corporations seeking to do a business which does not belong to the regulating power of Congress. The insurance business, for example, cannot be carried on in a State by a foreign corporation without complying with all the conditions imposed by the legislation of that State." *Crutcher v. Kentucky*, 141 US 47 (1890), p. 59. Several years later Justice Edward White reiterated the Court's position: "The business of insurance is not commerce. The contract of insurance is not an instrumentality of commerce. The making of such a contract is a mere incident of commercial intercourse...." *Hooper v. California*, 155 US 648 (1894), p. 655. The seminal case for these decisions was *Paul v. Virginia*, 8 Wall. 168 (1868). Also see E. Parmalee Prentice and John G. Egan, *The Commerce Clause of the Federal Constitution* (Chicago: Callaghan, 1898), pp. 46–47, and Charles Warren, *The Supreme Court in United States History* (Boston: Little, Brown, 1922), vol. 3, p. 348.

that their contracts with resident citizens or companies would be fulfilled.[109] In many cases, these regulations also (and not incidentally) impaired the competitive position of out-of-state companies vis-à-vis their resident counterparts. In 1879, for example, North Carolina required all fire insurance companies headquartered outside the state to deposit $10,000 in United States bonds with the state treasurer as a condition for transacting business. This deposit was intended to guarantee that judgments against out-of-state companies in the state courts would be satisfied.[110]

Many of the states that attempted to tax or otherwise regulate insurance contracts within their borders contained few resident insurance companies, and the burden of their levies or regulations thus fell heavily on out-of-state companies even when their laws did not discriminate in favor of resident firms.[111] In retaliation for such measures, the New York State legislature enacted a law that provided that insurance companies headquartered within the state (as most major insurance companies were) could not be compelled by the New York courts to pay benefits to claimants residing in states that discriminated against out-of-state firms. In practice, such retaliation was self-defeating because, once it became known that New York firms could

[109]   For analysis of state efforts to regulate out-of-state insurance companies, see Boudin, *Government by Judiciary*, pp. 424–430.

[110]   *Appleton's Annual Cyclopaedia of 1879* (New York: D. Appleton, 1886), p. 688. Some tax regulations openly discriminated against out-of-state or foreign firms. In 1889, for example, Missouri increased the taxes of all insurance companies and required out-of-state and foreign companies to pay a tax of 2 percent on their gross premiums, in addition to those taxes imposed upon in-state companies. After taking into consideration the impact of this discriminatory tax on premiums, many insurance companies reported that they experienced a net loss on the Missouri portion of their business. *Appleton's Annual Cyclopaedia of 1892* (New York: D. Appleton, 1893), pp. 473–474.

[111]   In many states in the South and Mountain West the insurance industry was dominated by out-of-state companies. The 1890 census data on insurance company income, for example, revealed that premiums paid by Georgia residents to joint-stock fire insurance companies were distributed as follows: Georgia (12.3% of all premiums were paid to firms located within the state); the states of the former Confederacy (including Georgia: 17.5%); and New England and the Middle Atlantic states (39.8%). British firms were major providers as well. Calculated from data in *Insurance Business in the United States: Fire, Marine, and Inland Insurance*, pt. 1 (Washington, D.C.: GPO, 1894), pp. 518–519, 542, and 672–674. From the point of view of the South, the terms of trade in insurance premiums probably worsened as the national market consolidated in subsequent decades. In 1919, for example, over 96 percent of all premiums paid on life and fire insurance policies in Georgia flowed to out-of-state companies. Over half of all premiums went to firms headquartered in just two cities, New York (39%) and Hartford, Connecticut (12%). Altogether, fire and life insurance companies in New England and the Middle Atlantic states drew 73 percent of all premiums paid by Georgia policyholders. Calculated from data displayed in Tables 1 and 3 in *Report of the Insurance Department of the State of Georgia for the Year Ending December 31, 1919* (Atlanta: Byrd Printing, 1920), pp. 20–23, 27–29.

not be compelled to honor contracts in states with discriminating regulatory frameworks, no one in those states would purchase policies from New York firms – thus perfecting the very object those discriminatory laws were intended to achieve in the first place.[112] Even so, this New York statute demonstrated one of the tensions then existing between the states over the extension and construction of the national market during the late nineteenth century.[113]

Although they were the most vulnerable, insurance companies were not the only targets of state regulation of out-of-state producers or merchants. Virginia, for instance, attempted to impose a licensing fee on out-of-state manufacturing companies while exempting in-state producers from the levy. When challenged by the Singer Sewing Machine company, headquartered in New York, this law was struck down as an unconstitutional violation of the interstate commerce clause.[114] Texas similarly attempted to discriminate against out-of-state liquor producers by exempting wines and beers produced by in-state residents from heavy taxes on alcohol. As in Virginia's case, this law too failed to survive court scrutiny.[115]

Other attempts to "Balkanize" the national market focused on the movement of labor into and out of the individual states. Several southern states, for example, imposed prohibitive taxes on agents when they tried to entice sharecroppers and tenant farmers to relocate to out-of-state plantations.[116]

---

[112] Noting that a bill to repeal this retaliatory measure had already been introduced in Albany, the *Commercial and Financial Chronicle* concluded that "the law is dead even without repeal and although not yet passed upon by the court of last resort. For this is a case where the law is worse than those to whom it relates." March 24, 1883.

[113] In the insurance sector, this tension usually assumed a form of aggressive reciprocity in which a state would mandate deposits or other requirements on out-of-state firms if their home states imposed such conditions on the first state's companies. In 1876, 26 states had passed such laws. Edward B. Whitney, "Commercial Retaliation between the States," *American Law Review* 19 (1885): 64 n. 5.

[114] *Webber v. Virginia*, 103 US 344 (1880). Some of the most important Supreme Court decisions involving construction of the commerce clause originated in state attempts to regulate peddlers of sewing machines. In addition to the present case, see *Welton v. Missouri*, 91 US 275 (1875); *[Howe] Machine Company v. Gage*, 100 US 676 (1879); and *Emert v. Missouri*, 156 US 296 (1894). Also see Charles W. McCurdy, "American Law and the Marketing Structure of the Large Corporation, 1875–1890," *Journal of Economic History* 38:3 (September 1978): 637–638.

[115] For brief descriptions of these cases and the general principles underlying their invalidation, see the *Commercial and Financial Chronicle*, July 2, 1881.

[116] In 1891, after emigration agents for several years had induced large numbers of sharecroppers and tenants to resettle on land in the western reaches of the cotton belt, the states of North and South Carolina retaliated by enacting laws that required each agent to pay $1,000 annually for a license within each county within which they operated. Georgia had previously enacted similar taxes on emigration agents in 1876 and 1877; Alabama had done so in 1877, 1879, and 1880. After the Supreme Court upheld the constitutionality of the Georgia statute in 1900, license

Pennsylvania went in the opposite direction when it passed a law in 1897 that required all employers pay into the state treasury three cents a day for every alien worker on their payroll. In practice, this levy would have barred many alien workers from employment within the state but was struck down as an unconstitutional violation of the equal protection clause of the United States Constitution.[117]

Many state efforts to regulate their relations with the national market targeted judicial review itself. In 1879, for example, the Indiana State legislature enacted a bill under which out-of-state corporations would forfeit their right to hold real estate or transact business in Indiana if, at any point, they sought to transfer litigation from the state courts into the federal courts. The purpose of the bill was to restrict such corporations to the state judicial system with reference to all litigation arising under Indiana laws.[118] By the turn of the century, numerous states had passed incorporation acts that required all nonstate corporations to pledge that they would not resort to the federal courts.[119] Another strategy for more effectively subjecting out-of-state corporations to state regulation was to require that they maintain a public office within the state.[120] Although corporations could threaten to leave if the regulations imposed by a state government became too onerous, there were few instances in which such threats were actually carried out.[121]

fees rapidly spread throughout the South. William Cohen, *At Freedom's Edge: Black Mobility and the Southern White Quest for Racial Control, 1861–1915* (Baton Rouge: Louisiana State University Press, 1991), pp. 233–238.

[117] *Appleton's Annual Cyclopaedia of 1898* (New York: D. Appleton, 1899), p. 621.

[118] *Appleton's 1879 Cyclopaedia*, p. 496.

[119] Tony A. Freyer, "The Federal Courts, Localism, and the National Economy, 1865–1900," *Business History Review* 53:3 (Autumn 1979): 349–350; Rogers M. Smith, *Civic Ideals: Conflicting Visions of Citizenship in U.S. History* (New Haven, Conn.: Yale University Press, 1997), p. 405.

[120] By amending its Corporation Act, the state of Illinois imposed such a requirement in 1897. For the text of the law, see the *Commercial and Financial Chronicle*, August 7, 1897.

[121] Describing the decision of the Standard Oil Company to move its headquarters and some portion of its operations out of Ohio because of the company's treatment as a "public enemy" by the state's attorney-general, the *Commercial and Financial Chronicle* commented, "We now and then get a glimpse of the way in which State hostility to the various forms of combined capital deprives any commonwealth engaged in such work of the benefits and use of all capital that is not so fixed that it cannot be transferred. Most of the harm such hostility does is impossible definitely to trace, for its action and movement are hidden. We know theoretically that floating capital is mobile and quickly deserts the locality where its burdens are unduly increased for one where they are lighter. But generally we can only gain evidences of its flight through long reaches of time; and where capital is more or less fixed, the movement is still more difficult to follow. The harm, though, done in all affairs of this kind to the material interests of the State is unquestionable." July 15, 1899.

In striking down such attempts to control the movement of goods or labor across state lines, the United States Supreme Court often declared its unqualified hostility to obstructions compromising the national market.[122] In an 1878 decision striking down a Pennsylvania law taxing the sale of out-of-state goods at auction, for example, Justice Samuel F. Miller wrote:

In granting to Congress the right to regulate commerce . . . the framers of the Constitution believed that they had sufficiently guarded against the dangers of any taxation by the States which would interfere with the freest interchange of commodities among the people of the different States, and by the people of the States with citizens and subjects of foreign governments.

The numerous cases in which this court has been called on to declare void statutes of the States which in various ways have sought to violate this salutary restriction, show the necessity and value of the constitutional provision. If certain States could exercise the unlimited power of taxing all the merchandise which passes from the port of New York through those States to the consumers in the great West, or could tax – as has been done until recently – every person who sought the seaboard through the railroads within their jurisdiction, the Constitution would have failed to effect one of the most important purposes for which it was adopted.

A striking instance of the evil and its cure is to be seen in the recent history of the states now compromising the German Empire. A few years ago they were independent States, which, though lying contiguous, speaking a common language, and belonging to a common race, were yet without a common government.

The number and variety of their systems of taxation and lines of territorial division necessitating customs officials at every step the traveller took or merchandise was transported, became so intolerable that a commercial, though not a political union was organized, called the German Zollverein. The great value of this became so apparent, and the community of interest so strongly felt in regard to commerce and traffic, that the first appropriate occasion was used by these numerous principalities to organize the common political government now known as the German Empire.[123]

---

[122] For a good overview of federal doctrine and citations to the leading cases during this period, see Freyer, "The Federal Courts, Localism, and the National Economy," pp. 343–363. By striking down state attempts to regulate interstate commerce, the federal courts simultaneously consolidated national judicial supremacy (over state sovereignty) and constructed a national marketplace. Beginning around 1880 and continuing into the twentieth century, southern and western congressmen responded by proposing to limit federal jurisdiction over cases involving corporations engaged in interstate trade; although such bills frequently passed the House of Representatives and, in at least one instance, the Senate, only one legislative limitation was ever enacted. This limitation made it more difficult for a corporation to demonstrate that local prejudice against its interests warranted removal of jurisdiction to the federal courts. For a review of congressional efforts to limit court jurisdiction, see pp. 357–361.

[123] *Cook v. Pennsylvania*, 97 US 566 (1878), pp. 574–575.

Eleven years later, while striking down a Michigan law regulating imported alcohol, Chief Justice Melvin W. Fuller firmly restated the Court's position:

We have repeatedly held that no State has the right to lay a tax on interstate commerce in any form, whether by way of duties laid on the transportation of the subjects of that commerce, or on the receipts derived from that transportation, or on the occupation or business of carrying it on, for the reason that such taxation is a burden on that commerce. . . . the power cannot be conceded to a State to exclude, directly or indirectly, the subjects of interstate commerce, or, by the imposition of burdens thereon, to regulate such commerce, without congressional permission. The same rule that applies to the sugar of Louisiana, the cotton of South Carolina, the wines of California, the hops of Washington, the tobacco of Maryland and Connecticut, or the products, natural or manufactured, of any State, applies to all commodities in which a right of traffic exists, recognized by the laws of Congress, the decisions of courts and the usages of the commercial world. It devolves on Congress to indicate such exceptions as in its judgment a wise discretion may demand under particular circumstances.[124]

As this passage suggests, the constitutional fulcrum for the political construction of the national market was the commerce clause. Quoting a leading constitutional authority, Justice Lucius Lamar elaborated the Court's interpretation of "commerce" as including:

the fact of intercourse and of traffic and the subject matter of intercourse and traffic. The fact of intercourse and traffic, again, embraces all the *means, instruments,* and places by and in which intercourse and traffic are carried on, and, further still, comprehends the act of carrying them on at these places and by and with these means. The subject matter of intercourse or traffic may be either things, goods, chattels, merchandise or persons.[125]

Judicial rulings on the commerce clause had begun with *Gibbons v. Ogden,* 9 Wheat. 1 (1824), closely followed by *Brown v. Maryland,* 12 Wheat. 419 (1827).[126] While both decisions firmly upheld federal authority over interstate commerce, the courts did not have many opportunities to further elaborate restrictions on state regulatory power prior to the Civil War (see Table 5.2). Before the railroad tied the United States together into one market, interstate commerce was so limited in the aggregate that the impulse on the part of the states to regulate its movement was weak. However, when the new consolidated manufacturing, commercial, and transportation corpora-

---

[124] *Lyng v. Michigan,* 135 US 161 (1889), pp. 166–167. Also see *Leloup v. Port of Mobile,* 127 US 640 (1887), p. 648.
[125] *McCall v. California,* 136 US 104 (1889), p. 108. Italics in the original.
[126] For a discussion of *Gibbons,* see Prentice and Egan, *Commerce Clause,* pp. 15–18. For a judicial history of the commerce clause, see pp. 1–42. The clause itself reads: "The Congress shall have power . . . To regulate commerce with foreign nations, and among the several States and with the Indian tribes."

Table 5.2. *State and Federal Cases Involving Construction of the Commerce Clause*

United States Supreme Court		All state and federal courts	
Founding to 1840	5	Founding to 1840	48
1840 to 1870	25	1840 to 1870	190
1870 to 1898	183	1870 to 1898	1,200

Note and source: Adapted from E. Parmalee Prentice and John G. Egan, *The Commerce Clause of the Federal Constitution* (Chicago: Callaghan, 1898), pp. 14–15. The number of state and federal cases involving the commerce clause for the last period is approximated. Supreme Court cases are included in the totals in the far right-hand column.

tions moved to the front of the national economy after the Civil War, the states repeatedly attempted to control and tax their activities. The United States Supreme Court responded by striking down the most aggressive of these state laws and otherwise crafting a set of principles through which state and federal regulatory boundaries might be policed. This effort, in fact, became a major judicial project consuming much of the Court's docket and intellectual energy.[127]

The centerpiece of the Court's interpretation of the commerce clause was the notion of "dual sovereignty," which divided trade into interstate and local components. The federal government was assigned exclusive sovereignty over interstate commerce, while the state governments were given equally exclusive control over what in effect became the residual, local economic activity. The boundary between them was determined by an often ritualized "act of consignment" in which a good or service was given over to interstate transportation. In 1888, for example, the United States Supreme Court upheld a state law prohibiting the manufacture of liquor even though the product was intended for sale in out-of-state markets. That decision held that congressional power to regulate interstate commerce did not include manufacturing, and for that reason, the production of alcohol fell exclusively within the police power of the individual states. In 1890, a second decision involving state authority over the interstate sale of liquor applied the concept of an "original package" as a limit on

---

[127] As the leading authorities in this period observed, "the commerce clause . . . presents the remarkable instance of a national power which was comparatively unimportant for eighty years, and which in the last thirty years has been so developed that it is now, in its nationalizing tendency, perhaps the most important and conspicuous power possessed by the Federal government." Prentice and Egan, *Commerce Clause*, p. 1. Also see Warren, *Supreme Court*, vol. 3, pp. 416–429.

local police power.[128] In this case, the Supreme Court ruled that as long as a product manufactured in one state was in its original package when entering into a second state that product remained in interstate commerce and could be regulated by no authority other than the United States Congress. As long as the product remained in the possession of the importer, this conceptualization of interstate commerce encompassed all characteristics and transactions associated with the product up to and including its sale.[129] Through this and similar decisions, the Court in effect created a boundary between the respective regulatory authorities of the individual states and the federal government, a boundary that required constant adjudication.[130]

Litigation over the commerce clause contested several very different policy dimensions: application of the original-package concept to various forms of interstate traffic, police power over health and related issues, local economic activity underpinning commerce generally, and federal attempts to regulate monopolies and trusts.[131] Some of the cases involving the

---

[128]   The notion of an "original package" first appeared in the opinion accompanying *Brown v. Maryland*: ". . . when the importer has so acted upon the thing imported, that it has become incorporated and mixed up with the mass of property in the country, it has, perhaps, lost its distinctive character as an import, and has become subject to the taxing power of the State; but while remaining the property of the importer, in his warehouse, in the original form or package in which it was imported, a tax upon it is too plainly a duty on imports to escape the prohibition in the constitution." 12 Wheat. 419 (1827), pp. 441–442. Almost three quarters of a century later, the Court observed that this "sentence contains in a nutshell the whole doctrine upon the subject of original packages, upon which so formidable a structure has been attempted to be erected in subsequent cases." *Austin v. Tennessee*, 179 US 343 (1900), p. 351. Also see Prentice and Egan, *Commerce Clause*, pp. 82–85.

[129]   To reach its verdict in *Leisy v. Hardin*, 135 US 100 (1889), the Court overturned *Peirce v. New Hampshire*, 5 How. 504. Because the decision threatened to vitiate state prohibition laws, the temperance movement was outraged and pressed Congress to restore to local governments the power to regulate the sale of liquor transported across state lines. Congress soon obliged with a law divesting such sales of their interstate character. Willard L. King, *Melville Weston Fuller: Chief Justice of the United States, 1888–1910* (Chicago: University of Chicago Press, 1967), pp. 167–169; *Appleton's Annual Cyclopaedia of 1890* (New York: D. Appleton, 1891), pp. 700–701. The Court upheld the law in *In Re Rahrer*, 140 US 545 (1890). In his majority opinion, Chief Justice Fuller stated, "Congress has now spoken, and declared that imported liquors or liquids shall, upon arrival in a State, fall within the category of domestic articles of a similar nature." P. 560. This law was later narrowed in its application by *Rhodes v. Iowa*, 170 US 412 (1897).

[130]   The case at hand was *Kidd v. Pearson*, 128 US 1 (1888). Schwartz, *History of the Supreme Court*, pp. 182–184.

[131]   For a general discussion of the principles distinguishing interstate from domestic commerce, Prentice and Egan, *Commerce Clause*, pp. 61–73, 82–106, 347–359.

concept of an original package involved its application to new forms of commerce. In *Western Union Telegraph Company v. James*, for example, the Supreme Court began by first confirming that telegraph messages transmitted across state lines were a form of interstate commerce and thus excluded from the police power of the individual states. State laws that attempted to regulate the delivery of messages sent by their residents to recipients residing in another state were, for that reason, an unconstitutional violation of the commerce clause. However, the court continued, state statutes regulating the delivery of telegraph messages that originated outside the state were upheld, provided that the enforcement mechanism did not itself unduly burden interstate commerce.[132]

Other decisions were minutely specific. In one case, a "station agent of the Burlington and Western [Railroad], in the discharge of his duties opened the door of the freight house and moved [a] box into a freight warehouse, which was about six feet from the platform." The unmarked box contained

---

[132] The decision upheld a 1887 Georgia statute requiring the diligent and impartial delivery of out-of-state messages to in-state residents. Under the law, the state had imposed a penalty of $100 against Western Union for failing to deliver a message confirming the sale of cotton on the same day that it had been sent from Eufaula, Alabama, to Blakely, Georgia. The principle underlying this penalty was important enough for the telegraph company to take the case through the court system, up to the supreme court of the state of Georgia and thence to the United States Supreme Court. For a detailed description of the case, see the *Commercial and Financial Chronicle*, May 30, 1896. For the decision itself, see *Western Union Telegraph Company v. James*, 162 US 650 (1895). The Court had earlier ruled, in *Western Union Telegraph Company v. Pendleton*, 122 US 347 (1886), that a state could not regulate the delivery of messages within the boundaries of another state. For other important decisions involving either state regulation or taxation of telegraph companies, see *Pensacola Telegraph Company v. Western Union Telegraph Company*, 96 US 1 (1877); *[Western Union] Telegraph Company v. Texas*, 105 US 460 (1881); *Ratterman v. Western Union Telegraph Company*, 127 US 411 (1887); *Massachusetts v. Western Union Telegraph Company*, 141 US 40 (1890); *Postal Telegraph Cable Company v. Adams*, 155 US 688 (1894); *Western Union Telegraph Company v. Taggart*, 163 US 1 (1895); *Adams Express Company v. Ohio State Auditor*, 165 US 194 (1896).

The leading railroad cases followed similar lines. See, for example, *Pickard, Comptroller v. Pullman Southern Car Company*, 117 US 34 (1885); *Wabash, St. Louis and Pacific Railway Company v. Illinois*, 118 US 557 (1886); *Fargo v. Michigan*, 121 US 230 (1886); *Smith v. Alabama*, 124 US 465 (1887); *Nashville, Chattanooga and St. Louis Railway v. Alabama*, 128 US 96 (1888); *Norfolk and Western Railroad Company v. Pennsylvania*, 136 US 114 (1889); *Pullman's Palace Car Company v. Pennsylvania*, 141 US 18 (1890); *Maine v. Grand Trunk Railway Company*, 142 US 217 (1891); *Ashley v. Ryan*, 153 US 436 (1893); *Reagan v. Mercantile Trust Company*, 154 US 413 (1893); *Pittsburgh, Cincinnati, Chicago and St. Louis Railway Company v. Backus*, 154 US 421 (1893); *Cleveland, Cincinnati, Chicago and St. Louis Railway Company v. Backus*, 154 US 439 (1893); and *New York, Lake Erie & Western Railroad Company v. Pennsylvania*, 158 US 431 (1894).

liquor that had been sent to Iowa from Illinois, and Iowa authorities had confiscated and destroyed the shipment. One of the issues the Supreme Court was asked to decide was whether or not the movement of the box across the platform constituted delivery of the original package and thus crossed the line between federal and state authority.[133]

Manufacturers and their agents soon adapted to the Court's decisions by making packages sent across state lines so small that they could be retailed to individual consumers. If allowed by the federal courts, this strategy would have entirely evaded the state's police power over goods moving across state lines. In one case, for example, cigarette manufacturers had reduced the size of their shipments to Tennessee to packages containing only ten cigarettes. The Court was not amused:

The real question in this case is whether the size of the package in which the importation is actually made is to govern; or, the size of the package in which *bona fide* transactions are carried on between the manufacturer and the wholesale dealer residing in different States. We hold to the latter view. The whole theory of the exemption of the original package from the operation of state laws is based upon the idea that the property is imported in the ordinary form in which, from time to time immemorial, foreign goods have been brought into the country. These have gone at once into the hands of the wholesale dealers, who have been in the habit of breaking the packages and distributing their contents among the several retail dealers throughout the State. It was with reference to this method of doing business that the doctrine of the exemption of the original package grew up. But taking the words "original package" in their literal sense, a number of so-called original package manufactories have been started through the country, whose business it is to manufacture goods for the express purpose of sending their products into other States in minute packages, that may at once go into the hands of the retail dealers and consumers, and thus bid defiance to the laws of the State against their importation and sale. . . .

The consequences of our adoption of defendant's contention would be far-reaching and disastrous. For the purpose of aiding a manufacturer in evading the laws of a sister State, we should be compelled to recognize anything as an original package of beer from a hogshead to a vial; anything as a package of cigarettes from an importer's case to a single paper box of ten, or even a single cigarette, if imported separately and loosely; anything from a bale of merchandise to a single ribbon, provided only the dealer sees fit to purchase his stock outside the State and import it in minute quantities.[134]

---

[133]   The Court said that the box remained in interstate commerce. *Rhodes v. Iowa*, 170 US 412 (1897), pp. 413–414. For related decisions involving the production, sale, and consumption of alcohol under the commerce clause, see *Tiernan v. Rinker*, 102 US 123 (1880); *Walling v. Michigan*, 116 US 446 (1885); *Bowman v. Chicago &c. Railway Co*, 125 US 465 (1887); *Kidd v. Pearson*, 128 US 1 (1888); *Leisy v. Hardin*, 135 US 100 (1889); *Lyng v. Michigan*, 135 US 161 (1889); *In Re Rahrer*, 140 US 545 (1890); and *Scott v. Donald*, 165 US 58 (1896).

[134]   *Austin v. Tennessee*, 179 US 343 (1900), pp. 359–360.

Other decisions taking up prohibitions on the importation of oleomargarine into a state worked out further details but generally sustained this interpretation of the commerce clause.[135]

Many of these ran up against the state's police power to regulate and protect the health and general well-being of society. Here the court attempted to balance competing claims. In an 1886 opinion written for the majority, Justice Joseph P. Bradley provided the best summary of the court's position:

> It is also an established principle ... that the only way in which commerce between the states can be legitimately affected by state laws, is when, by virtue of its police power, and its jurisdiction over persons and property within its limits, a state provides for the security of the lives, limbs, health, and comfort of persons and the protection of property; or when it does those things which may otherwise incidentally affect commerce, such as the establishment and regulation of highways, canals, railroads, wharves, ferries, and other commercial facilities; the passage of inspection laws to secure the due quality and measure of products and commodities; the passage of laws to regulate or restrict the sale of articles deemed injurious to the health or morals of the community; the imposition of taxes upon persons residing within the state or belonging to its population, and upon avocations and employments pursued therein, not directly connected with foreign or interstate commerce or with some other employment or business exercised under authority of the Constitution and laws of the United States; and the imposition of taxes upon all property within the state, mingled with and forming part of the great mass of property therein. But in making such internal regulations a state cannot impose taxes upon persons passing through the state, or coming into it merely for a temporary purpose, especially if connected with interstate or foreign commerce; nor can it impose such taxes upon property imported into the state from abroad, or from another state, and not yet become part of the common mass of property therein; and no discrimination can be made, by any such regulations, adversely to the persons or property of other states; and no regulations can be made directly affecting interstate commerce.[136]

But even this very clear statement of the problem could not resolve all the ambiguity between "noxious" goods and legitimate products.[137]

---

[135] The most important oleomargarine cases were *Plumley v. Massachusetts*, 155 US 461 (1894); *Schollenberger v. Pennsylvania*, 171 US 1 (1897); and *Collins v. New Hampshire*, 171 US 30 (1897). Prentice and Egan, *Commerce Clause*, pp. 49–54.

[136] *Robbins v. Shelby County Taxing District*, 120 US 489 (1886), pp. 493–494.

[137] The Court pondered just this problem in a later decision: "Cigarettes do not seem until recently to have attracted the attention of the public as more injurious than other forms of tobacco; nor are we now prepared to take judicial notice of any special injury resulting from their use or to indorse the opinion of the Supreme Court of Tennessee that 'they are inherently bad and bad only.' At the same time we should be shutting our eyes to what is constantly passing before them were we to affect an ignorance of the fact that a belief in their deleterious effects, particularly upon young people, has become very general, and that communications are constantly finding their way into the public press denouncing their use as fraught with great danger to

One of the easiest subjects to adjudicate involved the only area of concurrent jurisdiction over interstate commerce: that involving "those things
which may otherwise incidentally affect commerce, such as the establishment and regulation of highways, canals, railroads, wharves, ferries, and
other commercial facilities." Here the states were free to act as long as Congress did not legislate.[138] But otherwise the Court was quite aggressive in
policing the boundary between state and federal power over interstate commerce. Between 1877 and 1900, the Court under the commerce clause inval-
idated either in part or entirely statutes belonging to at least nineteen
states.[139]

Where the federal government, on the other side of the line, attempted
to regulate interstate commerce, the Supreme Court could be just as vigi-
lant. In 1898, for example, the Court held that transactions executed on
the Kansas City Live Stock Exchange, an association of commission agents
that effectively monopolized the marketing of livestock in that city, were

the youth of both sexes." *Austin v. Tennessee*, 179 US 343 (1900), p. 360. Also see
[Hannibal and St. Joseph] Railroad Company v. Husen, 95 US 465 (1877), pp.
473–474.

[138] As Charles Warren put it, "there was substantially but one class of cases affecting
interstate commerce in which the State powers were upheld, namely, those involving the right of the State to control its bridges, wharves and ferries." *Supreme Court*,
vol. 3, p. 353. See, for example, *County of Mobile v. Kimball*, 102 US 691 (1880).

[139] Alabama in *Leloup v. Port of Mobile*, 127 US 640 (1887); California in *McCall v.
California*, 136 US 104 (1889); Florida in *Pensacola Telegraph Company v. Western
Union Telegraph Company*, 96 US 1 (1877); Illinois in *Wabash, St. Louis and Pacific
Railway Company v. Illinois*, 118 US 557 (1886); Indiana in *Western Union Telegraph Company v. Pendleton*, 122 US 347 (1886); Iowa in three decisions: *Bowman
v. Chicago &c. Railway Co*, 125 US 465 (1887); *Leisy v. Hardin*, 135 US 100
(1889); and *Rhodes v. Iowa*, 170 US 412 (1897); Kentucky in *Crutcher v. Kentucky*,
141 US 47 (1890); Louisiana in *Hall v. DeCuir*, 95 US 485 (1877); and *Allgeyer v.
Louisiana*, 165 US 578 (1896); Maryland in *Guy v. Baltimore*, 100 US 434 (1879),
and *Corson v. Maryland*, 120 US 502 (1886); Michigan in three decisions: *Walling
v. Michigan*, 116 US 446 (1885); *Fargo v. Michigan*, 121 US 230 (1886); and *Lyng
v. Michigan*, 135 US 161 (1889); Minnesota in *Minnesota v. Barber*, 136 US 313
(1889); Missouri in *[Hannibal and St. Joseph] Railroad Company v. Husen*, 95 US
465 (1877); New Hampshire in *Collins v. New Hampshire*, 171 US 30 (1897); Ohio
in *Ratterman v. Western Union Telegraph Company*, 127 US 411 (1887); Pennsylvania in five decisions: *Cook v. Pennsylvania*, 97 US 566 (1878); *Philadelphia and
Southern Steamship Company v. Pennsylvania*, 122 US 326 (1886); *Norfolk and
Western Railroad Company v. Pennsylvania*, 136 US 114 (1889); *Brennan v.
Titusville*, 153 US 289 (1893); and *Schollenberger v. Pennsylvania*, 171 US 1 (1897);
South Carolina in *Scott v. Donald*, 165 US 58 (1896); Tennessee in two decisions:
Pickard, Comptroller v. Pullman Southern Car Company, 117 US 34 (1885); and
Robbins v. Shelby County Taxing District, 120 US 489 (1886); Texas in three deci-
sions: *Tiernan v. Rinker*, 102 US 123 (1880); *[Western Union] Telegraph Company
v. Texas*, 105 US 460 (1881); and *Asher v. Texas*, 128 US 129 (1888); and Virginia
in three decisions: *Webber v. Virginia*, 103 US 344 (1880); *Brimmer v. Rebman*, 138
US 78 (1890); and *Voight v. Wright*, 141 US 62 (1890).

not a part of interstate commerce even though most of the livestock coming into the yards had been transported across state lines.[140] However, the general principles underlying these decisions remained elusive.

Speaking for the court majority in 1877, Chief Justice Morrison R. Waite put the problem this way:

> The line which separates the powers of the States from this exclusive power of Congress is not always distinctly marked, and oftentimes it is not easy to determine on which side a particular case belongs. Judges not unfrequently differ in their reasons for a decision in which they concur. Under such circumstances it would be a useless task to undertake to fix an arbitrary rule by which the line must in all cases be located. It is far better to leave a matter of such delicacy to be settled in each case upon a view of the particular rights involved.[141]

The Court reiterated their continuing appreciation of the complexity of the problem in 1894:

> Owing to the paramount necessity of maintaining untrammelled freedom of commercial intercourse between the citizens of the different States, and to the fact that so frequently transportation and telegraph companies transact both local and interstate business, it has been found difficult to clearly define the line where the state and the Federal powers meet.[142]

In sum, even though the Court recognized that their often divided decisions over details in application would lead both the state and lower federal courts astray, the justices were nonetheless united on the importance of policing the boundary between state and federal authority:

> The difficulty of the subject is shown in the frequent and elaborate dissents in many of the cases. Still, it can be safely said that the differences of opinion thus manifested have not been so much upon fundamental principles, as upon questions of the construction and meaning of the various state statutes that have been under consideration.[143]

And the state courts obliged by striking down many laws even before they could enter the federal system on appeal.[144]

---

[140]   *Hopkins v. United States*, 171 US 578 (1898). A good description of the case and its practical implications can be found in the *Commercial and Financial Chronicle*, November 26, 1898. Federal prosecution was pursued under the Sherman Antitrust Act. For the leading livestock cases involving state statutes, see *[Hannibal and St. Joseph] Railroad Company v. Husen*, 95 US 465 (1877); *Kimmish v. Ball*, 129 US 217 (1888); *Minnesota v. Barber*, 136 US 313 (1889); and *Brimmer v. Rebman*, 138 US 78 (1890).

[141]   *Hall v. DeCuir*, 95 US 485 (1877), p. 488.

[142]   *New York, Lake Erie & Western Railroad Company v. Pennsylvania*, 158 US 431 (1894), pp. 437–438.

[143]   *Scott v. Donald*, 165 US 58 (1896), pp. 90–91.

[144]   For a sampling of such cases, see *Walling v. Michigan*, 116 US 446 (1885), pp. 457–458.

A second judicial doctrine, through which state regulation came under the scope of the Fourteenth Amendment, complemented dual sovereignty.[145] Under the Fourteenth Amendment, the states were prevented, among other things, from depriving "any person of life, liberty, or property without due process of law." In enforcing this clause, the Supreme Court gave due process a substantive interpretation under which any regulatory act that prevented a person or corporation from earning a reasonable return on invested capital was deemed a constitutional violation. To bring this construction fully to bear on the regulatory efforts of the individual states, corporations were ruled legally equivalent to persons.[146] In one of the first of these decisions, for example, the U.S. Supreme Court struck down two regulations imposed on local railroad operations by the Railroad and Warehouse Commission of Minnesota. Handing down both decisions in March 1890, the Supreme Court ruled unconstitutional the commission's attempts to reduce charges for switching cars in a Minneapolis railroad yard and to lower the rate by which milk was carried by rail into Minneapolis-St. Paul from smaller cities within the state. The majority opinion declared:

The question of the reasonableness of a rate of charge for transportation by a railroad company . . . is eminently a question for judicial investigation, requiring due process of law for its determination. If the company is deprived of the power of charging reasonable rates for the use of its property, and such deprivation takes place in the absence of an investigation by judicial machinery, it is deprived of the lawful use of its property, and thus, in substance and effect, of the property itself, without due process of law and in violation of the Constitution of the United States;

---

[145]   For general accounts of judicial interpretation of the due process clause in this period, see William M. Wiecek, *The Lost World of Classical Legal Thought: Law and Ideology in America, 1886–1937* (New York: Oxford University Press, 1998), pp. 124–126, 133–136; Boudin, *Government by Judiciary*, pp. 374–404. A brief survey of the cases associated with the development of the dual sovereignty doctrine can be found in Thorelli, *Federal Antitrust Policy*, pp. 104–107.

[146]   As Lawrence Friedman has observed, this interpretation transformed corporations into the legal equivalent of "flesh-and-blood people" and turned the Fourteenth Amendment, originally enacted in order to protect southern blacks, "into a stronghold for industrial corporations." *History of American Law*, p. 455. However, the answer to the question whether or not corporations were "persons" within the eyes of the law was never controversial. When counsel attempted to raise the issue before the Supreme Court in 1886, the Chief Justice announced: "The court does not wish to hear argument on the question whether the provision in the Fourteenth Amendment to the Constitution, which forbids a State to deny to any person within its jurisdiction the equal protection of the laws, applies to these corporations. We are all of opinion that it does." Schwartz, *History of the Supreme Court*, pp. 169–170. One of the unintended effects of this interpretation was to discourage trade unions from incorporating their organizations under state laws for fear that they "could . . . be sued as any other corporation [resulting] in a liability for actions which their funds would not warrant." *Industrial Commission: Capital and Labor*, vol. 7, pp. 6–8.

and in so far as it is thus deprived, while other persons are permitted to receive reasonable profits upon their invested capital, the company is deprived of the equal protection of the laws.[147]

In both these cases, the regulated activity lay wholly within the state of Minnesota. And in both cases, the Supreme Court concluded that, if the regulation were allowed to stand, the railroad would not be able to earn a reasonable return on its capital.

Contemporary observers immediately recognized the significance of these decisions. Condemning the decision in the strongest possible terms, the Farmers' Alliance of Minnesota called the ruling a "second Dred Scott decision" and asked the American people "to consider whether any other race would submit to have their liberties thus wheedled away from them on technicalities by a squad of lawyers sitting as a supreme authority high above Congress, the President and people.... In our anxiety to protect the rights of property we have created a machinery that threatens to destroy the rights of man...."[148] On the other side, the *Commercial and Financial Chronicle* praised the Court: "We were in imminent danger of permitting our great carrying interests to be irrevocably embarrassed by Socialistic legislation. ... The findings of our highest court are such as to put to rest these issues which had been so vigorously raised ... [thus] marking an epoch in the industrial and constitutional history of the country."[149] An even more prescient *Chronicle* might have also noted that this decision heralded the beginning of a period of judicial supremacy in the construction of the national market, unmatched either before or since.[150] From 1890 until the *Nebbia*

---

[147] From Justice Samuel Blatchford's majority opinion, *Chicago, Milwaukee and St. Paul Railway Company v. Minnesota*, 134 US 418 (1889), 458. The second, immediately following case was *Minneapolis Eastern Railway Company v. Minnesota*, 134 US 467 (1889). Both of these decisions, in effect, overruled interpretations by the Minnesota Supreme Court that had sustained the Commission's regulatory authority. Arnold M. Paul, *Conservative Crisis and the Rule of Law: Attitudes of Bar and Bench, 1887–1895* (New York: Harper Torchbooks, 1969), pp. 39–44. Although Justice Bradley, writing in dissent, may have slightly exaggerated when he said that the first decision "practically overrules" *Munn v. Illinois*, 94 US 113 (1877), which had granted the states the power to regulate businesses "clothed with a public interest," the ruling still constituted "one of the major turning points in the rise of the new constitutionalism." Ibid., pp. 9, 41–42. For Bradley's dissent, see *Chicago, Milwaukee and St. Paul Railway Company v. Minnesota*, 134 US 418 (1889), pp. 461–466. For an extensive discussion of the later attitude of the Court toward *Munn*, see *Budd v. New York*, 143 US 517 (1891), pp. 528, 538–548.

[148] Paul, *Conservative Crisis*, p. 42, n. 8.

[149] March 29, 1890.

[150] In 1894, the Supreme Court further defined the constitutional scope of state regulatory authority in two decisions consolidating earlier rulings. The Court first upheld North Dakota's power to regulate hundreds of grain elevators scattered across the state and thus expanded on *Munn v. Illinois* by extending legislative authority beyond national market centers (such as Chicago) to rural crossroads and rail

v. New York decision in 1934 and the *National Labor Relations Board v. Jones & Laughlin Steel Corp.* decision in 1937, federal application of this substantive interpretation of the due process clause, along with adjudication of the boundary between local and interstate commerce, made the United States Supreme Court the dominant force in the construction of the national market economy.[151]

In combination, the two new doctrines of substantive due process and dual sovereignty rendered many efforts to regulate economic activity impossible.[152] For example, many regulatory efforts to shape or restrain the national market ran afoul of "liberty of contract," a subsidiary principle gradually developed by the Supreme Court in the decades around the turn of the century. One of the most important of the cases under this new doctrine, *Allgeyer v. Louisiana*, 165 U.S. 578 (1896), struck down a state law that prohibited insurance contracts between Louisiana citizens and out-of-state companies. Ruling that such a prohibition violated the due process clause of the Fourteenth Amendment, the court majority went on to say:

The liberty mentioned in that amendment means not only the right of the citizen to be free from the mere physical restraint of his person, as by incarceration, but the term is deemed to embrace the right of the citizen to be free in the enjoyment of all his faculties; to be free to use them in all lawful ways; to live and work where he will; to earn his livelihood by any lawful calling; to pursue any livelihood or avocation, and for that purpose to enter into all contracts which may be proper, necessary and essential to his carrying out to a successful conclusion the purposes above mentioned.[153]

sidings. In the second decision, the Court struck down an entire schedule of railroad rates that had been imposed by the Texas railroad commission as "unreasonable." The net effect of these and other decisions was to preserve state authority to regulate activities related to the interstate transportation of products over the rail network while subjecting that regulation to substantive judicial review. Paul, *Conservative Crisis*, pp. 174–178.

151 Schwartz, *History of the Supreme Court*, pp. 165, 236–238.

152 Paul, *Conservative Crisis*, pp. 45–60; Wiecek, *Lost World*, pp. 156. Between 1889 and 1900, the Supreme Court struck down thirty-seven state laws, five municipal ordinances, and five federal acts. William F. Swindler, *Court and Constitution in the 20th Century: The Old Legality, 1889–1932* (Indianapolis, Ind.: Bobbs-Merrill, 1969), p. 344. Between 1897 and 1906, the due process clause was invoked in 297 cases decided by the Supreme Court. Edward S. Corwin, *The Twilight of the Supreme Court* (New Haven, Conn.: Yale University Press, 1934), p. 77.

153 Although this was the first Supreme Court decision in which a state law was struck down as a violation of substantive due process, the ruling in some respects merely confirmed trends that had taken hold in the state courts over the preceding decade. Schwartz, *History of the Supreme Court*, pp. 180–182. For a brief review of these earlier decisions, see Paul, *Conservative Crisis*, pp. 219–220. In addition to the reasons cited in the text, the Court grounded its decision in the commerce clause, contending that Louisiana's police power could not reach a contract written in New York between a Louisiana citizen and a company located in the latter state. *Allgeyer v. Louisiana*, 165 US 578 (1896).

However, constitutional barriers to economic regulation were sometimes erected only after judicial rulings had traveled a tortuous path. With respect to the constitutional standing of the great industrial trusts, for example, the courts began this journey in apparent hostility to the efforts of the great industrial corporations to consolidate operations and to thus control market conditions. In November 1889, the New York Supreme Court started off the run of cases with its decision in *People v. North River Sugar Refining Company*. Although not the first such case, the decision ultimately proved the most important, both because it was handed down in the home state of many of the nation's largest corporations and because it involved the Sugar Trust, one of the most openly aggressive attempts to control trade. When the court finally ruled, it decided against the Trust's absorption of the North River Refining Company, basing its opinion on two findings: first, that the merger tended to create a monopoly in the sugar industry and thus constituted a virtual conspiracy to uphold prices and destroy competition; and, second, that a corporation could not voluntarily surrender entire control of its operations to another corporation. With regard to the latter point, the decision was more narrowly construed, basing the court's ruling, at least in part, on the specific provisions of the corporate charter granted by the state of New York to the refining company.[154]

This decision was but one of a series of rulings handed down by the state courts, pronouncing unconstitutional trusts and other arrangements intended to restrict market competition. Handed down by courts in California, Illinois, Louisiana, Michigan, and Tennessee, most of these decisions invoked common-law principles and cited the state charters under which the corporations had been organized within their respective states. With respect to these charters, the courts relied on provisions that stipulated or implied that these corporations could not participate in agreements or organizational devices intended to restrain competition. Most of the decisions were written in the five-year period just prior to passage of the Sherman Antitrust Act in 1890. However, although the hostility of the state courts to the creation and operation of monopolistic combinations was clear, very few monopolies were dismantled.[155]

The common-law assault on trusts was largely ineffective because new forms of corporate organization were easily created as means of evading judicial rulings. Even before the New York Supreme Court had ruled in the North River case, for example, the state prosecutor hazarded a cynical prediction: "Of course the case will be appealed whichever way the decision

---

[154] *Commercial and Financial Chronicle*, November 9, 1889. For a summary of the subsequent decision by the New York Court of Appeals affirming this ruling, see the June 28, 1890, issue.

[155] Letwin, *Law and Economic Policy*, pp. 79–83; Chandler, *The Visible Hand*, p. 316. For a detailed discussion of antitrust prosecution by state governments, see Thorelli, *Federal Antitrust Policy*, pp. 42–50, 80–83, 155–156, 162, 259–267.

goes. In anticipation of an unfavorable decision, the trust, I have no doubt, will undergo a metamorphosis to escape the decision's effect. For example, each one of the companies might, in anticipation of an adverse decision, transfer its property to some other corporation or to individuals."[156] An even more important defect in the common-law approach to antitrust litigation was that state governments could not initiate suit but, instead, had to wait for an aggrieved private party to appeal to courts for remedy. In addition, most state interventions ran up against the constitutional prohibition on regulation of interstate commerce.[157]

Driven by the expansion of the national market, the steady decline of transportation costs, the development of more efficient but capital-intensive modes of production, and the maturation of financial markets as sources of investment capital, the consolidation of American industry into ever larger corporate organizations had begun well before the Civil War. The pace of consolidation, however, quickened perceptibly during the 1880s and thus generated the common-law cases through which state courts attempted to counter this trend. The first notable use of the trust for the facilitation of industrial consolidation was its adoption by the Standard Oil Company in 1882.[158] The Cotton Oil Trust followed suit in 1884, the Linseed Oil Trust in 1885, and in 1887 what had been a trickle threatened to turn into a flood: the Sugar, Whisky, Envelope, Salt, Cordage, Oil-Cloth, Paving-Pitch, School-Slate, Chicago Gas, St. Louis Gas, and New York Meat trusts all formed in that year.[159] This highly visible transformation of

---

[156] *Commercial and Financial Chronicle*, July 13, 1889. When the case was appealed, Mr. C. O. Foster, president of the Boston Sugar Refining Company and one of the trustees in the Sugar Trust, was reported as saying, "No matter what the decision of the Court may be, it will not affect the business of the trust. . . . If the Court says we are not doing business legally, why then we shall reorganize into a corporation, and our business will go on just the same. . . ." *Commercial and Financial Chronicle*, June 28, 1890. Equally important problems, according to Hans Thorelli, were that state attorneys-general lacked the resources to successfully prosecute large corporations, feared that antitrust suits would encourage the removal of industrial operations from their states, and were not encouraged by public opinion to pursue enforcement of antitrust legislation in the courts. *Federal Antitrust Policy*, pp. 155–156.

[157] Letwin, *Law and Economic Policy*, pp. 81, 84.

[158] Ibid., pp. 8–9, 55–59. For a description of the organization of the Standard Oil Trust, see Thorelli, *Federal Antitrust Policy*, pp. 76–78, 91–96.

[159] Letwin, *Law and Economic Policy*, pp. 69–70. Specifically mentioning the American Sugar Refining Company, the Cordage Company, the American Tobacco Company, and the Distilling & Cattle-Feeding Company as prominent examples, the *Commercial and Financial Chronicle* concluded that all "of the industrial companies, properly so-called, are the creations of the movement between 1886 and 1890 to restrict competition in various lines of industry through the amalgamation of separate concerns into national 'trusts.' Few of these companies, therefore, have yet enjoyed more than five or six years of corporate life." July 20, 1895.

the national marketplace engendered much public concern. The states were the first to respond; in 1889, Kansas, Michigan, and Nebraska passed antitrust laws intended to prevent corporate collusion on prices and production. And a year later the accelerating trend toward industrial consolidation provided the impetus behind passage of the Sherman Antitrust Act.[160]

The most significant passages in the act were those that directly addressed market competition.[161] The opening section declared every "contract, combination in the form of trust or otherwise, or conspiracy, in restraint of trade" to be illegal. This section was immediately followed by a second that made a crime any attempt "to monopolize or attempt to monopolize, or combine or conspire . . . to monopolize any part of the trade or commerce among the several states."[162] While the act armed the Attorney General of the United States for an attack on the great trusts, his lack of ammunition prevented much of an assault. To cope with a steadily increasing volume of routine government business, such as claims litigation, and other cases before the Supreme Court in which the Solicitor General played at least some part (180 in 1890 alone), the Department of Justice employed

[160] Friedman, *History of American Law*, p. 406. By 1890, twenty-one states had antitrust provisions in either their constitutions, statutory codes, or both. Thorelli, *Federal Antitrust Policy*, p. 155. Even after passage of the Sherman Act, the states continued to legislate against trusts. By 1900 fifteen states had enacted constitutional prohibitions and twenty-seven had banned them through statutory law. Most of these states were located in the southern and western periphery – almost none were in nation's manufacturing belt. On the whole, however, these state enactments had little or no impact upon the organization and development of industry. Edward C. Kirkland, *Industry Comes of Age: Business, Labor, and Public Policy, 1860–1897* (Chicago: Quadrangle Books, 1967), p. 315.

[161] What Congress intended to accomplish by passing the act is unclear. The legislative history can support a number of contradictory interpretations. Some scholars have argued, for example, that Congress was merely giving voice to a legislative consensus that laissez-faire needed, as a fundamental economic principle guiding American development, legal protection in order to maintain a thoroughly competitive marketplace. Others have noted that the Republican Fifty-first Congress which enacted this principle was dominated by many of the industrialists whose activities were to be monitored by an active antitrust policy. For this reason, they conclude that the act was a sham, intended to appease an aroused public and, at the same time, knowingly destined to vitiation by the courts. For summaries of the range of scholarly opinion, see Letwin, *Law and Economic Policy*, p. 52; Thorelli, *Federal Antitrust Policy*, pp. 214–221; Friedman, *History of American Law*, p. 298. In fact, even as the antitrust bill was on President Harrison's desk, awaiting his signature, the stock market was driving the prices of trust securities ever higher on heavy volume, leading the *Commercial and Financial Chronicle* to conclude that investors attached "little importance" to the measure. May 10, 1890.

[162] For succinct legislative histories of the law, see Letwin, *Law and Economic Policy*, pp. 87–95; Rudolph J. R. Peritz, *Competition Policy in America, 1888–1992* (New York: Oxford University Press, 1996), pp. 9–26. For a more comprehensive account, see Thorelli, *Federal Antitrust Policy*, pp. 166–214.

only eighteen lawyers in its central offices in Washington. And while there were federal district attorneys scattered about the remainder of the nation, they operated their offices largely beyond the control of the Attorney General.[163]

After a number of inconclusive preliminary cases, the Attorney General chose to prosecute one of the leading independent sugar refiners in the nation, E. C. Knight Company, for its entry into the Sugar Trust. Along with three other independent refiners in Philadelphia, E. C. Knight's share of the refined sugar market represented 33 percent of the national total. Before the combination with Knight and the other independents, the Sugar Trust controlled 65 percent of the market. Thus the combination gave the trust almost complete control of the nation's supply of refined sugar and, for that reason, came to represent an extremely important test of the effectiveness of the act in dismantling industrial combinations in restraint of trade.[164] In the years that intervened between the initial filing and the Supreme Court's decision in this antitrust suit, the government continued to win and lose cases, albeit without much pattern to the decisions. In its first effort to prosecute labor unions under the Sherman Antitrust Act, however, the government was clearly victorious.[165]

With the inauguration of Grover Cleveland in 1893, a new Attorney General took up prosecution of the Sugar Trust.[166] At this point, the ongoing Sugar Trust litigation was elevated in status, becoming the major test case for an exploration of the act's breadth and application. And the government lost as first the lower courts in 1894 and then the Supreme Court in the following year failed to convict. The latter opinion, which became the doctrine of the court, held that: (1) federal law could reach only commercial activities that lay within the scope of interstate commerce; (2) sugar refining as an industrial process lay wholly outside interstate commerce; and (3) the purchase of refineries was therefore a local transaction

---

[163] Letwin, *Law and Economic Policy*, pp. 103–106.

[164] Ibid., pp. 113–114. In the early 1890s, industrial mergers were occurring at such a rapid pace that the gobbling up of the Philadelphia companies attracted little comment. The *Commercial and Financial Chronicle*, for example, only said: "Consolidations go on, and this week we have the Tennessee Coal & Iron completed, and the Sugar Refineries absorbing two of the great Philadelphia concerns." March 19, 1892. Also see March 26, 1892.

[165] In this case, an injunction was issued against labor unions participating in a general strike in New Orleans. Letwin, *Law and Economic Policy*, p. 115.

[166] This was Richard Olney, whose law practice had included a number of corporate clients before he took up this position. There is some evidence that, however conscientiously Olney prosecuted cases under the Sherman Antitrust Act, he doubted the wisdom of the law and would have supported repeal. Letwin, *Law and Economic Policy*, pp. 118–120. For a full review of Olney's record, see Thorelli, *Federal Antitrust Policy*, pp. 383–394.

beyond the reach of federal law even if the Sugar Trust thereby monopolized interstate trade in refined sugar.[167]

During the remainder of Cleveland's administration, the Sherman Antitrust Act was used only sparingly, most notably in support of the government's prosecution of Eugene Debs and the American Railway Union in connection with the Pullman strike of 1894.[168] Although the act was not the only authority under which federal intervention in the strike was defended (the obligation to remove obstructions to the carrying of the mails was the central issue in the case), and although the Supreme Court formally excluded the law in reviewing the grounds for its decisions, the Industrial Commission, along with most contemporary observers, viewed the Sherman Antitrust Act as "the main reliance in the issue of injunctions and the punishment of strikers in connection with the railway strikes of 1894."[169]

---

[167] *United States v. E.C. Knight Company*, 156 US 1 (1894). Letwin, *Law and Economic Policy*, pp. 122–123, 161–167; Prentice and Egan, *Commerce Clause*, pp. 317–335; Thorelli, *Federal Antitrust Policy*, pp. 445–448. Arnold Paul described this decision as clearing "the way for a tremendous concentration of capital, unrestrained by fear of effective prosecution; by the time court views were modified in the next decade, 'bigness' had become entrenched in the economy." *Conservative Crisis*, p. 227.

[168] The crux of the Supreme Court's unanimous decision was made in the following passage, quoted with approval by the *Commercial and Financial Chronicle*: "We hold that the Government of the United States is one having jurisdiction over every foot of soil within its territory, and acting directly upon each citizen; that while it is a government of enumerated powers it has within the limits of those powers all the attributes of sovereignty; that to it is committed a power over inter-State commerce and the transmission of the mails; that the powers thus conferred upon the National Government are not dormant, but have been assumed and put into practical exercise by the legislation of Congress; that in the exercise of those powers it is competent for the nation to remove all obstructions upon highways, natural or artificial, to the passage of inter-State commerce or the carrying of the mail; that while it may be competent for the Government – through the executive branch and in the use of the entire executive power of the nation – to forcibly remove all such obstructions, it is equally within its competency to appeal to the civil courts for an inquiry and determination as to the existence and character of any alleged obstructions, and if such are found to exist, or threaten to occur, to invoke the powers of the courts to remove or restrain such obstructions." June 1, 1895. For a full account of this case, see Thorelli, *Federal Antitrust Policy*, pp. 389–394, 448–451.

[169] *Report of the Industrial Commission: Labor Organizations*, vol. 17 (Washington, D.C.: GPO, 1901), p. 593. In the decision, the Court stated that it entered "into no examination of the [Sherman Act] upon which the Circuit Court relied mainly to sustain its jurisdiction. It must not be understood from this that we dissent from the conclusions of that court in reference to the scope of that act, but simply that we prefer to rest our judgment on the broader ground which has been discussed in this opinion, believing it of importance that the principles underlying it should be fully stated and affirmed." *In Re Debs*, 158 US 564 (1894), p. 600. On the general application of the act to labor disputes, see Prentice and Egan, *Commerce Clause*, pp. 323–326.

The courts, both state and federal, also used common law principles to intervene in labor disputes, almost invariably on the side of employers. The basic principle in this expanding role for court injunctions was the concept of "civil conspiracy": the combined action of two or more persons who had confederated in order to pursue goals that had the effect of damaging the property of a third party. The latter could then, under the ordinary operation of the common law, sue in order to recover the damage. In cases where recovery was unlikely, the conspiracy might be injoined by the courts; a court injunction would be issued which would order that the activities of the conspirators cease. Beginning in the middle 1880s, the courts began to apply these principles to labor strikes and secondary boycotts in such a way that many of these actions became illegal. Because workers usually possessed little property, it was clear that whatever damage was done to the company was likely to be irrecoverable.

As support for an injunction, this common law principle was sound. That strikes and boycotts, if they caused damage to the company, could be interpreted as a conspiracy had a shorter and less well-developed legal tradition but was also fairly straightforward. However, what was often unclear was exactly what the concept of "company property" might encompass. The physical and financial assets held by the company were obviously within this definition of property; strikers who destroyed or threatened to destroy these assets were almost certain targets for an injunction. But the courts extended the concept of property to include commercial ties between a company, other businesses, and its customers – business connections that the company had built up over a number of years, in the ordinary course of events expected to continue, and were thus threatened by strikes and secondary boycotts. Along with the Sherman Antitrust Act and the Interstate Commerce Act, these new and expansive views on property encouraged a much broader application of injunctions to strikes and boycotts. The only practical method of reining in spreading use of court injunctions was the passage of laws abrogating the conspiracy principle in such a way that it no longer applied to labor disputes. But very few states passed such laws in the late nineteenth century.[170]

With respect to the Sherman Antitrust Act, the fact that the government was generally more successful in prosecuting labor unions than industrial combinations is both remarkable and somewhat paradoxical, particularly since one of the clearest themes in the legislative history was the notable

---

[170] Selig Perlman, "Upheaval and Reorganisation (since 1876)," in John R. Commons et al., *History of Labour in the United States*, vol. 2 (New York: Macmillan, 1918), pp. 504–509. John R. Commons and John B. Andrews, *Principles of Labor Legislation* (New York: Harper & Brothers, 1916), pp. 95–101. For a brief review of working-class legislation in the late nineteenth century, see Gerald Friedman, *Statemaking and Labor Movements: France and the United States, 1876–1914* (Ithaca, N.Y.: Cornell University Press, 1998), p. 93.

reluctance, even opposition, to including labor unions within the act's scope. Underscoring the unexpected nature of this use of the law was the fact that Samuel Gompers and the American Federation of Labor had been rather ambivalent toward passage of the Sherman Antitrust Act both because they felt that the emergence of trusts and industrial combinations was a more or less natural and inevitable development and because labor unions appeared, from the legislative deliberations and debate, to have been considered exempt from its provisions.[171] This ambivalence was reinforced by the generally favorable attitude of organized labor toward industrial consolidation.[172]

The Sherman Act nonetheless played a crucial role in the expanding role of the labor injunction as a judicial remedy for strike activity.[173] With respect to industry, the Sherman Antitrust Act became moribund under McKinley even as corporate mergers and combinations swept the American economy.[174] In a speech on the currency delivered in Boston,

---

[171]   At the time the Sherman Antitrust Act was passed, a large legislative majority, at least in the Senate, favored exempting labor unions from coverage. Thorelli, *Federal Antitrust Policy*, pp. 231–232. Thorelli, quoting Richard Olney, Cleveland's Attorney General, called use of the Sherman Act as an antistrike measure a "perversion of the law" (p. 389). For a brief synopsis of the Pullman strike litigation and labor union cases generally, see Paul, *Conservative Crisis*, pp. 104–158; Gustavus Myers, *History of the Supreme Court of the United States* (1912; rpt., New York: Burt Franklin, 1968), pp. 618–625; Letwin, *Law and Economic Policy*, pp. 97–98, 123–128, 155–161; *Industrial Commission: Labor Organizations*, vol. 17, pp. 592–601. Consistent with congressional intent and sentiment and, thus, in contrast to the experience of labor unions under the act, the law was successfully used in several cases involving "traffic associations" formed by railroads for the purpose of coordinating freight traffic and charges. *United States v. Trans-Missouri Freight Association*, 166 US 290 (1896); and *United States v. Joint Traffic Association*, 171 US 505 (1898). Also see Letwin, *Law and Economic Policy*, pp. 97–98, 130–137; Thorelli, *Federal Antitrust Policy*, pp. 452–462; MacAvoy, *Economic Effects of Regulation*, pp. 177–179, 187–188, 190–191. In fact, the *Commercial and Financial Chronicle* later concluded that "... under the construction placed upon the [Sherman Antitrust Act] by the Supreme Court the railroads are apparently the only parties engaged in inter-State trade who can with certainty be brought within the scope of the law...." November 26, 1898.

[172]   In his testimony before the Industrial Commission, for example, Samuel Gompers emphasized the productivity gains arising out of industrial consolidation, stated that government intervention against trusts would probably be counterproductive in that any legislation might end up being applied against labor, and stressed that the most effective remedy, in his opinion, was the emergence of an equally strong federation of workers as a counterweight to giant corporations. *Industrial Commission: Capital and Labor*, pp. 596, 648, 655–656.

[173]   Paul, *Conservative Crisis*, pp. 107–110; Thorelli, *Federal Antitrust Policy*, pp. 148–149, 232–233.

[174]   Letwin, *Law and Economic Policy*, pp. 137–142. For a detailed account of antitrust enforcement efforts under the Harrison, Cleveland, and McKinley administrations, see Thorelli, *Federal Antitrust Policy*, pp. 371–410.

McKinley's Treasury Secretary, Lyman Gage, incidentally alluded to trade combinations, saying:

Within the limits of half a life time industrial methods and processes have been revolutionized; combinations in labor, in trade, in manufacture have superseded to a degree the former processes of individual movement. It is philosophical to believe that they are all evolutionary – tending to a final and higher general good – but in their immediate effects they produce incidental injury in many directions. . . . Time will do much to restore, and the natural laws, everywhere operating, will bring in at last their compensation. In the meantime our statute laws must learn not to repress the operation of natural law, which is supreme over man-made laws, but they must learn to justly check and punish those who, grasping the new elements of power, pervert them into agencies of injustice and oppression.[175]

Despite passage of the Sherman Antitrust Act, the great industrial consolidations remained almost invulnerable to prosecution between 1890 and 1900, either because the Supreme Court applied the dual sovereignty doctrine of interstate commerce in such a way as to preclude application or because the Attorney General's office was hostile or indifferent to the goals embodied in the legislation itself.[176] As Andrew Carnegie testified some years later, "Nobody ever mentioned the Sherman Act to me, that I remember."[177]

Between the end of Reconstruction and the turn of the century the United States Supreme Court was dominated by justices who had been appointed by Republican presidents (see Table 5.3.) Indeed, for one six-year stretch from 1881 to 1887, the Supreme Court was entirely composed of Republican appointees.[178] And even when Cleveland was able to place Democrats

---

[175]   *Commercial and Financial Chronicle*, July 31, 1897.

[176]   The government's successful prosecution of collusive agreements between a number of cast-iron pipe manufacturers in 1899 was an exception that, in terms of judicial doctrine, weakened the implications of the sugar case. See, for example, Friedman's discussion of *Addyston Pipe and Steel Company v. United States*, 175 US 211 (1899), *History of American Law*, p. 408; Thorelli, *Federal Antitrust Policy*, pp. 466–470. However, the *Commercial and Financial Chronicle*, in lucid and convincing summaries of the decision, limited its impact to collusive arrangements peculiar to the iron pipe industry. February 19, 1898; December 9, 1899. Other combinations, such as the agreement entered into by 52 Fall River textile mills to restrict production and regulate cloth prices, apparently escaped prosecution altogether. *Commercial and Financial Chronicle*, October 14, 1899.

[177]   Earlier in his testimony, when told that the *Addyston Pipe* decision had strengthened the Sherman Antitrust Act in such a way that the law might apply to the U.S. Steel Corporation, Carnegie replied: "Do you really expect men engaged in an active struggle to make a living at manufacturing to be posted about laws and their decisions, and what is applied here, there, and everywhere?" U.S. House of Representatives, *Hearings before the Committee on Investigation of United States Steel Corporation* (Washington, D.C.: GPO, 1912), vol. 2, pp. 2433, 2455.

[178]   In at least two cases, Republican presidents appointed justices who belonged to the Democratic party: Stephen Field (Lincoln) and Howell Jackson (Harrison). Schwartz, *History of the Supreme Court*, p. 178.

Table 5.3. *Partisan Composition of the U.S. Supreme Court, 1877–1900*

| Year | New appointment | President | Party balance | | Appointed from Northeast/ Midwest |
			Republican	Democrat	
1877	Beginning of period:		8	1	7
1877	John Harlan (Ky.)	Hayes	8	1	6
1880	William Woods (Ga.)	Hayes	8	1	5
1881	Stanley Matthews (Ohio)	Garfield			
	Horace Gray (Mass.)	Arthur	9	0	5
1882	Samuel Blatchford (N.Y.)	Arthur	9	0	5
1887	Lucius Q. Lamar (Miss.)	Cleveland	8	1	5
1888	Melville Fuller (Ill.)	Cleveland	7	2	5
1889	David Brewer (Kan.)	Harrison	7	2	4
1890	Henry Brown (Mich.)	Harrison	7	2	5
1892	George Shiras (Pa.)	Harrison	7	2	5
1893	Howell Jackson (Tenn.)	Harrison	8	1	5
1894	Edward White (La.)	Cleveland	7	2	4
1895	Rufus Peckham (N.Y.)	Cleveland	6	3	5
1897	Joseph McKenna (Calif.)	McKinley	6	3	5

Source: Calculated from information in Bernard Schwartz, *A History of the Supreme Court* (New York: Oxford University Press, 1993), pp. 383–384. Party affiliation is that of the president who nominated the justice. See Table 2.1 for the states included under the heading "Northeast/Midwest."

on the Court, his nominees represented the most conservative wing of his party. In making the first appointment of a Democrat to the court in over a quarter of a century, Cleveland nominated Lucius Quintus Cincinnatus Lamar of Mississippi, a former colonel in the Confederate Army during the Civil War. While Lamar's Confederate credentials were impeccable, so were his views on monetary policy. A former professor of political economy, social science, and law at the University of Mississippi and a lawyer whose practice included many corporate clients, Lamar's opposition to free silver was so strong that he defied the adamant instructions of the Mississippi legislature in 1878 when he voted, as senator, to defeat the Bland bill.[179] As

[179] In response, the solidly Democratic Mississippi House of Representatives passed a resolution praising Senator Blanche Bruce, a black Republican, for his support of free silver while pointedly ignoring Lamar. Jefferson Davis also published a letter in the Jackson *Clarion* stating that it was the obligation of senators to follow a legislature's instructions in such matters. Albert D. Kirwan, *Revolt of the Rednecks: Mississippi Politics, 1876–1925* (New York: Harper Torchbooks, 1965), pp. 48, 50–51, 308. Schwartz, *A History of the Supreme Court*, p. 170.

Justice, Lamar wrote few dissenting opinions in his six-year career on the court and otherwise appeared comfortable with the staunchly conservative stance it assumed.

In 1888, Cleveland's second nomination went to Melville Fuller of Illinois, like Lamar, a stout advocate of sound money. In fact, when Bryan was nominated in 1896 on a free silver platform, he left the Democratic party. Over the next twenty-two years, Chief Justice Fuller facilitated many of the Court's most conservative decisions, writing many of them himself.[180] In 1895, after Lamar's death opened another vacancy on the Court, Cleveland again appointed a former Confederate, Edward White of Louisiana. Although he dissented from the Supreme Court's decision invalidating the income tax in 1895, White's views were sufficiently orthodox that a Republican president, William Howard Taft, later appointed him Chief Justice, elevating White over his Republican colleagues on the Court.[181] Cleveland's last nomination, Rufus Peckham of New York, became one of the principal theoreticians on the Court and a major reason why the Constitution became such an enduring barrier against government regulation.[182] If anything, then, Democratic appointments to the Court only reinforced a conservative tendency enthusiastically set by the Republican majority.[183]

Although many lawyers in this period had extensive corporate practices, the business connections of members of the Supreme Court were unusually dense.[184] Because railroad litigation was the primary staple of many a private lawyer's practice and because lawyers were so prominent in politics, railroad attorneys appeared at times to dominate American public life. Grover Cleveland, for example, appointed so many government servants with corporate ties that one scholar later called his regime "An Administration of Railroad Lawyers."[185] The Supreme Court was no exception. Many justices had an extensive railroad practice before their appointment to the court. In addition to generous fees and retainers, some had been given substantial blocks of stock in the companies and been placed on the boards

---

[180] King, *Melville Weston Fuller*, pp. 234–235.

[181] Schwartz, *History of the Supreme Court*, pp. 205–206.

[182] Ibid., pp. 175–176, 178–179.

[183] Along with Peckham, who was appointed late in this period, the intellectual core of the Court was composed of Republican appointees Samuel Miller of Iowa (1862–1890), Stephen Field of California (1863–1897), and Joseph Bradley of New Jersey (1870–1892). If regular dissenters are also included, then John Harlan of Kentucky would have to be named as well. Schwartz, *History of the Supreme Court*, pp. 162–163.

[184] See, for example, descriptions of the early careers of Noah Swayne, Stephen Field, William Strong, Joseph Bradley, Morrison Waite, Stanley Matthews, Horace Gray, Samuel Blatchford, Lucius Lamar, Melville Fuller, Henry Brown, George Shiras, Howell Jackson, and Rufus Peckham, in Myers, *History of the Supreme Court*, pp. 497–504, 517–524, 531–540, 556–565, 571–573, 582–589, 591–598, 625–634.

[185] Ibid., pp. 611–612.

of directors. As a result, most members of the court not only were aware of the kinds of arguments that large corporations would be expected to make before the bench, they could have easily written those arguments themselves.

Judges were not the only actors responsible for judicial construction of the national market; corporate counsel, in their efforts to evade and strike down encumbering regulatory legislation, provided much of the rationale and legal talent for this project. Court decisions, even at the national level, were often heavily dependent on the arguments of corporation lawyers for logic and evidence, as well as the dissemination of decisions through citation in other cases.[186] Furthermore, the Supreme Court's reinterpretation of the Constitution was not driven, for the most part, by an abstract conception of a free and unified national market. The common core of judicial interpretation in this period had much more to do with private capital accumulation in which, as it turned out, many of the states of the South and West came out short when the commercial books of the nation were balanced. The bottom line, when all these decisions are considered together, is that the Supreme Court unified the national marketplace in order to protect capital accumulation from claims arising within and forwarded by the states.[187] As one of the less conservative members of the court, Justice Henry Brown, concluded in his 1893 address to the American Bar Association:

The history of civilized society is largely a story of strife between those who have and those who have not . . . the desire of the rich to obtain the labor of the poor at the lowest possible terms, the desire of the poor to obtain the uttermost farthing from the rich. The cause and the result of it all is the unequal distribution of property. . . . There is, however, nothing unnatural or undesirable in this. . . .[188]

---

[186] For the ways in which corporate counsel and the Supreme Court jointly participated in the construction of the national market, see McCurdy, "American Law and the Marketing Structure of the Large Corporation," pp. 631–649.

[187] For a sectional interpretation of judicial interpretation in this period that is more or less consistent with this conclusion, see Boudin, *Government by Judiciary*, pp. 406–407. For slightly different perspectives that maintain that the intellectual climate of the period both enabled and compelled a conceptual equivalence between individual economic freedom and a democratic society, see Robert Gree McCloskey, *American Conservatism in the Age of Enterprise, 1865–1910* (New York: Harper Torchbooks, 1951); Paul, *Conservative Crisis*. For a discussion of these issues within the context of Stephen Field's career on the Court, see Charles W. McCurdy, "Justice Field and the Jurisprudence of Government-Business Relations: Some Parameters of Laissez-Faire Constitutionalism, 1863–1897," *Journal of American History* 51 (March 1975): 970–1005.

[188] Paul, *Conservative Crisis*, p. 85. In the midst of the Populist revolt in the West and rising strike activity throughout the manufacturing belt, the *Commercial and Financial Chronicle* took satisfaction in the attitude of the national judiciary, saying: "We have frequently referred to the decisions of the United States Courts as inevitably being fair and equitable and quite unbiased by popular clamor." February 3, 1894.

While the Supreme Court was the dominant agent in the political construction of the national market, Congress played a supporting, if mainly passive, role. In elaborating on the principles that limited state authority over interstate commerce, Justice Stephen Field clearly stated that the court privileged congressional authority even when the latter was dormant:

Of the former class [where Congress has exclusive authority over commerce] may be mentioned all that portion of commerce with foreign countries or between the States which consists in the transportation, purchase, sale, and exchange of commodities. Here there can, of necessity, be only one system or plan of regulations, and that Congress alone can prescribe. Its non-action in such cases, with respect to any particular commodity or mode of transportation, is a declaration of its purpose that the commerce in that commodity or by that means of transportation shall be free. There would otherwise be no security against conflicting regulations of different States, each discriminating in favor of its own products and citizens and against the products and citizens of other states.[189]

Viewed from another perspective, congressional inaction became the backstop against which state claims were pinned. But this doctrine only allowed the emergence of an unregulated national market as long as Congress failed to exercise its own authority over interstate commerce.

As it turned out, Congress was remarkably restrained in the last decades of the nineteenth century. Only six significant federal laws were passed. Two gave the states limited power over specific goods moving across state lines: an 1866 law allowing the states to either prohibit or otherwise regulate the movement of explosives, and the Wilson act, which similarly permitted the states to control alcohol.[190] Only four significant federal laws directly regulating commerce were passed before 1900: the 1887 Interstate Commerce Act, which addressed railroad competition and rates; the 1890 Sherman Antitrust Act; the 1893 Safety Appliance Act, requiring improved couplers and brakes on railroad rolling stock and locomotives; and the 1893 Harter Act, which limited the liability of water carriers.[191] While the Supreme Court, in liberating capital accumulation and expanding the national market, was certainly willing to strike down federal statutes along with state laws, Congress simply presented the bench with very few opportunities to do so.

---

[189]   *Webber v. Virginia*, 103 US 344 (1880), p. 351. Also see *Bowman v. Chicago &c. Railway Co*, 125 US 465 (1887). In the last decades of the nineteenth century, this interpretation subtly transformed the major constitutional issue in such cases from one involving an undue *burden* on interstate commerce to one of an *infringement* on congressional authority, thus moving from potential concurrent authority over interstate commerce to exclusive federal sovereignty.

[190]   Prentice and Egan, *Commerce Clause*, pp. 76–77.

[191]   Warren, *Supreme Court*, vol. 3, pp. 451–452; Prentice and Egan, *Commerce Clause*, pp. 304–313.

The general trend in American law between 1860 and 1900 was thus to allow increasing freedom to private corporations to do as they pleased in the marketplace. Where countertendencies surfaced, and they were weak, individual corporations or industries were regulated by statutory laws or ordinances passed at the state and local levels.[192] The one, very uneven, exception involved the railroads in which the regional locations of ownership and operation were often widely separated. The flow of eastern and European capital into western and southern railroad construction made the railroads alien institutions and thus exposed them to aggressive state-sponsored regulation. By regulating railroad rates for the carriage of agricultural produce, states outside the eastern manufacturing belt could partially redress the inequitable terms of trade otherwise imposed by the protective tariff and the gold standard. Because the railroads could not be moved, regulation of railroad rates often became confiscatory and settled, in some cases, at levels just sufficient to cover operating costs (providing little or nothing for the maintenance of right-of-way, equipment, or debt servicing). The hostility of the states to railroad interests was ultimately the source of much of the litigation brought before the Supreme Court with respect to due process and commerce clause limitations on state regulatory authority. In turn, these constitutional principles were largely the product of an intersectional struggle over the terms of trade within the national political economy. Because many of the large commercial and industrial corporations that emerged during this period also operated across state lines and were owned by eastern investors, the constitutional principles originally developed for railroad regulation were soon adapted for application to state regulation of "trusts" and other corporate combinations.

SUMMARY OF THE ORIGIN AND IMPACT OF THE NATIONAL MARKET

The national market was the product of several interrelated factors and processes. In the first instance, Union victory in the Civil War consolidated national sovereignty around a reinvigorated central government, retained the impoverished market and robust cotton exports of the South in the national political economy, and placed the interests most closely associated with northern industry and finance in control of the central state. All of these were immensely important to rapid industrialization in the late nineteenth century. In the second instance, the political construction of the national market provided the free economic space for the rise and maturation of the modern business enterprise. As constructed in the late nineteenth century, the national market probably exceeded the threshold size for pro-

[192] Friedman, *History of American Law*, pp. 446–447.

ducing the advanced corporate organizations that came to dominate American industrialization. For one thing, the extreme poverty of the southern market added little to the expanding consumer demand that drove the emergence of the large industrial combinations. If the national market had been restricted to just the North and West, everything else being equal, the United States could have still produced these corporate forms and thus exploited the immense economies of scale that were actually realized.

However, as a political project, failure to suppress southern separatism could have fragmented the remainder of the United States because southern independence would have strengthened centrifugal forces in the Plains and Mountain West, thus weakening the authority of the federal government. For that reason, a postsecession central state would have probably been a much less effective agent in the construction and maintenance of a national market and may even have been unable, in fact, to prevent further disintegration of the federal union.[193] Thus, even if the national market in the United States exceeded some theoretical minimum in terms of the emergence of the modern corporation, the political context dictated the outcome. Given the structure of the antebellum political economy, the United States was either going to over- or undershoot that theoretical minimum – there was no middle ground.

However, there are other reasons to believe that, everything else being equal, "bigger is always better" in terms of the size of the national market. Some of these reasons are very old. For example, a large national market provides a wide scope for internal free trade and, thus, for the efficient exploitation of comparative advantage between regions and varying forms of organization within their respective political economies. Of course, the political construction of such a free trade zone can become predatory, as it was in the American case, if most of the efficiency gained through regional specialization is siphoned off by particular groups and sectors. In the United States, the operation of the protective tariff, in conjunction with other features of the political economy, effectively skimmed off much of the gains arising from the internal construction of the national market and delivered them over to the northern manufacturing belt.

The North clearly captured most of these gains, so much so that the South was very likely worse off within the Union than it would have been as a separate nation. In that sense, the advantages of internal free trade were not national because the net gains were so unevenly shared among the regions (and we should consider the South, at least, a proto-nation). Although everything was not equal in the late nineteenth century and although the very concept of a "nation" was undercut by the structure of the political economy, internal free trade was, given the boundaries of the

---

[193] On the possible impact of southern independence on northern unity, see Bensel, *Yankee Leviathan*, pp. 60–64.

United States, still much better than the alternative. But as the adventure into imperialism in the last years of the century was to demonstrate, further additions to this free trade zone would come only at a very high political price that would prohibit their full economic incorporation.

More subtle is the impact of the national market on the pace of technological change. The general proposition is that free markets, regardless of size, are more likely to generate and adopt technological improvements in production and organization than command economies of equal breadth.[194] Within free markets, however, size probably matters. Resistance to the adoption of technological advances, it has been argued, primarily arises from the opposition of organized labor to the incorporation of machinery into industrial processes (because of the loss of employment through automation) or, alternatively, the repression of innovative advances by industrial producers that dominate their sectors (because of the loss of capital invested in potentially outmoded plants).[195] The larger and freer the market, the more difficult becomes the successful implementation of either of these strategies. In a large, highly differentiated, and unregulated economy, for example, national labor organizations are difficult to establish and consolidate. Since the gains from the incorporation of new technologies are often large, the entry of new firms, both unorganized by labor unions and freely exploiting new improvements in production and organization, becomes highly likely, if not inevitable. For that reason, whatever the claims made in the workplace, labor organizations are less likely to strongly resist the incorporation of new modes of production because such resistance would be, over the long run, futile.

For corporations that dominate their particular sectors, the situation is a little different. As long as the national market is truly unregulated, most of the means of repressing innovation are beyond the corporation's reach: licensing requirements (including some characteristics of patent enforcement), workplace and industrial process regulation, discriminatory taxation, and subsidization of older forms of production.[196] Although these strategies depend on government favor, they do not necessarily depend on the size of the national market. Instead, the impact of the sheer size of a national market is felt on those strategies available to a corporation through the exercise of its market power: the denial of capital to emerging

---

[194] Joel Mokyr, "Technological Inertia in Economic History," *Journal of Economic History* 52:2 (June 1992): 326–327. For a strong argument that the comparatively rapid growth in the American economy has been due to relatively high levels of investment in new machinery incorporating incremental advances in technology, see J. Bradford De Long, "Productivity Growth and Machinery Investment: A Long-Run Look, 1870–1980," *Journal of Economic History* 52:2 (June 1992): 307–324.

[195] Of these two sources of resistance, Mokyr has emphasized the importance of labor, particularly in the British case. "Technological Inertia," pp. 329, 336.

[196] Ibid., pp. 329–330.

competitors and, once competitors are established, the denial of access to consumer markets. In the latter case, dominant corporations can sometimes tie prohibitions on the purchase of competing products onto sale of their own production. As long as access to the dominant corporation's goods is necessary in order for distributors to service their own customers, such a linkage can stifle competition and, thus, technological advance. Market power strategies, however, depend on the level of diversification in the national political economy. Because competition within a large national market impedes the emergence of monopolies within commercial distribution, it also discourages attempts to control access to the consumer market by industrial producers. For all these reasons, a large national market, everything else being equal, probably encourages the rapid incorporation of technological advances into production.

The unification of the national market was a complex political project in which the fit between intent and outcome was not always close. One of the primary forces was, for example, the strong hostility toward government regulation in any form during the late nineteenth century. By default, this hostility implied an open national market because regional barriers to commerce and investment had to take the form of regulation by state and/or local governments. But as a means of constructing the national market, hostility to government regulation overshot the mark by prohibiting federal legislation as well. Whether such measures would have facilitated the construction of a national market or not will be endlessly debated (for example, with respect to the Interstate Commerce Commission). But federal controls could have been, at least theoretically, beneficial (e.g., by guaranteeing the security of interstate investment, adjudicating disputes between parties residing across state lines, etc.). And some aspects of the national economy, particularly the isolation of the South from national labor and capital markets, probably required intervention by the federal government as a remedy.

As a result of conflicting trends in constitutional interpretation and federal legislation at the end of the nineteenth century, state authority receded in the area of economic regulation, particularly of interstate corporations, while advancing in the areas of civil rights and elections.[197] In a

---

[197]   On the expansion of federal power, particularly the authority of the Supreme Court, over economic activity in the late nineteenth century, see Warren, *Supreme Court*, vol. 3, p. 347; L. H. Pool, "Judicial Centralization," *Yale Law Journal* 11 (1902): 246–255; Frederic P. Powers, "Recent Centralizing Tendencies in the Supreme Court," *Political Science Quarterly* 5 (1890): 389–410. On the retreat of federal authority over civil rights, see Smith, *Civic Ideals*, pp. 316–317, 327–337, 371–385. In the earliest important ruling in which civil rights and interstate commerce overlapped, the Supreme Court struck down a Louisiana law prohibiting racial discrimination in the assignment of cabins on steamboats plying interstate waterways. Chief Justice Morrison Waite wrote the opinion: "No carrier of passengers can

sense, these two trends can be seen as a complicated exchange in which autonomy over political and social affairs was extended to southern whites in return for a more or less wide-open field for the operations of corporations funded by northeastern capital.[198] While the language of the Fourteenth Amendment is very broad and was used to limit state regulatory authority over corporations, the Supreme Court tended to interpret its meaning very narrowly when applied to race segregation. In 1883, for example, the Supreme Court ruled that the national government, in measures such as the 1866 and 1875 acts, could ban racial discrimination only by the states in their role as governments and left discriminatory acts by private individuals and organizations beyond the scope of congressional authority.[199]

This decision brought to a halt most national efforts to guarantee civil rights in the South. At the end of the century, as a result of decisions such as *Plessy v. Ferguson* handed down in 1896, southern states were given the constitutional right to segregate the races as long as the separate institutions (such as public schools) met a very loose test of "equality."[200] After the *Plessy* decision, southern state governments were assured the national government could not overturn their segregationist measures as long as they followed a constitutional formula that conferred symbolically equal access and services to both races, a formula that almost always left nonwhites with materially inferior public facilities. In all these ways, uneven regional development provided the framework within which the principle of laissez-faire was easily defended, aligning the manufacturing belt against the remainder

conduct his business with satisfaction to himself, or comfort to those employing him, if on one side of a State line his passengers, both white and colored, must be permitted to occupy the same cabin, and on the other be kept separate." *Hall v. DeCuir*, 95 US 485 (1877), p. 489.

[198] One example of this type of compensated exchange occurred during legislative deliberations on the 1890 Force bill, a measure which was finally abandoned in the United States Senate after southern senators agreed to allow passage of a northern-sponsored revision of the tariff. The bill would have reimposed national enforcement of black voting rights upon the South. See Chapter 7.

[199] On the recession of federal authority over race discrimination and civil rights generally, see Warren, *The Supreme Court*, vol. 3, pp. 323–340. Warren concluded that two 1875 Supreme Court decisions, *United States v. Reese*, 92 US 214, and *United States v. Cruikshank*, 92 US 542, "entirely demolished" the possibility of protecting black rights through "direct federal legislation" (p. 324). By the early twentieth century, 42 of the 47 sections in the three major civil rights laws passed during Reconstruction (the Civil Rights Enforcement Act of 1870, the Civil Rights Act of 1875, and the Ku Klux Act of 1871) had "either been repealed directly [by Congress], or rendered obsolete by [other federal laws], or declared invalid by" the Supreme Court (p. 340).

[200] See, for example, Charles A. Lofgren, *The Plessy Case: A Legal-Historical Interpretation* (New York: Oxford University Press, 1987), pp. 196–208, and Joel Williamson, *The Crucible of Race: Black-White Relations in the American South Since Emancipation* (New York: Oxford University Press, 1984), pp. 249–56.

of the nation, particularly the South. And, as we see in the next two chapters, this same uneven pattern shaped support for the other two legs of the developmental tripod: American adherence to the international gold standard and tariff protection for industry.

6

Political Administration and Defense
of the Gold Standard

DURING the Civil War the United States abandoned the gold standard, allowing the dollar to fluctuate in value. Inflation subsequently reduced the purchasing power of the dollar to a fraction of its antebellum value. After the war ended in 1865, the nation pursued a deflationary policy that ultimately returned the country to gold in 1879. From that point until the mid-1890s, an expanding world economy and the growing number of countries joining the international gold community caused a global deflation in prices that, within the United States as in every other national economy adhering to gold, gradually but inexorably redistributed wealth from debtors to creditors.[1] Within the United States, given the very uneven pattern of regional development and distribution of investment capital, adherence to the gold standard thus heavily favored the industrial East over the capital-importing West and South. For this reason, one of the most important policy issues in national politics for most of the 1865–1900 period was whether the United States should adhere to gold or shift to some other standard, either paper money or silver, which would again inflate the currency.

POLITICAL UNDERPINNINGS OF THE GOLD STANDARD
AND MONETARY STABILITY

From a political perspective, the gold standard was extremely vulnerable for most of the late nineteenth century. In fact, the nation would have switched from gold to silver and, finally, to paper at several points had the policy been forced to stand alone. Among the reasons for this vulnerabil-

---

[1] On the global deflation between 1879 and 1897 in those countries maintaining the gold standard, see Milton Friedman and Anna Jacobson Schwartz, *A Monetary History of the United States, 1867–1960* (Princeton, N.J.: Princeton University Press, 1971), pp. 90–91, 137, 140.

ity were, most important, the demanding operating requirements imposed on the financial system by the gold standard itself. The federal government, for example, was compelled to carefully calibrate open-market transactions in order to keep the supply of gold in balance with the respective reserve requirements of the national treasury and the private banking system. The operation of the gold standard also compelled, within fairly narrow limits, a balancing of revenues and expenditures by the federal government and of exports and imports in the nation's trading relations with the rest of the world. These were stiff obligations for any developing nation in the late nineteenth century, but in the case of the United States, their severity was further compounded by the openness of the regime to democratic insurgency. What is truly remarkable about American membership in the international gold community is that the United States was both the most democratic of all the nations operating under the gold standard and the most straightforward follower, along with Great Britain, of the "rules of the game" under which the standard was supposed to operate. Most other members of the gold community, even with the advantage of more autocratic political insulation from popular insurgency, hedged their participation by imposing extraordinary protections for their gold reserves in one way or another.

The second major reason for the vulnerability of the gold standard lay in the stark association of class, wealth, and region with a hard-money policy. Finance capitalists, wealthy creditors, and the capital-exporting Northeast all favored gold in an alignment that clearly marked out the immediate and narrow benefits of the gold standard to their interests. Although American industrialization largely depended on the integration of the London and New York capital markets and, thus, on adherence to gold, the importance of this national benefit was largely discounted and even lost altogether when seen through the lens of sector, class, or region.[2] In a sense, there was no "national interest" underlying the gold standard because there was no "national economy" undergoing rapid development. Southerners and, for a time, westerners could very reasonably ask why a harsh monetary system that enriched their class and regional competitors while providing little or no tangible benefits to themselves was still, in any sense, in their larger interest as members of the American nation. For white southerners, in particular, such a connection between gold and a highly contentious "national interest" was counterintuitive. Finally, the impact of both demanding operating requirements and the stark divergence in regional benefits was compounded by the steady deflation that the gold standard imposed on the national economy until the last years of the century. Clearly and obviously benefiting creditors over borrowers, gold was not neutral during this period. It would have been difficult to justify the gold standard

---

[2] For the importance of the gold standard to industrialization, see Chapter 2.

to debtors even if there had been no impact upon prices other than the much-advertised stability. When, under deflation, its operation became a predatory weapon in the competition for advantage among sectors, classes, and regions, abstract arguments were rendered opaque to all but the most immediate beneficiaries.[3]

It was within the larger and complex interregional redistribution of wealth, then, that the gold standard had to be defended and, in fact, would probably have been abandoned if it had been forced to stand alone. And for the most part, it was within the logic of interregional redistribution that voters, guided by class, sector, and regional affiliations, conceived the operation gold standard to be either benign or perverse. The purpose of this chapter is to analyze roll call voting on bills and amendments directly affecting the structure of financial system in general and the gold standard in particular. This analysis begins with an analytical survey of the partisan landscape in the late nineteenth century, including the relationship between uneven regional development and party strength in Congress. The roll call analysis follows. A brief analysis of voting on issues affecting the national bank system concludes the chapter.

PARTY STRENGTH AND ECONOMIC DEVELOPMENT IN THE U.S. CONGRESS

The last quarter of the nineteenth century has often been described as the Republican era in national politics.[4] While there is some truth to that description, it must be heavily qualified. In the House of Representatives, for example, the Democrats actually organized the chamber in fourteen of the twenty-four years following the end of Reconstruction (see Table 6.1).

---

[3] Popular claims on the nation's financial system during the late nineteenth century often appear to have a self-defeating quality because, in an open market economy, impairment of the security of capital investment is almost inevitably met by capital flight. For that reason, Greenback and Populist proposals to abandon the gold standard and to regulate investment in ways that reduced the security and returns of lending appear paradoxical. Where the problem was a lack of access to capital markets, the destruction of existing capital markets, however inadequate they may be, does not in any way resolve the difficulty. Small farmers in the South and West instead should have accepted high interest rates and at least limited access to capital rather than proposing a radical reconstruction of the national financial system and abandonment of the gold standard. Articulated in a rhetoric of high hostility to capital-holders, both policies unambiguously threatened investment. However, the predation between regions (accentuated through operation of the gold standard and its primary political support, the protective tariff) was so severe that many southerners and westerners clearly preferred little or no economic growth to expansion on eastern terms.

[4] See, for example, Leonard D. White, *The Republican Era: A Study in Administrative History, 1869–1901* (New York: Free Press, 1958).

Table 6.1. *Party Membership in the U.S. House of Representatives,*
1877–1900

Congress	Members of the Republican party	Members of the Democratic party	Members of the Greenback or Populist parties	Other parties	Party organizing house
45th (1877–79)	136 (46.4%)	155 (52.9%)	—	2 (0.7%)	Democrats
46th (1879–81)	132 (45.1%)	141 (48.1%)	13 (4.4%)	7 (2.4%)	Democrats
47th (1881–83)	151 (51.5%)	128 (43.7%)	10 (3.4%)	4 (1.3%)	Republicans
48th (1883–85)	117 (36.0%)	196 (60.3%)	2 (0.6%)	10 (3.1%)	Democrats
49th (1885–87)	141 (43.4%)	182 (56.0%)	1 (0.3%)	1 (0.3%)	Democrats
50th (1887–89)	152 (46.8%)	167 (51.4%)	1 (0.3%)	5 (1.5%)	Democrats
51st (1889–91)	179 (53.9%)	152 (45.8%)	—	1 (0.3%)	Republicans
52nd (1891–93)	86 (25.9%)	238 (71.7%)	8 (2.4%)	—	Democrats
53rd (1893–95)	124 (34.8%)	218 (61.2%)	11 (3.1%)	3 (0.8%)	Democrats
54th (1895–97)	254 (71.1%)	93 (26.1%)	9 (2.5%)	1 (0.3%)	Republicans
55th (1897–99)	206 (57.7%)	124 (34.7%)	22 (6.2%)	5 (1.4%)	Republicans
56th (1899–1901)	187 (52.4%)	161 (45.1%)	6 (1.7%)	3 (0.8%)	Republicans

Source: Kenneth C. Martis, *The Historical Atlas of Political Parties in the United States Congress, 1789–1989* (New York: Macmillan, 1989), pp. 25, 437–466. Party designations are based on member affiliations at the time of their election. Greenback party members sat in the Congresses before 1891; Populist members attended after that year.

In the Senate, the Republicans were clearly the dominant party, organizing that chamber in eighteen years (see Table 6.2). However, in both the House and Senate, the parties were sometimes so closely matched that neither one had a clear majority (minor party and independent members comprising the balance).[5] The ascendant major party usually strengthened its hand by deciding the outcome of contested elections, tilting heavily in such decisions toward contestants belonging to its own organization. However, these addi-

[5] Because popular elections to the House were conducted under a plurality rule, there was always a victor. This meant that vacancies were relatively uncommon in the lower chamber. Senators, however, were elected under a majority rule by their respective state legislatures, an arrangement that could and did create prolonged contests during which the state's seat went unfilled. These deadlocks were particularly common during the Populist period in many western states because none of the parties possessed a clear majority in the legislature and acceptable compromise candidates were not available. Some of these contests went on for a year or more. The state of Washington, even with a clear Republican majority in the state legislature, could not elect a senator in 1893. Montana and Wyoming were also deadlocked throughout the same year, while Nebraska and South Dakota filled their seats with difficulty. For brief accounts of these contests, see *Appleton's Annual Cyclopaedia of 1893* (New York: D. Appleton, 1894), pp. 501, 503, 534–535, 754–755, 774. As a result of these deadlocks and

Table 6.2. *Party Membership in the U.S. Senate, 1877–1900*

Congress	Members of the Republican party	Members of the Democratic party	Members of the Populist party	Other parties	Party organizing senate
45th (1877–79)	40 (52.6%)	35 (46.1%)	—	1 (1.3%)	Republicans
46th (1879–81)	33 (43.4%)	42 (55.3%)	—	1 (1.3%)	Democrats
47th (1881–83)	37 (48.7%)	37 (48.7%)	—	2 (2.6%)	Democrats
48th (1883–85)	38 (50.0%)	36 (47.4%)	—	2 (2.6%)	Republicans
49th (1885–87)	42 (55.3%)	34 (44.7%)	—	—	Republicans
50th (1887–89)	39 (51.3%)	37 (48.7%)	—	—	Republicans
51st (1889–91)	51 (58.0%)	37 (42.0%)	—	—	Republicans
52nd (1891–93)	47 (53.4%)	39 (44.3%)	2 (2.3%)	—	Republicans
53rd (1893–95)	40 (45.5%)	44 (50.0%)	3 (3.4%)	1 (1.1%)	Democrats
54th (1895–97)	44 (48.9%)	40 (44.4%)	4 (4.4%)	2 (2.2%)	Republicans
55th (1897–99)	44 (48.9%)	34 (37.8%)	5 (5.6%)	7 (7.8%)	Republicans
56th (1899–1901)	53 (58.9%)	26 (28.9%)	5 (5.6%)	5 (5.6%)	Republicans

Source: Kenneth C. Martis, *The Historical Atlas of Political Parties in the United States Congress, 1789–1989* (New York: Macmillan, 1989), pp. 25, 437–466. Party designations are based on member affiliations at the time of their election. No Greenback party member sat in the senate. One seat remained vacant throughout the 56*th* Congress. In the 47*th* Congress, a Democrat served as president pro tempore from October 10 to 13, 1881. He was followed by David Davis, who had been originally elected from Illinois by a coalition of independents and Democrats. Davis served until March 3, 1883, the last day of the session. On that day, a Republican was elected to the post.

tions to the majority party were marginal and largely confined to the House of Representatives.[6]

The Republicans controlled the presidency in sixteen of these twenty-four years. Only Grover Cleveland interrupted Republican dominance in the period, serving two nonconsecutive terms in the White House. However,

the interim admission of new states (particularly in 1889), the distribution of party strength in the Senate at the beginning of a new Congress sometimes differed quite a bit from that reported in Table 6.2 (which only reports the distribution of party members among those who originally occupied each of the seats).

[6] Generally favoring more extensive federal control of congressional elections, Republicans used contests to reverse southern decisions shaped by fraud and violence. Decisions in Congresses when Republicans organized the House added, on the average, a little over five seats to their ranks. Democrats, who generally favored exclusive state control over congressional elections, were more reluctant to exercise partisan discretion in election contests; they added, on the average, only a little under two seats to their numbers when they controlled the House. See Richard Franklin Bensel, *Sectionalism and American Political Development, 1880–1980* (Madison: University of Wisconsin Press, 1984), p. 85.

Table 6.3. *Party Control of the Executive and Legislative Branches*

Congress	Legislative branch		Executive branch	Control of legislative and executive branches
	House	Senate		
45th (1877–79)	Democrats	Republicans	Republicans	Divided
46th (1879–81)	Democrats	Democrats	Republicans	Divided
47th (1881–83)	Republicans	Democrats	Republicans	Divided
48th (1883–85)	Democrats	Republicans	Republicans	Divided
49th (1885–87)	Democrats	Republicans	Democrats	Divided
50th (1887–89)	Democrats	Republicans	Democrats	Divided
51st (1889–91)	Republicans	Republicans	Republicans	Republicans
52nd (1891–93)	Democrats	Republicans	Republicans	Divided
53rd (1893–95)	Democrats	Democrats	Democrats	Democrats
54th (1895–97)	Republicans	Republicans	Democrats	Divided
55th (1897–99)	Republicans	Republicans	Republicans	Republicans
56th (1899–1901)	Republicans	Republicans	Republicans	Republicans

Note: See notes to Tables 6.1 and 6.2.

almost all of the presidential contests during the last quarter of the nineteenth century were close, with the Republicans even winning the 1876 and 1888 elections with fewer popular votes than the Democrats.[7] For the period as a whole, Republicans controlled both chambers in Congress and the White House in just six years between 1877 and 1900, while the Democrats did so in just two (under Cleveland from 1893 to 1895; see Table 6.3). The latter was the first time since the beginning of the Civil War that the Democrats controlled both the legislative and executive branches.[8]

Political-Economic Characteristics of the Party Memberships

The major parties rested on very different social bases and economic interests within American society. For example, each major party drew upon a different constituency in terms of relative economic development: per capita value-added in manufacturing, per capita patent filings, the average interest rate on mortgages, per capita wealth, and the proportion of adult males who were illiterate.[9] These have been calculated for each congressional dis-

---

[7] For a brief survey of national party competition from 1876 to 1892, see Paul Kleppner, *The Third Electoral System, 1853–1892: Parties, Voters, and Political Cultures* (Chapel Hill: University of North Carolina Press, 1979), pp. 34–35.

[8] Paul Kleppner, *Continuity and Change in Electoral Politics, 1893–1928* (Westport, Conn.: Greenwood, 1987), p. 59.

[9] For a full description of each of these characteristics and the construction of the developmental index, see Chapter 2.

trict for the twelve Congresses that served during the 1877–1900 period. The averages by party are reported here for five of the twelve.[10]

Over the course of the late nineteenth century, the overall distribution of districts along the five developmental dimensions did not significantly change (see the top section of Table 6.4).[11] Within the major parties, however, the distribution of districts varied quite a bit. For Democratic districts, for example, the average level of value-added in manufacturing peaked in the Fifty-second Congress after the 1890 landslide extended the party into many northern industrial areas previously out of reach to the Democrats. The trough came four years later after another landslide, this time favoring the Republicans, pushed the Democrats out of the manufacturing belt, restricting them almost entirely to their southern base. Reflecting the close intercorrelation between the five dimensions, the peaks and troughs on the other four developmental averages occurred in the same Congresses. For the Republicans, the peak in membership averages occurred in the Forty-sixth Congress, after the party had been all but eliminated from the states of the former Confederacy (only three Republicans were elected from that region in 1878) but before the admission of new states and reapportionment of members had increased the Plains and Mountain share of the Republican caucus. Unlike the Democrats, however, there was no clear trough for the Republicans in which the developmental composition of the membership fell significantly below the normal pattern.

Regardless of the variation between Congresses, the Republican caucus always scored much higher on each of the five developmental dimensions than did the Democrats. The differences between the parties were greatest in the Forty-sixth and Fifty-fourth Congresses. Reflecting the disproportionate share of their respective delegations arising out of rapidly settling

[10] Three of these Congresses were held before the 1894 election (which, along with the 1896 presidential contest, dramatically widened developmental differences between the parties): the Fifty-first Congress (1889–91), which had the greatest Republican majority in the House between 1877 and 1894; the Fifty-second Congress (1891–93), which had the greatest Democratic majority in that period; and the Forty-sixth Congress (1879–81) which had the closest balance between the Republican and Democratic memberships. The remaining two were held after the 1894 election: the Fifty-fourth Congress (1895–97), which had the greatest Republican majority between 1895 and 1900; and the Fifty-sixth Congress (1899–1901), which had the closest balance between the major parties in the same period. Because the Democrats were always a minority in the last years of the century, there was no Congress in the latter period upon which to calculate averages for a Democratic majority.

[11] With the exception of illiteracy (which uses 1900 data), the calculation of each of the developmental averages relies on 1890 or 1892 statistics. This reliance on one set of data for the entire period means that the overall development of the nation (e.g., increasing industrialization or decreasing illiteracy) is not reflected in the district averages when, for example, statistics from the Forty-sixth Congress are compared with the Fifty-sixth, held twenty years later. As discussed in Chapter 2, data on the respective developmental dimensions produced in the 1880, 1890, and 1900 censuses is either not comparable or simply not available.

Table 6.4. *Developmental Profiles of the Membership of the House of Representatives: Selected Congresses, 1877–1900*

	Developmental characteristics							Number of districts
	Manufacturing	Patents	Interest rate on mortgages	Wealth	Illiteracy	Average developmental level		
Congress								
46th (1879–81)	$66.33	3.14	6.83	$582.48	12.20	2.25		293
51st (1889–91)	63.62	3.09	7.02	590.51	12.07	2.16		332
52nd (1891–93)	63.67	3.09	7.02	589.32	12.07	2.16		332
54th (1895–97)	65.38	3.20	7.07	607.06	11.80	2.20		357
56th (1899–1901)	65.64	3.22	7.08	608.75	11.77	2.21		357
Average	64.93	3.15	7.00	595.62	11.98	2.20		
Democrats								
46th (1879–81)	42.88	2.00	7.23	471.84	17.92	1.44		141
51st (1889–91)	51.11	2.49	7.29	525.25	16.98	1.62		152
52nd (1891–93)	59.11	2.93	7.08	550.95	14.26	1.96		238
54th (1895–97)	37.68	1.73	7.86	404.88	23.07	0.96		93
56th (1899–1901)	51.36	2.56	7.40	515.29	17.90	1.57		161
Average	48.43	2.34	7.37	493.64	18.03	1.51		
Republicans								
46th (1879–81)	94.34	4.44	6.37	720.89	5.95	3.21		132
51st (1889–91)	74.56	3.61	6.77	648.16	7.83	2.63		179
52nd (1891–93)	80.97	3.64	6.73	691.52	6.83	2.79		86
54th (1895–97)	77.69	3.82	6.72	690.96	7.34	2.72		254
56th (1899–1901)	80.13	3.83	6.71	686.12	6.69	2.80		187

Average	81.54	3.87	6.66	687.53	6.93	2.83	13

Greenback/Populists							
46th (1879–81)	30.50	2.00	7.18	448.73	11.12	1.46	
51st (1889–91)							
52nd (1891–93)	13.29	1.90	8.40	632.32	3.19	1.37	8
54th (1895–97)	10.10	1.07	8.68	330.53	20.84	0.56	9
56th (1899–1901)	11.85	2.19	8.72	633.04	3.40	1.60	5
Average	16.44	1.79	8.24	511.16	9.64	1.25	
Other							
46th (1879–81)	77.07	3.54	7.01	592.55	16.99	2.00	7
51st (1889–91)	8.59	0.52	9.62	192.26	25.50	0.00	1
52nd (1891–93)							
54th (1895–97)	14.55	2.84	9.78	589.99	12.80	0.00	1
56th (1899–1901)	30.25	3.03	9.20	723.16	13.07	1.25	4
Average	32.61	2.48	8.90	524.49	17.09	0.81	

Note and source: Averages are the unweighted means for the party delegations elected to the five Congresses. Value-added in manufacturing calculated from data in the *1890 Census of Manufactures* and presented in dollars per capita. The figures on patents per capita. The figures on patents per capita are the number per 10,000 people, calculated from data in the *1892 Annual Report of the Commissioner of Patents*, pp. 1–411. The interest rate is the total interest paid in the congressional district on farm and home mortgages divided by the total principal. Calculated from data in *1890 Census Report on Farms and Homes: Proprietorship and Indebtedness* (Washington: GPO, 1896), Table 108. Wealth is the per capita wealth calculated for each congressional district. *1890 Census of Wealth, Debt, and Taxation* (Washington: GPO, 1895). Illiteracy is the percent of males over 21 who are illiterate. *1900 Census of Population* (Washington: GPO, 1901), pt. 1, pp. 971–1006. Each congressional district is assigned a developmental level according to the number of times its score on the five characteristics exceeds the national average (below in the case of interest rates and illiteracy). These levels are totaled for all districts in the decile and then divided by the number of districts. Congressional district boundaries taken from Kenneth C. Martis, *The Historical Atlas of United States Congressional Districts, 1789–1983* (New York: Macmillan, 1982).

Plains and Mountain districts, the Greenback (Forty-sixth Congress) and Populist membership displayed lower levels of development than the Democrats on three dimensions (manufacturing, patents, and interest rates) and higher levels on wealth and illiteracy. The rather motley collection of members in the "other" category also represented generally less developed districts.[12]

While the relationship between the two major parties and relative economic development was fairly consistent from one Congress to the next, the pattern within each Congress tended to be slightly curvilinear (see Table 6.5). For the Republicans, the pattern was single-peaked, with a pronounced bias toward the most advanced regions of the nation. The weakest decile for the party was that containing the least developed districts; in most Congresses, the Republicans held fewer than a fifth of these seats. From there, the proportion gradually rose with development. The peak appeared in the seventh decile in which, on the average, some four out of every five districts were represented by Republicans. From that point, the Republican percentage fell gradually to an average range of 60 percent or so.

The Democratic pattern was the inverse of the Republican. The Democratic percentage of the members in each decile first declined more or less steadily as industrial activity rose through the first seven deciles. Then the pattern reversed direction, with the Democratic percentage of each decile tending, albeit slowly, to rise in tandem with manufacturing over the course of the highest deciles. Viewed from the perspective of the Democratic party, this inversion in pattern was the result of three factors. One was the anomalous position of New York City within the national political economy, which placed the city (with its strong free trade predilections) firmly within the Democratic party despite its very advanced, overall level of economic development. Another was that the northern wing of the Democratic party tended to be more competitive in urban districts with large working-class populations than in rural areas. Since most of the moderately and highly advanced districts were northern, this tended to produce a weak bias toward the Democrats as manufacturing levels rose. Finally, Democrats were generally very weak in the Plains and Mountain states that held many of the districts that fell in the middle deciles. Viewed from a developmental perspective, this bipolar distribution presaged the split in the party following Bryan's nomination in 1896: both that the split would occur and that the program favored by the least developed regions would prevail. In contrast, the single-peaked distribution exhibited by the Republicans

---

[12] The seven members in this category in the Forty-sixth Congress were all "Independent Democrats." The lone members in the Fifty-first and -fourth Congresses were an Arkansas "Labor" member from the bottomlands along the Mississippi River and a "Silver" party member from Nevada, respectively. In the Fifty-sixth Congress, the Silver representative was joined by two "Silver Republicans" (from Colorado and Idaho) and an "Independent Populist" from North Carolina.

Table 6.5. *Value-Added in Manufacturing and Party Membership in the House of Representatives: Selected Congresses, 1877–1900*

Value-added in manufacturing (deciles)	Republicans and Democrats as percent of members in each decile											
	46th Congress (1877–81)		51st Congress (1889–91)		52nd Congress (1891–93)		54th Congress (1895–97)		56th Congress (1899–1901)		Average all congresses	
	Dem.	Rep.	Dem.	Rep.	Dem.	Rep.	Dem.	Rep.	Dem.	Rep.	Dem.	Rep.
Lowest	100.0	0	69.7	30.3	84.4	15.2	66.7	25.0	77.8	19.4	79.7	18.0
2nd	72.4	17.2	66.7	30.3	81.8	9.1	52.8	38.9	77.8	16.7	70.3	22.4
3rd	65.5	20.7	66.7	33.3	84.8	12.1	33.3	58.3	58.3	30.6	61.7	31.0
4th	48.3	44.8	54.5	45.5	81.8	12.1	31.4	65.7	51.4	45.7	53.5	42.8
5th	53.3	43.3	32.4	67.6	64.7	32.4	22.2	77.8	41.7	58.3	42.9	55.9
6th	46.7	40.0	52.9	47.1	73.5	26.5	5.6	94.4	27.8	72.2	41.3	56.0
7th	20.7	79.3	12.1	87.9	45.5	54.5	8.6	91.4	17.1	82.9	20.8	79.2
8th	27.6	65.5	33.3	66.7	66.7	33.3	11.4	88.6	25.7	71.4	32.9	65.1
9th	24.1	72.4	30.3	69.7	69.7	30.3	11.1	88.9	33.3	66.7	33.7	65.6
Highest	27.6	69.0	39.4	60.6	66.7	33.3	16.7	83.3	38.9	61.1	37.9	61.5

Source: Calculations by author. Party designations taken from Kenneth C. Martis, *The Historical Atlas of Political Parties in the United States Congress, 1789–1989* (New York: Macmillan, 1989).

suggests a much more compact membership, one in which the extremes were comparatively small and the bridging delegations in the middle ranges were relatively large. That distribution, combined with the strong general bias in the party toward the more advanced end of the developmental spectrum, foretold both the comparative unity with which the party would respond to Bryan and free silver and the embracing of gold in response to the Democratic turn to free silver at the 1896 convention.

The Executive Branch and the Gold Standard

Until 1896, the legislative and executive branches of the federal government were often at odds over whether and how the gold standard would be maintained. On the one hand, presidents, regardless of party, were staunch defenders of gold. On the other, Congress was usually controlled by majorities that were either indifferent to gold or openly backed greenback or silver alternatives. The primary reason for this striking institutional divergence originated in the anomalous position of New York City as both a fervent center of support for the gold standard and a hotbed of free trade sentiment. The city regularly returned a pivotal congressional delegation that toed the Democratic party line on tariff bills but broke with majorities over the gold standard. In presidential elections, the city's importance to the electoral vote cast by New York State made, for the Democrats, the nomination of a sound-money advocate an imperative necessity. This guaranteed, at least until Bryan's nomination in 1896, that the majority of Democrats in Congress and a Democratic president would be at loggerheads over monetary issues.[13]

During Republican presidencies, again until 1896 when the parties realigned nationally over monetary issues, a majority of the Republicans in Congress could usually be counted on to support the executive branch. However, in most years the size of the heterodox Republican minority was large enough, when combined with silver and greenback Democrats, to endanger passage of legislation supporting the gold standard. Thus, in both Republican and Democratic presidencies, the executive branch played a key role in keeping the nation on gold: first, by competently and consistently managing the day-to-day operation of the standard through the Treasury Department; and, second, by counterbalancing a legislative branch that was often either indifferent or openly hostile to the standard.[14]

[13]   On Cleveland's estrangement from congressional Democrats, see Ellis Paxson Oberholtzer, *A History of the United States Since the Civil War* (New York: Macmillan, 1931), vol. 4, p. 375; Allan Nevins, ed., *Letters of Grover Cleveland, 1850–1908* (Boston: Houghton Mifflin, 1933), pp. 376–377.

[14]   Although Cleveland was otherwise blessed with a heavily Democratic Congress and a vice-president elected on his own ticket, he nonetheless stood entirely alone in 1893 as the sole political barrier between the silverites and abandonment of the gold stan-

Throughout this period, presidents almost routinely sent messages to Congress urging policies that would protect and sustain gold payments. These messages, like the one Arthur sent in 1884 warning of an impending involuntary conversion to a silver standard, sometimes overstated the situation but did not exaggerate the general drift of federal policy from the end of Reconstruction until McKinley's victory in 1896.[15] The difficulty lay in the fact that the political compromises through which the executive branch was able to head off even more hostile congressional measures kept the United States at or near the brink of default on gold for most of this period. Although these compromise measures assumed a number of guises, they all had the effect of making administration of the gold standard much more difficult than would have been the case under a full-blooded, orthodox financial policy.

In addition, post-Reconstruction presidents labored under severe partisan constraints. One was the fact that the Treasury Department was simultaneously one of the chief sources of party patronage and the pivot around which the government conducted market operations in support of the gold standard. The secretary was responsible for administering the tariff and thus monitoring the nation's customs houses with their immense opportunities for fraud and corruption. That would have been an onerous task even if that were all that these officials were to do. But the most exacting responsibilities had to do with the financial operations of the Treasury, the execution of transactions that could, if poorly carried out, provoke a financial crisis through destabilization of the money market. These operations also entailed public defense of administration policy, a role always accompanied

---

dard. Realizing his vital role, Cleveland was even willing to endure extreme physical pain in order to maintain a façade of presidential stability. In June 1893, during the financial crisis over whether the United States would be able to maintain gold payments in the face of continuing revenue and trade deficits, a large and potentially malignant tumor was discovered in the roof of Cleveland's mouth. Since his vice-president, Adlai Stevenson, was sympathetic to silver and thus could not be counted on to continue Cleveland's gold policy, any appearance of weakness or possible mortality had to be avoided. For that reason, Cleveland arranged to have the tumor secretly removed, along with molars and his upper left jaw, while aboard a yacht sailing up the East River in New York City on July 1, 1893. Five days later, he left the boat at his summer home in Buzzard's Bay and, while there, was outfitted with an artificial jaw of vulcanized rubber. Cleveland's operation was kept secret, even after he returned to Washington for the opening of the special session of Congress at which he proposed repeal of the silver purchase act. H. Wayne Morgan, *From Hayes to McKinley: National Party Politics, 1877–1896* (Syracuse, N.Y.: Syracuse University Press, 1969), pp. 450–451; James Ford Rhodes, *History of the United States, 1850–1896* (New York: Macmillan, 1928), vol. 8, pp. 398–400; Oberholtzer, *History of the United States*, vol. 5, p. 260.

[15] For summaries of presidential messages to Congress supporting the gold standard and related financial policies, see Oberholtzer, *History of the United States*, vol. 4, pp. 366–367, 436–437; vol. 5, p. 146.

by calumny from that portion of the nation's press hostile to the gold standard. These dual economic and political roles often compelled presidents to select Treasury secretaries that combined, in some measure, prominence within their party and financial experience.[16] About half of the Treasury secretaries appointed in the late nineteenth century had been modestly successful small-town bankers or politicians before assuming office. The others, including John Sherman and John Carlisle, were already nationally prominent political or financial leaders.

Aggravating the situation was the tendency for Treasury secretaries to represent a large faction within the party that had been at odds with the president. Such was the case with Daniel Manning, who, before being appointed by Cleveland, had been chair of the Democratic party in New York and a close ally of Samuel Tilden. His ties to Tilden led to conflict with Cleveland over the appointment of the collector of customs for the port of New York – far and away the choicest patronage plum within the Treasury Department.[17] In this instance, the political assets Manning brought on board the administration sometimes impaired financial policy. A newspaperman by profession, Manning's understanding of finance was notoriously weak, although his opinions were utterly sound on gold.[18]

Other secretaries sometimes came to the post without even much sympathy for gold, accustoming themselves to its virtues at the same time they learned how to conduct the technical policies required of their post. In his second term, for example, Cleveland appointed John Carlisle to the post despite the fact that the former Speaker of the House had previously labeled the demonetization of silver in 1873 a "conspiracy which seems to have been formed here and in Europe to destroy by legislation and otherwise from three-sevenths to one-half of the metallic money of the world [resulting in] the most gigantic crime of this or any other age. The consummation of such a scheme would ultimately entail more misery upon the human race than all the wars, pestilences, and famines that ever occurred in the history of the world."[19] During the monetary crisis in early 1895, Cleveland depended heavily on Carlisle, "who had [now] mastered the principles governing public finance. The Secretary of the Treasury, who had commenced

[16] Civil War and Reconstruction presidents had previously faced very similar challenges in balancing policy requirements and party demands. Richard Franklin Bensel, *Yankee Leviathan: The Origins of Central State Authority in America, 1859–1877* (New York: Cambridge University Press, 1990), pp. 275–281.

[17] Oberholtzer, *History of the United States*, vol. 4, pp. 370, 461–463.

[18] In the end, however, both Manning and Cleveland earned the high respect of the financial community which saw them, as a team, as a bulwark against congressional radicalism. See, for example, the *Commercial and Financial Chronicle*, December 26, 1885.

[19] At the time he delivered these passages on the floor of the House, Carlisle was not Speaker. They were subsequently cited in *Congressional Record* 55:2:1280, January 31, 1898.

with little knowledge of the subject," now proceeded to fasten the gold standard on the United States despite the fervent opposition of party comrades he had left behind in the House.[20] By 1896, in fact, Carlisle was traveling throughout the nation "showing how the working classes would suffer under a depreciation in the standard of values" if the gold standard were abandoned.[21] Even with their often compromised political records, the financial community vastly preferred Secretaries of the Treasury to Congress.[22] As the *Commercial and Financial Chronicle* explained, looking back in 1881 at the record since the end of the Civil War, "in every financial emergency there has been a Secretary of the Treasury to stand between the people and ill-considered legislation. . . . Congress was generally a fractious body to be outmaneuvered when it could not be managed. It has tried – and at times apparently, that is for the moment, with success – to overset the best-laid plans for the re-adjustment of our finances. . . ."[23]

Like their secretaries, some presidents also had checkered histories with respect to monetary policy. McKinley himself, gold's advocate in the "Battle of the Standards," was perhaps the most notorious. Addressing an audience composed of former Greenbackers and silverites in Toledo, Ohio, in 1891, McKinley had criticized Cleveland for "dishonoring one of our precious metals, one of our great products, discrediting silver and enhancing the price of gold" during his first term. If returned to the presidency, McKinley predicted that Cleveland would "contract the circulating medium and

---

[20] Oberholtzer, *History of the United States*, vol. 5, p. 307.

[21] *Commercial and Financial Chronicle*, April 18, 1896.

[22] During debate on a free silver bill, Charles Crisp of Georgia noted that there "has never been a moment from the demonetization of silver [in 1873] until this hour that the Treasury Department, no matter by whom administered, has manifested a friendly feeling for silver as primary money." *Congressional Record* 54:1:1722, February 14, 1896. As a result of the executive branch's fidelity to an orthodox defense of the gold standard, relations between the Treasury Department and the nation's financial community were always officially and sometimes personally quite close. In the opinion of the *Commercial and Financial Chronicle*, the strongest Secretary of the Treasury may have been John Sherman of Ohio "whose name is destined to a high and conspicuous place in the annals of financial statesmanship and monetary reform in this country." July 24, 1880. In honor of Sherman's administration of the Treasury Department during the period leading up to resumption, the New York Chamber of Commerce commissioned the secretary's portrait, which was subsequently hung in the chamber's hall next to Alexander Hamilton. John Sherman, *Recollections of Forty Years in the House, Senate and Cabinet* (Chicago: Werner, 1896), pp. 576–577.

[23] May 14, 1881. At times, it was difficult to determine whether the *Commercial and Financial Chronicle* respected the executive branch in its own right or only by way of comparison with Congress. For example, commenting on the 1882 congressional election, the journal said that the "number of men in Congress who are really possessed or actuated by a feeling of official obligation and responsibility, may, we fear, be counted without taxing the arithmetic of the finger ends." November 11, 1882.

demonetize one of the coins of commerce, limit the volume of money among the people, make money scarce and therefore dear." McKinley was campaigning for the governorship of Ohio at the time and reversed his position once the Democratic candidate embraced free silver.[24] Both his opportunism in that campaign and sporadic defections from gold in his congressional voting record left some doubt concerning his commitment to financial orthodoxy – doubts that were assuaged only in 1896 once he formally accepted the Republican platform in a public letter embracing gold.[25]

In general, legislative proposals in Congress tended to address the gold standard from one of three perspectives. The first was quite hostile and involved the free coinage of silver at the prevailing statutory ratio of sixteen to one with gold. The practical effect of such a policy at any time in the late nineteenth century would have been abandonment of the gold standard in favor of silver. The greenback equivalent to free silver was a proposal to immediately monetize the national debt. The second perspective was much slower in its effect but had the same ultimate goal. This was the compulsory purchase and coinage of silver, usually at a fixed amount in either ounces or dollars per month. Higher quotas placed more stress on the federal budget and, thus, threatened the ability of the Treasury to maintain gold reserves as backing for the currency. Lower quotas were easier for the government to bear.[26] However, the usual question was whether or not to compel silver purchases and coinage by the Treasury, not how high or low the quota should be. From 1878 to 1890, the government was compelled to purchase silver under the Bland-Allison Act. From 1890 to 1893, the

[24] McKinley's victory in that race was subsequently interpreted as a triumph for "sound money." *Commercial and Financial Chronicle*, November 7, 1891. For running editorial commentary on the Ohio gubernatorial campaign from a free silver perspective, see *Financial and Mining Record*, August 8, 15, 22, October 24, November 7, 1891.

[25] Oberholtzer, *History of the United States*, vol. 5, pp. 144–145, 381; Rhodes, *History of the United States*, vol. 8, pp. 351–352. In reporting McKinley's acceptance of the nomination and the national platform, the *Commercial and Financial Chronicle* regretted that he chose to emphasize greater tariff protection, which the journal opposed, but nonetheless welcomed the unreserved endorsement of the financial plank. July 4, 1896. For commentary on McKinley's acceptance letter, issued later in the campaign, see August 29, 1896.

[26] Recognition of the impact of such measures was a commonplace in the popular press. For example, see the warning that continued coinage of silver dollars at $2 million a month would inevitably force the nation off gold and onto a silver basis in *Appleton's Annual Cyclopaedia of 1881* (New York: D. Appleton, 1882), p. 286. Also see John Sherman's account of the disruptive impact of passage of a free coinage bill by the House of Representatives upon bond negotiations by the Treasury Department in the winter of 1877–78, *Recollections of Forty Years*, pp. 507–512. Political attacks on the gold standard, when persistent and powerful as they were during the first half of the 1890s, seriously distorted what would otherwise have been the course of American economic growth. See, for example, Friedman and Schwartz, *Monetary History*, pp. 93, 104–119, 131–134.

Sherman Silver Purchase Act forced an even heavier burden on the Treasury. After 1893, no silver purchase policy was in effect. At several points during the fifteen years when the Treasury was buying millions of ounces of silver per month, the policy almost toppled the gold standard. But the Treasury always found a way to cope.

While silver purchases were a serious threat to the gold standard in economic terms, politically they were sometimes a refuge for those who in fact favored gold but found opposition to silver a serious threat to electoral survival. The third perspective from which legislation addressed the monetary policy was through the lens of an explicit endorsement of the gold standard. For most of this period between 1879 and 1900, the United States was in practice on a gold standard while formally pretending to support a bimetallic system in which both gold and silver would freely circulate at a fixed mintage ratio. Hostility in Congress to any attempt to confirm the gold standard as in fact the policy of the Treasury was so great that conservative members rarely brought up the issue and even more rarely pressed such proposals with any vigor. Only at the very end of this period, in 1900, did Congress finally enact a statute formally stating in law what had been invariable government practice for over two decades.

In terms of these three perspectives, the policy majorities in Congress can almost always be ascertained from the historical record (see Table 6.6). Both chambers voted fairly often on either free silver or compulsory coinage, as well as other aspects of the gold standard regime, and from those votes the general attitude of the majority of the members can usually be deduced. The only difficult case arose during the Fifty-third Congress, in which the Democratic majorities in both the House and Senate were publicly committed to (and, privately, also favored) continued silver purchases by the Treasury but, bowing to Cleveland's blunt use of the patronage and other presidential blandishments, voted to repeal the Sherman Silver Purchase Act. At the time, left to its own devices, the Senate would even had enacted a free silver policy. Other than this exception, congressional attitudes and legislative decisions corresponded with one another. Sentiment on monetary policy was extremely stable both within any particular Congress and across the period as a whole. The House of Representatives, for example, opposed free silver in all but the first Congress (1877–79). The Senate favored compulsory silver purchases and coinage in all but the last (1899–1901).

As can be surmised from Table 6.6, Congress was at best indifferent toward the maintenance of the gold standard and often outright hostile. The only factor that prevented the United States from switching from gold to silver or paper currency as the monetary standard was the unflinching position of the executive branch. The annual messages of presidents and Treasury secretaries, for example, often highlighted orthodox monetary reforms as administration policy priorities. As such, they attracted favor-

Table 6.6. *Congressional Sentiment toward Silver and Gold:*
By Chamber and Congress, 1877–1900

Congress	Opposition to free coinage of silver		Opposition to compulsory coinage of silver		Explicit endorsement of the gold standard	
	House	Senate	House	Senate	House	Senate
45th (1877–79)	No	Yes	No	No	No	No
46th (1879–81)	Yes	Yes	No	No	No	No
47th (1881–83)	Yes	Yes	Yes	No	No	No
48th (1883–85)	Yes	Yes	No	No	No	No
49th (1885–87)	Yes	Yes	No	No	No	No
50th (1887–89)	Yes	Yes	No	No	No	No
51st (1889–91)	Yes	No	No	No	No	No
52nd (1891–93)	Yes	No	No	No	No	No
53rd (1893–95)[a]	Yes	No	No	No	No	No
54th (1895–97)	Yes	No	Yes	No	No	No
55th (1897–99)	Yes	No	Yes	No	Yes	No
56th (1899–1901)	Yes	Yes	Yes	Yes	Yes	Yes

Note: These policies are arrayed from, on the left, a practical rejection of gold in favor of silver to, on the right, an explicit embrace of gold as a single standard. The middle policy, silver coinage under quota, was a threat to gold redemption but not an explicit rejection if accompanied by other financial measures (e.g., a substantial operating surplus in the federal budget). "Yes" for each policy indicates a general attitude on the part of the chamber favorable to gold. "No" indicates the opposite.
[a] Cleveland was able to repeal the Sherman Silver Purchase Act in 1893 despite intense congressional opposition. Without his very heavy-handed intervention, efforts to repeal the act would have failed and the Senate would have even supported free silver. Put another way, the institutional preferences of Congress with respect to the monetary system were more at variance with its actual legislative action in 1893 than at any other time.

able comment from the financial community, sometimes in the form of effusive praise and sometimes as a dialogue on the technical aspects of implementation.[27] Very rarely did the financial community openly criticize any

[27] The president's annual message and the annual report of the Treasury usually appeared during the first week in December, which was also the normal date for the convening of a new session of Congress. These communications were promptly reviewed in the financial press. See, for example, the *Commercial and Financial Chronicle*, December 11, 1880; December 10, 1881; December 9, 1882; December 8, 1883; December 6, 1884; December 12, 1885; December 11, 1886; December 7, 1889; December 12, 1891; December 10, 1892; December 9, 23, 1893; December 8, 1894; December 7, 1895; December 11, 1897; December 9, 1899.

administration.[28] Congressmen who favored silver or greenbacks, however, tended to view the executive branch with suspicion even when their party occupied the White House.

CONGRESSIONAL SUPPORT FOR THE GOLD STANDARD

The gold standard imposed several important fiscal requirements on the United States. For example, every revenue or spending bill affected to some extent the ability of the Treasury to maintain adequate reserves of gold. While a temporary deficit in the federal budget could be offset by bond issues, changes in major revenue or expenditure policies, such as the tariff and military pensions, carried a direct, material impact on the maintenance of gold payments. But these policies had their own political constituencies; in fact, these constituencies were often tied through the Republican party to the coalition supporting gold in complex ways that defied a strictly financial accounting of their merit. For example, the wasteful expenditure of federal funds on fraudulent claims for military pensions was, in a purely financial interpretation, a net drag on the fiscal health of the central government. But in political terms, military pensions and their recipients were probably necessary adjuncts to the policy coalition supporting the protective tariff. And the protective tariff, however constructed in terms of revenue, was probably indispensable to the policy coalition supporting maintenance of the gold standard.

There are thus several ways to interpret the impact of federal policy on maintenance of the gold standard. In economic terms, each policy can be evaluated in terms of its impact on the very onerous fiscal and trade requirements imposed by that monetary regime. One of the most stringent requirements concerned the subordination of Treasury revenues and expenditures to the maintenance of the gold reserve. From that perspective, the first priority of tariffs should have been the raising of revenue; federal spending, as on military pensions, should have been kept to a minimum. In political terms, these same policies can be interpreted as constituent elements underpinning the political coalition supporting gold payments. The prime goal, from this perspective, should have been to sustain that coalition's access to the policy instruments, such as those ensconced within the Treasury Department, through which the gold standard could be maintained. Seen this way, tariffs and pensions should have been con-

---

[28]   Early in Cleveland's first term, the *Commercial and Financial Chronicle* commented that the Democratic administration that had been "looked forward to with fear" because of its silver inclinations in Congress had, in fact, turned out well, "to the surprise of at least one-half the commercial classes the country has not suffered any harm. In fact, now that the business community has the new harness on, it rather likes it. . . ." August 22, 1885.

structed in such a way as to maximize political support for that coalition.

Taken alone, of course, neither of these strategies was viable. There is always a tension, in any nation, between the structural requirements of a policy and the political requirements for its sustenance against competing alternatives. In the case of the gold standard in the late nineteenth century, this tension was apparent to all observers for several reasons. First, whether or not the operating requirements for the gold standard were being met on any given business day was open to public inspection. Either the agent staffing the federal subtreasury window in New York City was redeeming all paper currency and silver dollars in gold on demand or he was not. If the former, then the United States was successfully meeting the prime test of adherence to the standard – no other policy at any other time in American history had such a clear and unambiguous test. If the subtreasury was refusing to redeem paper currency and silver dollars in gold, then the United States failed this test, and regardless of how the government might try to place a less negative interpretation on this failure, the nation had abandoned gold. Second, the monetary system and financial policy in general were one of the two most important policy questions in the nation's politics for most of the period. For that reason, the nature of the political requirements for sustaining the gold coalition was a constantly examined, interpreted, and tested question. Like the subtreasury window for redemption, the outcome of public elections periodically tested the viability of the gold coalition in a less ambiguous manner than for any other single policy question. Aside from the tariff, which structured much of major party competition, no other policy issue came close to the monetary system in political prominence. And for minor parties such as the Greenbackers and the Populists, the tariff was usually an unimportant, diversionary question. The primary difference between these two tests of the gold standard's viability, one economic and the other political, was that elections occurred much less frequently than the daily redemptions that took place at the subtreasury window. This introduced more play into political calculations in that the viability of political strategies was, in most cases, not immediately tested in an election.

The best way to interpret the impact of federal policy on the maintenance of the gold standard is to combine these economic and political elements into a single political economic analysis. In such an interpretation, both election outcomes and the size of the gold reserve are equally important tests or requirements underpinning adherence to the international gold standard. The tension between them is demonstrable in that strengthening the political coalition inevitably meant, in practice, weakening the fiscal basis for maintaining gold redemption and vice versa. Constructing a policy coalition that would successfully maintain gold payments meant striking a balance, if possible, between these competing economic and political requirements.

In the following section, congressional support for the gold standard is analyzed on thirty-four roll call votes cast between 1877 and 1900. These roll calls all involve the use of gold, greenbacks, and silver as alternative forms of money by the United States government. However, with few exceptions, arising at the very beginning and end of the period, these votes did not entail open endorsement or rejection of the gold standard itself. Instead, they either supported or undermined policies that were necessary to gold payments. (One of the most common proposals, for example, was for the unlimited coinage of silver, which would have, at most points in the period, effectively sabotaged the gold standard without addressing that policy directly.) These roll calls were generally selected for the clarity with which they implicated the gold standard. In some periods, such as the late 1870s and early 1890s, roll calls on issues closely related to gold were so abundant that their inclusion would have utterly overwhelmed the analysis. In those cases, only the clearest examples of congressional sentiment, involving the greatest participation by the membership, were selected. In other cases, such as the mid-1880s when financial legislation was seldom the subject of recorded votes, all roll calls have been included. This study is restricted to the House of Representatives, but since a parallel examination of the Senate would produce few differences, the findings can be generalized to Congress as a whole.

The roll call analysis and accompanying discussion demonstrates the consistently strong connection between the relative level of economic development within the nation's congressional districts and support for the international gold standard. In every single vote, the representatives of the most advanced districts in the nation cast much higher fractions of their votes in support of gold than did those representing the least developed regions. Districts with intervening levels of development usually reported appropriately higher or lower proportions of support than these extremes. In the vast majority of instances, the connection between development and gold held regardless of whether the entire House or separate party caucuses are examined. In all but two instances, involving votes on an explicit guarantee of gold interest and redemption of bond issues in 1895, the percentage of Republican members in the House that supported gold was higher than the percentage of Democrats. While it is not possible to provide a full legislative history of each of these bills, brief descriptions of each one, placing them in the political and economic context that accompanied their respective consideration, have been provided.

CONGRESSIONAL ALIGNMENTS ON MAJOR FINANCIAL PROPOSALS

In the fall of 1877, following the political settlement that placed Rutherford Hayes in the White House, the United States was still more than a year away from an anticipated return to the international gold standard. At that time, the nation's financial policy was governed by the 1875 Resumption Act under which the Secretary of the Treasury was authorized to issue federal bonds, using the proceeds to build up the gold reserve and retire a portion of the outstanding greenbacks. Both of these policies were intended to incrementally strengthen the currency in such a way that the greenback would slowly approach parity with the gold dollar; on January 1, 1879, the nation, as set forth under the Resumption Act, was to resume redemption of the greenback in gold.[29] In the intervening years after its passage and before resumption, many legislative attempts were made to repeal this act or to sabotage its execution. The most serious of these attacks involved a repeal proposal reported very early in the life of the Forty-fifth Congress. After almost a month of more or less constant debate in the House of Representatives, this proposal came to a vote on November 23, 1877 (see Table 6.7). Despite opposition from John Sherman, Secretary of the Treasury, who made almost daily trips to the Capitol, the measure passed the House and was sent on to the Senate.[30] At this point, on December 3, 1877, Hayes placed the full weight of his administration against repeal in his annual message to Congress. Sherman backed up the administration's position in the annual report of the Department of the Treasury.

While the Senate deliberated on the House bill, European investors began to liquidate their American holdings, turning in their bonds for gold.[31] This flight from American securities seriously undermined bond negotiations through which the Treasury was attempting to strengthen the government's gold reserve and thus threatened to wreck resumption even if the repeal bill was defeated in the Senate. In the meantime, the silver forces in the upper chamber passed a concurrent resolution providing that the principal and interest of all outstanding and future federal bonds could be paid in silver dollars. Since previous interpretations and practice had invariably honored

[29] For a legislative history and description of the provisions of the Resumption Act, see Irwin Unger, *The Greenback Era: A Social and Political History of American Finance, 1865–1879* (Princeton, N.J.: Princeton University Press, 1964), pp. 249–263.

[30] At the time, this vote was universally interpreted as a crucial test of congressional sentiment on resumption and financial policy generally. See, for example, *Appleton's Annual Cyclopaedia of 1877* (New York: D. Appleton, 1880), p. 291; described again in *Appleton's Annual Cyclopaedia of 1878* (New York: D. Appleton, 1879), pp. 175–195; and included in a list of "Votes on Coinage and Currency Legislation" compiled by Thomas C. McRae of Arkansas as part of a record of major votes on the gold standard, *Congressional Record* 56:1:2828–2843, March 13, 1900. For later descriptions of the vote, see Rhodes, *History of the United States*, vol. 8, pp. 97–98; Unger, *Greenback Era*, p. 355.

[31] The net repatriation of American securities, both government and corporate, from Europe was estimated at $100 million. Most of this substantial flow occurred during the early months of the year when congressional agitation over resumption was most intense. "Retrospect of 1878," *Commercial and Financial Chronicle*, January 4, 1879.

these obligations in gold, this legislation threatened to weaken the gold standard from another direction. The House, without debate, passed this concurrent resolution on January 28, 1878 (see Table 6.7).[32] After a few more weeks of maneuvering in the Senate, Republicans and gold Democrats were able to craft a compromise that effectively substituted limited remonetization of the silver dollar for both repeal of the Resumption Act and related proposals for the unlimited coinage of silver.[33]

Under what became known as the Bland-Allison Act, the Treasury was ordered to purchase at least two million dollars' worth of silver bullion a month to be coined into silver dollars which were given legal tender status. Faced with an almost certain override, President Hayes nonetheless vetoed this bill.[34] In his veto message, he contended: "The standard of value should not be changed without the consent of both parties to the contract. National promises should be kept with unflinching fidelity. There is no power to compel a nation to pay its just debts. Its credit depends on its honor." While inelegant in style, the president's concern with the nation's credit-worthiness was crystal clear. After hearing the president's message, the House voted without further debate to override the veto by a wide margin (see Table 6.7).[35] Two hours after Hayes sent his message and the bill back to the Capitol, the veto was overridden. Given the substantial surplus of revenues over expenditures in the government budget, silver purchases

---

[32] This measure was largely symbolic in that a concurrent resolution does not have the force of law and thus would not have compelled the Treasury to alter existing practice. However, as an expression of congressional sentiment regarding the gold standard, the message was emphatically hostile; the House of Representatives, for example, passed the resolution under suspension of the rules, a parliamentary motion requiring a two-thirds' majority. For a brief description, see A. Barton Hepburn, *A History of Currency in the United States* (New York: Macmillan, 1915), pp. 282–283. This roll call was included in McRae's 1900 list of "Votes on Coinage and Currency Legislation."

[33] Thirty-eight congressmen, all but two of them Republicans, voted for the Bland-Allison bill but against repeal of the 1875 Resumption Act. As in the Senate, these moderates represented the swing votes that made compromise possible. However, in the House, their position was too weak to have prevented either repeal or the even more radical adoption of a free silver bill during the Forty-fifth Congress. The Senate, although not a safe haven for gold, was more friendly than the House. For a list of the thirty-eight House moderates, see Unger, *Greenback Era*, p. 414.

[34] On the president's expectations concerning congressional reaction to his prospective veto, see Rhodes, *History of the United States*, vol. 8, pp. 95–96.

[35] Unger, *Greenback Era*, pp. 355–364; Morgan, *From Hayes to McKinley*, pp. 48–50; Hepburn, *History of Currency*, p. 281. This roll call was included in McRae's 1900 list of "Votes on Coinage and Currency Legislation." Describing the almost incessant speech-making on the resumption act during the years prior to 1879, Albert S. Bolles said: "On no financial subject in the last twenty-five years did so many small fishes talk like whales." *The Financial History of the United States* (1894; rpt., Augustus M. Kelley: New York, 1969), vol. 3, pp. 390–391. For the veto message, see *Congressional Record* 45:2:1418–1419, February 28, 1878.

Table 6.7. *Members Supporting the Gold Standard in the 45th Congress, 1877–1879* (%)

House membership category	Resumption act repeal (1877)	U.S. bonds payable in silver (1878)	Bland-Allison Act (1878)	Springer silver bill (1878)	Prohibit contraction (1878)	Greenbacks for duties (1879)
Full House	47.4 (253)	29.5 (268)	27.1 (269)	42.1 (242)	16.5 (212)	38.4 (198)
Republicans	76.7 (120)	42.7 (131)	39.2 (130)	66.7 (114)	27.5 (102)	69.1 (94)
Democrats	21.4 (131)	17.0 (135)	16.1 (137)	20.6 (126)	6.5 (108)	10.8 (102)
Other party	0.0 (2)	0.0 (2)	0.0 (2)	0.0 (2)	0.0 (2)	0.0 (0)
District level of development						
All members						
Highest	80.0 (40)	63.8 (47)	59.6 (47)	75.6 (41)	37.9 (29)	64.7 (34)
Middle high	75.8 (62)	45.2 (62)	42.9 (63)	67.9 (56)	31.5 (54)	62.0 (50)
Middle low	34.6 (104)	17.0 (106)	15.2 (105)	30.9 (94)	8.4 (83)	27.6 (76)
Lowest	10.6 (47)	5.7 (53)	3.7 (54)	7.8 (51)	0.0 (46)	5.3 (38)
Republicans						
Highest	81.0 (21)	58.3 (24)	53.8 (26)	81.0 (21)	40.0 (15)	83.3 (18)
Middle high	89.1 (46)	52.2 (46)	51.1 (45)	81.0 (42)	43.6 (39)	81.8 (33)
Middle low	61.7 (47)	28.3 (53)	23.1 (52)	48.9 (45)	11.9 (42)	55.3 (38)
Lowest	83.3 (6)	37.5 (8)	28.6 (7)	50.0 (6)	0.0 (6)	40.0 (5)

Democrats						
Highest	78.9 (19)	69.6 (23)	66.7 (21)	70.0 (20)	35.7 (14)	43.7 (16)
Middle high	37.5 (16)	25.0 (16)	22.2 (18)	28.6 (14)	0.0 (15)	23.5 (17)
Middle low	12.3 (57)	5.7 (53)	7.5 (53)	8.2 (49)	4.9 (41)	0.0 (38)
Lowest	0.0 (39)	0.0 (43)	0.0 (45)	2.3 (43)	0.0 (38)	0.0 (31)
Sectional stress	70.8	65.8	63.0	59.8	42.9	50.0

Note and sources: The roll-call position that accorded with support for the gold standard is indicated in parentheses: on passage of a bill to repeal the resumption act (nay); on approval of a Senate resolution affirming the right to pay principal and interest on federal bonds with silver dollars (nay); on passage of the Bland-Allison Act over the president's veto (nay); on passage of the Springer silver bill (nay); on passage of a bill to forbid further contraction of greenback currency (nay); and on adoption of an amendment providing that greenbacks would be accepted in payment of duties only as long as the nation remained on the gold standard (yea). The roll calls can be found in the *Congressional Record* 45:1:632–633, November 23, 1877; 45:2:627–628, January 28, 1878; 45:2:1420, February 28, 1878; 45:2:2014–2015, March 25, 1878; 45:2:2928–2929, April 29, 1878; 45:3:478–479, January 15, 1879. All congressional districts were divided into four categories according to their relative level of economic development: Highest (five on the index), middle high (three and four), middle low (one and two), and lowest (zero). See Chapter 2 for a description of the index. Sectional stress measures the degree of regional polarization on the roll call. For the formula, see Richard Franklin Bensel, *Sectionalism and American Political Development, 1880–1980* (Madison: University of Wisconsin Press, 1984), pp. 443, 449.

under the Bland-Allison Act were not an immediate threat to the gold standard because silver bullion purchased by the Treasury was simply coined and held in government vaults.[36] Few people demanded silver dollars for cash transactions because paper was more convenient and gold was safer. So, even when the government could place silver dollars in circulation, they rapidly returned to the Treasury and rejoined the ever-growing hoard.

In the following months, those congressmen opposed to resumption continued their efforts to prevent a return to gold payments. On March 25, 1878, less than a month after enactment of the Bland-Allison bill, the House entertained a motion to pass a free silver coinage bill (see Table 6.7). Free coinage would have flooded the mints with silver and thus destroyed any possibility of resuming gold payments. Without debate, a substantial majority voted in favor of this measure; however, the bill failed when fewer than two thirds of those voting supported the motion to suspend the rules (the required majority under the procedure under which the bill was considered). Even so, the House did pass a measure prohibiting any further contraction of the currency (a deflationary Treasury policy aiding resumption), passing a bill for that purpose under suspension of the rules by a margin of over five to one (see Table 6.7).[37] All of these and many more proposals intended to scuttle resumption were considered over the intervening months. Despite their continued popularity in the House of Representatives, the nation, as scheduled, resumed gold payments on January 1, 1879.

After that date, greenbacks were equivalent to gold for most purposes, although the law still required customs duties be paid in gold. A vestigial remnant of the Civil War era, this requirement had provided the gold necessary to meet interest payments on the vast debt with which the Union funded the northern war effort. Just weeks after resumption, the House took up a bill to make greenbacks, along with gold, receivable for import duties. James Garfield, the Ohio Republican who was to receive his party's presidential nomination in the following year, moved to stipulate that greenbacks could be received for customs only "so long as said notes shall be exchangeable at par in coin." This amendment would have protected the ability of the Treasury to pay interest on the bonded debt in gold in the event that the nation was forced off the gold standard at some point in the future. This was in no way a radical amendment; as long as the nation

---

[36] See, for example, the commentary and analysis in "Retrospect of 1878," *Commercial and Financial Chronicle*, January 4, 1879. Much more serious, from the *Chronicle*'s perspective, was the financial uncertainty and disruption of markets caused by constant congressional deliberations over whether or not the United States would resume gold payments or openly embrace silver.

[37] Unger referred to this measure but does not report the vote. *Greenback Era*, pp. 372, 374. Included in McRae's 1900 list of "Votes on Coinage and Currency Legislation." Bolles evidently referred to this measure when discussing a bill passed by Congress on May 31, 1878. *Financial History*, vol. 3, p. 297.

remained on gold, his amendment would have had no effect and, if the nation went off gold, his proposal merely mandated a return to the system that had prevailed from the Civil War until that time. Nonetheless, the House was impatient with any further discrimination against paper currency and emphatically rejected Garfield's safeguard by a margin of almost two to one (see Table 6.7) before going on to pass the bill.[38]

Drawing "a deep breath of relief" at the adjournment of the Forty-fifth Congress, the *Commercial and Financial Chronicle* noted that nothing had been done "towards taking the country out of the silver trouble, all the bills introduced relative to that subject, except one, having been of a sort which would only have made matters worse."[39] Indeed, of the six major votes on financial legislation, the House of Representatives recorded majorities hostile to the gold standard in every case (see Table 6.7). Although the Republicans were more favorable to gold than the Democrats, the party produced majorities on only three of the votes. In fact, fewer than 40 percent of voting Republicans supported their own president's veto of the Bland-Allison Act. The Democrats, however, established an even more hostile record; at no time did as much as a quarter of the party support positions friendly to the gold standard. Among members of both parties hailing from more developed districts, support for the gold standard was more or less regularly given, sometimes by quite lopsided majorities. The primary exception was on the bill to prohibit further contraction of greenbacks, but that was, in terms of its impact on gold, perhaps the least important of these votes. Among the less developed districts, however, member hostility to gold was very high. In the least developed districts in the nation – those which scored below the national average on all five developmental dimensions – more than nine out of every ten votes were regularly cast for policies antithetical to gold.

As a positive plan for the nation's financial system, these policies were not particularly coherent. The major tension arose between silver and greenbacks as alternative monetary standards. A shift to silver would have involved a one-time-only inflation of the monetary unit but would have otherwise retained a bullion basis. This basis would have continued to constrain national fiscal and financial policy in much the same way as did gold. Greenbacks, however, were a fiat currency; as proponents constantly

---

[38] In fact, because greenbacks were equivalent to gold under the gold standard, the customs houses already accepted them, as a practical convenience, in payment of duties. *Commercial and Financial Chronicle*, January 18, 1879. Terming House opposition as "conceived in the old unrelenting hostility to coin," the *Chronicle* strongly supported Garfield's amendment. The *Chronicle* also noted that the substance of the amendment had been endorsed by Secretary Sherman in a separate report to Congress. This bill, but not Garfield's amendment, was included in McRae's 1900 list of "Votes on Coinage and Currency Legislation."

[39] *Commercial and Financial Chronicle*, March 8, 1879.

emphasized, more dollars could be issued at any time in response to demands for increased circulation. Such a modulation of the currency was incompatible with proposals for a silver or any other bullion standard. While there were those who were completely devoted to either silver or greenbacks to the point of excluding the other as an alternative, most congressmen hostile to gold simply favored inflation of the currency. If silver provided enough inflation to relieve their constituents, then silver it would be. If not, then the shift to greenbacks would have been a logical next step. In this sense, Congress as a whole and the House of Representatives in particular were quite hostile to gold during the life of the Forty-fifth Congress but failed to demonstrate much commitment to a specific alternative. Even so, this somewhat diffuse sentiment for pure and simple inflation produced a challenge to the nation's hard-money policy that was not to be equaled again until the Fifty-third Congress.

The intervening years first saw a rapid decline in congressional interest in monetary issues until 1885 or so and then an equally rapid resurgence of inflationary sentiment. During this period, the gold standard became increasingly identified with financial orthodoxy in the business community, the academy, and in politics. In early 1880, one Illinois Democrat attributed the increasing ostracization of silver to "those charged with the financial department of this Government . . . and the money-lords of the East [who] have again and again denounced those of the West who have introduced measures of financial reform as dangerous agitators, demagogues, and lunatics."[40] Even so, elite conceptions of orthodoxy did not translate into political hegemony. And although the public would not use them, the Treasury was still compelled by law to mint silver dollars. As a Missouri congressman noted, the Treasury held "thirty-two thousand kegs, ordinary nail-kegs, of silver dollars now piled up in the vaults" as a result of passage of the Bland-Allison Act.[41] Every month's production of silver dollars

---

[40] *Congressional Record* 46:2:450, January 21, 1880. Speaking for the eastern financial community, the *Commercial and Financial Chronicle* contended that some "of our esteemed Congressmen . . . bring their ideas of finance fresh from their corn fields." December 6, 1879.

[41] *Congressional Record* 46:2:451, January 21, 1880. While always attempting to protect the gold reserve, the Treasury Department nevertheless constantly sought ways to put these silver dollars in circulation as an act of good faith toward the inflationists in Congress. But, as the *Commercial and Financial Chronicle* observed, "the Treasury puts the dollars out only to see them come in again in the form of duties. No one wants this 'stove-lid currency,' as the mechanics call it; it is never taken except under protest. Hence, whatever means the Secretary may devise for turning it over to the public, is only met by a counter influence pouring it back again, as constant and unfailing in its operation as the tide. And yet he must go on buying and coining two millions a month, and if the majority of the House of Representatives could have had its way, many millions more." The *Chronicle* then called for an end to compulsory mintage of the silver dollar – a request that the journal made hundreds of times during this period. July 12, 1879; also see July 26, 1879.

took up 534 cubic feet in the Treasury's storage rooms and added 120,000 pounds of silver bullion to the nation's holdings.[42] The *Chronicle* called this continued coinage of silver dollars "a dose of slow poison, which must finally involve the entire system in disease" by forcing the nation off gold.[43]

Prior to resumption, greenbacks had to be considered a realistic alternative to gold because, after all, they constituted the very basis of the financial system at that time. Silver was also an apparent alternative in that the metal was almost at par with gold and switching between the two would have been akin to changing trains going in about the same direction, at the same speed, and very close to one another. While not an entirely simple matter, adopting silver would have entailed much less disruption than later when the market price of the metal fell to less than half of par with gold (see Chart 6.1). In fact, although it was never presented in quite that way, the nation could have resumed on the antebellum silver standard more or less as easily it did in gold in 1879. At that time, the question was much more whether the United States should be integrated with the British financial markets under gold or more loosely tied under floating exchange rates as the market price of American silver fluctuated against the pound. The immediate inflationary impact of a silver standard at that time would have been slight. With resumption, however, gold became the embedded expectation in almost all trans-Atlantic and domestic commercial and financial transactions. Shifting back to greenbacks or forward to silver thus became increasingly unrealistic, both objectively and from the perspective of the nation's business community and professional economists.

Congressional support for inflation was tested very early in the Forty-sixth Congress when, on May 16, 1879, the House of Representatives overwhelmingly rejected a free silver amendment (see Table 6.8). Compared with the silver bill considered in the previous year, opposition to hard money declined by roughly 30 percent; this decline was more or less across the board, equally shared by the two major parties and tending to raise support for gold within each of the developmental levels. This vote was later followed by one of the most important roll calls on financial policy in this period, involving a confrontation between two congressmen who soon after became the presidential nominees of their respective parties. On April 5, 1880, James Weaver, an Iowa Greenbacker, moved to suspend the rules and pass a resolution that later became the basis of his party's national platform.[44] The resolution was offered in two parts:

---

[42] *Commercial and Financial Chronicle*, July 26, 1879.   [43] Ibid., October 25, 1879.
[44] For the text of 1880 Greenback platform, see Kirk H. Porter, *National Party Platforms* (New York: Macmillan, 1924), pp. 101–104. Hepburn, *History of Currency*, p. 289.

Table 6.8. Members Supporting the Gold Standard in the 46th and 48th Congresses, 1879–1881 and 1883–1885 (%)

House membership category	Free silver (1879)	Greenback planks (1880)	U.S. bonds payable in silver (1881)	Trade dollar (1884)	Suspend silver (1885)
Full House	72.1 (215)	58.2 (201)	55.8 (251)	47.6 (250)	43.7 (270)
Republicans	100.0 (100)	97.8 (89)	99.0 (104)	92.9 (95)	65.6 (93)
Democrats	53.0 (100)	30.2 (96)	28.2 (131)	25.7 (148)	32.2 (171)
Other party	13.3 (15)	6.2 (16)	0.0 (16)	28.6 (7)	33.3 (6)
District level of development					
All members					
Highest	93.7 (32)	80.0 (30)	86.4 (44)	71.1 (45)	86.0 (50)
Middle high	93.6 (47)	83.3 (48)	81.7 (60)	52.8 (53)	55.7 (61)
Middle low	67.0 (91)	53.2 (79)	45.7 (94)	48.0 (102)	33.3 (105)
Lowest	44.4 (45)	25.0 (44)	18.9 (53)	20.0 (50)	11.1 (54)
Republicans					
Highest	100.0 (24)	94.7 (19)	100.0 (28)	100.0 (16)	100.0 (18)
Middle high	100.0 (35)	97.3 (37)	97.7 (43)	86.2 (29)	79.3 (29)
Middle low	100.0 (37)	100.0 (30)	100.0 (31)	76.1 (46)	43.9 (41)
Lowest	100.0 (4)	100.0 (3)	100.0 (2)	75.0 (4)	40.0 (5)

Democrats					
Highest	85.7 (7)	55.6 (9)	66.7 (15)	55.6 (27)	77.4 (31)
Middle high	81.8 (11)	44.4 (9)	46.7 (15)	12.5 (24)	35.5 (31)
Middle low	46.8 (47)	27.3 (44)	21.1 (57)	24.5 (53)	25.8 (62)
Lowest	45.7 (35)	23.5 (34)	14.8 (44)	15.9 (44)	8.5 (47)
Sectional stress	30.0	53.6	59.5	52.9	66.1

Note and sources: The roll-call position that accorded with support for the gold standard is indicated in parentheses: on adoption of an amendment providing for the free coinage of silver (nay); on passage of resolutions that later became the basis of the national Greenback platform (nay); on adoption of an amendment that provided for the payment of silver for federal bonds (nay); on adoption of an amendment excluding the recoinage of trade dollars from quota under the Bland act (nay); and on adoption of a resolution providing for consideration of a bill, among other things, to suspend silver coinage (yea). The roll calls can be found in the *Journal of the House of Representatives*, 46th Cong. 1st sess., pp. 319–320 (May 16, 1879), and the *Congressional Record* 46:2:2142, April 5, 1880; 46:3:770–771, January 19, 1881; 48:1:2496, April 1, 1884; and 48:2:2210–2211, February 26, 1885.

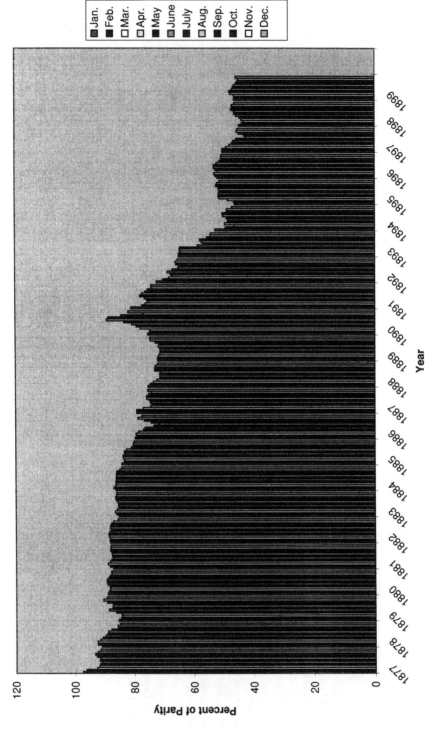

Chart 6.1. Price of silver as percent of parity with gold dollar, 1877–1900. *Source: Commercial and Financial Chronicle,* March 10, 1900.

Resolved, That it is the sense of this House that all currency, whether metallic or paper, necessary for the use and convenience of the people, should be issued and its volume controlled by the Government, and not by or through the bank corporations of the country; and when so issued should be a full legal tender in payment of all debts, public and private.

Resolved, That, in the judgment of this House, that portion of the interest-bearing debt of the United States which shall become redeemable in the year 1881, or prior thereto, being in amount $782,000,000, should not be refunded beyond the power of the Government to call in said obligations and pay them at any time, but should be paid as rapidly as possible, and according to contract. To enable the Government to meet these obligations, the mints of the United States should be operated to their full capacity in the coinage of standard silver dollars, and such other coinage as the business interests of the country may require.[45]

Soon to be nominated for the presidency by the Republicans, James Garfield of Ohio rose from his seat in order to speak as the primary opponent of Weaver's proposals. He began by noting that they had already "attained some historical importance by being talked about a good deal in the newspapers, and by blocking the other business of the House for some weeks." In his opinion, they raised three important issues. The first "is a proposition of the largest possible proportion, that all money, whether of coin or paper, that is to circulate in this country ought to be manufactured and issued directly by the Government. . . . [This is a measure that] makes the House of Representatives and the Senate, or the caucus of the party which happens to be in the majority, the absolute dictator of the financial and business affairs of the country. This scheme surpasses all the centralism and all the Caesarism that were ever charged upon the Republican party in the wildest days of the war or in the events growing out of the war." In saying this, Garfield not only defended the gold standard but also attempted to drive a wedge between the Democrats and Weaver's Greenback policies. Garfield implied that Democrats, given their strong inclination toward state's rights and local control, should be extremely wary of the centralizing impact of discretionary central state power over the supply of money.

The second issue, as Garfield saw it, was "that the Government of the United States shall pay all its public debts in this manufactured money, manufactured to order at the Treasury factory. Notwithstanding the solemn and acknowledged pledge of the Government to pay the principal and the interest of its public debt in coin, this resolution declares that in this legal-tender paper the public debt shall be payable." Embedded in this criticism were at least two old disputes. The first was whether the term "coin" was restricted to gold or, alternatively, included silver as well. This question was primarily applicable to the payment of interest on the federal debt. The second

---

[45] *Congressional Record* 46:2:2139, April 5, 1880.

was whether the repayment of the principal of that debt could be made in either silver or greenbacks, as opposed to gold. Garfield's attitude toward both questions reflected the conservative, hard-money position of the nation's financial community.

The last issue involved the funding of the $780 million in federal bonds which were to fall due over the next several years. Weaver's resolution called for the free coinage of silver as a way of turning that debt into circulating money but, as Garfield noted, his proposal did not explain how the government was to come by the resources to purchase silver. Although freely extrapolating, Garfield was undoubtedly correct when he contended that Weaver intended to purchase silver with greenbacks "manufactured at the Treasury." As a result, Weaver's solution to debt repayment was to "print it to death – that is the way to dispose of the pubic debt, says this resolution." As he ended his comments, Garfield called the resolution a "triple-headed monster of centralization, inflation, and repudiation . . . the last spawn of the dying party that thought it had a little life in it a year ago."[46] All but two Republicans joined Garfield, but in an indication of just how close the Democratic caucus was to Greenback principles, over two thirds of the Democrats voted to pass the proposal. The small Greenback delegation in the House, not surprisingly, unanimously backed Weaver.[47]

In the third session of the Forty-sixth Congress, the House returned to the question of whether federal bonds should be paid in silver. In the form of an amendment, the proposal would have required that the Secretary of the Treasury redeem maturing federal bonds in silver dollars and all gold in excess of a $50 million reserve; only after the silver dollars held in Treasury vaults had been exhausted could the government issue new debt as a way of refunding those maturing bonds. The practical result, had this amendment become law, would have been abandonment of the gold standard as the gold reserve was swamped with demands to redeem in gold these newly issued silver dollars. Unlike the 1878 vote (see Table 6.8), however, the nation was now on the gold standard and the bias in the membership was against the proposal. In fact, opposition to the amendment rose dramatically, placing the House by a comfortable majority in favor of gold redemption of bonds. The Republican party, which by a substantial margin had supported silver in the 1878 vote, now backed gold almost unanimously. The Democrats, however, remained firmly committed to silver, and as a result, the gulf between the parties over the money question widened substantially in this Congress. The net result was a Congress in which the gold standard was relatively secure – a rarity in the late nineteenth century.

---

[46] *Congressional Record* 46:2:2140, April 5, 1880. Included in McRae's 1900 list of "Votes on Coinage and Currency Legislation."

[47] At least two state Greenback parties, Minnesota and Tennessee, also endorsed Weaver's resolutions in their 1880 platforms.

The Forty-seventh Congress was equally or even more friendly to gold, so much so that some observers thought there may have been some possibility of suspending the coinage of silver dollars.[48] But this did not happen. Instead, whatever conservative sentiment existed was used to pass a bill that allowed the national banks to renew their charters.

The opening of the Forty-eighth Congress was received by the financial community with the usual mixture of trepidation and mild contempt.[49] The House of Representatives was dominated by the Democrats, who enjoyed their largest majority since the outbreak of the Civil War. At this time, most financial matters were safely in the hands of the administration, no further legislation being required in order to maintain gold payments. The exception was the continued coinage of silver. With respect to silver, the Democratic majority very early indicated their sympathies when Speaker John Carlisle of Kentucky appointed a prosilver enthusiast, Richard Bland of Missouri, as chair of the Committee on Coinage. With Bland at the head of Coinage, there was no possibility of bringing the minting of silver dollars to a halt.[50] However, there developed no serious threat to the gold standard itself.

Instead, the major legislative proposal emerging from the Committee on Coinage was for the redemption of trade dollars and their reminting into standard silver dollars. The trade dollar was a curious coin. They had been authorized as a means of exporting silver bullion to the Far East, in competition with Mexican eight reales which poured out of the mints south of the border. To match the Mexican coin, trade dollars were slightly heavier than silver dollars. While at first trade dollars had been made a legal tender in amounts of five dollars or less, this provision had been repealed in 1878 by the Bland-Allison Act. Thus their value rested purely on their bullion. As the value of silver declined against gold, the difference between the value of the trade dollar and other federal money widened. From almost the very day that the trade dollar was demonetized, brokers bought and sold trade dollars, speculating on the possibility that Congress would again award the coin legal tender status or provide for its redemption on an equality with the silver dollar. This speculative market was so active that prices were publicly posted on Wall Street. The difference between the bullion value and the speculative price was based on the prospects for full redemption and would have amply rewarded those enterprising enough to buy up trade dollars still circulating in the Far East, primarily China, and return them to the United States.[51]

Since the trade dollar saw hard use in the Far East and since bullion coin

[48] *Commercial and Financial Chronicle*, May 6, 1882.   [49] Ibid., April 19, 1884.
[50] Ibid., December 29, 1883.
[51] Ibid., May 24, 1879. For a later account of this market, see *Congressional Record* 48:1:2485, April 1, 1884.

was readily melted both for its metal and in order to be reminted into local money, many trade dollars had undoubtedly disappeared even before they were fully demonetized. The question was how many had disappeared. If only a few were gone, their recoining into silver dollars would have added substantially to the circulation, posing the same kind of threat to the gold reserve that compulsory production of silver dollars already presented. If many had already been destroyed in the melting pots of the Far East, then redemption would have been preferred, even by financial conservatives, to continued speculation.[52] After this became the announced position of the Treasury, legislative efforts to redeem the trade dollar were renewed.

At this time, the best estimates placed the number of trade dollars in the United States at about 20 million, or about ten months of silver dollar production under the Bland-Allison Act.[53] If trade dollars were treated as part of the quota under the act, purchases of newly mined silver would cease for that period as the mint was recoining those trade dollars into silver dollars. If trade dollars were considered an addition to the already existing monthly quota, then there would have been a sizable increase in silver coinage. This, not the extraordinary gain that would have accrued to speculators, was the major issue involved in trade dollar redemption.[54] George Cassidy, a Nevada Democrat, observed:

Every member on this floor who is opposed to silver, every member who is in favor of striking down the standard dollar and the closing of the doors of the mints against the further coinage of them, will be found voting to retain this obnoxious section [including the trade dollars in the monthly silver quota]. Watch the roll-call, and you will find every one of them recorded on that side. I especially warn Democrats, who are the friends of silver and of the people, to be careful of the vote they shall give on this important measure. The other side of the House will be found almost to a man in favor of destroying silver.[55]

But Cassidy's position was predictable on this issue – Nevada led the nation in per capita silver production. For members of both parties from the western mining states, the issue involved a straightforward economic question. In response, William "Pig Iron" Kelley, a Pennsylvania Republican, argued that a cessation of silver coinage would "force arrogant England, the persecutor of silver and silver-using nations, to sue for relief from her

---

[52] *Commercial and Financial Chronicle*, May 24, 1879. However, the size of some of the shipments back to the United States must have come as an unpleasant surprise to financiers otherwise favorable to redemption. In June and July of 1879, for example, just two steamers arriving from Southampton brought back 538,000 trade dollars between them. July 19, 1879.

[53] *Commercial and Financial Chronicle*, January 12, 1884.

[54] For commentary on the amendment, see ibid., April 5, 1884. For the debate in the House of Representatives, see *Congressional Record* 48:1:2351–2360, 2435–2452, 2476–2497, March 27, 31, April 1, 1884.

[55] *Congressional Record* 48:1:2479, April 1, 1884.

own arrogance by asking for the remonetization of silver" under a bimetallist standard. James Belford, a Colorado Republican answered:

Why did not the gentleman introduce a bill to protect arrogant England on the subject of pig-iron? [Great laughter.] The gentleman from Pennsylvania stands here and asks us people from the West to protect pig-iron, and I have voted to do it. New Jersey stands here and asks me to protect her silk interests. Connecticut says to me, "I want you to vote to protect my cutlery interests;" and Louisiana says, "I want you to vote to protect my sugar interests;" and I have always voted in that direction. Yet there is a settled, studied policy on the part of the monopolists of the East to discredit and injure and ruin the great industry of my state.[56]

In the House of Representatives, the vote that best tested silver sentiment occurred not on passage of the bill but on an amendment to exempt the reminting of trade dollars from the monthly quota of silver purchases mandated by the Bland-Allison Act. The House subsequently accepted the amendment, thus providing that redemption of the trade dollar would be in addition to the monthly silver quota, and passed the bill. But this legislation was lost in the Senate.[57] Similar proposals for the redemption of the trade dollar were repeatedly made over the next few years until, in 1887, President Cleveland allowed one of them to become law without his signature.[58]

By 1885, just over $200 million silver dollars had been coined under the Bland-Allison Act. Of those, only about a quarter were in circulation, the rest in storage. Still, Congress continued to compel their production. In 1888, the federal government coined 32,484,673 new silver dollars; during the same year, the Treasury was able to place only 39,000 of these in circulation.[59] There were so many coins that they were moved from place to

---

[56]   *Congressional Record* 48:1:2484, April 1, 1884. In his opening sentence, Belford was suggesting that Kelley propose to remove the tariff on pig iron in order to bring England to its knees in the same way that he proposed ceasing silver coinage. For a more general discussion of free silver as the rough equivalent of tariff protection for other commodities such as steel and cotton cloth, see *Financial and Mining Record*, July 18, 1891.

[57]   *Appleton's Annual Cyclopaedia of 1884* (New York: D. Appleton, 1888), pp. 216–219.

[58]   Oberholtzer, *History of the United States*, vol. 4, pp. 376–377, 438–439; Hepburn, *History of Currency*, p. 297; *Commercial and Financial Chronicle*, February 19, March 5, 1887. Under the operation of that law, about eight million trade dollars were redeemed and recoined into silver dollars or subsidiary denominations.

[59]   Noting the seemingly senseless coinage of silver but also realizing the Congress was not about to stop silver purchases, the Treasurer proposed that, at the least, he be allowed to hold the silver in bars. *Commercial and Financial Chronicle*, November 24, 1888. The *Chronicle* called this "undoubtedly a wise suggestion, but we are afraid it smacks too much of wisdom to be acceptable to our silver-loving Congressmen...." The real reason Congress still insisted on the coinage of all bullion purchases into silver dollars was that any change to bullion would have, in effect, carried an admission that the public did not want the coin.

place, sometimes over long distances, in search of storage room. In 1883, in fact, Congress had authorized $100,000 just to provide space by constructing and renting vaults at the local subtreasury offices. Two years later the Secretary of the Treasury gave notice that the fund was exhausted and that there was almost no room for more dollars. He reported that the San Francisco mint, although it now had three new vaults in place, was filled to capacity. The Carson City mint was almost full as well. Cincinnati reported that it had no space left and Boston had the room only that appeared once excess silver dollars had been sent on to Washington. In Philadelphia, the mint had been forced to haul 20 million newly minted silver dollars in canvas bags to the post office for storage.[60] Seven years later, the Treasury was still coining silver dollars, although under a different law (the 1890 Sherman Silver Purchase Act). By this time the government was storing 400 million silver dollars, a hoard that "was increasing at the rate of seven tons a day. It would make a column one foot in diameter six and a half miles high; it would fill 1,000 freight cars. If one man were assigned the duty of counting all the silver dollars in the government's vaults it would require his constant application working eight hours a day for a period of eleven years."[61]

In fact, the laws that compelled the purchase and coinage of silver bullion represented one of the most extraordinary episodes in American public policy. As their rapid accumulation in the Treasury's vaults amply demonstrated, the public would not take these silver dollars or, at least, would not take them for very long before exchanging them for paper or gold. The Treasury tried everything it could think of in order to move silver dollars out into remote sections of the nation where, it was hoped, the coin would be accepted. When these attempts failed, the Treasury tried to encourage the acceptance of silver certificates by the public. Although the circulation of paper representations of the silver dollar would not relieve the Treasury's vaults, it was hoped that at least the effort to push out silver-backed currency might somehow reduce the political agitation for continued coinage.[62]

---

[60] Oberholtzer, *History of the United States*, vol. 4, p. 366. The Philadelphia report came from the *New York Times*, May 8, 1886. The new vault in Washington, to which the Boston silver dollars had been sent, had room for forty million coins, less than two years production under the Bland-Allison quota. New Orleans also had a little space, although new silver dollars would have to be moved over long distances to reach it, and in any event, the room should be reserved for that mint's share of production. P. 367.

[61] The calculations were made by David A. Wells, a leading economist of the period. Oberholtzer, *History of the United States*, vol. 5, p. 145.

[62] In 1882, for example, the Treasury declared that it would deliver silver certificates free of charge anywhere in the country while requiring that other forms of money would move only at cost to the patron. At the same time, the printing of new gold certificates was delayed so that silver certificates would be the dominant form of

The reasons for the continued purchase and coinage of silver bullion were clear to everyone but rarely acknowledged by proponents. The United States, in effect, was operating a price-support program for silver producers, albeit a program with no set target price because it limited purchases and bought on the open market. However, such a program, favoring a particular sector, would have encountered much opposition had it not been partially disguised as an inflationary strategy. While a few congressmen were willing to talk, as did Belford, about the interests of their state's silver industry, most supporters of silver coinage interpreted the policy as tending to expand the nation's currency base and thus inflate the price structure. This inflationary event could happen only once (in a one-step-only inflation as the nation changed from the gold to a silver standard) and thus depended on abandonment of gold payments. Since the executive branch was committed to gold throughout the late nineteenth century, there was no direct way of switching silver for gold; any open legislative attempt to do so would be sure to meet a presidential veto and the silver forces in Congress did not have the votes to override the president. So the silver strategy became one of perseverance and subterfuge. The government would buy and coin silver until, it was hoped and anticipated, the growing hoard of silver dollars became too heavy for the budget to sustain.

As long as the Treasury ran a surplus of revenues over expenditures large enough to support the purchase of silver or could borrow money by issuing bonds for the same purpose, the gold standard was safe even with hundreds of millions of noncirculating silver dollars clogging government vaults. With the Treasury compelled by law to make monthly silver purchases, inflationists could also focus on the revenue side of this equation and attempted to further hamstring the government's ability to defend gold. Thus those favoring silver backed a reduction in the tariff and were hostile to the further issuance of government bonds, instead demanding their immediate recall and redemption in silver. Sooner or later compulsory silver purchases would force the government to switch monetary standards when the gold reserve was exhausted, but sooner would prevail if government ran a large deficit in its annual budget and was prevented from borrowing in the open money market.

Setting aside general fiscal policy for the moment, there were four primary positions on silver and gold in the late nineteenth century. The most inflationist was that openly embracing silver as the sole monetary standard for the nation. Although clearly displayed in some of the most contentious electoral contests of the period, particularly during the 1890s, bills embodying this position never reached a vote in the House of Representatives. Under

paper currency during the fall drain of currency to the interior that was part of the seasonal harvest cycle. *Commercial and Financial Chronicle*, September 2, October 28, 1882.

inflationist doctrine, the road to silver was through bimetallism, by way of which the nation could first enjoy the use of both gold and silver under a fixed ratio. That ratio would be based on the historic sixteen to one ratio under which the nation had coined both silver and gold before 1873 and, by substantially overvaluing that silver in comparison to gold, would thus rectify the injustice done to the former metal. Bimetallists contended that unlimited purchases of both gold and silver by the United States government would first serve to raise the price of silver and then stabilize the world market at the historic ratio. Some inflationists may have actually believed that the United States could have accomplished this end, even when a tide of silver flowed into this country in response to the undervaluation of gold. But most probably did not.[63] In any event, the greed of international financiers would have been blamed for the failure of the bimetallist experiment and thus a silver standard would have been safely reached without an explicit rejection of bimetallism.

Aside from an open embrace of a single silver standard, the second most inflationist position was that favoring unlimited coinage of silver. "Free silver" as this position was known, would have opened the mints to silver on the same terms as gold under the prevailing ratio of sixteen to one. This was, in a formal sense at least, clearly the bimetallist position. In practical effect, the end result would have been a single silver standard as gold left the Treasury and silver took its place. This alternative was proposed in literally hundreds of bills and amendments to bills throughout the period, some of which are examined above. Less inflationary in its implications, because the Treasury could counter its impact, was the limited coinage of silver under compulsory statutes. This third position on silver and gold is also discussed above. In terms of public debate over the

[63]   At one point in this period, the *Commercial and Financial Chronicle* tried to distinguish sincere bimetallists from silver producers: "... it must be remembered that there are two silver parties in this country and they should not be confounded. One is purely selfish, having not a suspicion, no not even the aroma of patriotism or humanitarianism attaching itself to a thread of one of its garments; this is the 'silver-mine-party' which believes in silver only because by stacking it away in Government vaults it gives the wealthy owners of silver mines a higher price for their product. ... The other silver party are honest bi-metallists, who believe that the two metals having been used together as currency by the world ever since the first recorded commercial transaction; having been the twofold basis under which the world's exchanges have developed to their present proportions and present values been built upon; – must not now and cannot now without infinite wrong be divorced." November 21, 1885. However, most of the time the journal more realistically assumed that most silverites in Congress simply sought abandonment of the gold standard as their primary goal. Commenting on a Senate debate over silver early on in the Forty-ninth Congress, for example, the *Chronicle* asserted that "the desire among [those senators agitating the silver question] is not bi-metalism at all, but mono-metalism and that metal silver, and the lower its bullion value the better they would like it...." January 23, 1886.

monetary standard, limited purchases of silver was a bit odd. The policy both failed to place silver on an equality with gold (and thus appeared to endorse gold) and encouraged speculation that silver would replace gold as the nation's monetary standard (and thus undercut Treasury efforts to strengthen the stability of the nation's financial system). At times, this policy was the best that the silverites could obtain. At other times, when silver sentiment was stronger, it was the best that supporters of gold could hope for. At all times, silver purchases endangered the gold standard without cleanly demarcating the fundamental issues separating the two metals.

The fourth and last of the primary positions on the monetary standard was, of course, an open embrace of the gold standard. The resumption policy that produced the 1879 return to gold payments was in a sense an open endorsement of the gold standard but lacked a formal statutory declaration to that effect. In addition, resumption was accompanied by passage of the Bland-Allison Act, which, in 1878, mandated compulsory but limited silver coinage. The combination tended to qualify the impact of resumption as an endorsement of gold. Proposals to clearly endorse gold as the single monetary standard were quite rare and came to a vote only at the turn of the century. Like the silverites, gold supporters tended instead to camouflage their favorite in bimetallist clothing. In their case, the possibility of an international agreement on remonetizing silver was held out as a necessary precondition for bimetallism. If there were gold supporters who actually believed that the European powers, particularly Great Britain, would seriously entertain such a possibility, they were as rare as those silverites that honestly contended that the United States could, acting alone, peg the price of silver on the world market.[64]

In the Forty-eighth Congress, as usual, most of the debate was over the two middle policies, free silver and compulsory but limited silver coinage. Because the Committee on Coinage was openly hostile to gold, the only way a proposal for suspending silver purchases could come to the floor was by means of some extraordinary parliamentary maneuver. In

---

[64] When speaking in floor debate over repeal of the Sherman Silver Purchase Act, Leonidas Livingston, a Georgia Democrat, ridiculed the possibility that silver coinage might be resumed under an international agreement "with Germany, England, indeed with all Europe committed against silver and in favor of a single gold standard, they being creditor nations, we a borrowing nation, [such a proposal] is equivalent to 'going to hell for justice and the devil sitting as judge.'" *Congressional Record* 53:1:3064, November 1, 1893. On the unlikely prospects for European participation in an international bimetallic agreement, see *Appleton's 1881 Cyclopaedia*, pp. 287–289. Most economists and historians have maintained that international bimetallism, if ever viable, was politically impossible after the 1870s. See, for example, Marc Flandreau, "The French Crime of 1873: An Essay on the Emergence of the International Gold Standard, 1870–1880," *Journal of Economic History* 56:4 (December 1996): 890.

the actual event, the tactic chosen involved a motion to suspend the rules and pass a Sundry Civil Appropriations bill providing for expenditures in support of the World's Industrial and Cotton Exposition and, much more important, a suspension of silver coinage. The Exposition was to be held in New Orleans and, thus, would have provided at least some political cover for southern congressmen as they otherwise voted to suspend silver coinage, not a popular position in the region. As it turned out, almost 90 percent of southern congressmen opposed the bill. This motion required a two-thirds' majority and was thus simply a test of House sentiment – no one expected the measure to actually pass. In fact, the proposal failed to even produce a majority, confirming the position of the chamber as favoring continued silver purchases and coinage (see Table 6.8).[65] This vote was a great disappointment to the financial community, which had been hoping for at least a brief suspension of silver coinage before the end of the Forty-eighth Congress.[66] Just days after the vote, Cleveland was inaugurated, and while the financial community was very pleased by the new president's firm public declaration in favor of the gold standard, the *Commercial and Financial Chronicle* mused: "[W]hether the administration will be able to lead its party to adopt the same views, is (judging from the vote on suspending silver coinage), a question of some doubt...."[67]

The most serious challenge to the gold standard during the Forty-ninth Congress came early in 1886 when Richard Bland attempted to pass a free silver bill in the House of Representatives. Although a majority of the Committee on Coinage, Weights and Measures had adversely reported the bill, the committee had also instructed Bland, as the chair, to bring the bill to the floor.[68] This he did on March 16 when he offered a resolution to place

---

[65] The debate on this measure was very brief. *Congressional Record* 48:2:2209–2211, February 26, 1885.

[66] The *Commercial and Financial Chronicle* lamented that "the vote in Congress ... indicates that the financial policy of the United States is to be dictated for the present by the representatives from Texas, Missouri, Colorado, &c." February 28, 1885. For other commentary on the significance of this vote, see *Appleton's Annual Cyclopaedia of 1885* (New York: D. Appleton, 1889), pp. 246–250; Rhodes, *History of the United States*, vol. 8, pp. 255–256; Hepburn, *History of Currency*, p. 293.

[67] March 7, 1885. Cleveland's declaration came in a reply to a public request by almost a hundred western Democrats that he not announce his hostility to silver in his upcoming inaugural address. For the text, see Nevins, ed., *Letters of Grover Cleveland*, pp. 56–57. Also see Hepburn, *History of Currency*, p. 293; Morgan, *From Hayes to McKinley*, pp. 265–266.

[68] The New York *Nation* referred to the Missouri Democrat as a "financial lunatic" whose fervent advocacy of then very popular free silver proposals nonetheless compelled Speaker Carlisle to reappoint him as chairman of the Committee on Coinage at the beginning of the Forty-ninth Congress. The remainder of the committee was somewhat more conservative. Oberholtzer, *History of the United States*, vol. 4, p. 371.

the bill on the legislative docket as a special order. His motion easily secured the two-thirds' majority necessary under suspension of the rules and thus seemed to indicate a hefty majority for the bill itself, although there was substantial doubt that the membership would override an expected presidential vote if the free silver bill passed (see Table 6.8). The ensuing debate was long and bitter. In the end, the House first turned away a feeble attempt to suspend silver coinage before narrowly defeating the free silver measure (see Table 6.8).[69] Thus the status quo, continued purchase and coinage of two million dollars' worth of silver per month, remained in place.

The next move by the silverites was to attack the Treasury's gold reserve. Ever since resumption of the gold standard in 1879, the practice of the Treasury had been to maintain a reserve for the redemption of greenbacks of at least $100 million, often much more than that. While not large enough to redeem all greenbacks in circulation, this reserve still guaranteed that the United States could maintain gold payments against almost any emergency. What the size of the gold reserve should be was a matter of judgment, however, not fact. Those supporting the gold standard almost universally tended to place a high figure on an adequate reserve. Those supporting silver thought a much smaller reserve or none at all would be preferable. In the summer of 1886, the silverites in the House attempted to compel the Secretary of the Treasury to substantially reduce the gold reserve by spending any surplus over $100 million on government bonds eligible for redemption. At the time, the Treasury held some $200 million in gold as backing for the currency. Since the Democrats enjoyed a sizable majority in the House of Representatives and since the joint resolution ordering the reduction in the reserve had been reported favorably by the Ways and Means Committee, this was a measure for which the Democratic party was responsible. There was no surprise in the fact that a majority of that party would wish to trim the reserve since many of them would have been quite pleased to have abandoned gold payments entirely. However, with Cleveland in the White House and with the reserve under the entire discretionary control of the Treasury, the congressional Democrats were attempting to hamstring a friendly administration. And Cleveland himself left no doubt as to his opposition to the resolution.[70]

During floor debate, William McKinley of Ohio, the future victor in the great "Battle of the Standards" in 1896, sardonically commented on relations between the congressional and executive branches of the Democratic party:

[69] Also see Oberholtzer, *History of the United States*, vol. 4, p. 375. Both the vote on the amendment suspending coinage and the final one on passage of the free silver bill were included in McRae's 1900 list of "Votes on Coinage and Currency Legislation."

[70] *Congressional Record* 49:1:6878, July 13, 1886. Also see Cleveland's letter of July 14 to Samuel Randall, Nevins, ed., *Letters of Grover Cleveland*, pp. 115–116.

If this is a mere play of politics, if it is a mere play for position, you are welcome to it, gentlemen; when your own Secretary of the Treasury solemnly tells the chairman of the Committee on Ways and Means, in an official communication, that if this resolution passes it will impair the public credit, will shake public confidence, will destroy the good financial name which we have enjoyed so long, thanks to Republican fidelity, that it will leave no working balance for the great transactions of the Government, if that is any solace or comfort in your affliction we cheerfully grant it to you. . . . If there is anything upon which the majority of this House and the President are in accord, I would like to know it.[71]

When the resolution finally came to a vote, the nation was treated to an extremely rare spectacle in which a huge majority of Republicans backed a Democratic president over the opposition of an equally large majority of his fellow Democrats (see Table 6.9).[72]

The following December, the *Commercial and Financial Chronicle* said that Cleveland's annual message "about the white metal will have just as much influence on Congress as it will have on the inhabitant of the moon. . . ."[73] However, the fratricidal nature of the conflict over silver, combined with the realization that Cleveland could and would effectively veto any silver measure, convinced the Democratic leadership in the House that squelching inflationist proposals was the better part of party valor. As a consequence, no measure of any importance came to a vote during the entire life of the Fiftieth Congress. However, there is no reason to suppose that the balance between silver and gold sentiment in the membership had changed; quite the contrary, the positions held by members probably hardened over the last two years of Cleveland's administration.

In the 1888 general election, Benjamin Harrison narrowly defeated Cleveland and the Republicans returned to the White House. In the same election, Republican majorities were sent to both chambers of Congress and, for the first time since the end of Reconstruction, the Republicans controlled both the legislative and executive branches. Because the election had been primarily fought over the tariff, these partisan majorities were predictably decisive with respect to trade; in 1890, Congress enacted and the new

---

[71] *Congressional Record* 49:1:6935, July 14, 1886.
[72] For House debate on the resolution, see *Congressional Record* 49:1:6877–6888, 6921–6946, 7983–8005, July 13–14, August 4, 1886. The vote included in Table 6.9 was taken on a motion to recommit the resolution with instructions to add a section providing clear statutory authority for a gold reserve of $100 million. That motion was rejected and the resolution was then adopted by an overwhelming margin (207–67). On the latter vote, many Republicans abandoned Cleveland's position, although almost half still stood by the administration. Cleveland's support from the Democratic majority remained under 10 percent of those voting. Although the Senate later made the resolution more palatable to gold advocates, Cleveland nevertheless pocket-vetoed the bill. *Commercial and Financial Chronicle*, August 7, 1886. Also see Oberholtzer, *History of the United States*, vol. 4, p. 376.
[73] December 4, 1886.

Table 6.9. *Members Supporting the Gold Standard in the 49th and 51st Congresses, 1885–1887 and 1889–1891 (%)*

House membership category	Free silver resolution (1886)	Free silver (1886)	Gold reserve (1886)	Free silver (1890:A)	Free silver (1890:B)
Full House	32.7 (266)	56.4 (289)	43.6 (273)	54.7 (256)	53.0 (287)
Republicans	60.7 (117)	75.6 (123)	91.4 (116)	90.1 (141)	85.5 (152)
Democrats	10.2 (147)	42.1 (164)	7.7 (155)	11.4 (114)	16.4 (134)
Other party	50.0 (2)	50.0 (2)	50.0 (2)	0.0 (1)	0.0 (1)
District level of development					
All members					
Highest	69.2 (52)	91.8 (49)	76.6 (47)	94.3 (35)	94.0 (50)
Middle high	43.6 (55)	72.6 (62)	61.4 (57)	69.4 (62)	73.3 (60)
Middle low	23.1 (108)	45.0 (120)	40.2 (112)	52.8 (106)	46.2 (119)
Lowest	3.9 (51)	32.8 (58)	5.3 (57)	15.1 (53)	10.3 (58)
Republicans					
Highest	89.3 (28)	100.0 (21)	100.0 (24)	100.0 (28)	100.0 (32)
Middle high	63.9 (36)	80.5 (41)	94.6 (37)	88.9 (45)	88.9 (45)
Middle low	44.9 (49)	64.9 (57)	86.5 (52)	87.1 (62)	77.9 (68)
Lowest	25.0 (4)	50.0 (4)	66.7 (3)	83.3 (6)	71.4 (7)
Democrats					
Highest	43.5 (23)	85.2 (27)	50.0 (22)	71.4 (7)	83.3 (18)
Middle high	5.3 (19)	57.1 (21)	0.0 (20)	17.6 (17)	26.7 (15)
Middle low	5.2 (58)	27.4 (62)	0.0 (59)	4.5 (44)	3.9 (51)
Lowest	2.1 (47)	31.5 (54)	1.9 (54)	6.5 (46)	2.0 (50)
Sectional stress	51.7	56.3	50.4	62.1	65.9

Note and sources: The roll-call position that accorded with support for the gold standard is indicated in parentheses: on adoption of a resolution providing for the consideration of a free silver bill (nay); on passage of the free silver bill (nay); on adoption of an amendment supporting maintenance of the gold reserve (yea); on a motion to recommit with instructions to report a free silver bill (nay); and on adoption of an amendment to provide for the free coinage of silver (nay). The roll calls are in the *Congressional Record* 49:1:2418–2419, March 16, 1886, 49:1:3300–3301, April 8, 1886; 49:1:6945, July 14, 1886; 51:1:5813–5814, June 7, 1890; 51:1:6503–6504, June 25, 1890.

president signed the heavily protectionist McKinley Tariff. In terms of monetary policy, however, Republican control of the machinery of government was as nominal and confused as it had been under the Democrats and Cleveland. Strengthened by an influx of new members from the recently admitted states of Idaho, Montana, North Dakota, South Dakota, Washington, and Wyoming, the silver forces now enjoyed a clear majority in the Senate. Free silver proposals would have probably passed the chamber with ease had Harrison been willing to sign them. On occasion silver senators passed them anyway so that no outside observer could mistake their position. In the House of Representatives, the admission of the new but sparsely populated western states made little difference. Sentiment in that chamber remained about where it had been under Cleveland, favorable to continued coinage but marginally opposed to free silver.[74] Had the Senate been in a position to insist on free silver, the House may have well capitulated. But Harrison's hostility made insistence pointless.

While the situation was discouraging for silverites, it was still fraught with danger for hard-money Republicans. As a way of "doing something for silver," as the phrase went, the party leadership proposed to increase the government's purchases of silver by replacing the two-million-dollar compulsory monthly quota under the Bland-Allison Act with a new, equally compulsory quota to be fixed in terms of ounces of silver.[75] With its much more structured parliamentary organization, the House of Representatives was able to move first. On June 5, under a harsh whip, the Republicans passed a special order providing for consideration of the bill by one vote.[76] When the measure subsequently came to the floor, the Republican representative from Nevada called the measure a continuation of the "great battle of the standards" that "has agitated the public mind for some fifteen or twenty years."[77]

In one of the most articulate floor speeches of the period, Horace Bartine then dismissed charges that a silver standard would "Mexicanize the

---

[74] On silver sentiment in Congress, see Rhodes, *History of the United States*, vol. 8, p. 355; Sherman, *Recollections of Forty Years*, pp. 827–828; Hepburn, *History of Currency*, pp. 300–301.

[75] As an example of the ubiquitous use of the phrase, see "Can the United States Alone Do Anything for Silver?," in the *Commercial and Financial Chronicle*, February 21, 1891.

[76] The roll call, as officially recorded, exhibited a three-vote margin because one Democratic member changed his vote from "Nay" to "Yea" after the first roll call revealed that the resolution would pass. By changing his vote, that member was then in a position, under parliamentary rules, to move to reconsider, thus testing Republican strength a second time. The motion to reconsider was tabled (killed) by a six-vote margin. *Congressional Record* 51:1:5645–5653, June 5, 1890.

[77] *Congressional Record* 51:1:5791, June 7, 1890. This may have been one of the first public appearances of the phrase later made famous as a description of the Bryan-McKinley presidential contest in 1896.

country" or place the United States on the "Chinese level." Instead, the Nevada congressman insisted, "people seem to forget that we are no longer in a dependent colonial position" and should no longer wish "to occupy the proud position of a golden tag on the tail of [England's] financial kite." Then addressing the Republican commitment to trade protection, Bartine noted that his colleagues often soared "aloft in a flight of inspired eloquence denunciatory of the free-trade dogmas of England, as enunciated through that pernicious Cobden Club literature, and at the same time [swallowed] the financial nostrums with as keen a relish as if they were chocolate caramels or homeopathic pills." The result of this obsequious policy, Bartine argued, could be seen throughout his section. "In every gulch and upon every mountain-side throughout our great Western mineral belt we may behold in the abandoned shafts, tunnels, and prospect holes and in the ruins of deserted towns the most conclusive evidence of wrecked fortunes and blasted hopes." Directing his attention then to eastern members of his party, he complained that

since taking my seat upon this floor it has frequently been said to me, "Why, of course you far Western people are all for free coinage; you want a market for your silver," the tone implying that we stand upon just about the same equitable plain as if we were demanding the free coinage of galvanized iron. . . . We who live in the wilds of the far West buy the iron and steel of Pennsylvania, the cotton and woolen goods of Massachusetts, the clocks and wooden nutmegs of Connecticut, and all the highly protected products of the Empire State. In every political campaign we march shoulder to shoulder with you in the great battle for protection to American industry, but when we ask you to do justice by our silver – a product upon which our very existence depends – you shrink from us as if we were unclean things. . . . the advocate of the silver dollar is regarded as a sort of cross between a bandit and a three-card-monte dealer – a man wholly without conscience, and whose noblest ambition is to rob the unsophisticated money-lender of New York and New England.[78]

Under the special order, there was only one opportunity for the opposition to offer a free silver alternative to the bill. This arose just before passage when Richard Bland of Missouri proposed to recommit the bill to the Committee on Coinage, Weights and Measures, "with instructions to report back a bill for the free coinage of silver." The House turned back this motion by a narrow but comfortable margin of twenty-four votes (see Table 6.9) and sent the bill on to the Senate.[79] When the bill came back to the House, the Senate had transformed it into a free silver measure.[80] When the

---

[78] *Congressional Record* 51:1:5796–5798, June 7, 1890.
[79] Hepburn, *History of Currency*, p. 302. This vote was included in McRae's 1900 list of "Votes on Coinage and Currency Legislation."
[80] For the legislative history of the Sherman Silver Purchase Act, see Sherman, *Recollections of Forty Years*, pp. 822–831; Morgan, *From Hayes to McKinley*, pp. 343–345; Oberholtzer, *History of the United States*, vol. 5, pp. 112–116.

Republican Speaker attempted to refer the amended bill to the Committee on Coinage, Weights and Measures, the free silver members appealed his decision and subsequently embroiled the chamber in a volatile mixture of arcane distinctions of parliamentary law and broad issues of monetary policy. Although this debate was one of the most intense and prolonged contests over a parliamentary ruling in the history of House, almost all members ultimately made their position on free silver the decisive factor in deciding whether or not to support the Speaker's decision.[81] When the Senate amendment finally came to a vote, the House of Representatives turned down free silver for a second time, although the margin was a little narrower (see Table 6.9).[82] In the end, after a conference committee had crafted a compromise, what became known as the Sherman Silver Purchase Act passed both chambers. This law changed the compulsory monthly quota from two million dollars' worth of silver to four and a half million ounces of silver.[83] At prevailing market prices, the act increased the minimum amount of silver that the Treasury was compelled to purchase by over 50 percent, thus substantially increasing the risk associated with the policy. The Republican leadership in Congress supported this increase only because free silver might have been the result had the party chose to resist all silver legislation. Sherman himself said later:

> The situation at that time was critical. A large majority of the Senate favored free silver, and it was feared that the small majority against it in the other House might yield and agree to it. The silence of the president on the matter gave rise to an apprehension that if a free coinage bill should pass both Houses he would not feel at liberty to veto it. Some action had to be taken to prevent a return to free silver coinage, and the measure evolved was the best obtainable. I voted for it, but the day it became a law I was ready to repeal it, if repeal could be had without substituting in its place absolute free coinage.[84]

In the middle of January 1891, about one and a half months into last session of the Fifty-first Congress, the Senate again passed a free silver bill and sent it on to the House. The financial markets reacted, predictably, with declines in the stock market and the American dollar, the latter bringing the United States very close to the exporting point for gold in a season during which the nation usually imported the metal.

The Senate was still favorable to free silver as the new Fifty-second Congress organized for business; for its part, the House of Representatives was

[81]   For the debate over the Speaker's referral, see *Congressional Record* 51:1: 6261–6285, 6310–6324, 6352–6365, June 19–21, 1890.
[82]   *Appleton's Annual Cyclopaedia of 1890* (New York: D. Appleton, 1891), p. 233; Hepburn, *History of Currency*, p. 303. This vote was included in McRae's 1900 list of "Votes on Coinage and Currency Legislation."
[83]   Kirkland, *Industry Comes of Age*, pp. 38–39.
[84]   Sherman, *Recollections of Forty Years*, pp. 829–830.

only marginally opposed to unlimited coinage. With the Republicans slightly weaker in the Senate and utterly decimated in the House as a result of the Democratic landslide in the 1890 election, only President Harrison stood between the nation and abandonment of the gold standard. His public commitment to gold, however, would produce vetoes.[85] While, as the election returns demonstrated, the Sherman Silver Purchase Act had not provided much political cover for representatives who opposed free silver, it was still in force and silver purchases were continuing at the increased rate mandated under the law. Although dangerous, this status quo seemed the best that could be hoped for by gold advocates. As the *Commercial and Financial Chronicle* noted, "there is a new force working in the United States which cannot be ignored in any currency discussion now-a-days, and which will of necessity have a share in shaping a new system. What we refer to is to be found embodied in Farmers' Alliances and in their demands for currency issues – demands that are not without reason, for they have their origin in the changed condition which our Western and Southern country has entered into in the last ten years." However, the journal disputed the belief held by the Farmers' Alliances that free silver would alleviate the currency shortage in remote sections of the nation.[86] The *Chronicle* noted that "London at present is about six days off from New York by steam and six minutes by cable. The two financial centres are therefore next-door neighbors. More than that, commerce has made them one, tying them together so closely that the floating capital of London cannot help moving to New York when by so doing it secures the opportunity to earn more than it can earn staying at home." But the silver crusade, the journal feared, was

---

[85] *Commercial and Financial Chronicle*, August 22, 1891.
[86] December 6, 1890. Also see "Our Currency and Farmers' Needs," ibid., November 29, 1890. After a long disquisition on the limits to currency inflation under a silver standard, the journal asked, "Does it not follow from what has been said that an inflation of the currency would be impossible with *free* coinage? We leave this last question for our friends in the Farmers' Alliances, who write us so many letters, to answer." January 17, 1891. At this time the *Chronicle* was the leading national source of supply and price information on commodity markets and thus widely read in small market towns and villages throughout the nation. Whether or not the hard-money views and opinions the journal expressed led many of these readers to cancel their subscriptions was never reported, but the *Chronicle* consistently treated the heretical proposals of the Farmers' Alliances with more courtesy than those made by Democratic politicians such as Representative Richard Bland of Missouri or Senator James Beck of Kentucky. When "Sockless" Jerry Simpson, a newly elected Populist representative from Kansas, outlined his unorthodox views in an interview with a New York newspaper, the *Chronicle* reported that he "appears to be a man of much more intelligence than has been represented . . . he is really a man of thought, of observation and of ideas. Of course his opinions on financial subjects are not of Eastern growth, and in good part would not be acceptable to people in this neighborhood; but we notice that he always has a reason for the remedial legislation he proposes. . . ." March 14, 1891.

rapidly unraveling these closely intertwined financial markets. One symptom was the new practice, then one or two years old, of including a gold clause for the payment of principal and interest in all loan contracts. Such clauses insulated the lender from the inflationary impact of a possible switch from gold to a silver standard. Reflecting the apprehension of foreign financiers that abandonment of the gold standard was more than a remote possibility, the appearance of these clauses in loan contracts had become mandatory; without them, American borrowers simply could not draw upon European capital.[87]

When the Fifty-second Congress convened, the Democrats controlled more than 70 percent of the seats in the House of Representatives. While most Democrats were strong supporters of free silver, northeastern delegations were willing to defy their party's leadership in order to defend the gold standard. This marked the beginning of what became a party-rending struggle. As George Williams of Massachusetts put it, "a day of reckoning . . . will come to those Democrats who are trying to make a Farmers' Alliance party out of the Democratic party; but let me assure you that you have got to decide between one of two things – either the Farmers' Alliance of the South or a Democratic alliance with the North."[88] Williams addressed the House during debate over a special order bringing to the floor a free silver bill. When the bill was considered in its own right, the proceedings attending the roll calls on procedural motions demonstrated a very close balance in the chamber between those favoring and those opposing free silver.[89] On one of the roll calls, for instance, the Speaker first reported to the House that a motion to reconsider had been lost in a tie vote, 148 on each side of the question. However, the chamber was so chaotic that the Speaker agreed to a recapitulation of the vote which, to the immense consternation of the silver bloc, revealed a slight majority favoring the motion (for an analysis of this vote, see Table 6.10). Both motions were directed at an original proposal to table the free silver bill which had been defeated by a single vote. Because, under the special order, the bill had to be passed that day, the silver bloc with the assistance of the Speaker kept the House

---

[87] *Commercial and Financial Chronicle*, August 23, 1890. The first references to these gold clauses in the *Chronicle* appeared in the spring of 1889 when they were described as "a recent feature in time contracts." May 25, 1889. Also see "Features of New Railroad Mortgages" in the September 1889 number of the *Investors' Supplement* to the *Chronicle*.

[88] *Congressional Record* 52:1:1830, March 7, 1892.

[89] One of these roll calls was included in McRae's 1900 list of "Votes on Coinage and Currency Legislation." The same vote was described as an early "the test of strength" between the silver and gold forces in *Appleton's Annual Cyclopaedia of 1892* (New York: D. Appleton, 1893), pp. 207–208. A slightly different roll call the same day was chosen for analysis in Table 6.10. That roll call was recorded under conditions of even greater stress than the vote listed by McRae and described in the *Cyclopaedia*.

Table 6.10. Members Supporting the Gold Standard in the 52nd and 53rd Congresses, 1891–1893 and 1893–1895 (%)

House membership category	Table free silver (1892)	Senate free silver (1892)	Free silver amendment (1893)	Repeal silver purchase (1893:A)	Repeal silver purchase (1893:B)
Full House	50.3 (298)	53.1 (290)	64.4 (351)	68.9 (347)	67.4 (288)
Republicans	87.0 (77)	87.0 (69)	89.7 (126)	80.8 (125)	79.5 (88)
Democrats	39.0 (213)	44.1 (213)	52.6 (211)	64.9 (208)	64.4 (188)
Other party	0.0 (8)	0.0 (8)	14.3 (14)	21.4 (14)	25.0 (12)
District level of development					
All members					
Highest	92.0 (50)	96.1 (51)	100.0 (59)	100.0 (59)	100.0 (54)
Middle high	73.8 (65)	81.0 (63)	83.5 (85)	83.1 (83)	82.4 (68)
Middle low	40.6 (128)	38.4 (125)	58.3 (139)	65.9 (138)	63.9 (108)
Lowest	7.3 (55)	11.8 (51)	22.1 (68)	29.9 (67)	25.9 (58)
Republicans					
Highest	100.0 (13)	100.0 (14)	100.0 (20)	100.0 (20)	100.0 (16)
Middle high	93.1 (29)	88.9 (27)	94.0 (50)	85.7 (49)	86.1 (36)
Middle low	78.8 (33)	84.0 (25)	83.0 (53)	71.7 (53)	64.7 (34)
Lowest	50.0 (2)	33.3 (3)	75.0 (3)	33.3 (3)	50.0 (2)
Democrats					
Highest	89.2 (37)	94.6 (37)	100.0 (37)	100.0 (37)	100.0 (36)
Middle high	58.3 (36)	75.0 (36)	75.0 (32)	83.9 (31)	82.8 (29)
Middle low	29.9 (87)	29.3 (92)	47.4 (78)	68.8 (77)	70.1 (67)
Lowest	5.7 (53)	10.4 (48)	20.3 (64)	30.2 (63)	25.0 (56)
Sectional stress	70.9	65.4	56.0	48.1	55.3

Note and sources: The roll-call position that accorded with support for the gold standard is indicated in parentheses: on a motion to reconsider a motion to table the free silver bill (yea); on adoption of the Bland free silver amendment to the bill to repeal the silver purchase act (nay); on passage of the Senate free silver bill (nay); on passage of the repeal of the silver purchase act (yea); and on concurring in the Senate amendment to the repeal of the silver purchase act (yea). The roll calls can be found in the Congressional Record 52:1:2546, March 24, 1892; 52:1:6133, July 13, 1892; 53:1:1004, August 28, 1893; 53:1:1008, August 28, 1893; and 53:1:3066–3067, November 1, 1893.

in session late into the night despite the very close balance within the membership and despite the intensity of the contest. At one point, the Speaker even directed that the Sergeant-at-Arms impose order by carrying the mace around the chamber as members retook their seats.[90] Ultimately, so many members left the hall from sheer exhaustion that the leadership allowed the House to adjourn and the bill was lost.[91]

Because a solid majority in the Senate favored free silver, attention then turned to the upper chamber.[92] After the Senate passed its own free silver bill, the House prepared to take up the issue once more. Although this occurred at about the same time as the violence between Pinkerton agents and strikers at the Carnegie plant in Homestead, Pennsylvania – one of the most important events in American labor history – the *Commercial and Financial Chronicle* reported that "efforts made in the House of Representatives to hasten to a vote the Senate Free Coinage bill . . . [had] proved a much more disturbing influence in business circles."[93] The Senate bill arrived back in the House just three weeks after the Democratic national convention had adopted a money plank that fell far short of immediate and unqualified free silver coinage. Citing the inconsistency between the policy advocated in the national party platform and the Senate bill, several Democrats now changed their positions.[94] The chamber then defeated the Senate free silver measure by a margin slightly greater than it had some four months earlier (see Table 6.10).[95] When Congress finally adjourned a few weeks later, the *Commercial and Financial Chronicle* gave a great sigh of relief: "a kind of restful feeling will no doubt pervade trade circles when our Government legislators are actually homeward bound, for a more irritating legislative body, threatening so many industrial interests by its proposed laws, never within our memory held its sittings at Washington. . . ."[96]

With respect to their announced positions on monetary policy, the finan-

---

[90] *Congressional Record* 52:1:2549, March 24, 1892.
[91] The *Commercial and Financial Chronicle* hailed defeat of the bill but apparently misinterpreted the parliamentary situation that produced this outcome. Because of the confused nature of the proceedings, the *Chronicle* focused on the tie vote on the original motion to table the bill as decisive when, in fact, the silver forces prevailed in that vote (ties defeat a motion). March 26, 1892.
[92] Ibid., April 2, June 4, July 2, 1892. Sherman, *Recollections of Forty Years*, pp. 893–895.
[93] July 9, 1892.
[94] See the debate in *Congressional Record* 52:1:6128–6129, July 13, 1892.
[95] Also see *Appleton's 1892 Cyclopaedia*, p. 208; Hepburn, *History of Currency*, p. 345; and Rhodes, *History of the United States*, vol. 8, p. 383. The roll call was included in McRae's 1900 list of "Votes on Coinage and Currency Legislation." The *Commercial and Financial Chronicle*, as a matter of course, praised the outcome. July 16, 1892.
[96] August 6, 1892.

cial community was satisfied with both Harrison and Cleveland as the major party nominees. For its part, the *Commercial and Financial Chronicle* stated that "there was no great financial question involved" in the national Republican convention, and that, as the party's nominee, "there is probably as much confidence in President Harrison's soundness on financial matters as there is in any other person" who might have been a candidate. Two weeks later the journal similarly reported that the "nomination of Mr. Cleveland for President had a favorable effect on the market, because of Mr. Cleveland's known sound views on financial questions."[97]

Despite the relatively placid campaign, at least from the financial community's perspective, both the economy and the monetary position of the nation were rapidly weakening under the operation of the Sherman Silver Purchase Act. Sensing the growing uncertainty of gold payments by the United States, European investors had been repatriating American securities for some time, more rapidly during the progress of silver measures through Congress and with less alacrity when Congress was out of session.[98] But, almost always, the flow of capital and gold was out of the United States back toward Europe. The hypothetical possibility that drove this movement had as its central element a scarcity of gold as backing for bank reserves and the redemption of government securities. The possible impact of a subsequent run on these dwindling reserves was described by the London *Statist* in its July 23 number, issued days after the House had rejected the Senate free silver bill:

to begin with there must be a run firstly upon the banks and secondly upon the Treasury for gold. The metal must be hoarded and must go to a premium. All that would imply such a state of panic as could hardly fail to result in disaster. . . . The crisis upon the stock Exchange . . . would be very serious, because as we have been showing, Europe has been clearing out its American investments for fully two years now. It shows no inclination to take them back, and the inclination would not be increased if a crisis were to come. Of course *at a price* Europeans would buy; but then who can say beforehand what the price would be? . . .

[97] June 11, 25, 1892. Toward the end of the campaign, the *Chronicle* said that "the country has seldom, if ever, engaged in a Presidential contest with less interruption to business occurring. . . ." October 29, 1892. Somewhat surprisingly, the *Chronicle* paid almost no attention during the campaign to the Populist platform or ticket, although they were clearly, from the journal's perspective, thoroughly unsound on monetary issues. In its lengthy commentary on "The Election and Its Industrial Results," for example, the journal did not once, even in passing, mention the Populist campaign. November 12, 1892.

[98] The *Commercial and Financial Chronicle* frequently connected congressional proceedings on monetary policy to the movement of gold into and out of the United States, as well as the temper of financial markets generally. See, for example, July 2, 9, 1892. On the larger impact of financial uncertainty on general economic conditions, see "Effect on the Price of Cotton of a Free Inflow of Capital," August 20, 1892.

[S]ince the middle of 1890 the withdrawals of capital employed in the United States by great houses and the sales of securities by European holders have been on such a scale that the United States have had to remit *immense amounts* of gold. ... It follows ... very clearly that everywhere throughout the Union the banks are practically boycotting silver and are increasing to the utmost of their power their gold holdings.[99]

As can be seen in the annual figures presented in Table 6.11, the financial uncertainty associated with the movement toward a silver standard provoked the most prolonged and severe export of gold from the United States during the late nineteenth century.[100] As a major gold-producing nation, the United States always enjoyed a privileged position; even in most years when gold exports exceeded imports, the United States was usually able to add to its domestic stock through additions from mining activity. Aside from gold production from mines, which was comparatively stable over the period, the net movement of gold was remarkably responsive to the ebb and flow of monetary politics. Resumption of gold payments in 1879, for example, eliminated a major source of financial uncertainty and was followed within a year or so by a vast influx of bullion from Europe. This movement was exceeded only by the flow of gold toward the United States that followed McKinley's victory in the 1896 presidential election, a similarly stabilizing political factor in monetary policy. On the other hand, the onset of renewed silver agitation in 1889 was followed by six more years of adverse gold movements.[101] In fact, between 1889 and 1895, when silver sentiment clearly and consistently dominated Congress, the outflow of gold was so great as to entirely counterbalance all additions from mining. And since the United States consistently exported more products than it imported, Europeans paid for this gold by repatriating American securities and thus reclaimed prior capital investment in the United States. These developments had the twin results of throwing the nation into what became a prolonged depression and threatening the stability of the financial system (by draining the banking system and the Treasury of gold reserves).

Underlying both economic depression and financial insecurity were the continuing purchases of silver; compelled by law, the Treasury bought millions of ounces even though the federal budget was now deeply in the red. Thus draining the gold reserve, silver purchases had an obvious and direct impact on the ability of the Treasury to maintain gold payments. In

[99]   Quoted in ibid., August 6, 1892.
[100]   For similar data and a graph of net gold flows into and out of the United States, see Jeffrey G. Williamson, *American Growth and the Balance of Payments, 1820–1913: A Study of the Long Swing* (Chapel Hill: University of North Carolina Press, 1964), pp. 165–166.
[101]   "Gold Imports and the Currency," *Commercial and Financial Chronicle*, October 17, 1896.

Table 6.11. *Annual Production, Exports, and Imports of Gold,*
1877–1900

Year	Exports	Imports	Production	Net addition to or subtraction from national supply
1877	27	26	42	+41
1878	9	13	36	+40
1879	5	6	34	+35
1880	4	81	31	+108
1881	3	100	29	+126
1882	33	34	28	+29
1883	12	18	27	+33
1884	41	23	24	+6
1885	8	27	25	+44
1886	43	21	29	+7
1887	10	43	32	+65
1888	18	44	29	+55
1889	60	10	32	−18
1890	17	13	29	+25
1891	86	18	31	−37
1892	50	50	31	+31
1893	109	21	33	−55
1894	77	72	39	+34
1895	66	36	47	+17
1896	112	34	51	−27
1897	40	85	54	+99
1898	15	120	59	+164
1899	38	89	62	+113
1900	48	45	66	+63
Total				+998

Source: Includes both coin and bullion, in millions of dollars. The ounces reported in this source were multiplied by their dollar value under the gold standard ($20.6718). For gold imports into and exports from the United States, see *Historical Statistics of the United States, Colonial Times to 1970* (Washington, D.C.: GPO, 1975), pt. 2, series U 187–200, p. 885. For gold production by year from 1877 to 1900, see Orris C. Herfindahl, "Development of the Major Metal Mining Industries in the United States from 1839 to 1909," in National Bureau of Economic Research, *Output, Employment, and Productivity in the United States after 1860* (New York: Columbia University Press, 1966), pp. 323–324.

this situation, abandonment of the gold standard could be averted only if the government were able to successfully float new bond issues that, in practice, allowed the Treasury to balance its spending and revenue accounts. But the success of such bond issues, in turn, depended on investor confidence that the government would be in a position to honor the commitments as to interest and principal that they entailed. Since these commitments had to be made in terms of gold and since these bond issues were, in effect, public admissions of extreme stress in the Treasury's gold reserve, the Treasury was between the proverbial rock and a hard place. If it maintained a stiff upper lip by refusing to enter the bond market, the gold reserve would continue to decline. If it issued bonds, the admission of weakness in the Treasury's position might undercut whatever confidence investors still had, thus stimulating such a run on the remaining reserve as to entirely counterbalance whatever benefit might be gained by floating the bonds. The Gordian knot was, of course, the silver purchase law and its repeal, long a goal of the financial community, thus assumed new and increasing urgency.[102]

On the western plains, the monetary depression of the early 1890s became intertwined with the collapse of the land boom of the late 1880s in a way that made the unwinding of bad real estate investments all but impossible. Kansas may have been the most distressed of the states west of Mississippi. Although many of the state's some 400 banks possessed seriously impaired assets, the Kansas bank commissioner permitted them to continue operation: the "problem was not what banks should be closed but how to prevent a stampede of creditors which would wipe out half the banks in the state." By the end of October 1893, however, the commissioner estimated that banks in Kansas had lost half of all the deposits they had held the previous April. In all, forty-one banks, approximately one in ten of those that had operated at the beginning of the year, went into involuntary liquidation during 1893. Although this was by far the worst period, banks and mortgage companies weakened by the crisis continued to fail in 1894 and even later. But the frequency of failures and the gravity of the threat to the state's financial system clearly peaked just before Congress, under Cleveland's strong leadership, repealed the Sherman Silver Purchase Act.[103]

---

[102] See, for example, ibid., October 8, December 24, 31, 1892; January 21, 28, February 11, 18, March 11, May 27, 1893, and, in particular, "Gold Shipments – The Responsibility Rests with Congress," December 17, 1892.

[103] Jennie Small Owen and Kirke Mechem, eds., *The Annals of Kansas, 1886–1925* (Topeka: Kansas State Historical Society, n.d.), vol. 1, pp. 82, 83, 112, 116, 117, 119, 123, 149, 150, 153, 154, 155, 158, 160–161, 176, 178, 183, 209, 235, 238, 273, 279, 292. In Colorado, like Kansas, the banking system similarly teetered on the edge of complete disintegration during the last part of July. R. G. Dill, *The Political Campaigns of Colorado* (Denver: Arapahoe Publishing, 1895), pp. 216–217. In

The general elections in 1892 had given, for the first time since the outbreak of the Civil War, the Democrats control of both chambers of Congress and the presidency. Early readings of congressional sentiment, taken just after the election, strongly suggested a free silver majority in the Senate and a possible one in the House.[104] In the period intervening between the election and Cleveland's inauguration, Congress conducted a lame-duck session in which repeal of the silver purchase law failed to pass the House.[105] During debate on this proposal, William Jennings Bryan, then a Democratic congressman from Nebraska, clearly laid out the rather peculiar attitude of the free silver members toward the Sherman Silver Purchase Act, as well as the depth of hostility to gold on the western plains:

The Sherman law is the child of the opponents of free coinage. But they have given it to us, and we will hold it as hostage until they return to us our own child, "the gold and silver coinage of the Constitution." [Loud applause.] They kidnapped it twenty years ago, and we shall hold their child, ugly and deformed as it is, until they bring ours back or give us something better than the makeshift which we now have. . . . If we who represent them consent to rob our people, the cotton-growers of the South and the wheat-growers of the West, we will be criminals whose guilt cannot be measured by words, for we will bring distress and disaster to our people. In many cases such a vote would simply be a summons to the sheriff to take possession of their property. [Loud applause.][106]

As Bryan implied, the continuation of silver purchases during this period carried with it the strong probability that gold payments would have to be abandoned in the near future. Never at any point during the late twentieth century was compulsory but limited silver purchase so obviously the back door through which the gold standard would be expunged from the nation's financial system.

Cleveland entered the White House in March 1893, just as the financial crisis brought on by the nation's silver policy was working its worst havoc on the economy. In response, commercial associations in the nation's heartland began to call for an end to silver purchases, joining by the end of May

the nation as a whole, almost 600 banks were forced to close during 1893. Kleppner, *Continuity and Change*, pp. 97–98. For a day-by-day listing of important events of the year, from which the progress of the panic can be traced in market disturbances and bank suspensions, see *Appleton's 1893 Cyclopaedia*, pp. 286–293. For a good, summary history of the silver crisis, see "Is It the Balance of Trade or the Silver Law?," *Commercial and Financial Chronicle*, August 5, 1893.

[104] *Mercantile and Financial Times: Devoted to Money, Finance, Insurance, and the Commercial Interest of the United States* 12:78 (December 24, 1892): 7.

[105] The special order that would have allowed the House to take up the bill was recommitted to the Committee on Rules without instructions, a motion that had almost the same effect as tabling the proposal. The division was not close, 150 favoring recommittal and 83 opposed. *Congressional Record* 52:2:1382–1383, February 9, 1893. Also see *Appleton's 1893 Cyclopaedia*, pp. 207–209.

[106] *Congressional Record* 52:2:1380, February 9, 1893.

what had been the long held position of their eastern counterparts.[107] At the end of June Cleveland called Congress into special session and, after the House and Senate had organized in early August, issued a strong demand for the "prompt repeal" of the Sherman Silver Purchase Act. With Treasury gold reserves dropping through the $100 million dollar mark, the imminent abandonment of gold was blamed by the new administration for the collapsing economy.[108] Wielding every political club and blandishing every favor that his position as president and party leader provided him, aided by the suffering of millions of people caused by the financial crisis, Cleveland expeditiously worked repeal through both chambers of Congress. The president's use of the patronage, in particular, changed many free silver Democrats into administration loyalists, thus transforming substantial soft-money majorities in both chambers into narrow hard-money victories on official votes.[109] The measure passed the House on August 28 and the Senate on October 30.[110]

In the House of Representatives, silver advocates led by Richard Bland of Missouri attempted to amend the repeal measure by attaching a free coinage amendment. If adopted, the effect of the amendment would have been simultaneously to repeal the Sherman Silver Purchase Act and to open the doors to unrestricted coinage. The influence of the president's lobbying efforts were clearly evident in the almost two to one majority recorded against free silver (see Table 6.10). Later the same day, August 28, 1893, the repeal bill passed the House by an even larger majority. The Senate subsequently amended this bill and sent it back to the House where the Senate amendment was concurred in by a majority of over two to one.[111] Ninety minutes later Cleveland signed the bill into law.[112] Floor debate on the latter

---

[107] These public resolutions and declarations were warmly welcomed by the *Commercial and Financial Chronicle*. May 27, June 10, 17, 24, 1893.

[108] The gold reserve appears to have dropped below $100 million for the first time on April 25. After that, the reserve moved back up to the mark in May only to go below a $100 million once more early in June. Ibid., April 22, May 6, June 3, 1893.

[109] In a letter written August 20, 1893, Cleveland urged delay on appointments to office of those recommended by "Senators who are inclined to be mean, as well as opposed to what we want [and] especially desire . . . we ought not to incur too much fatigue in our efforts to gratify at this time those who bitterly oppose our political attempts to help the country and save our party." Nevins, ed., *Letters of Grover Cleveland*, p. 331. On application of the patronage in the Senate by Cleveland, where free silver sentiment was stronger than in the House, see Rhodes, *History of the United States*, vol. 8, pp. 403–404, 412.

[110] Kleppner, *Continuity and Change*, pp. 99–100. For legislative histories of the repeal bill, see Sherman, *Recollections of Forty Years*, pp. 919–929; Oberholtzer, *History of the United States*, vol. 5, pp. 254–272; *Appleton's 1893 Cyclopaedia*, pp. 226–244; Morgan, *From Hayes to McKinley*, pp. 447–460.

[111] This vote was included in McRae's 1900 list of "Votes on Coinage and Currency Legislation."

[112] *Commercial and Financial Chronicle*, November 4, 1893.

was comparatively unremarkable except for two addresses by Bryan, the first of which foreshadowed in some ways his "Cross of Gold" speech to the 1896 Democratic national convention:

> So far as the laborer has been heard from, he has denounced unconditional repeal; so far as the farmer has been heard from he has denounced unconditional repeal. Who gave the Eastern capitalists the right to speak for these men[?] It is a contest between the producers of wealth and those who exchange or absorb it. We have heard a great deal about business interests and business men demanding repeal. Who are the business men? Are not those entitled to that name who are engaged in the production of the necessaries of life? Is the farmer less a business man than the broker, because the former spends three hundred and sixty-five days in producing a crop which will not bring him over a dollar a day for his labor, while the latter can make ten times the farmer's annual income in one successful bet on the future price of the farmer's product? I protest, Mr. Speaker, against the use of the name business men in such a way as to exclude the largest and most valuable class of business men in the country.

In the second, much shorter speech, Bryan concluded general debate on repeal with this passage comparing repeal to the crucifixion and silver to Christ:

> You may think that you have buried the cause of bimetallism; you may congratulate yourselves that you have laid the free coinage of silver away in a sepulchre, newly made since the election, and before the door rolled the veto stone. But, sirs, if our cause is just, as I believe it is, your labor has been in vain; no tomb was ever made so strong that it could imprison a righteous cause. Silver will yet lay aside its grave clothes and its shroud. It will yet rise, and in its rising and its reign will bless mankind.[113]

Late in the following winter, silver once more reared its head. This time silver advocates resorted to a rather unusual and roundabout ploy for forcing the abandonment of gold. Their strategy involved coinage of the "seigniorage" that had theoretically accrued to the Treasury's accounts when silver was purchased at a market price below its nominal value when coined into a silver dollar. With silver far below parity at sixteen to one with gold, as it had been for years, the total difference between the market cost of silver and its nominal value as coin had reached some $55 million. During the Senate debate on repeal of the Sherman Silver Purchase Act, one compromise alternative had surfaced in the form of a proposal to coin this silver seigniorage. But Cleveland's strong opposition to anything but an absolute end to silver purchases and coinage quickly squelched the idea.[114] However, while Cleveland could keep the proposal out of the repeal bill,

---

[113] *Congressional Record* 53:1:3062, 3066, November 1, 1893.

[114] At the time, the *Commercial and Financial Chronicle* wrote that its "epitaph, if written in full, would read – born Saturday, struggled through Sunday, and died Monday." October 28, 1893.

he could not prevent Congress from considering the idea in its own right. This the House proceeded to do early in 1894. Because part of the plan was to coin silver already held by the Treasury, thus simply converting bullion to coin without any other change, the impact of the proposal, in terms of the Treasury's ability to maintain gold payments, was a little unclear. But that the implications for gold that would attend enactment were negative, no one doubted. On the House floor, an attempt was made to eliminate the second section which would have required coinage of the entire stock of bullion (see Table 6.12). The silver bloc prevailed on that vote and the proceeded to pass the measure (see Table 6.12).[115] When the Senate concurred, Cleveland immediately vetoed the bill, setting up a third important House vote on override. Unlike repeal of the Sherman Silver Purchase Act the previous fall, Cleveland did not need a majority to support his position, and thus, although the House supported an override by a sizable margin, the administration prevailed as the bill fell short of the required two-thirds' majority (see Table 6.12).[116]

While repeal of the Sherman Silver Purchase Act and the failure of the seigniorage bill were very important victories for the gold standard, the gold reserve maintained by the Treasury remained under severe stress. The proximate problem was the continuing excess of expenditures over revenue in federal accounts. That imbalance, in the first instance, forced currency out into circulation where it increased potential claims on the gold reserve. These increasing claims heightened distrust in the financial system, leading, among other things, European investors to further liquidate their American investments. To pay for repatriated American securities, investors drew down their bank balances and exported gold to Europe. Thus, the liquidation of European holdings tightened credit and, in turn, dampened activity in the American economy. The accompanying depression tended to reduce tax income to the government and thus started another cycle of red ink,

[115] When the proposal passed the House, the *Commercial and Financial Chronicle* welcomed the event by referring to it as "[t]hat stupendous embodiment of ignorance known as the 'Seigniorage Bill'" and, in another section of that issue, quoted with approval descriptions of its purpose as to "coin a vacuum" or "to coin the negative quantity on the side of the vacuum." March 3, 1894. Also see *Appleton's Annual Cyclopaedia of 1894* (New York: D. Appleton, 1895), p. 223. This vote was included in McRae's 1900 list of "Votes on Coinage and Currency Legislation."

[116] When a committee appointed by the president of the New York Chamber of Commerce offered to travel to Washington in order to advise the president on his options, Cleveland's personal secretary telegraphed back that this would not be necessary. *Commercial and Financial Chronicle*, March 24, 1894. For Cleveland's veto message, see March 31, 1894. The vote on override was included in McRae's 1900 list of "Votes on Coinage and Currency Legislation." For brief accounts of the seigniorage bill, see Oberholtzer, *History of the United States*, vol. 5, pp. 281–282; Friedman and Schwartz, *Monetary History*, pp. 116–117; Hepburn, *History of Currency*, pp. 356–357; *Appleton's 1894 Cyclopaedia*, p. 748.

Table 6.12. *Members Supporting the Gold Standard in the 53rd Congress, 1893–1895 (%)*

House membership category	Strike section two seigniorage (1894)	Passage of seigniorage bill (1894)	Veto override seigniorage (1894)	Bryan amendment gold bonds (1895)	Passage of gold bonds (1895)	Passage of gold contract (1895)
Full House	47.4 (274)	43.4 (297)	44.2 (258)	56.9 (295)	45.5 (297)	41.8 (287)
Republicans	76.7 (73)	79.0 (100)	76.6 (77)	84.3 (102)	43.6 (101)	34.4 (96)
Democrats	38.3 (188)	26.1 (184)	31.2 (170)	44.2 (181)	48.9 (184)	48.3 (180)
Other party	15.4 (13)	15.4 (13)	18.2 (11)	16.7 (12)	8.3 (12)	0.0 (11)
District level of development						
All members						
Highest	100.0 (41)	89.4 (47)	94.3 (35)	97.9 (47)	91.5 (47)	92.7 (41)
Middle high	71.6 (67)	69.9 (73)	69.1 (68)	75.0 (68)	56.5 (69)	50.7 (71)
Middle low	33.3 (105)	31.3 (115)	31.6 (98)	54.2 (118)	37.0 (119)	31.3 (115)
Lowest	9.8 (61)	0.0 (62)	5.3 (57)	11.3 (62)	14.5 (62)	16.7 (60)
Republicans						
Highest	100.0 (8)	92.9 (14)	100.0 (5)	100.0 (15)	75.0 (16)	76.9 (13)
Middle high	85.3 (34)	88.4 (43)	86.5 (37)	84.6 (39)	48.6 (37)	43.6 (39)
Middle low	65.5 (29)	68.3 (41)	61.8 (34)	80.0 (45)	28.9 (45)	14.6 (41)
Lowest	0.0 (2)	0.0 (2)	100.0 (1)	66.7 (3)	33.3 (3)	0.0 (3)
Democrats						
Highest	100.0 (31)	87.1 (31)	92.9 (28)	96.8 (31)	100.0 (30)	100.0 (28)
Middle high	63.3 (30)	48.1 (27)	53.6 (28)	63.0 (27)	70.0 (30)	65.5 (29)
Middle low	23.2 (69)	11.9 (67)	17.2 (58)	43.1 (65)	47.0 (66)	45.5 (66)
Lowest	10.3 (58)	0.0 (59)	3.6 (56)	8.6 (58)	13.8 (58)	17.5 (57)
Sectional stress	66.2	69.0	72.8	66.1	57.0	52.5

Note and sources: The roll-call position that accorded with support for the gold standard is indicated in parentheses: on adoption of the Outhwaite amendment to strike section two of the seigniorage bill (yea); on passage of the bill to coin the silver seigniorage (nay); on passage of the seigniorage bill over Cleveland's veto (nay); on adoption of the Bryan amendment to the bill providing for bonds to replenish the gold reserve (nay); on engrossment and third reading of the bill to provide bonds to replenish the gold reserve (yea); and on engrossment and third reading of the bill defining "coin" to mean "gold" in the bond contract (yea). The roll calls can be found in the *Congressional Record* 53:2:2522–2523, March 1, 1894; 53:2:2524–2525, March 1, 1894; 53:2:3460, April 4, 1894; 53:3:1923–1924, February 7, 1895; 53:3:1926, February 7, 1895; and 53:3:2201, February 14, 1895.

liquidation, economic contraction, and decreasing tax revenue. To maintain the gold reserve, the Treasury issued bonds at two points during 1894. The Treasury announced an issue of $50 million in ten-year, 5 percent bonds, payable in coin on January 17, and a similar issue was offered for sale on November 13.[117] Both of these bond issues were made under authority granted the Treasury by the resumption act of January 14, 1875, and did not require new congressional approval. In fact, given the preponderance of silver sentiment in Congress at the time, such approval would not have been forthcoming.[118]

These bonds only postponed the redemption crisis that the continuing drain on the gold reserve would make inevitable. On January 28, 1895, Cleveland sent a special message to Congress urgently requesting relief for the Treasury.[119] His appeal was ignored. At this point, the president turned to J. P. Morgan and August Belmont, then the most prominent bankers in the United States, for assistance in floating yet another bond issue. Cleveland met with Morgan on February 5 and 8. With the Treasury's condition now critical, the administration came to terms with the bankers on a negotiated contract in which they would take the bonds, provide for their sale in Europe for gold, deposit the gold in the Treasury, and guarantee that the bonds would not return to the United States and thus renew gold exports. One key element in the contract depended on the provision for redemption. If the government guaranteed that the bonds would be repaid in gold, the interest rate would be 3 percent; if the government guaranteed only that they would be repaid in "coin," a contentious euphemism for gold, the rate would be 4 percent.[120]

Just before these negotiations were concluded, the House of Representatives took up a bill that would have explicitly provided for a new bond issue to bolster the gold reserve and, most important, would have provided for its repayment in gold. Many Republican members objected to this bill because, in explicitly requiring gold, it seemed to implicitly allow the term "coin" to include silver. Since that term had been used in all prior bond issues, the bill, in their view, seemed to weaken the case for the redemption of those bonds in gold alone. In response, the Republicans offered their own substitute that replaced "gold" with "coin" in such a way as to make this new issue conform with previous practice. To this substitute, William

---

[117] For both commentary and description of these issues, as well as their relationship to the gold reserve, see the *Commercial and Financial Chronicle*, January 6, 20, 27, February 3, 10, April 14, June 23, 30, July 28, November 17, 24, December 1, 22, 29, 1894; January 5, 19, 26, February 2, 9, 16, 23, 1895.

[118] Oberholtzer, *History of the United States*, vol. 5, pp. 283–284.

[119] For the text of this message, see *Commercial and Financial Chronicle*, February 2, 1895.

[120] For a description of some of the issues involved, see "Are Government Bonds Payable in Gold?," ibid., February 16, 1895.

Jennings Bryan offered an amendment that said, in effect, that the term "coin" did include silver.[121] Cleveland's supporters in the Democratic party and the Republicans managed to combine and defeat this amendment; however, when the Republican substitute itself was rejected, many Republicans opposed the president's bill on final passage, thus dooming the measure (see Table 6.12).[122] On the next day, February 8, Cleveland sent a message to Congress announcing the necessity of a new bond issue, this one for $62.4 million at 4 percent and a thirty-year term.[123] As the contract allowed, Cleveland then went back to Congress and again requested that "gold" be specifically endorsed as the money of repayment, pointing out that this would save the government over $16 million over the life of the loan because the interest would accrue at 3, not 4, percent.[124]

Even if the Republicans had been sincere in their original rejection of the president's proposal on February 7, many of them were clearly opportunistic when this new measure came before the House on February 14. With the president unshakably committed to a defense of the gold standard and, though more doubtfully, able to maintain gold payments without new legislation, congressional Republicans were free to take partisan advantage of the disarray within the Democratic party. For example, one otherwise dependable gold member, Ohio Republican Charles Grosvenor, sounded more like a Populist as he described the terms of the bond contract Cleveland had negotiated:

The Rothschilds, who have held empires and kingdoms and republics of the Old World by the throat, come here and say to you, "Your system is obnoxious to us, and we want a different system. We are taking great interest in you these days, you Republic of America, something rather unusual for us, but we have concluded to do it, and we want you to change your system to conform to our notions. Tear up this old pod-auger, effete way you have of doing business. Get rid of this popular idea that a nation can be run on the patriotism and integrity of its people. Abolish

---

[121] For the text of Bryan's amendment, see *Congressional Record* 53:3:1920, February 7, 1895.

[122] This vote was included in McRae's 1900 list of "Votes on Coinage and Currency Legislation." The motion on which the vote actually occurred was to provide for the engrossment and third reading of the bill, usually a pro forma stage in the proceedings.

[123] For the text of the bond contract between Morgan, Belmont, and the government, see *Congressional Record* 53:3:2183, February 14, 1895.

[124] To the great dismay of the silver advocates, even state and local governments in their own constituencies quite often included gold clauses in contracts. For reports of such contracts involving Jacksonville, Florida; the state of Idaho; Montgomery, Alabama; and Beaumont, Texas, see *Congressional Record* 53:3:2196, February 14, 1895; *Appleton's Annual Cyclopaedia for 1895* (New York: D. Appleton, 1896), p. 352; *Commercial and Financial Chronicle*, February 2, 1895; *Appleton's Annual Cyclopaedia for 1896* (New York: D. Appleton, 1897), pp. 9–10; *Commercial and Financial Chronicle*, March 20, 1897; February 26, December 3, 1898.

this whole notion of yours that bimetallism can ultimately be upheld in this country. Strike it all out; and if you will, so deeply interested are we in your future happiness and your future prosperity that we will actually give you sixteen and a half millions of dollars in payments of a little over $500,000 a year. We will put you on our pension roll; we will pension you for thirty years at $500,000 a year, if you will just fix the terms of your financial system to suit us. It is disinterestedness on our part, of course, and everybody understands that."[125]

A little later in the debate, "Sockless" Jerry Simpson, the Kansas Populist, tried to pull off this Republican disguise:

One of the greatest evils that ever has come to this country, I think, is that which makes it possible for the Republicans to stand here to-day masquerading as the friends of the free coinage of silver, pretending that they want these obligations payable in coin, so that you can avail yourselves of silver. They do not mean it. They do not wish that these obligations shall be redeemable in anything but gold; and one of the greatest calamities that is upon us is that it gives the Republican party a chance to return to power and continue the same policy that has brought us to the present evil.[126]

Notwithstanding the transparency of the veil cloaking their tactics, most Republicans deserted Cleveland on this bill, and like the previous attempt, this one also went down to defeat (see Table 6.12).[127] When the bonds were finally floated, without the gold clause, they were still a decided success; the New York allotment sold out in twenty minutes, the somewhat larger London subscription lists were filled in two hours.[128] Shaking once more its editorial head, the *Commercial and Financial Chronicle* welcomed the adjournment of the Fifty-third Congress because "further crude and consequently disturbing financial legislation and agitation being no longer possible, the chief obstacle to business development has been removed."[129]

---

[125] *Congressional Record* 53:3:2184, February 14, 1895. August Belmont, one of the American bankers involved in the contract, represented Rothschild interests in the United States. A pod-auger was a primitive hand tool for boring holes that had largely disappeared by 1800. In the late nineteenth century, the term "pod-auger days" referred to life before the invention of machinery.

[126] *Congressional Record* 53:3:2188, February 14, 1895. For the text of a national Populist declaration on this bond issue, signed by Populist representatives and other leaders of the party, see pp. 2194–2195.

[127] This vote was included in McRae's 1900 list of "Votes on Coinage and Currency Legislation." As was the case with the first bill, the motion on which the vote actually occurred was to provide for the engrossment and third reading of the measure.

[128] *Commercial and Financial Chronicle*, February 23, 1895. The alacrity with which the bonds were taken up by investors was undoubtedly due to the skill and reputation of the underwriters, as well as the uncompromising stand of the administration in support of gold. For its part, Congress did little but undermine confidence in the issue.

[129] March 9, 1895.

The 1894 election had produced a titanic landslide in which the Republicans added 130 new members in the House of Representatives while the Democrats lost 125. Gaining control of the chamber for the first time in four years, the Republicans now held over 70 percent of the seats. In the intervening period between the adjournment of the Fifty-third Congress in March and the meeting of the Fifty-fourth in December, 1895, the Treasury continued to teeter on the brink of repudiation. In May, the Supreme Court struck down the income tax that had been attached to the Wilson Tariff in the previous year. By ruling the tax unconstitutional, the court in effect wiped out the entire surplus expected for the 1895 calendar year; that surplus had been counted on as part of the effort to rebuild the Treasury's gold reserve. In the short run, the gold provided by the Morgan-Belmont Syndicate, in exchange for the bonds sold in New York and London, bolstered the Treasury reserve, returning the net holdings to the benchmark $100 million level.[130] By the beginning of September, however, the reserve had again fallen below the $100 million mark.[131] Just after this, rumors of yet another bond issue started to surface, indicating the reemergence of anxiety over the Treasury's ability to maintain gold payments.[132] Although the Republicans had large and confident majorities in both chambers of the new Fifty-fourth Congress, the Senate was still in the hands of a very committed free silver bloc. With the House now tilting toward gold, the difference in monetary stance between the House and Senate was wider than at any other point in the late nineteenth century; the crucial factor was the disproportionate weight given to western state senators in the upper chamber.[133]

Recognizing that gold sentiment was weak in the South and West where a disproportionate number of Senate seats were located, the *Commercial and Financial Chronicle* advocated a direct intervention by the financial community:

It is . . . highly desirable that efforts [be made] to encourage those who are engaged in the contest for sound money, especially in the South. . . . The work New York

---

[130] *Commercial and Financial Chronicle*, June 8, 29, July 6, 1895. Reflecting both the intense interest that foreign bankers took in American finance and the wonderment with which they viewed the nation's politics, an officer of the Bank of Montreal commented, "God is good to his little children, to drunken men and to the people of the United States, or they would have gone to eternal smash long ere this." June 15, 1895.

[131] Ibid., September 7, 1895.

[132] Ibid., September 14, 21, 1895. On the importance of the $100 million mark "as the line of demarcation between safety and danger," see *Congressional Record* 54:1:348, December 27, 1895.

[133] As the *Commercial and Financial Chronicle* saw it, the Senate had a "preponderance of members from frontier States in the infancy of commercial intelligence," while in the House "the people are heard in virtue of their population and industrial progress." May 30, 1896.

has to do is more necessary than ever and cannot be completed until the elections that are to determine the character of the State legislatures which are to choose new United States Senators have been held. . . . The seats of several United States Senators are being contested in the South that might possibly be gained for advocates of a stable currency by a little judicious assistance on the part of the North. We cannot vote there, but we can send money, by means of which the work of educating the people could be continued – a work that is most effectively done in that section by public speaking at political meetings. The question we want to ask is, why should not the sound-money candidate in each State, the one who appears to offer the best promise of success, be furnished the means for conducting his canvass? This action is made the more imperative because there is a lack of capital in the South, and because the silver-mine owners always have an abundance of funds for those who are willing to follow their beck and call. . . .[134]

The journal suggested that a committee of the New York City Chamber of Commerce undertake the task of funding hard-money candidates in the South. A few of the journal's readers were appalled at the idea of using wealth to influence elections outside the home region of the donor. To them, the *Chronicle* responded by claiming that such contributions were a routine feature of national politics, implying that the contest would otherwise be one-sided:

Conducting a canvass is an expensive matter – a single public meeting costs money. When the desire is to educate States on the subject of finance and to hold numerous and attractive meetings in every school district, attractive enough to bring out the people, it costs a large amount of money. . . . About all the "free-silverite" needs is an "orator" with a loud voice and free action, capable of saying "gold-bug," "Wall Street," "Vanderbilt," and now, with special emphasis, "Pierpont Morgan, the Prince of Gold-bugs."[135]

Following up on this remarkable admission as to the popular sentiment of the South and West, the *Chronicle* declared that "men of wealth do not live up to their duty if they fail to help in every legitimate way to rid our Senate Chamber of those men who have destroyed business during the past year talking and voting for free silver and obstructing all sound money legislation." This declaration marked a turning point in the politics of the monetary standard, a decisive shift from the siege mentality that had dominated the financial community for almost twenty years to an aggressive countercampaign of propaganda and other means of utilizing the advantages of wealth. However, partisan politics still prevented a clear and unambiguous contest of strength between gold and silver forces.

As the gold reserve fell below $80 million, European investors again began a massive liquidation of their American investments, producing panic

---

[134] "A Sure Way to Defeat Free Silver," June 22, 1895.   [135] July 13, 1895.

on the stock exchange and credit contraction throughout the financial system. At this point, Cleveland again requested legislation to replenish the gold reserve and thus reestablish confidence in the Treasury.[136] As Marriott Brosius, a Pennsylvania Republican, described the situation, "the Treasury of the United States is in distress. The white flag is out." Noting that greenbacks, when redeemed at Treasury offices, drew down the gold reserve, he called paper money "the auriferous tapeworm that wriggles back and forth between Wall street or London and the Treasury of the United States."[137] Carefully responding to the situation in a way that recognized both the free silver predilections of the Senate and the opportunistic political advantages associated with condemnation of Cleveland's bond issues, the Republican leadership in the House crafted a bill made up of two parts. In the first, a new fifteen-year bond, bearing 3 percent interest, was to be made available to the Treasury, adding an option to those already available. This new bond was to be distributed through popular subscription, thus barring closed negotiations with a banking syndicate.

In the second section, the bill authorized $50 million in temporary loan certificates, thus making available a short-term measure for Treasury relief. The major difference between this bill and the administration's position was the failure of the measure to specify that bonds would be paid in gold. While the differences were not great, Cleveland's Secretary of the Treasury indicated his disappointment in the bill.[138] As a sleight-of-hand, its commitment to Treasury relief only half-heartedly disguised by distinguishing itself from the administration's policy, the proposal drew criticism from Republicans as well as Democrats. As William Bowers of California put it, "I want to talk to Republicans – I have no desire to talk to Democrats [laughter]; they seem to be going all right on this bill – every one of you Republicans, when upon the stump addressing your constituents, has denounced the President for doing exactly what you propose to do in indorsing this bill." After noting that even this measure faced certain defeat in the Senate, Bowers stated that every Republican voting for this doomed measure would thereby be forced to explain "why you did this; why, at this time, you sought refuge under the umbrella of Grover Cleveland, who has gathered you in as a hen gathers her chickens under her wings."[139] There was little doubt as to the urgency of the Treasury's condition. As one member noted, "already, in expectation of another bond issue under secret contract to favorite individuals or syndicates, the agents of the Rothschilds,

---

[136] Oberholtzer, *History of the United States*, vol. 5, pp. 316–317.
[137] *Congressional Record* 54:1: 381, 383, December 28, 1895.
[138] *Congressional Record* 54:1:396, December 28, 1895.
[139] *Congressional Record* 54:1:373, December 27, 1895.

the Morgans, and the Belmonts are crowding the little offices of the great hotels of this city, waiting like vultures for an opportunity to again light upon their prey, as they did last spring."[140] The House voted separately on the two sections of the bill; only votes on the first section were recorded. Once that section passed easily, the second part of the bill passed by a voice vote.

Just a week after this decision, the Secretary of the Treasury announced a new bond issue at 4 percent and for $100 million to be distributed through popular subscription.[141] At this point, J. P. Morgan dissolved his syndicate, the financiers that had belonged to his group thereafter acting as individuals.[142] When the bids were opened in early February, about a third of the bonds were taken by Morgan's firm, which had put in a bid for the entire amount.[143] At the same time, the Senate, as had been predicted, substituted a free silver proposal for the House bill. When the bill arrived back in the House, Henry Turner of Georgia, one of the few southern Democrats who was ambivalent toward silver, remarked, "They might just as well have put a protective tariff in place of the measure we sent them. They might just as well have put in place of our bill, and as a substitute for it, the abandoned subtreasury bill of the Populists. So far as germaneness is concerned, they might just as well have substituted a scheme for the annexation of Mexico, silver and all."[144] The House showed little patience with the Senate proposal, rejecting a motion to concur in the upper chamber's amendment by a margin of over two to one (see Table 6.13).[145] On the last day in January, the gold reserve had declined to $50 million, about half of the minimum that investors and the government thought sufficient to discourage a run on the Treasury. As a result of this last bond issue, which, like the others, Congress refused to endorse, the gold reserve increased to $124 million. Although the gold standard would still face a stiff challenge in the fall presidential election, the fiscal position of the Treasury now took a turn for the better, and extreme measures, in which the executive branch was compelled to defend gold alone, were to prove unnecessary in the future. In all, Cleveland issued more than a quarter of a billion dollars in new,

---

[140] *Congressional Record* 54:1:390, December 28, 1895. Aside from rhetorical flourishes, the rumors on which this report was based turned out to be remarkably accurate, as to both participants and the terms of the negotiation. See, for example, *Commercial and Financial Chronicle*, December 28, 1895. Also see January 4, 1896.

[141] *Commercial and Financial Chronicle*, January 11, 1896.

[142] Ibid., January 18, 1896.

[143] In all, there were 4,640 individual bids, totalling some $568 million. Ibid., February 8, 1896. Oberholtzer, *History of the United States*, vol. 5, p. 320.

[144] *Congressional Record* 54:1:1726, February 14, 1896.

[145] *Appleton's 1896 Cyclopaedia*, pp. 189–199. This vote was included in McRae's 1900 list of "Votes on Coinage and Currency Legislation." The *Commercial and Financial Chronicle* praised the decision in the House as a "good tonic" for the "16 to 1 idiocy." February 15, 1896.

Table 6.13. *Members Supporting the Gold Standard in the 54th and 55th Congresses, 1895–1897 and 1897–1899 (%)*

House membership category	Gold reserve (1895)	Senate silver amendment (1896)	Bryan platform (1897)	U.S. bonds payable in silver (1898)
Full House	55.7 (307)	70.5 (305)	57.5 (226)	57.6 (314)
Republicans	78.7 (216)	88.5 (208)	100.0 (128)	99.4 (179)
Democrats	1.2 (84)	34.4 (90)	1.1 (88)	1.8 (111)
Other party	0.0 (7)	0.0 (7)	10.0 (10)	4.2 (24)
District level of development				
All members				
Highest	83.6 (55)	100.0 (47)	94.1 (34)	92.5 (53)
Middle high	70.0 (70)	82.7 (75)	78.4 (51)	76.4 (72)
Middle low	55.1 (127)	74.0 (123)	56.4 (94)	56.6 (129)
Lowest	10.9 (55)	25.0 (60)	10.6 (47)	6.7 (60)
Republicans				
Highest	97.9 (47)	100.0 (41)	100.0 (31)	100.0 (47)
Middle high	75.4 (65)	85.1 (67)	100.0 (39)	100.0 (55)
Middle low	72.9 (96)	87.2 (94)	100.0 (53)	100.0 (73)
Lowest	62.5 (8)	66.7 (6)	100.0 (5)	75.0 (4)
Democrats				
Highest	0.0 (8)	100.0 (6)	0.0 (2)	20.0 (5)
Middle high	0.0 (4)	71.4 (7)	10.0 (10)	0.0 (13)
Middle low	0.0 (29)	33.3 (27)	0.0 (35)	0.0 (44)
Lowest	2.3 (43)	22.0 (50)	0.0 (41)	2.0 (49)
Sectional stress	64.7	58.9	67.7	65.4

Note and sources: The roll-call position that accorded with support for the gold standard is indicated in parentheses: on passage of legislation providing for bond issues to protect the gold reserve (yea); on adoption of the Senate amendment to restore the coinage of silver dollars (nay); on a motion to recommit a monetary commission bill with instructions to report back legislation embodying the financial plank of the 1896 Democratic platform (nay); and on passage of a concurrent resolution stating that U.S. bonds are payable in silver (nay). The roll calls can be found in the *Congressional Record* 54:1:400–401, December 28, 1895; 54:1:1735, February 14, 1896; 55:1:2971, July 24, 1897; 55:2:1309–1310, January 31, 1898.

long-term debt between 1894 and 1896 – all of it in defense of the gold standard.[146]

---

[146] Oberholtzer, *History of the United States*, vol. 5, p. 321. Cleveland's staunch defense of the gold standard during this period earned him the enduring respect of many Republicans. For example, a few months after repeal of the Sherman Silver Purchase Act, Horace White, editor of the Chicago *Tribune*, reported a conversation with

By the end of March 1896, the financial community and the nation had begun to turn its attention to the campaigns for presidential nominations.[147] About this time, the Republican state conventions in New York and Minnesota adopted strong endorsements of the gold standard in their platforms.[148] Other conventions in the East soon followed. In reply to these expressions of support for sound money, the Colorado Republican convention committed the state party to a bolt of the national campaign if the platform did not endorse free silver. At that convention, a former congressman went even further, suggesting that Colorado secede from the Union if the nation continued to subordinate silver to gold.[149] Congressional deliberations degenerated into a squabble between the free silver Senate and sound-money House as members used their respective chambers as soap boxes. When Congress finally adjourned in early June, the *Commercial and Financial Chronicle* called its closing "the most welcome act in its career" for which "all business interests will feel grateful."[150]

Just back from London, J. P. Morgan, a man who seldom spoke to the press and even more rarely took public stands in politics, strongly urged that the Republican national platform "should be for sound money, with no compromise and no straddle, but out and out for gold. European investors are watching the situation here closely. They will not invest in American securities until they know in what kind of money we propose to pay our debts. A single gold standard is the only basis for sound money."[151] At about the same time, Cleveland's Secretary of Agriculture, J. Sterling Morton of Nebraska, said:

> If the Republicans will come out squarely, flatly and positively for a single gold standard ... their ticket will get a great deal of support from sound money Democrats, and there will be a heap of vest-pocket voting for the Republican ticket by those Democrats who do not wish openly to divorce themselves from their party. ... The silver sentiment is universal all over the West, and it is growing. ... There is no hope of electing gold candidates anywhere in the West, and right there in San Francisco,

Republican Senator William Allison of Iowa in which the latter "said it was God's mercy to the country that [Cleveland was] elected President in 1892 instead of Harrison or any Republican because no Republican President could have procured the repeal of the Sherman Silver Act, however strongly he might have tried. He added his belief that no other Democrat than yourself *would* have done it. It was his opinion that if that act had not been repealed we should now be a ruined people." Nevins, ed., *Letters of Grover Cleveland*, p. 350. Years later, just after the 1900 general election, Theodore Roosevelt wrote Cleveland praising him for "the very great service you had rendered to the whole country [as president] by what you did about free silver ... doing for the American public in this matter of free silver what at the time no other man could have done. ... you are entitled to thanks and congratulations." P. 541.

147   See, for example, the *Commercial and Financial Chronicle*, March 28, April 4, May 9, 1896.
148   Ibid., April 25, 1896.   149   Ibid., May 23, 1896.   150   June 13, 1896.
151   Ibid. This, of course, was also the position taken by the journal. See, for example, June 20, 1896.

where they have more than a hundred millions of gold coin in the vaults of their banks, where deposits are paid in gold by specific contract, and where greenbacks have never been good enough for them, the people are crying for 50-cent silver dollars. . . . In Missouri they are wilder than Texas steers, and in Illinois pretty near all the Democrats have gone crazy, and are following Altgeld into anarchy and free silver. . . . The most serious part of the thing is that the extraordinary victories of the silver men in Kentucky, Ohio and elsewhere are likely to frighten European investors, who will dump all their American securities upon the home market and create a panic.[152]

By the end of June, the *Chronicle* had given up hope of even a waffle as a monetary plank at the Democratic convention, instead reporting to its readers that at least two thirds of the delegates would favor free silver and that most of those had been selected in state conventions in which "frenzied hate" was the only sentiment expressed toward gold.[153] When the Democratic platform was adopted in a form that confirmed the *Chronicle*'s worst fears, the journal called the document "the political work of . . . anarchists" who favor "radicalism and lawlessness of the worst sort" and thereby "write themselves down as no better than thieves and robbers."[154] Countering the silver crusade with a jihad of its own, the journal declared that what "is needed now is not simply to elect the Republican candidate for President and to elect none but sound-money men for members of Congress, but to give such an overwhelming vote against the Silver and Anarchists' party as to close and settle forever this free-silver coinage agitation in the United States. . . ."[155]

Within a week or so of the Democratic convention, reports of gold hoarding began to appear as the financial community and citizens generally began to monitor the presidential race. At the same time, the eastern wing of the Democratic party began to break up as gold Democrats bolted the national ticket, creating their own organizations for the election and ceding control of their respective state parties to those willing to endorse Bryan.[156] Foreign exchange rapidly moved to the gold-exporting point as well when investors began to shift their assets abroad in anticipation of a possible Democratic victory.[157] When Vermont and Maine, which voted in September instead of November, delivered Republican majorities much greater than had been expected, the stock market and foreign exchange steadied somewhat.[158] By

---

[152] *Finance and Commerce: A Standard Weekly Review of Current Events* 5:23 (June 8, 1896): 502.

[153] June 27, 1896. The journal added, "A great party that gets so low as to train under the Populist Generals, ex-Governor Tillman of South Carolina and Governor Altgeld of Illinois, seems grievously to need discipline and reorganization."

[154] Ibid., July 11, 1896. After the Populist national convention endorsed Bryan, the *Chronicle* added that hereafter "[a]ll criminals of every description will be among his partisans." August 1, 1896.

[155] "The Chicago Convention and Its Results." July 11, 1896.

[156] *Commercial and Financial Chronicle*, July 18, 1896.

[157] Ibid., July 25, 1896.   [158] Ibid., September 5, 19, 1896.

the middle of October the financial community was fairly optimistic, giving McKinley a much better than fifty-fifty chance of victory, but gold continued to be hoarded and short-term interest rates were very high, reflecting much unease and a consequent unwillingness to lend. Gold was at a premium to currency in much of this period and interest rates supporting commodity trades were almost extortionate.

In response to the extraordinary return offered by these rates, gold reversed direction and moved from Europe to the United States in large quantities.[159] On the day before the election in November, a long line of men and women who had withdrawn their savings from banks waited outside the federal subtreasury offices in New York in order to exchange currency for gold. Others went to bullion brokers or bought foreign exchange in order to protect their assets against the adverse consequences of a Bryan victory. On Wednesday, the first business day following the election, the demand for currency at the subtreasury was so great that officials turned away requests to deposit gold. The premium on gold in the bullion market disappeared, and the stock market, buoyed in part by surging demand from London investors who had liquidated their American holdings prior to the election, welcomed McKinley's victory with booming prices.[160] As a result, business conditions immediately turned for the better, but the economic crisis that attended Bryan's nomination and the subsequent presidential campaign continued to take its toll in insolvent banks and bankrupt companies that had been weakened during the four months between June and November.[161]

In January, 1897, speculation on the calling of a special session of Congress to reform the tariff began to surface. As always, the idea of congressional deliberations raised the specter of renewed silver agitation and, thus, apprehension in financial circles.[162] When Congress met in special session during the spring and early summer, the major item on the legislative agenda was the tariff. However, a bill authorizing the appointment of a commission to study the monetary system was also considered at McKinley's request.[163] This proposal passed the House but not the Senate. In the House, an attempt was made to amend the bill by instructing the proposed commission to "proceed along the line laid down in the financial plank of the

---

[159] Ibid., October 17, 24, 31, 1896.

[160] Ibid., November 7, 1896. For a summary of the impact of Bryan's candidacy and McKinley's victory on the domestic economy, see *Appleton's 1896 Cyclopaedia*, pp. 276, 280–281.

[161] *Commercial and Financial Chronicle*, January 2, 1897. The crisis in Chicago had been so severe that the stock exchange in that city closed its doors on August 4 and did not reopen them until November 5.

[162] Ibid., January 2, 1897.

[163] For the text of the president's message to Congress, see *Congressional Record* 55:1:2958, July 24, 1897.

Democratic platform adopted at Chicago in 1896, and it shall especially include the restoration of the system of bimetallism by the free, independent, and unlimited coinage of both gold and silver at the ratio of 16 to 1."[164] This amendment produced an almost party-line roll call, the first of a string of such votes that closed out the century (see Table 6.13). The Bryan campaign, even in defeat, had succeeded in turning the gold standard into a strongly partisan issue by destroying the hard-money wing of the Democratic party.

Just as the congressional alignment on the gold standard was becoming almost exclusively partisan, orthodox monetary theory was becoming increasingly hegemonic in the nation's leading educational institutions and cultural centers. Even on the western plains support for free silver was believed to be waning in inverse proportion to the rising price of wheat. However, "schooled as it has been by experience to believe that the [opening of the coming session] inevitably opens a Pandora box full of evils, each a disturbing influence to industrial interests," the financial community remained wary of Congress.[165] One of the dark clouds cluttering the horizon was Cuba and the increasing bellicosity of American congressmen and senators with respect to the island's struggle for independence from Spain. Still, to the *Chronicle* and apparently to the administration also, the time had come for a thorough reform of the nation's financial system along orthodox lines. The administration announced its reform program in the annual report of the Secretary of the Treasury, who subsequently met with the House Banking and Currency Committee before the Christmas recess.[166] Early in the new year, the Monetary Commission of the Indianapolis Convention, a privately organized group of chambers of commerce, commercial clubs, and boards of trade from throughout the United States, issued its report.[167] Although the details differed in many respects from those in the administration's proposal, the substance of the plan was similar in that both sought an explicit endorsement of the gold standard as a foundation for the nation's financial system and desired more elasticity in the relationship between gold reserves and the circulation of money.

However reassuring these proposals were to the financial community, the Senate was still not ready for them.[168] In that chamber they were met by a

---

[164] *Congressional Record* 55:1:2971, July 24, 1897.
[165] *Commercial and Financial Chronicle*, August 28, September 11, and October 30, 1897.
[166] "The Elections – What They Mean," ibid., November 6, 1897. Also see December 11, 18, 25, 1897.
[167] See *Report of the Monetary Commission of the Indianapolis Convention* (Chicago: University of Chicago Press, 1898).
[168] The *Commercial and Financial Chronicle*, while strongly preferring the House of Representatives to the Senate in terms of financial policy, still believed that the upper chamber had been improved as a result of the recent election. "The Senate: Past,

proposal, sponsored by Senator Teller of Colorado, to repay federal bonds in silver. Teller's proposal came in the form of a concurrent resolution that was intended to express the opinion of Congress without possessing the force of law. As such, the proposal also did not require the president's signature (which, of course, would not have been forthcoming). Teller chose as his text the language of a concurrent resolution which had passed Congress some twenty years earlier.[169] The Senate Finance Committee promptly and favorably reported the resolution. At this point, on January 27, McKinley announced his opposition to the proposal in an address to the National Association of Manufacturers at the Waldorf-Astoria Hotel in New York City, saying, "Nothing should ever tempt us – nothing ever will tempt us – to scale down the sacred debt of the nation through a legal technicality. Whatever may be the language of the contract, the United States will discharge all its obligations in the currency recognized as the best throughout the civilized world at the times of payment."[170] The Senate nonetheless passed the resolution the following day and sent it on to the House of Representatives.

In the House, however, the Committee on Ways and Means promptly but unfavorably reported the proposal with a recommendation that it be defeated.[171] It is exceedingly rare in the history of Congress for recorded votes to be taken on identical proposals separated by the lapse of a single year, let alone two decades. That the same issues could be raised over this expanse of time demonstrates the durability of monetary issues in the late nineteenth century, in both form and saliency. In fact, the reason for reintroducing the concurrent resolution, originally sponsored by Stanley Matthews in 1878, was to embarrass major Republican politicians who had in the earlier year voted for silver but now stood for

Present and Future," March 6, 1897. The journal was even more optimistic when Kentucky, after a deadlock in the state legislature that lasted over a year, finally elected a gold Republican. May 1, 1897.

[169]   The text of the resolution read: "*Resolved* . . . , That all the bonds of the United States issued or authorized to be issued under the said acts of Congress hereinbefore recited are payable, principal and interest, at the option of the Government of the United States, in silver dollars of the coinage of the United States containing 412 1/2 grains each of standard silver, and that to restore to its coinage such silver coins as a legal tender in payment of said bonds, principal and interest, is not in violation of the public faith nor in derogation of the rights of the public creditor." *Congressional Record* 55:2:1267, January 31, 1898.

[170]   A Tennessee Democrat described the dinner as "a feast [given McKinley] by the multimillionaires, members of the gold-bug trust, amidst the clink of cut glass, the sparkle of champagne, and the glare of electric lights. . . ." Later this banquet was described by a California Democrat as the "new Belshazzar's feast . . . a $15,000 dinner in a $10,000,000 hotel, surrounded by a billion-dollar gathering of money kings." *Congressional Record* 55:2:1264, 1275, 1303, January 31, 1898. Also see *Commercial and Financial Chronicle*, January 22, 29, 1898.

[171]   *Congressional Record* 55:2:1260, 1278, January 31, 1998.

gold.[172] In addition, many senators wished to demonstrate that their free silver predilections were as strong as ever, despite Bryan's defeat. But, for gold advocates in the House of Representatives, this was also an opportunity to disassociate the lower chamber from the heterodox doctrines of the Senate. Overturning the vote on the resolution twenty years earlier, the House soundly defeated the proposal (see Table 6.13).[173]

Comparison of the two votes, separated by twenty years of agitation over silver, reveals the radical change that took place in the late 1890s (compare Tables 6.7 and 6.13). In the full House, support for gold redemption of federal bonds almost doubled, from 29.5 percent in 1878 to 57.6 percent in 1898. Republican support for gold more than doubled, from substantially less than half of the party caucus in 1878 to near-unanimity two decades later. The Democrats, however, traveled in the opposite direction. The destruction of that party's northeastern gold wing was confirmed by the steep decline in support for gold among members hailing from the most developed districts in the nation, as well as the fact that there were only five such members in the party's House delegation in 1898 where there had been twenty-three in 1878. In both years, there was a high correlation between relative economic development and member support and opposition to silver, but the gradient underlying that pattern was somewhat steeper in the later vote. The general result was a much stronger connection between party affiliation and divisions over the monetary standard – a pattern in which only 1 percent of the members of the two major parties voted against their colleagues in 1898, sharply contrasting with the almost 30 percent who had done so twenty years earlier (when, in fact, both parties had prosilver majorities). Despite the destruction of the gold wing of the Democratic party and the sharp increase in partisan polarization over the monetary standard, the level of sectional stress on the two roll calls was almost identical (and extremely high in both cases).[174]

Coming as it did a year after enactment of the Dingley Tariff, the now open commitment of the administration to the gold standard confirmed the manufacturing belt's domination of the national political economy; this ascendancy became only stronger over time. As one Louisiana Democrat lamented, under "the gold standard and a high protective tariff, the twin

---

[172] Republicans targeted in this way included Joseph Cannon of Illinois, who became Speaker of the House five years later; McKinley, who as a member of the House had voted for the resolution in 1878; Senator William Allison of Iowa; and Charles Grosvernor of Ohio, who chaired the House Republican Caucus. *Congressional Record* 55:2:1263, 1283–1284, 1291, 1299, January 31, 1898.

[173] This vote was included in McRae's 1900 list of "Votes on Coinage and Currency Legislation."

[174] Compared with the House, the shift in the Senate toward gold was relatively slight because the interim admission of many new Plains and Mountain states disproportionately strengthened the silver bloc in the upper chamber. "The First Vote on the Currency," *Commercial and Financial Chronicle*, February 5, 1898.

fetishes of Republican ignorance and greed, the Southern cotton planter is between the upper and nether millstones of legislative oppression – by the one the value of his product is decreased, and by the other the articles which he must necessarily buy are increased in price."[175]

This was the season, also, of the Spanish-American War, but when the *Commercial and Financial Chronicle* spoke of "peace," the journal was often referring to the much more reassuring political prospects for gold: "We have not been in the possession of such a peace as we have now in prospect since the current decade began. . . . From [1890] to this our industries have never been free to enjoy six continuous months of uninterrupted development. The silver advocates, by getting possession of the Senate, have kept the country, and particularly the enterprising and commercial classes, in a state of constant unrest. . . . Under these circumstances what does peace mean? It means a gold standard now and for all time."[176] The midterm congressional elections were quite favorable to gold, although the Republican majority in the House was slim; more important, Republican majorities were recorded in state legislatures throughout the North, implying the possibility of a gold majority in the Senate as well. Immediately recognizing the possibilities of the situation, the *Chronicle* began to advocate a strong campaign for an open endorsement of the gold standard, urging that the euphemism "coin" be explicitly defined as "gold."[177] On January 21, 1899, in the waning weeks of the lame-duck Fifty-fifth Congress, the Committee on Coinage, Weights and Measures favorably reported a measure openly declaring gold to be the standard of value. But the late date and continuing hostility of the Senate forestalled action.[178] Instead, the House and Senate Republican Caucuses agreed to appoint separate committees to examine and recommend monetary legislation to the incoming Fifty-sixth Congress. This harbinger of favorable action on the gold standard was matched, outside Washington, by what were reported to be the first gold-denominated bonds ever issued in the state of Kansas.[179]

Just about a week before the Fifty-six Congress assembled in December,

---

[175] Samuel Baird, *Congressional Record* 55:2:1277, January 31, 1898.

[176] August 13, 1898. However, the pro-silver Senate remained a worry. August 20, 1898.

[177] This election, as the *Chronicle* recognized, turned as much or more on the imperialist implications of the territorial possessions wrested from Spain as it did on the money question. Most important, the popularity of expansionism in the Plains and West appeared to have strengthened the Republicans in areas where pro-silver Democrats and Populists had previously been dominant. "The Elections," November 12, 1898.

[178] *Commercial and Financial Chronicle*, January 28, 1899.

[179] These bonds were issued by Topeka and appear to have been accepted, through private negotiation with the Treasurer of the Atchison, Topeka & Santa Fe Railway, on particularly advantageous terms to the city because of their precedent-setting terms. *Commercial and Financial Chronicle*, February 4, 18, May 27, 1899.

the committee appointed by the House Republican Caucus made its report, favorably endorsing an open declaration of gold as the monetary standard.[180] Both the House and Senate went to work immediately, turning out slightly different bills but with clearly similar intent.[181] In the House, the bill was awarded the designation "H.R. 1," the number given to the first measure introduced in the chamber and usually reserved for the controlling party's highest legislative priority. On December 8, 1899, the Rules Committee reported a special order moving the bill to the floor even though it had not yet been referred to a committee. After brief debate, the House narrowly approved this special order on a straight, party-line vote (see Table 6.14). Ten days later the House passed the bill. Again the Republicans were united, but on this vote, a little over a third of the Democrats from the most advanced districts in the nation joined them.[182] On March 13, 1900, the House of Representatives approved the conference report on H.R. 1, finally establishing gold as the declared monetary standard for the United States and ending a struggle over the design of the national financial system that had dominated American politics since the end of Reconstruction. On this vote the Republicans remained united and there was a slight increase in the proportion of supporting Democrats from advanced districts.[183] Six months later McKinley again faced Bryan in the 1900 presidential election. The relief felt in financial circles by the now-expanded margin of victory for the Republican candidate was reflected in an enthusiastic frenzy that drove volume on the New York exchange to record levels.[184]

[180] The committee also recommended a number of changes in the operation of the national bank system. For the text of this report, see *Commercial and Financial Chronicle*, December 2, 1899.

[181] Ibid., December 9, 1899.

[182] Measures of high priority to the Speaker and the majority party were sometimes voted on before committee assignments were made, in order that dissidents might be punished for their defections. Such was the case for the gold standard bill. Immediately following passage, without any intervening business whatsoever, the Speaker announced the new committee memberships for the Fifty-sixth Congress in an unambiguous display of organizational power. *Congressional Record* 56:1:573–574, December 16, 1899. This vote was included in McRae's 1900 list of "Votes on Coinage and Currency Legislation."

[183] Demonstrating the continuing intimate linkage between the banks and the gold standard, the bill also contained a number of provisions affecting the national bank system, including a section expanding bank notes to the full par value of bonds deposited with the Treasury and another allowing the organization of national banks with $25,000 capital in towns of 2,000 population or less. This vote was included in McRae's 1900 list of "Votes on Coinage and Currency Legislation." On the general importance of this measure, see, for example, *Appleton's Annual Cyclopaedia of 1900* (New York: D. Appleton, 1901), p. 218.

[184] As in 1896, American brokerage houses in both Chicago and New York remained open throughout the night of the election so as to take orders for stocks that could then be placed on the London stock exchange via the trans-Atlantic cable. Oberholtzer, *History of the United States*, vol. 5, p. 649.

Table 6.14. *Members Supporting the Gold Standard in the 56th Congress, 1899–1901 (%)*

House membership category	Rules resolution (1899)	Passage of the gold standard (1899)	Conference report on gold standard (1900)
Full house	53.2 (308)	55.9 (340)	58.0 (286)
Republicans	100.0 (164)	100.0 (179)	100.0 (155)
Democrats	0.0 (138)	7.2 (152)	8.7 (126)
Other party	0.0 (6)	0.0 (9)	0.0 (5)
District level of development			
All members			
Highest	65.3 (49)	72.1 (61)	75.9 (54)
Middle high	76.1 (71)	78.5 (79)	77.9 (68)
Middle low	59.2 (125)	58.8 (136)	61.3 (111)
Lowest	6.3 (63)	6.2 (64)	7.5 (53)
Republicans			
Highest	100.0 (32)	100.0 (35)	100.0 (32)
Middle high	100.0 (54)	100.0 (60)	100.0 (51)
Middle low	100.0 (74)	100.0 (80)	100.0 (68)
Lowest	100.0 (4)	100.0 (4)	100.0 (4)
Democrats			
Highest	0.0 (17)	34.6 (26)	40.9 (22)
Middle high	0.0 (17)	11.8 (17)	11.8 (17)
Middle low	0.0 (46)	0.0 (51)	0.0 (39)
Lowest	0.0 (58)	0.0 (58)	0.0 (48)
Sectional stress	60.4	57.3	58.3

Note and sources: The roll-call position that accorded with support for the gold standard is indicated in parentheses: on adoption of the rules resolution providing for consideration of the gold standard bill (yea); on passage of the gold standard bill (yea); on adoption of the conference report on the gold standard bill (yea). The roll calls can be found in the *Congressional Record* 56:1:163, December 8, 1899; 56:1:572–573, December 18, 1899; 56:1:2863–2864, March 13, 1900.

SUMMARY DISCUSSION OF VOTING ALIGNMENTS ON GOLD, 1877–1900

Thirty-four roll calls on one aspect or another of the gold standard are analyzed in this chapter. All were cast in the House of Representatives between 1877 and 1900 on issues that involved the purchase and coinage of silver, the redemption of federal bonds, or the Treasury's ability to maintain gold payments in the face of budget deficits. These issues were often,

Table 6.15. *Members Supporting the Gold Standard, Summary,*
1877–1900 (%)

House membership category	First period resumption (1877–88)	Second period silver crisis (1889–96)	Third period gold supremacy (1897–1900)	Overall (1877–1900)
Full House	43.6	54.5	56.4	50.3
Republicans	71.8	77.4	99.9	78.4
Democrats	23.0	37.9	3.8	26.6
Other party	16.5	9.0	2.8	11.2
District level of development				
All members				
Highest	74.0	95.1	80.0	84.2
Middle high	62.1	72.8	77.5	69.1
Middle low	39.9	47.6	58.5	46.0
Lowest	13.9	14.4	7.5	13.2
Republicans				
Highest	84.4	96.2	100.0	91.9
Middle high	78.4	81.5	100.0	83.0
Middle low	60.4	68.4	100.0	69.8
Lowest	56.9	48.4	95.0	58.7
Democrats				
Highest	63.2	87.7	19.1	67.5
Middle high	30.0	56.9	6.7	38.5
Middle low	15.5	31.7	0.0	20.3
Lowest	10.4	11.9	0.4	9.6
Sectional stress	55.2	62.1	61.8	59.2
Number of roll calls in period	14	15	5	34

Note and sources: This table summarizes the roll calls analyzed in Tables 6.7–6.9, 6.11–6.14. The number of roll calls entering into the averages calculated for each period is given in parentheses.

in fact, intertwined, as in the case of silver purchases and budget deficits. The individual roll-call patterns previously reported are summarized in Table 6.15. The votes have been divided into three periods that generally correspond with the larger context in which they were recorded. In the first period, for example, the successful resumption of gold payments was the primary concern of the Treasury with opposition arising from both the Greenback party and silver Democrats. Although these opponents of the gold standard subscribed to conflicting monetary principles, the general context in which their proposals were made presumed a compatibility between paper currency and silver coinage. This was also a period in which the price of silver was comparatively close to gold; thus a shift between the metals would have been much less inflationary than was the case afterward. Although inflation was still the chief motive behind opposition to gold, the recent experience with a greenback basis for the financial system during the Civil War and Reconstruction and the narrow price discrepancy between gold and silver gave a more practical cast to debate between gold and silver advocates than was the case in later years.

The second period was ruled by the silver crisis brought on by continuing purchases of silver, growing budget deficits, and rising apprehension that the United States would be forced off gold.[185] During these years, congressional debate between proponents of the two metals was much less grounded in pragmatic considerations and much more millennial in character. By this point the subtleties of greenback theory had been largely discarded, along with fading memories of the paper system in use before 1879. Despite the (often inconsistent) sponsorship of greenback theory by a minority of the Populist party, rather simple panaceas based on silver dominated most discussions of alternatives to gold. This dominance was accompanied by a rapidly increasing gap between the price of the two metals that would have made a potential shift from gold to silver much more abruptly inflationary. The sharp price differential portended an apocalyptic disruption in capital investment and the banking system if the United States were ever forced off gold. However theorized, a shift to silver was largely beyond practical experience and so extreme in its implications as to turn most discussions between advocates of the two metals into heated ideological disputes, long on rhetoric and short on pragmatic policy distinctions.

In the last period, after McKinley's victory in the 1896 presidential election, gold supporters were able to consolidate their position in the national political economy, substantially aided by the global inflationary trends that set in after the gold strikes in the Yukon and the Rand.[186] Although silver

---

[185]   For political reasons, the boundary between the first and second periods is more pronounced than otherwise might be expected. In Cleveland's first term (1885–89), most congressional Democrats who favored free silver restrained their activity; to have passed a silver bill during those years, against the president's strong opposition, would have disrupted the party. Once a Republican had returned to the White House, however, congressional Democrats again declared open season on gold. As Daniel Kerr, an Iowa Republican, noted, Richard Bland "has been as silent as a church mouse on that subject almost for the last four years. [Laughter and applause.] But now when the Republican party has come into power and it is no longer a criticism of his own administration, his clarion voice is again heard in the land. [Laughter.]" *Congressional Record* 51:1:927, January 28, 1890.

[186]   For a general overview of the importance of these discoveries, see George E. Roberts, "The New Golden Era and Its Influence," which originally appeared in *The Forum* (February 1899) and was subsequently republished widely, in this case in *The Conservative* 2:4 (August 3, 1899), pp. 4–7.

advocates kept up their agitation, albeit at much lower decibel levels, the dominant theme of this relatively short period was how to most firmly commit the United States to gold without reopening political opportunities for silver.

The similarities in the patterns of congressional support across these three periods far outweigh the differences. In drawing out these similarities we should set aside the general level of House support for the gold standard: first, because one motive in selecting these roll calls was the fact that they were closely contested (and thus it comes as no surprise that the average support hovers around 50%); and, second, because the policy controversies within each period differed quite a bit in their implications for maintaining the gold standard. For example, the votes in the House on repealing the Sherman Silver Purchase Act in 1893 were absolutely necessary to maintaining gold payments, while roll calls on free silver over much of the late nineteenth century were largely symbolic (because all congressmen anticipated that inevitable presidential vetoes could not be overridden). In the last period, also, roll calls on explicitly adopting gold as the standard of value, while certainly a positive endorsement of the metal as the foundation of the monetary system, could have been adverse without materially endangering the Treasury's ability to pay out gold. For all these reasons, it is the changing differences between relative support by the various groups in the House of Representatives that are most meaningful, not the absolute levels of support they delivered to gold.

Perhaps the most striking difference is the relatively greater support given to the gold standard by Republicans compared with Democrats. In the first period, the percentage of Republicans backing gold is three times as great as that for Democrats. Primarily as a result of Cleveland's discriminating control of federal patronage, support among Democrats rises in the second period, narrowing the margin between the two parties to slightly over two to one. With Bryan's nomination in 1896, the Democratic party is formally committed to silver, while the Republican party moves to an open endorsement of gold. As a result, roll calls on monetary policy become overtly partisan as the two major party delegations become more or less internally homogenous with respect to the gold standard. At all points, third-party members delivered less support to gold than either of the major parties, suggesting that the electorate's hostility to gold was even greater than the response of the Democratic party would otherwise indicate. For most of the late nineteenth century, the challenge presented to both major parties was to somehow satisfy one of the polarized constituencies within the nation while also attracting the relatively small number of voters in the middle of the electorate (who might support their candidates for other reasons). For the Republicans, the problem was thus to satisfy gold advocates while attracting marginal voters who were more oriented toward tariff protection, military pensions, or other parts of the party platform. For the Democrats, the problem was to satisfy inflationists while attracting marginal voters on free trade or states' rights issues.

Of the two parties, the Democrats were faced with the stiffer challenge in that a compact, major stronghold of their organization, New York City, was simultaneously free trade and gold. Further moves toward silver would compel losses in New York City that would also produce losses in New York State, which, because of its size and crucial strategic position in presidential races, meant defeat in presidential elections. Failure to move further toward silver, however, was a contributing factor in the rise of the Greenback and Populist parties which eroded party support in the nation's periphery. The resulting stress between the demands associated with New York and the rising political insurgency in the periphery is reflected in the contrasting trends in Democratic and third-party support for gold. Between the first and second periods, Democratic support for gold increased by almost 15 percent, while expanding insurgent delegations from the South and West almost halved third-party support for gold. The admission of new states in the late 1880s and the reapportionment of the House in 1892 accelerated third-party expansion along monetary issues and, finally, gave the Democratic party a compelling opportunity to respond by explicitly embracing silver in its national platform. The certain loss of New York State in such a campaign was to be made up by gains in the Plains and Mountain states, many of which were newly admitted and all of which had been rapidly growing before the collapse of the land boom in 1887.

Regardless of party, support for the gold standard was strongly related to relative levels of economic development. Among the most advanced districts, for example, the percentage of members supporting the gold standard in each of the three periods was never less than five times as great as the support given by members hailing from the least advanced districts in the nation. The consistency of the patterns across the roll calls both individually and grouped within the three periods demonstrates the foundational influence of uneven regional development on monetary policy. Another way of viewing these developmental differences is through the relative integration of the regions into the national financial system and their relative position as creditors or borrowers. Delegations from trade areas that both exported capital to the remainder of the nation and contained one of the five primary intermediating financial centers (New York, Boston, Cleveland, Cincinnati, and Chicago) gave the highest level of support for the gold standard in thirty of the thirty-four roll calls analyzed in this chapter. Three of these exceptions were recorded in 1899 and 1900 after Bryan's candidacy had shifted a portion of the (much reduced) New York City Democratic delegation toward silver. Delegations from capital-exporting trade areas lacking an intermediating financial center generally supported the gold standard less than those in the first group; however, on every roll call, delegations from capital-exporting regions, regardless of whether they contained a primary financial center or not, provided more support for gold than capital-importing trade area delegations.

When these latter trade areas are divided into those which were well-integrated, heavy capital-importing regions and others which were, by comparison, poorly integrated, light capital-importing trade areas, the pattern is equally striking (see Table 6.16). On thirty of the thirty-four roll calls, support for the gold standard was greater among members from the well-integrated, borrowing regions than among those from more isolated areas. Trade areas in both categories suffered equally from high interest rates and a local shortage of capital, but for communities in the well-integrated regions capital was at least available, and thus the abandonment of the gold standard, with accompanying disruption in the intersectional movement of investment, carried real and immediate adverse consequences. For those who had already borrowed funds and who were encountering difficulty in carrying their obligations, these consequences were relatively unimportant; thus, when compared with capital-exporting regions, a low level of support for the gold standard was to be expected throughout the period. However, there were still important interests, in the form of national banks and commercial institutions, which were dependent on the continuing flow of investment into the Plains and Mountain states. These interests account for the relatively greater support for gold compared with the poorly integrated, light capital-importing trade areas. In the latter, communities literally had almost nothing to lose from an abandonment of the gold standard – their delegations produced hostile majorities on every single vote.

Returning again to the summary percentages in Table 6.15, a number of secondary trends can now be identified. For example, the particularly notable divergence between the trends exhibited by members from the "middle low" and "low" developmental categories can be accounted for by the varying consequences for their constituents as the price of silver dropped relative to gold. In the first period, when the market price of silver was relatively close to the historic sixteen to one ratio, the consequences for intersectional capital investment from an abandonment of gold were comparatively slight, and thus the percentages for the two membership groups were separated by only 26 percent (39.9% and 13.9%, respectively). In the second period, with the price of silver much lower and the consequences from a shift in monetary standards much more severe, support for the gold standard increased in the "middle low" grouping of members, many of whom represented Plains and Mountain districts, while remaining steady for districts in the lowest developmental category (almost all of which were southern). When rising gold production in the last years of the century relieved the adverse deflationary implications of support for the gold standard, support in the "middle low" group increased still more while decreasing among members from the least advanced regions of the nation. At that

Table 6.16. *Support for the Gold Standard: Trade Areas and Interregional Capital Flow*

	Capital-exporting with significant intermediating roles	Capital-exporting with no significant intermediating role	Well-integrated heavy capital-importing	Poorly integrated heavy capital-importing
Resumption (1877)	75.9 (58)	52.2 (92)	50.0 (38)	9.2 (65)
U.S. bonds (1878)	56.5 (62)	37.1 (97)	7.1 (42)	7.5 (67)
Bland bill (1878)	56.5 (62)	33.7 (95)	4.7 (43)	5.8 (69)
Springer bill (1878)	71.9 (57)	54.1 (85)	20.5 (39)	11.5 (61)
Contraction (1878)	40.5 (42)	19.7 (76)	5.1 (39)	1.8 (55)
Duties (1879)	70.0 (40)	46.9 (81)	26.7 (30)	4.3 (47)
Free silver (1879)	95.6 (45)	81.5 (81)	76.5 (34)	36.4 (55)
Greenbacks (1880)	86.0 (43)	67.2 (67)	58.3 (36)	25.5 (55)
U.S. bonds (1881)	86.0 (57)	64.4 (87)	56.1 (41)	18.2 (66)
Trade dollar (1884)	72.2 (54)	63.5 (85)	25.5 (47)	21.9 (64)
Suspend silver (1885)	70.6 (51)	65.3 (101)	10.9 (46)	15.3 (72)
Silver resolution (1886)	66.7 (57)	40.4 (94)	16.7 (48)	4.5 (67)
Free silver (1886)	82.8 (58)	73.2 (97)	39.7 (58)	27.6 (76)
Gold reserve (1886)	66.7 (54)	56.2 (96)	50.0 (50)	5.5 (73)
Free silver (1890:A)	86.0 (43)	71.8 (85)	50.0 (58)	18.6 (70)
Free silver (1890:B)	81.8 (55)	74.5 (94)	43.3 (60)	14.1 (78)

Free silver (1892:A)	80.7 (57)	70.5 (105)	41.0 (61)	6.7 (75)
Free silver (1892:B)	87.0 (54)	76.0 (104)	34.5 (55)	11.7 (77)
Free silver (1893)	93.0 (71)	88.5 (113)	48.1 (77)	25.6 (90)
Repeal silver (1893:A)	98.6 (71)	89.2 (111)	45.5 (77)	39.8 (88)
Repeal silver (1893:B)	98.4 (62)	87.4 (95)	41.1 (56)	36.0 (75)
Seigniorage (1894:A)	84.6 (52)	69.6 (79)	33.3 (63)	12.5 (80)
Seigniorage (1894:B)	77.6 (58)	68.5 (92)	29.9 (67)	1.2 (80)
Seigniorage (1894:C)	80.8 (52)	69.6 (69)	35.0 (60)	3.9 (77)
Bryan amendment (1895)	94.2 (52)	80.2 (96)	42.3 (71)	15.8 (76)
Gold bonds (1895)	70.4 (54)	69.1 (97)	21.1 (71)	20.0 (75)
Gold contract (1895)	73.1 (52)	60.0 (90)	17.1 (70)	21.3 (75)
Gold reserve (1895)	76.9 (65)	85.4 (96)	47.1 (70)	7.9 (76)
Senate amendment (1896)	98.4 (61)	95.8 (95)	60.6 (71)	26.9 (78)
Bryan platform (1897)	90.2 (41)	81.9 (72)	51.0 (51)	12.9 (62)
U.S. bonds (1898)	87.3 (63)	85.7 (98)	47.9 (73)	8.7 (80)
Gold standard (1899:A)	68.3 (60)	75.0 (96)	65.3 (72)	5.0 (80)
Gold standard (1899:B)	73.0 (74)	77.8 (108)	64.4 (73)	5.9 (85)
Gold standard (1900)	76.3 (59)	80.4 (92)	65.6 (64)	7.0 (71)

Note: For the classification of trade areas into these four categories, see Table 2.11 of Chapter 2 and the accompanying text.

point, in the third period, the difference between the averages reported by these two groups had risen to over 50 percent.

Within the groups of members from more advanced districts, the trends were more partisan in nature. The most striking change is the comparative decline in support for the gold standard within the most developed category between the second and third periods – a decline driven entirely by the decimation of the northeastern gold wing of the Democratic party following Bryan's nomination in 1896. When separated out by party, the relationship between relative development and support for the gold standard is evident within each of the caucuses of the House. Within both parties, the disparities in support across the four developmental categories are strong in the first period, become even stronger in the second, and almost entirely disappear in the last. The Republican pattern was produced by the plunging price of silver with corresponding increasingly severe consequences for capital movement between the regions. As would be anticipated, only Republicans from the least developed districts failed to increase their support for gold between the first two periods. In the last, the party's open declaration for gold aligned the entire party with support for that metal. The Democratic pattern for the first two periods mimics that for the Republicans except that the increases in relative support, driven in part by Cleveland's patronage during his second term, are comparatively greater than in the Republican party. And as has been noted, Bryan's nomination almost destroyed support for the gold standard within the party after 1896. There are thus significant partisan influences and themes that play out over the period, but the terrain on which they move is the radically uneven pattern of regional development that characterized the American political economy of the late nineteenth century. Conforming to the general pattern, the average level of sectional stress underlying the roll call alignments in each of the three periods was almost constant (and extremely high, both historically and in comparison to other policy areas in the period).

The roll-call record on the gold standard starkly divides the nation along sectional lines (see Map 6.1).[187] At one extreme, many of the counties in New England and New York were never represented by a congressman who voted against the gold standard, no matter how the issue was framed. The *Commercial and Financial Chronicle*, in fact, described Boston as "the most

---

[187] To depict roll-call behavior over this twenty-four-year period, the votes of individual congressmen were recorded by the counties that composed their respective congressional districts, as opposed to the districts themselves. This procedure allowed for changes in district lines – always a fairly common occurrence over any lengthy time period – by making the county the unit of analysis. This was particularly effective in the late nineteenth century since relatively few counties were divided between two or more districts. Isolated counties that were exchanged between adjacent districts on one or more occasions could thus have slightly different roll-call records than, as in western Iowa or central Indiana, their neighbors.

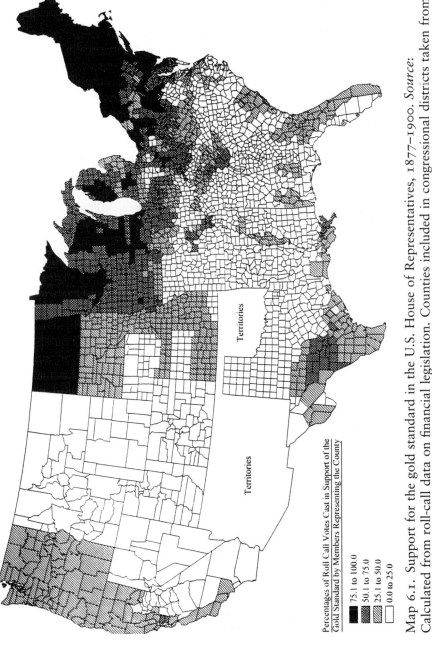

Percentages of Roll Call Votes Cast in Support of the
Gold Standard by Members Representing the County

75.1 to 100.0
50.1 to 75.0
25.1 to 50.0
0.0 to 25.0

Territories

Territories

Map 6.1. Support for the gold standard in the U.S. House of Representatives, 1877–1900. *Source:*
Calculated from roll-call data on financial legislation. Counties included in congressional districts taken from
Kenneth C. Martis, *The Historical Atlas of United States Congressional Districts, 1789–1983* (New York:
Macmillan, 1982).

conservative city of the country" in terms of financial attitudes and poli-cies.[188] The lower portion of the Northeast was slightly less friendly to gold. Congressmen from the interior of Pennsylvania often favored greenbacks over gold during the late 1870s and early 1880s. Their record, despite later almost monolithic support for the standard, produced the weak regions dis-played in that state. Of the five developmental dimensions (value-added in manufacturing, interest rates, wealth, patents, and literacy), the spatial pattern that most closely mimicked support for the gold standard was, not surprisingly, relative interest rates (see Map 2.5). Aside from pockets of rel-atively strong support for gold in North Dakota and northern portions of Michigan, Minnesota, and Wisconsin, as well as relative weakness in Kentucky, Tennessee, and Virginia, the two patterns are almost a match. As has already been discussed, these variations can be explained, at least in part, by the relatively high integration into the national capital market of the former areas; for the relatively weak congressional support given by the latter states, the correspondingly poor integration into the national capital market, along with little importation of investment, accounts for their devi-ation from what might otherwise be expected. Put another way, relative interest rates best account for congressional support for the gold standard when combined with both the direction and size of intersectional capital movements.

CONGRESSIONAL SUPPORT FOR THE GOLD STANDARD AND PRESIDENTIAL ELECTION RETURNS

The best fit for support for the gold standard, however, is not with purely economic dimensions in late nineteenth century society but with presiden-tial politics. Regional support both for the Populist party in 1892 and for Bryan in 1896 was highly correlated with congressional support for the gold standard (compare Map 6.1 with Maps 4.4 and 4.5). This tight fit, of course, arose out of the respective stances on monetary policy of these presidential campaigns and the consistency with which voters responded to those stances based on their region's position in the national political economy. The patterns are so strikingly similar that they are worth exam-ining in more detail. In 1892, for example, the Populist vote in those counties whose congressmen most frequently supported gold was a minus-cule 1.8 percent, probably less than the Prohibition vote if it were separated out from the other third party returns. For those counties whose congres-sional representatives supported gold on from just over half to three-quarters of recorded votes, electoral support for the Populist party rose

[188]　November 26, 1881.

Table 6.17. *Presidential Election Returns in 1892 and Congressional Support for Gold*

Counties categorized by the percentage of votes cast by their representative in favor of the gold standard	Percentage of votes cast in the 1892 presidential election for				Total number of votes cast
	Democrat	Republican	Populist	Other	
Category 1 (75.1–100%)	46.5	48.6	1.8	3.1	4,352,344
Category 2 (50.1–75%)	45.5	47.8	3.7	3.0	2,480,400
Category 3 (25.1–50%)	39.4	42.4	16.0	2.2	2,134,950
Category 4 (0–25%)	49.7	32.0	17.5	1.2	2,979,022

Notes and sources: All counties, with the exception of those in Louisiana, were categorized by the percentage of the votes cast by their congressman in support for the gold standard between 1877 and 1900. The percentages in the table are for the proportion of the aggregate vote cast for each party by voters in each of the four categories. Louisiana was excluded because the fusion arrangement in that state between the Republicans and the Populists makes it difficult to assign the vote to either of the two parties. For 1892 election returns, see W. Dean Burnham, *Presidential Ballots, 1836–1892* (Baltimore: Johns Hopkins University Press, 1955). All calculations were done by the author.

slightly to just under 4 percent (see Table 6.17). The big break in pattern appears when the votes are tabulated for those counties whose representatives were comparatively hostile to gold, where the Populist percentage jumps to 16 percent, and for those counties whose congressmen were most hostile to gold, where it settles at 17.5 percent. With a financial conservative, Grover Cleveland, at the head of a ticket leading an overwhelmingly silver congressional party, Democratic support in 1892 was comparatively unrelated to congressional voting. However, the Republican ticket, with a gold nominee for president and a financially conservative congressional party, drew significantly more electoral support from counties whose members tended to favor gold than from those whose members opposed the metal.

Support for Bryan was equally well correlated with congressional support for the gold standard (see Table 6.18). Already in 1888, there was some connection between congressional support for gold and major party strength in presidential returns. Cleveland, the Democratic candidate that year, grew progressively stronger as congressional support for gold declined. Given Cleveland's well-known commitment to gold, this pattern can be

Table 6.18. *Major Party Support in the 1888 and 1896 Presidential Elections and Congressional Support for Gold*

Counties categorized by the percentage of votes cast by their major representative in favor of the gold standard	Total vote cast for major party candidates (%)							
	1888 presidential election			1896 presidential election			Change in party support	
	Total number of votes	Democrat	Republican	Total number of votes	Democrat	Republican	Dem.	Rep.
Category 1 (75.1–100%)	4,087,290	45.4	51.7	4,873,552	35.5	61.2	–9.9	+9.5
Category 2 (50.1–75%)	2,439,382	45.9	50.7	3,012,980	43.3	54.6	–2.6	+3.9
Category 3 (25.1–50%)	1,983,568	47.3	48.6	2,283,540	49.3	48.8	+2.0	+0.2
Category 4 (0–25%)	2,862,876	56.4	39.5	3,334,091	62.3	36.3	+5.9	–3.2

Notes and sources: All counties were categorized by the percentage of the votes cast by their congressman in support for the gold standard between 1877 and 1900. The percentages in the table are for the proportion of the aggregate vote cast for each party by voters in each of the four categories. Election returns from states admitted between 1888 and 1896 were excluded because they would have impaired the calculation of relative percentage changes between the two elections. For 1888 election returns, see W. Dean Burnham, *Presidential Ballots, 1836–1892* (Baltimore: Johns Hopkins University Press, 1955). For most states, the source for 1896 election statistics was Edgar Eugene Robinson, *The Presidential Vote, 1896–1932* (Stanford, Calif.: Stanford University Press, 1947). The Bryan vote in 1896 combines the Democratic and People's party tickets. In all but Texas, the source for the combined vote was the *1898 Boston Journal Almanac* (Boston: Boston Journal, 1898). In Texas, the source was the *1899 World Almanac* (New York: New York World, 1899). All calculations were done by the author.

explained only by the underlying political economic base of the Democratic party in Congress, a base as committed to silver as Cleveland was to gold and as relatively underdeveloped as Cleveland's home state of New York was comparatively advanced. Before Bryan's nomination, the Democratic party named presidential candidates who could compete with the Republicans in New York and thus took their periphery base in the South for granted. When the Populists offered a silver alternative in 1892, the silver predilections of the periphery drew enough Democratic votes away from Cleveland that the connection between congressional support for gold and his electoral strength almost disappeared (see Table 6.17). When Bryan was nominated in 1896, the disjunction between the silver commitments of the Democratic party in Congress and the party's strategy in presidential elections was eliminated, and electoral support for the major parties shifted dramatically. These shifts made the difference between the highest and lowest categories of counties, in terms of congressional support for the gold standard, much larger than they had been in the earlier election. In 1888, the difference in Cleveland's support between the counties in the highest and lowest categories was 11 percent; for Bryan in 1896, the variation was almost 27 percent. The change was only slightly less striking for the Republicans. Few changes in national party platforms have had such a strong electoral impact; even fewer have been so clearly discernible in the policy alignments characterizing congressional voting.[189]

---

[189] These connections must be carefully specified. Most important, it should be noted that much of congressional voting on the gold standard was recorded after the 1888, 1892, and 1896 elections, although only five votes occurred after the latter contest. Viewed in purely political terms, congressional alignments were certainly influenced by these contests. For example, after his election in 1892, Cleveland used presidential patronage to move the Democrats toward gold. Four years later, Bryan's nomination both decimated the northeastern wing of the Democratic party and moved the survivors toward silver. So presidential elections clearly mattered in congressional voting patterns, and including roll calls cast after an election, as has been done here, undercuts the utility of congressional alignments as an indicator of policy leanings within the nation's counties when analyzing a particular presidential contest. Thus the decision to stick with the same set of roll calls for analyzing all of these election returns must be justified on pragmatic grounds because it is clearly incorrect theoretically. Three justifications can be offered. In the first instance, all the solutions would have involved complex explications, arising out of the varying sets of roll calls used in the analysis; in the end, methodological rigor would have been purchased at the cost of a complex and murky discussion. Second, most areas of the nation, regardless of who occupied the White House or what period was under examination, voted very consistently on gold. The political effects, in terms of executive influence on that underlying pattern, turn out to be relatively minor. Finally, those political effects, because they operated on congressmen in directions contrary from what their constituencies preferred, tend to disrupt the expected overall pattern. For example, Bryan made silverites out of Tammany Democrats despite New York City's strong preference for gold. Their post-1896 voting record was thus substantially different from the city's prior, overwhelming commitment to

THE NATIONAL BANK SYSTEM AND
THE GOLD STANDARD

In strictly economic terms, the national bank system was not essential to the operation of the gold standard. In many respects, in fact, the system was an ill-fitted, even clunky holdover from the Union mobilization during the Civil War. Some of its features, such as the deposit of federal bonds with the Treasury in exchange for national bank notes, had been originally conceived as a means of attracting investor interest in the debt that funded the war effort. Although ingeniously connected to the safety of the national bank currency, other policy devices would have served this purpose as well or better. Other characteristics, such as the inelasticity of bank notes in response to the seasonal fluctuations in the demand for currency and the pyramiding of deposits culminating in their concentration in New York City, were more or less obvious flaws that drew proposals for reform from the financial community throughout the late nineteenth century.

However, for better or worse, the national bank system did exist and was therefore closely linked with Treasury operations under the gold standard. Their intertwined political destinies can be viewed from several perspectives. First, the national banks were in a creditor relationship with both private borrowers and, more important, the federal government. As with bankers almost anywhere and at any time, their investments strongly encouraged them toward financial conservatism and, in particular, hostility to inflationary policies. This was reinforced by the illiquid nature of the bonds deposited with the Treasury as backing for their notes; in the event of an impending abandonment of the gold standard, the national banks would not be able to retrieve these bonds before the government shifted to a new standard because the process of recalling the bank notes that the bonds secured often took months.[190] For this major portion of most national bank portfolios, there was thus no practical way to hedge against a change in monetary standards. Of all institutions within the financial community, the national banks were far and away the most vulnerable in such an event. So they had abundant motive to favor gold.[191]

---

hard money. Omitting the post-1896 votes would thus only strengthen, for New York and much of the nation, the tendency for high congressional support for gold to result in heavy shifts against the Democratic party in 1896.

[190] For a detailed but narrow discussion of the procedure by which the national banks might withdraw their circulation and reclaim their bonds from the Treasury, *Commercial and Financial Chronicle*, June 25, 1881. Also see *Appleton's 1881 Cyclopaedia*, pp. 127, 290–291.

[191] The national banks well understood their interests in maintaining gold payments. For the negotiations between the Secretary of the Treasury, the United States Treasurer, and the sixty-six member banks of the New York Clearing House under which

The national banks also had political clout. In 1886, some 220,000 individuals owned shares in one or more national banks. Their distribution throughout the country mimicked the geographical pattern of support for the gold standard – a pattern that, as political agents, they played a substantial role in generating. Over 40 percent of all shareholders resided in New England alone. Another 30 percent lived in the other northeastern states, most of them in New York. Shareholders were comparatively hard to find in the remainder of the country, particularly the South. In the Plains and Mountain states, however, the presence of numerous, small national banks tended to plant at least some gold sentiment in soil that otherwise was very predisposed to favor silver. Many of these banks were established by eastern investors, and their local agents transmitted eastern gold sentiment throughout the trans-Mississippi West. The South, in contrast, was relatively unaffected by such institutional factors in its politics because, in local politics, they simply did not exist.[192] And shareholders in national banks were the very antithesis of their archenemies in the Greenback and Populist movements – members of a wealthy, urban, and sophisticated elite instead of a poor, rural, and rough-hewn underclass. As a compact, elite body that well understood its interests and how to promote them within national politics, bankers projected influence that far exceeded their

the banks agreed to accept subsidiary silver in return for gold as a means of rescuing the government from an otherwise impending abandonment of the gold standard, see *Commercial and Financial Chronicle*, May 23, 30, June 6, July 18, 25, August 8, 1885. This rescue was immediately followed by the annual convention of the American Bankers' Association in Chicago which emphatically condemned silver purchases under the Bland-Allison Act as a policy endangering the Treasury's ability to maintain an adequate gold reserve. September 26, 1885. This condemnation was repeated the following year, combined "with a plain appeal to boards of trade, and mercantile and political associations of every kind, to labor against the continued coinage of silver dollars. . . ." August 14, 1886. And again in 1887. October 15, 1887. In addition to the national banks, chambers of commerce, boards of trade, and other financial and commercial organizations bombarded Congress with appeals for the suspension of silver purchases and coinage. See, for example, the February 27, 1886, issue, where the *Chronicle* reports a petition "signed by the presidents and cashiers of all the savings banks in the State of New York, who represent 1,165,000 working men and women," as well as a resolution passed by the Milwaukee Chamber of Commerce and a second petition from "sixty-six leading mercantile firms, &c., of Norfolk, Virginia." During the Battle of the Standards a decade later, commercial and banking organizations were among the very few opponents of silver in the nation's periphery, and for that reason, their resolutions were warmly acknowledged by the *Chronicle*. May 30, 1896.

[192] For the distribution of national bank shareholders, see *Commercial and Financial Chronicle*, December 11, 1886. In 1876 the number of shareholders had been 208,486, slowly rising to 281,225 by 1897. Kirkland, *Industry Comes of Age*, p. 30. For a general description of the national bank system and its role in the movement of capital from east to west, see Chapter 2.

numbers.[193] One Ohio Democrat, for example, complained during House debate that passage of the gold standard bill was "for the benefit of the 3,600 national banks, who constitute a secret society that has more power than the million Masons, the million Odd Fellows, and the half million Knights of Pythias combined. No secret society on the face of the earth ever wielded such influence and such power."[194]

Such charges were plausible for a number of reasons, one of which was the complexity of financial policy and the relative absence of expertise within the government. But the most important reason was the presence of numerous national bank shareholders among members of Congress.[195] Although the full extent of such interests within the membership is not known, more than a third of all members of the House may have owned shares.[196] There were also partisan differences with respect to national bank investments, with Republicans more likely to hold shares than Democrats.[197] Regardless of the extent of share-holding among members of Congress, the national banks as institutions were often very politically active in their own right.[198] In fact, the policy linkages between national

---

[193]   The unity of the national banks rested on their common interests in politics, not on an organizational centralism in their commercial activities. As the *Commercial and Financial Chronicle* put it, "banking has become a great power in the country and all over the commercial world. Banking and transportation are probably the most important of commercial powers. . . . [And yet there] is hardly a guild or trade class in the country, from transportation companies down to trades unions, which uses so much independence of action and is so little governed by an organized central authority from within, as that of the banks." July 23, 1881.

[194]   Rep. John Jacob Lentz, *Congressional Record* 56:1:548, December 16, 1899.

[195]   As investments, national bank shares were long on relative safety and rather short on real return on capital. In 1897, for example, average dividends per share were estimated at somewhat less than 5 percent of invested capital and surplus. Kirkland, *Industry Comes of Age*, p. 30. Shares were also widely dispersed, indicating a high level of passive investment. *Commercial and Financial Chronicle*, August 12, 1882. Such characteristics were probably attractive to men of wealth who, like members of Congress, spent a good portion of their time away from what would have been their place of business. For a discussion of the profitability of national banks, including interest on bonds deposited with the Treasury, state and federal taxes, and other income and expenses, see *Commercial and Financial Chronicle*, December 4, 1880.

[196]   For an important debate on the extent of national bank shareholding among members of the House of Representatives, see *Congressional Record* 46:3:764–769, January 19, 1881.

[197]   Republican Roswell Horr of Michigan: "There are some Democrats who are national bankers, perhaps not so many as there are Republicans, but that grows out of the fact that the large majority of the business men of the country are Republicans." *Congressional Record* 46:3:733, January 18, 1881. However, members, if they revealed any aspect of their holdings (which was not often), almost always denied holding any kind of stake in the national bank system.

[198]   For example, William Hatch, a Missouri Democrat, reported during debate on Cleveland's bond contract that the "House has been flooded with petitions from national banks and boards of trade asking members to vote for this bill." *Congres-*

banks and the monetary standard were so tight that bills for the purpose of making policy in one area sometimes became the vehicle for changes in the other.[199]

The downside to all this influence was the tendency in much of American society to regard the interests and policy pronouncements of bankers with deep suspicion. During debate on a bill to refund the federal debt, for example, an Iowa Republican complained that

the great bug-bear about this thing is the cry as to the national banks. They are the troublesome element in this matter. There are gentlemen upon this floor of intelligence, of integrity, of standing, not only here but at home, who rush to the front with as much velocity and ferocity whenever you name "national banks" as the wildest bull that ever came from the mountains of Andalusia would rush upon a red flag ... with your insane ferocity you rush upon this national banking system; yes, and you would rush on the thick bosses of Jehovah's buckler if you thought that there was a national bank behind it and destroy it if possible.[200]

In response, James Weaver replied, "The National Bankers' Association is here in force, are literally overrunning the lobby, and have eaten up everything in the House restaurant ... the war has begun, and it will never stop until these undemocratic, dangerous, and hostile institutions are swept from existence and the people shall have forever reclaimed their sovereign right to issue the money of the country. This is the old Jacksonian battle over again, of the people against the banks."[201] In fact, in that Jacksonian spirit, bankers in the United States were often described as English toadies, as in the following excerpt from House debate some thirteen years later – this time on a resolution to allow repayment of federal bonds in silver:

Bankers are but money lenders and money changers. The greatest bankers of this country are but agents for the greater bankers of Europe, and the bankers of Europe are but agents for the greater bankers of London – creditor of creditors, source of all financial sources, the concentrated power and clearing house of the financial world. The bankers of England who control this source and ultimate of financial

---

sional Record 53:3:2195, February 14, 1895. In turn, Secretaries of the Treasury found the annual meetings of banking associations almost irresistible as platforms for their own policy initiatives. Secretary Sherman, for example, addressed the 1880 American Bankers' Association convention in Saratoga, New York. *Commercial and Financial Chronicle*, July 24, 1880.

[199] In 1893, for example, what was originally a national bank measure was unsuccessfully transformed into a bill calling for repeal of the Sherman Silver Purchase Act. *Congressional Record* 52:2:1377–1383, February 9, 1893.

[200] Hiram Price. *Congressional Record* 46:3:2323, March 1, 1881. It might be noted that Price was the president of the First National Bank of Davenport, Iowa, in addition to his congressional vocation.

[201] *Congressional Record* 46:3:2324, March 1, 1881.

power are the greatest money experts on earth from the standpoint of the bankers and money lenders' interest in the money question.[202]

All of these factors – the policy linkages between the national bank system and Treasury management of the government's finances, the interests of the banks in maintaining gold payments, the prominence of bankers as lobbyists and political agents in their own right, and the vulnerability of financiers as a cosmopolitan elite within a very parochial popular culture – produced a direct connection between the national bank system and defense of the gold standard that permeated almost all political debate over monetary policy. Responding to the simple prejudices and lack of financial sophistication in the popular culture, political rhetoric often conflated the national banks, support for the gold standard, and orthodoxy in economic theory into the same, undifferentiated ball of demonic greed.

Not surprisingly, for that reason, voting alignments on national bank policy were almost indistinguishable from patterns characterizing gold standard roll calls (compare Table 6.19 with Table 6.15). The five votes analyzed here were chosen both for the variety of policy features they addressed and their wide distribution throughout the period. However, most were recorded during the greenback era when hostility to banks was most intense and policy alternatives to the existing system were most entertained. For example, the first vote was taken on a proposal to retire national bank notes and issue in their place an equivalent number of greenbacks. Given that the issuance of bank notes was the primary reason that financiers organized national banks, this bill would have dismantled the system had it been enacted. A more complex issue was raised in a second vote that year when a resolution was offered that would have compelled the national banks to accept silver dollars as legal tender. The problem for the banks was that only greenbacks could serve as a reserve for their deposits under federal law. Compelling the banks to accept silver dollars could thus endanger bank reserves if, for any number of reasons, the public preferred greenbacks to silver and thus could force the banks to perform the switch. This simple resolution, which would not have had the force of law but would have instructed the Committee on Banking and Currency to report the necessary legislation, failed only because the motion required a two-thirds' majority.

The third and fourth votes in Table 6.19 were taken on the National Bank Extension Act, which permitted the institutions to renew their charters, many of which were expiring at that time. One of these roll calls was on an amendment offered by Richard Bland, the Missouri Democrat, to compel national banks whose charters expired to involuntarily liquidate their institutions, replacing bank notes with Treasury notes. Had it been adopted, this amendment would have abolished the national bank system.

---

[202] James McGuire, a California Democrat, *Congressional Record* 55:2: 1303, January 31, 1898.

Table 6.19. *Members Supporting the National Bank System,*
1877–1900 (%)

House membership category	Retire bank notes (1878)	Accept silver dollars (1878)	Abolish bank system (1882)	Bank extension act (1882)	Repeal tax on state banks (1894)
Full House	50.9 (224)	37.3 (241)	66.0 (209)	58.2 (189)	62.8 (274)
Republicans	87.6 (113)	61.9 (118)	98.3 (115)	97.0 (101)	100.0 (89)
Democrats	13.8 (109)	14.0 (121)	22.6 (84)	15.1 (79)	41.7 (175)
Other party	0.0 (2)	0.0 (2)	60.0 (10)	0.0 (9)	100.0 (10)
District level of development					
All members					
Highest	71.9 (32)	74.4 (39)	92.1 (38)	76.7 (30)	90.9 (44)
Middle high	78.3 (60)	55.0 (60)	87.8 (49)	88.4 (43)	92.2 (64)
Middle low	45.2 (84)	27.4 (95)	64.6 (82)	51.9 (79)	66.7 (105)
Lowest	12.5 (48)	4.3 (47)	17.5 (40)	21.6 (37)	4.9 (61)
Republicans					
Highest	75.0 (20)	85.7 (21)	100.0 (27)	100.0 (19)	100.0 (15)
Middle high	93.3 (45)	68.2 (44)	97.5 (40)	94.6 (37)	100.0 (32)
Middle low	87.8 (41)	47.9 (48)	97.8 (45)	97.5 (40)	100.0 (39)
Lowest	85.7 (7)	40.0 (5)	100.0 (3)	100.0 (5)	100.0 (3)
Democrats					
Highest	66.7 (12)	61.1 (18)	70.0 (10)	36.4 (11)	85.7 (28)
Middle high	33.3 (15)	18.7 (16)	44.4 (9)	50.0 (6)	82.8 (29)
Middle low	4.7 (43)	6.4 (47)	17.2 (29)	6.1 (33)	41.7 (60)
Lowest	0.0 (39)	0.0 (40)	8.3 (36)	11.5 (29)	0.0 (58)
Sectional stress	71.8	62.2	54.9	58.2	73.5

Note and sources: The roll-call position that accorded with support for the national bank system is indicated in parentheses: on a bill to retire national bank notes (nay); on a bill to compel national banks to accept silver dollars (nay); on an amendment to abolish national bank system (nay); on a bill to extend national bank charters (yea); and on repeal of the federal tax on state bank notes (nay). The roll calls can be found in the *Congressional Record* 45:2:4872–4873, June 19, 1878; 45:3:63, December 9, 1878; 47:1:4088, May 18, 1882; 47:1:5852, July 10, 1882; and 53:2:5891–5892, June 6, 1894.

Several months later, after long debate and further consideration of the bill, the House of Representatives passed the conference report and the banks were permitted to renew their charters.[203]

[203] Under existing law, the Comptroller of the Currency could and did continue the operation of national banks even though their charters had expired. Thus, the authority embodied in the extension bill was technically unnecessary when a friendly

The last vote in Table 6.19 was recorded on what was, at that time, one of the oldest issues raised by the national bank system. In 1865, two years after creation of the national bank system, the federal government in effect took away the ability of state-chartered banks to issue their own notes by placing a prohibitive 10 percent annual tax on their value. Ever since the end of the Civil War, proposals had been made for the elimination of that tax so that the states could charter banks of issue on their own authority. But the question was not pressed with much vigor until the depression of the early 1890s brought the Democrats into power at the White House and in Congress on a platform that committed the national party to repeal. The regional center of this campaign was the South, where the national bank system was extraordinarily weak and the national capital market had little or no presence. For that region, the reemergence of state-chartered banks of issue promised to aid economic development and, at the same time, strengthen local political and economic autonomy. When the bill came to the floor, however, the repeal that it carried was only temporary. In response, Nicholas Cox, a Tennessee Democrat, offered an amendment to make repeal permanent. The vote analyzed in Table 6.19 was recorded on that amendment. Although the Speaker, Charles Crisp of Georgia, asked the clerk to call his name in order that he might cast a vote in support (a rare event in that the Speaker seldom votes except in the case of ties), the amendment was soundly defeated. The bill itself was later lost in an unrecorded, voice vote.

The voting alignments on these five national bank decisions almost precisely followed those on the gold standard (compare Tables 6.15 and 6.19). The Democrats, for example, were always less sympathetic to the banks than the Republicans. Minor party members were also less sympathetic in most cases, although Greenback members opposed the 1882 amendment to abolish the national bank system because the federal currency that would have replaced national bank notes would not have had legal tender status. In 1894, also, the Populists opposed repeal of the federal tax on state-chartered bank notes because they opposed bank notes in all forms, even those issued by state banks. In both cases, doctrinal differences between Democratic and Greenback financial policy were displayed to an extent not usually evident on decisions more directly related to the gold standard. On all five votes, the relative degree of economic development within congressional districts was an important factor aligning both the parties and the House membership on national bank policy. Within the Republican party, however, support for the national bank system tended to be so high

official occupied the Comptroller's office. However, the operations entailed by this alternative procedure were, at best, cumbersome and, at worst, endangered the financial system. *Congressional Record* 47:1:3473, May 1, 1882. For the text and a description of the Bank Extension Act, see the *Commercial and Financial Chronicle*, July 15, 1882.

throughout the caucus that the differences in support with regard to development were small to nonexistent. Within the Democratic party, however, they were quite striking, particularly on repeal of the tax on state-chartered bank notes which pitted an almost unanimous faction from the underdeveloped South against an almost equally monolithic delegation from the advanced regions of the Northeast. Regional polarization within the full House membership, as measured by sectional stress scores, was generally as high as that on the gold standard decisions; in both policy areas, these scores were among the highest ever recorded on any policy issue in the House of Representatives.

CONCLUSION

Along with the gold standard, the protective tariff was both a major feature of the policy framework within which industrialization proceeded and a major factor in the steady redistribution of wealth from the southern and, to a lesser extent, western periphery to the core manufacturing areas of the Northeast. The strictly economic impact of protection was to accentuate the accumulation of capital in heavy industry (particularly iron and steel) by redistributing wealth from commodity agriculture (particularly cotton and wheat). Since both sectors were highly concentrated within different regions, this redistribution of wealth was between sections, closely overlapping with the pattern produced by the gold standard.

In the pure logic of abstract economic theory, there was little reason for support for the gold standard to coincide with support for the protective tariff. On one hand, the gold standard had little direct impact on the profitability of industrial corporations. The role of gold was to integrate the capital markets of New York and London in such a way as to facilitate the flow abroad of federal, state, and municipal bonds, along with railroad securities. In addition, the integration of these two markets under the discipline of the gold standard served to encourage the retention of capital otherwise accruing to industrial corporations out of profits. But industrial securities were not directly exchanged in the international capital market until very late in the nineteenth century, and, thus, the profitability and capitalization of industrial corporations was only tangentially affected by the gold standard. Instead, gold tended to encourage the reinvestment of industrial profits in expanded production in the United States by stabilizing the currency and providing access to European capital for developing the transportation network and urban infrastructure. Without this stabilization and infrastructure development, a larger portion of the corporate profits generated from industrial operations would have been invested abroad, but the net return to industrialists would have probably been little affected. In sum, the gold standard was fundamentally important to the pace of industrialization (because it underpinned the availability of investment in social and transportation infrastructure, as well as encouraging the reinvestment of industrial profits) but was much less important to individual industrialists (since they had investment opportunities abroad).

On the other hand, finance capitalists, although vitally interested in the preservation of gold payments, had little direct stake in tariff protection since industrial securities played but a small role in the markets they managed or the portfolios they held. Thus, when viewed as separate sectors within the American economy, finance capitalists and industrialists potentially had very different interests with respect to protection and gold. Finance capitalists, otherwise strongly committed to a defense of the gold standard, could have viewed the tariff question with relative indifference, while industrialists dependent on tariff protection could have viewed the money question with relative equanimity. In fact, these two sets of policy positions more or less accurately describe the opinions held by sizable fractions of both sectors in the period between the Civil War and resumption in 1879. In those years, for example, industrialists held but small investment portfolios and often entertained expansive monetary opinions that favored a greenback-based currency.[204] As industrial corporations matured, internal expansion of their operations could not absorb all of the capital they generated through profits. As industrialists diversified their portfolios by investing in other enterprises, they became rentier capitalists, ever more committed to defense of the gold standard. But it was in their relatively new and partial role as rentier capitalists, not industrial entrepreneurs, that the connection to gold emerged.[205]

For finance capitalists, the road was different but converged on the same result. Until very late in the century, when industrial stocks and bonds finally claimed an important role on the major exchanges, finance capitalists favored free trade for two reasons. The primary reason was the tendency of tariff protection to reduce the volume of exports and imports (and thus the need for the services of finance capitalists in carrying and organizing international trade). Only slightly less important was the derangement of "natural," competitive prices as a direct result of the imposition of

---

[204] Unger, *Greenback Era*, pp. 49–62.

[205] Perhaps the archetypal example of such a transformation was Andrew Carnegie, who, when interviewed just as he embarked for Europe in the spring of 1896, declared that "no man should be either a Republican or a Democrat, but a patriot, and insist that this coming [presidential] campaign shall settle for all time the question of a standard of value in this country. . . . Capital at home equally with capital abroad has become alarmed. It has run into its hole and will not come forth to embark in enterprises which create prosperity until it is established that the American people borrowing a dollar in gold will return a dollar, and not seek to defraud its creditor by returning a dollar worth only fifty cents." *Commercial and Financial Chronicle*, May 23, 1896.

customs duties. Financiers also bemoaned the destabilization of market expectations (and thus stock prices) whenever legislative deliberations on the tariff were under way; congressional debate on revision always increased investor uncertainty as to the market prospects for important industries and the economy as a whole.

Over the course of the late nineteenth century, however, several trends increased the favor with which finance capitalists viewed tariff protection. The first was economic and relatively minor: As industrial securities increased their share of transactions on the major financial markets, finance capitalists began to view continuity in tariff policy as more important than the abstract virtues that would have attended "free trade" reform. Since protection, by and large, was the prevailing policy during this period, finance capitalists increasingly tended to see that position as the one offering the best chance of minimizing market uncertainty. The second trend was political and more important: The decreasing support for gold in national politics, particularly after 1889 when the admission of many western and plains states dramatically strengthened the silver forces in the Senate, drove finance capitalists into the arms of protectionists out of necessity. After 1896, when the Democrats in their national convention broke with gold altogether, this convergence was complete.

For all these reasons, then, the interests of finance capitalists and industrialists drew together over the course of the late nineteenth century. As their interests converged, both groups strengthened their commitment to the Republican party. In fact, the leaders of the Republican party managed this convergence of interests in several ways. First, the overlapping pattern of wealth redistribution between the sections produced a convergence of policy interests within electoral constituencies much earlier and more completely than that arising out of the melding of the two sectors in market institutions. Within congressional districts, wealth holders tended to have overlapping stakes in both the financial system and industrial expansion, both of which benefited from a largely identical pattern of intersectional redistribution. Outside New York City, for example, dense communities of industrialists and finance capitalists tended to concentrate within the same regions. For this reason, it was fairly easy for Republicans within the manufacturing belt to support both the gold standard (the strong preference of finance capitalists) and tariff protection (the strong preference of industrialists) even when the two sectors were indifferent or even opposed to each other's position. Within such districts, in addition, the concentration of industrial workers and commercial interests dependent on the general prosperity of the manufacturing belt also tended to knit together the two policies into a unified Republican platform. This district-level coincidence of support for protection and gold was elaborated into a much larger and more intricate Republican program for industrial development in the late nineteenth century – a program that rested on the spatial distribution of their constituent economic interests as much or more than it did on an abstract theory of the developmental process. Still, even though the political bases of support for the protective tariff and the gold standard became intimately intertwined within the Republican party, the two policies inhabited distinct realms with partially autonomous dynamics.

7

Tariff Protection and the Republican Party

STANDING at the very center of the Republican coalition that guided late nineteenth-century industrialization, the tariff most immediately benefited industrial manufacturers who were directly exposed to foreign competition. But the benefit conferred on these producers was not enough to politically sustain the tariff. For that reason, the tariff coalition was broadened by protecting selected agricultural products as well. Because the United States exported vast amounts of grain, cotton, and other agricultural products, the list of farm goods that could be enlisted into the tariff coalition was a short one, with raw wool at the head. Sugar, which enjoyed a domestic market robust enough to withstand very high duties on imports, generated much of the revenue from the tariff and, incidentally, often attracted Louisiana congressmen to the coalition.

The revenue generated from protection, in turn, supported a vast pension system for Union veterans who, through the Grand Army of the Republic, subsequently enlisted in the tariff coalition. Further underpinning Republican dominance within the manufacturing belt, the combination of protection and pensions gave American industrialization a particularly nationalist flavor.[1] In addition, by extending the tariff coalition into the western plains, the pension system probably postponed and ultimately weakened western revolt against the "gold and protection" developmental path followed by the United States. "Voting as they had shot," Union veterans refought the Civil War, this time as a conflict over pension benefits and northern industrialization.[2] Finally, the tariff secured the principal and interest payments

---

[1] See, for example, H. Wayne Morgan, *From Hayes to McKinley: National Party Politics, 1877–1896* (Syracuse, N.Y.: Syracuse University Press, 1969), pp. 170, 318–319.

[2] For a sampling of the thick and enduring connections between the Grand Army of the Republic, military pensions, the protective tariff, and the Republican party, see Mary R. Dearing, *Veterans in Politics: The Story of the G.A.R.* (Baton Rouge: Louisiana State University Press, 1952), pp. 287–288, 364–367, 377, 381–382,

on federal bonds by raising revenue; in fact, in most years, customs duties provided most of the government's income. In sum, Republican management of the tariff coalition spawned a vast, interrelated policy complex in which the original impulse to protect emerging industrial sectors became embedded in an extended system of alliances and working arrangements between widely separated groups in the national political economy. In the process, the tariff lost whatever coherence it might have had as a national economic policy and became a political instrument for regional industrialization of the Northeast and Great Lakes littoral. In that and other roles, the tariff was also transformed into the political foundation for the Republican developmental coalition. The tariff certainly had economic effects, some of them very important, but the importance of protection for national development lay primarily in its politics, operating through the larger policy complex constructed by the Republican party.

THE IMPACT OF THE TARIFF ON INDUSTRIAL DEVELOPMENT

The tariff mediated between the American domestic economy and the international economy, determining which goods and, as well, which nations gained access to American consumers. As such, the tariff could have been a strong, discriminating device in the conduct of foreign policy. If outward-directed, a relaxation of customs duties can be used to reinforce political alliances through a closer integration of their respective domestic markets. Conversely, rising trade barriers can be used to exclude competitors whose interests and expansionist tendencies conflict with the ambitions of the home nation. Such possibilities tend to make tariffs and trade relations generally less economic and more political by subordinating the domestic market to international power politics.[3] However, the American tariff system of the late nineteenth century was almost entirely inward-directed in that external politics rarely played anything but a trivial role in the construction of schedules and the determination of external market relations.

As a set of domestic demands to which politicians responded, the tariff

---

384–385, 389, 397–398, 451. These connections were perhaps strongest during the great struggle over the tariff in the 1888 presidential campaign when "most Grand Army assemblies were quietly managed Republican rallies." Pp. 385, 469. At other times, the links between the Republican party and the GAR were so close that the latter was sometimes described as "Generally All Republicans." P. 496.

[3] See Kenneth A. Oye, *Economic Discrimination & Political Exchange: World Political Economy in the 1930s and 1980s* (Princeton, N.J.: Princeton University Press, 1993), esp. chap. 1. Jonathan Kirshner and Rawi Abdelal, "Strategy, Economic Relations, and the Definition of National Interest," *Security Studies* 9:1 (Autumn 1999): 119–156.

was almost unrelentingly economic in nature. The position of industries, sectors, and regions was determined by careful calculation of the advantages and disadvantages both of the particular schedules that most directly affected their respective markets and of the entire tariff as a pastiche of hundreds of individual duties. From the perspective of individual schedules, such calculations were fairly simple. Current producers would benefit most. Those who produced goods that could be substituted for the protected item were also advantaged, but less certainly and completely. Those who consumed that good as a raw material in their own operations were clearly disadvantaged, sometimes seriously if they could not substitute unprotected alternatives. And everyone else more or less suffered a comparative loss of income determined by the degree to which they consumed the products in their daily lives. Then as now, the benefits of a tariff on a particular good, if produced in the domestic economy in any significant amount, were concentrated on a fairly small number of industries, sectors, and regions while the liabilities tended to be widely distributed but relatively minor.

As political economists have repeatedly noted for more than a century, this concentration of benefits and wide distribution of liabilities has encouraged the organization of interest groups and their legislative lobbies. From that perspective, the protective tariff stimulated the political organization of American business into industrial and commercial associations more than any other government policy in the late nineteenth century. These groups, as well as their individual members, petitioned and testified before Congress by the thousands whenever tariff revision became a serious political possibility. Their demands strongly reinforced both the domestic perspective within which the tariff was constructed and the economic perspective within which interests were defined and acted on. Given the way interests were mobilized before the central government, it might be expected that politicians would have merely served as independent brokers for the industries, sectors, and regions that could, either as constituents or otherwise, influence their behavior. In fact, some scholars have viewed late nineteenth-century tariff construction in exactly that frame – as a highly decentralized process in which individual congressmen acted on behalf of private interests at every stage save final passage. At final passage, party loyalty superseded the almost impossible summary accounting for the hundreds of individual schedules, and congressmen avoided complex economic calculations of advantage by simply aligning with their party. This interpretation explains both the very messy process through which tariffs were constructed and the very stark, almost ritualized, display of party divisions on final passage.[4]

---

[4] For a clear and rather extreme example of this perspective on tariff politics in the United States in the late nineteenth century, see Daniel Verdier, *Democracy and International Trade: Britain, France, and the United States, 1860–1990* (Princeton, N.J.: Princeton University Press, 1994), pp. 69–70, 73, 79, 82.

Far less persuasive has been the international or developmental interpretation of late nineteenth-century tariff policy. Accepting the "infant industry" arguments of contemporaries, this interpretation contends that tariff protection promoted the expansion of manufacturing within the American economy when most technological advantages lay with foreign, particularly British, producers. Without tariff protection, this interpretation contends, American industrialization would have expanded much more slowly than was actually the case as British producers penetrated and reshaped the domestic market to their own advantage. This perspective views nations as possessing a unified interest in the world system that is shaped by their relative development compared with foreign competitors.[5]

This national interest is viewed as a lodestone for domestic politics that determines the outcome of tariff construction and other developmental policies, at least in cases where national policy is not compromised by foreign intervention of one sort or another. For example, late nineteenth-century American tariff policy exploited the position of the United States in the world system by protecting the domestic market from the major hegemon in the international political economy while permitting that same hegemon, Great Britain, to provide the necessary international security within which the United States could concentrate on domestic industrial development. In sum, the United States turned the terms of trade between itself and Great Britain to its own advantage while allowing Great Britain to bear the military costs of imposing order and stability on international markets.[6]

In this case, the analytical problem presented by the very messy political construction of tariff politics is simply assumed away as mere detail. Instead, the perspective interprets the national interest as an overriding and obvious policy goal to which parties must subscribe or be consigned to the political wilderness. Thus, protection was almost predestined to survive even the most serious political challenges, including a sustained Democratic attempt to dismantle trade barriers when the party controlled both Congress and the executive branch. The strong aspects of this interpretation have been its robust yet simple model of national interest within the international political economy. However, the model depends on several dubious assumptions: first, that some notion of the national interest was on display as an universally acknowledged guide to government policy, and, second,

---

[5] For an outline of the general theory and its application to the United States in the late nineteenth century, see David A. Lake, *Power, Protection, and Free Trade: International Sources of U.S. Commercial Strategy, 1887–1939* (Ithaca, N.Y.: Cornell University Press, 1988), pp. 19–65. For acceptance of the "infant industry" interpretation, see pp. 42–44.

[6] On the symbiotic relationship between the United States and Great Britain and the very favorable position of the former within that relationship, see ibid., pp. 92–98.

that the operation of the protective tariff actually encouraged American industrialization when the impact of all the individual schedules is taken into account.

A third interpretation contends that American industrialization was the product of domestic economic processes that were so powerful that tariff policy was simply irrelevant. Here, government policy presented nothing but trivial obstacles to the expansion of the modern business enterprise – obstacles that were, in every case, almost immediately overrun by minor adjustments in the formal organization of corporations that left their economic imperatives largely unaffected. For this perspective, the protective tariff was nothing but noise in the system, a source of some uncertainty in corporate calculations but no more than that. Politics simply does not appear on the interpretive screen. Government policy was so unimportant that the analysis neither assumes the correct construction of appropriate measures nor implies a dynamic through which politics was prevented from adopting seriously constraining alternatives.[7]

These three interpretations can be given labels. The first, because it stresses the decentralized lobbying activities of individual industries, might be termed the "interest group" perspective. Its strengths are on the politics side of the tariff equation but it leaves the economic impact of the tariff almost unaddressed and, with that omission, neglects external linkages and developmental impacts. Even with respect to politics, the processes through which one of the parties comes to be almost universally aligned with protection while the other stands opposed is left unexplained. While the tariff was often the most salient policy dispute in major party competition, the "interest group" perspective, with its indeterminate summary accounting of the impact of hundreds of individual schedules, cannot begin to explain why party loyalty on this issue should even exist, let alone govern much of the legislative mobilization of party energy and influence.

The second interpretation is widely recognized as a variant of "international political economy." Its strengths lay in the recognition of the world system as a dynamic, changing environment within which domestic economies are situated and in its explicit acknowledgment of the impact of foreign political and economic policies on the positioning of the national market in the international economy. However, domestic politics and the economic impact of tariff protection are assumed to have delivered the requisite outcomes for the international analysis – in the first instance, because domestic political actors recognized and acted on the national interest and, in the second place, because the protective tariff actually encouraged American industrialization. Because both of these outcomes are assumed, not

---

[7]   The foremost example is Alfred D. Chandler, Jr., *The Visible Hand: The Managerial Revolution in American Business* (Cambridge, Mass.: Harvard University Press, 1977), pp. 374, 494–495.

demonstrated, most of impact of the tariff on either domestic politics or economic development is unexamined.

The last perspective might be labeled "economic history" in the sense that the interpretation dominates that field. The major strength is the precise explication of an economic dynamic that ultimately conferred on the United States a developmental advantage over the other industrializing nations of the world. As political analysis, however, the approach has almost nothing to offer except things to be explained. The most important of these are the existence of the preconditions of the rise of the modern business enterprise: the unrestricted national market, the retention and reinvestment of domestically generated profits from industrial operations, and the mobilization of popular support for the facilitating government policies that underpinned these two features of American economic development.

The following analysis indirectly draws on all three of the above approaches but usually as foils and rarely as supporting analyses. For example, the interest group interpretation tends to view all claims for tariff protection as relevant or important to the construction of the resulting coalition in rough proportion to their economic size in the domestic economy. For that reason, party coalitions are seen as "bottom up" constructions of interest group blocs that, in a sense, are determined only at the last stage of tariff deliberations when the entire bill is approved or rejected. The problem with this interpretation is that not all schedules within the tariff were politically equal, regardless of their economic impact. Iron and steel, for example, were the central core of the Republican-led tariff coalition. Republican construction of a new tariff always began with highly protectionist schedules for these industries and then proceeded to include other sectors.[8] But industrial protection, on its own, could not attract enough legislative support for passage. In the recruitment of congressional allies from the dominant agricultural producers of the nation, the Republicans added protection for raw wool. This extended the tariff coalition into the Mountain West and the Pacific Coast but obviously hampered the competitive position of wool manufacturers. In turn, the latter were offered compensating protection for their own production.

Protection was not the only aspect of the tariff that was politically salient. Much of the federal government's revenue came from customs duties and much of that arose from the sugar schedule. The largest part of tariff revenue, in turn, was spent on pensions for Union veterans in such a way as to further extend the tariff coalition throughout the North and West. All of these relationships between the tariff and political blocs were well rec-

---

[8]   Iron and steel also stood at the center of the northern industrial economy. The *Commercial and Financial Chronicle*, for example, used weekly reports on the number of iron and steel furnaces in and out of blast, as well as the price of steel rails, as the most important barometers of economic conditions, once even explicitly referring to the "iron market" as a "barometer of industrial improvement." November 21, 1885.

ognized by congressional leaders at the time and predetermined, before committees even began to deliberate on tariff reform, much of the outcome. In that sense, much of the tariff in the late nineteenth century was "top down" in that the Republican party attempted to balance the interests of coalitional blocs within a very familiar and consistent policy template while the Democratic party attempted to dismantle that same coalition by drawing one or more of these same blocs toward free trade. There is no question that many of the schedules in the tariff were the product of interest group lobbying and influence, but the overarching frame within which those schedules were enacted was the product of very conscious party-led construction. In a very real sense, the Republican party thus produced and managed a developmental coalition within a strategic context even while many of the schedules were left to tactical decisions by individual members of congressional committees.

However, even though the tariff underpinned the Republican developmental coalition, protection did little to directly promote American industrialization. Much of the political popularity of the tariff rested, for example, on substantial side payments to sheep raisers and Union veterans, which were, at best, clearly irrelevant to industrial expansion in economic terms. In fact, these side payments should be viewed as net costs that detracted from whatever benefits the industrial schedules provided.[9] And many of the industrial schedules themselves were indeterminate in their impact.[10] High duties on steel rails, for example, retarded `the expansion of the national market by restraining the development of the railroad network.[11] For these reasons, the automatic assumption that tariff protection accelerated national industrial expansion is at least problematic.[12] The best case that can be made is that tariff protection redistributed

---

[9]　F. W. Taussig, for example, consistently condemned the tariff on raw wool: "So strong and so clear are the objections to duties of this kind that hardly another civilized country, whatever its general policy, attempts to protect wool." *The Tariff History of the United States* (New York: G. P. Putnam, 1903), p. 240.

[10]　For a review of the literature on the impact of the tariff on the growth of the American iron and steel industry, see Bennett Baack and Edward Ray, "Tariff Policy and Comparative Advantage in the Iron and Steel Industry, 1870–1929," *Explorations in Economic History* 11 (Fall 1973): 6–8. Contrary to some earlier studies, the authors concluded that the tariff played "a significant part in promoting production." P. 23.

[11]　During the great railroad construction boom of 1881 and 1882, the *Commercial and Financial Chronicle* reported that the tariff on steel rails made "the profits of the manufacturers for a time . . . fabulous." November 25, 1882.

[12]　Protectionism has always fared badly in economic theory. In the late nineteenth century, in particular, many American financiers and economists were hostile to tariff protection both in the abstract and, especially, as practiced by the Republican party. See, for example, the address of David A. Wells setting out the views of the National Free-Trade Conference held in Detroit in the spring of 1883. *Appleton's Annual Cyclopaedia of 1883* (New York: D. Appleton, 1884), p. 776. For a particularly

income from the southern cotton plantation to the northern factory, thus promoting capital accumulation in the coffers of industrial corporations. While this redistribution undoubtedly accelerated industrial development of the Northeast and Great Lakes littoral, the impact on the southern economy was correspondingly devastating.

Because the tariff lacked almost all coherence as a developmental policy (industries were simply protected from or exposed to international competition on the basis of their influence with individual congressmen or salience within the Republican coalition), protection had little net impact on overall national growth or income. However, by protecting American industry from foreign competition, the agricultural exporting regions of the West and, particularly, the South were forced to buy manufactured goods in a protected domestic market while receiving prices set by an openly competitive world market. The terms of trade under this tariff policy were thus set heavily against the South and West. Coming at the expense of the agricultural sector, the ensuing redistribution of wealth may have spurred on industrialization at a faster rate than otherwise would have been the case. However, tariff policy was a zero-sum game in which one region's loss was another region's gain. It was from this perspective that Representative Hilary Herbert, an Alabama Democrat, poignantly described the consequences of tariff protection:

If the farmer in the Northwest and in the South will ponder upon these things he will understand why it is that in America there are so many rich manufacturers, who pile in money to swell the corruption fund in political campaigns, who give dinners in America that eclipse the world in extravagance, who ride in bedizened coaches and four over the turnpikes of Europe, who rent castles in Scotland and on the Rhine, and whose highest ambition seems to be, spurning the plain ways of the American people, to marry their daughters to those seedy scions of spendthrift aristocracy who are ever on the watch to trade their titles of nobility for the fortunes of foolish American women; and they will understand, too, how it is that there are so many impoverished American farmers.[13]

emphatic attack on protection, see the testimony of Edward Atkinson, a prominent Boston economist and leading figure in the insurance business, before the Industrial Commission. *Report of the Industrial Commission: Trusts and Industrial Combinations*, vol. 13 (Washington, D.C.: GPO, 1901), pp. 517–551. For a general survey of free trade thought, see Joanne Reitano, *The Tariff Question in the Gilded Age: The Great Debate of 1888* (University Park: Pennsylvania State University Press, 1994), pp. 57–62. The *American Economist*, a weekly published by the American Protective Tariff League, admitted to its readers that "the majority of college presidents are Free-Traders, or Tariff Reformers of various grades, and the same is true of the political economy professors." 11:23 (June 9, 1893): 218–220. On the potential benefits of a more open trade policy achieved through lower duties, see *Commercial and Financial Chronicle*, February 17, December 29, 1883; May 10, 1884; March 22, 1890; August 18, 1894.

[13] His remarks were made during debate on what became the McKinley Tariff. *Congressional Record* 51:1:5040, May 20, 1890.

Any conclusion as to whether or not the United States as a whole gained from protection thus requires a calculation of benefits to the manufacturing belt from which the damage to the South and much of the Plains and West must be subtracted. While such calculations would be difficult and contentious, the result under most reasonable assumptions would probably be slightly negative or, at best, nothing at all. There is no question that tariff protection benefited northern industrialization – in fact, that was the precise intent of the policy. Because the international political economy perspective simply assumes a net national benefit from the tariff, the approach implicitly identifies northern industrialization with the national interest, an identification that effectively depoliticizes analysis of late nineteenth-century tariff policy. In turn, only such an identification of national interest with regional development can save the assumption of benefits from the operation of the protective tariff.[14]

In terms of national development, tariff policy was never an end unto itself. Instead, protection was the primary pillar for the Republican party in popular politics. In turn, the Republican party became the primary policy support for both the gold standard and the expanding national market. The latter two carried much less popular appeal than protection but were much more central to national industrial expansion.[15] These interrelationships, operating through the Republican party, made tariff protection the most important political bulwark of economic development even though its own economic contribution was ambiguous. In fact, the lack of an economic

[14]   For a close analysis of the general models underlying Republican and Democratic positions in the 1894 deliberations on the tariff, see Richard C. Edwards, "Economic Sophistication in Nineteenth Century Congressional Tariff Debates," *Journal of Economic History* 30:4 (December 1970): 802–838. In his analysis, Edwards repeatedly privileged a national or macro-economic focus on benefits and costs as comparatively "sophisticated." He then noted that this orientation was infrequently assumed by members of the House of Representatives, who, instead, favored micro-economic explanations of the relative impact of tariff protection. In addition, both parties tended to falter at precisely the same point, the relationship between tariff protection and real industrial wages. From the point of view of party competition, this is not at all surprising since this was the pivotal group in national party competition over the tariff and both parties thus strained their arguments in describing ostensible benefits to industrial workers. In other words, where Edwards perceived a lack of rigor in economic theory among congressmen, political analysts might perceive the necessities of coalition maintenance. While very interesting as an exercise in extracting the implicit models of economic relationships that underlay political rhetoric, Edwards also omits any discussion of the major theme in this and all congressional debates over the tariff in the late nineteenth century: the redistribution of wealth from export-oriented agriculture to import-protected industry.

[15]   In a letter to President Cleveland during the silver crisis in the spring of 1893, Andrew Carnegie, the steel magnate, wrote, "if I were called upon to vote for a Free-Trade Democrat who supported sound money, or a Tariff Republican who was not sound upon money, I should vote for the former." Allan Nevins, *Letters of Grover Cleveland, 1850–1908* (Boston: Houghton Mifflin, 1933), p. 323.

"performance test" for the tariff meant that policy could be left to Congress while the much more salient economic policies associated with daily management of the gold standard and the judicial imposition of the unregulated national market became the responsibility of the more insulated executive and judicial branches.[16]

But it was the Republican coalition that gave purpose to these branches as they created and implemented the developmental policies so neatly assumed by economic historians. The latter are correct when they stress the ambiguous impact of tariff protection on American development only if they blindly isolate the tariff from party politics and thus from the very developmental policies they otherwise assume into existence. The tariff was not essential to American industrialization in its own right but it was absolutely indispensable as the ground on which the Republican developmental coalition was constructed – and, in that way, to the expansion of the national market and to the maintenance of the international gold standard.

Thus, the classic economic question – whether or not the high-tariff policies of the period, in strictly economic terms, ultimately impeded or facilitated the development and expansion of particular sectors of American industry – is rather unimportant.[17] What is significant is that protectionism

[16]   Many leading industrialists, in fact, probably preferred stability in tariff rates at relatively low levels to the uncertainty that accompanied revision, even revision upward. In his testimony before the Industrial Commission, for example, the president of the National Association of Manufacturers lamented that "our principal depressions in business here have resulted from change of policy by the National Government. . . . Tariff policy has been a most frequent cause of trouble. Whether the change is for a higher tariff or for a lower tariff it always causes a period of depression, very frequently a panic, resulting from the change. . . ." *Report of the Industrial Commission: Capital and Labor Employed in Manufactures and General Business*, vol. 7 (Washington, D.C.: GPO, 1901), p. 129. On the Association's attitudes toward the tariff generally, see Paul Wolman, *Most Favored Nation: The Republican Revisionists and U.S. Tariff Policy, 1897–1912* (Chapel Hill: University of North Carolina Press, 1992), pp. 19–37.

[17]   And, for the most part, unanswerable. Even after more than a century of debate, conclusions concerning the actual impact of tariff protection remain quite contentious. See, for example, Edward C. Kirkland, *Industry Comes of Age: Business, Labor, and Public Policy, 1860–1897* (Chicago: Quadrangle Books, 1967), pp. 187–189. On one side of the question is the stimulation that rather minor sectors received as a result of protection, among them woolen goods, tin plate, and silk cloth. F. W. Taussig, *Some Aspects of the Tariff Question* (Cambridge, Mass.: Harvard University Press, 1915), pp. 176–177, 217–218, 336. On the other side stand the undeniable costs to consumers and the forsaken opportunities that would have been available through free trade exploitation of the comparative advantage of the United States in other areas, most of them quite a bit larger than those in which the tariff may have operated favorably. Taussig, who possibly remains the most often cited scholar in this area, concluded: "To judge a very moderate measure like that of 1894 [Wilson Tariff] by its visible fruits is so difficult as to touch the bounds of the impos-

was probably an essential element in broader, political economic terms. This is so for several reasons. Most important, the protective tariff redistributed wealth from the agricultural sector into American industry and thus helped to fund industrialization without heavily relying on foreign or domestic capital markets. This independence from outside investment was probably a contributing factor in the early and subsequently pervasive adaptation of the modern business enterprise in the United States.[18] In addition, protectionist policies generated government revenue that could be diverted into military pensions for Union veterans. These pensions, within the coalition politics of the Republican party, broadened support for the protective tariff and the maintenance of an unfettered national market by appealing to many groups in the electorate that would have otherwise had little or no reason to support these policies.[19] For that reason, tariff protection for American industry should not, from a developmental perspective, be considered in isolation from the entire package of measures proposed and carried out by the Republican party. In addition, whatever the direct impact of the tariff on the pace of industrialization, again in strictly economic terms, this impact was probably much more favorable during the early years of this period and much less so at the turn of the century.[20] As a factor sustaining the Republican party coalition, the primary political agent of American eco-

---

sible. The effects on any particular industry – which are but a fragmentary bit of evidence as to the promotion of general prosperity – are sufficiently difficult to trace. . . . Even after the lapse of time, there could hardly be such an unmistakable result one way or the other as to prevent doubt and dispute." *Tariff History*, pp. 318–319.

[18] Or so it would seem, given both the dominance of British investment in the flow of foreign capital into the United States and the reluctance of the British to accept more efficient corporate organizational forms within their own economy. On the dominant role of British investment, see Jeffrey G. Williamson, *American Growth and the Balance of Payments, 1820–1913: A Study of the Long Swing* (Chapel Hill: University of North Carolina Press, 1964), pp. 11–14, 90–101. On the reluctance of the British to adopt the modern corporate form, see Alfred D. Chandler, Jr., *Scale and Scope: The Dynamics of Industrial Capitalism* (Cambridge, Mass.: Harvard University Press, 1990), pp. 291–294, 334–336, 389–392. The passive participation of foreign investors, through investment in government and industrial bonds as opposed to stocks, may thus have been a blessing.

[19] Richard Franklin Bensel, *Sectionalism and American Political Development, 1880–1980* (Madison: University of Wisconsin Press, 1987), pp. 62–73.

[20] In 1899, Charles Smith of Pennsylvania, McKinley's Postmaster General, recognized the changing nature and position of American industry in the world economy when he admitted: "The tariff is not an issue of the same importance as in the past. The policy of protection aimed to build up our industries to a point where they could stand independent on their own feet. This object has been accomplished. Protection has established the complete industrial independence of this country. More than that: it may fairly be said that it has substantially established our industrial supremacy. This truth has been demonstrated within the past two years, as we are now beating the products of the Old World on their own grounds." *The Conservative* 2:3 (July 27, 1899): 9.

nomic expansion, the political importance of the protective tariff paralleled its economic significance (with the caveat that protectionism was always more important politically than economically).[21]

CONGRESSIONAL COALITIONS AND TARIFF LEGISLATION IN THE LATE NINETEENTH CENTURY

While late nineteenth-century tariff protection was an economic policy (in that it protected American industry from foreign competition), it was one of the most politically managed policies in American history. The goal was not and never could be to simply exclude all foreign competition from American markets.[22] Because the tariff so starkly redistributed wealth

[21]   As Edward Stanwood put it, "[a]ll tariff acts for many years have been to a large degree political measures, chiefly designed by their promoters to further the ends of party, and secondarily to benefit the country and advance its prosperity." *American Tariff Controversies in the Nineteenth Century*, vol. 2 (Boston: Houghton, Mifflin, 1903), p. 359. As a fairly staunch protectionist, Stanwood's conclusion was all the more significant.

[22]   Tariff bills can be arrayed along a single dimension defined by the extent to which they protected American producers. Among the possible constructions of such a dimension, one alternative uses the ratio of the value of goods on the free list, compared with the value of those subjected to import duties. Another relies on the ratio of duties collected to the total value of imported goods. Yet a third method calculates duties as a percentage of the value of only those goods subjected to a tariff. See, for example, Taussig, *Tariff History*, Table 1: Imports, Duties, and Ratio of Duties to Imports, 1860–189[7], p. 411. For an extension of this table, see U.S. Bureau of the Census, *Historical Statistics of the United States: Colonial Times to 1970* (Washington: GPO, 1975), pt. 2, "Value of Merchandise Imports and Duties: 1821 to 1970," p. 888. For a graph of annual tariff revenue as a percentage of the total value of dutiable imports, possibly the most popular way of evaluating the extent of tariff protection, see *Atlas of the World*, vol. 2: *United States* (Chicago: Rand, McNally, 1895), p. 301. These different constructions, however, give varying answers as to which of the tariffs constituted, in fact, the most effective barrier to foreign competition in the period between the end of Reconstruction and 1900. According to the first conception, the ratio of goods on the free list to those subjected to tariffs, the schedules in effect between 1877 and 1883 were the most protective. According to the second, the ratio of duties to the total value of imports, the tariff in effect between 1883 and 1890 holds that honor. According to the third, the ratio of duties to the value of protected imports, the tariff in effect between 1897 and 1900 would be nominated. While part of the problem lies in the lack of a precise definition of tariff protection, as conceived as a bundle of schedules with varying effects on trade, the fact is that the United States pursued heavily protectionist policies throughout the period. The earlier schedules were broader in scope in that they included a larger number and variety of goods (thus the larger ratio of protected to total imports). The later schedules were more selective but contained higher, often prohibitive, tariffs (thus the higher ratio of duties collected to the total value of protected imports). The choice of the kind of tariff to enact was much more a matter of politics, in particular the building of legislative coalitions, than a close economic calculation of impact on domestic production.

between the sections and because the socio-economic bases of the two parties almost exactly divided the electorate into winners and losers under protection, reform was almost always somewhere on the congressional policy agenda. However, because the tariff was so deeply embedded in major party competition, significant changes in the law were possible only when one of the two parties controlled both chambers of Congress and the presidency: The 1890 McKinley Tariff, the 1894 Wilson Tariff, and the 1897 Dingley Tariff all passed in years when either the Republicans or Democrats controlled both the legislative and executive branches.

The sole exception was the Tariff of 1883, enacted when the parties divided control of the branches, the Republicans dominating the House and the presidency while the Democrats organized the Senate. However, the Senate was so closely balanced between the two major parties that formal control of the chamber actually passed to the Republicans on the last day of the Congress, the day after the chamber approved the tariff.[23] Only one Congress, the Fifty-sixth (1899–1901), held coinciding House and Senate party majorities, along with control with the White House, but failed to pass a general revision of the tariff. That Congress, however, immediately followed the Fifty-fifth in which the Dingley Tariff had been enacted and the Republicans had no reason to alter the schedules. Seen from the other direction, only one of the eight Congresses in which party control was divided produced a successful revision of the tariff, and as already discussed, that exception came very close to proving the rule.

In terms of tariff politics, the late nineteenth century can be divided into two periods, the first preceding and the other following President Grover Cleveland's frontal assault on protection in 1888. Before 1888, a large majority of the Democratic party in Congress opposed tariff protection but party loyalty was not enforced. After Cleveland's attack, the Democrats made reduction of duties a party principle, particularly in the House of Representatives. Although differences between the two periods can easily be

---

[23]   The situation in the Senate was actually more confused than the text indicates. Until March 3, 1883, David Davis of Illinois had served as president pro tempore, the presiding officer of the Senate when the vice-president is not present. Although largely a ceremonial post with little real power, the majority party in the Senate has always awarded the position to one of its own members. However, during the Forty-seventh Congress no party controlled a majority in the Senate; furthermore, Davis, who had originally been a Republican, had been elected to the Senate by a coalition of independents and Democrats. For that reason, his election to the post did not clearly indicate that, in the absence of a formal party majority, the Democrats practically controlled the Senate. While George Edmunds of Vermont, who replaced Davis on March 3, 1883, had impeccable Republican credentials, his elevation took place the day after the tariff bill passed the Senate. To further complicate matters, Republican majorities appear to have been appointed to most, but not all, the important committees in the chamber. See *Congressional Directory for the Forty-seventh Congress, Second Session* (Washington: GPO, 1882), pp. 81–85.

Table 7.1. *Economic Development and Roll Call Alignments on Tariff Legislation, 1877–1887*

House membership category	Support for tariff protection on major bills (% of members voting)				
	1878	1883	1884	1886	Average
Full House	52.5 (255)	56.7 (268)	50.6 (314)	52.9 (297)	53.2
Republicans	94.3 (122)	91.0 (144)	96.5 (115)	96.8 (126)	94.6
Democrats	14.5 (131)	14.2 (113)	21.2 (189)	20.1 (169)	17.5
Other party	0.0 (2)	45.5 (11)	80.0 (10)	50.0 (2)	43.9
District level of development					
All members					
Highest	59.1 (44)	74.5 (47)	58.9 (56)	71.7 (53)	66.0
Middle high	76.7 (60)	83.1 (65)	78.3 (69)	80.6 (62)	79.7
Middle low	55.3 (103)	50.5 (107)	50.8 (126)	50.4 (119)	51.7
Lowest	10.4 (48)	18.4 (49)	12.7 (63)	14.3 (63)	13.9
Republicans					
Highest	100.0 (23)	93.3 (30)	100.0 (19)	96.2 (26)	97.4
Middle high	95.2 (42)	96.2 (52)	100.0 (37)	100.0 (40)	97.8
Middle low	94.0 (50)	83.6 (55)	92.3 (52)	94.5 (55)	91.1
Lowest	71.4 (7)	100.0 (7)	100.0 (7)	100.0 (5)	92.8
Democrats					
Highest	14.3 (21)	37.5 (16)	34.3 (35)	46.2 (26)	33.1
Middle high	33.3 (18)	30.8 (13)	53.1 (32)	45.5 (22)	40.7
Middle low	18.9 (53)	11.4 (44)	16.2 (68)	12.7 (63)	14.8
Lowest	0.0 (39)	2.5 (40)	0.0 (54)	6.9 (58)	2.3
Sectional stress	60.3	55.2	54.8	61.4	57.9

Note and sources: For the roll calls, see *Congressional Record* 45:2:4154–4155, June 5, 1878; 47:2:3742, March 3, 1883; 48:1:3908, May 6, 1884; 49:1:5830, June 17, 1886.

overdrawn, the net effect of Cleveland's attack on the tariff was to discipline Democratic opposition to protection, placing it on much the same footing as Republican support had assumed all along (compare the party percentages in Tables 7.1 and 7.2). Other than this increasing cohesion within Democratic ranks, the two periods exhibit very similar voting patterns.

Between the end of Reconstruction and the turn of the century, eight general revisions of the tariff came to a vote in the House of Representatives (see Tables 7.1 and 7.2). The first attempt took place in 1878 when the Democrats proposed a general reduction in duties levied on manufactured goods. Falling with particular severity on the woolen industry, the proposed reductions might have utterly destroyed both carpet and

Table 7.2. *Economic Development and Roll Call Alignments on Tariff Legislation, 1888–1897*

House membership category	Support for tariff protection on major bills (% of members voting)				
	1888	1890	1894	1897	Average
Full House	47.9 (311)	53.6 (306)	40.7 (344)	62.7 (327)	51.2
Republicans	97.9 (146)	99.4 (165)	100.0 (122)	100.0 (198)	99.3
Democrats	2.5 (159)	0.0 (140)	8.2 (208)	4.1 (123)	3.7
Other party	33.3 (6)	0.0 (1)	7.1 (14)	33.3 (6)	18.4
District level of development					
All Members					
Highest	52.0 (50)	63.5 (52)	50.0 (56)	90.2 (61)	63.9
Middle high	73.9 (69)	72.2 (72)	61.4 (83)	80.3 (76)	71.9
Middle low	53.5 (127)	59.0 (122)	39.6 (134)	64.3 (126)	54.1
Lowest	6.2 (65)	11.7 (60)	11.3 (71)	12.5 (64)	10.4
Republicans					
Highest	95.8 (24)	100.0 (33)	100.0 (19)	100.0 (54)	98.9
Middle high	100.0 (50)	100.0 (52)	100.0 (49)	100.0 (61)	100.0
Middle low	98.5 (68)	100.0 (72)	100.0 (50)	100.0 (78)	99.6
Lowest	75.0 (4)	87.5 (8)	100.0 (4)	100.0 (5)	90.6
Democrats					
Highest	12.0 (25)	0.0 (19)	25.7 (35)	0.0 (6)	9.4
Middle high	5.3 (19)	0.0 (20)	6.2 (32)	0.0 (13)	2.9
Middle low	0.0 (55)	0.0 (50)	4.0 (75)	6.5 (46)	2.6
Lowest	0.0 (60)	0.0 (51)	4.5 (66)	3.4 (58)	2.0
Sectional stress	51.0	54.4	42.1	60.7	52.0

Note and sources: For the roll calls, see *Congressional Record* 50:1:6660, July 21, 1888; 51:1:5112–5113, May 21, 1890; 53:2:1796–1797, February 1, 1894; 55:1:557, March 31, 1897.

cloth manufacturers by denying them protection from British competition. However, because the Senate and the executive branch were controlled by Republicans, this attempt was doomed from the start. In the actual event, the House of Representatives struck out the enacting clause, killing the measure even before a vote was taken on passage. When added to Republican ranks, a minority of northern Democrats, led by Samuel Randall of Philadelphia, provided enough votes for defeat of the bill.[24] Philadelphia was the center of the woolen industry in the United States and would have been devastated by this measure. A strong protectionist,

[24] Stanwood, *American Tariff Controversies*, vol. 2, pp. 197–198. Most of these Democrats came from Maryland, New Jersey, and Pennsylvania.

Randall was also Speaker of the House, having been elected by the Democratic majority; his opposition underscored the impossibility of tariff reform in this Congress, particularly along the lines his party attempted.[25]

Congressional deliberations on this bill were rather typical in several respects, particularly in the crucial role played by the woolen industry and the stress trade liberalization imposed on Democrats from the more advanced regions of the nation. The Republicans managed what might appear to have been a jerry-rigged complex of policies surrounding and supporting protection – superficially, at least, very vulnerable to segmented assault on one or more of the mutually supporting elements. In fact, seven Republicans, almost all from very rural districts, bolted to the Democrats on this bill. However, Democratic efforts to exploit latent divisions within Republican ranks usually uncovered, instead, even deeper fractures within their own party, particularly between the cotton-exporting South and northern industrial districts.

In the years following resumption of gold payments in 1879, abundant revenue from the tariff pushed the Treasury deeply into the black. Despite a vast federal debt (which provided a "sink" for excess revenues), the resulting budget surpluses became more than an embarrassment to the Republicans. In response, President Chester Arthur proposed the creation of a commission to "thoroughly investigate all the various questions relating to the agricultural, commercial, mercantile, manufacturing, mining, and industrial interests of the United States, so far as the same may be necessary to the establishment of a judicious tariff, or a revision of the existing tariff, upon a scale of justice to all interests." Arthur appointed nine members to this commission, most of them representing one of the separate elements of the Republican-led tariff coalition. John L. Hayes of Massachusetts, Secretary of the National Association of Wool Manufacturers, was chosen as the commission's chair. He was joined by a Pennsylvania iron manufacturer, Henry W. Oliver, Jr.; an Illinois sheep raiser and president of the National Association of Wool Growers, Austin M. Garland; and a Louisiana sugar planter, Duncan F. Kenner. As party representatives, Arthur selected three former members of the House of Representatives. The Republican was Jacob A. Ambler from Ohio, who also held executive positions in a steel wire and nail company and a bank. As Democrats, Arthur selected two former Confederate veterans: John Underwood of Georgia, a lawyer, and Alexander R. Boteler of West Virginia, who had served on Stonewall Jackson's staff and, later, in the Confederate Congress sitting in Richmond. Two government officials, one a statistician formerly employed by the Census Office and the other an officer in the New York Custom House, rounded out the commission by providing technical advice and support.

---

[25] For a colorful description of Randall's protectionist attitudes and his relations with his Philadelphia constituents, see Morgan, *From Hayes to McKinley*, pp. 81–82.

While all the members have been reported as favoring "the principle of protection," the most likely opponents were clearly marked and isolated by their Confederate histories.[26] Rarely have the coinciding economic bases of partisan politics, industrial development, and central state policy been so starkly displayed as in the appointments to this commission.

The commission made its report in December 1882, just after the start of the second session of the Forty-seventh Congress. Coming after the 1882 elections but before the new members took office the following March, this was a lame-duck session. In what turned out to be complex and sometimes confused legislative deliberations, involving such questions as whether or not the Senate could originate a tariff bill under the Constitution, tariff reform became combined with a revision of the internal revenue system. In the end, almost all of the reduction of revenue was effected through the elimination of a host of excise taxes, although liquor and tobacco levies remained in place. Tariff rates, although amended in many particulars, remained largely as they were.[27] Like ships passing in the night, the extreme protectionists in both parties bolted their organizations. Led by William McKinley of Ohio, thirteen Republicans voted against the conference report because duties, as they saw the matter, were set too low. Seven of the dissidents represented Ohio districts while four more held districts in western Pennsylvania.[28] These members, however, were more than offset by Randall's band of Democratic protectionists who cast sixteen votes supporting the report. Twelve of these came from New Jersey, New York, and Pennsylvania.[29]

These movements can largely be explained by the construction of the new schedules. Although the bill generally reduced duties on woollen goods, the rates were still so high as to constitute effective barriers to foreign competition. What is more, other changes in the woollen schedules increased the

[26] For descriptions of the commission and brief accounts of its deliberations, see Stanwood, *American Tariff Controversies*, vol. 2, pp. 202–207; Paul H. Tedesco, *Patriotism, Protection, and Prosperity: James Moore Swank, the American Iron and Steel Association, and the Tariff, 1873–1913* (New York: Garland, 1985), pp. 104–105, 111–113. These descriptions were supplemented by the individual entries of former members of Congress taken from the *Biographical Directory of the American Congress, 1774–1971* (Washington: GPO, 1971).

[27] Referring to the new law, the chair of the tariff commission, John L. Hayes, wrote in a business publication devoted to wool manufacturing: "Reduction in itself was by no means desirable to us; it was a concession to public sentiment, a bending of the top and branches to the wind of public opinion to save the trunk of the protective system. In a word, the object was *protection through reduction*. We were willing to concede only to save the essentials both of the wool and woolens tariff.... We wanted the tariff to be made by our friends." Taussig, *Tariff History*, p. 249 n. 1. Emphasis in the original. On the impact of the 1883 tariff generally, see pp. 249–250.

[28] Tedesco, *Patriotism, Protection, and Prosperity*, p. 117.

[29] For an account of the legislative deliberations on this bill, see Stanwood, *American Tariff Controversies*, vol. 2, pp. 207–218.

protective impact of the tariff; it is these revisions that explain the satisfaction with which Randall and his band viewed the new law. On the other hand, the new schedules made reductions on higher grades of raw wool and steel rails, which appeared to portend new openings for foreign producers in supplying the American market. Although these changes turned out to be unimportant, the schedules still providing an effective barrier to foreign competition, the lower rates enacted under the new law explain the opposition of Ohio and Pennsylvania Republicans.[30]

Immediately after the 1883 tariff bill was signed into law, the Forty-seventh Congress passed into history and, with it, the Republican majority in the House of Representatives. In the new Forty-eighth Congress the Democrats held an advantage of some eighty seats over the Republicans and they immediately began work on their own revision. One of the most important factors aiding their labors was the continuing budget surplus.[31] However, the Republicans had by now clearly established a majority in the Senate and Arthur still held the presidency. For these reasons, whatever the Democrats might have accomplished in the House was probably doomed once it left that chamber.[32]

As reported to the floor by the Committee on Ways and Means, the Democratic revision was very simple. All duties on three items (salt, coal, and lumber) were removed. The duties on liquor and silk manufactures were unchanged. Ceilings were imposed on duties for cotton goods (40% of imported value), woollen goods (60%) and metals (50%). Other than these exceptions, all duties were to be reduced to 80 percent of existing tariffs with the proviso that no rate would be lower than the corresponding schedule imposed in the 1861 Morrill Tariff. Thus, the basic principle underpinning the proposed revision was an across-the-board, "horizontal" reduction in duties. Randall was no longer Speaker; he had been rejected by the Democratic caucus in favor of John Carlisle of Kentucky, whose hostility to tariff protection was long-standing and placed him squarely in the mainstream of his party.[33] Even so and despite the large Democratic major-

[30]   For an anaylsis of the 1883 act, comparing the new schedules with what had been the status quo, see Taussig, *Tariff History*, pp. 233–250.

[31]   On the fiscal difficulties caused by the continuing surplus, see *Commercial and Financial Chronicle*, February 17, March 3, November 17, 1883; February 9, April 5, and June 7, 1884.

[32]   Ellis Paxson Oberholtzer, *A History of the United States since the Civil War* (New York: Macmillan, 1931), vol. 4, p. 159.

[33]   The contest for the Democratic nomination for Speaker turned almost entirely on the tariff, with Randall representing protection and John G. Carlisle of Kentucky, along with Samuel S. Cox of New York, favoring a tariff for revenue only. Despite Randall's past service as Speaker, Carlisle easily defeated him in the party caucus, 106 to 52. Cox received thirty votes. This contest in some ways marked the passing of the torch from the northern Democrats, who had dominated the party during the Civil War and Reconstruction when the South was out of the Union, to the south-

ity in the chamber, Randall and his band were able to strike the enacting clause from the bill and thus kill the measure. With the proposed decreases in the raw wool, woollen, and iron schedules providing abundant political cover, forty Democrats followed him. Most represented districts in New Jersey, Ohio, and Pennsylvania.[34]

In 1886, House Democrats tried once more to revise the tariff through a general reduction of duties. Since, despite the elimination of most excise taxes, the surplus was still large and growing, even the Republicans had committed themselves to a reduction in tariff revenue in the 1884 election. Cleveland's victory, however, had placed a Democrat in the White House and, although the Senate was still in Republican hands, the initiative lay with his party. The bill reported by the Ways and Means Committee placed lumber, raw wool, salt, and other raw materials on the free list and reduced the duty on woollen and cotton goods, along with sugar. However, Randall again led his band of protectionists into opposition. This time tariff revision was killed almost at the source as the chamber refused even to resolve the House into the Committee of the Whole for general debate. The almost solid Republican ranks were joined by thirty-four Democrats, two-thirds of them from New Jersey, New York, Ohio, and Pennsylvania. Blamed for the bill's defeat, Randall was bitterly excoriated by his party and, although he served in the House for four more years, never recovered from these attacks.[35]

In 1888, the last year of Cleveland's first term, the Democrats attempted once more to revise the tariff. Laboring under a continuing budget surplus, the Treasury found it difficult to dispose of revenue fast enough to prevent cash shortages from endangering the financial system. In response to this challenge, Cleveland now committed his party to a radical reduction of schedules. In his annual message to the Fiftieth Congress, Cleveland inveighed against protection, citing both the need for revenue reduction and traditional free trade principles of equity and efficiency.[36] In response, Speaker Carlisle appointed southern Democrats to five of the eight positions on the Ways and Means Committee. The chair of the committee was given to Roger Q. Mills of Texas, a former Confederate colonel who had been wounded three times during the Civil War. Excluding Republican

ern wing which had, by 1883, returned to Washington in force, again providing much of the leadership and direction for the party as it had during the antebellum period. *Appleton's Annual 1883 Cyclopaedia*, pp. 776–777.

[34]   Stanwood, *American Tariff Controversies*, vol. 2, pp. 220–221.

[35]   Ibid., pp. 225–226. In explaining why the bill died, the New York *Times* claimed that Randall's opposition was but an example of "the slavish work for which he is retained by the Republicans of Pennsylvania, the payment of the service for which he is permitted to hold his seat." June 18, 1886. Quoted in Oberholtzer, *History of the United States*, vol. 4, p. 378n. Also see vol. 5, pp. 2, 7.

[36]   For a narrative account of Cleveland's call for a tariff reform, see Oberholtzer, *History of the United States*, vol. 4, pp. 473–487.

members of the committee from their deliberations, the Democrats reported a revision that placed raw materials (most important, wool) on the free list, substituted in many cases ad valorem for specific duties, and generally reduced tariff schedules.[37] As this bill was being debated on the floor, the national Democratic convention met in St. Louis, renominated Cleveland for the presidency, and unanimously passed a resolution endorsing the "early passage of the bill for the reduction of the revenue now pending in the House of Representatives." Lengthy debates accompanied all tariff legislation in the late nineteenth century, and the 1888 bill was no exception. Over 150 speeches, just under one for every two members of the House, were delivered on this occasion so that congressmen could "convince their constituents of their economical learning."[38] When the measure finally came to a vote, only four Democrats, three from New York and one from Pennsylvania, opposed passage. Randall opposed the bill but was not present. Although Cleveland and his allies permanently destroyed the Democratic high tariff bloc in the House, the bill itself died when the chamber refused to consider the protectionist amendments adopted by the Republican Senate.[39]

The ensuing 1888 presidential and congressional campaigns were waged primarily on the tariff.[40] Before this election, party platforms at the state level had often revealed clear differences between Republicans and Democrats – in fact, since the end of Reconstruction, the tariff had been the most common platform plank for both parties, and almost invariably, they assumed opposing positions on the issue.[41] But at the national level, party differences had been less sharp, and in Congress, dissent had been toler-

---

[37]   For a detailed review of the bill, see George B. Curtiss, *The Industrial Development of Nations* (Binghamton, N.Y.: George B. Curtiss, 1912), vol. 3, pp. 73–90.

[38]   Oberholtzer, *History of the United States*, vol. 4, p. 489.

[39]   Stanwood, *American Tariff Controversies*, vol. 2, pp. 226–242; John Sherman, *Recollections of Forty Years in the House, Senate and Cabinet* (Chicago: Werner, 1896), pp. 776–777; Morgan, *From Hayes to McKinley*, pp. 273–281, 308–310. On Cleveland's recognition of Randall's influence in the House as the most important obstacle to tariff reduction, see Nevins, ed., *Letters of Grover Cleveland*, pp. 157–159. On Randall's actual role in tariff deliberations, see Reitano, *Tariff Question*, pp. 48–50, 104.

[40]   Oberholtzer, *History of the United States*, vol. 5, pp. 1–56. During this contest, "free trade" was constantly associated with an alleged fawning affection for Great Britain (see pp. 12, 39–40, 48, 55–56, 60). *Judge*, a weekly magazine with a strong protectionist bias, ran a remarkable political cartoon in which Britain, as John Bull, discovered an infant Cleveland in a small basket floating among the bulrushes. "Ah," said he, "this is the Moses that will open the American Land of Milk and Honey to the products of my Pauper Labor." January 7, 1888. This was one of three full-page color cartoons that *Judge* printed every week with the one in the center a double-page spread. In the twenty-six issues printed between January and June 1888, twenty-one had the tariff as a major theme in one or more of these cartoons, several of them picturing a corpulent Cleveland clothed in a British uniform.

[41]   For detailed analysis of these and other state platforms, see Chapter 3.

ated. Cleveland's attack on protection, however, mobilized interests within the tariff coalition into an unprecedented frenzy of activity. The American Iron and Steel Association, for example, distributed well over a million "educational" pamphlets during the struggle over the Mills bill in Congress and the subsequent presidential contest.[42]

While Cleveland won a plurality of the popular vote in 1888, the Republicans, under Benjamin Harrison, took the White House through the count in the electoral college. While not a sweeping victory by any means, the Republicans also gained control of the House of Representatives while retaining the Senate. Thus both chambers of Congress and the White House were in their hands during the Fifty-first Congress that convened in December 1889.

Harrison promptly called for a thorough revision of the tariff in his annual message to Congress, and the battle was joined. Just a week into the session, the newly elected Speaker, Thomas Reed of Maine, appointed a Ways and Means Committee studded with major figures from both parties.[43] Six of the eight Republicans represented districts in the northeastern and midwestern manufacturing belt. The two exceptions hailed from Iowa and California. William McKinley of Ohio was appointed chair of the committee. While none of the Republicans were southerners, three of the five Democrats represented districts that lay within the bounds of the former Confederacy with one more from Kentucky. In April 1890, the committee reported a bill to the House, a measure that passed five weeks later on what was, with the exception of a lone Republican from Louisiana, a straight party-line vote. After hundreds of changes in the Senate, many of which were approved by the House, this bill became law on October 1.

To reduce the revenue that was then accumulating so rapidly in Treasury vaults, the new tariff removed all duties from unrefined sugar. The sugar schedule had historically provided more revenue than any other part of the tariff, but Congress now substituted federal subsidies for the protection from foreign competition that domestic producers had previously enjoyed. This change moved sugar from the credit to the debit side of the federal ledger in one fell swoop, thus justifying, at least on revenue grounds, the reinforcement of protection on other favored goods.[44] In addition, the tariff on tin plates was intentionally raised. Stimulating the emergence of a tin plate industry in the American economy where none had existed previously, this change clearly expanded on the historic protection of infant industries

---

[42]   For a description of the pamphlets and their use, see Tedesco, *Patriotism, Protection, and Prosperity*, pp. 120, 168–169, 281.

[43]   Stanwood, *American Tariff Controversies*, vol. 2, p. 260.

[44]   For the fiscal impact of the abolition of sugar duties and the creation of the bounty system, see ibid., p. 297; *Appleton's Annual Cyclopaedia of 1892* (New York: D. Appleton, 1893), pp. 424, 714.

by adding planned development of entirely new sectors to the purposes of the tariff.[45] Although limited to sugars, molasses, coffee, tea, and hides imported from abroad, the Republicans also initiated a policy of reciprocity through which bilateral reductions of duties might be used to gain entry to markets in other nations. Many agricultural items were added to the tariff for the first time, although the impact of these duties, apart from communities near the Canadian border, was negligible.[46]

The McKinley Tariff immediately became the major issue in the fall congressional campaigns. Widely advertising the "opportunity" to purchase goods before the new duties forced them to raise prices, retailers incidentally highlighted the cost of the new tariff to consumers. While this was extremely effective as a marketing ploy, it was also devastating to the Republicans as free political advertising for the free-trading Democrats.[47] Republicans went down in droves everywhere in the nation, ending up with just over a quarter of the seats in the new House of Representatives. However, because they still controlled the Senate and the presidency, tariff reform was an impossibility for the new and large Democratic majority in the House.

The 1892 general elections renewed Democratic control of the House of Representatives, delivered the Senate into Democratic hands, and brought Cleveland once more into the White House. With control of both chambers and the presidency, the Democrats had the same opportunity to revise the tariff that the Republicans had exploited in 1890. Charles Crisp of Georgia, who continued as Speaker, appointed William Wilson of West Virginia as chair of the Ways and Means Committee. A college professor before entering the House of Representatives, Wilson held strong free trade views that were grounded in economic theory as well as practical politics.

Moving with dispatch, Wilson and his committee reported a bill to the House on December 19, 1893. The proposed tariff put many raw materials on the free list, among them wool, iron ore, coal, and lumber, and

---

[45] In the ten years following adoption of the McKinley Tariff, the tin-plate industry blossomed in the United States, subsequently turning into a trust (the American Tin Plate Company). On the indispensability of the tariff to the industry, see *Report of the Industrial Commission: Preliminary Report on Trusts and Industrial Combinations*, vol. 1 (Washington, D.C.: GPO, 1900), p. 189 (and, more generally, pp. 24, 187–188, 854, 856–858, 878); Naomi R. Lamoreaux, *The Great Merger Movement in American Business, 1895–1904* (New York: Cambridge University Press, 1985), p. 39.

[46] For legislative deliberations on the McKinley Tariff, as well as a discussion of its provisions, see Stanwood, *American Tariff Controversies*, vol. 2, pp. 259–287; Morgan, *From Hayes to McKinley*, pp. 336–339, 349–354; Harry J. Sievers, *Benjamin Harrison, Hoosier President: The White House and After* (Indianapolis: Bobbs-Merrill, 1968), pp. 163–172.

[47] Sievers, *Benjamin Harrison*, pp. 175–176.

reduced many duties on manufactured goods. Sugar was to remain on the free list, and after adoption of an amendment from the floor, the subsidy paid to domestic producers was to cease on July 1, 1894. This would have exposed the current and all future sugar crops to withering foreign competition. Another amendment created a federal income tax as a new source of income for the government.[48] Because the burden of the tariff, even after reform, would still fall disproportionately on their regions, southern and western members welcomed the income tax as an equitable adjustment of fiscal responsibilities. The capital-rich manufacturing districts of the East, however, vehemently denounced the amendment as unconstitutional and worse. When the House finally voted on the first of February, seventeen Democrats joined a solid phalanx of Republican opponents, but the bill still passed handily and went on to the Senate. With but one exception, the Democratic bolters all hailed from wealthy eastern or Louisiana sugar districts. While they could not defeat the bill in the House, their counterparts in the Senate played a decisive role in changing what had been a pragmatic, free trade measure into merely another set of tariff schedules – a milder version of protectionism than a Republican majority would have enacted, but protectionism all the same.

The Republicans held thirty-seven seats in the Senate, the Populists four, and the Democratic majority forty-four. Of the latter, the two Louisiana senators would not vote for any bill that did not contain a duty on raw sugar. One of the Democratic senators from New York would not vote for any bill that contained an income tax; however, the Populists would not vote for any bill that did not contain that levy. So the New York vote was lost. The other New York Democrat quietly insisted on protection for his state's leading industries, particularly linen collars and cuffs, as the price of his support. Other Democrats from Alabama, Maryland, and West Virginia demanded reimposition of imposts on iron ore and coal. Taking the House bill as their vehicle, about a dozen Democratic senators forced the reinstatement of many duties, among them raw sugar, iron ore, and coal, and increases in the tariff on many more goods. Raw wool remained on the free list, along with lumber. By the time the bill was sent back to the House, the Senate had attached over 600 amendments, almost all of them more protective in character than the original schedules passed by the other chamber. On July 2, the day before the Senate finished action on the bill, Cleveland sent Wilson a letter expressing great disappointment in the upper chamber's work. With Cleveland's permission, Wilson subsequently produced this letter during the long struggle in the conference committee between the House and Senate. Hamstrung by the delicate and

---

[48] For the first time in many years, the federal budget was running a deficit, primarily because of increased payments for silver purchases and military pensions which coincided with a general depression in the national economy.

complex nature of the agreements that had enabled them to pass the bill in the upper chamber, the Senate conferees could not budge from their work, however severely flawed as a free trade measure it might be. In the end, the House capitulated, adopting the Senate bill without change, 600 amendments and all. Cleveland allowed the bill to become law without his signature.

Despite the many opportunistic amendments added by the Senate, the Wilson Tariff still managed to make a number of significant changes. First and foremost were the abolition of duties on raw wool and corresponding downward adjustments in protection offered to woolen goods.[49] However, the reductions in the latter schedules were so slight that Taussig described the attitude of Democrats as one of "marked tenderness" toward woolen manufacturers.[50] Duties on coal and iron ore were reduced but not significantly. The steel rail and pig iron schedules were also lowered, but as Taussig pointed out, these reductions followed the decreasing cost of domestic production in such a way as to leave untouched their protective impact. This had been the case in the prior 1883 and 1890 reductions as well.[51] The truth was that the iron and steel industry was rapidly outgrowing the need for protection, and with that trend, the centerpiece of the Republican tariff coalition was breaking up.[52] The Wilson Tariff also reduced the duty on tin plate but the industry was still protected. A tariff on raw sugar was reinstituted and, with it, the bounty on produc-

---

[49] John Sherman, for example, called the removal of protection for raw wool "the culminating atrocity" of the Wilson Tariff. *Recollections of Forty Years*, p. 938. Although Chester Whitney Wright thought the overall impact of the tariff on the historical development of sheep raising in the United States had been relatively "slight," he attributed the collapse of flocks in the East and Midwest after 1894 to the Wilson Tariff. *Wool-Growing and the Tariff: A Study in the Economic History of the United States* (Cambridge: Harvard University Press, 1910), pp. 314, 322–326.

[50] Taussig, *Tariff History*, p. 294.

[51] The iron and steel industry was the first sector to work out the details of modern factory management, adopting its characteristic "systematic practices and procedures" on the shop floor in response to the difficulties attending the processing of metals. Chandler, *The Visible Hand*, p. 258. However, this modern management structure and the design and implementation of new processing plants evolved over many years. Thus, although the metal-making and metal-working industries were the first to adopt a modern form of factory management, they subsequently lagged other sectors in its perfection. This lag explains, in part, why the efficiency of American mills increased over many decades as opposed to reaching a plateau in a much shorter time.

[52] By the 1890s, the United States appears to have been competitive with the British in pig-iron production. Baack and Ray, "Tariff Policy and Comparative Advantage," p. 9. Robert Allen similarly placed the date of American competitiveness with the British at 1895. "International Competition in Iron and Steel, 1850–1913," *Journal of Economic History* 39 (December 1979): 928.

tion was abolished. This switched sugar back from the debit to the credit side of the federal ledger.[53] Finally, the Wilson Tariff enacted a new federal income tax that would have replaced some of revenue lost in the other schedules. However, the Supreme Court subsequently struck down the income tax as unconstitutional. All in all, the new tariff law mildly but inconsistently reduced duties in a way that left industrial protection substantially intact.[54]

The 1894 election, in which both free silver and the Wilson Tariff played prominent roles, brought on a Republican landslide as large as the one produced for the Democrats by the McKinley Tariff in 1890. With control of Congress and the White House divided between the parties, however, there was no opportunity to change the schedules in the second half of Cleveland's term.[55] The two major parties joined the 1896 campaign on different terms, with the Republicans at the outset nominating McKinley and stressing trade protection as the primary issue and the Democrats addressing the Populists by emphasizing free silver with only passing mention of the tariff.[56] While Bryan and the Democrats successfully turned the election into a contest over alternative monetary standards, they lost the election. Accompanied by a large House majority and operating control of the Senate, McKinley thus entered the White House on a platform that stressed the tariff as the coalitional basis of the Republican party but the gold standard as the clearest public mandate. With the gold standard secure for the time being, the party immediately turned its atten-

[53] Despite the reinstatement of the tariff, the abolition of the sugar bounty and the consequent elimination of what had been expected to be some $16 million in compensating federal payments to Louisiana sugar growers sparked a political revolt by what had hitherto been one of the most loyal elements of the state Democratic party. *Appleton's Annual Cyclopaedia of 1894* (New York: D. Appleton, 1895), pp. 444–445.

[54] For legislative histories of the Wilson Tariff, see Stanwood, *American Tariff Controversies*, vol. 2, pp. 319–354; Taussig, *Tariff History*, pp. 288–316; Oberholtzer, *History of the United States*, vol. 5, pp. 273–281; Morgan, *From Hayes to McKinley*, pp. 460–465, 473–476. For a detailed comparison of duties under the McKinley and Wilson Tariffs, see Curtiss, *Industrial Development of Nations*, vol. 3, pp. 276–280.

[55] The House of Representatives did pass a bill in December 1895 reinstating a tariff on raw wool and making an across-the-board increase of 15 percent on a wide number of manufactured goods. However, this bill was almost entirely symbolic in character with no attempt made to adjust differences within the Republican party either in the House or in the Senate. In fact, the Senate Committee on Finance substituted a free silver measure for the House tariff bill. Stanwood, *American Tariff Controversies*, vol. 2, pp. 372–373.

[56] By 1896, McKinley was thoroughly and completely identified with protectionism. After the election, the *American Economist*, published by the American Protective Tariff League, called him "the greatest exponent of Protection that the world has ever seen." 19:20 (May 14, 1897): 269.

tion to the tariff.[57] For some years the federal budget had been running a deficit, although a narrowing one. Tariff reform promised to put the Treasury in the black and, thus incidentally, make management of gold payments all the easier.

Just two days after his inauguration, McKinley called Congress into special session in order to revise the tariff. Four days into this special session, the newly appointed Ways and Means Committee, under the leadership of Nelson Dingley of Maine, reported a tariff bill to the House. On the last day of March, less than a month after McKinley entered the White House and barely two weeks after the opening of the new Congress, the House passed the tariff bill and sent it on to the Senate.[58] Most Populists abstained while five Democrats voted for the bill. The latter, three from Louisiana and two from Texas, were attracted by the sugar and raw wool schedules, respectively. Every Republican who voted backed the measure. In the Senate, the Committee on Finance deliberated the bill for a little over a month, and debate on the floor of the Senate consumed another two months or so. In early July, the bill was sent back to the House with almost 900 amendments. As in the House, Populists abstained. One Democrat from Louisiana voted for passage. Both chambers agreed to a conference, the result of which was a general increase in duties, often beyond those contained in either the House or Senate bills. McKinley signed the new Dingley Tariff into law on July 24, 1897, the same day that the conference report was finally approved by the Senate.[59]

The most important change made by the Dingley Tariff was the reimposition of duties on raw wool.[60] Although corresponding adjustments were

---

[57] As they had been throughout their party's history, congressional Republicans were far more united behind protectionism than they were on hard money. By transforming gold into Republican orthodoxy, as opposed to a party predisposition, the 1896 election so heightened tensions between the silver and gold wings that, at least in the Senate, passage of the Dingley bill was threatened. The *American Economist* left no doubt as to the policy priorities of the tariff coalition: "We are sorry to note, in some of the Republican papers of the country, a tendency to abuse certain United States Senators because of their belief in the policy of 'Free Silver.' . . . There are several so-called 'Silver' Senators who are strong and ardent friends of the American policy of Protection. This fact alone is proof enough of their Americanism, even though they should disagree with other Protectionists upon facts relating to questions of finance. . . . By abusing them we may make them our enemies. . . . It does no good to call names. That is not argument. It is schoolboyish. Stop it." 19:20 (May 14, 1897): 268.

[58] The Republicans in the House of Representatives had actually been at work on the tariff bill for months, starting just after McKinley's election victory. Oberholtzer, *History of the United States*, vol. 5, pp. 459–460.

[59] For a legislative history of the Dingley Tariff, see Stanwood, *American Tariff Controversies*, vol. 2, pp. 378–389.

[60] The *Commercial and Financial Chronicle* considered the changes in the wool and woolen schedules "extreme, and as we view the situation unwise." And the journal

made to protect woolens, manufacturers vehemently protested against the new duty. Their experience with free wool under the Wilson Tariff had demonstrated how detrimental duties on their primary raw material were to their overall position in the domestic market. Unlike prior negotiations between producers and manufacturers, the Republicans were consequently unable to close the gap between them by tweaking the various schedules. However, Bryan's surprising, sometimes overwhelming, strength in the Mountain states in the 1896 election made duties on raw wool imperative for the Republicans. In that region, the wool tariff was the party's major answer to free silver.[61] On the whole, the new schedules reenacted the McKinley Tariff duties with marginally higher rates for manufactured wool. Important revisions were made with respect to the iron and steel industry as well. While duties on iron ore, pig iron, and steel rails were left unchanged or even, as in the last case, lowered, the new rates left the sector

also noted that many viewed the Republican "vote last November [as] certainly first of all for sound money, with the tariff as a secondary issue [but] we are not only getting the tariff first without the accompaniment of sound money but no movement at all is being made towards currency reform." Nevertheless, the *Chronicle* assumed a position of benign resignation: "We are not inclined to take issue with the Administration over the question raised by the early introduction of a protective tariff bill. Protective duties are what we consider the independent voter consented to when he helped elect Mr. McKinley as President. . . . On the financial question the President's party had pronounced for gold money and the other party for silver money. That presented a definite issue of deeper importance than any kind of a tariff measure could raise. . . ." With that much broader view in mind, the journal could not "see how a tariff for protection could have been framed without taking wool off the free list." Thus, those who supported the gold standard as the primary issue in the 1896 election had thereby signed onto tariff protection (because that was a fundamental element in the Republican coalition) and, specifically, should now be expected to accept a tariff on raw wool (because that duty was essential to passage of a Republican tariff). In effect, this was an open admission that the tariff on raw wool was necessary to maintenance of the gold standard. "Tariff Legislation and Currency Reform," March 20, 1897. Almost all contemporary and subsequent analysis has conceded the political centrality of raw wool in the construction of the measure. Oberholtzer, for example, described the Dingley bill as "built around a tariff on wool." *History of the United States*, vol. 5, p. 381. Also see the description of Senate revisions in the House bill in the *American Economist* 19:20 (May 14, 1897): 266.

61 Western Republicans, in fact, made higher duties on wool, along with fruits and hides, the price of their support for any tariff bill. *Commercial and Financial Chronicle*, April 10, 1897. However, the Wool-Manufacturers' Association maintained that the plight of relatively high-cost wool producers in the East was the real motivation behind the reinstitution of duties. The large, comparatively efficient sheep ranches of the West, they contended, could and did take care of themselves, even when subjected to free trade. But faced with both increasing domestic competition from the West and foreign competition, particularly from Argentina, the older regions of Michigan, Ohio, and Pennsylvania were in decline. In effect, the Association maintained, the reinstitution of duties meant but mere survival for eastern producers while providing western producers with windfall profits. Taussig, *Tariff History*, p. 330 n. 1.

well protected as domestic producers continued to improve their operating efficiency at a much faster rate than foreign competitors.[62] In fact, along much the same lines as the McKinley Tariff, many of the iron and steel schedules extended protection that effectively prohibited all foreign competition. The duty on raw sugar was doubled, primarily to raise revenue.[63] Finally, reciprocity, which had been abolished under the 1894 act, was reinstituted and the executive branch was once more permitted to negotiate bilateral reductions of trade barriers with other nations.[64]

Seven of the eight tariff bills just described found the major parties divided along expected lines, with the Republicans supporting greater protection for the home market and the Democrats backing comparative trade liberalization. The exception, a partial one, was the rather inconclusive adjustment of rates in the 1883 law, a measure that was primarily intended to reduce the budget surplus and did so mainly by abolishing internal excise taxes. In analyzing the voting pattern on the 1883 tariff, passage has been interpreted as supporting protection because the alternative method of reducing revenue would have been a general reduction in customs duties (see Tables 7.1 and 7.2). The Democratic party initiated five of these measures (in 1878, 1884, 1886, 1888, and 1894) and the Republicans three (1883, 1890, and 1897). While all three of the Republican bills were enacted, only one Democratic measure, the 1894 Wilson Tariff, reached the statute books. In fact, several of the Democratic bills never reached an up or down vote on passage in the House. The 1878 and 1884 bills, for example, died when the House struck the enacting clause from the texts, well before parliamentary debate on the measures had been completed. The votes analyzed here took place on those motions to strike, with "yea" votes supporting protection. The 1886 bill was killed when the House refused to even enter the Committee of the Whole for the purposes of general debate. A "nay" vote on that roll call supported protection. Both the 1888 and 1894 roll calls, as well as those on the 1890 and 1897 Republican measures, were recorded on initial passage of the House bill. The 1883 roll call was taken on approval of the conference report.

These roll calls have been grouped chronologically into two sets, recorded

---

[62] For a comparison of American and British prices for steel rails and pig iron between 1870 and 1900, along with the duties imposed by the various tariff acts, see Tedesco, *Patriotism, Protection, and Prosperity*, pp. 272–273. Although the steel industry at the turn of the century was exporting a sizable proportion of its product, leading financiers and steel executives still insisted on the necessity of tariff protection. *Industrial Commission: Trusts and Industrial Combinations*, vol. 13, pp. 110–111, 456; *Industrial Commission: Preliminary Report on Trusts and Industrial Combinations*, vol. 1, pp. 193, 199, 204, 947, 1013.

[63] In describing the tariff's impact on the federal budget, the *Commercial and Financial Chronicle* concluded that "[n]o one can fail to see the urgency existing for more revenue." March 13, 1897.

[64] For a close analysis of the Dingley Tariff, see Taussig, *Tariff History*, pp. 328–356.

either before or after Cleveland formally committed the Democratic party to a reduction of duties. As can be seen by comparing Tables 7.1 and 7.2, the major result of Cleveland's initiative was to slightly tighten party lines on protection. The immediate impact was the repression of the small band of protectionist Democrats in the House (but not, as Cleveland was to learn in 1894, in the Senate). His action thus probably enabled passage of the 1888 bill, which would have otherwise failed in the House. The increase in Republican cohesion was comparatively insignificant, arising primarily from a small decline in the number of party members from the South and the termination of the Minnesota delegation's irregularity on the issue.[65] In terms of trade policy, those who bolted party lines were primarily motivated by the impact of proposed schedules on their individual constituencies. From that perspective, the duties on raw wool, woolen goods, and iron and steel were the most difficult problems that party managers faced in constructing general revisions of the tariff, for it was these that most often sparked defections from party regularity. Before 1888, when managers could hope to attract bolters from the other party to compensate for their own dissidents, party lines were more fluid and voting alignments tended to more closely follow regional interests. This explains the slightly higher sectional stress scores for the four votes recorded in the earlier period, compared with the later period when party discipline was applied more forcefully.

On the whole, however, the alignments on these eight tariff bills compellingly demonstrate the intimate connection between the very uneven pattern of regional economic development and congressional support for tariff protection. For example, members representing the least developed districts in the nation opposed protection by wide margins in every instance. Reflecting their political dependence on the northern wing of their party, southern Republicans were but a minor exception, usually providing protectionists with a majority of their votes. In contrast, southern Democrats, who represented similar districts but were free of entangling party ties, voted almost unanimously against protection. Only the sugar areas of Louisiana and, later, the Birmingham steel region in Alabama produced protectionist votes among southern Democratic delegations. In the House as a whole, support for protection generally rose coincidentally with the level of economic development, but the increase was particularly steep between the bottom rungs of the developmental scale and leveled off or even declined slightly at the top. Almost all the correlation between development and protection was the result of the disproportionately large

---

[65] On the defection of Minnesota Republicans in the 1884 tariff vote, see Oberholtzer, *History of the United States*, vol. 4, p. 379. The apostasy of the Minnesota Republicans made their state a special target of the "educational" activities of the American Iron and Steel Association. Tedesco, *Patriotism, Protection, and Prosperity*, pp. 146–150.

percentage of districts represented by Republicans at the upper end of the developmental scale while Democrats dominated districts grouped at the lower end. Thus most of the correspondence was the result of district pre-dispositions to select one party over another, not divisions within the parties themselves.

These broad patterns reflected several general characteristics of tariff policy in the late nineteenth century. First, protection was the product of a Republican-managed coalition that involved substantial side payments to groups and interests outside the manufacturing belt, most important, wool producers and the recipients of military pensions. These side payments broadened the support for tariff protection in a way that generalized support throughout the Republican party and throughout the North, thus reducing the disparity between protection and development that otherwise might have obtained and almost eliminating any correspondence within the Republican party. Second, the Democrats were unable to split the Republican coalition, even when the party controlled the House and could craft its own alternative. Even more to the point, Democratic defections before 1888 were consistently heavy and disproportionately distributed across the upper rungs of the developmental spectrum. Even when the Republicans were in the minority, the policy complex that they had created was durable enough to fatally undermine Democratic efforts to significantly reduce protection. When the Democrats began to discipline their northern wing on tariff votes, the districts that had previously been represented by dissidents, such as Randall's Philadelphia district, tended to return Republicans instead so that no net gain for tariff reduction arose, over the long term, from enforcing party regularity.

Within the most advanced districts of the nation, New York City always stood out as relatively hostile to protection (see Table 7.3). Until 1897, Democrats usually controlled the New York City delegation, in most cases by a large margin. Their votes were only very slightly more likely to be cast against protection than the votes of party colleagues from similarly advanced areas of the nation. However, in every Congress, Republicans represented a much smaller proportion of New York City districts than other highly advanced regions of the nation. This fact, combined with the strong tendency of all members to cohere with their party organizations, meant that most of the differential tendency of New York City votes to be cast for free trade positions operated between the parties, not within them. New York City Democrats and Republicans, for example, were no more prone to disloyalty on tariff measures than their party colleagues in other very advanced districts. But because the New York City delegation was far more Democratic compared with other advanced metropolitan regions, the delegation as a whole cast a far smaller percentage of its votes for protection (36.5% vs. 72.2% in the rest of the country). The explanation for this pattern, including the city's inclination to elect Democrats to Congress, was

Table 7.3. *Comparison of Voting by Members from New York City and Other Advanced Districts on Tariff Legislation, 1878–1897*

Tariff bill	Democrats (% of members supporting protection)		
	New York City	Other advanced districts	All advanced districts
1878	0.0 (7)	21.4 (14)	14.3 (21)
1883	28.6 (7)	44.4 (9)	37.5 (16)
1884	12.5 (8)	40.7 (27)	34.3 (35)
1886	55.6 (9)	41.2 (17)	46.2 (26)
1888	20.0 (10)	6.7 (15)	12.0 (25)
1890	0.0 (10)	0.0 (9)	0.0 (19)
1894	45.5 (11)	16.7 (24)	25.7 (35)
1897	0.0 (4)	0.0 (2)	0.0 (6)
Average	20.3	21.4	21.2

Tariff bill	All members (% of members supporting protection)		
	New York City	Other advanced districts	All advanced districts
1878	22.2 (9)	68.6 (35)	59.1 (44)
1883	44.4 (9)	81.6 (38)	74.5 (47)
1884	22.2 (9)	66.0 (47)	58.9 (56)
1886	54.5 (11)	76.2 (42)	71.7 (53)
1888	25.0 (12)	60.5 (38)	52.0 (50)
1890	9.1 (11)	78.0 (41)	63.5 (52)
1894	45.5 (11)	51.1 (45)	50.0 (56)
1897	69.2 (13)	95.8 (48)	90.2 (61)
Average	36.5	72.2	65.0

Note: New York City districts include Brooklyn. For the purpose of this table, advanced districts are those that ranked five (the highest level) on the index of relative development. All New York City districts ranked five on the index throughout the late nineteenth century.

New York City's unique role as the major entrepôt for the national political economy.[66]

The final element shaping the broad pattern of tariff roll calls was the isolation of the South. The Republican-led tariff coalition supplemented industrial support for protection with side payments to several groups in American society, most important, wool producers and military pensioners.

[66] See Chapter 2.

With the partial exception of sheep ranchers in west Texas, very few south-erners belonged to either group.[67] Thus, almost all the benefit from side payments was felt outside the South. Of course, because the South was far and away the least developed region of the nation, the direct influence of industrial protection was strongly negative; for the most part, the price of manufactured goods was simply raised with no offsetting benefit to regional producers. Furthermore, the export-oriented markets of the cotton economy were hampered by the tariff in that foreign nations found it more difficult to pay for American products when many of their own goods were prohibited from entering the country. Since the South was the most export-dependent region in the United States, the impact was comparatively strong and negative here as well. Viewed in the broadest perspective, there was simply nothing in the tariff policy complex for the South but tiny scraps falling from the lavishly provided protectionist table. Southern congress-men responded by regularly casting 90 percent or more of their votes for tariff reduction and, at times, proposing unvarnished "free trade" aban-donment of both protectionist and revenue-raising duties.[68]

ANALYSIS OF THE COALITION THAT ENACTED THE MCKINLEY TARIFF

The Republicans managed the tariff as the policy foundation of the party's national coalition. Most of that management occurred out of view, in private correspondence and conversations that were not intended to see the light of day or behind committee doors that locked out Democrats and everyone else. And although the tariff was managed by party leaders, there

[67]   Even the Spanish-American War did little to nationalize the pension system. In 1910, almost half a century after the Civil War, per capita federal expenditures on military pensions stood at $4.08 in Maine, $4.04 in Vermont, $3.96 in Kansas, $3.90 in Indiana, and $3.36 in Ohio. In the South, spending was minuscule: $0.19 in South Carolina, $0.21 in Georgia, $0.29 in Alabama, $0.30 in North Carolina, $0.37 in Texas, $0.42 in Mississippi, and $0.57 in Louisiana. William H. Glasson, *History of Military Pension Legislation in the United States* (New York: Oxford University Press, 1918), p. 269.

[68]   The isolation of the South in national trade policy was an artifact, nonetheless real, of the political economy created by the Republican party during and just after the Civil War. As C. Vann Woodward put it, "the tariff menace to the region's welfare had loomed vastly larger since the restraining combination of South and West had been broken during the Civil War, and tariff rates had mounted higher and higher. The immemorial pattern of colonialism – the dependence upon the sale of cheap raw materials on a world market and upon buying back manufactured goods from pro-tected industrial and commercial areas – continued to hold sway in the South despite the much-vaunted 'industrial revolution.'" *Origins of the New South, 1877–1913* (Baton Rouge: Louisiana State University Press, 1967), p. 186.

was constant interaction with the rank and file in Congress. Construction of a tariff, in terms of the myriad of detailed schedules for various goods and commodities, was, for the most part, a bottom-up process in which member preferences were constantly consulted. Only on the central elements of the tariff – those necessary to maintaining the backbone of the party coalition – was leadership influence decisive. From that perspective, the most important schedules were those protecting iron and steel from foreign competition. These were the duties that made owners and workers in the great iron and steel foundries of Pennsylvania, Ohio, and Illinois the single most important element in the Republican coalition. In size and, at least in the earlier part of the period, material benefits received from protection, iron and steel were far and away the most significant industrial sector sheltered from foreign competition.

A wide variety of other manufacturing sectors were also offered protection – some of them, in fact, would not have existed but for the tariff – but two agricultural schedules were much more strategically important in gluing together the Republican coalition. The first imposed duties on the importation of wool and ultimately made sheep-raising in much of the United States dependent on Republican rule. The second laid a duty on foreign sugar and similarly made sugar cane production in Louisiana dependent on tariff protection. Unlike the wool tariff, however, the sugar schedules were a major revenue stream for the federal government and could not easily be abandoned by either party. Heavy federal expenditures by the Republican party, necessitated by side payments to Union veterans and, later, by military intervention abroad, maintained the sugar schedules at relatively high rates under which Louisiana producers could prosper. Democratic party efforts to impose "economy" on federal spending, on the other hand, carried an implicit possibility of lower sugar duties.

Two other dimensions rounded out the tariff policy complex: wool manufacturers and recipients of federal military pensions. Even without duties on their primary raw material (wool), most wool manufacturers would have required protection in order to turn a profit. But duties on raw wool made protection an absolute necessity. Since these manufacturers – the vast majority located in northeastern cities – were heavily Republican with close ties to finance capital, their interests could not be ignored in the construction of a general tariff. But the schedules on manufactured wool could not be simply declared; instead, they had to be calibrated with those on raw wool in such a way that manufacturers were compensated for the increase in price of their primary raw material. This calibration, in turn, introduced an interdependency between the raw and manufactured wool schedules that often required the attentions of the Republican leadership.

Spending the revenue raised by the tariff, Union pensions extended the tariff coalition into areas and social groups that otherwise would have had little or no reason to support protection. Military pensions, of course, were not formally addressed in tariff bills; instead they were considered in general legislative acts establishing eligibility and benefits and in hundreds of private bills that simply declared that particular individuals would be placed on the pension rolls. Involving expenditures instead of revenues and individuals instead of economic sectors, military pensions were about as different from the tariff as any federal policy could be. But the political connection between them may have been closer than any other two free-standing policies of the period.

There were thus at least five important dimensions to the tariff policy complex: iron and steel producers, wool manufacturers, sugar cane growers, sheep raisers, and Union veterans.[69] Sugar cane growers were not a major force in the Republican party coalition for two reasons. First, the duties on sugar were much more important as a revenue schedule than as a discretionary grant or benefit to that sector of the economy. As a result, sugar cane growers were either free-riding beneficiaries of protection when revenues were short or likely casualties when revenues were abundant. Either way, there was often relatively little they could do to shape their fate. Second, sugar cane growers were primarily located in Louisiana, a southern state with no other tangible stake in tariff protection. Even if every sugar grower became a loyal member of the party, Republican candidates would have lost the large majority of elections in Louisiana after the end of Reconstruction. During the consideration of general tariff bills, the votes of Louisiana congressmen and senators were sometimes important at the margin of the Republican coalition, but the commitment of the party to sugar and the corresponding commitment of sugar to the party was always weak.

The other four dimensions of the tariff policy complex easily divide into two categories: those that directly involved protection for American industry and those that extended the tariff coalition into other sectors of society. The iron and steel and wool manufacturing sectors were obviously industrial in nature. With respect to them, the tariff clearly aided industrial expansion by redistributing wealth from other parts of the economy. The Republicans also contended that the tariff raised the wages of industrial labor because corporate owners shared their tariff-enhanced revenue with workers.[70] In some highly protected industries, the tariff almost certainly

---

[69]   For example, omitting only Union veterans, Tedesco named these groups as the leaders of the "protectionist campaigns in the United States" during the 1880s. *Patriotism, Protection, and Prosperity*, p. 95.

[70]   Many labor leaders were persuaded by this Republican argument and campaigned actively for the party's presidential nominees. For their activities in the 1888 contest, see Selig Perlman, "Upheaval and Reorganisation (since 1876)," in John R. Commons et al., *History of Labour in the United States*, vol. 2 (New York: Macmillan, 1918), pp. 468–469.

benefited labor because agreements between workers and employers contained what amounted to profit-sharing clauses.[71] In fact, industrial combinations that enjoyed effective tariff protection from foreign competition and a dominant position in the domestic market were often at least neutral toward unionization of their employees, while some actively favored their organization.[72] In less-protected industries, an impact on wages was likely but would be difficult to prove.[73]

[71] See, for example, the testimony of James Campbell, chief factory inspector of the state of Pennsylvania, ex-president of the Glass Workers of America, and former member of the general executive board of the Knights of Labor, before the Industrial Commission. Asked, "Is it a fact that your scale of wages and arrangements with the proprietors are conditioned considerably by national tariff legislation?," Campbell replied: "When there is tariff agitation there has always been a clause inserted in the scale that in case of a reduction of the tariff there will be a rearrangement of the wages." Asked whether that clause was "agreed to by both parties," he answered: "That has always been the case when there is any agitation on the tariff subject. If there is an advance the workmen get an advance." When asked to explain why he thought "wages are better now than they ever have been, considering the purchasing power of money, in the glass-workers' trade," Campbell replied, "Organized labor and a protective tariff." *Industrial Commission: Capital and Labor*, vol. 7, pp. 44–47. For a description of the "sliding scale" that connected wages to the market price of iron and steel products, see the testimony of Mahlon Garland, former president of the Amalgamated Association of Iron and Steel Workers of America, pp. 89–90, 92–94. At the time of his testimony, Garland was the "surveyor of customs" in Pittsburgh, having been appointed to the post by McKinley. There was also extensive cooperation between manufacturers and the Glass Bottle Blowers' Association of America in which most employers hired only union labor in order to standardize wage costs between them. However, the employment by a few owners of nonunion labor evidently undercut the ability of the industry as a whole to share the benefits of protection with workers. *Industrial Commission: Capital and Labor Employed in Manufactures and General Business*, vol. 7, p. 108. Adolph Strasser, ex-president of the Cigar Makers' International Union, one of the most important in the American Federation of Labor, testified that tariff protection was necessary for the employment of workers in his trade. Pp. 266–267. For additional testimony as to the probable impact of the tariff in the form of higher wages in the rubber, tobacco, and cotton thread industries, see *Industrial Commission: Trusts and Industrial Combinations*, vol. 13, pp. 83, 85–86, 328, 351.

[72] *Industrial Commission: Preliminary Report on Trusts and Industrial Combinations*, vol. 1, pp. 30–31. This was particularly the case in the glass industry. P. 927.

[73] This inherent ambiguity, however, did not prevent Republicans from advocating a "scientific" tariff based on relative labor costs. John Sherman, for example, was probably sincere in claiming, "[I] never was an extreme protectionist. I believed in the imposition of such a duty on foreign goods which could be produced in the United States as would fairly measure the difference in the cost of labor and manufacture in this and foreign countries. This was a question not to be decided by interested capitalists, but by the careful estimate of business men." *Recollections of Forty Years*, p. 775. For a theoretical analysis of tariff protection that supports the Republican argument that the working class benefited from the tariff, along with industry, see Wolfgang Stolper and Paul Samuelson, "Protection and Real Wages," *Review of Economics and Statistics* 9 (November 1941): 58–73. Their analysis also implies, when

In general, of course, Republicans could point to higher wage scales in the United States, as compared with those prevailing in Europe, and the massive flow of immigrants as evidence for the tariff's benefits to workers. However, unrestricted immigration clearly undercut the argument because workers, unlike corporations, were unprotected from foreign competition. In addition, the cost of living was probably higher in the United States (in part because of the tariff) so that the differences in wage scales were more apparent than real. All in all, the tariff probably raised wages paid to industrial workers but the impact was uneven and, in some cases, may have been perverse. Despite the ambiguity, Republicans constantly contended that "Protection and Prosperity," McKinley's slogan during the 1896 presidential contest, were inseparable. And, just as clearly, it was the votes of workers in industries such as iron and steel and wool manufacturing, not the minuscule number of ballots cast by their employers, that enabled the Republicans to dominate the manufacturing belt. For these workers, particularly in the iron and steel industry, protectionist sentiment at times even moved beyond politics and became a force for social organization and identity.[74] For them, as for the *American Economist*, "why the Free-Traders should care so much more for foreign workmen than for American workmen [was] a puzzle."[75]

Because sheep-raising farmers and military pensioners resided, for the most part, in rural areas, their inclusion in the tariff policy complex extended the protectionist coalition to other parts of the country. During deliberations on what became the McKinley Tariff, Rep. Alexander Dockery, a Missouri Democrat and certainly no friend of Republican policy, only articulated prevailing political wisdom when he said: "Wool . . . is the keystone of the arch which binds the great body of agriculturists to the protective system. If it were possible to protect the farmer in any aspect or degree by a tariff it must be in respect to this one product . . . wool offers the only basis upon which the Western farmer can indulge the hope of sharing the benefits of protection, as it is apparent that foreign competition

applied to late nineteenth-century United States, that the remainder of the nation suffered a net loss of income through redistribution and, in addition, that the tariff imposed a net drag on the national income in the aggregate.

[74] In Pittsburgh, for example, the first spring reunion of the Amalgamated Association of Iron and Steel Workers in 1880 was organized as a public demonstration of support for a higher tariff. Subsequent gatherings, held annually, brought together huge crowds of workers and their families ranging in size from 15,000 to 25,000 people. David Montgomery, *The Fall of the House of Labor: The Workplace, the State, and American Labor Activism, 1865–1925* (New York: Cambridge University Press, 1987), p. 33.

[75] *American Economist* 19:20 (May 14, 1897): 270.

with any other product of the Western farm is a *prima facie* absurdity, tariff or no tariff."[76]

With respect to military pensions, there was no logical reason why these pensioners could not also be industrialists or industrial workers. However, most pension recipients tended to be disproportionately rural or small-town residents. Many industrial centers held large foreign-born communities whose residents had only recently immigrated to the United States; for that reason, Union veterans were often comparatively scarce in many northern cities. In the Mountain West, both immigrants and the comparative youth of the population also reduced the percentage of pensioners. And because Confederate soldiers were not eligible, all parts of the South had very few pensioners. As a result, Union pensioners were disproportionately concentrated in northern rural areas that had been settled before the war broke out. Thus both the duties on raw wool and military pensions extended the benefits of tariff protection to societal groups outside the manufacturing belt and the industrial sector.[77]

In political terms, these four dimensions of the tariff policy complex had several attractive characteristics. First, they did not overlap much in terms of geography and thus, since geography is the basis of congressional representation, did not waste policy resources through redundancy. In Table 7.4, the top 10 percent of all districts in terms of iron and steel production, wool manufacturing, raw wool production, and pension recipients, respectively, have been cross-tabulated with one another. Of the thirty-three districts with the highest per capita iron and steel production, to take just one example, only three were in the top thirty-three districts in terms of wool manufacturing. Only five stood among the top districts in raw wool production; only one showed up on the list of top pension districts. One intersection, raw wool with wool manufacturing, had

---

[76] *Congressional Record* 51:1:4311–4312, May 8, 1890. Taussig cited the wide but shallow distribution of raw wool production as a major economic reason why the duty should be reduced: ". . . reduction of a duty of this kind can take place with exceptional ease. Wool is not produced, as a rule, in large quantities, by persons who devote themselves exclusively to this as a business. It is mainly produced by farmers, whose chief income comes from other sources, and on whom a reduction of duty and a fall of price would fall with comparatively little weight." *Tariff History*, p. 241. However, this wide but comparatively shallow distribution of sheep-raising was precisely the reason the duty was attractive to the Republican party. James Ford Rhodes, for example, noted that Cleveland's recommendation that the tariff on raw wool be abolished "made of every farmer who owned a sheep a protectionist." *History of the United States, 1850–1896* (New York: Macmillan, 1928), vol. 8, p. 307.

[77] However, the economic impact of the tariff still remained very important. In his *Tariff History*, for example, Taussig concluded that the "schedules in the tariff which have [had] the greatest effect on the welfare of the country are those fixing the duties on iron and wool. . . . " P. 239.

Table 7.4. *Constituency Characteristics and the Tariff Policy Complex:
51st Congress, 1889–1891*

Constituency characteristic	Intersection of constituency characteristics (% of districts in each category)			
	Iron and steel production	Wool manufacturing	Raw wool production	Recipients of military pensions
Iron and steel production	xxxx	9.1	15.2	3.0
Wool manufacturing	9.1	xxxx	0.0	9.1
Raw wool production	15.2	0.0	xxxx	21.2
Recipients of military pensions	3.0	9.1	21.2	xxxx
Represented by Republicans	75.8	84.8	72.7	78.8

Percentage of Republicans in the House of Representatives Who Represented a Leading District with Respect to at Least One of the Four Dimensions in the Tariff Policy Complex: 47.5 (179)

Percentage of Democrats in the House of Representatives Who Represented a Leading District with Respect to at Least One of the Four Dimensions in the Tariff Policy Complex: 18.4 (152)

Note and Sources: The leading districts with respect to each of the four dimensions in the tariff policy complex were those that ranked in the top 10 percent. The number of cases in each cell in the upper two parts of the table is thus 33 in each instance (10% of 332, the number of members in the House of Representatives during the 51st Congress). Iron and steel production was measured in tons per capita by congressional district. This group also includes one iron ore district from the Upper Peninsula of Michigan and one coal district from the Connellsville coke region of Pennsylvania. For data on production, see *1890 Census of Mineral Industries* (Washington: GPO, 1892), p. 393. Wool manufacturing was measured by the per capita total value produced in five basic categories: woolen, hosiery, knitting, carpet, and worsted mills. State data on wool manufacturing for each of these five was taken from *1890 Census of Manufacturing*, pt. 3 (Washington: GPO, 1895), pp. 98, 106, 116, 118, 120, 122, 128. The hosiery and knitting mill data was adjusted for wool content. The state data was prorated by district on the basis of the number of establishments of each type. Data on mill locations was taken from *The Manufacturers of the United States for Domestic and Foreign Trade: 1887* (New York: Armstrong and Knauer, 1886), "List of Manufacturers in Prominent Trades," pp. 522–523 (carpets), 624–625 (hosiery), 640–642 (knit goods), 784–789 (woolen goods), and "Index to Articles," pp. 478–479 (worsted goods). Raw wool production was measured in per capita total pounds of wool shorn in the fall of 1889 and spring of 1890. The data source was the *1890 Census of Agriculture* (Washington: GPO, 1895), pp. 237–273. Recipients of military pensions were measured in percentage of the district population receiving benefits. The data on recipients was taken from *Executive Documents of the House of Representatives for the First Session of the Fiftieth Congress*, serial no. 2542 (Washington: GPO, 1889), Table 20, pp. 1090–1108.

no overlap at all.[78] Despite the lack of overlap at the top of these distributions, all four types of districts tended to elect Republicans – the tendency was strongest among wool manufacturing districts, where over five of every six districts were held by members of the party. Seen another way, almost half of all Republicans in the House represented a district falling within the top 10 percent of one or more of the four distributions; the corresponding percentage for the Democrats was less than one in five. Thus these four dimensions of the tariff policy complex provided a broad, northern foundation for the Republican party, both in elections when people voted and in the halls of Congress when legislation was passed.[79]

The McKinley Tariff passed the House of Representatives in 1890 with but one dissenting vote among the Republicans; every Democrat opposed passage. Thus, aside from the few absences and abstentions, the partisan breakdown on the roll call is easily analyzed (see Table 7.5). Republican members voted for the bill regardless of whether their district was at the top or the bottom of the pension distribution (representing districts with thousands of pensioners or dozens). The Democrats similarly voted against the bill, regardless of the composition of their district. However, when all House members are analyzed, the connection between the density of military pensioners and relative support for the McKinley Tariff emerges with

[78]   On the changing distribution of sheep-raising in the United States, see Wright, *Wool-growing and the Tariff*, particularly chaps. 7 and 8; Rodman W. Paul, *The Far West and the Great Plains in Transition, 1859–1900* (New York: Harper & Row, 1988), pp. 207–219. On the varying regional distributions and concentrations of sheep-raising and wool manufacturing, see *Report of the Industrial Commission: Distribution of Farm Products*, vol. 6 (Washington, D.C.: GPO, 1901), pp. 322–336.

[79]   This very general analysis treats all four distributions as if they had the same relative concentration across the congressional districts of the United States. This was not the case. Iron, steel, and, particularly, wool manufacturing were highly concentrated in the top 10 percent of their respective distributions with little or no presence in the remaining districts. In contrast, sheep-raising was far more general in the United States with every district, even those in the Deep South, containing at least some flocks. However, even here significant concentration was evident in the very high sheep densities of the Far West and states like Ohio and Michigan. Military pensions were even more widely distributed among the nation's districts, at least in the North. The point here is that the tips of the four distributions analyzed in Table 7.4 probably had very different political implications for the tariff: The industrial distributions described highly concentrated, intensely interested groups of districts while the others reflected much broader, less vitally interested blocs (from the standpoint of the average member). It was the broad distributive characteristics of the latter that gave them their foundational qualities; they tended to bind together members who otherwise represented very disparate districts. However, like the others, the tails of these distributions lay in the South where they tended to heavily overlap. Thus the intensity of opposition to the tariff, spawned in part by the lack of any district interest in the policy complex, was impotently concentrated in the largely Democratic congressional districts of the former Confederacy.

Table 7.5. *Members Supporting the McKinley Tariff*
by the Tariff Coalition (%)

	All parties	Republicans	Democrats
Recipients of military pensions/% of district population			
1: Under 0.2	6.8 (59)	100.0 (4)	0.0 (54)
2: 0.2–0.3	37.5 (48)	94.7 (19)	0.0 (29)
3: 0.4–0.6	59.6 (57)	100.0 (34)	0.0 (23)
4: 0.7–0.8	66.7 (39)	100.0 (26)	0.0 (13)
5: 0.9–1.1	75.5 (53)	100.0 (40)	0.0 (13)
6: Over 1.1	84.0 (50)	100.0 (42)	0.0 (8)
Raw wool districts/pounds per capita			
1: Under 0.11	47.1 (51)	96.0 (25)	0.0 (26)
2: 0.11–0.40	50.0 (48)	100.0 (24)	0.0 (23)
3: 0.41–0.90	34.5 (55)	100.0 (19)	0.0 (36)
4: 0.91–1.70	58.0 (50)	100.0 (29)	0.0 (21)
5: 1.71–3.25	56.0 (50)	100.0 (28)	0.0 (22)
6: Over 3.25	76.9 (52)	100.0 (40)	0.0 (12)
Wool manufacturing districts	87.1 (31)	100.0 (27)	0.0 (4)
Iron and steel districts	83.9 (31)	100.0 (26)	0.0 (5)

Note: For sources and definitions, see Table 7.4.

a vengeance: the percentage of members supporting the tariff invariably rising with increases in the density of pensioners. The explanation for this pattern, of course, lay with the varying propensity to elect Republicans or Democrats.[80] In the lowest tier of districts, Democrats were preferred by a margin of about thirteen to one over Republicans. In the highest tier, Republicans were preferred by a margin of over five to one. Thus almost the entire connection between pensions and the tariff in 1890 lay in the electoral arena where, clearly, military pensions played a large role in major party competition.

When the vote on the McKinley Tariff is analyzed with respect to raw wool production, a similar but more irregular pattern emerges. Again, the connection lay in the electoral arena where districts with high concentrations of sheared wool tended to prefer Republicans to Democrats, but that

---

[80] It should be noted that one third-party member also voted in the lowest tier (against the bill).

propensity is an important factor only in the top tier of districts (those with wool yields of more than three and a quarter pounds per capita). Compared with military pensions, raw wool production was clearly a more marginal factor in the policy basis of major party competition, with effects that rapidly tailed off lower down in the distribution. Put another way, pensions often, on their own, determined the votes of the electorate, while raw wool was an auxiliary reason or justification Republicans could offer for their tariff position. As can also be seen in Table 7.5, the vast majority of members from the top 10 percent of the industrial distributions voted for the McKinley Tariff. Again, this heavy support was due to the strong tendency of these districts to prefer Republicans to Democrats.

The McKinley Tariff raised the duty on raw wool by 10 to 20 percent, depending on the grade.[81] As compensation for this increase, the Republicans also raised the duty on the various grades and types of manufactured woolen goods. However, this adjustment of schedules still stressed the tariff coalition. In general, sheep raisers needed a tariff on woolen goods in order to create a domestic market for their raw wool; without that market, protection would have been useless to them. Woolen manufacturers, on the other hand, always had an interest in free trade in wool, their primary raw material.[82] The protectionist bargain within the tariff policy complex was protection for both raw wool and woolen goods. To arrive at this balancing of interests, sheep raisers sometimes threatened, without much credibility, to withhold support for duties on woolen goods.[83] This threat was clearly limited by the fact that the sheep raisers needed a protected domestic market for their wool. That economic constraint was matched, on the manufacturers' side, by the apparent political reality that protection for raw wool was a major underpinning for protectionist legislation; without the duty on raw wool, the entire policy complex might be pulled down, duties on woolen goods included. As Robert La Follette of Wisconsin warned during floor debate on the 1890 tariff bill, "when [woolen manufacturers] start [their] looms on free wool they will weave their own winding sheet

[81] For a comparison of the 1883 and 1890 wool schedules, see Wright, *Wool-Growing and the Tariff*, p. 346; and, more generally, Stanwood, *American Tariff Controversies*, vol. 2, pp. 284–286. For a comparison of the woolen schedules, see Taussig, *Tariff History*, pp. 256–266.

[82] As the *Commercial and Financial Chronicle* put it, "[t]o suppose that any wool manufacturer would advocate a tariff on his raw material, except in fear and duress of the menace so boldly uttered by Mr. McKinley of Ohio and others, that free wool shall mean free goods likewise, is to suppose him destitute of common sense." March 17, 1888.

[83] Commenting on demands for protection of raw wool during the 1888 tariff debate, the *Commercial and Financial Chronicle* recalled that sheep raisers had, in 1867, used the slogan "either full protection to raw wool or no protection to wool manufacturers" in order to cow the latter "into submission and combination" on a tariff that protected both their interests. March 17, 1888.

for their own burial."[84] Thus, retaliatory threats by manufacturers also lacked full credibility, although they were more believable than the ones made by sheep raisers.[85] Constituting a third element in this calculus was the potential substitution of cotton goods for woolens. As prices on woolen cloths and carpets rose, increasing numbers of consumers would switch to cotton products. Some of this substitution would, in fact, occur within the factories themselves where manufacturers could increase the cotton content of blended goods or even switch over completely from wool to cotton production. And because the United States exported more than half of its cotton crop, there was no way, under the tariff, to construct a higher price for cotton as a raw material in manufacturing.[86] There was thus, over the long term, a practical ceiling to the protection that could be imposed on woolen goods (and, indirectly, raw wool).[87]

During consideration of the tariff bill in the House of Representatives, the Ways and Means Committee recommended a level of protection to woolen manufacturers that more than compensated them for the prospective increase in duties on raw wool. Seizing an opportunity to divide the tariff coalition, Democrats were only too happy to point out that, even under the committee's own estimates, the rates proposed for woolen goods in the bill were much higher than the new duties on raw wool required.[88] The Democrats subsequently demanded recorded votes on the duties recommended for woolen goods. On two separate roll calls, dissident Republicans joined with a solid phalanx of Democrats to rebuff the committee. An analysis of the second of these votes, chosen because of the slightly lower number of abstentions and absences, is displayed in Table 7.6.

---

[84]   *Congressional Record* 51:1:4475, May 10, 1890.

[85]   In its summary of proceedings at the thirty-first annual convention of the National Association of Wool Manufacturers, *The Textile Manufacturers' Review and Industrial Record* reported that the industry recognized the tariff on raw wool as "the popularly regarded keystone of the arch of protection." 29:3 (January 18, 1896): 36. In economic terms, despite their relative subordination to sheep raisers within the tariff coalition, wool manufacturers may actually have reaped disproportionate benefits from the alliance. Wright, *Wool-Growing and the Tariff*, pp. 313–314.

[86]   For a general discussion of competing economic interests and legislative strategies with respect to the tariffs on raw wool and woolen manufactures, see Wright, *Wool-Growing and the Tariff*, pp. 289–292, 296–297.

[87]   During floor deliberation on what became the McKinley Tariff, a petition opposing duties on raw wool, signed by several hundred woolen manufacturers, was printed in the *Congressional Record* 51:1:4505–4506, May 10, 1890. The last paragraph in the petition stressed the importance of cotton cloth as an upper bound on tariff protection for wool: "As the only civilized country in the world . . . which levies a duty on raw wool, we ask that American industry may be relieved of this unnatural burden, and that our domestic wool interests may now be put upon the same wholesale basis as the cotton manufacturing industry with free raw material."

[88]   For floor debate on the committee's recommendations, see *Congressional Record* 51:1:4787–4789, May 16, 1890.

Table 7.6. *Members Supporting a Higher Duty on Wool Cloth*
by the Tariff Coalition (%)

Coalition partner	All parties	Republicans	Democrats
Military pensions	79.3 (29)	100.0 (23)	0.0 (6)
Wool producers	74.1 (27)	100.0 (20)	0.0 (7)
Wool manufacturers	86.7 (30)	100.0 (26)	0.0 (4)
Iron and steel	80.6 (31)	96.2 (26)	0.0 (5)
All coalition districts	78.0 (100)	98.7 (79)	0.0 (21)
All other districts	34.4 (189)	85.5 (76)	0.0 (112)

Note: The vote analyzed in this table occurred on an amendment to the McKinley Tariff bill printed in *Congressional Record* 51:1:5110, May 21, 1890. For sources and definitions of the district categories, see Table 7.4. The percentages calculated for "all coalition districts" are adjusted to exclude double-counting for members representing constituencies in more than one coalition category.

As can be seen in the table, Democrats, regardless of whether they represented districts normally within the Republican tariff coalition, voted against the higher duties on wool cloth recommended by the Ways and Means Committee. Thus, all the interesting aspects of the vote are contained in the patterns for the Republicans and the House of Representatives as a whole. Of the seventy-nine Republicans representing districts within the core of the tariff coalition, only one, Abner Taylor of Illinois, defected from the committee position. While unanimity may not have been surprising with respect to members representing wool manufacturing and raw wool districts, the loyalty of those from high-pension districts should be underscored; because they involved expenditures, not revenue, military pensions were not directly addressed in any section of the bill. Thus, the loyalty of these members to the committee, which had no jurisdiction over pension legislation, was purely programmatic. However, when all the votes were tallied, eleven of the seventy-six Republicans outside the core of the tariff coalition defected to the Democrats; these defections were enough to turn the tables against the committee.

The pattern for the entire House is even more clear. Members representing wool manufacturing districts were the most loyal group, followed by iron and steel, military pensions, and wool producers, in that order. Of the 100 members representing districts within one or more of these groups, seventy-eight followed the Ways and Means Committee in pursuit of higher duties on wool cloth. Of the 189 members representing districts outside the core of the tariff coalition, only 34 percent supported the committee. As can be seen in the table, most of this difference originated between, not within, the parties; with respect to the voting membership of the House on this roll call, 79 percent of all tariff coalition districts were represented by Republicans, while slightly over 59 percent of all districts outside the policy basis of the tariff coalition were represented by Democrats. It is within this overarching partisan and policy framework that the dissenting Republicans must be placed; they were particularly stressed by the combination of extraordinarily high duties suggested by the committee and the fact that their districts were not as clearly ensconced in the tariff policy complex as those of their more favored colleagues.

THE POLICY FOUNDATION OF THE REPUBLICAN
COALITION: CIVIL WAR PENSIONS,
TARIFF PROTECTION, THE GOLD STANDARD,
AND SOUTHERN BLACKS

During a period of about nine weeks in the spring of 1890, a series of crucial roll calls were recorded on four major Republican policies: the Force bill, the Dependent Pension Act, the McKinley Tariff, and the Sherman Silver Purchase Act (see Table 7.7).[89] The voting alignments illustrate how these policies were integrated, as political practice, into the Republican coalition. Much of the politics of this era was crude by modern standards, but, apparently without exception, such has been the case with every comparable period of rapid economic development anywhere in the world. What should be clear from this analysis is the great sophistication and complexity of the unfolding coalitional strategies of the Republican party as it grappled with the problem of integrating short-term, material benefits for its constituent groups with the long-term developmental requirements of rapid industrialization. The analysis of these votes also suggests why black suffrage in the South was the odd man out as the party pursued northern economic development.

In terms of economic development, the most important of the four was the gold standard because adoption of a free silver policy would have severely restricted capital investment in the United States. The gold standard, however, was also the most politically vulnerable of the four policies, requiring extensive support from other elements of the Republican program. From a political perspective, the most important of the four was the tariff. This was the primary foundation upon which the Republicans

[89] For a description of the Sherman Silver Purchase Act, see Chapter 6. Because consolidation of the national market was almost exclusively centered in the judiciary branch, Congress rarely voted on that issue and such was the case in 1890. The one important measure that implicated the national market, the Sherman Antitrust Act, was passed by an overwhelming margin; only later, after the Supreme Court began to hand down decisions based on that act, did the two parties split over just what the law was intended to accomplish.

Table 7.7. *Members Supporting Dependent Pensions, the McKinley Tariff, the Gold Standard, and the Force Bill in the 51st Congress, 1889–1891 (%)*

House membership category	Dependent pensions (April 1890)	McKinley Tariff (May 1890)	Gold standard (June 1890)	Force bill (July 1890)
Full House	71.6 (250)	53.6 (306)	53.0 (287)	51.0 (304)
Republicans	99.3 (142)	99.4 (165)	85.5 (152)	98.7 (156)
Democrats	35.2 (108)	0.0 (140)	16.4 (134)	0.0 (147)
Other party	— (0)	0.0 (1)	0.0 (1)	100.0 (1)
District level of development				
All members				
Highest	93.5 (46)	63.5 (52)	94.0 (50)	59.2 (49)
Middle high	93.5 (62)	72.2 (72)	73.3 (60)	73.1 (67)
Middle low	76.6 (94)	59.0 (122)	46.2 (119)	56.1 (123)
Lowest	12.5 (48)	11.7 (60)	10.3 (58)	12.3 (65)
Republicans				
Highest	100.0 (31)	100.0 (33)	100.0 (32)	96.7 (30)
Middle high	100.0 (44)	100.0 (52)	88.9 (45)	100.0 (49)
Middle low	100.0 (60)	100.0 (72)	77.9 (68)	100.0 (69)
Lowest	85.7 (7)	87.5 (8)	71.4 (7)	87.5 (8)
Democrats				
Highest	80.0 (15)	0.0 (19)	83.3 (18)	0.0 (19)
Middle high	77.8 (18)	0.0 (20)	26.7 (15)	0.0 (18)
Middle low	35.3 (34)	0.0 (50)	3.9 (51)	0.0 (54)
Lowest	0.0 (41)	0.0 (51)	2.0 (50)	0.0 (56)
Trade areas (capital movements)				
Exporting (Intermediating)	93.1 (58)	62.9 (62)	81.8 (55)	59.6 (57)
Exporting (No-Intermediating)	90.6 (85)	69.2 (107)	74.5 (94)	65.4 (104)
Heavy importing	83.7 (49)	72.4 (58)	43.3 (60)	72.1 (61)
Light importing	12.1 (58)	11.4 (79)	14.1 (78)	11.0 (82)
Sectional stress	66.2	54.9	65.9	59.7

Note and sources: For definitions of categories used in this table, see the notes to Tables 2.11 and 6.7. These roll calls were taken on passage of the Dependent Pension bill; on passage of the McKinley Tariff bill; on an amendment to provide for the free coinage of silver (nay votes supported the gold standard); and on passage of the Force bill. The roll calls can be found in the *Congressional Record* 51:1:4062–4063, April 30, 1890; 51:1:5112–5113, May 21, 1890; 51:1:6503–6504, June 25, 1890; 51:1:6940–6941, July 2, 1890. "Intermediating" indicates those trade areas with an intermediating financial center for capital exports. "No-Intermediating" indicates those trade areas lacking such a center.

ran their campaigns throughout the late nineteenth century and enjoyed enthusiastic support throughout the manufacturing belt and much of the West. Because military pensions distributed much of what would have been a politically embarrassing and economically destabilizing revenue surplus, the expansion of Union beneficiaries under what became the Dependent Pension Act was intimately linked to tariff protection both programmatically and politically.[90] In economic terms, Civil War pensions were a nullity – any number of alternatives would have reduced the surplus produced by the tariff without the waste and corruption that attended the pension system. Politically, however, Union pensions were almost the perfect auxiliary to the Republican development program because they simultaneously distinguished the party as the loyalist alternative to the Confederate-tainted Democrats, enjoyed the active support of a large and vigorous popular organization (the Grand Army of the Republic), and created a large clientele interest in keeping tariff rates high – a clientele interest that could tangibly and unambiguously trace their interest in tariff protection to their monthly benefits. The last of the four policies, represented by the Force bill, had been a central element in the Republican program during Reconstruction, when the installation of a loyalist element in the Confederate South had been a pressing requirement for political stability. By 1890, however, the impulse to intervene in southern elections had become a vestige of history. While consideration of the Force bill may have generated more political heat than any other policy during the Fifty-first Congress, the measure had nonetheless become a minor element in the Republican program.[91] In the end, the Force bill was used to intimidate southern Democratic senators in order to permit passage of the McKinley Tariff and later by western Republicans as trade material in their bargaining with southern Democrats over free silver proposals.

These policies, not surprisingly, starkly divided the major parties. The roll calls on the tariff and southern suffrage were almost party-line decisions, with one Republican dissenter in the first case and two in the

[90] Under the 1890 act, any Union veteran who could demonstrate some disability, regardless of whether or not it was related to their service in the Civil War, was entitled to $144 a year ($12 per month). All that was required was that they be incapable of performing manual labor. In addition, their widows were entitled to benefits whether or not their husband's death could be traced to an injury or condition arising out of their military service. Finally, the legislation required only three months' service and an honorable discharge as a trigger for veteran's benefits. Dearing, *Veterans in Politics*, pp. 399–400. Also see, Glasson, *History of Military Pension Legislation*, pp. 234–238.

[91] The intensity of southern hostility to this bill can hardly be overstated. Both the Alabama and Arkansas state legislatures, for example, postponed action on bills to provide for state exhibits at the upcoming 1893 World's Columbian Exposition while Congress was considering the Force bill. Viewing both the Exposition and the Force bill as expressions of nationalist sentiment and thereby linked, both legislatures refused to appropriate funds even after the elections bill had died. *Appleton's Annual Cyclopaedia of 1891* (New York: D. Appleton, 1892), pp. 7, 31.

second. The lone defector on the tariff, Hamilton Coleman of Louisiana, opposed the bill because he believed that the sugar bounty would ultimately be abandoned by his party, thus leaving producers with neither protection nor a compensatory subsidy.[92] The Democrats were united on both roll calls.

Both the pension bill and the free silver amendment, however, split Democratic ranks. Northern and western Democrats found the popularity of the Civil War pensions hard to resist, and a large majority of the party outside the South supported expansion of the system. All southern Democrats, many of whom were in fact Confederate veterans, opposed expansion of benefits to former Union soldiers and their dependents. In that sense, the connection between economic development and support for pensions displayed in the table is somewhat specious; the battle lines on this policy were largely drawn up in the same way and for largely the same reasons as they were during the Civil War. However, because both the Civil War and divisions over the course of industrialization had similar origins in the pattern of uneven regional development, the federal pension system was thoroughly embedded, from both directions, in the partisan politics of an overarching sectional redistribution of wealth. The clearest connection with relative economic development, however, appeared on the free silver vote; both parties as well as the House as a whole displayed consistent differences across the developmental spectrum. When trade area delegations are categorized by their position within the national capital market, these developmental alignments are more or less replicated. Not surprisingly, the gold standard decision produced the cleanest fit between interregional capital flows and roll-call votes, followed by pensions, the tariff, and southern suffrage.[93] Sectional stress scores were very high across the board but slightly higher for both pensions and the gold standard.[94]

In most legislative debate, the tariff, military pensions, trusts, and

---

[92]   Coleman noted that he had been "a Confederate soldier, a private in Lee's army of Northern Virginia for nearly four years," but, having resumed loyalty to the "Stars and Stripes," he now served his state and nation in order "to protect the industries of the American people all along the line. From the lime in Maine to the sugar and rice in Louisiana; from the glass lamp-chimneys of New York and Pennsylvania to the wool of Ohio and Iowa and borax of California; also Michigan lumber and Wisconsin beer. [Laughter and applause.] And now, fair play demands that you do not forsake the sugar interests of Louisiana, from which State I was elected a Republican member of Congress. [Loud applause.]" *Congressional Record* 51:1:5005–5006, May 20, 1890. Coleman was also one of the two Republican defectors on passage of the Force bill; the other was Herman Lehlbach of New Jersey.

[93]   These voting patterns also closely followed the sectional alignments revealed by policy positions in state party platforms. See Chapter 3.

[94]   For both the tariff and the Force bill, the sectional pattern was slightly marred by the hostility of the relatively large Democratic delegation from New York City; for the House as a whole, their votes substantially reduced support in the highest developmental category. Within the Democratic caucus, of course, there was no relationship at all with development; the party cast all of its votes against both bills.

monetary policy were discussed separately on their own terms. But congressmen and senators implicitly recognized that they were interlocking aspects of a unified Republican program. When Senator James Beck, a Kentucky Democrat, took the floor in early March of 1888, for example, he ran them all together in a way that defied easy summary. In assessing Beck's argument, John Sherman, then a senator from Ohio, illustrated how these different policies meld together in the heat of political combat:

> ... the other day ... the Senator from Kentucky started off against a bill intended to grant pensions to certain disabled soldiers of the Union Army. He extended from that point until he got upon the tariff, very naturally, perhaps; he thinks so at least, because every road leads to the tariff with him. When the tariff got to be a little tiresome he commmenced talking about trusts and said that the great trusts were caused by the tariff. I ventured in a mild-mannered way to suggest to him a doubt whether trusts were caused by the tariff; whether trusts did not exist in domestic as well as foreign productions, and he answered promptly that tariff was the great cause of all. I named to him the whisky trust, the oil trust, the cotton-seed trust, and other trusts of that kind, and wanted to know how they grew out of the tariff. Thereupon the Senator changed his ground and got onto the silver question, and then he commenced assailing me for the coinage act, and said I had been responsible for the coinage act of 1873.[95]

Several years later, in his first speech of the 1890 campaign, Sherman himself listed the Sherman Antitrust Act, the Dependent Pension Act, the Sherman Silver Purchase Act, and the McKinley Tariff as the four most important issues facing the electorate.[96] His omission of the Force bill was notable, not only because Congress had failed to enact the measure but because it was an indication that black voting rights had become so unpopular that northern Republicans could use it only to threaten southern Democrats.

Even as a mere threat, the political costs were high.[97] Richard Clarke, an Alabama Democrat, favored conducting the national campaign in 1892 on that very issue, long after the election bill was dead:

[95] *Congressional Record*, 50:1:2015, March 13, 1888.
[96] Sherman, *Recollections of Forty Years*, p. 843.
[97] In the form that the bill passed the House, most provisions were administrative in nature, providing for popular petitions from the citizenry which could invoke supervision of elections by the federal judiciary. However, in the case of local resistance, the president could call out federal troops in order to compel compliance – hence the name "Force bill." For maneuvering in the Senate that subordinated the election bill to both the tariff and free silver, albeit by radically different elements of the Republican party, see Vincent P. De Santis, *Republicans Face the Southern Question* (New York: Greenwood Press, 1969), pp. 208–209, 212–213; Stanley P. Hirshon, *Farewell to the Bloody Shirt: Northern Republicans & the Southern Negro, 1877–1913* (Chicago: Quadrangle Books, 1968), pp. 226, 228–230, 232–233; Oberholtzer, *History of the United States*, vol. 5, pp. 116–117, 137–138; Rhodes, *History of the United States*, vol. 8, pp. 363–364.

[The] Republican party by its platform, by the declarations of its two national candidates, by the writings and utterances of its leaders, by its sectional hate, stands pledged to the enactment of the force bill, carrying in its train race hatred, confusions, bloodshed, race war, the absolute wiping out of Northern capital invested in the South, and the destruction of a magnificent home market for Northern manufacturers, Eastern merchants, and Western mules, bacon, wheat, and corn.[98]

But even people outside the South were often appalled by the measure's implications. For example, Terence Powderly, who led the Knights of Labor, told his membership that there was "more intimidation contained in four lines of that [proposed] law than in all the Southern outrages that have taken place since the war."[99]

All four policies – the tariff, pensions, southern suffrage, and the monetary standard – were quite tangible in the late nineteenth century. Each had a material presence with which the electorate could relate and somehow, often erroneously or simplistically, bring abstract policy questions down to earth. Pensions, for example, placed monthly stipends in the hands of Union veterans. However the policy might be wrapped in patriotic cloth as a reward for service in the Civil War, the practical impact of the policy was this stipend. And that was the way Congress divided: regions in which stipends were numerous voted for pensions, those in which pensioners were scarce voted against them.

In the case of the tariff, customs duties clearly and unambiguously raised the price of imported foreign goods. The law deployed customs agents and armed them with tariff schedules for that very purpose. That the tariff had the effect of raising the income of protected domestic producers was also fairly clear. The real question was whether the tariff raised wages. The Republicans contended that the tariff raised wages throughout the economy, not only for protected industries but for all other sectors as well. The Democrats were skeptical. And this was the major fault line on which the issue was fought outside the South; few argued that the tariff had anything but a negative impact on that region. Monetary policy had its own material pivots. One was the clear connection between deflation and the interests of long-term creditors, particularly those holding federal bonds. Another was between inflation and the interests of borrowers, particularly those who had entered into long-term mortgages. These immediate interests, as the evidence in this chapter indicates, were easily expanded into the

---

[98] In Clarke's opinion, that issue and the tariff, the two policies on which Democrats in and out of Congress stood united, should have been the principles on which the election should be fought. Silver was too divisive and should be set aside. *Congressional Record* 52:1:6128–6129, July 13, 1892.

[99] Quoted in David Montgomery, *Citizen Worker: The Experience of Workers in the United States with Democracy and the Free Market during the Nineteenth Century* (New York: Cambridge University Press, 1993), p. 155.

policy predispositions of regions, depending on how they stood within the national capital market.

The odd man out was southern suffrage. During Reconstruction, the Republican party attempted to make such a connection between federal intervention in southern elections and the personal self-interest of northerners. However, this connection steadily waned as it became increasingly clear that southern Democrats, however obstreperous they might otherwise be, were no longer a threat to national sovereignty. Southern white loyalty to the United States government remained weak but there was little occasion to test southern patriotism beyond the simple condition that federal laws were obeyed (and, since there were few federal laws that directly reached southern citizens, particularly after Reconstruction, this was almost no test at all). Despite the suspect loyalty of southern whites, federal intervention in southern elections became more and more unlikely as northerners increasingly distinguished black voting in the South from their own material interests. In the end, those most directly affected by federal intervention, southern blacks, were not strong enough to act as their own agents in what was a very individualistic world.

CONCLUSION

The programmatic underpinnings of the gold standard were primitive compared with the rich texture of the policy complex supporting the tariff. Protection for northern industry was clothed in side payments to major groups in the electorate through duties on raw wool and pensions for Union veterans in such a way that benefits were distributed in almost every northern and western district while liabilities fell heavily on the South. The tariff policy complex thus broadened the redistributive impact of industrial protection while narrowing, albeit also intensifying, the opposition. In addition, the auxiliary policies that accompanied the industrial schedules of the tariff softened the impact of protection by pointing to benefits other than simple and massive redistribution of wealth from agriculture and industry. For all these reasons, tariff protection became the broad policy backbone of the Republican developmental coalition.

Like the tariff, the gold standard was one of the three major developmental policies of the late nineteenth century (the other being the expansion of an unregulated national market). But where the tariff was, in sheer economic terms, fairly unimportant in American industrialization, the gold standard was central, even essential. And where the impact of industrial protection was clothed in distracting, even if substantively important, duties on raw wool and pension payments, the redistributive impact of the gold standard was on naked display. No late nineteenth-century voter could fail to discern the interests of northeastern bondholders and rentier capitalists in maintaining gold payments. And from this tightly knit group, the interests of sound money were easily projected onto the broader communities of finance capitalists and capital-exporting regions. There were no side payments to unrelated groups, and the most important extensions of the gold community into the South and West tended to be the hirelings of northeastern financiers, hardly a promising base on which to build a party coalition in those regions. The gold standard, in political terms, was a very expensive dependent within the Republican developmental coalition, subsidized by votes drawn on the much more popular accounts kept by the tariff policy complex. In short, the protective tariff supported the rather lame gold standard in politics, while gold provided much of the substantive economic basis for the industrial expansion that was, ostensibly, the real purpose of protection.

The foundation interests on which these policies were formulated were quite primitive in the sense that individual self-interest, as expressed and evidenced in immediately experienced material relationships, dictated much of political conflict. For that reason, most political strategy focused on either reinforcing or disrupting the logic of these relationships. One of the most powerful of these strategies was the use of nationalism. Tariff protection and nationalism, for example, went hand-in-glove. When Union pensions were added to the equation, the tariff reinforced strong internal claims on national loyalty as well. The direct policy benefits to groups within the Republican coalition was cemented, in nationalist terms, by every encampment of the Grand Army of the Republic where, inevitably, the connection between tariff revenue and liberal pensions was unambiguously laid out for all to see. The industrial tariff, from this angle, placed American interests above those of Britain by protecting the home market and, in that way, appeared to pay for the well-earned pensions of the boys in blue. The boys in gray were mere unworthy bystanders in a nationalist drama that only slightly disguised, if it did so at all, the pariah status of the South in the American political community.

But while the tariff could easily be promoted on nationalist grounds, the gold standard was a much harder, even impossible, sale. For those who supported hard money, the most common nationalist argument was that the United States should belong to the elite, culturally advanced community of nations subscribing to the gold standard as compared with the impoverished, struggling countries laboring under silver. This interpretation both encompassed the cosmopolitan characteristics of the American financial community and invited citizens to view monetary policy as social ethics, albeit written on a global scale. Against this contention, the silverites placed the image of an indigenous American virtue, an ethics capable of creating a tailored financial system just as it molded immigrants into a distinctive national community. The gold standard, in this perspective, was an alien product of British design. The Populists, for example, connected alien ethics and foreign interests in what they called "The Gold Bug's Prayer":

Our Father who art in England, Rothschild be thy name, thy financial kingdom come to America, thy will be done in the United States as it is in England. Give us this day our bonds in gold, but no silver; give us plenty of men's votes to keep monopoly in power, and its friends in office. We know our Father we have done wrong; we have robbed the honest poor, and brought distress to many a door. We know it was wrong to refund the bonds and make them payable in gold coin; we know it was wrong to water our railroad stock, but thou knowest we make money by that. Thou knowest our Father that we are above politics, it is the same to us whether the republicans or democrats rule. Thou Oh! Father, knowest we are able to sway all political jobs in our favor, lead us not, Oh! Father into the ways of strikes, and Oh! Father deliver us from the insane Knights of Labor and Farmers' Alliance. Oh! Father subdue this People's party that we may have the kingdom, bonds, interest, power, and gold until the Republic shall end. Ah men![100]

But such connections were not only drawn by the Populists. Both silver Democrats and silver Republicans were quite capable of Anglophobia as well.[101]

While silver promised to establish an American financial system, free from foreign influence, tariff protection encouraged the development of national industry and thus economic independence from British producers. Thus the pure nationalist combination of the two policies was silver and protectionism. But while both free silver and protectionist sentiment were both widespread in the late nineteenth century, they were not positions that were often held by the same person, in or out of Congress. For reasons that have their origin in uneven regional development, protection and the gold standard had become the twin economic principles underlying the Republican coalition in national politics, much as free trade and silver had come to dominate the Democratic party. Neither party could make Anglophobia into an overarching political principle without sacrificing one of its princi-

---

[100]   Taken from the Ketchum *Keystone* and reprinted in William Joseph Gaboury, *Dissension in the Rockies: A History of Idaho Populism* (New York: Garland, 1988), p. 65. For a slightly different version, entitled "Jay Gould's prayer," published in the Winfield, Kansas, *American Nonconformist and Kansas Industrial Liberator*, April 12, 1888, see Jeffrey Ostler, *Prairie Populism: The Fate of Agrarian Radicalism in Kansas, Nebraska, and Iowa, 1880–1892* (Topeka: University Press of Kansas, 1993), p. 80.

[101]   After quoting a plank in the 1896 national Democratic platform ("Gold mono metallism is a British policy and its adoption has brought other nations into financial servitude to London. It is not only un-American but anti-American"), the *Commercial and Financial Chronicle* observed that "the speeches and newspaper articles of the adherents of silver abound in similar references. The word 'gold' in the thoughts and discussions of these people is always allied with the adjective 'British,' and they work themselves into a frenzy denouncing this 'British gold policy.'" "Has the Gold Standard Hurt Us and Benefited Great Britain?," August 15, 1896.

ples: for the Republicans, the gold standard; for the Democrats, free trade. As a result, although the United States was intensely involved in a world economy dominated by the British, Anglophobia remained, for the most part, the very restricted prerogative of western Republicans and Populists, both of whom could combine silver with at least a friendly indifference toward protection. And when the United States began to aggressively expand abroad in the last years of the century, the British chose to stand aside. This decision, along with the cross-cutting implications of the tariff and gold, produced a highly nationalist combination of internal development and intervention abroad in which neither major political party identified a consistent and powerful foreign opponent. In other words, the very structure of development policies and the national political economy of the United States encouraged a nationalism rooted in American self-affirmation, as opposed to a militarist jingoism that equated patriotism with the defeat of a foreign enemy.

8

Conclusion

THE POLITICAL ECONOMY of American industrialization carries two very different implications for comparative development, one economic and the other political. In economic terms, development must attract and retain capital – a requirement that usually demands fairly high rates of return and a disciplined focus on productive efficiency. In the American case, given the conservative ideological orientation of the industrial and financial elite, deciding what public policies might provide these conditions was rather simple: An unregulated national market provided the impetus to technological innovation (and thus productivity), while adherence to the gold standard guaranteed that the resulting profits would not be impaired by inflation or exchange rate instability. Because the political agent for constructing these policies became the Republican party, the political viability of industrialization depended to a large extent on the party's electoral success. Viewed in economic terms, the national market and the gold standard were the most fundamental developmental policies; viewed politically, the tariff was far more central to development because protection underpinned the Republican coalition.

From a comparative perspective, the important point is that successful developmental programs must be both economically and politically viable; because both conditions must be met, scholars cannot choose between them. This was particularly evident in the United States because the political and economic preconditions for industrialization were so distinct. On the one hand, there was an economic process that required a national market and monetary stability. On the other, there was a democratic process in which the developmental party had to prevail in electoral politics. From a comparative perspective, there is no reason that the same policies will both promote development as a dynamic economy and serve the electoral needs of the developmental party as agent; in fact, as this book has demonstrated, there are good reasons why these separate policy preconditions are likely to conflict. In many instances, the economic and political preconditions for development are so far apart that no party can emerge as a viable developmental agent, a situation implying that either rapid development will not occur or democracy must be abandoned. Seen that way, an explanation for the compatibility of democracy and development in the United States can be reduced to a fortuitous intersection of preconditions, the inclination of a politically viable Republican party, resting on the protective tariff, to impose an unregulated market and the gold standard on the national economy.

However, this partial explanation raises more questions than it puts to rest. Many of these fall under four broad headings. First and foremost, what were the institutional connections between developmental policies and popular politics? Government policies must somehow stimulate development even while exposed to popular control and influence. The basic arrangement in the American case was to ensconce the most essential economic policies within the most insulated government institutions; those policies most politically essential to maintaining the viability of the Republican party were assigned to the most socially responsive institutions. A second question immediately follows: In what way were policies assigned to the various branches of the central government? For example, how did the Supreme Court, the most insulated branch, come to dominate political construction of the national market, the most important, in economic terms, of the primary developmental policies? The answer here lies in institutional repertoires, such as legal doctrine, that are instrumentally adapted to developmental requirements, such as repression of state and local attempts to regulate commerce. In turn, both of these explanations raise a third question: What kept the Republican party focused on the preconditions for industrialization, in its role as institutional agent, while much of the clamor in the larger electoral arena called for abandonment of the party's developmental program? The easy (and inadequate) response is that, by and large, industrial expansion was good politics. The more complete answer is that the party discovered ways to concentrate most of the losses from industrialization on a minority of the electorate (southerners) while distributing at least some of the benefits among the remainder of the nation. That raises the fourth and last question: What made that concentration of losses and broad distribution of benefits both feasible and persuasive as a popular ideology or developmental vision? The answer is that the radically uneven topography of the American economy made design of such policies possible while the political inheritance of the Civil War provided abundant warrant for their implementation. Each of these four aspects of the political economy of American industrialization is taken up below.

THE INSTITUTIONAL CONTEXTS OF THE GREAT
DEVELOPMENTAL POLICIES

American industrialization in the late nineteenth century was grounded in three great developmental policies: unregulated commercial movement and exchange within an emerging national market, tariff protection for heavy industry, and adherence to the international gold standard.[1] The first of these policies was largely in the custody of the federal judiciary, particularly the United States Supreme Court, and enabled the full exploitation of economies of scale otherwise made possible by the emergence of the modern business enterprise as an organizational form. The tariff was centered in Congress (with only occasional and ineffectual intervention by the president) and, while not essential to industrialization in economic terms, was politically vital as a policy extending and deepening the Republican coalition. The gold standard, both administratively and politically, became the assignment of the executive branch, with the president often struggling with a hostile Congress over this issue. Thus all three legs of the developmental tripod, each necessary to the Republican-led industrial program in one way or another, was defended and promoted by the party within a different branch of the federal government.

The tariff was centered in Congress, deep in the log-rolling and deal-making legislative processes where the abstract principles of trade protection assumed a concrete form as developmental policy. When the tariff emerged from congressional committee rooms, festooned with side payments to sheep raisers, Union veterans, and other interests, the primary purpose underlying the policy was no longer industrial expansion but, instead, the maintenance and extension of the Republican coalition. When the Democrats were in power, they began the task of tariff revision with a strong inclination to reduce duties on everything except Louisiana sugar and usually ended up decorating their own proposals with numerous exceptions and side issues such as a federal income tax. The Democrats, in effect, were compelled to emulate Republican coalition-building practices as the only means of achieving tariff reduction of any sort. In the end, the political primacy of the tariff to both parties (but particularly to the Republicans) made discussions of its developmental impact both academic and inconclusive. Rather than enter the fray on policy terms, minor parties chose to view the tariff as either a major party intrigue with business or a political charade in which the major parties deluded voters into thinking that they had important interests at stake. What minor parties would have done with the tariff had they won office is a mystery and a rather large one at

---

[1]   These three policies were the most politically contested of the major economic policies undergirding industrialization. Other policies, such as private property, were just as important in economic terms but far less challenged in politics.

that, since protection was the single most prominent policy dispute in late nineteenth-century politics.

With respect to an unregulated national market, the broad consensus between the parties was broken only by their differences over railroad and antitrust regulation.[2] In contrast to the tariff where the parties consistently and strongly divided, Republicans and Democrats were able to compromise their differences over the Interstate Commerce Act in 1887 and the Sherman Antitrust Act in 1890; the final votes in both cases were almost unanimous. However, the unwillingness of the major parties to effectively control market expansion subsequently forced conflict into the federal courts where most regulatory efforts were frustrated by hostile decisions. As a result, railroad regulation and antitrust enforcement were almost complete policy failures before the turn of the century.

The emerging national market divided the nation fairly cleanly into agrarian regions that looked to the East for consumer goods and capital and the manufacturing belt for which market expansion increased employment in industry. This division, along with the consolidation of industry into ever larger corporate combinations, made the market an arena of predation between the East, on the one hand, and the South and West, on the other. However, there were two other aspects to the national market. First, eastern consumers consumed much of the commodity production of the Plains and Mountain West. For that reason, much of the resistance to market consolidation in the latter regions was highly selective. The conflict between the West and the East was over the terms of interregional trade, not whether there should be trade. However, for the South the question was the trade itself; the export-oriented cotton economy would have been at least as well off, if not more prosperous, had the South been entirely independent of the industrial system of the North. But this broad, hostile stance toward the national market attracted few allies in the remainder of the nation.

The second aspect of the market counterbalanced interregional exploitation with rapid improvements in industrial productivity; in fact, railroad rates and consumer prices rapidly declined throughout the period even as the profits of trusts and other combinations rose exponentially. Even allowing for the deflationary impact of the gold standard, the general price trend for most manufactured goods was so clear that market expansion was to some extent depoliticized. While this did little to stem demands for an adjustment of the terms of interregional trade, it did mean that the consolidation of the national market was, with the exception of the South, not seriously threatened in the late nineteenth century. The federal courts were

[2] After the turn of the century, major party differences over the construction of the national market rapidly widened and, in fact, became a major theme in both policy-making and electoral competition. See, for example, Elizabeth Sanders, *Roots of Reform: Farmers, Workers, and the American State, 1877–1917* (Chicago: University of Chicago Press, 1999).

left with the task of putting out brush fires ignited by state and local governments while conflagrations over the tariff and monetary standard ranged throughout popular politics.

The gold standard and the tariff appeared to be, in many ways, the inseparable twins of American industrialization. In their political impact on the major parties, however, they could not have been more different. Where the tariff brought together the different party factions, the gold standard often tore apart state Republican organizations, either feeding them to Democratic and Populist wolves in local elections if they followed the national party line or forcing them into opposition to Republican presidential administrations if they dissented. When Grover Cleveland, a Democrat, was responsible for administering the gold standard, western Republicans could freely embrace silver without much stress. But when Republicans occupied the White House, the cost of dissent was much higher, risking ostracization within Congress and other national party councils.

On the Democratic side, hostility to gold was so universal that excommunication was risked by those who supported Cleveland's orthodox monetary policies. Cleveland's hard-money predilections were tolerated only because they appeared necessary to carry New York in a presidential election; before the admission of new states in the Plains and West, the southern-based Democrats could win a national contest only with New York on board. But once the party had placed a hard-money Democrat in the White House, the congressional wing utterly abandoned the new administration by embracing silver. And in 1896, the party finally gambled on an exclusively regional coalition of the South and West and drove the eastern gold wing entirely out of the temple.

In Congress, the major parties were more flexible and free-floating on monetary policy than on the tariff, with interparty coalitions forming and dissolving on both sides of the dispute over the gold standard. In the executive branch, however, presidents of both parties were unshakably devoted to gold, however costly that policy might be politically. In one sense, this devotion was due to the construction of national coalitions in presidential races which tended to privilege the interests of the capital-exporting East where electoral votes could be had in large blocs under the headings of states such as New York, Pennsylvania, and Massachusetts. However, managing the gold standard involved administrative tasks of high complexity with implications for expenditures, revenues, bond issues, and seasonal Treasury interventions in the money market. Of necessity, these tasks required a much more thorough and sustained policy commitment than did, by comparison, the tariff which worked its political magic even if poorly designed as a purely developmental policy. For that reason, the presidential commitment was much more than a simple policy declaration; presidents and their subordinates actively administered the gold standard on a daily basis. There is thus little doubt that presidents in the late nineteenth century sincerely believed that the gold standard was the optimal monetary basis for economic development and that this commitment ran far beyond the interest-brokering design of national party platforms. In this sense, where the tariff was often a cynical and opportunistic construction of political favors in Congress, the gold standard was a far more substantial policy commitment by the executive branch.[3]

Throwing up a complex, alternative monetary theory in their own platform declarations, Greenbackers and Populists strongly challenged the nation's commitment to the gold standard. Greenback theory required discretionary control of the money supply by the federal government. That discretion, in turn, required abandonment of all metallic standards of value, silver as well as gold. However, as the foundation of the financial system, the public viewed silver much more favorably than fiat currency. In fact, beyond the recruitment of a cadre of party activists, a fully elaborated greenback theory may have been a net political liability. For that reason, Greenbackers and Populists almost routinely included a plank calling for the free coinage of silver. But while these free silver demands often gained the parties a hearing for the rest of their platforms, they also deranged the otherwise carefully arranged tenets of greenback theory in such a way as to make the program practically unworkable. For their part, Republican and Democratic presidents often walked a tightrope between political compromise with silverites and the operating requirements of the gold standard. While their administrative record clearly demonstrated their overriding commitment to gold, their rhetoric, with its expressions of sympathy for silver and promises of concessions to soft money, often appeared both theoretically incoherent and deceptive. Yet the skill required to administer the gold standard necessitated a theoretical understanding of the monetary system at least as great as that explicitly laid out in minor party platforms. In sum, the Greenbackers and Populists took advantage of their out-party status to openly construct a financial theory they could not politically implement, while major party presidents practiced an equally complex financial orthodoxy they could not openly acknowledge.

We can now summarize the differing relationships between the three great developmental policies and American industrialization (see Table 8.1). Tariff protection was politically irreplaceable because of the interior strength it lent to the Republican coalition. In economic terms, however, the tariff could have been easily jettisoned from the developmental program. The unregulated national market reversed these roles; market-expanding policies were both economically essential to industrialization and a net political liability for the Republican party. So, while rhetorically acknowledging the possible need for restraints on market expansion, the Republi-

---

[3] For a similar conclusion concerning the tilt of presidents toward the gold standard and the interests of finance capital generally, see ibid., pp. 395–396.

Table 8.1. *Political, Economic, and Administrative Characteristics of the Major Developmental Policies*

Development policy	Economic role and impact	Political role and impact	Administrative characteristics
National market	*Economically necessary.* Underpinned rise of the modern business enterprise and, ultimately, the comparative advantage of the United States in the international political economy.	*Net liability.* State and local opposition to market consolidation cost the Republican party much support in the Plains and West, particularly with respect to antitrust policy and railroad regulation.	*Dominated by the U.S. Supreme Court.* Congress seldom acted. When it did, the laws were eviscerated by the judiciary. Presidents were a little more active (e.g., antitrust prosecutions) but the Court frustrated their weak initiatives as well.
Tariff protection	*Economically unessential.* Redistributed wealth from agriculture to industry and from South and West to the eastern manufacturing belt. But, otherwise, tariff schedules lacked developmental logic or purpose.	*Politically necessary.* The tariff policy complex, comprised of protected industries, Union army pensioners, and northern and western sheep raisers, provided the backbone of the Republican coalition in national politics.	*Dominated by Congress.* The construction of tariff laws was primarily driven by interest group politics with only moderate intervention by party leaders. The role of presidents was weak. The role of the courts was almost nonexistent.
Gold standard	*Economically important.* Stabilized American exchange rates and thereby encouraged foreign investment and retention of domestic profits in the industrial sector. However, in terms of economic theory, other monetary systems might have better achieved these ends. The problem was that none of these alternatives was sponsored by a credible agent (i.e., political party).	*Politically ambiguous.* In Congress, the gold standard was a net political liability; most members opposed gold for that reason. In presidential races, however, the gold standard was much more favorably positioned. On the whole, the gold standard survived because the tariff provided enough political rent for the Republican party to offset its congressional losses on gold.	*Dominated by the executive branch.* Although Congress challenged the standard throughout most of the late nineteenth century, presidents retained just enough authority to prevent abandonment of gold. Day-to-day administration of the gold standard required intensive and competent management by Treasury secretaries as well. The role of the courts was almost nonexistent.

cans turned most of the implementation of laissez-faire principles over to
Republican judges on the Supreme Court who, well insulated from popular
influence, could turn back state and local attempts to Balkanize the national
market.

Neither economically nor politically irreplaceable, the gold standard lay
somewhere in between the tariff and the market.[4] While a greenback system
that credibly guaranteed a stable exchange rate would probably have been
superior to the gold standard in economic terms, the problem was that no
government anywhere in the world would have been given exchange rate
credibility in the absence of a firm commitment to the gold standard. In the
United States, in particular, there was little or no reason for neutral
observers to believe that either the Greenbackers or the Populists with their
angry denunciations of financiers and loud demands for inflation would
have been credible to foreign or domestic capital-holders. And if they had
won, the ensuing capital flight would have been disastrous to industrial
expansion. On this score, Bryan's one-step devaluation of the dollar to a
silver standard, involving a halving of its value against the British pound,
might have been slightly more credible than greenbackism but not much
less damaging to industrial development.

In terms of administration, Congress, often under Republican leadership,
gave the executive branch just enough discretion and just enough leeway in
other areas so that presidents could conduct a defense of the gold standard
that was just adequate to the task. The emphasis is on the word "just." In
political terms, the gold standard involved great costs everywhere outside
the East, but there the Republicans, when the Democrats finally embraced
silver under Bryan, reaped benefits beyond their wildest dreams. Money
flowed like water into the national party under McKinley, so much so that
the campaign was hard-pressed to find a use for all the funds raised by
Bryan's threat. This political advantage had been largely neutralized in
previous races when Cleveland and other Democratic nominees had been
equally committed to hard money. But in an open contest in which the

[4] From a counterfactual perspective, these three policies can be distinguished as follows:
Little industrialization would have occurred in the United States, for economic
reasons, if the national market had been fragmented by state and local regulation;
little industrialization would also have occurred, for political reasons, if the
Republican party had not exploited the tariff as an electoral underpinning to its coalition; and, finally, little industrialization would have occurred, for both political and
economic reasons, if the gold standard had been abandoned. In economic terms, other
constructions of the national financial system were certainly feasible in theory but, in
political terms, the operating requirements for those alternative systems (such as fiat
currency) were out of reach. There was simply no politically viable agent (i.e., party)
that could both take the United States off gold and maintain monetary stability. Put
another way, the gold standard was the only financial policy that, in the real world
of the late nineteenth century, fell within the conjunction of possible political and economic solutions to the developmental problem.

national parties clearly differed on gold, the political benefits were clearly revealed. Even so, the Republican party would have much preferred to run against Bryan on the tariff; that, in fact, was the primary reason McKinley, with his somewhat checkered monetary record in Congress, was chosen as the nominee.

THE ASSIGNMENT OF DEVELOPMENTAL POLICIES TO GOVERNMENT INSTITUTIONS

As the political agent promoting industrial expansion, the Republican party decided what would be the relationship between the three great developmental policies and their respective branches of the federal government. With respect to the political construction of the national market, the United States Supreme Court, dominated by Republican appointees, instrumentally created the legal doctrines that suppressed both state and federal regulation of commerce. As constitutional principles, dual sovereignty and substantive due process were cut from cloth woven well after the Civil War. This deliberate accommodation of constitutional interpretation to the requirements of industrial expansion extended to a fine distinction between the federal government's ability to control the great industrial trusts (in most cases, it could not) and its capacity to repress, through injunction, strike activity by labor unions (in most cases, it could).[5] No other branch of the government could have reached the individual states, save through formal amendment of the Constitution. However, the juridical creativity that went into the construction of an unregulated national market and the consistently facilitating orientation of Republican justices evidence the strong commitment of the party to this, the central economic pillar of American industrialization. The party did not choose to assign the national market, as a developmental project, to the court but it did choose to make construction of a national market economy one of the highest policy priorities the party would pursue. In this case, the mechanism through which choice was effected involved the careful selection of accommodating federal justices.

The gold standard involved a similar party commitment. Complex seasonal and fiscal influences on financial activity imposed stiff administrative responsibilities on the government with respect to the maintenance of gold reserves; because neither Congress nor the Court could have carried out

---

[5] The Supreme Court also calibrated a careful exchange between a receding federal jurisdiction over southern race relations and politics, on the one hand, and an increasing nationalization of federal authority over market relations, on the other. This exchange pragmatically mitigated opposition to judicial activism by placating southern hostility to civil rights legislation and election oversight while, almost simultaneously, risking popular resistance with aggressive rulings on government regulation of the economy.

these responsibilities, facilitating administration of fiscal policy necessarily became an executive branch task. The pivot for monetary policy therefore became the presidency, the office responsible for both administering and politically defending the gold regime. The Republican party thus did not choose to assign the monetary system to the executive branch but it did choose to make the gold standard a high priority in the party program. In this case, the principle mechanism was the nomination of presidential candidates at the party's quadrennial conventions.

Unlike the construction of a national market and the gold standard, the tariff did involve a deliberate institutional choice. If Congress had decided to assign discretionary authority for the tariff to the executive branch, probably by way of negotiated agreements with other nations, protection might have had some theoretical coherence and, thus, might have played a more positive role in late nineteenth-century economic development.[6] In the actual event, the Republican party chose to sacrifice an economically coherent and efficacious trade policy by assigning almost all responsibility to Congress. Tariff protection, from a developmental perspective, was important to American industrialization almost solely for the political rent it conferred on the Republican party. Here the mechanism of choice was the interest-group driven construction of the tariff in Congress.[7]

Thus, when allocating the major developmental policies among the federal branches, the Republican party acted under rather severe constraints. Given the nature of the American polity, the construction of the national market could only be a project centered in the courts, and the administration of the gold standard had to be handled by the executive branch. There was some leeway on the tariff but, because this policy ended up as the foundation of the Republican coalition, it was no surprise that

[6] Such a possibility hinges on two assumptions: first, that a properly constructed protectionist policy would have been preferable to free trade and, second, that the executive branch would have been willing and able to implement such a trade policy through negotiated agreements with other nations.

[7] The transfer between the tariff (rich with political rent) and the gold standard (necessary for industrial expansion) was anchored by the ties of Republican representatives to two very different constituencies. On the one hand, Republican politicians were popular representatives compelled to cater to mass sentiment and rituals such as torchlight parades and large open conventions. This constituency drew them toward the tariff policy complex and away from the national market and the gold standard. On the other hand, these same politicians drew on the commercial and financial elite for financial contributions, an elite that generally placed as much, if not more, emphasis on the national market and the gold standard as the tariff. In fact, many members of this elite were either indifferent or hostile to protection. In addition, many Republican politicians were both drawn from this elite before entering politics and returned to it after leaving office. They thus often shared the elite consensus on gold and market both as social orthodoxy and professional norm (e.g., as lawyers, bankers, journalists). See Chapter 7 for a discussion of congressional deliberations on the tariff and the limited opportunities for executive influence.

Congress dominated the politics of protection. The tariff was the quintessential distributive policy, almost infinitely divisible with only weak limitations in terms of coherence and interdependency.[8] To have assigned such a policy to the executive branch where the benefits and losses would have tended to balance out would have sacrificed much of the political rent otherwise available. Congress was a much better choice because each member of the protectionist coalition could claim a particular benefit for a major group in his constituency, efficiently collecting the rent available from each important sector benefited by the tariff pastiche.

Unlike the tariff, however, both the national market and the gold standard had clear performance tests in the economy at large. In the first case, the test was whether or not attempts to regulate economic activity were suppressed, thus allowing industrial consolidation to effectively exploit the economies of scale available in an unregulated national market. In turn, this unregulated market, by encouraging experimentation in corporate forms and the design of industrial processes, provided the most important preconditions for the rise of modern business enterprise. The performance test for the gold standard was even simpler: The United States was either on or off, depending on whether or not the federal Treasury was able to redeem federal currency in gold on demand.

For all these reasons, the institutional relationships within which the three great developmental policies evolved were almost preordained. The tariff, the most political of the three, would be a project carried out in Congress, the most socially responsive and least centralized of the federal branches. The gold standard had to be an executive policy, given the complex administrative tasks it required. And the national market, in order to simultaneously avoid both local Balkanization and congressional regulation, clearly required heavy, even exclusive, intervention by the Supreme Court.

THE REPUBLICAN PARTY AS DEVELOPMENTAL AGENT

All of this, however, raises another question: To what extent was the Republican party an intentional agent with the capacity to plan the political economy of industrialization? This question neatly divides into two parts: How cohesive was the party, and what kept the party focused on economic development as a political project? Because the individual state parties dominated politics, the Republican party was, of course, not a monolithic organization.[9] The influence of uneven regional development, working through these state parties, tended to fragment the national party into competing factions. This was counterbalanced to some extent by the centripetal pull

---

[8] See Theodore J. Lowi, "American Business, Public Policy, Case-Studies, and Political Theory," *World Politics* 16:4 (July 1964): 677–715.

[9] See Chapter 3 for a discussion of state party platforms and regional fragmentation.

of presidential conventions (with their national platforms and high electoral visibility), presidential patronage (reinforcing loyalty to Republican executives), and congressional discipline (working through Republican Speakers with control over choice committee assignments). However, all of the latter still rested on consent within the collective party organization. And that, in turn, permitted dissenting party members to have at least some voice in what policies were followed. What ultimately gave the Republican party coherence as a policy-making organization was the emergence of a national party coalition centered in the manufacturing belt that exploited the distributive benefits available through tariff protection while articulating a broad vision of development with respect to interstate commerce and the gold standard. While loyalty to this program could not be imposed, the uneven topography of the national political economy naturally encouraged Republican party cohesion, even within a pluralistic democratic system in which Democrats and minor party insurgencies constantly battered the Republican coalition from almost all directions.

POPULAR CLAIMS ON WEALTH

As with conservative parties generally, the Republican program was most vulnerable when class conflict over income shares became salient issues in popular politics. While class-conscious claims rarely found a place in national politics, intense struggles over wealth and market position often drove much of the politics within each of the three great sections of the country: (1) within the northeastern and midwestern manufacturing belt, the focus was on the wage bargain in industrial production and the tens of thousands of strikes that accompanied rapid industrialization; (2) within the southern plantation economy, the regional base of the Democratic party, local politics often revolved around the struggle for control of the cotton crop by merchants, planters, and sharecroppers; and (3) within the vast grain-producing plains of the West, class conscious political conflict emphasized the commercial and marketing connections between commodity producers and the larger national economy.

With respect to these regional conflicts over different kinds of market transactions, one of the most distinctive features of the American political economy in the late nineteenth century was the simultaneous existence of militant action in the industrial workplace and broad apathy on the part of labor toward social democratic political movements. The explanation for this apathy lay in the structure of uneven regional development that systematically redistributed wealth, through the tariff and other federal policies, from the cotton-exporting South into investment in industrial production in the Northeast and Midwest. Although other cleavages also shaped labor's position in the northern party system, the tariff and gold standard policies of the Republican party drew many workers into its ranks and, in the end, effectively removed conflict over the industrial wage bargain from national politics even while strike activity rose to some of the highest levels ever recorded in world history. Thus, in the North, a combination of mass suffrage and violent, direct claims on wealth in the workplace coexisted with broad support for the national Republican party – the major vehicle of capital accumulation, adherence to the gold standard, and corporate consolidation.

In the plantation South, on the other hand, struggle over disposition of the cotton crop finally resulted in disfranchisement of poor whites and blacks – the latter supporters of the Republican party and, thus, Republican-led industrialization.[10] Within the American political economy of the late nineteenth century, even a radical redistribution of wealth among the major contenders for control of the cotton crop would probably have had little impact on capital accumulation in northern industry. This is true for several reasons. In the first place, even the upper classes of the rural South were too poor to invest much money in local economic development. Thus, even in the best of all possible worlds, very few late nineteenth-century southerners would have been able to invest outside their region. Second, the major forms of interregional redistribution were underpinned by national policies, such as tariff protection, that were beyond the authority of state and local governments. Such national policies would have redistributed wealth from the South and into northern industrialization regardless of who dominated state and local southern governments.

Thus, the intense struggle over the cotton crop was irrelevant to the northern worker's focus on the wage bargain in industry because it involved very different institutional and market relationships, and it also was irrelevant to the process of capital accumulation and investment that underpinned rapid industrialization in the North. In sum, any change in the distribution of wealth *within* the South would not have had much impact on northern industrialization because the region was extremely poor and already marginalized within the national political economy.

---

[10] One of the most ironic byproducts of the sectional organization of the nation party system was the position of southern blacks. By far the poorest, most economically oppressed group in the nation, southern blacks nonetheless supported a northern Republican industrial program that made their situation materially worse. When disfranchising legislation was passed in the late nineteenth century, southern blacks were the first target of the movement. From the point of view of the compatibility of democracy and development during this period, disfranchisement of the poorest group in American politics actually weakened electoral support for private capital formation in the industrial sector. With reference to this group, the developmental problem was thus not too much democracy, but too little, because their insertion into the national political economy placed them in a position of dependence on the northern wing of the Republican party.

Table 8.2. *General Model of American Party System, 1877–1900*

	Democrats	Republicans
South	Plantation elite/allied middle class	Freedmen/minority of hill country whites
North	Immigrant labor/subsistence farmers	Industrial-financial elite/native labor/prosperous agricultural producers

Unlike local claims on wealth in the industrial North and plantation South, agrarian insurgency in the grain-producing Plains and West swiftly and easily moved into national politics. These agrarian claims generated redistributive proposals to inflate the currency, regulate railroad rates, and provide government facilities for marketing commodity crops. All of these claims became important parts of the national Populist party program which also attracted widespread support in the South from sharecroppers and poor yeoman farmers. Here was the basis, at least, for an interregional alliance that was to repeatedly surface in the decades around the turn of the century. On the other hand, this agrarian focus on market linkages and facilities was either irrelevant to northern workers or, with respect to its hostility to the gold standard, a possible threat to their interests in continued industrial expansion.

The coalitional bases of the two major parties made the emergence of broad claims on wealth difficult because they divided both economic elites and the lower classes along sectional lines (see Table 8.2). In the North, the Republican party represented the interests of industrial and financial elites, while the Democrats drew support from immigrant workers and subsistence farmers. In the South, however, the Republicans were aligned with freedmen and poor mountain whites and the Democratic party was dominated by the planter elite.[11] This cross-sectional inversion of class alignments made the emergence of insurgent class claims in national politics impractical since an attack on economic privilege could be made only by sacrificing the elite interests of at least one of the two major parties.

During the late nineteenth century the American party system repeatedly presented to the national electorate three different visions of economic development. In the dominant vision, the Republican party advocated maintenance of the international gold standard, tariff protection, and an unreg-

---

[11] For more on the class alignments of the American party system within the North and South, see Richard Franklin Bensel, *Yankee Leviathan: Origins of Central State Authority in America, 1859–1877* (New York: Cambridge University Press, 1990), chap. 7, and *Sectionalism and American Political Development, 1880–1980* (Madison: University of Wisconsin Press, 1984), pp. 368–402.

ulated national market, thus presenting to the electorate an extremely harsh program of interregional redistribution from the South to the North that was very attractive to the industrializing East and Midwest. In terms of popular claims on wealth during the period, the national party recognized only the demands of southern blacks for electoral rights (and, even then, gave little more than lip service to those claims). Like the Republicans, the Democratic party also supported gold in presidential elections (until 1896) but opposed tariff protection and most national government support for industrial expansion. Instead, the Democratic program favored the export-oriented southern cotton economy and recognized its role as a supplier of raw material to European (primarily British) textile producers, as well as a consumer of domestic and foreign manufactures. It thus envisioned development as an improvement in the interregional terms of trade both within the United States and with the rest of the world economy, a program very attractive to the commodity-exporting South and some parts of the West. The national Democratic party recognized popular claims on wealth to a greater extent than did the Republicans, particularly after Bryan's nomination in 1896 aligned the party with yeoman farmers in Plains and West and industrial workers in the East.

Third-party agrarian insurgency rejected the gold standard in favor of currency inflation, advocated more sweeping regulation of corporate consolidation and operations than the other parties, rarely mentioned the tariff, and proposed government intervention in the marketing of agricultural commodities (particularly warehouses, commodity exchanges, and transportation). As a national program, these policies were most identified with and attractive to the commodity-producing West, with substantial appeal in the cotton South as well. This was the only vision that successfully incorporated popular claims on wealth into a broader developmental program.

The tariff was always a salient issue in national politics because protection so clearly and radically redistributed wealth from agriculture to industry and from the South to the North. The gold standard became a salient issue because it also redistributed wealth from the capital-importing regions of the South and West to the capital-rich manufacturing belt. Emphasizing inflation as a means of redressing the terms of trade between the sections, silverites attempted, almost by sleight of hand, to unite southern sharecroppers and western yeomen in one insurgent movement. Hoping to broaden the national class basis of this insurgency, silverites also offered the northeastern worker a fairly progressive labor agenda. In the end, however, northern workers supported gold because they viewed both silver and greenbacks as threats to industrial expansion. For that reason, industrial labor turned, first, against the Populists and, then, against the Democratic party after it took up the Populist banner under William Jennings Bryan. For the sharecropper and the yeoman farmer silver was not enough to build an enduring alliance – particularly after the gold strikes in the Klondike and the South African Rand began a secular inflation that continued well into the twentieth century.

Thus, what kept the Republican party focused on economic development, even under the stress of intense party competition, was the salience of a continuing interregional redistribution of wealth through the operation of the tariff, the gold standard, and the national market. American industrialization was thus a regional project with national pretensions. This regionally biased development program, for example, allowed the Republican party to proclaim itself the agent of national prosperity while displacing the popular claims of the factory worker that otherwise would have undercut industrial development. Despite its complex and effective design, however, this system was more a response to opportunities and demands in popular politics than it was the product of elite intent and control.

COMPATIBILITY OF DEMOCRACY AND DEVELOPMENT

A political system as complex as the American nation in the late nineteenth century is not easily summarized in terms of a few fundamental factors and their derivative implications. At the risk (and a substantial one it is) of oversimplifying and distorting the actual case, the compatibility of democracy and development in the United States can be outlined in the following way.

(1) Because of its diversity and size, the American economy was very unevenly developed throughout the nineteenth century. This uneven development was a major factor behind southern separatism and the Civil War. In turn, Union victory imposed a political patina on regional economic conflict that further isolated the South from effective inclusion in national coalitions.

(2) For both economic and political reasons, then, the American party system became firmly rooted in conflict over the interregional transfer of wealth between the industrializing North and the cotton South. Most industrial workers backed Republican-led development in national politics because the party program promoted capital investment and production in eastern industry.

(3) Because the major parties were organized in a way that inverted their respective class bases in the North and South, they rarely addressed claims on wealth arising on the cotton plantation or the factory shop floor. Effectively taking one of what might have been the most important popular claims on wealth out of democratic politics, this was the major reason that industrial strikes seldom affected the policy basis of national party competition.

(4) Popular claims on wealth in the South placed black freedmen in an unholy alliance with the national Republican party, an alliance that traded northern support for black political rights for southern backing of the northern industrial program. Within this framework, both major parties largely ignored the struggle over control of the cotton crop within the South. While the market-oriented claims of western agrarians did enter into national politics by way of state party organizations, these demands influenced only the margins of the national party programs. Failure by the major parties – with the exception of Bryan's Democrats – to address these claims produced, in turn, the rural-periphery base from which most insurgent, radical parties drew their strength.

(5) Finally, all of these factors, along with the sectional organization of the major party system, made formal democratic institutions and rapid industrial development more or less compatible in the late nineteenth century. The characteristics of the major developmental policies, institutional repertoires, party programs, popular claims on wealth, and uneven economic topography all combined in such a way as to leave the citizenry free to contest rapid accumulation of wealth in the industrial sector without impeding the flow of capital into corporate expansion and consolidation.

Thus, American industrialization presents one of the most striking examples of compatibility between electoral democracy and rapid economic development in comparative experience, not because there were no struggles over income shares, wealth, and streams of capital investment; not because the electorate wore ideological blinders that deflected attention from their class exploitation; not because the central state stepped in and repressed insurgency; *but because the extreme disparity in economic development within the United States gave rise to government policies and, through them, political party coalitions that made intersectional redistribution the most important factor in American politics.*

Many scholars, particularly those who discern a hegemonic "liberalism" as the major force in American political development, tend to view the combination of democracy and development in the late nineteenth-century United States as more or less inevitable. Scholars writing within that perspective often downplay the very real threats to national unity and the very uneven regional pattern of development during industrialization.[12] Instead, they criticize what they view as the weakness of the American central state – failing to see that successful suppression of southern separatism and the creation of a national market free from local barriers were, in fact, truly stupendous accomplishments. In addition, they tend to cite policies, such as universal education and religious tolerance, as the more-or-less benign

---

[12] See, for example, Louis Hartz, *The Liberal Tradition in America* (New York: Harcourt, Brace, 1955), and Samuel P. Huntington, *Political Order in Changing Societies* (New Haven, Conn.: Yale University Press, 1968), chap. 2.

lessons that the Third World should take away from American development. While universal education and religious tolerance are good things, they are by no means the only or even the most important lessons to be drawn from American history during the late nineteenth century. Instead, aside from the compatibility of democracy and development, the most striking features of the American experience are the massive redistribution of wealth from southern agriculture to northern industry and the brutal repression of lower classes throughout the nation. While an effective combination of robust democratic institutions and rapid industrial development is a rare accomplishment, the American case demonstrates that it may not be entirely benign in its consequences.

Index

Adams, Charles Francis, 311
Addyston Pipe and Steel Company v. United States, 344n
agriculture, 457; diversification of in the East, 223–224; topic of state party platforms, 161–163
Alabama, 21; accumulated wealth in, 40; and convict labor, 154, 155; and distribution of national bank capital, 62n; Greenback party strong in, 273; illiteracy in, 34, 35; letters mailed per capita, 305; manufacturing in, 25; patent filings in, 31; pension payments in, 488n; reaction to Force bill, 502n; relative development in, 50; senators and Wilson Tariff, 479; state Democratic convention, 104–105; state Democratic platform, 171n, 173; state legislature instructs federal representatives and senators, 111n; state Populist platform, 143n; state Republican convention, 112n; state Republican platform, 126, 156n; strikes in, 216; taxation of labor agents, 323
Albany, New York, 61, 70, 71, 77n
Allgeyer v. Louisiana, 336
Allison, William, 424n, 429n
Altgeld, John P., 425n
Amalgamated Association of Iron, Steel and Tin Workers, 122n, 491n, 492n
Ambler, Jacob A., 472
American Bankers' Association, 447n, 449n
American Bar Association, 347
American Bell Telephone Company, 32n, 55
American Cotton Seed Oil, 55n, 318, 338

American Economist, 464n, 481n, 492
American Federation of Labor, 491n; ambivalent toward Sherman Antitrust Act, 343; endorses silver in national conventions, 269n; maintains labor organizers in South, 209n; officially neutral in 1892 and 1896 election, 151n, 269n; and strikes, 210n; supports restriction of Chinese immigration, 150
American Iron and Steel Association, 477, 485n
American Pig Iron Storage, 55n
American Protective Association, 182
American Protective Tariff League, 464n
American Railway Union, 148, 341
American Sugar Refining Company, 337–338, 340–341
American Telegraph Company, 306
American Tin Plate Company, 122n, 478n
American Tobacco Company, 55n, 338n
Anglophilia, 126–127, 507–509
Anthony, Kansas, 63–64, 70n
antitrust regulation: rulings in state courts on, 337–338; state legislation enacting, 339; topic of state party platforms, 121–124, 190, 193; see also Sherman Antitrust Act
Appalachians, 27; illiteracy in, 36; railroads in, 300; strikes in, 215
Appalachicola, Florida, 217, 301
Appleton's Annual Cyclopaedia, 112
Arizona, 59; and distribution of national bank capital, 62n; Socialist party strong in, 280

529